THE PAPERS OF
WOODROW WILSON

VOLUME 53
NOVEMBER 9, 1918-JANUARY 11, 1919

SPONSORED BY THE WOODROW WILSON
FOUNDATION
AND PRINCETON UNIVERSITY

THE PAPERS OF

WOODROW WILSON

ARTHUR S. LINK, *EDITOR*

DAVID W. HIRST, *SENIOR ASSOCIATE EDITOR*

JOHN E. LITTLE, *ASSOCIATE EDITOR*

FREDRICK AANDAHL, *ASSOCIATE EDITOR*

MANFRED F. BOEMEKE, *ASSISTANT EDITOR*

DENISE THOMPSON, *ASSISTANT EDITOR*

PHYLLIS MARCHAND AND MARGARET D. LINK,
EDITORIAL ASSISTANTS

Volume 53
November 9, 1918-January 11, 1919

PRINCETON, NEW JERSEY

PRINCETON UNIVERSITY PRESS

1986

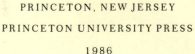

Note to scholars: Princeton University Press subscribes to the Resolution on Permissions of the Association of American University Presses, defining what
we regard as "fair use" of copyrighted works. This Resolution, intended to encourage scholarly use of university press publications and to avoid unnecessary applications for permission, is obtainable from the Press
or from the A.A.U.P. central office. Note, however, that
the scholarly apparatus, transcripts of shorthand, and
the texts of Wilson documents as they appear in this
volume are copyrighted, and the usual rules about the
use of copyrighted materials apply.

Publication of this book has been aided by a grant
from the National Historical Publications and Records
Commission.

Printed in the United States of America
by Princeton University Press
Princeton, New Jersey

INTRODUCTION

THIS volume, which opens upon the eve of the Armistice, finds Wilson engrossed in last-minute details concerning the signing and publication of the document that will bring to a conclusion the greatest war in history to this date. A few hours after the agreement is signed at Compiègne, Wilson goes before a joint session of Congress, reads the military and naval terms, and announces: "The war thus comes to an end." Messages of congratulation come pouring in upon Wilson, such as (from Colonel House): "Autocracy is dead. Long live democracy and its immortal leader" and (from Newton D. Baker): "You have done this great thing! May God's blessing rest on it and on you."

Meanwhile and during the weeks following the Armistice, Wilson is largely preoccupied with all the preliminaries to the peace conference, which, it has been agreed, will meet in Paris—protocols for the organization of the conference, the date of its convocation, the size of various delegations, and, above all, the appointment of the American commissioners. Contrary to the advice of most of his principal counselors, Democratic leaders in Congress, and his friends, Wilson, on November 18, declares that he will go to Paris as the head of the American delegation. Then, on November 29, Wilson announces the names of the other peace commissioners—Robert Lansing, Henry White, Colonel House, and Tasker H. Bliss.

At the same time, the vast machinery created for wartime mobilization begins to dissolve in what can only be described as a process of voluntary dismantlement. Some cabinet members, heads of war agencies, and businessmen plead with Wilson to plan carefully for the conversion from war to peace, but he pays little attention to these suggestions because his mind is so preoccupied with the coming peace conference. Wilson does, however, give strong support to Herbert Hoover's plans for a program for American relief to war-ravaged Europe.

Wilson delivers his Annual Message to Congress on December 2. Two days later, he and a large company of State Department personnel and "experts" from The Inquiry sail from Hoboken on the *U.S.S. George Washington* for what will become the most important involvement of the United States in world affairs to this date. Wilson, by this time highly suspicious of the Allied premiers, goes to Europe full of grim determination, if not of high hopes. Affected, no doubt, by what seems to be an almost universal approval of his international ideals and objectives, Wilson, in remarks to members of The Inquiry aboard ship on December 10, declares that he alone represents the hopes and aspirations of the common people of the world. "Tell me what's right and I'll fight for it," he says; "give me a guaranteed position."

Events in western Europe soon after Wilson's arrival in France on December 13 seem to bear out his convictions that he, representing the New World, has come to redeem the Old World. He is greeted by virtually the entire population of Paris on December 14. Then, while French and British leaders dally, Wilson makes tours of England and Italy, where he is again hailed by vast throngs and words of adulation. Back in Paris on January 7, Wilson draws up what is known as the first Paris draft of the Covenant of the League of Nations. In this document, Wilson, impressed by the ideas of General Jan C. Smuts, reveals one of the most momentous shifts in his thinking that has yet occurred—his conversion from the idea of a loose confederation of nations to a plan for a League of Nations with explicit guarantees for security and peace.

Our introduction to the Peace Conference Volumes follows.

THE PEACE CONFERENCE VOLUMES

We now come to the period of the supreme testing of Wilson's leadership on the world stage—the preliminaries to and meetings of the conference of nations in Paris during the first half of 1919 for the purpose of concluding a treaty of peace with the Central Powers and of laying the foundations of a new international order. Of the nearly 1,200 boxes and volumes in the Papers of Woodrow Wilson in the Library of Congress, 256 relate to the Paris Peace Conference. We have organized all of our materials chronologically, and we have not found them to be unmanageable in spite of their bulk. Perhaps fortunately for us—and, we think, also for our readers—Wilson saw only a small portion of the documents for this period. For example, tens of thousands of admirers and well-wishers sent messages of adulation and encouragement to Wilson as the hope of the future in late 1918 and early 1919. Among others, thousands of French school children and virtually all the municipal councils of Italian towns and cities poured out their praise to the man who was to bring security to and a bright future for the world. It was of course impossible for Wilson to see, much less to read, correspondence of this sort, even though his secretaries must have described it to him. We print only a highly selective representation of these letters and telegrams, which we hope will convey some understanding of Wilson's stature at this time and the way in which he seemed to embody the universal yearning for an orderly, just, and peaceful world order.

In selecting documents for the Peace Conference Volumes, we have always tried to bear sternly in mind the fact that we are editing the *Wilson* Papers, not the Papers of the Paris Peace Conference, large and important portions of which have been published by others. We continue, therefore, to select only those documents which Wilson himself generated, which had a significant impact on his thought and action, or which yield important information about his activities from day to day. Moreover, as has always been our practice, we print everything which we think is important, regardless of its length or whether it has been printed before.

At this writing, we are working intensively in the documents to about April 1, 1919, and our best estimate now is that we will be able to cover the Paris Peace Conference and its preliminaries in seven volumes. However that may be, we are deeply enough into the events of this period to be able to describe for our readers the major categories of the contents of these volumes; and we have also had sufficient experience in dealing with them to comment upon our method in presenting them. The categories, with comment on method, follow:

1. *Political and diplomatic correspondence.* This constitutes the major part of the Peace Conference Volumes and includes, among a great variety of other things, the hitherto neglected correspondence between Wilson and departmental and congressional leaders in Washington about problems of demobilization and domestic reconstruction. We reproduce the great bulk of this correspondence *verbatim et literatim*, and we beg our readers to believe that inconsistencies in spelling, capitalization, enumeration, and minor misspellings in these and in all documents in this series are *sic* in the original manuscripts. However, we silently correct words with transposed letters or obvious typographical errors in typed copies of telegrams and other typed documents. We make other corrections in square brackets.

We have encountered some problems in dealing with the telegrams between Wilson and Colonel House and between Wilson and Joseph P. Tumulty. Tumulty not only wrote frequently on his own initiative; he also sent messages from departmental and congressional leaders to Wilson on the White House wire. Wilson, House, and Tumulty all used private codes. These codes appear to have been very difficult for the decoders at Wilson's end—Wilson, Mrs. Wilson, Charles L. Swem, and Gilbert F. Close—to put into English. As a result, most of the telegrams that Wilson actually read were garbled, sometimes beyond comprehension. It is obviously essential for the reader to see telegrams and radiograms in the exact form in which Wilson saw them. Thus, whenever possible, we print the copies that Wilson sent (he often wrote them on his own typewriter) and the telegrams, etc., *as he read them.* It is also important for the reader to see telegrams and radiograms in the exact form in which House and Tumulty sent them. We fortunately possess senders' copies of most of their communications. If there are only minor mistakes in the received copies, we print them *verbatim et literatim.* If the decode in the Wilson Papers is garbled, we reproduce the garbled decode and, wherever possible, correct it from the sender's copy in square brackets immediately following blank spaces or garbled words and phrases. If, as rarely happens, a decoded telegram is garbled beyond repair, we print that version and, in a footnote, the sender's copy also. We follow the same method in reproducing telegrams from Wilson to House and Tumulty. Thus the reader can see the telegram, cablegram, or radiogram both as it was sent and as the receiver read it or tried to read it.

As the reader will soon discover, the difficulties in communication in code affected most seriously the interchanges between Wilson and House and, most particularly, the communications from House to Wilson. Swem decoded most of the telegrams from House and from the White House. His method was to write the decode out in shorthand and then type it up, but frequently without sufficient regard for meaning or coherence.

2. *Debates and discussions in various councils.* Wilson played a prominent role in the discussions and debates in the Supreme War Council, the Council of Ten, the Council of Four, and the plenary sessions of the conference, and we print all the minutes of the meetings in which Wilson participated in any significant way. We reproduce the typescripts of the minutes kept by Sir (later Lord) Maurice Hankey, Secretary of the British delegation, whose minutes were accepted as the official text by the American and other delegations. Since we leave out certain portions of these minutes, the reader should know that they are printed in full in the State Department's *Papers Relating to the Foreign Relations of the United States, 1919: The Paris Peace Conference* (13 vols., Washington, 1942-47). The editors of that series silently corrected the few typographical errors and misspellings of names in Hankey's typescripts, and we have done the same. It might be added that the text in the State Department's Peace Conference Series is on the whole a very faithful rendition of the original typescripts. To date, we have read the text in this series against Hankey's typescripts through March 22, 1919, and have discovered only one serious error: Volume IV, p. 379, line 17, should read "the 22nd of January" not "the 2nd of January."

Because the Big Four decided for a time not to have a formal record made, Hankey was not present at their sessions (with some exceptions) from March 24 to April 16, 1919. Fortunately for historians, Professor Paul Mantoux, official translator of the conference, began to keep stenographic records of his own of the Council of Four on March 24 and continued to do so until June 28, 1919. Professor Mantoux published transcripts of his notes in 1955 in two volumes under the title *Les Délibérations du Counseil des Quatre (24 mars-28 juin 1919)* (2 vols., Paris, 1955). We have translated both volumes into English. For those sessions when Hankey was absent, we print our translations of the Mantoux minutes as discrete documents. For those sessions when both Hankey and Mantoux were present, we regard the Hankey transcripts as the basic texts because his record is longer and more complete than Mantoux's. However, we do print most of Mantoux's notes at their appropriate place along with Hankey's notes. The latter usually supplement and do not repeat Hankey's version.

In addition, for a short time, until January 24, 1919, Joseph C. Grew, Secretary of the American delegation, prepared, or had prepared, his own minutes of the Supreme War Council and the Council of Ten. We reproduce them, wherever appropriate, in footnotes to Hankey's minutes.

Both Hankey's and Mantoux's minutes were obviously based on stenographic records, and they appear to have been faithfully transcribed. However, Hankey was keeping minutes that were distributed day by day, and he naturally edited them to mute passionate controversy and to delete all derogatory personal remarks made by one participant about another. Mantoux's stenographic notes were destroyed soon after his two volumes were published. One can only assume that he deleted all derogatory personal remarks from his published record on grounds of taste. For example, we know from contemporary sources that Clemenceau, during a furious debate over the Saar Valley on March 28, 1919, said that Wilson was pro-German. Wilson retorted that, if Clemenceau was not willing to abide by solemn agreements, he, Wilson, might as well go home. Mantoux kept the minutes that day (Hankey was not present), and Mantoux omitted this exchange from the record. Wilson often related to other people the tenor and contents of the debates in various councils; these persons, in turn, recorded Wilson's accounts in their diaries. Our impression from Wilson's own comments is that both Hankey and Mantoux recorded most conversations in full and paraphrased others in less forceful language than was actually used.

The same observations apply even more importantly to the minutes of the Commission on the League of Nations, which record little of the debates in this body. To see a glaring example of what was *not* recorded in the official record, the reader may compare the minutes printed at March 22, 1919, with the extracts from the diaries of Lord Robert Cecil and David Hunter Miller printed at the same date.

All important matters relating to the peace settlement and the reconstruction of Europe eventually found their way to the forums in which Wilson participated. Thus, the Hankey and Mantoux minutes, in particular, give us a marvelous view of all the important issues as they were fought out and brought to settlement.

3. *Wilson's speeches.* We include all of Wilson's speeches during the period covered by the Peace Conference Volumes, except for a few brief remarks which Wilson made on his English tour in December 1918. In reproducing Wilson's speeches, we have followed our usual practice of reading Swem's transcripts against his shorthand notes and what other transcripts of Wilson's speeches we could find. As in the past, this method has proved invaluable. For example, Swem left out one whole paragraph in his transcript of Wilson's speech in Boston on February 24. The omission is not monumentally important, but it was in the speech as Wilson delivered it. Moreover, we have also modernized archaic spelling in contemporary transcripts, and we have supplied punctuation wherever we think that it belongs in speeches.

4. *Diaries and letters of contemporaries.* Many of the participants in the drama being played out in Paris realized that they were involved in one of the most important events in history and kept diaries or wrote letters to their families at home about it. Dr. Grayson's diary, published in these volumes for the first time through the courtesy of James Gordon Grayson and Cary T. Grayson, Jr., is a detailed intimate record; indeed, so informative is it about Wilson and the events that swirled around him that it might well be regarded as the centerpiece of our Peace Conference Volumes. It is a typed manuscript, which begins with Wilson's departure for Europe and breaks off with Wilson's presentation of the Versailles Treaty to the Senate on July 9, 1919. It resumes on September 3, 1919, with Wilson's departure for his western tour, and it ends on September 28, 1919, the day of Wilson's return to Washington.

The typescript of the Grayson diary is obviously based on an earlier source or sources—a daily diary or notes dictated to or taken by a secretary. For example, Grayson's account of Wilson's press conference with the representatives of the three news services aboard the *George Washington* on December 11, 1918, could only have been based upon notes by a shorthand stenographer. There can be no doubt about the credibility of the Grayson diary. We have checked out all his accounts and have found only such minor errors as would confirm the authenticity of the document. There is simply no way that Grayson could have remembered with such accuracy all the vast detail of his diary, nor could he conceivably have invented it. Moreover, Wilson said the same things to various people who kept diaries. As the reader will note, they repeat, sometimes in almost the same words, Wilson's conversations as recorded in the Grayson diary. Compare, for example, Wilson's description of General Allenby in the extract from the Grayson diary printed at March 19, 1919, with Wilson's comment on Allenby as recorded in the entry from the diary of Ray Stannard Baker printed at the same date.

At some unknown time, but perhaps in 1921-1922, Grayson prepared, or had someone prepare, the version which we now possess. He obviously at first intended to publish the diary and added a few prospective portions, along with indications that Wilson's speeches and other documents were to be included in the published version. Dr. Grayson was unusually discreet; he obviously decided that the contents of his diary, if published, might damage the reputations of many persons still alive, and he set the diary aside, where it lay unknown until his sons discovered it about 1965.

In reproducing the Grayson diary, we have silently corrected its few typographical errors and misspelled names; we have also eliminated those portions which are obviously prospective in nature and the instructions to an editor to include copies of Wilson's speeches and other documents.

Ray Stannard Baker began to keep a diary in earnest when he returned to Europe with Wilson on the *George Washington* in early March 1919. It is a handwritten document, kept daily, and is second in importance for these volumes only to the Grayson diary. In spite of its significance, the Baker diary, which has been available for many years in Mr. Baker's papers in the Library of Congress, has never been printed and has rarely been used by historians. Perhaps many of them gave up in despair when they tried to read Baker's atrocious script. The same might be said about Mrs. Wilson's weekly letters to her family!

The most disappointing diary for the peace conference is the one kept by that inveterate diarist and recorder of events, Colonel House. House had influenza for several weeks, and there are no entries in his diary at all between November 21 and November 30, 1918. However, he seems to have recovered substantially by the time Wilson arrived in Paris. House busied himself with many projects and engaged in a very active social life, unusual for him, once the peace conference began, hence he may not have had much time to devote to his diary. For whatever reason, it is, on the whole, skimpy for the entire period of the peace conference. For example, it really tells us nothing about what House did during the period of Wilson's absence from Paris, and it omits all references to actions which caused Wilson gradually to lose confidence in House.

Extracts from numerous other diaries and letters to families at home provide an intimate running account of events, and particularly of Wilson's conversations and actions. For example, the accounts of Wilson's meeting with his advisers on board the *George Washington* on December 10, 1918, when read together, present a definitive and memorable record of this event.

5. *Memoranda, reports, etc., to Wilson*. We have printed all important memoranda and reports to Wilson by his military and naval advisers. Not only are these documents extremely valuable in their own right, but they also reveal the extraordinary degree to which Wilson relied on these advisers in helping to work out the military and naval terms of the Versailles Treaty. In addition, we print or summarize in notes all important position papers on such matters as boundaries, the terms of reparation, and relations with Russia.

6. *Materials relating to the Covenant of the League of Nations*. To our knowledge, we have printed all documents which illustrate Wilson's leadership and participation in the drafting of the Covenant of the League of Nations. These include all of Wilson's own drafts of the Covenant, his correspondence, statements, and conversations about it, and the complete minutes of the Commission on the League of Nations, which have heretofore been printed only in David Hunter Miller, *The Drafting of the Covenant* (2 vols., New York and London, 1928). Copies of the minutes of this commission are extremely rare, and we were fortunate to find complete sets in the Wilson Papers and the Swem Collection.

7. *Personal letters*. In spite of the unrelenting pressure of affairs of state, Wilson somehow managed to maintain an ongoing correspondence with members of his family and his many friends and admirers. We have included most of these letters in these volumes; they reveal a person who, even though under great stress, was a compassionate friend.

These, then, are the major categories of materials which the reader will find in our Peace Conference Volumes. Perhaps it would not be amiss to explain our method in arranging them.

Our first rule has been and remains the rule of chronology. We print the documents as they unfold from day to day, since this is the only way to show events as they actually occurred, that is, to use Ranke's immortal phrase, *wie es eigentlich gewesen ist*. We begin the documentation for each day with the Grayson diary and extracts from other diaries which give an overarching view of the events of the day. We then follow with documents that record, in as much a chronological manner as is possible, Wilson's activities of the day. Having concluded our documentation for Wilson's activities in Paris, we then devote the balance of the documents for a particular day to letters, telegrams, etc., relating to the administration of the government and affairs at home.

We have tried to accomplish in these Peace Conference Volumes what no one else has attempted to do, that is, to bring together in one series all important documents which shed light on Woodrow Wilson and the larger arena in which he strove so hard to bring about a just and lasting peace to a world deeply wounded by the blood-letting, passions, and hatred of the previous four and a half years. Persons will continue to argue whether Wilson failed or succeeded in Paris. Others will continue to ponder the meaning and consequences of events at the Paris Peace Conference. The record is all here in these volumes, at least that part of the record that Wilson helped to make.

We would be remiss if we did not acknowledge our deep indebtedness to memoirs by contemporaries; to such published collections as the State Department's Peace Conference Series, David Hunter Miller's massive and rare collection known as *My Diary at the Conference of Paris, with Documents* (21 vols. with one box of maps, New York, 1924-26), Ray Stannard Baker's *Woodrow Wilson and World Settlement* (3 vols., Garden City, N.Y., 1922-23), and Philip M. Burnett's excellent *Reparation at the Paris Peace Conference* (2 vols., New York, 1940); and the hundreds of excellent scholarly works on the Paris Peace Conference by historians in many different countries.

We are especially indebted to John Milton Cooper, Jr., William H. Harbaugh, August Heckscher, Richard W. Leopold, and Betty Miller Unterberger for reading the first two Peace Conference Volumes with great care, and for their helpful criticisms of this introduction at a meeting of the Editorial Advisory Committee in Princeton on May 24 and 25, 1985. It goes without saying that we, not they, are responsible for any errors that may have crept into these volumes.

"VERBATIM ET LITERATIM"

In earlier volumes of this series, we have said something like the following: "All documents are reproduced *verbatim et literatim*, with typographical and spelling errors corrected in square brackets only when necessary for clarity and ease of reading." The following essay explains our textual methods and review procedures.

We have never printed and do not intend to print critical, or corrected, versions of documents. We print them exactly as they are, with a few exceptions which we always note. We never use the word *sic* except to denote the repetition of words in a document; in fact, we think that a succession of *sics* defaces a page.

We usually repair words in square brackets when letters are missing. As we have said, we also repair words in square brackets for clarity and ease of reading. Our general rule is to do this when we, ourselves, cannot read the word without having to stop to puzzle out its meaning. Jumbled words and names misspelled beyond recognition of course have to be repaired. We correct the misspellings of names in documents in the footnotes identifying those persons.

However, when an old man writes to Wilson saying that he is glad to hear that Wilson is "comming" to Newark, or a semiliterate farmer from Texas writes phonetically, we see no reason to correct spellings in square brackets when the words are perfectly understandable. We do not correct Wilson's misspellings unless they are unreadable, except to supply in square brackets letters missing in words. For example, he consistently spelled "belligerent" as "belligerant." Nothing would be gained by correcting "belligerant" in square brackets.

We think that it is very important for several reasons to follow the rule of *verbatim et literatim*. Most important, a document has its own integrity and power, particularly when it is not written in perfect literary form. There is something very moving in seeing a Texas dirt farmer struggling to express his feelings in words, or a semiliterate former slave doing the same thing. Second, in Wilson's case it is crucially important to reproduce his errors in letters which he typed himself, since he usually typed badly when he was in an agitated state. Third, since style is the essence of the person, we would never correct grammar or make tenses consistent, as one correspondent has urged us to do. Fourth, we think that it is very important that we print exact transcripts of Charles L. Swem's copies of Wilson's letters. Swem made many mistakes (we correct them in footnotes from a reading of his shorthand books), and Wilson let them pass. We thus have to assume that Wilson did not read his letters before signing them, and this, we think, is a significant fact.

We think that our series would be worthless if we produced unreliable texts, and we go to considerable effort to make certain that the texts are authentic.

Our typists are highly skilled and proofread their transcripts carefully as soon as they have typed them. The Editor sight proofreads documents once he has assembled a volume and is setting its annotation. The Editors who write the notes read through documents several times and are careful to check any anomalies. Then, once the manuscript volume has been completed and all notes checked, the Editor and Senior Associate Editor orally proofread the documents against the copy. They read every comma, dash, and character. They note every absence of punctuation. They study every nearly illegible word in written documents.

Once this process of "establishing the text" is completed, the manuscript volume goes to our editor at Princeton University Press, who checks the volume carefully and sends it to the printing plant. The galley proofs are read against copy in the proofroom at the Press. And we must say that the proofreaders there are extraordinarily skilled. Some years ago, before we found a way to ease their burden, they queried every misspelled word, inconsistencies in punctuation and capitalization, absence of punctuation, or other such anomalies. Now we write "O.K." above such words or spaces on the copy.

We read the galley proofs at least three times. Our copyeditor gives them a sight reading against the manuscript copy to look for remaining typographical errors and to make sure that no line has been dropped. The Editor and Senior Associate Editor sight read them against documents and copy. We then get the page proofs, which have been corrected at the Press. We check all the changes three times. In addition, we get *revised* pages and check them twice.

This is not the end. The Editor, Senior Associate Editor, and Assistant Editor give a final reading to headings, description-location lines, and notes. Finally, our indexer of course reads the pages word by word. Before we return the pages to the Press, she comes in with a list of queries, all of which are answered by reference to the documents.

Our rule in the Wilson Papers is that our tolerance of error is zero. No system and no person can be perfect. There may be errors in our volumes. However, we believe that we have done everything humanly possible to avoid error; the chance is remote that what looks at first glance like a typographical error is indeed an error.

THE EDITORS

Princeton, New Jersey
June 5, 1985

CONTENTS

Personal correspondence
  From Wilson to
    Newton Diehl Baker, 54
    Bernard Mannes Baruch, 213, 334
    Herbert Edward Douglas Blakiston, 162
    Edward Booth, 524
    Louis Dembitz Brandeis, 55
    Andrew Carnegie, 67
    Homer Stillé Cummings, 244
    Earl Curzon of Kedleston, 161
    D. C. Heath and Company, 45
    Cleveland Hoadley Dodge, 68
    Edward Graham Elliott, 45
    Solomon Bulkley Griffin, 251
    Henry Morgenthau, 3
    The Norman Foster Company, 205
    Alice Wilson Page, 491
    Walter Hines Page, 203
    John Joseph Pershing, 473
    May Randolph Petty, 221
    Edith Kermit Carow Roosevelt, 625
    Jessie Woodrow Wilson Sayre, 68
    Edward Wright Sheldon, 167
    John Howell Westcott, 129
  To Wilson from
    Herbert Henry Asquith, 542
    Newton Diehl Baker, 46
    Bernard Mannes Baruch, 209, 309
    Louis Dembitz Brandeis, 46
    An extract by Louis Dembitz Brandeis from "The Bacchae" by Euripides,
      47
    Andrew Carnegie, 32
    Homer Stillé Cummings, 242
    Edward Parker Davis, 243
    Cleveland Hoadley Dodge, 46
    Mary Owen Graham, 31
    Solomon Bulkley Griffin, 241
    Eleanor Foster Lansing, 584
    The Norman Foster Company, 159
    Frank Mason North, 718
    William Cardinal O'Connell, 274
    Walter Hines Page, 189
    John Joseph Pershing, 432
    Georges Roth, 261
    Jessie Woodrow Wilson Sayre, 21, 212, 436
    Edward Wright Sheldon, 126
    John Howell Westcott, 235
    Theodore Wright, 394

Interviews
  A memorandum by Stockton Axson about a White House conference on the
    creation of an international Red Cross organization, 301

Collateral Materials

ILLUSTRATIONS

Following page 384

ABBREVIATIONS

AL	autograph letter
ALI	autograph letter initialed
ALS	autograph letter signed
BL	Breckinridge Long
CC	carbon copy
CCL	carbon copy of letter
CCLI	carbon copy of letter initialed
CCS	carbon copy signed
EBW	Edith Bolling Galt Wilson
EMH	Edward Mandell House
FKL	Franklin Knight Lane
FLP	Frank Lyon Polk
FR	*Papers Relating to the Foreign Relations of the United States*
FR-WWS 1917	*Papers Relating to the Foreign Relations of the United States, 1917, Supplement, The World War*
FR-WWS 1918	*Papers Relating to the Foreign Relations of the United States, 1918, Supplement, The World War*
FR-1918, Russia	*Papers Relating to the Foreign Relations of the United States, 1918, Russia*
FR-1919, Russia	*Papers Relating to the Foreign Relations of the United States, 1919, Russia*
HCH	Herbert Clark Hoover
Hw, hw	handwriting, handwritten
JD	Josephus Daniels
JPT	Joseph Patrick Tumulty
MS, MSS	manuscript, manuscripts
NDB	Newton Diehl Baker
PPC	*Papers Relating to the Foreign Relations of the United States, The Paris Peace Conference, 1919*
RG	record group
RL	Robert Lansing
T	typed
TC	typed copy
TCL	typed copy of letter
TI	typed initialed
TL	typed letter
TLI	typed letter initialed
TLS	typed letter signed
TS	typed signed
TWG	Thomas Watt Gregory
WCR	William Cox Redfield
WGM	William Gibbs McAdoo
WHP	Walter Hines Page
WW	Woodrow Wilson
WWhw	Woodrow Wilson handwriting, handwritten
WWsh	Woodrow Wilson shorthand
WWT	Woodrow Wilson typed
WWTL	Woodrow Wilson typed letter
WWTLI	Woodrow Wilson typed letter initialed
WWTLS	Woodrow Wilson typed letter signed

ABBREVIATIONS FOR COLLECTIONS AND REPOSITORIES

Following the National Union Catalog of the
Library of Congress

AFL-CIO-Ar	American Federation of Labor-Congress of Industrial Organizations Archives
AzU	University of Arizona
CSt-H	Hoover Institution on War, Revolution and Peace
CtY	Yale University
DARC	American National Red Cross
DGU	Georgetown University
DLC	Library of Congress
DNA	National Archives
EBWP, DLC	Edith Bolling Galt Wilson Papers, Library of Congress
FO	British Foreign Office
JDR	Justice Department Records
KyU	University of Kentucky
LDR	Labor Department Records
MdBJ	The Johns Hopkins University
MH	Harvard University
MoHi	Missouri State Historical Society
MoU	University of Missouri
NjP	Princeton University
NN	New York Public Library
NNC	Columbia University
OClW	Case Western Reserve University
PRO	Public Record Office
RSB Coll., DLC	Ray Stannard Baker Collection of Wilsoniana, Library of Congress
SDR	State Department Records
TDR	Treasury Department Records
ViU	University of Virginia
WC,NjP	Woodrow Wilson Collection, Princeton University
WP, DLC	Woodrow Wilson Papers, Library of Congress

SYMBOLS

[January 3, 1919]	publication date of published writing; also date of document when date is not part of text
[*December 18, 1919*]	composition date when publication date differs
[[January 6, 1919]]	delivery date of speech if publication date differs
**** ***	text deleted by author of document

THE PAPERS OF

WOODROW WILSON

VOLUME 53

NOVEMBER 9, 1918–JANUARY 11, 1919

THE PAPERS OF
WOODROW WILSON

To Henry Morgenthau

My dear Morgenthau: The White House 9 November, 1918.

I am warmly obliged to you for the first copy of the book,[1] and I want you to know how deeply and sincerely I appreciate the generous dedication to me.[2] I am looking forward with keen interest to reading the volume aloud to Mrs. Wilson at such little intervals as we get in the evenings to be together and enjoy something that takes our thoughts away from the pressing matters of the day. Mrs. Wilson has already read portions of the book as published elsewhere[3] and has whetted my appetite for it by telling me some part of what she has read.

    With best wishes from us both,
            Cordially and sincerely yours,   Woodrow Wilson

TLS (WP, DLC).
    [1] Henry Morgenthau, *Ambassador Morgenthau's Story* (New York, 1918). There is a copy of this book in the Wilson Library, DLC.
    [2] "TO WOODROW WILSON THE EXPONENT IN AMERICA OF THE ENLIGHTENED PUBLIC OPINION OF THE WORLD, WHICH HAS DECREED THAT THE RIGHTS OF SMALL NATIONS SHALL BE RESPECTED AND THAT SUCH CRIMES AS ARE DESCRIBED IN THIS BOOK SHALL NEVER AGAIN DARKEN THE PAGES OF HISTORY."
    [3] See H. Morgenthau to WW, June 11, 1918, n. 1, Vol. 48.

Three Telegrams from Edward Mandell House

[Paris, Nov. 9, 1918]

[No. 8][1] In conversation with French Prime Minister this morning he stated that it was his purpose to work in harmony with the United States in all things. He asked French Minister for Foreign Affairs who was present to be a witness to the promise that he would not [never] bring up any matter at the peace conference that he had not first discussed with us, and the inference was clear that if we disagreed he would yield to our wishes and judgment.

He declared that it was not our financial and economic assistance that France wanted as much as our moral approval. He thought we had opened a new and more splendid ethical era and France wished to stand with us in upholding it. He thought the United

States and France were the only nations willing to make an unselfish settlement.

He begs that this conversation and promise be held in confidence.

T transcript of WWsh decode (WP, DLC).
  ¹ Additions and corrections in square brackets in this and all following telegrams between Wilson and House from the copies in WP, DLC, and in the the House Papers, CtY. Significant differences between texts as sent by Wilson and decoded by House, and vice versa, will be noted usually in footnotes or, wherever necessary, by printing telegrams as Wilson or House decoded them.

Paris November 9, 1918.

Number 72. Secret. For the President and The Secretary of State.

At a conference with Clemenceau this morning I stated that the United States was inclined to favor Versailles as the meeting place for the peace conference. He assured me that if it was finally determined to have the conference at Versailles all possible facilities would be extended to the United States representatives, such as living accommodations and communication service. He begged me not to ask him for any particular thing but to rest assured that anything we wanted would be made available to us. He said that he would prefer to have the conference almost any place than in Geneva even going so far as to say that he would prefer London or Washington if it were not possible to agree on Versailles. No final decision can be reached until I have had an opportunity to communicate with both George and Orlando inasmuch as before these gentlemen left Paris we had tentatively agreed on Geneva. Orlando stated, however, that any place the United States was in favor of would be satisfactory to Italy. As soon as the matter is agreed upon I shall take the necessary steps to secure appropriate accommodations. It would greatly assist me to receive from you a definite approval of secrecy plan respecting communications set forth in my number 51.[1]   Edward House.

  ¹ EMH to RL, Nov. 5, 1918, T telegram (WP, DLC).

Paris. November 9, 1918.

Number 74. Secret for the President and Secretary of State.

I have just received the following communication from the French Foreign Office: "The President of the Council, Minister of War, to Colonel House. In case the Germans should refuse the armistice nothing will be published. But I regard it as almost certain that they will accept *is* (it?). If they were to communicate the clauses of the armistice to the foreign newspapers we would allow the newspapers to reproduce them, reserving to the Chamber of Deputies the news of the signing when that shall take place. I have just seen Foch who has communicated to me the minutes of the proceedings which I shall address to you as soon as they shall be typewritten. They have made no remark either as to the bridgeheads or as to the fleet. Their theme is to say that they will succumb to Bolshevikism if we do not help them to resist and that after them we ourselves will be invaded by the same scourge. They have asked that they be permitted to retire more slowly from the left bank of Rhine saying that they required the means of forming an army to combat Bolshevikism and reestablish order. Foch replied to them that they could form this army on the right bank. They likewise objected that we were taking from them too many machine guns and that they would have none left to fire upon their fellow citizens. Foch replied to them that they would have their rifles left. They also asked what we wanted to do on the left bank of the Rhine. Foch replied to them that he did not know and that it was none of his business. Finally they asked to be reprovisioned by us, saying that they were going to die of hunger. Foch replied to them that it would suffice them to put their merchant marine into our programs [pool] and that in this way they could be reprovisioned. They replied that they preferred to be given permits for their vessels. They complained that we were taking much too many locomotives, in view of the fact that theirs were scattered everywhere. Foch replied to them that we were asking only what they had taken from us. They are very much depressed. From time to time a sob escaped the throat of Winterfeld.[1] Under these conditions, the signing does not appear to me a matter of doubt, but the present situation in Germany brings us face to face with the unknown. It is the interest of the armies that we should have a few days for our military action. This eventually must be taken into account because the signature of a government which might not (?) [be obeyed] could only increase the confusion. It seems moreover that we are already at that point, because it is the impossibility of finding military authorities who can get obedience in the German lines which has indefinitely delayed the messenger who carried the clauses of the armistice to the German great headquarters. As long as he does not find in front of him an authority capable of definitely regulating the matter, Foch will continue his march forward. Signed Clemenceau."

Edward House.

T telegrams (WP, DLC).
[1] Maj. Gen. Hans Karl Detlof von Winterfeldt, formerly the liaison officer between the German High Command and the Imperial Chancellor, at this time the army representative on the German commission to negotiate an armistice.

From Robert Lansing, with Enclosure

My dear Mr. President: Washington November 9, 1918.

Here is Mr. Bullitt's memorandum on "The Bolshevist Movement in Western Europe." (November 8th)

I am sending it to you because of the recommendation which I have marked on page 4[1] and which I consider worthy of consideration.

While there is a certain force in the reasoning as to the peril from extreme radicalism under the leadership of such men as Liebknecht and the Independent Socialists, who affiliate with the Bolsheviks, the danger of compromise with any form of radicalism and the unwisdom of giving special recognition to a particular class of society as if it possessed exceptional rights impress me as strong reasons for rejecting such a proposal.

Kerensky's experience in compromise and the results which have followed the exaltation of a class at the expense of the rest of society, (whether the class be aristocratic, land owning or labor) are not encouraging to adopting the course suggested.

Faithfully yours,   Robert Lansing

TLS (WP, DLC).
[1] Recommendation No. 2.

ENCLOSURE

November 8, 1918.

Memorandum for the Secretary:
Subject: The Bolshevist Movement in Western Europe

My dear Mr. Secretary:

With great rapidity evidence accumulates indicating that immediate action by the United States and the Allies is necessary to prevent famine and economic disorganization from driving Austria and Hungary to Bolshevism.

1. Mr. Stovall, under date of November 7, reports that the Swiss Political Department has submitted to all Allied Missions the following request: The Commander of the Army of the Tyrol,[1] who was forced to order the troops on Monday last in South Tyrol not to retire northwards because of lack of food, urgently begs the Governments of the Entente to occupy the Tyrol and to provide for the subsistence of the population and the army. The National Council of the Tyrol expresses the same request, feeling that such action

will be the only means of saving the army and the population from a death which threatens them by famine and starvation.

2. The Papal Nuncio at Vienna[2] called together a conference on November 1 to request the neutrals to intervene in favor of the provisionment of Vienna which will have food only until November 14.

3. The German population of Vorarlberg—the district of Austria which lies immediately to the East of the St. Gall district of Switzerland and South of Wurtemberg—has begun a movement for incorporation with Switzerland. Austrian soldiers returning from the front have been guilty of such excesses that portions of the population are attempting to escape to Switzerland and it is reported that a provisional Republic has been established.

4. In regard to Vienna, Mr. Stovall expresses the following opinion under date of November 5:

The agitation in Vienna in favor of the formation of red guards and soldiers' committees is evidence of the Bolshevik danger which will increase greatly with the return of the demobilized troops and which, I fear, may triumph unless the Allies have food to offer and forces to maintain order throughout the centers of population of Austria.

5. In regard to Hungary, Mr. Stovall expresses the following opinion, under date of November 5:

The complexion of Karolyi's cabinet is extremely radical and a step further to the left could mean the acceptance of Bolshevism.[3] Karolyi realizes the critical position of his Government and is making every possible concession to the laboring and soldier classes, favoring a republic, announcing the surrender of Hungary in order to secure an immediate end of hostilities, raising the pay of the soldiers, promising agrarian reforms and universal suffrage, including woman suffrage and the dissolution of the present Parliament, if it refuses to accept. It is still a question whether Karolyi will be able to hold his own against the Bolshevik movement.

6. The mutiny at Kiel[4] has shown the potential strength of the Liebknecht-Mehring group, which has formed a working alliance with the Russian Bolsheviki. Until the past few weeks this ultra radical "Spartacus group" has been a negligible factor in the political life of Germany. But during the past fortnight it has gained adherents with the same rapidity which distinguished the growth of the Bolsheviki in Russia. Those leaders of the Independent Socialists who are opposed to Bolshevism, to wit, Haase and Ledebour, have apparently formed a working agreement with the Majority

Socialists led by Scheidemann, Ebert and David in order to combat the Liebknecht-Bolshevist menace.

7. The latest reports, which are as yet unverified, indicate that not only Kiel but also Hamburg, Bremen, Rostock, Warnemuende and Luebeck are in the hands of workmen's, soldiers' and sailors' councils, and that an appreciable portion of the German fleet is under control of mutineers.

8. Further information is at hand in regard to the organization of the propaganda bureau of the Bolsheviki in Switzerland.

In view of all these facts and of a host of others in regard to Scandinavia, the Baltic Provinces, Italy and France, which it seems superfluous to recite again, the conclusion is inescapable that social democracy throughout the continent of Europe is inevitable and that the question still before the world is only whether the evolution to social democracy shall be orderly and peaceful under the leadership of the moderate leaders of the working classes, or shall be disorderly and bloody under the dominance of the Bolsheviki.

It is distinctly doubtful whether or not any action which may be taken by the United States or the Allies can save Europe from a bath of Bolshevism. But it is respectfully submitted that the course of action which gives the greatest promise of success is the following, (which was suggested in less detail in a memorandum submitted on November 2):[5]

1. If economic factors permit, Mr. Hoover should be sent at once to Berne to undertake the provisioning of the Tyrol, Vienna and Bohemia. The announcement of his coming should be issued as soon as possible; for Mr. Hoover's name carries such prestige throughout the world that the people of Austria will trust in his ability to perform the impossible, and will be inclined to await his coming before turning in despair to Bolshevism.

2. It should be suggested to Colonel House that he should consider the advisability of asking Mr. Lloyd George and M. Clemenceau to call into consultation the labor leaders and moderate socialists of their countries with a view to establishing a basis of cooperation against Bolshevism. It is respectfully submitted that the Governments of the world should not and cannot with safety draw the line at all socialists and labor leaders. If the Governments of the world form a holy alliance against social democracy in Europe and attempt to suppress it by force in opposition to the moderate socialists as well as the Bolsheviki, the entire moderate socialist group, comprising Albert Thomas, Renaudel, Henderson, Webb, Scheidemann, David, Haase, Victor Adler, etc., etc., will stand with the Bolshevist forces against their Governments. For example, after

the surrender of Germany, if the Allies should attempt to march into Russia to destroy Bolshevism by force, the indispensable South Wales coal miners would strike at once, and the Longuet section of the French Socialist Party probably would call a general strike. To a struggle with the moderate socialists on the side of the Bolshevists there could be but one issue: definite class war and the ultimate bloody triumph of Bolshevism. If, on the other hand, the Governments of the world meet the demands of Henderson, Albert Thomas and their supporters, an alliance can be formed which may be able to combat Bolshevism successfully.

3. It is respectfully submitted that famine and economic disorganization are the parents of Bolshevism in Russia just as they are the parents of Bolshevism in Western Europe, and that the roots of Bolshevism can be cut only by food and restoration of economic life, and not by arms.

In this connection, the appended article by the correspondent of Gorky's newspaper in Petrograd[6] is of more than usual interest.
                    Very respectfully submitted,   William C. Bullitt

TS MS (WP, DLC).
  [1] Field Marshal Alexander, Baron von Krobatin.
  [2] The Most Rev. Theodore Valfré di Bonzo, titular Archibishop of Trebizond.
  [3] Although Károlyi's cabinet included two Social Democrats and a member of the so-called "Radical party," it is now generally considered to have been moderate in its political orientation, similar in nature to Kerenskii's government in Russia, and "radical" only in contrast to the royal governments which had preceded it. See Gábor Vermes, "The October Revolution in Hungary: from Károlyi to Kun," in Iván Völgyes, ed, *Hungary in Revolution, 1918-19: Nine Essays* (Lincoln, Neb., 1971), pp. 31-51, and Peter Pastor, *Hungary Between Wilson and Lenin: The Hungarian Revolution of 1918-1919 and the Big Three* (Boulder, Colo., 1976), pp. 30-48.
  [4] See EMH to WW, Nov. 1, 1918 (second telegram of that date), n. 1, Vol. 51.
  [5] Bullitt's memorandum is printed at Nov. 2, 1918, Vol. 51.
  [6] The newspaper was *Novaia Zhizn (New Life)*. The enclosed article is missing.

From Edward Nash Hurley

My dear Mr. President: Washington, November 9, 1918.

I agree heartily with your suggestion[1] that it will be well for us on the other side to listen a great deal, to say little, and to promise nothing.

When the war ends there is bound to be considerable confusion if the governments relax their present shipping regulations. If the shippers are given free sway they will ship their goods not to the points where they are most needed, but where they will get the best prices. Such a condition would result in chaos.

I am well aware that you understand this problem better than any of us, but there is one thought, which is subject to such wide application, that I would like to submit it to you for immediate consideration.

For a long time there have been suggestions, made here and in England, that we will not be able to operate our new merchant fleet because of the higher and costlier standards imposed by the La Follette Seaman's Act.

From Chambers of Commerce, Trade Boards and Maritime Exchanges I am constantly receiving the suggestion that we should either repeal that law or amend. I need hardly tell you that I am strongly opposed to either course.

The La Follette law does impose higher standards. The wage scale paid under it is higher than the wage scale of England, France, Norway and all other nations. The requirements with respect to living conditions are higher. The operating costs naturally are higher.

The law, however, is humane. Living conditions on merchant ships throughout the world always have been poor. A seaman's life closely approximates the proverbial "dog's life."

If the right sort of arguments are presented, I believe it will be possible to induce foreign governments to accept the standards of the La Follette law.

The position you have taken with respect to the freedom of the seas can be given concrete vindication by an agreement among the leading maritime nations to adopt the standards of the Seaman's law which you advocated and signed.

We can and should go further. We should advocate international uniformity of freight rates. The lines of international communication thus would be freed from any nation's domination. With uniform freight rates and uniform wages to seamen, the trade would go to the efficient manufacturer, and not to the favored manufacturer. It would be similar to an application of the American Interstate Commerce law to the world's free seas.

If this program were adopted, it would be applauded by America unanimously, and, while it might be opposed by shipping interests abroad, it would certainly have the grateful approval of the seamen in all foreign countries. It would, I believe, solve the problem of trade wars. It would give reality and force to the "freedom of the seas."

I have been making a personal study of the question, from the angle indicated, and have been collecting data in support of the agreement. I have reached the point where I am convinced that if we take such a position, it will be regarded as sound, the whole effect of it being in the direction of bringing foreign shipping standards up to ours.

As I view it, the European nations naturally may be reluctant to give up what they regard as an advantage, even though it may be an unfair advantage. However, this country is now a factor of such importance in the realm of shipping that our efforts to raise the common level for the benefit of the seamen of all countries will, I am confident, be accorded proper weight.

It seems to me that we have a great opportunity for service to the world in this matter. You have probably given some thought to it yourself. If you think it advisable, I can put Colonel House in touch with the situation when I go to the other side, but I will feel more assured if I can have your frank expression of opinion. My own thought is that the time is ripe to lay the ground-work for such a move.   Faithfully yours,   Edward N. Hurley

TLS (WP, DLC).
  ¹ Apparently made orally.

From Newton Diehl Baker

My dear Mr. President: Washington. November 9, 1918.

Representatives of the State Councils of Defense have been invited to Washington to meet the War Industries Board on Monday. The purpose of the invitation was to enlist the agencies of the State Councils of Defense in aid of the inquiries, industrial and economic, which the War Industries Board undertakes to keep itself informed. This use of the State Councils of Defense was suggested by the War Industries Board and cordially approved by the Council of National Defense.

In view of the pending armistice and possible suspension of the war program, it seems that the War Industries Board has decided to change the character of the meeting on Monday and to take up with the representatives of the State Councils the problem of industrial and economic reconstruction. A dinner has been arranged for Monday evening at which these problems are proposed to be discussed. Invitations to several of us in the Council have been extended, indicating phases of the reconstruction problem which it is desired to have us discuss at the dinner. Secretary Houston and I this morning discussed the question with considerable anxiety and agreed that the matter ought to be called to your attention for fear that embarrassment might arise out of it.

The Council of National Defense has for some time been collecting the data on and literature of reconstruction, but of course has not formulated a comprehensive policy, and equally, of course, would not announce any such policy without first submitting it for your approval. If at the dinner on Monday night plans for and theories of industrial reconversion, labor employment, army demobilization, etc., are discussed, quite active discussions in the newspapers will of course follow, and it may well be that the administration will be assumed to have determined on courses of action which have not yet been worked out and do not form any part of a program which you have as yet adopted. It might also meet with the suggestion that various emergency instrumentalities are designed to continue under fresh legislation for post-war activity, and suggest to the Congress agitating jealousies which may not be necessary if, in fact, upon mature consideration you do not decide to seek legislation retaining all of the instrumentalities in question.

It may well be that part of the anxiety which Secretary Houston and I feel on this subject is because neither of us feel that we have seen far enough into the perplexing problems of reconstruction to talk safely about it, and that we are therefore distrustful of the wisdom of their being any talk which, coming from official persons, may look like a settled program on a subject yet to us filled with deep uncertainties.

In any case, both of us felt that we ought to call this matter to your attention so that you could, if you felt it wise, get Mr. Baruch to indicate his whole thought in the matter to you and be restrained by your judgment in the themes and extent of the discussion at the dinner.   Respectfully yours,   Newton D. Baker

TLS (WP, DLC).

From Thomas Watt Gregory

Dear Mr. President: Washington, D. C. November 9, 1918.

Mr. Tumulty has referred to this Department a letter addressed to you by Mr. George Foster Peabody, in regard to the sentence of Roger M. Baldwin.[1] I called for a report from one of my most valued assistants, and it is as follows:

"Replying to your memorandum of today concerning the case of Roger M. Baldwin, I have the honor to advise you that Baldwin came to the attention of the Department about the time that war started.

"He is an active pacifist, has been opposed to the Selective Service Act, is opposed to war and I believe is genuinely disloyal. He is a very intelligent, well educated man, a graduate of Harvard and has a very pleasing personality. He was the director of the National Civil Liberties Bureau, and in connection with its operation, in the judgment of the Department, has violated the Selective Service Act by deliberately working to create conscientious objectors of a type not entitled to relief from the performance of full military service by the Selective Service Act.

"His conversations over the telephone have indicated his opposition to the course of the Government in the war and incidentally has shown that instead of being a person of high morals, as many of his friends believe, is not leading a moral life. He is a member of the National Executive Committee of the Peoples Council which is an organization which undertook to unify all of the radical anti-war organizations, is a member of the National Executive Committee of the Fellowship of Reconciliation, a peace and anti-war organization, is a member of the Advisory Board of the Collegiate Anti-Militarism League, is a member of the Executive Committee of the American Union against Militarism. He is in sympathy with the I.W.W. and is a member of perhaps forty or fifty radical organizations, some of them good, some of them bad and most of them of probably not much consequence.

"He was indicted for a violation of the Selective Service Act in that he wilfully refused to file a questionnaire after having registered in deference to certain of his associates, but contrary to his own personal inclinations. He plead guilty and was sentenced to a year in jail—allowance being made for some few days he had spent in jail.

"As above stated, the Department believes he has been guilty of other offenses in addition to that for which he has been convicted, to wit, the preventing of other persons from performing their duties under the Selective Service Act. In my judgment the punishment which has been imposed upon him is hardly sufficient and unless the quick termination of the war may make a different course advisable, it seems to me that further indictments should be brought against him. I am satisfied that any sympathy for him or any feeling that he is a martyr to his principles is misplaced and that he should at least serve the full sentence which has been imposed upon him."

I herewith return Mr. Peabody's letter to you and a newspaper clipping which accompanied it.[2] If the newspaper clipping correctly quotes Baldwin's remarks to the court, they furnish additional reason why no clemency should be extended. In my judgment, Baldwin is one of a very dangerous class of persons, most of whom are at large in this country and from whom I fear we may hear a good deal in the future. I consider the punishment visited on him exceptionally light.   Faithfully yours,   T. W. Gregory[3]

TLS (WP, DLC).

¹ See G. F. Peabody to WW, Oct. 31, 1918, Vol. 51.
² Clipping from the New York *Evening Post*, Oct. 30, 1918.
³ Tumulty sent a copy of this letter to Peabody in JPT to G. F. Peabody, Nov. 11, 1918, TLS (G. F. Peabody Papers, DLC).

Two Letters from Herbert Clark Hoover

Dear Mr. President: Washington *9-November-1918*

In enlarging the functions of the Belgian Relief Commission to cover the entire reconstruction and relief programme for Belgium, I would like to suggest for your approval the following matters:

1. To strengthen the C.R.B. organization I propose to set up a new executive committee, under my chairmanship, comprising representatives of the Food Administration, the Belgian Relief Commission, the War Industries Board, the Shipping Board, the War Trade Board and the Treasury; during my absence Mr. Edgar Rickard, who has been associated with the Relief Commission from the beginning, to act for me as chairman of this executive committee.

2. Any programme will require an assurance of at least $200,000,000 to pay for the food and reconstruction materials necessary to be shipped from the United States, pending the restoration of trade conditions and of possible legislation providing money for definite reconstruction and credit relations to Europe. It is necessary that we should have at once an assurance of at least this sum of money under the present legislation and resources of the government. It would probably only be required over a period of from 8 to 10 months. In addition to this I have hopes of establishing some commercial credits for Belgian Banks with our banks, to take care of any programme over and above the amount outlined. In other words, to press the Belgians to use all the self help that they can find.

3. Under the present powers of the government, the Treasury is able to make advances to the Allied governments for purposes of the war, and it has, as you know, made very considerable advances to the Belgian government for the purposes of the relief and direct war expenditure. It would seem to me a right interpretation of the law for the Treasury to undertake to furnish $200,000,000 to the Belgian government and stipulate that the money is to be used for expenditures in the United States through the Relief Commission. It appears to me that the prevention of starvation and disturbances in this population is vital to the making of the status quo during armistice, and is therefore a perfectly legitimate advance under the present law. In case peace should come suddenly, in order to avoid a debacle in the relief, it seems to me necessary that the Treasury

should take a commitment to furnish this sum of money at once; otherwise, we shall have a lot of liabilities out in the United States and be entirely unable to fulfill them. I would propose that these advances should be subject to the Belgian Government finding from other governments all monies necessary to pay transportation charges on any materials shipped from here and to find monies from other quarters for all purchases made outside the United States.

4. Another feature of this matter which appeals greatly to Mr. Baruch and myself is the fact that with the armistice we will at once be closing a large number of factories on war work and if we can at once place in their hands orders for material from such sources as this, we will have contributed in a very large measure to prevent industrial difficulties in the United States, and that an assurance of such orders will be of profound value just at the present juncture.

I would be very glad indeed to have your views in the matter.

Faithfully yours,   Herbert Hoover

Dear Mr. President: Washington 9 *November 1918*

In the matter of feeding the liberated peoples of Austria, Serbia, Bulgaria, Turkey, et cetera, I have had conferences with Messrs. Hurley and Baker and our own staff and, as a result, I have to propose to you the following measures, which meet with approval on all sides:

1. That the Army should hand to us certain cargo boats at once which we will load with foods at their expense. This food will be of a character than can be used by the American Army or the Allies in any event, and will be despatched in the first instance to Bordeaux for orders.

2. In order to secure an organization to carry on the work during my own and Mr. Hurley's absence, and to co-ordinate the various branches of the government concerned, I would like your authority to set up a committee under my chairmanship and to comprise Mr. Theodore Whitmarsh of the Food Administration, who would act as my alternate when away; Mr. Julius H. Barnes of the Food Administration Cereal Division and Mr. F. S. Snyder[1] of the Food Administration Meats Division; Mr. John Beaver White of the War Trade Board; Mr. Prentiss N. Gray[2] representing the Shipping Board and someone to be selected by Mr. Baker representing the War Department; Mr. William A. Glasgow of this department to act as counsel.

3. It appears to me that it will be absolutely necessary to secure

an appropriation for the handling of this enterprise. It is entirely probable that I can make such arrangements in Europe that will permit of the sale of the food, but, in the present disorganized conditions, it will be almost hopeless to secure rapid enough implementing of credits to solve the situation and that, for some preliminary stages at least, this relief enterprise would have to revolve on advances from our government. I should also, when I arrive in Europe, ask all the Allied governments if they wish to participate in the enterprise. It appears to me with the state of mind of the well-thinking people of this country that the government could agree to appropriate $200,000,000 for the feeding of the liberated populations in Europe,—such a sum to be placed at your disposal. In the ordinary course of events, I would not think that much of this money would be lost, for, at least, obligations could be obtained from municipalities and governments for its ultimate re-payment.

It is my view that the critical moment is right now to carry over the period pending the rehabilitation of trade and that if we can worry through the next four or five months we will have solved the problem. It is not necessary for me to mention how fundamental it appears to me that this is, if we are to preserve these countries from Bolshevism and rank anarchy.

Yours faithfully,   Herbert Hoover.

TLS (WP, DLC).
   [1] Frederic Sylvester Snyder, president of Batchelder & Snyder Co., a wholesale food company of Boston; chairman of the national board of directors of the Institute of American Meat Packers; member of the U. S. Food Purchasing Board; and chief of the Division of Coordination of Purchase for the U. S. Food Administration.
   [2] Prentiss Nathaniel Gray, chief of the Marine Transportation Division of the U. S. Food Administration.

From George Creel, with Enclosure

My dear Mr. President: Washington, D. C. November 9, 1918.
   This may be of interest to you.

Respectfully,   George Creel

TLS (WP, DLC).

ENCLOSURE E[1]

Sept. 24, 1918

(This report may throw some light on the present and future policy and possible action of the Vatican. It is based on intimate conversations with high officials in the papal secretariate of state. These pretend to and apparently do represent the pontifical point of view. In connection with the Vatican's pyschological argument it may be interesting to note that generally reliable clerical circles report the Pope to have been in full pyschological accord with the President, as far as "the time and timeliness" of his reply to the recent Austrian note were concerned.)

The Pyschological Moment for Peace Should be Watched for and Seized. Reliable clerical authorities in close touch with Vatican affairs declare that the Pope is a constant and perfect pyschologist and that his mind and diplomacy reason as follows:

Peace, it is said and said truly, can come *too soon*, but it can also come *too late.* In either case the world could and would have *"The peace that is not peace." "When will the President decide to make peace?"* can be a far more vital question for humanity than was the question, *"when will the President decide to make war?"*

History is largely a study in applied pyschology. There will be a single pyschological moment when the Wilsonian peace terms can have their fullest acceptance and triumph. This pyschological moment may be almost unmixed with military factors. It can and apparently will be more largely and essentially dependent upon the anarchistic ferment and the Bolscevik tendencies in both the Central Powers and the Entente countries. Nationalistic prospects and mutual and centuries'-old jealousies and suspicions of friends and foes alike can also enter into it very, very deeply.

This ferment can naturally or artificially explode and these tendencies stretch or be stretched to the breaking point, perhaps almost in the twinkling of an eye. By such natural means as war weariness, hunger and pest,—and of the last there seems to be already a sharp indication—or by the artificial devices of politics, international finance and impulsive and indeliberate or subtle and deliberate betrayal, these things could come or be brought about.

It therefore should be the President's study to know the exact pyschological instant, suitable for America's peace, with which the Pope feels that he is in substantial agreement. Logic and prudence seem to advise that this moment be seized by Wilson, when it comes and used to its fullest possible advantage. A second's hesitation could jeopardize the Wilsonian program, in its entirely [entirety] or its greater part and throw much of Europe and in the end probably the greater part of Europe into the lawlessness and terro[r]ism of anarchy and Bolscevism.

The Pope is convinced that the American President today is the greatest, living force, standing between fighting Europe and Bolscevism, and will be so effective for a certain but not an indefinite time to come. The pyschological moment will arrive, he believes, when to use a paradox only peace—and not war—will bring about peace. On watch for this moment, the President, it is sincerely thought, should keep his hand on the pulse of the morale of Europe and the world. The moment come, quick action will not merely be most important but absolutely necessary, it would seem, or Europe will become chaos, corrupting democracy and civilization and immeasurably pushing back true progress in tragic and terrifying ways.

The germs of Bolscevism with its anti-war and drop-arms positivism are more numerous and widely spread than the world apparently imagines. The contagion—and it is a contagion—is not slow to affect ignorance, and the sections of the popular mass of the fighting countries on this side of the ocean, which are and have been affected by the germs are becoming increasingly larger. Of all these countries France seems at present to be the most free of and safe from these germs. But even here there are signs of limit to France's comparative immunity. The Pope in deep concern believes that Bolscevism can spread or be spread throughout Europe and is convinced that the spirit of the more ignorant popular mass is almost everywhere, in Europe, ripening towards it.

Writer's Memorandum: The above report complements and should be read in connection with Hearley's[2] several other reports on Vatican and clerical tendencies, which are going forward under the same cover. It is not impossible that these observations of the Vatican are affected in part, at least, by the reflections of Bolscevism in Italy, reflections which are atheistic and anti-Catholic in their nature.

T MS (WP, DLC).
    [1] The following unsigned memorandum was probably written by Charles E. Merriam.
    [2] John Hearley, Merriam's assistant.

From Harry Andrew Wheeler

Sir: Washington, D. C. November 9, 1918.

The War Service Executive Committee of the Chamber of Commerce of the United States has been in session here this week giving special consideration to questions which are coming from business interests in every direction, as to the cancellation of war contracts and the transfer from war to peace conditions. It has learned with much satisfaction of the thought which is being given to this problem and the plans you have in mind for maintaining centralized control, during the period of readjustment.

As you are doubtless aware, the cancellation of contracts by some government agencies during the last ten days has caused a great deal of apprehension and disturbance, the extent of which, fortunately, has not attracted public attention because the war news has so greatly overshadowed it. The developments incident to the cancellations referred to indicate the difficulties we will have to face unless the transition is gradual and the vast labor and financial interests involved are most carefully safeguarded. The stoppage of work in the small number of instances where steps have already been taken is causing uneasiness among the banks which in almost every case are extending credit to the contractors, and is likewise affecting the credit of large numbers of sub-contractors who are supplying materials to the principals.

The alarm apparent in other industries is, however, the most serious incident of the matter as indicated by the information reaching our Committee from various business interests. The statements of plans proposed to deal with these difficulties now being made public will have a tendency to allay this apprehension, but our Committee desires to suggest the advantage of the earliest possible announcement of a comprehensive scheme for meeting the emergency and preventing the possibility of panic.

In creating new machinery, or adjusting that now in existence, full consideration will no doubt be given to the necessity of harmonizing the policies of the various departments engaged in war work in their action on the cancellation of contracts and the matters affected thereby.

It seems to us that it is possible to work out certain common principles which should obtain in all government departments in affecting settlements on contracts now to be stopped and adjusting them on a fair basis. We realize, of course, that no policy can be fixed which will apply in all cases. Nevertheless, we believe that the principles recognized in all departments should be consistent so far as possible. If one bureau, or department, follows its own ideas and another pursues a different course it seems to us that it will lead to endless controversy and confusion. For this reason we believe the agencies set up in the various bureaus and departments to deal with the question should be controlled by some common authority in order to prevent great difficulty.

Pending the development of an adequate organization, we earnestly hope that a clearance committee may be appointed at once to which will be referred all proposals to cancel contracts, with instructions to all departments that cancellations shall not be made without the approval of this committee, in order that raw materials which will be released by the stoppage of war production may be allocated to industries able to use them immediately for peace-time needs. We are of the opinion that war contracts should not be canceled until provision is made for the absorption of these raw materials.

Another serious situation is that involving the protection of values in stocks of raw materials on hand, which a very large number of manufacturers engaged on government work purchased at the high prices which have prevailed and are now carrying. If, through sudden cancellations, these stocks are now freed and no arrangement is made for their utilization in some other direction, there is likely to be a very great decline in prices temporarily at least, until demands in other directions assert themselves.

We are sure from the statements already made public that most of these matters are receiving earnest consideration, but the inquiries made of our Committee have been so general and insistent that by direction of the Committee I am venturing to convey to you thoughts concerning some phases of the problem which are causing general concern among business men just now.

Very truly yours,   Harry A. Wheeler

TLS (WP, DLC).

From Grant Squires[1]

My dear Mr. President: New York. November 9th 1918.

You spoke with a rare and true insight into the near future, when you predicted to me a few weeks ago,[2] of the dangers of Bolshevikism, likely to show themselves in this Country as well as abroad.

Agreeably to your permission to send to you direct any evidence of this which I might acquire along these lines for your information, I am enclosing herewith an advance copy of a printed issue of "The Labor Defender" which is in "dummy" form, showing closely how it will appear next Wednesday or Thursday. It bears date, November 15, and points the way to violence on the part of its readers from the front page and throughout.[3] Although less than four months old, it circulates all over the country.

Tomorrow, I am promised the names of a number of preachers of violence and disorder now in our midst, which is the offering of a Russian who has lately come to live in this country and has conceived the greatest admiration of the way in which you are handling problems affecting the laboring people. Of course, the Bureau of the War Department, with which you know I have been acting since the war began, will report through the usual channels what it learns and what it does, yet I deemed it in accord with your wishes that I send you this direct. The enclosure has not been off the press more than a few hours.

Would you be willing to do me a favor? Two months ago, I was asked by my chief here to apply for a commission as Captain in the Army. I did so, and all the requisites complied with over a month ago, but the commission still lies unacted upon in the Adjutant General's office, which is overwhelmed doubtless with more important matters. I should naturally prefer the commission issue before the conclusion of an armistice, so am turning to you for any aid to expedite it you may be willing to extend.

I remain,   Faithfully yours,   Grant Squires

TLS (WP, DLC).

[1] Lawyer of New York, at this time involved in counterintelligence work in the New York office of the Military Intelligence Division of the United States Army. Squires had become acquainted with Wilson through his handling of the interest payments on the mortgages on properties in the Bronx which Wilson had bought from Mary Allen Hulbert in 1915 (about which see Horace H. Clark to WW, July 28 and August 6, 1915, Vol. 34).

[2] At the White House on October 16.

[3] *The Labor Defender*, I (Nov. 15, 1918). This periodical was published by the Industrial Workers of the World. The cover illustration (p. 1) of this issue carried the caption "Labor's Crucifixion" and depicted a Christlike figure nailed to a cross, with an elegantly gowned woman and a little fat man with a money bag for a stomach, who presumably represented the exploiting classes, peering up at the martyr. The contents of the sixteen-page issue consisted of brief articles or news items, each of which was written from a militantly socialistic point of view. Typical headlines were "The Capitalist vs. Eugene Debs," "American Bolsheviks Get Twenty Years," "General Strike to Free Mooney," and "Outlawing the Parasite." Other items hailed various actions of the Bolshevik regime in Russia and other radical organizations in the United States and elsewhere.

From Jessie Woodrow Wilson Sayre

Dearest, dearest Father,   [New York] Nov. 9, 1918

How the time runs on. It seems only yesterday that Frank and I went with Margaret to see "Tea for three" and then in a perfectly casual and unemotional sort of way rolled down to the quiet deserted dock at about midnight and deposited Margaret in the Davids' care. It was impossible to realize that she was sailing for Europe for there were no signs of departure; it didn't even look like a ship, some how, at that time of night. And I was planning to write you all about it at once! And now she has landed and begun her career and still I haven't told you about her going!

So many exciting things have happened in between, too. It is impossible to describe New York when the fake news[1] struck here, and I saw only this comparatively quiet corner of it up here. Those who went down town could hardly get back or move at all, and I didn't try to join them!

All runs smoothly with us in our airy corner. Colds, yes, but no signs of the dreaded influenza and this heavenly weather makes us feel most serene and happy—if only those wretched elections were not so. I can't bear to think of the dastardly trouble they will make you and how they may prevent our clinching and making sure of all we have fought for. Oh well I can't bear to talk about it.

We have had a kind of transient hotel since we saw you but now that we have a guest whom we hope may stay a while we shall expect to settle down a bit.

We took dinner with Mrs. Page and Katherine last week. Mr. Page has only just recovered consciousness for the first time except during fleeting moments, for the last six weeks.

Wardlaw Miles of Princeton[2] has been wounded, one leg gone. He is a Captain and made a private carry him on his back till a rather critical action was completed. Several Princeton people expressed a wish that old Madame Miles,[3] one of your most ardent and devoted admirers and supporters might have a little note from you. I wouldn't promise to even let you know so as to leave you quite free to do so or not.[4]

Catherine[5] is proud and happy over him, and glad he is able to come home again. She is a real soldier's daughter.[6]

Frank and I spent our engagement anniversary in Princeton with the Vreelands. We saw only Adeline Scott and Ruth Hall[7] and their babies and a few of the old friends of the Vreeland circle. It was perfect weather and loads of fun. I had not been there since our wedding.

What a lot of changes. The eating hall,[8] the park and so many more homes. The military goings on made it all seem very unfamiliar and therefore not as sad as it might be.

Dearest Father, a whole heartful of love for you and dear Edith from us both.   Your devoted daughter   Jessie.

ALS (WC, NjP).

[1] The false Armistice, about which see S. Gompers to WW, Nov. 7, 1918, n. 1, Vol. 51.

[2] Capt. Louis Wardlaw Miles, formerly Instructor and Preceptor in English at Princeton University. He had been wounded in an action near the Aisne-Marne Canal in France on September 14 and was later awarded the Congressional Medal of Honor for his heroism on that occasion.

[3] Jeanie Wardlaw (Mrs. Francis Turquand) Miles.

[4] There is nothing in WP, DLC, to indicate that Wilson wrote to her.

[5] Katharine Wistar Stockton (Mrs. Louis Wardlaw) Miles.

[6] She was the daughter of the late Col. Samuel Witham Stockton of Princeton, who had served with distinction in the Civil War.

[7] That is, Ruth Preble Hall Smith.

[8] Madison Hall, erected in 1916.

A Memorandum by Joseph Patrick Tumulty

THINGS TO BE ATTENDED TO AT ONCE.

9 November 1918.

PROGRAM FOR 1920.

1st. SUFFRAGE.

The votes of Senator Shields of Tennessee; Senator Pollak of South Carolina and Senator Gay[1] of Louisville will determine this question. The policy of the Democratic Party should be to put it over now and thus obtain the credit for it. If we wait, the Republicans will surely put it over in March and we will have the name of defeating it. Our program should be as follows.

The President should send for Senators Shields, Pollak and Gay at once and tell them, as southerners that they ought to help to consummate this thing. The President should speak to them as a Southerner who fears the effect upon the South of a refusal to help in this great progressive movement. The important thing is speed in this matter. If, after talking to the senators, the President will let it be known, unofficially, that these gentlemen would vote our way, through carefully handled publicity we could get this impression to the country, without embarrassment to the senators and then Key Pittman, in charge of suffrage, should be advised of the progress we are making in the matter, so that he may make a statement and force an early vote.

The President should also send for Senators Simmons, Overman and Martin and urge them to support him or at least, to urge Senator Martin not to block its passage to [in] the Senate, as leader of the Democratic majority.

In the matter of the selection of a minority leader. There is no disputing the fact that one of the issues in the campaign just closed, was Claude Kitchin. All over the country, the argument used was that a vote for the Democratic candidates was a vote in support of Kitchin and everything for which he stood, viz.:

1st. Opposition to the war, which Kitchin voted against;
2d. Opposition to conscription;
3d. Opposition to appropriations for a large navy;
4th. Harrassing business by unjust tax legislation;
5th. *Antagonizing the newspapers and magazine[s] by unjust charges for mailing second class mail matter, etc.*

I think that the President, for the sake of the south and the Democratic Party's future, has got to throw down the gauntlet to

Kitchin and oppose his selection as leader. If Kitchin be selected, his selection will become a national issue in 1920. The President ought to let it be known now, unofficially, that he is opposed to Kitchin and we should be asked to line up our friends against him.

Senators Pittman and Gerry, with reference to newspapers and magazines, should confer at once with Senator Simmons, Burleson and the President. If we do not straighten this matter out, the Republicans will do it for us. The Postmaster General ought to be told just what the situation is. Mr. Tumulty will see Senators Sommons [Simmons] and McKeller.

In the matter of Labor. Dinsmore,[2] of the Labor Board, should be sent for and told about the manipulation by the Republicans in the various states.

Suffrage;
Publicity.

Unofficial committee, composed of Pittman, Bob Wooley, Hollister, Jameson, Gerry, Ferris and Mr. Tumulty to meet every week. Outline what should be discussed. Our weaknesses; our strength with labor; foreign vote; business vote; finances. President's attitude on certain questions. Trips by President, to be in closer touch with the people. Consider the question of the establishment of a foreign bureau; woman's bureau; labor bureau; speakers' bureau. Possible trip of President to _____. Prepare for ovation when he returns; trip out west. President's message in December; what it should contain on reconstruction. Efforts of the Democrats in the Senate should be given to bringing about a split in the Republican Party. Attacks on Penrose, as Chairman of Finance Committee, should be begun. Every attack we make in the Senate should have a definite purpose. Consider appointment of a special committee to prepare data for congressmen and senators.

Prepare a letter to the President, showing the real situation throughout the country; discuss our weaknesses and our strength. Call attention to: 1st. The use of money in campaigns; 2d. The use of Publicity; 3d. The subtle character of the campaign carried on by the Republicans.

Our weakness in various states—like Kansas, New Jersey, Illinois, Indiana, Pennsylvania; complaints and criticisms directed against various departments—for instance, the Post Office Department; the War Department; Agricultural Department. Lack of publicity with reference to the work being done by farmers; the necessity for the President getting out more among the people; lack of personal contact; impression the President is a great intellectual machine. The great vote in New York City showed the virtue of public appearance by the President and letting the people see him personally. Necessity for a trip out west and New England, especially after the results of the peace conference. Discussion by the President, of the plans for reconstruction. "We are living in a new world." Old slogans are being cast aside. Party catch-words are no longer to be considered. Kitchin, Dent and Clark are great liabilities. Too much southern domination. Failure to fix the price of cotton. *We must fight Kitchin. We must fix the price of cotton.*

T MS (J. P. Tumulty Papers, DLC).
   [1] Edward James Gay of Louisiana, not Louisville, who had been elected to fill the vacancy created by the death of Robert F. Broussard.
   [2] John B. Densmore, director general of the United States Employment Service.

Two Telegrams from Edward Mandell House

[Paris, Nov. 10, 1918]

[9.] I would suggest that when the Armistice is signed that you read the terms to Congress and use the occasion to give another message to the world. You have the right to assume that the two great features of the armistice are the defeat of German military imperialism and the acceptance by the Allied powers of the peace the world has longed for. Steadying note seems to me necessary at this time. A word of warning, a word of hope should be said. The world is in ferment, civilization itself is trembling in the balance.

10. In view of the Republican resentment against Governor McCall's attitude in the elections[1] and in anticipation of a hostile Senate would it not be well to increase the British [membership of the] delegation [delegates] and include another Republican of standing and influence of Root? In the event that for any reason you should not find possible to name any members of cabinet other than Lansing may I suggest Sharp as a desirable delegate.

T transcript of WWsh decode (WP, DLC).
   [1] Samuel Walker McCall, although a Republican, had consistently supported Wilson's war policies.

To Edward Mandell House

To House. XII.   The White House [Nov. 10, 1918].

With reference to the peace conference will it not be wise and necessary to postpone it until there are governments in Germany and Austria-Hungary which can enter into binding agreements? I feel obliged not to leave before delivering my annual message to the Congress on the second of December. I could leave immediately after that and hope that it will be possible to fix the date of meeting accordingly. Would a preliminary visit to England be wise if I could not visit Italy also beforehand? Nelson Page will tell you how busy the English propagandists are destroying our prestige and building up their own in Italy.

Referring to your number 66,[1] our judgment corresponds with yours. Hoover is coming over immediately to discuss the matter and propose our method of handling it.

Referring to your number 51[2] the plan of secret codes is being worked out between the Departments of State and Navy.

Referring to your number eight,[3] please express to the French Prime Minister my deep pleasure and great encouragement. He may rest assured that we will not take advantage of his generous promise unreasonably and I am sure that between us we can serve the world in the noblest way.

Do not think it would be wise to increase delegation to seven. That would involve similar increase in other delegations. Better to make another Republican selection.

WWT telegram (WP, DLC).
    [1] EMH to WW, Nov. 8, 1918 (second telegram of that date), Vol. 51.
    [2] EMH to RL, Nov. 5, 1918, T telegram (WP, DLC).
    [3] EMH to WW, Nov. 9, 1918 (first telegram of that date).

Five Telegrams from Edward Mandell House

Paris Nov 10, 1918

Number 76, Secret for the President. Your number 24,[1] November 9, 4 pm. As soon as Armistice is signed I will advise you in a message which will have priority over all others. I will inform you whether terms as heretofore cabled you are the same as those finally signed. If there are minor changes I will send these in the same cable. If changes are considerable I will send them in following cable. I will advise you the time when the terms of the Armistice will be made public in Europe and you can make terms public in the United States in advance thereof provided United States censor does not permit any mention of publication of terms to leave United States before publication here.   Edward House.

    [1] It is missing in all collections.

Paris Nov 10, 1918

Number 82. Secret for the President. Following has just been sent me by Clemenceau:

"I learn from Basle that a telegram from Berlin gives the conditions of the Armistice. If I receive them this evening as it appears to me certain, I will give them to the Press and invite you to do likewise. If contrary to our anticipations the text does not arrive until tomorrow morning I will post it up immediately in the Chamber of Deputies and in the Senate because a direct communication with Parliament seems to me to be useless if I do not know either that the Armistice has been signed or has been refused." I understand this to mean that if it appears that Germany has published the terms of the Armistice Clemenceau intends to publish them also. If Germany has not published them he will after the expiration of the time set for the signing of the Armistice, that is, eleven o'clock Monday morning, go before Parliament and read the terms announcing at the same time either, one, that Germany has signed the Armistice or two, that she has refused to sign the Armistice.

Edward House.

Paris, Nov. 10, [1918]

Number 83. Secret for the President.

The following has just been received by me from Colonel Mott:[1]

"The German Government has announced by wireless that they accept the terms of the armistice. The signing of the armistice as far as we know has not taken place. No information has yet come from Marshal Foch that any paper has been signed."

Edward House

[1] That is, Thomas Bentley Mott.

[Paris, Nov. 10, 1918]

No. 11. In view of the enormous claims which the French [and Belgian Governments] will make on Germany I think we should get our engineers to make an approximate estimate for our guidance. If you have any reason [If you approve] I can have this begun at once.

[Paris, Nov. 10, 1918]

No. 12. Lord Curzon tells me that by now you should have received a letter written by him some two weeks ago[1] in behalf of Oxford University in which they offer you the Department [sic] degree of D.C.L. and asking you to deliver the Romanes (?) lecture when it is conferred upon you. He assures me you will have the warmest welcome both in England and on this occasion [at Oxford].

He suggests that you might be interested in making democracy your theme and give [giving] your interpretation of what the world might hope for under its benign influence when properly directed. Politics of a conventionalized [controversial] nature are frowned upon.

T telegrams (WP, DLC).
  ¹ Earl Curzon of Kedleston to WW, Nov. 3, 1918, ALS (WP, DLC). Curzon was Chancellor of the University of Oxford.

From Albert Sidney Burleson, with Enclosures

My dear Mr. President,   The White House [c. Nov. 10, 1918].

I think you should see the attached papers. Mr. Tumulty can explain the situation as it presents itself at this time.
                                        Faithfully   Burleson

ALS (WP, DLC).

E N C L O S U R E   I

NIGHT LETTER   Raleigh, N. C., October 25, 1918.

Hon. William H. Taft, President,
League to Enforce Peace,
Yale University,
New Haven, Connecticut.

The repeated assaults of Mr. Roosevelt on the basic principles of the League to Enforce Peace call for a vigorous reply from you as President of the League if our organization is expected to live. Every utterance of Mr. Roosevelt on the subject would have fitted well the mouth of the Kaiser five years ago. In a recent speech Mr. Roosevelt said that we should so develop our military powers that no nation would dare to look cross-eyed at the United States. This is the very militarism against which the conscience of the world is today in arms. It would be Potsdamism enthroned at Washington. In a recent editorial in the Kansas City Star Mr. Roosevelt endeavors to relegate the League to Enforce Peace to the innocuous position of a mollycoddle motto and insists that when the real affairs of nations are to be settled a gun still is, and of right ought to be God. Today in a telegram to Washington he makes war on the fourteen articles of peace enumerated by the President before Congress in January, and thereafter elaborated at Mt. Vernon on July 4th, and in New York on September 27th. When the President of the United States proclaimed these principles and conditions of peace they

were treated with ill-concealed contempt by the Imperial Government of Germany, but were hailed with joy by all the peoples of
our Allies. Time and again these wise and just principles have been
endorsed by our Allies until they have come to be regarded as a
new Magna Charta for the whole world. But as victory comes to
our arms in the field and when it is perfectly plain that the German
people will take their Government into their own hands, or that our
armed forces will grind to powder the military masters of Germany,
Mr. Roosevelt comes forward and asseverates that the American
people have never spoken, and that the now world famous fourteen
articles should be treated as scraps of paper, and that only ham-
mering of guns should be heard when we come to settle the peace
of the world for all time. This is Prussianism to the bone. I would
undertake to reply to Mr. Roosevelt but I endeavor to retain the
sense of proportion, and this advises me that you, and not myself,
are the proper person to defend the life of the League. You are its
President, and as Chairman of the North Carolina Division, I urge
you to telegraph to Washington your withering condemnation of
the utterances of Mr. Roosevelt, and call upon Congress to stand
solidly behind the President in his high and Holy purpose to make
the League of Nations the most vital part of the great treaty that
will be written when the German people, having swept clean their
own house, shall accept the terms and conditions of peace that
have already been dictated or when military masters of Germany
shall have been forced into complete and unconditional surrender.

T. W. Bickett,
Governor and
Chairman of the N. C. Division of the
League to Enforce Peace.

TC telegram (WP, DLC).

E N C L O S U R E   I I

William Howard Taft to Thomas Walter Bickett

My dear Governor: Washington, D. C. October 30th, 1918.

I have your telegram and I think I ought to answer it, though
not for publication unless you think it necessary. The truth is that
the President does not favor our League to Enforce Peace. He told
President Lowell, of Harvard, and me that fact last March.[1] The
truth is that Mr. Roosevelt has come around to favoring the League
to Enforce Peace, provided it does not mean universal disarmament.
I find myself in general agreement with Mr. Roosevelt on this

subject, indeed more than I would with President Wilson, who having announced his complete acquiescence in the principles of the League advised us in the conversation to which I referred that he had changed his mind. So far as Mr. Roosevelt's opinion is concerned on the fourteen points of January 8th, I am largely in sympathy with him. I think those fourteen points cannot be made the safe basis of a treaty of peace. They are too vague and indefinite. They would give rise to as many disputes as the present war. They do not embrace all that our Allies have the right to demand and they embrace some things that our Allies would not concede. Mr. Wilson has not consulted our Allies as he should. He refuses to call them Allies. For that reason I am sincerely hopeful that a Republican Congress will be returned and an answer given to his unrepublican and undemocratic appeal for uncontrolled and despotic power during the life of the next Congress. His reflection on the Republican minority is most unjust.

Now my dear Governor these are my personal opinions. Therefore I did not answer your telegram and I am not quite sure whether you expected an answer. Whether it was not in the sending of the telegram that the importance lay.[2] You are at liberty to publish this if you choose, but I don't insist on it.

Sincerely yours,   Wm. H. Taft.

TCL (WP, DLC).
  [1] See the memorandum by W. H. Taft printed at March 29, 1918, Vol. 47.
  [2] This sentence *sic*.

E N C L O S U R E   I I I

Thomas Walter Bickett to William Howard Taft

My dear Mr. Taft: Raleigh November 2nd, 1918.

I thank you for your very kind and courteous letter of the 30th of October in reply to my telegram of recent date.

I confess that the letter comes to me as a distinct surprise, for prior to its reception I would have gone on the witness stand and testified that the greatest enemy of the League to Enforce Peace is Mr. Roosevelt, based upon his editorial of October 16th of this year in the Kansas City Star, and I would have further testified on oath that the greatest friend of the League to Enforce Peace is Mr. Wilson, based upon his New York speech of September 27th. In the recent discussion of the Fourteen Articles I have not seen any intimation that Mr. Wilson intended to recede from the position that he took in his New York speech, in which he said he proposed to form a league of nations as part and parcel of the treaty of peace.

To my mind this is the vital question, for unless the league of nations is made a part of the treaty then, in my opinion, it will be relegated for the next ten years to academic discussions on Chatauqua platforms and in high school debating societies.

Of course, I can understand how differences may exist as to just how far we should go, but if we want to get anywhere it seems to me that the thing to do is to line up behind the President. The processes of disarmament will necessarily be slow, but that is the ultimate end sought. As I understand it, the purposes of our League is to put war out of business, and you cannot do that with nations armed to their teeth. The one reason for the existing war is the fact that Germany was armed. If she had not been armed she would not have dreamed of fighting. You cannot train a nation of men to fight without their fighting, and it is my opinion that we ought to go just as far towards disarmament as practical considerations will admit. Of course it cannot be done in a day nor in a generation, but we can set that up as the ultimate goal. In my opinion the one great work before this century is to make the public conscience as sensitive as that of the individual, and to compel nations to observe in their dealings with each other the principles of the Ten Commandments and the Sermon on the Mount. I may do him an injustice but, judging from his public utterances, Mr. Roosevelt is today closer kin to the Kaiser than any other living man.

You will pardon me for adding that, with the profoundest respect for your opinion, I find myself in utter disagreement with Mr. Roosevelt, and I think his attack upon Mr. Wilson is born of the same jealous selfishness as his attack upon you when you were nominated for president the second time in Chicago.

With much respect, I beg to remain,

Sincerely yours,   T. W. Bickett

TCL (WP, DLC).

From Mary Owen Graham

My dear Mr. Wilson,   Raleigh, North Carolina Nov. 10, 1918.

Your note,[1] received several days ago with your words of appreciation of my brother's friendship and of his work, is greatly valued.

I feel that the world is too full of sorrow to put my individual sorrow upon it. Your words of sympathy hearten me for the task which is before me.

I know that the epoch-making and inspirational work you are doing stimulated my brother in many of his endeavors.

How strange it is that avenues of friendship and of understanding open up between families of succeeding generations. Your father was the honored pastor of my father and mother[2] in Wilmington, N. C., and other near & dear kinspeople his church officers and friends.

We think down here that you, Mr. Wilson, have "come to the kingdom for such a time as this."

May you be blessed and cheered in your endeavors.

With highest regards,

Cordially & sincerely yours,   Mary Owen Graham.

ALS (WP, DLC).
  [1] WW to Mary O. Graham, Oct. 29, 1918, Vol. 51.
  [2] Archibald Graham and Eliza Owen Barry Graham.

From Andrew Carnegie

Dear Mr President   New York November 10th 1918.

Now that the world war seems to be practically at an end I cannot refrain from sending you my heartfelt congrat[ulat]ions upon the great share you have had in bringing about its successful conclusions.

The Palace of Peace at the Hague would, I think, be the fitting place for dispassionate discussion regarding the destiny of the conquered nations and I hope your influence may be exerted in that direction.

Mrs Carnegie[1] rejoices with me in the realization of your ideals and we both send our affectionate regards.

Yours ever   Andrew Carnegie

ALS (WP, DLC).
  [1] That is, Louise Whitfield Carnegie.

From the Diary of Josephus Daniels

November Sunday 10 1918

Telegram came from Solf, Minister of Foreign Affairs, who said "We are forced to accept armistice," but looked to President Wilson to prevent millions from starving. Objected to blockade provision because it would deny opportunity to secure food.[1] Took it to Lansing who thought it ought not to be given out

Went to White House. WW said House had introduced resolution in Austrian matter that allies would co-operate to secure food for people of conquered country. WW is writing message & expects to appear before Congress to announce result when armistice is signed. Will touch upon food also. Must first of all support our soldiers.

Food must go to prevent bolshevikism & anarchy & help preserve the people. Danger of no government is call for our help

Hw bound diary (J. Daniels Papers, DLC).
    ¹ The enclosure with RL to WW, Nov. 13, 1918, TLS (WP, DLC).

Four Telegrams from Edward Mandell House

Paris Nov 11, 1918

Number 85, November 11, 3 am. Secret for the President. Mr. Clemenceau has just communicated to me the following reply [radio] sent by the German Government to the plenipotentiaries "The Supreme Command of the German Army to the Plenipotentiaries at the High Command of the Allies. The German Government communicates to the Supreme Command of the Army the following for Secretary of State Erzberger.¹ Your Excellency has full power to sign an Armistice. Kindly make the following declaration in your process verbal. The German Government will undertake the execution of the conditions laid down with all its force but the undersigned consider it their duty to point out that the execution of certain points of the conditions will introduce famine into that part of Germany which is not to be occupied. The abandonment of all the stores of provisions in the regions to be evacuated which were destined for the feeding of troops, the curtailment of the means of operating the transport service taking place at the same time as the limitation of transport service, the blockade remaining in force would render revictualling impossible as well as any organization for its distribution. The undersigned consequently ask for power to negotiate any modification of the points in question susceptible of rendering revictualling possible. The Supreme Command of the German Army charges General Von Winterfeld to notify it of the signature of the Armistice in referring to the points communicated this afternoon. The German Government to the German Plenipotentiaries at the High Command of the Allies. The German Government accepts the conditions of the Armistice which have been submitted to it the eighth of November. Signed the Chancellor of the Empire. Please acknowledge receipt." Mr. Clemenceau informs me at the same time that he believes that we should consider this signature good in accepting the marginal note regarding revictualling. I have replied to Mr. Clemenceau that I entirely agree with him.   Edward House.

¹ Matthias Erzberger had been named Secretary of State without Portfolio on October 4. Prince Max placed him in charge of propaganda activities on October 21. He was appointed Armistice Commissioner on November 6. See Klaus Epstein, *Matthias Erzberger and the Dilemma of German Democracy* (Princeton, N. J., 1959), pp. 261-71.

Paris, November 11, 1918.

Number 86, November 11, 6 a.m. Secret for the President. Armistice signed five o'clock this morning. Hostilities to cease eleven a.m. today. We have no information as yet as to whether terms were in any way changed but we shall know definitely concerning this within three hours and will promptly cable.

Edward House.

Paris, November 11, 1918.

Number 87, November 11, 8 a.m. Secret for The President. Clemenceau has just now eight a.m. Greenwich mean time sent me word that the armistice has been signed and he has requested that this be kept secret until four o'clock this [Monday] afternoon Greenwich mean time when he will appear before the Chamber and announce the signing of the armistice and read *them* there [the terms thereof]. If you have already announced that armistice has been signed I earnestly request [that] our censor be instructed under no circumstances to permit any news of this character to leave the United States until after announcement is made here.

Edward House.

T telegrams (WP, DLC).

[Paris, Nov. 11, 1918]

[No. 13] Autocracy is dead. Advance [Long live] democracy and its immortal leader. In this great hour my heart goes out to you in pride, admiration and love.   Edward House

EBWhw and WWhw decode (WP, DLC).

A Statement

The White House [c. Nov. 11, 1918]

A supreme moment of history has come. The eyes of the people have been opened and they see. The hand of God is laid upon the nations. He will show them favour, I devoutly believe, only if they rise to the clear heights of His own justice and mercy.

Woodrow Wilson

WWhw MS (Waters-Butterfield Coll., NN).

From the Diary of Henry Fountain Ashurst

November 11, 1918.

Senate Sergeant-at-arms 'phoned me the President would address the two Houses in joint session this day.

The Senators led by the Vice-President went to the House. At one pm President Wilson appeared and shook hands with Vice-President Marshall and with Speaker Clark. The galleries were filled and many celebrities occupied seats. The faces of Lansing, Sec. of State, McAdoo of Treasury, Baker of War and Daniels of Navy, beamed, whilst Lane, Sec. of Interior, sat an unreadable sphinx. The Chief Justice of the United States accompanied by the Associate Judges sat in a semi-circle around the rostrum where the President stood. Hon. Charles Evans Hughes, former Governor of New York, former Associate Justice of the Supreme Court and lately Republican nominee for President, led the applause. Senator La Follette who usually remains quiet joined in the applause. This dauntless little giant from Wisconsin, this man of keen intellect and phenomenal industry has borne with much fortitude the insults and the lampoons which his attitude toward the War brought him.

The President used but few words by way of preface, and at once read the Terms of the Armistice, signed by Germany; he had read but a few sentences, when out rolled the statement that Alsace-Lorraine must be evacuated. The pent-up emotions of his auditors whose nerves were at high tension, then broke loose. Tumultuous shouts seemed to rive the stained-glass roof; the portraits of Washington and LaFayette to the right and left respectively of the President, seemed to smile benignantly.

The President read the message (which took 30 minutes) without rhetorical effort, dramatic pose or note of triumph. "The war thus comes to an end" was the only sentence he emphasized.

After the joint session my wife and I entertained the Ambassador of France and Madame Jusserand at lunch at the Senate Restaurant and the brilliant diplomat wept from joy.

T MS (AzU).

An Address to a Joint Session of Congress

Speaking Copy,—11 Nov., 1918.

Gentlemen of the Congress: In these anxious times of rapid and stupendous change it will in some degree lighten my sense of responsibility to perform in person the duty of communicating to you some of the larger circumstances of the situation with which it is necessary to deal.

The German authorities who have, at the invitation of the Supreme War Council, been in communication with Marshal Foch have accepted and signed the terms of armistice which he was authorized and instructed to communicate to them. Those terms are as follows:

I. Military Clauses on Western Front.

One. Cessation of operations by land and in the air six hours after the signature of the armistice.

Two. Immediate evacuation of invaded countries: Belgium, France, Alsace Lorraine, Luxemburg, so ordered as to be completed within fourteen days from the signature of the armistice. German troops which have not left the above mentioned territories within the period fixed will become prisoners of war. Occupation by the Allied and United States forces jointly will keep pace with evacuation in these areas. All movements of evacuation and occupation will be regulated in accordance with a note annexed to the stated terms.[1]

Three. Repatriation beginning at once and to be completed within fourteen days of all inhabitants of the countries above mentioned, including hostages and persons under trial or convicted.

Four. Surrender in good condition by the German armies of the following equipment: Five thousand guns (two thousand five hundred heavy, two thousand five hundred field), thirty thousand machine guns; three thousand minenwerfer;[2] two thousand aeroplanes (fighters, bombers—firstly D; Seventy-threes and night bombing machines.) The above to be delivered in Simmstu [situ] to the allies and United States troops in accordance with the detailed conditions laid down in the annexed note.

Evacuation by the German armies of the countries on the left bank of the Rhine. These countries on the left bank of the Rhine shall be administered by the local authorities under the control of the allied and United States armies of occupation. The occupation of these territories will be determined by allied and United States garrisons holding the principal crossings of the Rhine, Mayenee [Mainz], Coblenz, Cologne, together with bridgeheads at these points in thirty kilometer radius on the right bank and by garrisons similarly holding the strategic points of the regions. A neutral zone shall be reserved on the right of the Rhine between the stream and a line drawn parallel to it forty kilometers to the east from the frontier of Holland to the parallel of Gernsheim and as far as practicable a distance of thirty kilometers from the east of stream from this parallel upon Swiss frontier. Evacuation by the enemy of the

---

[1] The "annexures" to the Armistice agreement were conveyed in EMH to WW, No. 97, Nov. 12, 1918, T telegram (WP, DLC).
[2] That is, trench mortars.

Rhine lands shall be so ordered as to be completed within a further period of eleven days, in all nineteen days after the signature of the armistice. All movements of evacuation and occupation will be regulated according to the note annexed.

Six. In all territory evacuated by the enemy there shall be no evacuation of inhabitants; no damage or harm shall be done to the persons or property of the inhabitants. No destruction of any kind to be committed. Military establishments of all kinds shall be delivered intact as well as military stores of food, munitions, equipment not removed during the periods fixed for evacuation. Stores of food of all kinds for the civil population, cattle, etc., shall be left in situ. Industrial establishments shall not be impaired in any way and their personnel shall not be moved. Roads and means of communication of every kind, railroad, waterways, main roads, bridges, telegraphs, telephones, shall be in no manner impaired.

Seven. All civil and military personnel at present employed on them shall remain. Five thousand locomotives, fifty thousand wagons and ten thousand motor lorries in good working order with all necessary spare parts and fittings shall be delivered to the Associated Powers within the period fixed for the evacuation of Belgium and Luxemburg. The railways of Alsace-Lorraine shall be handed over within the same period, together with all pre-war personnel and material. Further material necessary for the working of railways in the country on the left bank of the Rhine shall be left *in situ*. All stores of coal and material for the up-keep of permanent ways, signals and repair shops left entire *in situ* and kept in an efficient state by Germany during the whole period of armistice. All barges taken from the allies shall be restored to them. A note appended regulates the details of these measures.

Eight. The German command shall be responsible for revealing all mines or delay acting fuses disposed on territory evacuated by the German troops and shall assist in their discovery and destruction. The German command shall also reveal all destructive measures that may have been taken (such as poisoning or polluting of springs, wells, etc.,) under penalty of reprisals.

Nine. The right of requisition shall be exercised by the Allied and the United States armies in all occupied territory. The up-keep of the troops of occupation in the Rhine land (excluding Alsace Lorraine) shall be charged to the German Government.

Ten. An immediate repatriation without reciprocity according to detailed conditions which shall be fixed, of all Allied and United States prisoners of war. The Allied Powers and the United States shall be able to dispose of these prisoners as they wish.

Eleven. Sick and wounded who cannot be removed from evacuated territory will be cared for by German personnel who will be left on the spot with the medical material required.

II. Disposition Relative to the Eastern Frontiers of Germany.

Twelve. All German troops at present in any territory which before the war belonged to Russia, Roumania or Turkey shall withdraw within the frontiers of Germany as they existed on August first, 1914.

Thirteen. Evacuation by German troops to begin at once and all German instructors, prisoners, and civilian as well as military agents, now on the territory of Russia (as defined before 1914) to be recalled.

Fourteen. German troops to cease at once all requisitions and seizures and any other undertaking with a view to obtaining supplies intended for Germany in Roumania and Russia (as defined on August 1, 1914).

Fifteen. Abandonment of the treaties of Bucharest and Brest-Litovsk and of the supplementary treaties.

Sixteen. The allies shall have free access to the territories evacuated by the Germans on their eastern frontier either through Danzig or by the Vistula in order to convey supplies to the populations of those territories or for any other purpose.

III. Clause Concerning East Africa.

Seventeen. Unconditional capitulation of all German forces operating in East Africa within one month.

IV. General Clauses.

Eighteen. Repatriation, without reciprocity, within a maximum period of one month, in accordance with detailed conditions hereafter to be fixed, of all civilians interned or deported who may be citizens of other Allied or Associated States than those mentioned in clause three, paragraph nineteen, with the reservation that any future claims and demands of the Allies and the United States of America remain unaffected.

Nineteen. The following financial conditions are required: Reparation for damage done. While such armistice lasts no public securities shall be removed by the enemy which can serve as a pledge to the allies for the recovery or repatriation for war losses. Immediate restitution of the cash deposit, in the National Bank of Belgium, and in general immediate return of all documents, specie, stock, shares, paper money together with plant for the issue thereof, touching public or private interests in the invaded countries. Restitution of the Russian and Roumanian gold yielded to Germany or taken by that power. This gold to be delivered in trust to the allies until the signature of peace.

V. Naval Conditions.

Twenty. Immediate cessation of all hostilities at sea and definite information to be given as to the location and movements of all German ships. Notification to be given to neutrals that freedom of navigation in all territorial waters is given to the naval and mercantile marines of the Allied and Associated Powers, all questions of neutrality being waived.

Twenty-one. All naval and mercantile marine prisoners of war of the Allied and Associated Powers in German hands to be returned without reciprocity.

Twenty-two. Surrender to the Allies and the United States of America of one hundred and sixty German submarines (including all submarine cruisers and mine laying submarines) with their complete armament and equipment in ports which will be specified by the Allies and the United States of America. All other submarines to be paid off and completely disarmed and placed under the supervision of the Allied Powers and the United States of America.

Twenty-three. The following German surface warships which shall be designated by the Allies and the United States of America shall forthwith be disarmed and thereafter interned in neutral ports, or, for the want of them, in allied ports, to be designated by the Allies and the United States of America and placed under the surveillance of the Allies and the United States of America, only caretakers being left on board, namely: Six battle cruisers, ten battleships, eight light cruisers, including two mine layers, fifty destroyers of the most modern type. All other surface war ships (including river craft) are to be concentrated in German naval bases to be designated by the Allies and the United States of America, and are to be paid off and completely disarmed and placed under the supervision of the Allies and the United States of America. All vessels of the auxiliary fleet (trawlers, motor vessels, etc.,) are to be disarmed.

Twenty four. The Allies and the United States of America shall have the right to sweep up all mine fields and obstructions laid by Germany outside German territorial waters, and the positions of these are to be indicated.

Twenty five. Freedom of access to and from the Baltic to be given to the naval and mercantile marines of the Allied and Associated Powers. To secure this the Allies and the United States of America shall be empowered to occupy all German forts, fortifications, batteries and defense works of all kinds in all the entrances from the Categat into the Baltic, and to sweep up all mines and obstructions within and without German territorial waters without any question of neutrality being raised, and the positions of all such mines and obstructions are to be indicated.

Twenty six. The existing blockade conditions set up by the Allies and Associated Powers are to remain unchanged and all German merchant ships found at sea are to remain liable to capture.

Twenty seven. All naval aircraft are to be concentrated and immobilized in German bases to be specified by the Allies and the United States of America.

Twenty eight. In evacuating the Belgian coasts and ports, Germany shall abandon all merchant ships, tugs, lighters, cranes and all other harbor materials, all materials for inland navigation, all aircraft and all materials and stores, all arms and armaments, and all stores and apparatus of all kinds.

Twenty nine. All Black Sea ports are to be evacuated by Germany; all Russian war vessels of all descriptions seized by Germany in the Black Sea are to be handed over to the Allies and the United States of America; all neutral merchant vessels seized are to be released; all warlike and other materials of all kinds seized in those ports are to be returned and German materials as specified in clause twenty eight are to be abandoned.

Thirty. All merchant vessels in German hands belonging to the Allied and Associated Powers are to be restored in ports to be specified by the Allies and the United States of America without reciprocity.

Thirty one. No destruction of ships or of materials to be permitted before evacuation, surrender or restoration.

Thirty two. The German Government shall formally notify the neutral Governments of the world, and particularly the Government[s] of Norway, Sweden, Denmark and Holland, that all restrictions placed on the trading of their vessels with the Allied and Associated Countries, whether by the German Government or by private German interests, and whether in return for specific concessions such as the export of shipbuilding materials or not, are immediately canceled.

Thirty three. No transfers of German merchant shipping of any description to any neutral flag are to take place after signature of the armistice.

VI. Duration of Armistice.

Thirty four. The duration of the armistice is to be thirty days, with option to extend. During this period, on failure of execution of any of the above clauses, the armistice may be denounced by one of the contracting parties, on forty eight hours previous notice.

VII. Time Limit for Reply.

Thirty five. This armistice to be accepted or refused by Germany within seventy two hours of notification.

The war thus comes to an end; for, having accepted these terms of armistice, it will be impossible for the German command to renew it.

It is not now possible to assume the consequences of this great consummation. We know only that this tragical war, whose consuming flames swept from one nation to another until all the world was on fire, is at an end and that it was the privilege of our own people to enter it at its most critical juncture in such fashion and in such force as to contribute in a way of which we are all deeply proud to [of] the great result. We know, too, that the object of the war is attained: the object upon which all free men had set their hearts; and attained with a sweeping completeness which even now we do not realize. Armed imperialism such as the men conceived who were but yesterday the masters of Germany is at an end, its illicit ambitions engulfed in black disaster. Who will now seek to revive it? The arbitrary power of the military caste of Germany which once could secretly and of its own single choice disturb the peace of the world is discredited and destroyed. And more than that—much more than that—has been accomplished. The great nations which associated themselves to destroy it have now definitely united in the common purpose to set up such a peace as will satisfy the longing of the whole world for disinterested justice, embodied in settlements which are based upon something much better and much more lasting than the selfish competitive interests of powerful states. There is no longer conjecture as to the objects the victors have in mind. They have a mind in the matter, not only, but a heart also. Their avowed and concerted purpose is to satisfy and protect the weak as well as to accord their just rights to the strong.

The humane temper and intention of the victorious governments has already been manifested in a very practical way. Their representatives in the Supreme War Council at Versailles have by unanimous resolution assured the peoples of the Central Empires that everything that is possible in the circumstances will be done to supply them with food and relieve the distressing want that is in so many places threatening their very lives; and steps are to be taken immediately to organize these efforts at relief in the same systematic manner that they were organized in the case of Belgium. By the use of the idle tonnage of the Central Empires it ought presently to be possible to lift the fear of utter misery from their oppressed populations and set their minds and energies free for the great and hazardous tasks of political reconstruction which now face them on every hand. Hunger does not breed reform; it breeds madness and all the ugly distempers that make an ordered life impossible.

For with the fall of the ancient governments which rested like an incubus upon the peoples of the Central Empires has come political change not merely, but revolution; and revolution which seems as yet to assume no final and ordered form but to run from one fluid change to another, until thoughtful men are forced to ask themselves, With what governments, and of what sort, are we about to deal in the making of the covenants of peace? With what authority will they meet us, and with what assurance that their authority will abide and sustain securely the international arrangements into which we are about to enter? There is here matter for no small anxiety and misgiving. When peace is made, upon whose promises and engagements besides our own is it to rest?

Let us be perfectly frank with ourselves and admit that these questions cannot be satisfactorily answered now or at once. But the moral is not that there is little hope of an early answer that will suffice. It is only that we must be patient and helpful and mindful above all of the great hope and confidence that lie at the heart of what is taking place. Excesses accomplish nothing. Unhappy Russia has furnished abundant recent proof of that. Disorder immediately defeats itself. If excesses should occur, if disorder should for a time raise its head, a sober second thought will follow and a day of constructive action, if we help and do not hinder.

The present and all that it holds belongs to the nations and the peoples who preserve their self-control and the orderly processes of their governments; the future to those who prove themselves the true friends of mankind. To conquer with arms is to make only a temporary conquest; to conquer the world by earning its esteem is to make permanent conquest. I am confident that the nations that have learned the discipline of freedom and that have settled with self-possession to its ordered practice are now about to make conquest of the world by the sheer power of example and of friendly helpfulness.

The peoples who have but just come out from under the yoke of arbitrary government and who are now coming at last into their freedom will never find the treasures of liberty they are in search of if they look for them by the light of the torch. They will find that every pathway that is stained with the blood of their own brothers leads to the wilderness, not to the seat of their hope. They are now face to face with their initial test. We must hold the light steady until they find themselves. And in the meantime, if it be possible, we must establish a peace that will justly define their place among the nations, remove all fear of their neighbours and of their former masters, and enable them to live in security and contentment when they have set their own affairs in order. I, for one, do not doubt their purpose or their capacity. There are some happy signs that they know and will choose the way of self-control and peaceful accommodation. If they do, we shall put our aid at their disposal in every way that we can. If they do not, we must await with patience and sympathy the awakening and recovery that will assuredly come at last.

Printed reading copy (WP, DLC).

Three Telegrams from Edward Mandell House

Paris. Nov. 11, 1918.[1]

Number 89. For the President.

Italian affairs. If you decide to recognize the national council of Zagreb as representative of the Serbo-Croat-Slovene nation, or the territory formerly belonging to the Austro Hungarian monarchy it would be well to assure *the affairs*. If you decide in a very guarded way that the question of their territorial aspirations is a matter to be decided by the peace conference. This action is advised in order to reassure them in the face of the Italian occupation of the Dalmatia coast along the line of the convention of London, against which I protested and consented only upon the explicit promise that this territory should have the same status as the territory to be occupied under the terms of the German armistice. It is to the interest of Italy also that the conditions of the armistice be not made the pretext for presaging this most difficult territorial question. United States now is in a position to speak (?) caution since France and Great Britain are committed by the Pact of London. A statement that its frontiers would be determined in the interests of all concerned and in accordance with principles accepted by all the Allies would be reassuring to all small nationalities who are now in a state high tension. Edward House.

T telegram (WP, DLC).
[1] The copy of this telegram in the House Papers reads as follows: "For the President Number 89 PRIORITY. Concerning Jugo-Slav Italian affairs STOP If you decide to recognize the national council of Zagreb as representative of the Serbo-Slovene nation in territories formerly belonging to the Austro-Hungarian monarchy it would be well to assure the Jugo-Slavs in a very guarded way that the question of their territorial aspirations is a matter to be decided by the peace conference STOP This action is advisable in order to reassure them in the face of the Italian occupation of the Dalmatian coast along the line of the convention of London, against which I protested and consented only upon the explicit promise that this territory should have the same status as the territory to be

occupied under the terms of the German Armistice STOP It is to the interest of Italy also that the conditions of the armistice be not made the pretext for pre-judging this most difficult territorial question STOP United States alone is in a position to speak a word of caution since France and Britain are committed by the pact of London STOP A statement that its frontiers would be determined in the interests of all concerned and in accordance with principles accepted by all the allies would be re-assuring to all small nationalities who are now in a state of high tension. Edward House." EMH to WW, Nov. 11, 1918, T telegram (E. M. House Papers, CtY).

Paris, Nov. 11, 1918.

90A. SECRET FOR THE PRESIDENT

I believe it is essential that you land in England. You could arrange to visit Italy later and during some interim. I shall count on your sailing December third. This would enable you to land December eleventh and remain in England the twelfth and thirteenth reaching Paris night of fourteenth. The peace conference will probably be called for December sixteenth but there need be no active sessions for a week or ten days. This time could be used for inter-allied conferences. Please let me know whether I can plan according to this schedule.   Edward House.

T telegram (SDR, RG 59, 033.1140/247, DNA).

Paris. Nov. 11, 1918.

Number 91. For the President.

Hunter [Hughes], Australian Premier, in a letter to the TIMES of November 9, 1918, states that he has remained London for the purpose of representing Australia in the settlement of the terms of peace. He says: "The first intimation I received that the terms of peace had been discussed at Versailles was conveyed in the document which I received which notified me that they had been definitely settled. Neither imperial war cabinet nor the individual representatives of the dominions, or at any rate of Australia, were consulted in any way." To this the British Government press bureau in the same copy of TIMES replies: "The terms of peace were exhaustively discussed by the war cabinet and communicated to the Australian Government before the conference at Versailles and nothing had been agreed upon at that conference inconsistent with the general conclusion of the war cabinet." There is no denial that the terms of peace have been effectively outlined.

Leading editorial of TIMES November 9th discusses the American elections, pointing out that their importance is psychological rather than concrete. "They will not change the President's policy but they will, to some extent, affect the atmosphere by removing certain misapprehensions and strengthen the 'united front' and will help to bring the President's ideals into still closer touch with opinions in America and in all allied countries."

Edward House.

T telegram (WP, DLC).

To Henry French Hollis

My dear Senator: [The White House] 11 November, 1918.

All your letters are helpful and enlightening.[1] I get a side-light on things that I would not otherwise hear about not only, but also a direct light on a great many important matters, and I am certainly your debtor for taking the trouble to keep me apprised of the currents that are running both inside and outside official circles.

With warm appreciation,

Sincerely yours, Woodrow Wilson

TLS (Letterpress Books, WP, DLC).
[1] H. F. Hollis to WW, Oct. 2, 6, 13, and 23, 1918, all in Vol. 51.

To Edward Graham Elliott

My dear Edward: [The White House] 11 November, 1918

I have approved the revised statement for "The State" on International Law[1] and am today sending it to D. C. Heath and Company. Thank you warmly for letting me have a look at it. It is a comfort to know that the book is in your hands.

We think of you very often in these exciting and perplexing days, and I hope with all my heart that you are all well.

With affectionate messages from us all,

Affectionately yours, Woodrow Wilson

TLS (Letterpress Books, WP, DLC).
[1] See E. G. Elliott to WW, Oct. 31, 1918, and the notes thereto, Vol. 51.

To D. C. Heath and Company

My dear Sirs: [The White House] 11 November, 1918.

At the request of Dr. Edward Elliott, who is engaged in revising "The State," I am sending you the enclosed revision of paragraphs 1457 and 1458 concerning International Law. With slight changes of phraseology, I have approved it.

Sincerely yours, Woodrow Wilson

TLS (Letterpress Books, WP, DLC).

From Newton Diehl Baker

My dear Mr President:　　　　　　Washington November 11, 1918

I cannot let this historic moment pass without sending you a word of appreciation and congratulation. You have done this great thing! May God's blessing rest on it and on you.

May I add too a word of gratitude for your patience with all of us who have had parts in the execution of your great vision. For myself I can only say that your constant support and confidence and forbearance have been at once my comfort and my courage whenever the task seemed either long or hard.

　　　Gratefully and respectfully yours　　Newton D. Baker

ALS (WP, DLC).

From Cleveland Hoadley Dodge

My dear Friend & President　　　New York. November 11th, 1918

As the whole world turns to you today, you will be flooded with letters[1] & I will only write a line to congratulate you from the depths of my heart for the glorious result of all your efforts & the complete justification of your policies

You must be a happy man today when you realize what you have wrought. May God who has so far lead you all the way, continue to guide you in all the coming days, with the great issues which will engage you.

　　　Mrs Dodge joins me in much love & hearty wishes for Mrs Wilson & yourself

　　　Most thankfully & aff'ly　　　Yours　　Cleveland H Dodge

ALS (WP, DLC).
　[1] Wilson was indeed flooded with letters and telegrams of congratulation and greeting from all over the world—from kings and queens, ministers of state, friends, school children, and so on. We have included only a few samples of this correspondence.

From Louis Dembitz Brandeis, with Enclosure

My dear Mr. President:　　　　Washington, D. C. November 11/18

Throughout the war I have refrained from burdening you with communications. Today, I venture to send you some lines from Euripides.　　　　　　Most cordially　　Louis D. Brandeis

ALS (WP, DLC).

ENCLOSURE

FROM "THE BACCHAE"—BY EURIPIDES.
(Translation by Gilbert Murray)

Chorus.

O Strength of God, slow art thou and still,
   Yet failest never!
On them that worship the Ruthless Will,
On them that dream, doth His judgment wait.
Dreams of the proud man, making great
   And greater ever,
Things which are not of God. In wide
   And devious coverts, hunter-wise,
He coucheth Time's unhasting stride,
   Following, following, him whose eyes
Look not to Heaven. For all is vain,
The pulse of the heart, the plot of the brain,
That striveth beyond the laws that live.
And is thy Faith so much to give,
Is it so hard a thing to see,
That the Spirit of God, whate'er it be,
The Law that abides and changes not, ages long,
The Eternal and Nature-born—these things be strong?

What else is Wisdom? What of man's endeavour
   Or God's high grace so lovely and so great?
   To stand from fear set free, to breathe and wait;
   To hold a hand uplifted over Hate;
And shall not Loveliness be loved for ever?

T MS (WP, DLC).

From Bernard Mannes Baruch

My dear Mr. President: Washington November 11, 1918.

Mr. Wheeler of the Chamber of Commerce came to see me this morning, and has sent me a copy of a letter which he addressed to you.[1]

Most of the suggestions in his letter have already been taken care of. I have already suggested to the Army, Navy and Shipping Board that they should come to a common agreement regarding the methods of handling the adjustment of contracts. The Army is already well organized for this, and the Navy have the matter in hand. The matter of a clearance committee on page three of this letter has already been established in the War Industries Board, in order that when and if any contracts are cancelled, raw materials should be released to the industry. Arrangements have also been made with the Departments, wherever raw materials are the property of the Government that they will only be re-sold through the agency of the War Industries Board and with little, if any disturbance to the general business situation.

I am sending this to you as you may want to use these facts in answering his letter.

Yours very truly,   Bernard M Baruch

TLS (WP, DLC).
¹ That is, H. A. Wheeler to WW, Nov. 9, 1918.

From William Cox Redfield

My dear Mr. President: Washington November 11, 1918.

There are two phases of our commerce so vital and one of them at least so urgent that I am venturing to offer suggestions for your thought respecting them.

In the near future and continuing for perhaps two or even three years we shall be called upon both by desire and necessity to furnish large supplies of raw materials not only to the nations that have been associated with us in the war but possibly to some extent to the people of the former central empires. This demand will certainly be so large as to tax our power to meet it. It cannot but have direct effects upon our own industries. It seems to me essential not only that our supply of raw materials should be equitably rationed among other nations and for our own use but that the rationing, so far as it may affect others, should be done in consultation with an international group comprising representatives of the countries which we must thus supply.

It is equally certain that for a somewhat similar period we must be called upon to finance the commercial operations resulting from the supplying of these materials and it is probable we shall have to furnish credits in other directions to large amounts to assist in the reconstruction work of our injured friends. It seems certain, therefore, that we must ration our credits, also, and that this therefore should have the consideration of an international body, though possibly separate from the more directly commercial transactions dealing with materials.

Following the so-called reconstruction period will come, let us hope, the time when the nations may resume more normal lives. What the United States will do during this period may and, I think, will fix her future standing and influence in the world. Perhaps I should say the spirit in which she deals with the opportunity that will then open will fix her place in the world. We have almost suddenly discovered that we have a giant strength financially and otherwise. Other nations have discovered it with something of a shock, also. The way in which we are to use this strength is of deep interest to them and, of course, important to ourselves. Shall we enter anew upon a form of competition in which we shall seek to grasp all we can get of the world's trade, with the spirit of seeking only our own profit, or shall we retain our idealism in commerce and make it our hand-maiden of mutual service to the world?

If we answer the first question affirmatively we may prosper thereby in a material sense with the risk of losing our national soul and with the certainty of becoming deservedly hated and suspected. Indeed this is the way, I think, that leads to future wars.

If we prefer an affirmative answer to the second question we may not be as rich in economic wealth but we may become and remain the leader of the moral forces of the world even in commerce.

This future period presents so many problems, the questions coming up concerning it are so difficult and in their present forms so novel that it seems to me they could best be studied, discussed and perhaps settled by an international commercial conference. Such a body would take up the broad question as to what the equities in international commerce are; what is fair trade between the nations; how can each play its part and live its life and expend its energies while helping, rather than hindering, the others?

I seem to catch a glimpse of the possibility of international commerce which is neither indolence and neglect upon the one hand nor selfish warfare on the other, which acts upon the principle "he that would be chief among you, let him be the servant of all" and which offers ample room for the economic power of our country in ways that are consistent with the full play of its moral forces.

I have written too long but the point is and my recommendation is that you give earnest thought to the wisdom of an international commercial conference with which may be connected, if you think well, the financial phase suggested and that this body seek to determine ways by which we can avoid such a conduct of our international trade as will invoke reprisals and the hostility that comes with such a contest.

May I say that my purpose in writing a letter of this nature to you is known to Dr. Taussig of the Tariff Commission, Mr. Colver of the Federal Trade Commission, Mr. Robertson[1] representing the Shipping Board, Mr. Miller of the Federal Reserve Board, and Mr. Cutler,[2] chief of the Bureau of Foreign and Domestic Commerce, and the viewpoint suggested has their approval?

                    Yours very truly,   William C. Redfield

TLS (WP, DLC).
[1] He meant Henry Mauris Robinson, lawyer and businessman of Los Angeles, at this time associated informally with the United States Shipping Board.
[2] Burwell Smith Cutler.

From Key Pittman, with Enclosure

My dear Mr. President: [Washington] November 11, 1918.

It would afford me great happiness to see you in person so that I might express to you the feeling of pride and moral elation your message stimulated in my mind and soul for our country and for our President. It invincibly arms us all in our now fixed will to fight with you patiently and against every obstruction and harrassment and without counting the temporary cost until your great ideals become realisms. I know, however, that it would be inconsiderate in me to ask even a moment of your time, so I must content myself with these poor expressions of my feelings. I am enclosing a copy of a statement that I have given to the press.

There is another matter that disturbs me greatly, with regard to which I trust that you will briefly advise me. Since the beginning of the war I have desired deeply to view the situation with my own eyes. Partly it is true from natural curiosity, but partly for a higher purpose. I am confident that your principles will be adopted—I hope not reluctantly by the Peace Conference. Some of these principles have already been denounced by Republican leaders, and I have no doubt that any treaty embracing them will be fought upon the floor of the Senate. These principles, in the very nature of things, will affect every phase of our life. I had hoped to watch and listen to the actions and arguments of the statesmen and business men of the countries with whom we must deal. I desired the local atmosphere for my own information and for the prestige that it might give me in the debates in the Committee on Foreign Relations and upon the floor of the Senate.

Mr. Hoover, with whom I have cooperated on a number of occasions, on last night told me of his intended departure, and was kind enough to urge that I go upon the same steamer. I realize the danger of a member of the legislative body going to Europe at this time. I understand that the giving of any interviews might be embarrassing to the Executive. This matter, however, does not concern me, as I take no extraordinary pleasure in advertisement. The question in my mind is whether I could be of more value in the support of your Administration by remaining here or going to Europe. I am not on the Finance Committee, yet I might be of some assistance if I remain here in presenting to the individuals, or such as are my friends, your view of the situation. This, however, could probably be done by members of the committee in a far more effective way than could be accomplished by me.

I trust, Mr. President, that you will not take the trouble to answer this letter by mail but will have me notified of your views over the telephone.   Sincerely,   Key Pittman.

TLS (WP, DLC).

E N C L O S U R E

Nov. 11, 1918.
Statement from Senator Key Pittman of Nevada,
    member of the Foreign Relations Committee:
The Armistice is a full compliance with the demands made by the President. It has accomplished everything that could have been accomplished by forcing an unconditional surrender to our armies upon the field. Germany has been placed in a position where she is powerless to again renew the fight. The President's determination that the German people should have a democratic government has been accomplished. Militarism in Germany has not only been defeated but destroyed. The very roots of arbitrary government have been torn from the soil of Europe. The President's matchless diplomacy is now clear to the world. It was his dominating statesmanship and will that placed our overwhelming army and resources in Europe. It was his diplomacy that precipitated the internal dissolution of the Imperial German Empire and its allies. He will sit at the peace table in person because there is no man who is qualified to represent him, and from that conference will come the establishment of the principles that he has advocated and which will mean an enduring peace. He will not again be charged with the disposition to surrender to Germany. His diplomacy will never again be charact[e]rised as mischievous and treacherous. The American people will not again be deceived and they will back him as a man in his fight for the principles that he will maintain at the peace conference.

T MS (WP, DLC).

Remarks to State Food Administrators

12 November, 1918.

I am very glad, Mr. Hoover, to meet these gentlemen. It is a pleasure to have a chance to shake their hands and say how sincerely we are obliged to them for the work they have done. Because, gentlemen, I think one of the benefits of this war—for some benefits have come out of it—is that we have learned a new kind of cooperation and fellowship and a new view of national interests and a way to promote them by cooperation. We know each other better than we used to. We know how to cooperate, and we know what there is to cooperate in, which was not always the case.

Mr. Hoover has just said, or intimated, that this is the end of your function, but I am not so sure that it is. I am not so sure that we won't continue for some time to come to need your advice and cooperation, because the world has to be revictualed, as you know better than I do, and not all the aspects and problems of that revictualing are revealed. I would not like to promise you that we can let you off, and I would not like to feel that we might not still have your advice and active assistance in solving these problems. For war is a definite problem which can be learned, though you may not at the outset have wished to learn it, but peace is very much more complicated than war, and the problems of peace are very much more variegated than the problems of war. I feel for my part that we are standing at the threshold of a period which has yet to disclose the variety of work which it is going to impose upon us, and it is going to impose much of it upon us because we came out of this war the freest nation that has been engaged. I am not speaking of political freedom, but the freest to help, the freest to advise and back up our advice with assistance. And it fills me with enthusiasm when I think of the result of being a friend to the world. It will result in giving America the greatest influence that any one nation has ever had, and I for one am so sure of the ideals and standards of thoughtful men in America that I am proud to believe that that assistance will be beneficial to the world, and that they will like us better for what they have got from us. It is a fine thing to be looked to by all the world to do disinterested things, and I am sure that you feel, as I do, that we must be very careful that what we do is disinterested.

I am very much obliged to you, gentlemen, for the compliment of this call and the privilege of saying to you how much I appreciate what you have done.

T MS (WP, DLC).

To Key Pittman

My dear Senator: The White House 12 November, 1918.

You put a hard question up to me in your letter of yesterday—hard because I can see between the lines of your letter how eager you are to go with Hurley,[1] and because I must say that I think that our full fighting force will be necessary here in the Senate in the few months that remain for the present Congress.

For one thing, there is going to be an effort on the part of some members on the Republican side to cut down the figures of the revenue bill, which would certainly bring bigger loans upon the country and very serious financial embarrassments, inasmuch as their thought that we can suddenly rapidly curtail expenditures is based upon ignorance and the failure to consider the enormous tasks of readjustment.

This is only a sample of the things that will be attempted, and I hope with all my heart you will stay on the firing line.

With warmest regard,

Cordially and faithfully yours,   Woodrow Wilson

TLS (K. Pittman Papers, DLC).
[1] Actually, Hoover.

From George V

[London, Nov. 12, 1918]

At this moment of universal gladness I send you, Mr. President, and the people of your great Republic, a message of congratulation and deep thanks in my own name and that of the people of this empire.

It is indeed a matter of solemn thanksgiving that the peoples of our two countries, akin in spirit as in speech, should today be united in this greatest of democracy's achievements. I thank you and the people of the United States for the high and noble part which you have played in this glorious chapter of history and freedom.

[George R.I.]

Printed in the *New York Times*, Nov. 14, 1918.

To George V

[The White House] 12 November, 1918.

Your generous and gracious message is most warmly appreciated, and you may rest assured that our hearts on this side of the Atlantic are the more completely filled with joy and satisfaction because we know the great partnership of interests and of sentiments to which we belong. We are happy to be associated in this time of triumph with the government and people upon whom we are so sure we can count for cooperation in the delicate and difficult tasks which remain to be performed in order that the high purposes of the war may be realized and established in the reign of equitable justice and lasting peace.   Woodrow Wilson

T telegram (Letterpress Books, WP, DLC).

To Newton Diehl Baker

My dear Baker: The White House 12 November, 1918

Your note of yesterday has touched and moved me. I wonder if you know how genuinely and entirely I have trusted and believed in you and how happy I am that the trust and belief have been absolutely justified by the result. It has therefore cost me no effort to support you, and any help I have given is more than repaid by such generous confidence as you have in me.

Cordially and sincerely yours,   Woodrow Wilson

TLS (WC, NjP).

To Jouett Shouse

My dear Mr. Shouse: The White House 12 November, 1918.

Your letter of the seventh[1] has given me peculiar pleasure. It breathes a fine spirit, which I have come to regard as characteristic of you.

There is nothing to discourage us in the recent elections. Very definite tasks are now to be performed as the adjustments of peace are attempted, and the Republicans are going to take a very serious responsibility, which public opinion will assist them to exercise.

Cordially and sincerely yours,   Woodrow Wilson

TLS (J. Shouse Papers, KyU).
[1] See J. Shouse to WW, Nov. 7, 1918, Vol. 51.

To Louis Dembitz Brandeis

[The White House]

My dear Mr. Justice Brandeis: 12 November, 1918.

I have read the extract from Euripides with such emotions as you may imagine, and I am warmly obliged to you for thinking of me and affording me the stimulation of such a passage at this time.

Cordially and sincerely yours,   Woodrow Wilson

TLS (Letterpress Books, WP, DLC).

To Grant Squires

[The White House]

My dear Mr. Squires: 12 November, 1918

I have taken up the matter of the commission and will soon know, I hope, what the difficulty is. I take it for granted it is merely a congestion of business.

I have examined with painful interest the copy of "The Labor Defender" which you have sent me in dummy. It will be necessary to be very watchful and united in the presence of such danger signals.   Cordially and sincerely yours,   Woodrow Wilson

TLS (Letterpress Books, WP, DLC).

To Albert Sidney Burleson

My dear Burleson: The White House 12 November, 1918.

I am sure the enclosed[1] will interest you as painfully as it has interested me.

Cordially and faithfully yours,   Woodrow Wilson

TLS (A. S. Burleson Papers, DLC).
[1] Presumably G. Squires to WW, Nov. 9, 1918, with its enclosure.

To William Cox Redfield

My dear Mr. Secretary: [The White House] 12 November, 1918

Your letter of yesterday dwells upon matters which have engaged my thought very seriously and, I may say, very constantly for many months past. I doubt whether it would be wise just at this venture or very soon to call together a commercial conference to discuss the best method by which the resources of the world, our own included, can be correlated in order to render the best service in the critical times now at hand. Happily, there are international agencies of conference and cooperation now in existence growing out of the war which not only can be used but are already being used to consider cooperation. There is no one matter which has come up more often for discussion in my Wednesday conferences with the little war board I have gathered about me, and I have been delighted to find the spirit of service which prevailed in all our discussions. We have not yet risen to the task, but I think we are rising to it.

Cordially and faithfully yours,   Woodrow Wilson

TLS (Letterpress Books, WP, DLC).

From Edward Mandell House

Paris Nov 12, 1918

Number 99. Secret for the President. Referring further to our number 61.[1] I beg to suggest the following:

The whole problem of securing political intelligence, establishing an adequate counter espionage organization and providing protection for you and for the personnel, papers, and property of the American representatives at the Peace Conference should be dealt with, I believe, along the following lines:

One. Political Intelligence.

At the present time the United States officials in Europe charged with considering political and economic questions presented by the termination of the war are receiving practically no dependable information concerning political and economic conditions in the following countries: Poland, Bohemia, Ukraine, Austria, Servia, (including Yugo-Slavia), Hungary, Bulgaria, Albania and Turkey. From Roumania and Greece some information is obtained but it is very incomplete. I consider it essential that we at once set up instrumentalities in these localities which will furnish us with information concerning political conditions in these countries and that this information should come to us through American eyes. I do not think it will be difficult promptly to set up an organization for this purpose and I suggest that I be authorized to proceed along the following lines:

Sub paragraph A. After conferring with Hoover and learning his plans for relief, to select men from among the United States military and naval forces now in Europe and from any other available sources, who shall be appointed for the time being, agents of the Department of State. These men to constitute the basis of a "political intelligence section" of the American delegation to the Peace Conference.

Sub paragraph B. To despatch the men so selected as soon as practicable to do so, to points such as Warsaw, Lemberg, Posen, Prague, Berne (Moravia) Budapest, Vienna, Innsbruck or Salzburg, Belgrade, Agram, Serajevo, Sofia, Bucharest (and some point in Transylvania), Kief, Scutari, Constantinople and Odessa. One agent should be sent to each place and he should take with him one code clerk with codes, one stenographer and if necessary one interpreter. A courier service also will shortly have to be established to operate between the United States and[2] individual agents and their base from which messages could be forwarded by telegraph to Paris.

Sub paragraph C. These agents so selected not to be in any sense accredited to the countries in which they are located. The military and naval men will of course not wear their uniforms. So far as possible the Governments in the localities to which they are sent will be requested to give them assistance in the conduct of their work. These men would work in close cooperation with any relief (arrangements?) [agencies] set up by Hoover.

Sub paragraph D. To set up at some point in the Balkans, such as possibly Bucharest, a central office to which these agents can forward (probably for the President by courier only) their reports for transmission to the United States via Paris.

Sub paragraph E. To establish at Paris for the assistance of the American delegation at the Peace Conference a "political intelligence section" under the direction of Grew and such other persons as the State Department may send to help him to which would be forwarded all reports from these agents and from other agents of the Department of State already constituted in European countries.

Two. Counter espionage organization.

I have conferred with General Nolan[3] the head of the United States Military Intelligence in Europe and I believe that this work should be handed over to him and I suggest that a civil official of the Department of State who has an appreciation of the duty of work desired done should be associated with him.

Three. The protection of the President and of the American delegation at the Peace Conference and their (*) [papers] and property.

I suggest that the most practical method of handling this problem is through the use of the military authorities working under the direction of General Nolan who is entirely familiar with the peculiar conditions presented by this kind of work in France.

Almost all of the personnel to do the work outlined in paragraph one can be obtained here in Europe. I should very much appreciate an expression of your views respecting this important matter. If the plan as outlined is promptly approved it can be put into operation before the Peace Conference is called.   Edward House.

T telegram (WP, DLC).
   [1] EMH to WW, Nov. 8, 1918 (first telegram of that date), Vol. 51.
   [2] "United States and" not in House's copy.
   [3] Brig. Gen. Dennis Edward Nolan.

From William Gibbs McAdoo

Dear Mr. President,   Washington Nov. 12. 1918

Now that an armistice has been signed and peace is at hand, I feel at liberty to apprise you of my desire to return, as soon as possible to private life.

I have been conscious, for a long time, of the necessity for this step but of course I could not consider it while the country was at war.

For almost six years, I have worked incessantly under the pressure of great responsibilities. Their exactions have drawn heavily on my strength. The very burdensome cost of living in Washington and the inadequate compensation allowed by law for the office I hold, have so depleted my personal resources that I am obliged to reckon with the facts of the situation.

I do not wish to convey the idea that I am ill or that I am threatened with illness because such is not the case. As a result of long overwork I need a reasonable period of genuine rest. But more than this I must, for the sake of my family, get back to private life to retrieve my personal fortunes.

I cannot secure the required rest nor the opportunity to look after my long neglected private affairs unless I am relieved of my present responsibilities.

I am giving you this early notice in order that there may be ample time to arrange for my retirement with as little inconvenience to yourself as possible. It would gratify me if this could be effected shortly after the New Year.

I hope you will understand, my dear Mr. President, that I would permit nothing but the most imperious demands to force my withdrawal from public life. Always I shall cherish as the greatest honor of my career the opportunity you have so generously given me to serve the country under your leadership in these epochal times.

Affectionately Yours   W G McAdoo[1]

ALS (WP, DLC).
   [1] McAdoo wrote an expanded version of this letter, for publication, to Wilson on November 14, 1918. It is printed at that date.

From Herbert Clark Hoover, with Enclosure

Dear Mr. President: Washington. 12 November 1918.

Please find enclosed herewith a memorandum agreed this morning between Mr. Baker, Mr. Hurley and myself.

I should be glad to know if it meets with your approval.

Yours faithfully,   Herbert Hoover.

TCL (Hoover Archives, CSt-H).

E N C L O S U R E

MEMORANDUM OF ARRANGEMENTS WITH REGARD TO PROVISIONING THE POPULATIONS WHICH ARE NOW OR HAVE BEEN UNDER THE DOMINATION OF THE CENTRAL EMPIRES.

12 November 1918

1. Mr. Hoover, as United States Food Administrator, will proceed at once to Europe to determine what action is required from the United States and what extensions of the Food Administration organization or otherwise are necessary in order to carry out the work of the participation of the United States Government in this matter, and to take such steps as are necessary in temporary relief.

2. In order to expedite the movement of foodstuffs towards Europe, the War Department will undertake to purchase in the usual coordination through the Food Administration during the next twenty days, 120,000 tons of flour and from 30,000,000 to 40,000,000 pounds of pork products. These foodstuffs to be shipped by the diversion of Army tonnage at the earliest possible moment that the Shipping Board arranges and to be consigned to French ports for re-consignment or storage.

3. This foodstuff and any other suitable surplus supplies of the Quartermaster in Europe to be made available for distribution at Mr. Hoover's direction, it being understood that if it proves infeasible to re-ship or re-direct the steamers to the territories lately held by the Central Empires, Mr. Hoover will make arrangements for the re-sale of the foodstuffs to the Allied governments or, alternatively, to the Belgian Relief.

4. In order to facilitate administration in Washington, Mr. Hoover will set up a preliminary committee to assist the Food Administration, comprising—

Mr. Theodore Whitmarsh, of the Food Administration, who will act as Chairman in Mr. Hoover's absence.

Mr. F. S. Snyder, of the Meat Division of the Food Administration.

Mr. Julius H. Barnes, of the Cereal Division of the Food Administration.

General R. E. Wood,[1] Quartermaster General, representing the
War Department.

Mr. John Beaver White, representing the War Trade Board.

Mr. Prentiss N. Gray, representing the Shipping Board.

These gentlemen to take in hand the general directions of those
operations through the various government agencies concerned.

5. The War Department is to purchase, inspect, pay for, load and
ship these foodstuffs in the usual manner of transmission of Quartermaster's supplies and upon transfer from the Quartermaster's
Department in Europe they are to be paid for by the buyer.

6. The American representatives in Europe are to be at once instructed by cable that the whole of the matter of the American food
supplies and the establishment of a more permanent organization
are to be settled by Mr. Hoover on his arrival in Europe and that
the United States will take no participation in any arrangements
made pending that time.

Approved Woodrow Wilson[2]

T MS (Hoover Archives, CSt-H).
[1] Brig. Gen. Robert Elkington Wood.
[2] WWhw.

From Key Pittman

My dear Mr. President: Washington, D. C. November 12, 1918.

Your kind and frank reply to my letter settles my mind with regard
to my duty. I will prepare for the fight and stay upon the firing line.
We are all solicitous that your health and strength may continue
under the great burdens that are cast upon you, but we look forward
with the utmost confidence to the perfect consummation of your
great program. Our hearts go with you in your great fight.

Sincerely yours,   Key Pittman

TLS (WP, DLC).

From Joseph Patrick Tumulty, with Enclosure

Dear Governor: The White House 12 November 1918.

The attached is a letter from Congressman Stephens which you
ought to read. I beg to suggest that you drop him a line of appreciation.   Sincerely,   J P Tumulty

TLS (WP, DLC).

ENCLOSURE

Dan Voorhees Stephens to Joseph Patrick Tumulty

My dear Mr. Tumulty: Fremont, Nebraska, Nov. 9, 1918

You may be interested in an analysis of the vote here in Nebraska. Postmortems are always more or less interesting to us who are directly involved in the results. The swing of this State from 40 thousand for the President in 1916 to about 20 thousand for the Republican ticket in 1918 is quite remarkable. In my judgment it shows clearly we are not exactly what we seemed to be. It shows I think an anti-war vote, not all of which was in the ranks of the German-Americans. I base that statement on the vote of '16 under the slogan "He kept us out of war," and in '18 under a pro war slogan. The German-American vote in this State was largely democratic. We lost about half of it two years ago and this year we lost it all.

The cause for the defeat of the Administration by the failure of the people to return a Democratic Congress are roughly summarized as follows:

1st. The German-American vote which, in this State at least, went almost solidly for the straight Republican ticket. This was by far the largest single factor. Anyone of 3 German Counties in my District would have elected me by giving me my normal democratic majority.

2nd. The anti-war vote which must have existed in a much larger degree than we had suspected when we consider the 40 thousand majority given the President two years ago against the 20 thousand or more given Senator Norris this year.

3rd. The natural gain for the Republican ticket from the disgruntled, namely, the man peeved because he was short of help, the man opposed to the draft, the man forced to buy bonds and contribute to war activities against his will, and the man pinched by the income tax and hoping the Republicans will put it on consumption. All these made a factor second only to the pro-German loss.

4th. The dissatisfaction among the farmers due to a refusal to increase the wheat price, largely manufactured by Republican agitators. My own losses were sustained largely in the country outside of incorporated towns and cities.

5th. The tremendous fight against the Administration made by the Republicans everywhere. It was a strange spectacle quite apart from what we had expected. The main excuse for it was our alleged pretense of adjourning polit[i]cs. They used the President's appeal to the American people in the most malicious and criminal fashion, absolutely misrepresenting the President everywhere. I deny the Republican claim that the President's letter caused the landslide. It afforded partisans who never intended to support us an excuse to bawl about it. It may have made some votes for the Republicans as a result of their open work, but in my judgment we greatly profitted in the net results. The great mass of people are not partisans and the President's letter was worth a great deal to them. I think the landslide would have been greater without it.

The above summary constitutes the principal reasons for our loss of the State.

I hope the President will submit to Congress a program of reconstruction that we can put thru before March 4 next, so our war record can be practically made complete before the Republican Congress comes into being.

I fully expect the Republican Congress will approve what we have forecasted, viz, that it would in effect split the Government by attempting to hamstring the Commander in Chief. The leaders are right now planning how they can overcome the President. I prophesy that before the Presidential Election comes around the people will be sick of their bargain.

The President's record as leader of the Allied Nations and of his Party is so admirable and sound in every particular that I have the fullest confidence in the recoil that is sure to follow this election. I have never been prouder in victory than I am now in defeat. I class it a glorious defeat because it is the result of being 100% American. I made the first speech in Congress against the Embargo on Arms and Ammunition, February 2, 1915, and lost 6 thousand German-American democratic majority in the following election in 1916. My vote for every single war measure of every kind and character since merely increased that opposition. I feel that we have really made a sacrifice for our Country. I am proud of the President and want to assure him that he is to be congratulated upon the character of the opposition that appears to have delivered us a staggering blow. To me it is a signal for a great endorsement two years hence.

With kindest regards to you and the President, I am,

Yours very truly,   Dan V. Stephens

TLS (WP, DLC).

From George Mason La Monte

My dear Mr. President Wilson: New York November 12, 1918.

I thank you very much for your cordial note of the eighth,[1] and am glad you feel about the Election as you do. If we had had another week we could have won out, but on account of the Influenza we did not have a single open meeting in New Jersey, and notwithstanding that fact wherever the Edge record was exposed we "beat him to it." I am told from various sources he is very much chagrined at the comparatively small vote which he received.

I confess I became ambitious to have some part in the reconstruction work which is now upon us and it will be a terrible thing if reactionary forces should control. Having won the war we must not now lose it by letting things settle back in the old way—there must be no old way.

I thank you most sincerely for your continued interest in the case of Miss Pollok, and I want to suggest that as we are now beyond certain points of trouble it may be more easily possible for you to do something which you could not have done heretofore. This sentence is somewhat involved but I think you will understand exactly what I mean.

Yours very sincerely,   George M. La Monte

TLS (WP, DLC).
[1] WW to G. M. La Monte, Nov. 8, 1918, Vol. 51.

Hans Sulzer to Robert Lansing

Handed me by Swiss Min.
Nov 12/18 RL.

Sir: Washington, D. C. November 12, 1918.

By direction of my Government, I have the honor to transmit the following cable:

"The German Government urgently requests the President of the United States to inform the German Chancellor Ebert,[1] by wireless, whether he may be assured that the Government of the United States is ready to send foodstuffs without delay if public order is maintained in Germany and an equitable distribution of food is guaranteed."

Accept, Sir, the renewed assurances of my highest consideration.

Hans Sulzer

TLS (SDR, RG 59, 862.48/37, DNA).
[1] Prince Max of Baden had announced the abdication of William II as German Emperor in Berlin shortly before noon on November 9. William, then at Supreme Headquarters

at Spa, Belgium, had strongly objected to this action and declared that he would stay with the army. However, later that day, General von Hindenburg informed William that he could no longer guarantee the security of his person from mutinous troops, and he decided to flee to the Netherlands. William crossed the Dutch border in the early morning of November 10 and was granted asylum by the government of the Netherlands later that day. He then took up temporary residence at the estate of Count Godard Bentinck at Amerongen. After the safe arrival from Germany of Empress Augusta Victoria on November 28, William, on that day, signed a formal act of abdication both as German Emperor and King of Prussia.

Immediately after Max, on November 9, announced William's abdication, the Prince offered the chancellorship to Friedrich Ebert, leader of the Majority Socialists in the Reichstag. Actually, Ebert held the chancellorship only one day. On November 10, Ebert formed a provisional government, the Council of Peoples' Representatives, composed of three Majority Socialists and three Independent Socialists. This coalition broke up on December 28, and Ebert formed a new council composed exclusively of Majority Socialists. It was the central government of Germany until the German constitutional convention met at Weimar on February 6 and elected a new government headed by Philipp Scheidemann, a Majority Socialist. The Weimar Assembly elected Ebert as the first President of the German Republic on February 11, 1919.

Robert Lansing to Hans Sulzer

Sir: [Washington] November 12, 1918.

I have the honor to acknowledge the receipt of your note of to-day, transmitting to the President the text of a cable inquiring whether this Government is ready to send foodstuffs into Germany without delay if public order is maintained in Germany and an equitable distribution of food is guaranteed.

I should be grateful if you would transmit the following reply to the German Government:

"At a joint session of the two houses of Congress on November 11th, the President of the United States announced that the representatives of the associated governments in the Supreme War Council at Versailles have by unanimous resolution assured the peoples of the Central Empires that everything that is possible in the circumstances will be done to supply them with food and relieve the distressing want that is in so many places threatening their very lives; and that steps are to be taken immediately to organize these efforts at relief in the same systematic manner that they were organized in the case of Belgium. Furthermore, the President expresses the opinion that by the use of the idle tonnage of the Central Empires it ought presently to be possible to lift the fear of utter misery from their oppressed populations and set their minds and energies free for the great and hazardous tasks of political reconstruction which now face them on every hand.

"Accordingly the President now directs me to state that he is ready to consider favorably the supplying of foodstuffs to Germany and to take up the matter immediately with the Allied Governments, provided he can be assured that public order is being and will continue to be maintained in Germany, and that an equitable distribution of food can be clearly guaranteed."

Accept, Sir, the renewed assurances of my highest consideration.

Robert Lansing

CCL (SDR, RG 59, 862.48/37, DNA).

From the Diary of Josephus Daniels

November Tuesday 12 1918

Baker said he had cable that Am. soldiers held their watches & fought till 11 o'clock, the time of the armistice.

Discussed bringing troops home. How many will we need? Baker thought 600,000.

Burleson wished to abolish censorship—said it had never done any good. Lansing dissented & said War Trade Board needed it. France & GB continued theirs and we should do likewise until conditions were normal, say until peace terms were agreed upon.

McAdoo thought could pass 6 billion dollar bill & no 8 bil dolls. He and Burleson urged economy WW said must not stop so hurriedly that labor will be idle.

Wheat discussion. Houston said Hoover never said same thing twice. Told him farmers ought to go slow increasing production & that he told others there would not be enough food. McAdoo thought price of wheat would go down & the Treasury would have to make up deficit to wheat growers, who all voted R ticket because price of wheat too low

WW will go to Peace Conference.

Approved Sims & Gleaves[1]

[1] That is, their promotion to admiral and vice-admiral, respectively, effective December 4. Gleaves was Albert Gleaves.

A Memorandum by Robert Lansing[1]

WILL THE PRESIDENT GO TO THE
PEACE CONGRESS?

November 12, 1918.

I had a conference this noon at the White House with the President in relation to the Peace Conference. I told him frankly that I thought the plan for him to attend was unwise and would be a mistake. I said that I felt embarrassed in speaking to him about it because it would leave me at the head of the delegation and I hoped that he understood I spoke only out of sense of duty. I pointed out that he held at present a dominant position in the world, which I was afraid he would lose if he went into conference with the foreign statesmen; that he could practically dictate the terms of peace if he held aloof; that he would be criticized severely in this country for leaving at a time when Congress particularly needed his guidance, and that he would be greatly embarrassed in directing domestic affairs from overseas.

The President did not like what I said. His face assumed that harsh, obstinate expression which indicates resentment at unacceptable advice. He said nothing, but looked volumes. If he goes, he will some day be sorry. He will probably not forgive me, and may even decide not to make me a delegate. However I have done my duty. I believe that I have told him the truth. My conscience is clear.

T MS (R. Lansing Papers, DLC).
    [1] This memorandum might well have been written *ex post facto*. Neither the White House Diary nor the Executive Office Diary mentions a meeting between Wilson and Lansing at noon on November 12. Indeed, the former says that Wilson worked in his study all morning and had no luncheon guests.

To Edward Mandell House

[The White House, Nov. 13, 1918]

To House. No. XIV. I hope that it is understood that my coming to the peace conference depends upon the prime ministers, the actual directing heads of the other governments, being also delegates. I assume also that I shall be selected to preside. I have decided that the selection of McCall would be unwise and expect to appoint Justice Day if he is well enough.

Referring to your number 100 [12],[1] no letter from Curzon about an Oxford degree has reached me. Of course I cannot decline the degree but it will be impossible for me to prepare an address which I would be willing to deliver on the Romanes foundation.

Referring to your number 89,[2] my position must of course be that the boundaries of Italy and the whole Adriatic settlement is to be decided by the peace conference in the general interest.

WWT telegram (WP, DLC).
    [1] EMH to WW, Nov. 10, 1918 (fifth telegram of that date).
    [2] EMH to WW, Nov. 11, 1918 (first telegram of that date).

To Andrew Carnegie

My dear Mr. Carnegie: The White House 13 November, 1918.

It was very delightful to receive your letter. I know how your heart must rejoice at the dawn of peace after these terrible years of struggle, for I know how long and how earnestly you have worked for and desired such conditions as I pray God it may now be possible for us to establish. The meeting place of the Peace Conference has not yet been selected, but even if it is not held at The Hague, I am sure that you will be present in spirit.

Cordially and faithfully yours,   Woodrow Wilson

TLS (A. Carnegie Papers, DLC).

To Joseph Patrick Tumulty

Dear Tumulty: [The White House] 13 November, 1918

Will you not assure these gentlemen that this is a matter that I have very much at heart and am not likely to forget or neglect if I have any opportunity to act.[1] You might ask them also if they have in mind any practicable present measures.

The President

TL (WP, DLC).
    [1] Wilson was responding to Louis Marshall and Julian W. Mack to WW, Nov. 11, 1918, T telegram (WP, DLC). This telegram warned of the imminent danger of pogroms directed against the Jews of all eastern European countries, but especially those of Poland and Rumania, and provided some evidence to support this assertion. Similar events, the writers warned, might be expected in Germany and the former territories of Austria-Hungary unless "strong and immediate preventive measures" were taken. They did not state what these measures should be, but they did urge Wilson to take some action to prevent the expected massacres. They suggested that the recognition of such new nations as Poland should depend upon their safeguarding the rights of Jews and other minority groups.

To Dan Voorhees Stephens

My dear Mr. Stephens: [The White House] 13 November, 1918

Tumulty has been kind enough to let me see your interesting letter to him of November 9th, and I want you to know with how much interest I have read it not only, but how deeply I appreciate the whole spirit and purpose of it. We must not allow the results of the recent election to disturb us in any way. Anybody who gets in the way of the proper measures of reconstruction and reform will, I am sure, be the worse for wear when the struggle is over.

Cordially and sincerely yours,   Woodrow Wilson

TLS (Letterpress Books, WP, DLC).

To Key Pittman

My dear Senator: The White House 13 November, 1918.

Your letter of November 12th is characteristic of you, and I am happy to have such an associate.

Cordially and faithfully yours,   Woodrow Wilson

TLS (K. Pittman Papers, DLC).

To Cleveland Hoadley Dodge

My dear Cleve: The White House 13 November, 1918.

This is just a line of deep affection and gratitude. Your letter has made me very happy, but I do not know how to answer it except to bless you.   Affectionately yours,   Woodrow Wilson

TLS (WC, NjP).

To Jessie Woodrow Wilson Sayre

My dear little girl: [The White House] 13 November, 1918

It was a real joy to get your letter. With Margaret gone, I feel peculiarly bereft of my dear daughters, and any news you can send me of yourself and your dear ones is not only welcome, but makes me very happy, particularly when it is good news such as this letter brings.

Margaret seems to have plunged into the midst of intensely interesting things in France, and I am sure that they will all feel that she is a breath of fresh air out of the West. We are all well. I am very tired, but not too tired, and not at all dismayed or disheartened by the recent elections. I think the Republicans will find the responsibility which they must now assume more onerous than joyful, and my expectation is that they will exercise it with some circumspection. I shall see to it that they are put in a position to realize their full responsibility, and the reckoning in 1920 may hold disappointing results for them.

Edith and I have been wondering if while Helen is there you could not steal down to see us, without the children if you thought there was any danger to their health in bringing them, or with them if you could bring them. We are extremely hungry for a glimpse of you.

Edith joins me in warmest love to you, my dear, dear litle girl, and to Frank and the babies. I need not tell you that my own love for you is without measure.

Your loving father, [Woodrow Wilson]

CCL (WP, DLC).

Three Telegrams from Edward Mandell House

Paris. Nov. 13, 1918.

Number 100. For the President.

Lord Derby, British Ambassador called today and presented me the following telegram from Mr. Balfour: "If you think invitation would be acceptable will you please express to the President the sincere hope of His Majesty's Government that should he decide to come to Europe in connection with negotiations for peace he will honor this country by landing here. I need hardly assure you of the warm welcome he will receive. Oxford University would, I know, be proud to offer him a degree. Cambridge has already done so, gladly violating in his honor its immemorial practice. I hope he *would* find time to visit both." Edward House.

Paris, November 13, 1918.

Number 101. For The President.

The Allied Governments are waiting to know the approximate date of your arrival so that plans for the preliminary and final conferences can be made. I hope it will be possible to have your answer today.

Edward House.

T telegrams (WP, DLC).

Paris. Nov. 13, 1918.

Number 105. Secret for the President.

Clemenceau informs me that the Allies feel, now that the armistice is signed, that the German authorities should address their official communication to them rather than to the United States exclusively. It is a small matter, but under the circumstances I believe it would be wise for you to give the German authorities an intimation that better feeling could more easily be brought about if they would do this. I would suggest that you inform the Allied

Ambassadors as to any action you take so that they may inform their governments.   Edward House.

T telegram (SDR, RG 59, 763.72119/9132, DNA).

To Edward Mandell House

[The White House, Nov. 13, 1918]
[No. 13.] I expect to sail December 3rd.

T transcript of WWsh telegram (WP, DLC).

From Charles Evans Hughes

My dear Mr. President: [New York] November 13, 1918.
Absence from New York has prevented an earlier acknowledgment of the receipt of your letter with respect to the aircraft inquiry.[1] I am deeply gratified to receive this expression from you, as it was my constant aim to make the investigation, within the range described in the report, as thorough as possible and to give the country an exact and impartial statement of the facts.
I have the honor to remain
Very sincerely yours,   Charles E. Hughes

TLS (WP, DLC).
[1] See WW to C. E. Hughes, Nov. 7, 1918, Vol. 51.

From the Diary of Josephus Daniels

1918 Wednesday 13 November
War Council
Shall we annul contracts?
      "   "   continue to fix prices?
WW. Gradual. Do not disturb conditions   better make more shells than we need
Shall Gov. own and run ships? Or let them go back   WW own them
McAdoo thought there must be some dislocation,   prices stimulated must go down
Treasury cannot finance on present scale

To David Lloyd George

[The White House] 14 November 1918.

May I not express my sincere admiration of the admirable temper and purpose of your address of the eleventh just reproduced in part in our papers.[1] It is delightful to be made aware of such community of thought and counsel in approaching the high and difficult task now awaiting us.   Woodrow Wilson.

T telegram (Letterpress Books, WP, DLC).
[1] Lloyd George had spoken to a meeting of members of the Liberal party at No. 10 Downing Street on November 12, not the 11th. He declared that one of the principal issues at the coming general election would be the nature of the peace settlement. He called for a peace based upon right and justice rather than upon vengeance and avarice. He stated his belief that a league of nations was "absolutely essential to permanent peace" and said that the British delegation would go to the peace conference to guarantee that the league became a reality. He also discussed domestic and imperial affairs. He argued that the victory in the war should be the impetus for thoroughgoing reform at home rather than for the kind of reactionary movements which had followed other wars. The revolutionary spirit abroad in the world needed wise direction to lead it into constructive channels. For a summary of Lloyd George's speech, see "Coalition to Continue," London *Times*, Nov. 13, 1918. A briefer account is "Lloyd George Against Vengeance Peace," *New York Times*, Nov. 14, 1918.

To Daniel Calhoun Roper

My dear Mr. Roper: [The White House] 14 November, 1918.

I am sincerely obliged to you for your letter of November 13th.[1] It concerns a matter with which as you naturally assume my thoughts have been very much concerned, and I am obliged to you for a very thoughtful suggestion.
                    Cordially and sincerely yours,   Woodrow Wilson

TLS (Letterpress Books, WP, DLC).
[1] D. C. Roper to JPT, Nov. 13, 1918, TLS (WP, DLC). Roper warned that the Republicans were about to take up the issue of economy and retrenchment in federal governmental activities now that the war had ended. He urged that Wilson preempt this issue by immediately appointing a committee to survey the present activities of the government and bring about "effective coordination . . . in contracting the activities and reducing the expenditures and appropriations proportionately."

From Edward Mandell House

Paris Nov 14, 1918

107. Secret for the President.

If the Peace Congress assembles in France Clemenceau will be presiding officer. If a neutral country had been chosen you would have been asked to preside.

Americans here whose opinions are of value are practically unanimous in the belief that it would be unwise for you to sit in the Peace Conference. They fear that it would involve a loss of dignity and your commanding position.

Clemenceau has just told me that he hopes you will not sit in the Congress because no head of a state should sit there. The same feeling prevails in England. Cobb cables that Reading and Wiseman voice the same view. Everyone wants you to come over to take part in the preliminary conferences. It is at these meetings that peace terms will be worked out and determined just as the informal conferences determined the German and Austrian armistices. It is of vital importance I think for you to come as soon as possible. For everything is being held in abeyance.

John Davis who is here gives as his offhand opinion that you need not be present the opening of Congress. However I *am* [planning] *for your* sailing December third but hoping you will consider it possible to come at an early [earlier] date. Clemenceau believes that the preliminary discussion[s] need not take more than three weeks. The peace conferences he believes may take as long as four months.

We will not know until we have a meeting to discuss the method of procedure just how many delegates each country may have but I am inclined to think that they will adopt my suggestion and appoint seven with only five sitting at one time. I believe it would be well to have seven delegates with two republicans and one of those Root and the other McCall. This may avoid criticism and opposition. I doubt whether Justice Day would satisfy the republicans any better than McCall and he would not be as useful. I believe it would be a mistake not to have labor represented.

If you do not deliver the valedictory [Romanes] lecture at Oxford I would suggest coming directly to France and going to Italy and England later. Pending your arrival we will take up the question of the method of procedure but Clemenceau promises me that no questions concerning peace terms will be brought up. He insists that you become the guest of the nation and in my opinion you cannot avoid this.

In announcing your departure I think it important that you should not state that you will sit in at the Peace Conference. That can be determined after you get here. There is reason enough for your coming because of the impossibility of keeping in touch and exercising a guiding hand at such a distance.

The French, English and Italian Prime Ministers will head their delegations.   House.

T telegram (WP, DLC).

Two Letters from Josephus Daniels

My dear Mr. President: [Washington] November 14, 1918.

I trust that in your message to Congress you will urge the authorization of the three year building program for new naval construction. I have talked to Chairmen Padgett and Swanson and they are both in hearty accord, but in view of the opposition that may arise along the line of immediate reduction before the Peace Conference, I feel sure a word from you will insure adoption.

Sincerely yours,   [Josephus Daniels]

CCL (J. Daniels Papers, DLC).

Dear Mr. President: Washington. Nov. 14, 1918.

You will recall that some days ago, in discussing the personnel of the Peace Commission, I expressed the hope that you would name Mr. Bryan. He is in perfect accord with the spirit and letter of your declarations and your large purposes. His convictions as to the means to make permanent peace are in line with those you entertain. It is true that many regard him as a pacifist, and in a sense he is, but during the entire war his support of every measure for its prosecution has been genuine and sincere, and in the early days it was helpful when ultra-militarists were criticizing and hindering the programme.

Mr. Bryan, as you said in your speech in Washington in 1912,[1] has rendered lasting service in pointing out deep rooted evils and in fighting them when many others did not see and warn. As a stout champion of the rights of the people he is a world figure and his devotion is appreciated by those who labor.

It is the crowning ambition of his life to have the opportunity of rendering this service and I trust you will feel that you can name him as one of the commissioners. I know there are thousands—very many—who would be gratified at his selection

With the earnest hope that this suggestion (and you know I would not make it if [I] did not feel deeply it would strengthen the principles for which you stand) may meet your approval, I am,

Sincerely yours,   Josephus Daniels

ALS (WP, DLC).
[1] Wilson's address is printed at Jan. 8, 1912, Vol. 24.

From William Gibbs McAdoo

Dear Mr. President: Washington. November 14, 1918.

Now that an armistice has been signed and peace is assured, I feel at liberty to apprise you of my desire to return, as soon as possible, to private life.

I have been conscious, for some time, of the necessity for this step, but of course I could not consider it while the country was at war.

For almost six years, I have worked incessantly under the pressure of great responsibilities. Their exactions have drawn heavily on my strength. The inadequate compensation allowed by law to Cabinet Officers (as you know I receive no compensation as Director General of Railroads) and the very burdensome cost of living in Washington have so depleted my personal resources that I am obliged to reckon with the facts of the situation.

I do not wish to convey the impression that there is any actual impairment of my health because such is not the fact. As a result of long overwork I need a reasonable period of genuine rest to replenish my energy. But more than this, I must, for the sake of my family, get back to private life to retrieve my personal fortunes.

I cannot secure the required rest nor the opportunity to look after my long neglected private affairs unless I am relieved of my present responsibilities.

I am anxious to have any retirement effected with the least possible inconvenience to yourself and to the public service but it would, I think, be wise to accept now my resignation as Secretary of the Treasury, to become effective upon the appointment and qualification of my successor so that he may have the opportunity and advantage of participating promptly in the formulation of the policies that should govern the future work of the Treasury. I would suggest that my resignation as Director General of Railroads become effective January 1, 1919, or upon the appointment of my successor.

I hope you will understand, my dear Mr. President, that I would permit nothing but the most imperious demands to force my withdrawal from public life. Always I shall cherish as the greatest honor of my career the opportunity you have so generously given me to serve the country under your leadership in these epochal times.

Affectionately yours,   W G McAdoo

TLS (WP, DLC).

From Herbert Clark Hoover

Dear Mr. President: Washington *14 November 1918*

The general food situation in Europe looms more strongly hour by hour through the various reports and telegrams that we are receiving.

In accordance with the arrangements made with your approval, the War Department is to give us shipping for 140,000 or 150,000 tons at once which foodstuffs they will advance to carry into French stocks or southern European ports for re-distribution on methods that may be determined on my arrival.

In addition to this, and in view of the serious situation in Northern Europe, I am—in accordance with our discussions of yesterday—instructing the Grain Corporation to purchase and ship to English ports for re-direction, another 125,000 to 140,000 tons of food to be used, probably in Northern Europe. We can finance this through the Grain Corporation up to the point of sale.

The ability to perform the measure will depend of course on our ability to secure the shipping. Mr. Hurley is making arrangements to divert to us if possible some boats outside of the Army programme but if this should fail I am anxious that the Army should make other sacrifices of its munitions programme to enable this to be carried out at once. I am confident that if we can have started to Europe 350,000 to 400,000 tons of food for these special purposes within the next ten or fifteen days and I can inform the various governments—especially some of the Northern Neutrals—of positive arrivals that will be placed at their disposal, it would enable them to increase rations from their present stocks and probably keep their boats from rocking.

I have had an opportunity this morning to discuss with a group of Senators the question of the provision of an appropriation for working capital to cover these operations. Some of them, especially Senators Pittman and Kellogg, are prepared to place themselves at your disposal, to forward any appropriation for this purpose. On the other hand, I find that amongst some of them bitterness is so great that they would raise strong opposition to raising an appropriation that they thought might be used for feeding Germany. I do believe that appropriation of a revolving fund could be obtained for providing food to the liberated peoples and neutrals and that it might be well to limit this legislation to these purposes; because through such agencies as the Army and the Grain Corporation, with perhaps your Presidential fund, we could probably manage to handle the German problem in itself.

While it should be clear in such appropriation that it is not a gift, but to provide a revolving fund to enable us to carry on relief commerce, it should have a special provision that the foodstuffs may be used for philanthropic purposes if necessary, for the populations of Belgium and Serbia.   Yours faithfully,   Herbert Hoover

TLS (WP, DLC).

From Herbert Clark Hoover, with Enclosure

Dear Mr. President: Washington 14-November-1918

I enclose herewith copy of the cablegram which I have dispatched to Mr. Cotton in accordance with your suggestion.
                              Faithfully yours,   Herbert Hoover

TLS (WP, DLC).

E N C L O S U R E

Copy of Cablegram

With regard to various telegrams yourself and Cravath on relief to areas lately under German control on further consultation with President he authorized the following further statement to be made to our officials in Europe for their guidance but not for communication and asks that a copy should be sent to Colonel House and Cravath Statement begins We consider ourselves as trustees of our surplus production of all kinds for the benefit of the most necessitous and the most deserving We feel that we must ourselves execute this trusteeship that we are not unmindful of the obligation which we have to the sustenance of those who have fought with us against Germany and that together with the necessities of those populations released from the German yoke we feel that they may well deserve a priority in our distribution On the other hand we cannot undertake any cooperative arrangements that look to the control of our exports after peace and furthermore and equally important that the interallied councils hitherto set up in Europe were entirely for the purpose of guiding interallied relations during the period of the war and that any extension of their functions either by way of their control of our relations to other nations or the extension of their present functions beyond peace cannot be entertained by us All relationship involving the use of American food or credit for the people of other nations than the Allies themselves must await Mr Hoovers arrival in Europe so far as any such supplies or interest of the United States is concerned in which we will coordinate in every proper way (end of Statement) You can inform Sir Worthington Evans[1] that the form of organization involving coordination of the United States Government for distributing its food commodities arising in the United States through the various parts of Europe lately under German subjection can only be settled upon my arrival that the United States Food Administration is taking steps to at once largely increase the volume of American food stores at various points in Europe in order that the material may be available and that we have every desire for proper coordination of all efforts　　　　　　　　　Herbert Hoover

TC telegram (WP, DLC).
[1] Sir Worthington Laming Worthington-Evans, Minister of Blockade and Parliamentary Undersecretary in the British Foreign Office.

From Joseph Patrick Tumulty

Dear Governor:　　　　　　The White House 14 November, 1918.

The attached clipping, entitled "E. H. Gary Warns of Industrial Panic,"[1] shows the necessity for some statement from you on the industrial situation. Something along these lines would help:

"This is a time for self-control and calm thinking on the part of the business men of America. No one need fear the readjustments that must inevitably follow as a result of peace. In preparing ourselves to enforce our ideas America has demonstrated her great power and marvelous originality in a way to challenge the admiration of the world. Turning away from the activities of war to the business of peace, if done violently and hurriedly, is bound to injure the tender fabric of business as a whole. In considering the processes of readjustment we must consider business as a whole, so that whatever changes are found to be necessary to bring business back to the normal bases of peace must be done gradually and with a due regard to business as a whole.

"Nobody need fear for the business future of America. During the war instrumentalities for helpful cooperation between government and business have been fully developed and can be now called into action. The Federal Reserve Act, which has done such marvelous work in stabilizing the credit of the country, can be further utilized as a helpful instrument not only in helping business in a domestic way, but in aiding it further in developing foreign markets for American Business.

"The period of exclusiveness for American business is past. The development of our merchant marine will open up markets to American genius and initiative never before dreamed of. Agencies like the Webb Act,[2] the Rural Credits Act, and other instrumentalities placed at our disposal by the acts of Congress will now be given full rein and a newer vigor. No one need be afraid that any step taken by the government in this transitional stage will be taken without knowledge of all the facts of the situation. Justice to every interest, both of capital and labor, will characterize every step and every forward movement. America has only to retain her self-control and poise if she would be successful in all these great enterprises."

Sincerely yours,   Tumulty

TLS (WP, DLC).
   [1] It is missing.
   [2] He meant the Webb-Pomerene Act, which became law on April 10, 1918. It exempted business associations entered into for the sole purpose of engaging in export trade from prosecution under the antitrust laws. 40 *Statutes at Large* 516.

From William Rufus Day

My dear Mr. President: Washington, D. C. November 14. 1918.

I am deeply appreciative of the honor which you have conferred upon me in the offer of a place upon the Peace Commission.[1]

I wish it were practicable for me to accept this opportunity for service. I am, however reluctantly, constrained to forego this privilege.

Wishing you continued success in the great work before you,
   I am, with high regard,

Sincerely yours,   William R. Day

ALS (WP, DLC).
   [1] Wilson's letter to Day is missing in WP, DLC, and in the W. R. Day Papers, DLC.

From Morris Sheppard and Kenneth Douglas McKellar

Dear Mr. President: [Washington] 14 November 1918.

We have noted with great interest and approval your statement that foodstuffs would be shipped to the suffering European peoples.[1] It was suggested at a conference of Senators from cotton growing states that the need of these peoples for clothing would doubtless be equally as great or nearly as great as the need for food. We were requested to write to you respectfully suggesting that you look into the advisability of permitting shipments of cotton to these peoples at the earliest practicable date.

Under present conditions cotton cannot be exported to these peoples at all unless specific permission or license is given by the

War Trade Board. The fact that such permission is not being given by the War Trade Board is causing cotton to accumulate and congest in the Southern states, when it could be used to such good effect abroad.

This condition is having an adverse effect on the price of cotton, and is causing the banks and other financial institutions to be severely overloaded. Therefore, as a matter of justice both to the people abroad and to our own people, we bring this matter to your attention.

It has been stated by someone connected with the Shipping Board that no ships would be available for the transportation of cotton abroad, and this is a further factor in depressing the price and causing congestion of cotton in this country.

We have been asked to bring to your attention this situation, and the further suggestion that the ships which go to Europe to bring our soldiers home could be utilized, in part at least, in carrying cotton there. We also understand that other ships under control of the Shipping Board could be made available for the transportation of cotton.

With highest regard, we are

Very sincerely yours,   Morris Sheppard
Kenneth McKellar

TLS (WP, DLC).
[1] That is, in his address to a joint session of Congress printed at Nov. 11, 1918.

From Louis Marshall

The President,   New York November 14, 1918.

On the 7th instant I submitted to you on behalf of the American Jewish Committee a communication relative to the status of the Jews of Poland,[1] which I followed on the 11th instant by a telegram which set forth the terms of a cablegram received from Copenhagen which contained alarming information concerning threatened attacks upon the Jews of Poland and Roumania.[2]

In my letter I suggested a number of principles the acceptance of which it was hoped might be made conditions precedent to the establishment of the new Poland. They were presented under the stress of urgency, in order that you might have before you in general terms the ideas which most Jews entertain on the subject. They have been revised as to phraseology, after conference with a number of gentlemen who are deeply concerned in the proper solution of the problems affecting the Jews of Poland. I now take the liberty of bespeaking for them in their amended form your favorable consideration. They are as follows:

(1) All inhabitants of the territory of the Polish State, shall for all purposes be citizens thereof, provided, however, that such as have heretofore been subjects of other states, who desire to retain their allegiance to such states or assume allegiance to their successor states, to the exclusion of Polish citizenship, may do so by a formal declaration to be made within a specified period.

(2) All Polish citizens, without distinction as to origin, race or creed, shall enjoy equal civil, political and religious rights, and no law shall be made or enforced which shall abridge the privileges or immunities of, or impose upon any citizen any discrimination, disability or restriction whatsoever, on account of race or religion, or deny to any person the equal protection of the laws.

(3) At no election for members of any legislative, administrative or judicial body, whether national, district, municipal or local, at which the electors are to choose more than two members of any such body, shall any elector vote for more than two-thirds of the members thereof to be voted for at the election.

(4) Polish shall be the official language, but no law shall be passed restricting the use of any other language, and all existing laws declaring such prohibition are repealed.

(5) The Jews shall be accorded autonomous management of their own religious, educational, charitable and other cultural institutions.

(6) Those who observe the seventh day as their Sabbath shall not be prohibited from pursuing their secular affairs on any other day of the week so long as they shall not disturb the religious worship of others.　　　Faithfully yours,　Louis Marshall

TLS (WP, DLC).
[1] L. Marshall to WW, Nov. 7, 1918, Vol. 51.
[2] See WW to JPT, Nov. 13, 1918, n. 1.

From William Graves Sharp

My dear Mr. President,　　　　　　　Paris, November 14, 1918.

The momentous events occurring within the past week have hastened the coming of a time to which I have long looked forward, as determining me to tender to you my resignation from the post with which you honored me and which I have filled during now four years.

Beginning my service almost coincident with the breaking out of the war, I have consistently thought to end it approximately with its close. Now that that time has come, I have not altered my mind from my original purpose. I would be pleased, therefore, if you would kindly accept my resignation, to take effect soon after the beginning of the coming new year—say, at some time within the month of February.

Regretting for many reasons, as I shall, to lay down the work which, arduous at times though it has been, nevertheless has always been agreeable to me on account of its pleasing associations and the important character of its duties, yet, after such a long absence from home, I feel that I must now give my attention to my business affairs. I am led to believe that by the time set for my departure, we shall all have the satisfaction of seeing at least the most important of the large questions settled by the Peace Conference.

The acquiesance in principle by all the Allies as well as by the Central Powers of the fourteen conditions enunciated by you last January has indeed done much to prepare the way for the solution of such questions. But I am persuaded that if the assurance of a lasting peace is sought, then emphatically the condition imposed in No 4 calling for a reduction of national armaments—they should ultimately cease to exist except for enforcing domestic order—and the principle of the League of Nations involved in No 14 must be written in ineffac[e]able letters in the Treaty. These alone can guarantee the performance of all the other conditions so wisely laid down by you for governing the future relations of peoples toward each other.

I cannot thus tender my resignation—that you may have suffic[i]ent time in which to consider the selection of my successor—without expressing to you my deep appreciation for the words of confidence and good-will which you have sent over to me. They have been very precious to me and have afforded that kind of encouragement that every man needs at times in order to go ahead with the desired assurance.

I must also express to you my admiration for the remarkable vision displayed by you from the very beginning of the war in forecasting the events which have so transformed old conditions and for the high order of constructive ability which you have shown in shaping such events to their final fruition. You have made the world your debtor as no other man in history.

With every good wish for the unbounded success of all your undertakings and for the vouchsafing to you of good health for the completion of the high mission for which Providence has appointed you, I am, believe me, my dear Mr. President,
Very sincerely yours, Wm. G. Sharp.

TLS (WP, DLC).

From George Weston Anderson

My dear Mr. President: Boston. November 14th, 1918.

The fact that Senator Lodge is prospectively Chairman of the Foreign Relations Committee I think justifies me in making sure that you have what appears to be a verbatim copy of the speech that he made before a representative audience at the City Club on Tuesday night.[1]

As you know, the Boston Transcript is read by "all our best people." I need not point out that Senator Lodge did not mention the League of Nations or any form of international organization substantially different from that which was mapped out at the Congress of Vienna a century ago. He would have found Count Mettinich [Metternich] a most congenial associate.

Permit me to add that, after taking some pains to sense the public feeling in this community, I am satisfied that on an issue properly presented, your policies for a peace with justice based upon some sort of international organization, would command the support of at least two-thirds of the voters of New England. Confused as were the issues in the minds of the voters on November 5th, Massachusetts did better through the election of Senator Walsh than almost any other place in the country. For your type of democracy, New England is a good field to cultivate. I hope you have not forgotten that if 30,000 Republicans, rightly divided, had two years ago voted the Democratic ticket, you would have carried all of New England.

I enclose also clipping from the Boston Post urging Governor McCall for the Peace Commission.[2] The Post has, I suppose, the largest Democratic circulation of any paper in New England.

Please do not spend one minute of your valuable time in acknowledging this letter. But I should like to feel at liberty from time to time to report such indications as seem to be worth while, of the condition of public sentiment here on the great issues of the foundation of a permanent peace.

Perhaps I may add that I am one of the Trustees of the World Peace Foundation, which has the income of about $1,000,000 for this purpose. I was counsel for Mr. Edwin Ginn and worked into legal shape his plans for getting the world so organized as to prevent what has now (since his death) happened. He, more than any— perhaps all—others, was responsible for Mr. Carnegie's contribution of $10,000,000. Both of these endowments[3] ought now to be put to active use in creating a public sentiment which shall back you in your plans for a world order.

Sincerely yours,   George W. Anderson

TLS (WP, DLC).

¹ "Lodge Warns Against Pacifist Sentimentality in Making Peace Terms," *Boston Evening Transcript*, Nov. 13, 1918. As the headline suggests, Lodge, in his speech to the Boston City Club on November 12, called for a severe peace settlement with Germany and her allies, one designed to guarantee that Germany could never again wage war effectively against her neighbors. The German people, he declared, had supported the Imperial government and its war effort to the bitter end and thus shared in the guilt of the war. The only way to insure that Germany would not again run amuck was to surround her with physical barriers. To this end, he called for the return of Alsace-Lorraine to France, the award of *Italia Irredenta* to Italy, the breakup of the Austro-Hungarian and Turkish empires and the restoration or creation of independent states out of their various nationality groups, and the establishment of a great Polish nation, with access to the sea at Danzig. Lodge also argued that Germany could pay, and should be forced to pay, heavy indemnities, not only to Belgium, France, England, and the United States, but even to neutral nations such as Norway, which had lost much of their shipping on account of submarine attacks. Finally, Lodge said that Germany should not receive back her former colonial possessions. He warned the American people to stand firm against attempts by "a pacifist movement" to modify and make easy the peace terms with Germany.

² "Hardly Root," *Boston Post*, Nov. 14, 1918.

³ That is, the World Peace Foundation and the Carnegie Endowment for International Peace.

To Newton Diehl Baker

Dear Baker,   [The White House, c. Nov. 14, 1918]

Senator Pittman wants to get ahead of Smoot in this.¹ What do you think of it.   W.W.

ALI (N. D. Baker Papers, DLC).
¹ Pittman had proposed to introduce a resolution authorizing the President "to cause to be struck bronze medals commemorating the winning of the world's war and the valor of our military forces and to distribute and present such medals to the officers and men of our land, sea, and air forces." *Cong. Record*, 65th Cong., 2d sess., p. 11578.

From Newton Diehl Baker

Dear Mr. President: Washington. November 15, 1918.

I return the enclosed papers. The idea seems to me eminently proper and I would suggest that Senator Pittman be asked to introduce the resolution at once.

Respectfully yours,   Newton D. Baker

TLS (WP, DLC).

To Frank J. Hayes

My dear Mr. Hayes: [The White House] 15 November 1918.

Were there no other reason, the extraordinary record made by the mine workers of the United States in mining coal during the past eventful months would lead me to consider the appeal contained in the telegram of November 1st, signed by you and others representing the United Mine Workers of America.[1]

I have examined with care the matter involved in your request and believe that the course pursued by Mr. Garfield not only deals justly with the bituminous mine workers today but that this course together with the firm adherence of the United Mine Workers to the arrangement made with me last year constitute a long step in the direction of stabilizing wages.

I am satisfied that only by pursuing this course will we escape the unfortunate results which otherwise and at other times have characterized the change from war to peace, a process which unregulated would press with the greatest severity upon labor.

By the time peace is promulgated, I am hopeful that the application of this principle will complete the transition of the nation's industries from war to peace with the least possible disturbance, suffering and loss.

Cordially and sincerely yours,   Woodrow Wilson

TLS (Letterpress Books, WP, DLC).
[1] See F. J. Hayes and Others to WW, Nov. 1, 1918, Vol. 51.

To Joseph Wingate Folk

My dear Governor: [The White House] 15 November, 1918.

I am deeply disappointed in the result in Missouri.[1] I had looked forward with real pleasure to being associated with you here in a new and vital way, but I think I understand in some part at least the results, and you may be sure I am not repining.

With the warmest good wishes,
Cordially and sincerely yours,   Woodrow Wilson

TLS (Letterpress Books, WP, DLC).
[1] Wilson was replying to J. W. Folk to WW, Nov. 11, 1918, TLS (WP, DLC). Folk had lost to Selden Palmer Spencer, Republican, in the race in Missouri to fill the unexpired term of the late Senator William Joel Stone.

Two Telegrams from Edward Mandell House

Paris. Nov. 15, 1918.

Number 108. For the President. I send for your information following telegram from Clemenceau to Lloyd George. "The coming of President Wilson naturally changes some of our plans in preparing for the conference. It seems to me that we cannot begin the work before the President arrives. We ought to be unanimous in this respect. Besides, I think it is not a bad idea to let the German revolution settle down for a while in order that we may know before proceeding what we have before us. I would suggest to you that we draw up some preparatory memoranda, either in London or in Paris. I am ready to accept all your suggestions in this respect. If we should proceed thus, the President on arriving could make his observations without any delay and the task would find itself advanced. I expect to see Mr. Sonnino this afternoon. I do not doubt that he will assent. A particularly serious question is to know whether the President intends to take part in the conference. I ought not to hide from you that in my opinion this seems to be neither desirable nor possible. Since he is chief of state he is consequently not on the same level as ourselves. To admit one chief of state without admitting all seems to me an impossibility."

Edward House.

T telegram (SDR, RG 59, 763.72119/9133, DNA).

Paris. Nov. 15, 1918.

Number 110. For the President.

I have just received the following communication from Lord Derby: "Copy of telegram from Mr. Balfour to Lord Derby of November 15th. Very urgent. Personal. Please convey following message from the King to Colonel House for transmission to the President of the United States. 'I am delighted to hear that you contemplate shortly coming to England on your way to France. It would give the Queen and myself the greatest pleasure if you and Mrs. Wilson will be our guests at Buckingham Palace during your stay in London.' "

Edward House.

T telegram (WP, DLC).

Edward Mandell House to Robert Lansing[1]

Number 109.   Paris, November 15, 1918.

Following are remarks made by the French Foreign Office on previous peace conferences:

[1] There is a copy of this telegram in SDR, RG 59, 763.72119/9121, DNA. The telegram printed below was retyped, and Wilson's comments were typed in red ink. Wilson wrote "Peace Conference" at the top of the document, which signified that he intended to take it with him to Paris. He answered the urgent questions in WW to EMH, Nov. 18, 1918 (first telegram of that date).

"ONE

The offices of President and Secretary are both of great importance and appertain invariably to the power where the plenipotentiaries are assembled.

(NOTE: President, yes.

Secretary, ?

TWO

The plenipotentiaries for each power are few in number in order to facilitate negotiations, avoid lengthy discussions and diversion of views between delegates of the same power and indiscretions.

THREE

The representatives of the states are either the Chancellor or Prime Minister or the Minister of Foreign Affaires."

NOTE: I do not understand this.

FOLLOWING is scheme of procedure as suggested by French Foreign Office:

"SCHEME OF PROCEDURE

A. The Peace Congress is composed of representatives of the belligerent powers which have taken actual part in the war. Exceptionally other powers may be convened in so far as questions interesting them directly may be made the subject of debates there at and only in regard to such questions.

NOTE: Japan? Brazil? Portugal?

B. The Powers shall be exclusively represented at the Congress by plenipotentiary delegates to the maximum number of three, the latter may be accompanied by technical counsellors.

NOTE: Does this mean at the sittings? If so, is there no limit as to numbers?

I favor 5 commissioners and a limit on advisers.

C. The order of precedence among the members of the Congress is the French alphabetical order of the powers (rule consecrated by custom).

NOTE: Approved.

D. The Congress shall be opened under the provisional presidency of the President of the Council of Ministers of the country where it is sitting, the verification of the powers of the members of the Congress shall be proceeded with immediately by a committee composed of the first plenipotentiary of one of the Allied or

Associated powers and of the first plenipotentiary of one of the adverse powers.

NOTE: Approved.

E. Following the verification of the powers of the members the Congress shall nominate its permanent President and two vice Presidents.

NOTE: Shall not the Government where the meeting is held name the President?

How are the vice-Presidents to be named?

F. A secretarial bureau designated of the members of Congress shall be presented to the latter's approval by the President who shall assume control and responsibility thereof. The office of this bureau shall be to establish the protocol of the sitting, to file the archives and provide the administrative organization of the Congress and generally assume the regular and punctual working of the services entrusted to it.

The chief of this bureau will be given the guardianship and responsibility of the protocols and archives of the Congress which shall always be accessible to the members thereof.

NOTE: Approved.

G. The press reports of the progress of the Congress shall be assured daily, official communiques prepared by the Secretariat and published each day at the same hour. The members of the Congress undertake formally not to give out any other communications concerning the operations of the Congress.

NOTE: General approval, provided there is opportunity for complaint and change in the event it is not satisfactory.

H. The French language is recognized as the official language for the deliberations and the acts of the Congress. The members thereof are free to present their remarks or verbal communications in any language they may choose subject to their giving out immediately a French translation thereof.

NOTE: I think that this is probably necessary, provided English as well as French stenographers report the oral statements and oral French statements are put at once into English.

Personally I favor both French and English be declared official languages.

I. All documents destined to be included in the protocols shall be written out and read by the members of the Congress who shall have had the initiative thereof; when not made out in French they shall be accompanied by a translation; no proposition can be presented to the Congress otherwise than by one of the plenipotentiaries and on behalf of the power represented by him.

NOTE: generally approved.

J. The members who may be desirous of submitting propositions must do so by writing and deposit same at the previous sitting in order to facilitate discussion thereof, except where amendments are concerned and not material propositions.

NOTE: I think that the rule should be to deposit at a previous meeting or at least 48 hours before a sitting with Secretary who shall deliver copies to all delegates 24 hours before sitting.

K. Petitions, missions, remarks or documents addressed to the Congress by persons other than the plenipotentiaries shall be received, classified and summarized by the Secretary who shall deposit same in the archives of the Congress.

NOTE: Rules as to printing and distributing should be made.

L. The discussion of questions will be preceded by a first and second reading in order to establish first, the agreement upon the principles, and subsequently, allow the definition of details.

NOTE: I do not understand this.

M. Subject to the acceptance of the Congress, the plenipotentiaries are entitled to authorize their technical counsellors to present directly technical explanations upon any particular question when such explanations may be deemed expedient. The technical: any particular question may be entrusted by the Congress to a committee composed of technical advisers of the plenipotentiaries charged with the mission of presenting a report to the Congress and of proposing solutions.

NOTE: Approved.

N. All the decisions of the Congress shall be taken unanimously, except in regard to question of, unless in that second the minority should put on record a formal protestation.

NOTE: Query.

O. The protocol drawn up by the secretarial bureau shall be printed and distributed as provisional agreement proofs to the plenipotentiaries; this previous communication will take the place of the first reading and in the event of no modification being demanded, the text thereof shall be considered as approved.

Some determination must also be taken in regard to our Allies who have treated with the enemy (without our recognizing these treaties): Roumania, Russia.

What form of representation shall we accept for the states in formation, non-recognized by us: Yugo-Slavs, Finns, Ukrainians, Lithuanians, Esthonians, Lettons, Arabs, Armenians, Jews of Palestine?

Certain regulations interesting neutrals having to be examined by the Congress, it is expedient to provide for the presentation and protection of their interest: Norway, Sweden, Denmark, Netherlands, Luxemburg, Switzerland, Spain, Persia, Ethiopians, Mexico, Argentine, Chile, and other neutral American states, (Bolivia, Peru, Uruguay, Ecuador—in a state of severance of diplomatic relations— and Colombia, *Dominican Republic*, Paraguay, San Salvador, Venezuela.)

NOTE: Query?

Finally, the enemies: Germany, Bulgaria, Turkey, Bavaria, German-Austria, Magyarie.

Evidently there can be no idea of allowing neutrals to discuss territorial rearrangement, indemnities and guarantees but on the other hand it is impossible to exclude them from the debates concerning the future international organization to which their adhesion is desired.

NOTE: Ought not claims of neutrals against belligerents to be provided for in some way? Otherwise full justice will not be done.

NOTE: Should not protocol be passed upon at next meeting by Congress.

P. A committee shall be formed to record the acts adopted by the Congress. This committee shall only have cognizance *of the* (*) *settled by* the Congress and shall be solely in charge of the recording of the text of the decisions adopted and of presenting same to the approbation of the Congress. It shall be composed of six members each forming part of the plenipotentiaries and comprising, one Frenchman, one of English tongue, one of Italian tongue, one of Portuguese tongue, one of Slav tongue, one of German tongue.

NOTE: How is committee to be named?

Two. Representation of the Powers and of the States.

The question of the participating powers in the Congress present certain delicate problems. First of all, the belligerents shall form part thereof, properly speaking: France, Great Britain, Italy, United States, Japan, Belgium, Servia, Greece, Portugal, Montenegro.

A place must also be reserved to the theoretical belligerents: China, Brazil, South American States (Cuba, Panama, Guatemala,

Nicaragua, Costa Rica, Haiti, Honduras, which might be represented by the United States to avoid crowding,) Liberia.

Then will come the question of the new States recognized by the Allied Powers: Poland, Bohemia.

THREE. PROCEDURE AND ORGANIZATION OF THE OPERATIONS.

Provision will have to be made for a first unofficial examination by the great powers (Great Britain, France, Italy, United States) of the questions to be discussed, examination which will lead to the preparation between them of the preliminaries of peace and the whole mechanism of the Congress of peace.

NOTE: This has the old element of danger which existed in the Concert of Powers, and yet to prevent confusion some method of the sort must be adopted.

It smacks of "secret diplomacy" and will doubtless invite that criticism by the smaller countries.

The work should evidently be divided among preparatory commissions formed only by plenipotentiaries (with the assistance of legal experts, financial, geographic, military, naval, industrial, and commercial experts, possessing consultative vote.)

NOTE: Is this work limited to the four powers?

It may be foreseen that the three general plenipotentiaries who will deal with the settlement proper of the war will appoint as assistants one or two representatives more particularly qualified to study the principles of the league of nations, that is to say, the stipulations of general public law which shall constitute the second great task of the Congress.

The three general plenipotentiaries (in accordance with the precedents mentioned herein above) might be for France: The Prime Minister, the Minister for Foreign Affairs, the Generalissimo.

The necessity of defining and limiting the delegations of the powers is imperative in order to avoid for instance the individual representation claimed by the important English colonies (a principle which cannot be allowed, for why should not a similar claim be presented by each of the different states composing the federation of the United States.)

NOTE: I quite agree as to this in principle, and I have the impression that the suggestion of 7 members originated with the British, so that Canada, Australia and South Africa might each have a representative, though Great Britain would maintain the majority of 4 members.

FOUR. PRINCIPLES AND BASES OF NEGOTIATIONS.

Similarly to the Congress of Vienna, leading principles should be proclaimed:

A. Right of peoples to decide their own destinies by free and secret vote (combined with the principle of a certain homogeneousness of the states, principally applicable to Bohemia, Tyrol, Istria, Dalmatia, Luxemburg as aforesaid.) In other regions, sectionings will have to be carried out in view of the discordance between the administrative frontiers and the limits of the peoples which they divide: A. such is the case for the Polish countries incorporated in Prussia or Austria, for the Lithuanian countries incorporated in Prussia or Russia in Europe, for the countries incorporated in the Ottoman Empire, on account of the confluence of the ethnical and religious groups, and of the difficulty of applying the criterion of equal and secret vote.

NOTE: Does not this also apply to Alsace-Lorraine, the Russian provinces &c.?

B. Release from treaties concluded between them of such groups of states which by the fact of their admission to the Congress shall waive their right thereto: This principle is entirely in accordance with the ideas of President Wilson.

NOTE: This applies as I read it to all agreements made prior to or during the war—Russia, Italy, Japan and Great Britain in regard to Pacific Islands.

Such a declaration has the advantage of freeing the allies from any previous imperialist aims. The necessity of abolishing the agreements with Russia (which would comprise the cession of Constantinople to that power) would in itself (assure?) the adoption of such a measure.

As to Italy, should she not adhere thereto, it would be difficult to see how she could be admitted into the discussion: having previously to her entry into the war presented to the Allies minutely detailed conditions for the advantages she desired to derive therefrom, she would only be entitled to discuss the affairs of the others if she herself allowed discussion upon her own extensions.

NOTE: We must not forget the hostility and jealousy between France and Italy, and that this is France's plan.

Finally, this Congress, like all those which have preceded it, should adopt a basis of discussion. It cannot, like the previous ones, lean upon the stipulations of a treaty, inasmuch as hitherto the Powers have only concluded armistices (with Bulgaria, Austria-

Hungary, Turkey and Germany, which cannot serve as a basis discussing a peace treaty.)

One single basis seems to exist at the present time: it is the solidary decision of the Allies upon their war aims, formulated January tenth 1917, in answer to the question of President Wilson, but it is rather a program than basis of negotiations.

It would therefore seem indispensable that the Prime Ministers and the Ministers for Foreign Affairs of the four great powers meet previously at Versailles to settle between them the affairs which the Congress shall have to deal with (that is to say, the preliminaries of peace) and the order in which they shall be discussed as well as the condition of the sittings of the Congress and its operations.

In a general way the questions to be discussed are segregated in two main series: First settlement proper of the war, second, elaboration of the league of nations.

This distinction would limit to the parties really interested the discussion of the essential and immediate questions to be settled and, wards the interest of a large number of states to discuss the general principles of the organization of the world to which their participation has been co[n]vened.

A. SETTLEMENT OF THE WAR.

One. Political stipulations.
A. New states. One, already recognized (Poland, Czecho-Slovaks). Two, in course of formation (Yugo-Slavs, Russian countries, etc.)
B. Territorial questions (restitution of territories, territories neutralized for the purpose of protection).
NOTE: What does the last clause refer to? Protectorates? Neutral States?

First. Alsace-Lorraine, (eighth Wilson proposition); Belgium, (seventh Wilson proposition); Italy, (ninth Wilson proposition).
Second. Frontiers (France, Belgium, Servia, Roumania, etc.)
Third. International status of means of communication, in particular those of Central Europe, rivers, railroads, canals, ports.
C. Oriental question, (twelfth Wilson proposition); Turkey, Armenia, Syria, Palestine, Arabia.
D. Colonies, (fifth Wilson proposition).
E. Extreme east, (Kiaochou, etc.)
NOTE: Does this cover Pacific Islands? Two. German owned concessions in China?

Two. Military and naval stipulations.
Military guarantees on land and sea, number of troops, disman-

tling of fortifications, reduction from war factories, territorial occupations etc.
NOTE: Is this disarmament? If so, how about naval forces? Sec. 5
    under B ("League of Nations")

Three. Stipulation of indemnities preparation of war damage on
land and sea, restitutions, re-constitutions, compensations in kind,
reimbursement of expenditure illegally imposed (C.R.B.)[2]
Four. Economic and financial stipulations: raw material, economic regime, settlement of accounts.
Five. Stipulations of private law. Settlement of private credits.
Liquidation of sequestrations.
Six. Reestablishment of the conventional regime upset by the
war.

B. LEAGUE OF NATIONS. (Stipulations of general public law)
One. League of nations (fourteenth Wilson proposition).
Two. Freedom of the seas (second Wilson proposition).
NOTE: Does this include a revision of the Rules of War on land,
    on sea, and in the air?

Three. International economic regime (third Wilson proposition).
NOTE: Should there not be some arrangement for codifying the
    principles of international law?

Four. Publicity of treaties (first Wilson proposition).
NOTE: Should not the subject of international arbitration be re-
    viewed in connection with a league of nations?

Five. Limitation of armaments (fourth Wilson proposition)."

I should appreciate very much if you will be good enough to
telegraph me as soon as practicable any modifications, additions or
suggestions you may care to make to me upon the above scheme
of procedure.   Edward House.

T MS (WP, DLC).
    [2] That is, the Commission for Belgian Relief.

From Key Pittman

My dear Mr. President: [Washington] November 15, 1918.
On yesterday you honored Senator Gerry and myself by seeking
our opinion with regard to the general impression of the necessity
of your attending the Peace Conference. I then unhesitatingly replied that I believed that the necessity was recognized by a large
majority of the members of the Senate. I now discover that there

is a grave diversity of opinion with regard to the effect that such action on your part might have and it has occur[r]ed to me that you would possibly be interested in a frank recital of these various expressions.

Last night I had the pleasure of assembling at a dinner with about thirty of your closest and strongest political supporters. The assembly involuntarily and spontaneously resolved itself into an unofficial and temporary committee upon the welfare of yourself and the Democratic party. It might seem presumptuous that any Democrat should take the liberty of even suggesting the effect of the future conduct of one who has always been intuitively right and whose success has not only been beyond that of his party but supreme throughout the world. The debate and the suggestions, Mr. President, came from no presumption, but from the love that each man there has for you and the hopes that are wrapped up in your career. The following are some of the points urged most strongly by those who believe that it would be a mistake for you to attend the Peace Conference, namely:

1. That you are now held in a sacred reverence by all the people of Europe and are looked upon as a superman residing afar off in a citadel of power beyond that of all nations, and that your association at the peace table with well-understood statesmen, who are but frail men long subject to criticism and even suspicion by certain classes of peoples, would lower your dignity, mar your prestige, and encourage resistence to any ultimatum that you might find it necessary to submit to the Peace Conference.

2. That you would be involved by the numerous petty questions and details and that your position with regard to the great principles that you maintain would be obscured.

3. That in these debates and decisions upon lesser questions you would lose the moral support of peoples that you may now confidently look to in your effort to establish the great principles of international justice.

4. That our own country itself is now in the immediate and gravest period of reconstruction, and that without your guiding hand upon the rudder at all times our government may be shipwrecked.

5. That congress is in session; that your advice and your executive action may be required at any minute.

Those who believe that it will be necessary for you to attend the Peace Conference expressed these views:

1. That the adoption and establishment of your program is essential to the liberty, the peace, and the happiness of the world, and that such accomplishment is of more importance than the temporary glory of any man or group of men.

2. That there are certain facts bearing upon the diplomacy of the greater nations that may be only told verbally, and that you alone have the power to speak them with sufficient verity to give them the fullest force.

3. That it would be unnecessary for you to wear away the strength of your armor and of your sword upon lesser questions and in minor debates; that these simpler but more tedious questions and other preliminaries could be disposed of by the Peace Conference before the great questions which will start the contest of great nations come before the Peace Conference. And that even then you need not attend the conference until it has reached such a stage of open and hopeless rupture that your dominating presence, personality and power are required to force the cessation of debate and the adoption of the only program that this country will ever stand for.

4. That it is unnecessary at this time to either declare that you will or will not attend the conference, as nothing but events can determine the necessity of the case.

5. That if the adoption of your program should ultimately require your presence at the peace table then all other considerations, both personal and political, should be cast aside.

You know, of course, that the latter expressions were mine as well as the expressions of a number of other supporters of yours who attended the dinner. I must say, however, that I have the very highest regard for the opinions of those who expressed contrary views. I have again this morning, when visiting several of the Departments, listened to similar arguments, both pro and contra. Should you desire at any time to speak to any of these gentlemen with regard to the matter, I will, of course, feel at perfect liberty to submit to you their names.

Personally, I hope that if you do go to the Peace Conference you will not come back until your program is adopted. Then I know that you will come back with the recognition that you have won and are entitled to, a recognition that will not only reflect glory upon you but upon your party which hangs and depends upon you.

Very sincerely yours,   Key Pittman

TLS (WP, DLC).

A Thanksgiving Proclamation

[Nov. 16, 1918]

It has long been our custom to turn in the autumn of the year in praise and thanksgiving to Almighty God for His many blessings and mercies to us as a nation. This year we have special and moving cause to be grateful and to rejoice. God has in His good pleasure given us peace. It has not come as a mere cessation of arms, a mere relief from the strain and tragedy of war. It has come as a great triumph of right. Complete victory has brought us, not peace alone, but the confident promise of a new day as well in which justice shall replace force and jealous intrigue among the nations. Our gallant armies have participated in a triumph which is not marred or strained by any purpose of selfish aggression. In a righteous cause they have won immortal glory and have nobly served their nation in serving mankind. God has indeed been gracious. We have cause for such rejoicing as revives and strengthens in us all the best traditions of our national history. A new day shines about us, in which our hearts take new courage and look forward with new hope to new and greater duties.

While we render thanks for those things, let us not forget to seek the Divine guidance in the performance of those duties, and Divine mercy and forgiveness for all errors of act or purpose, and pray that in all that we do we shall strengthen the ties of friendship and mutual respect upon which we must assist to build the new structure of peace and good will among the nations.

Wherefore, I, WOODROW WILSON, President of the United States of America, do hereby designate Thursday, the twenty-eighth day of November next as a day of thanksgiving and prayer, and invite the people throughout the land to cease upon that day from their ordinary occupations and in their several homes and places of worship to render thanks to God, the ruler of nations.

In Witness Whereof I have hereunto set my hand and caused the seal of the United States to be affixed.

Done in the District of Columbia this 16th day of November in the year of our Lord one thousand nine hundred and eighteen and of the independence of the United States of America the one hundred and forty-third.   Woodrow Wilson

CC MS (WP, DLC).

To Edward Mandell House

[The White House, Nov. 16, 1918]

No. 15 Your 107 upsets every plan we had made. I infer that French and English leaders desire to exclude me from the Conference for fear I might there lead the weaker nations against them. If I were to come to the seat of¹ the Conference and remain outside I would be merely the centre of a sort of sublimated lobby. All weak parties would resort to me and there would be exactly the same jealousy that was excited by the Germans addressing themselves exclusively to me. I play the same part in our government that the prime ministers play in theirs. The fact that I am head of the state is of no practical consequence. No point of dignity must prevent our obtaining[2] the results we have set our hearts upon and must have.[3] It is universally expected and generally desired here that I should attend the conference, but I believe that no one would wish me to sit by and try to steer from the outside. I am thrown into complete confusion by the change of programme. The program[4] proposed for me by Clemenceau, George, Reading, and the rest seems to me a way of pocketing me. I hope you will be very shy of their advice and give me your own independent judgment after reconsideration.

WWT telegram (WP, DLC).
 [1] "the seat of" not in House's copy.
 [2] "must prevent our obtaining" transcript of WWsh.
 [3] This sentence in House's copy: "I object very strongly to the fact that dignity must prevent our obtaining the results we have set our heart on."
 [4] "program" transcript of WWsh.

To Newton Diehl Baker

PERSONAL

My dear Baker: The White House 16 November, 1918.

I have read the enclosed[1] (which by the way I have not yet acknowledged) with the consciousness that there is a great deal of truth in it, and yet I want to put before you very frankly this thought: As a matter of fact, because we were obliged to commit the selection of the State Councils of Defence to the Governors of the several States, they have very generally been made in effect political organizations, and presiding as they have over the formation of local units, they have covered the country with a network of organizations which were, I believe, most actively useful to the Republican party in the last campaign. I would therefore be very much obliged to you if you would tell me whether you think this impression is correct and would tell me what your judgment is as to the continuation or dissolution of these agencies.

Cordially and faithfully yours,   Woodrow Wilson

TLS (N. D. Baker Papers, DLC).
 [1] G. B. Clarkson to WW, Nov. 14, 1918, TLS, enclosing G. B. Clarkson, "Council of Defense System and its Relation to Reconstruction Work," Nov. 8, 1918, CC MS, both in N. D. Baker Papers, DLC. Clarkson in both documents urged that the existing network of some 184,400 state and local councils of defense be utilized in the coming work of

reconstruction, especially as a means of conveying information from the national to the state and local levels. He outlined in considerable detail the various functions which the network might carry out.

To Josephus Daniels

PERSONAL AND CONFIDENTIAL

My dear Daniels: The White House 16 November, 1918.

I am sure you know my own cordial personal feeling towards Mr. Bryan, but I would not dare, as public opinion stands at the present moment, excited and superheated and suspicious, appoint Mr. Bryan one of the Peace Commissioners, because it would be unjustly but certainly taken for granted that he would be too easy and that he would pursue some Eutopian scheme.

As I have said, this would be unjust, but I am sure you agree with me that it would be thought, and the establishment of confidence from the outset in the processes of the Peace Conference on the part of our people, now too much in love with force and retribution, is of the utmost importance.

Cordially and faithfully yours,   Woodrow Wilson

TLS (J. Daniels Papers, DLC).

To Jean Jules Jusserand

[The White House]
My dear Mr. Ambassador: 16 November, 1918.

I need not tell you how deeply gratified I have been by Monsieur Clemenceau's little message to me,[1] which you were so kind as to send through Mr. Tumulty. It was very delightful to feel that we are drawing so close together on the two sides of the water that we take the same view of the great public interest of the world with which we are dealing, and that I can count with such certainty on entering into complete cooperation with Monsieur Clemenceau, for whom I have the highest regard and with whom it will, I am sure, be a pleasure to work in every way.

Cordially and sincerely yours,   Woodrow Wilson

TLS (Letterpress Books, WP, DLC).
[1] It is missing.

To Cordell Hull

My dear Mr. Hull: [The White House] 16 November, 1918

I have read your letter of November 14th[1] with a great deal of interest and am inclined to agree with its conclusions, though I must admit that my mind has been so much engrossed in other directions that I have not given any study to the matter. I am going to take the liberty of sending your letter to the Secretary of the Treasury in the hope that he may think it wise to suggest definite legislation along the lines you indicate.

Cordially and sincerely yours,   Woodrow Wilson

TLS (Letterpress Books, WP, DLC).
    [1] The Editors have not found Hull's letter in the C. Hull Papers and W. G. McAdoo Papers, both in DLC. However, Hull, in his memoirs, says that the letter concerned the establishment of an adequate sinking-fund plan to reduce the national debt, and he quotes from the letter, as follows:
"Such action would include desirable sinking-fund arrangements, authority to refund into lower rates of interest as the opportunity arises, and also authority to purchase bonds from any surplus in the Treasury and their cancellation. These steps, in my opinion, should be taken to as full extent as possible at this stage." Cordell Hull, *The Memoirs of Cordell Hull* (2 vols., New York, 1948), I, 99.

To William Gibbs McAdoo

My dear Mac: [The White House] 16 November, 1918

It seems to me that the suggestions of the enclosed letter are very sensible. Perhaps you have it already in mind, but if you have not, do you not think it would be well to set somebody to work formulating legislation along the lines Mr. Hull suggests, so that we might attempt at least to get it enacted before the fourth of March next?   Affectionately yours,   Woodrow Wilson

TLS (Letterpress Books, WP, DLC).

To Louis Marshall

My dear Mr. Marshall: [The White House] 16 November, 1918

I have your letter of November 14th, and you may be sure I shall keep the highly important matter with which it deals constantly in my thought whenever I have the opportunity to deal with it.

In unavoidable haste,

Cordially and sincerely yours,   Woodrow Wilson

TLS (Letterpress Books, WP, DLC).

To Leo Stanton Rowe[1]

My dear Mr. Secretary: [The White House] 16 November, 1918

It was thoughtful of you to write me your letter of November 13th.[2] All such facts are pertinent in the deepest sense to the tasks that lie ahead of us, and I am grateful to you for telling me what you have heard of popular sentiment abroad. It is astonishing how utterly out of sympathy with the sentiments of their own people the leaders of some of the foreign governments sometimes seem.

Cordially and sincerely yours,   Woodrow Wilson

TLS (Letterpress Books, WP, DLC).
  [1] At this time Assistant Secretary of the Treasury.
  [2] L. S. Rowe to WW, Nov. 13, 1918, TLS (WP, DLC).

To Morris Sheppard

My dear Senator: [The White House] 16 November, 1918

I have your letter of November 14th, which is signed also by Senator McKellar. I need not tell you that I appreciate the gravity and importance of the matter of which it speaks.

As a matter of fact, the question is one of shipping and ship-space more than anything else, and I am sure that you can take it for granted that the War Trade Board will release its restrictions as rapidly and as liberally as it is possible to do so. Of course, the people on the other side must first have food.

In haste,

Cordially and sincerely yours,   Woodrow Wilson

TLS (Letterpress Books, WP, DLC).

Three Telegrams from Edward Mandell House

Paris. Nov. 16, 1918.

Number 114. Secret for the President.

I suggest that you send me a cable which I can show to the heads of British and French Governments for the purpose of obtaining from them the entire suspension of the present political censorship upon American press despatches. Military necessity can no longer be invoked as a defense of the drastic censorship now being exercised. There seems to be in my opinion no adequate reason why the character of the political information supplied to the American people should be dictated by the French and British Governments.

Edward House.

T telegram (WP, DLC).

Paris. November 16, 1918.

No. 15. In reply to your number 15 my judgment is that you should sail for France December 3rd and determine upon your arrival what share it is wise for you to take in the proceedings. As Commander in Chief of the armed forces you have ample grounds for coming in order to solve the important questions connected with their return home. This can only be done here intelligently.

When here you will be in a position to assess the situation properly. It is impossible to do so from Washington through cables from me.

As far as I can see all the Powers are trying to work with us rather than with one another. Their disagreements are sharp and constant.

There is a tendency to delay not only the preliminary conferences but the final one. This I think is unfortunate. The sooner you announce your purpose of sailing December 3rd the better. Until then no plans can be made.   Edward House.[1]

[1] There is a WWsh decode of this telegram in WP, DLC. A typed transcript, also in WP, DLC, conforms very closely to this version.

Paris, November 16, 1918

No. 16 To be more explicit as to my own opinion as to the advisability of your sitting in the Peace Conference let me say that I have constantly contended that you should do so, but Sharp is practically the only one who has agreed with me. I see no need of reaching a decision until you arrive.

I notice in the memorandum which the French Foreign Office gave me yesterday concerning procedure and which I cabled to the Secretary of State[1] that they recommend only three delegates for each country. This is misleading for nothing has yet been determined and I think George and Clemenceau have different views.

Edward House.

T telegrams (E. M. House Papers, CtY).
[1] That is, EMH to RL, No. 109, Nov. 15, 1918.

From Newton Diehl Baker

Dear Mr. President: Washington. November 16, 1918.

As your letter of November 12[1] inquiring whether the appointment of Mr. Grant Squires as a captain in the Army cannot be expedited was evidently written under the impression that the policy of making no more appointments in the Army had not been announced, I am taking the liberty of asking for further instructions before taking any further action in this case.

As soon as the armistice was signed the policy was adopted of making no further appointments or promotions in the Army for the period of the emergency, as it is believed that there will be no further military need therefor. Public announcement of this policy appeared in the press on the morning of the twelfth. Since then great pressure has been exerted from all directions to force exceptions. At the time this policy was adopted there were in the hands of The Adjutant General several thousand approved cases. In many of these the individuals concerned had closed up their business, purchased uniforms and equipment and in some instances submitted to voluntary induction as privates upon the assurance that they would be immediately commissioned. It is of course unfortunate that these patriotic citizens should be disappointed or put to considerable expense and inconvenience. This, however, is only one of the fortunes of war and is a small price to pay as compared with the sacrifices others have made.

There is nothing to indicate that the War Department has obligated itself to Mr. Squires to as great an extent as it has done to many hundreds of others. Should this appointment be made it will be extremely difficult to withstand the importunities in many other cases. It is manifestly impracticable to continue to issue commissions in the Army indefinitely now that the military need no longer exists.   Very sincerely,   Newton D. Baker

TLS (WP, DLC).
  [1] WW to NDB, Nov. 12, 1918, TLS (Letterpress Books, WP, DLC).

From James Cardinal Gibbons

My dear Mr. President: Baltimore. November the 16th, 1918.

I have just received a cablegram from His Eminence the Cardinal Secretary of State,[1] by which he, in the name of the Holy Father, requests me to make known to you the extremely grave food situation in Germany and that the population of that country implore you to provide for them at once in order to save them from sertain [certain] death.

In communicating to you this message of the Holy Father, I beg to say that I have just informed him that this Government is sending Mr. Herbert Hoover as Food Administrator to Europe to look into this very question of providing food for the suffering peoples there, that this country is fully alive to the seriousness of the situation and what it considers its duty in the matter.

I hope that you have received my letter addressed to you on the fifth instant.[2]

With sentiments of the most profound respect, I am, my dear Mr. President,   Yours very sincerely,   J. Card. Gibbons.

TLS (WP, DLC).
[1] That is, Pietro Cardinal Gasparri.
[2] See J. Cardinal Gibbons to WW, Nov. 5, 1918, Vol. 51.

From Peter Goelet Gerry

My dear Mr. President,   [Washington] November 16th, 1918.

Since seeing you the day before yesterday, The Secretary of the Treasury has appeared before the Finance Committee and greatly clarified our taxation policy. He advocated a six billion dollar revenue bill for the year 1918 with a two billion dollar reduction effective the following year. This would mean that the country would be put on a peace basis of taxation by the present Congress.

The Republicans are evidently dismayed by this plan, as they expected to obtain much political advantage by a reduction of the taxes following the organization of the Republican Congress recently elected. With a six billion dollar revenue bill in force, they felt it would be absolutely necessary for you to call an extra session of Congress soon after the 4th of March. Opportunity would then be taken of framing not only a new revenue but also a new high tariff bill which you would be forced to approve or, in the alternative, to veto, thus leaving the country upon a war basis of taxation. I anticipate, to this policy of the Secretary, no serious objection from the Democrats but rather very satisfying support both in the Committee and the Senate itself. Difficulties may occur when the bill goes to conference, then your leadership will be necessary to bring about a speedy adjustment of the divergent views. This will be one of the many very important matters that will undoubtedly arise this session and there is unquestionably a feeling among the Democrats that if a division or serious difficulty in our party is to be avoided, our Senate and House leaders must often secure your counsel and advice. Having in mind this view of the situation, they feel some doubt of the advisability of your leaving to attend the Peace Conference. I have also heard the hope expressed that if you do decide to go, it will not be until after preliminary questions and matters have been agreed upon and when your presence would enable you to speak with the most telling effect. In that event, it is expected that it would not be necessary for you to be long absent from Washington. On the other hand, there does not seem to be much doubt that your presence would give the United States a prestige and a force that would make it the dominating power at the Council table.

I have written this letter on the theory that it was your desire to hear the different opinions that are being expressed at this time by members of our party and wish to add this to the many that you are receiving from all sections of the country.

Very sincerely yours,   Peter G. Gerry.

TLS (WP, DLC).

From Louis Marshall

The President,   New York November 16, 1918.

Under date of November 13th I am in receipt of a letter from Mr. Tumulty, in which, referring to the telegram of November 11th which Judge Mack and I forwarded to you, he conveys your gratifying message that the matter to which we have referred is one which you have very much at heart, and that you have inquired whether I have in mind any practicable present measures whereby the alarming threats of pogroms against the Jews of Poland and Roumania may be averted.

Although I fully realize the practical difficulties presented by the extraordinary conditions which now exist in eastern Europe, I am strongly persuaded that a public announcement by you, which will unquestionably be heeded by all the world, in which you would give expression to your abhorrence of these outbreaks of religious and racial prejudice, will go far to thwart the plans of those who may seek to profit, politically or otherwise, by these wanton attacks upon the Jews. Poland and Roumania are seeking to enlarge their boundaries and to secure political independence. To accomplish that end they must rely on the good-will of our country, as represented by you, and on that of our co-belligerents. Hence any intimation that persistence in anti-Semitic activity will be regarded as creating an obstacle to the giving of the recognition desired, cannot fail to make a deep impression.

Roumania expects the annexation of Transylvania and other territory and is seeking an outlet on the Black Sea. Yet it continues to withhold from the Jews, many of whom have lived there for centuries, the rights of citizenship, and is subjecting them to oppressive and discriminatory laws of the same character as those which during the reign of the Czar rested upon the Jews of Russia. All this is in direct violation of the terms of the Treaty of Berlin, to which Roumania owes its existence as a separate State.

In Poland there has been in continuous operation since 1912 an economic boycott, directed solely against the Jews, of such virulence as to impoverish the entire Jewish population and to threaten it with literal annihilation. As I sought to show in my communication to you of November 7th,[1] to which there was annexed a report of a conversation which I had on October 6, 1918, with Mr. Roman Dmowski, President of the Polish National Committee, which has been for some purposes recognized by our Government, he and his party frankly avow responsibility for the creation and the continuance of this boycott, as does Mr. Paderewski, the American representative of that Committee. On Tuesday last they made the same concession [confession] to Hon. Oscar S. Straus, Judge Julian W. Mack and others, who were present at a conference at which we presented to them the same cablegram which was called to your attention in the telegram of November 11th forwarded to you. We indicated our desire to cooperate with them in helping the cause of Poland, but urged as a condition precedent that they should at once take the necessary steps to terminate the boycott and to issue an appeal to the people of Poland setting forth their desire that henceforth their relations to the Jews should be friendly. We also requested that they give their approval to the clauses which we had formulated for insertion in the Constitution of the new Poland and which I communicated to you in my letter of the 14th instant. Thus far we have received no favorable response from them.

Would it not be a practicable thing to let these gentlemen understand that their aspirations for a new Poland cannot receive sympathetic consideration until they first give evidence that they are possessed with that spirit of justice and righteousness which is essential to the establishment of a free and independent government? Should they not be persuaded of the necessity of putting an end to the intolerable condition which now confronts the Jews of Poland, for which the party which they, Messrs. Dmowski and Paderewski, represent is directly responsible? I am convinced that a mere suggestion from you to them that they shall, without delay, act as they have been requested by us to act, will relieve the tension and in all probability put an end to the massacres which are imminent and to the intense suffering for which the boycott is principally responsible. Only then can the world regard the establishment of the new State without misgivings; for it is inconsistent with the grant of the political independence that one part of the inhabitants of a State shall be the victims of the hate, prejudice and intolerance of a majority.

With deepest gratitude for your expressions of sympathy, I am
                    Cordially yours,   Louis Marshall

TLS (WP, DLC).
  [1] L. Marshall to WW, Nov. 7, 1918, Vol. 51.

From William Gibbs McAdoo

My dear Mr. President: Washington November 16th, 1918.

In the matter of Mr. F. J. H. von Engelken,[1] I am satisfied that he has been very unjustly suspected of disloyalty. Having already gone over this matter with you personally, it is not necessary for me to repeat the reasons for this conclusion. The very full report of the Secret Service Division has been carefully examined, not only in this Department but in the War Department. Under date of November 1st, Secretary Baker wrote to Mr. Norris:[2]

"So far as I can discover, alike from the investigation made by the War Department and those made by the Department of Justice and the Treasury Department, there is no reasonable doubt of Mr. von Engelken's entire loyalty and zeal as a patriotic American citizen."

Secretary Baker added that if the future needs of the Department required Mr. von Engelken's services "no objection will be interposed because of any speculative doubts as to his entire loyalty to the United States."

Mr. von Engelken admits frankly that for a certain length of time after the outbreak of the war he was prejudiced in favor of Germany as against her European antagonists, and he was probably indiscreet in certain utterances made at that time. There is no charge against him of any disloyal act, and I have reached the same conclusion which Secretary Baker reached in an independent investigation, that "there is no reasonable doubt of his entire loyalty and zeal as a patriotic American citizen." I think that he belongs to the class to which you referred in your letter of April 8th, 1918, in which you said:

"You may be sure that I sympathize with you and shall co-operate in every effort to see to it that the loyal residents of the United States of German birth or descent are given genuine proof of the sincerity of our institutions.

"It distresses me beyond measure that suspicion should be attached to those who do not deserve it, and that acts of injustice and even violence should be based upon the suspicion."[3]

The suspicions which have been cast on Mr. von Engelken's loyalty have almost closed to him the doors of public and private service, and have subjected him to social ostracism in his neighborhood, and to serious pecuniary loss and inconvenience. I think that if you would address a letter to him which he would be at liberty to use it would be an act of justice, and would completely rehabilitate him.

He may be addressed at The Marlborough, 917 Eighteenth Street, N.W., Washington, D. C.   Cordially yours,   W G McAdoo

TLS (WP, DLC).

[1] Friedrich Johannes Hugo von Engelken, German-born American citizen who had been Director of the Mint from September 1916 to February 1917 and president of the Federal Land Bank, Columbia, South Carolina, from February 1917 through September 1918. He had been accused of disloyal conduct following the entrance of the United States into the war. Despite the fact that he had been intensively investigated and found innocent of all charges by several governmental departments and agencies, the taint of his alleged disloyalty had led to the loss of his government position, the denial of an officer's commission in several branches of the army, and the closure of his bank accounts. His alleged disloyalty was also the most probable cause of suspected arson in the burning of a building on his property. He had strongly appealed to Wilson to do something to restore his reputation. F. J. H. von Engelken to WW, Oct. 11, 1918, TLS (WP, DLC).

[2] George Washington Norris of the Federal Farm Loan Board.

[3] WW to Otto H. Butz, April 12 (not 8), 1918, Vol. 47.

From Andrew Furuseth

Mr. President: Washington, D. C., Nov. 16, 1918.

On behalf of the Seamen of America for whom I am commissioned to speak and on behalf of the seamen of the World, whose feelings I believe, that I am expressing, I thank you for your prompt intervention with the Shipping Board.[1] We believe now that all danger is passed. With the Shipping Board following the advice of Secretary Wilson we know that we shall be permitted to continue in the service of America without discrimination. We feel also that this service will be more effective because the advice will include the vitalizing of such sections of the Seamens' Act as so far have had no opportunity to function.

I now beg your permis[s]ion to lay before you in this letter an im[m]inent danger to the future sea-power of America.

The coming Peace Conference will in some way seek to either wholly or partly nullify the Seamens' Act.

The power that will try it, secretly or openly, will be Great Britain. Her statesmen understand this act perfectly. They know that with this act standing unmutilated and fully enforced the United States will become a very dangerous rival on the ocean.

The language clause properly enforced will practically exclude the Orientals from European or American vessels and will thus preserve the sea-power to the white race. The legal and economic freedom will keep sea-labor so fluid that equalization of wage-cost will inevitably follow.

This was fully understood by the British and Germans working together at the Conference of safety of life at sea in London in 1913. The effort was then to prevent the United States from adopting this law. The effort at the coming Peace Conference will be to nullify this law and thus shut out a very serious competitor on the ocean.

There are comparatively few men high enough in Public Life to be considered as possible Peace Commissioners. There are still fewer of those who understand the economic aspect of this law and who can therefore see its National aspect. Commissioners who fail in this will be overreached and might be made to agree to some International Agreement which would nullify this law and thus deprive the United States of the only possible material benefit that can reasonably flow from the war.

The most astute appeals to class interests will be used to disguise the National interests behind the efforts made and the Commissioners ought to be specifically instructed on this subject as well as there should be among them some man who can see and understand. Such men are known to you.

Of course I am not thinking only of the interests of the United States, though I hope that you will believe, that such is my first thought. I am thinking of the seamen also who may be again made unfree and deprived of all hope. Feeling that you will understand and forgive me for addressing you on this subject, I am,

Most respectfully and gratefully yours,

Andrew Furuseth.

TLS (WP, DLC).
¹ See A. Furuseth to WW, Nov. 4, 1918; WW to A. Furuseth, Nov. 5, 1918; and WW to C. R. Page, Nov. 5, 1918, all in Vol. 51.

From Edward Mandell House

Paris. November 17, 1918.

No. 17. You have not replied to my No. 11 about our getting some sort of estimate as to the damage done in France and Belgium. Shall I proceed or are there objections?   Edward House.

T telegram (E. M. House Papers, CtY).

Two Telegrams to Edward Mandell House

[The White House, Nov. 18, 1918]

Number 16. I am issuing the following announcement: The President expects to sail for France immediately after the opening of the regular session of the Congress, for the purpose of taking part in the discussion and settlement of the main features of the treaty of peace. It is not likely that it will be possible for him to remain throughout the sessions of the formal peace conference, but his presence at the outset is necessary in order to obviate the manifest disadvantages of of [sic] discussion by cable in determining the greater outlines of the final treaty, about which he must necessarily be consulted. He will, of course, be accompanied by delegates who will sit as the representatives of the United States throughout the conference. The names of the delegates will be presently announced. End quote. It would not be wise for me to come as if on another errand. There is only one errand our people would approve. If the French prime minister is uneasy about the presidency of the conference I will be glad to propose that he preside. I urge that the larger delegations be limited to five. Two other messages go to you through the State Department. I approve of your plan to employ experts on the assessment of damage done

[Woodrow Wilson]

WWT and WWhw telegram (WP, DLC).

Washington, November 18, 1918.

42 FOR COLONEL HOUSE: Your number 114. November 16, 10 pm.

Following reply from the President: QUOTE: Please express to the French and British authorities our hope and expectation that they will entirely remove the present political censorship upon American press dispatches. Now that the argument of military necessity no longer obtains, there can be no good reason why the character of the political information supplied to our people should be determined by the British and French Governments and there is danger of a very serious revulsion of feeling on this side of the water, if such a censorship is continued. I hope that you will press the matter very earnestly and very promptly. UNQUOTE.   Lansing

TS telegram (SDR, RG 59, 851.731/118, DNA).

To Robert Lansing

CONFIDENTIAL

My dear Mr. Secretary: [The White House] 18 November, 1918.

Will you not be kind enough to transmit in code the following message to Mr. House in Paris, requesting that he transmit it to His Majesty, the King of England?

"The kind invitation from Your Majesty and the Queen, which Mr. House has transmitted, has given Mrs. Wilson and me the greatest gratification. If we were coming at once to England, we would accept it with pleasure. It now seems to be my duty, however, to go directly to France and there await the developments of the great business in hand, before making any personal plans. We hope that we shall later be able to cross the channel and have an opportunity to thank you and the Queen in person for your generous courtesy."[1]   Faithfully yours,   [Woodrow Wilson]

CCL (WP, DLC).
    [1] There is a WWsh draft of this message in WP, DLC.

To George Weston Anderson

My dear Judge: [The White House] 18 November, 1918.

Thank you for your letter of November 14th sending me a copy of Lodge's speech. I share your views about the Senator and am looking forward with genuine anxiety to the part he is likely to play as Chairman of the Foreign Relations Committee of the Senate.
    In haste,
            Cordially and sincerely yours,   Woodrow Wilson

TLS (Letterpress Books, WP, DLC).

From Josephus Daniels

My dear Mr. President: Washington. November 18, 1918.

Just before I went abroad I had a talk with Mr. Hurley about the proposed purchase by Great Britain of the International Merchant Marine.[1] Both of us thought that until the Peace Conference settled all these problems, it seemed unwise for Great Britain to be buying corporations owned entirely by Americans, and while the course pursued by Americans of building the ships and putting them under British registry, this has always seemed to me justified only because our Government has paid no attention to securing a large merchant marine, which would guarantee to us a part of the world's trade. They were undoubtedly actuated by this largely because they could get cheaper labor and have conditions which were not conducive to the health and proper care of the seamen; but under the Seamens' Bill, whose passage you secured, this will ultimately raise the standard of conditions and pay for seamen. Of these 800,000 tons of shipping, built by Americans, they would be purchased with money which we loaned to the British Government, and these facts give us concern, and Mr. Hurley and I felt that the matter should be laid before you so that you could take action promptly if you desired to prevent this arrangement.
    The price to be paid for these ships is $88.00 per ton. This is far

less than ships can be built for now, or at any time in the near future. It seems to us that no change in the ownership of these ships should be made until the peace treaty has been signed.

I have looked into the mattter somewhat, and find if a transfer should be made, there are,

First. 3750 shares of Oceanic Steam Navigation Company, which is the entire capital stock. This company owns thirty steamers, of 405,678 tons gross.

Second. The Atlantic Transport Company, 50,000 shares of stock, all owned by Americans. This company has eleven steamers, of 70,699 tons gross.

Third. The British and North Atlantic Steam Navigation Company, with 45,687 shares, and all but five shares owned by Americans. This has seven steamers, of 52,825 tons gross.

Fourth. The Leyland Line, 118,463 ordinary shares, and all but 1500 of this class of stock owned by Americans; 58,703 shares of preferred stock. This company owns twenty-nine steamers of 181,064 tons gross.

Of course if these ships should be bought, they will then be put under British registry, and we do not see how we can stop their transfer, for that would not be for the benefit of Americans if they are to go there. If you desire to take action to prevent this transfer, I think it must be done at once, as Mr. Franklin[2] has been in communication about the matter and he understands the Government is not opposed to it. I have no idea upon what his understanding is based.   Sincerely yours,   Josephus Daniels

TLS (WP, DLC).
    [1] The Cunard Line had sold a number of steamships, totaling about 800,000 tons, to the International Mercantile Marine Corporation, a concern controlled by J. P. Morgan & Co., in 1901. The ships had remained in British registry and had been requisitioned by the British government early in the war. At this time, because of alleged harassment by the British government, the I.M.M.C. was contemplating a resale of the vessels to Cunard. See Jeffrey J. Safford, *Wilsonian Maritime Diplomacy, 1913-1921* (New Brunswick, N. J., 1978), p. 165.
    [2] That is, Philip Albright Small Franklin, vice-president of the I.M.M.C.

To Bainbridge Colby, with Enclosure

My dear Colby: [The White House] 18 November, 1918.

I do not know to whom it is formally correct for me to turn in a matter regarding shipping in Mr. Hurley's absence, but after all what I want to write is not a piece of business for the Shipping Board but something which ought to be personally attended to.

The enclosed will explain itself. I am emphatically of Mr. Mc-

Adoo's opinion that if we can prevent it, we ought not to permit the sale of these ships to any British interest, official or other, but that we should insist that the ownership be retained in this country. My own judgment is that if any purchasing is done, it should be done by the government through the Shipping Board.

I am therefore writing to you to ask if you will not personally look into this matter and gain access to the parties concerned, in order to express to them this earnest judgment of mine, and in order also to ascertain what kind of transaction would be legitimate and effective in protecting our national interests.

I am assuming that the Fleet Corporation itself could purchase these interests. Am I right?

Cordially and faithfully yours,   [Woodrow Wilson]

CCL (WP, DLC).

ENCLOSURE

From William Gibbs McAdoo

Dear Mr. President: Washington November 16, 1918.

The enclosed letter from Mr. Henry Walters[1] presents a very important question mentioned at the last Wednesday meeting. While I do not agree with all of Mr. Walters' conclusions and inferences, I am in full accord with him about the fundamental question, namely, the transfer of British ships owned by the American corporation, the International Mercantile Marine, to the British Government. I believe that this Government should not permit these ships to be transferred but should insist that their American ownership, although under British registry, should be preserved. I believe that strong representations to the British Government will result in their recognition in the justice of such a request. I think we should go further and secure the transfer of those American owned ships of British registry to American registry.

As you know, we have been extending liberal credits to the British Government, and as a result of the relief America has afforded in this way, Great Britain is now in a position to buy these ships. It would requite us in an extraordinary way if Great Britain should take advantage of the strength we have imparted to her to strike this blow at America's essential ocean transportation system.

I do not know who, if anyone, is giving attention to this matter, but I earnestly recommend that you request the State Department to have some prompt exchanges with the British Government on this subject. The transaction at least should be delayed until we have had full opportunity to consider it in all of its aspects.

Cordially yours,   W G McAdoo

TLS (Letterpress Books, W. G. McAdoo Papers, DLC).
[1] Capitalist of Baltimore, at this time associated with McAdoo in the Railroad Administration representing shipping interests.

To Philip Albright Small Franklin

My dear Mr. Franklin: [The White House] 18 November, 1918.

With regard to the sale to the British Government of the International Merchant Marine, may I not request that no action be taken in the matter until the views of this government are fully presented and considered?

Sincerely yours,   Woodrow Wilson

TLS (Letterpress Books, WP, DLC).

To Josephus Daniels

My dear Daniels: The White House 18 November, 1918

You may be sure I will not forget the three-year programme when I write my message.

In haste,   Faithfully yours,   Woodrow Wilson

TLS (J. Daniels Papers, DLC).

To Friedrich Johannes Hugo von Engelken

[The White House]
My dear Mr. von Engelken: 18 November, 1918.

My attention has been called to the very distressing experiences you have recently had, and I have acquainted myself very fully with the real facts of the case. It affords me real pleasure, therefore, to say that the fullest investigation having been made, there can be no reasonable doubt of your entire loyalty and zeal as a patriotic American citizen. I am glad to have an opportunity to tell you that this is my own unhesitating opinion and that I hope the clouds that have gathered about you will presently clear happily away.

Very sincerely yours,   Woodrow Wilson

TLS (Letterpress Books, WP, DLC).
[1] Von Engelken fades out of sight in the documents at this point. In *Who's Who in America* in the 1918-1919 editions, he said that he was assisting in the promotion of farm-loan bonds.

To Andrew Furuseth

My dear Mr. Furuseth: [The White House] 18 November, 1918.

Thank you for your letter of the 16th. You may be sure I will keep the danger you mention in mind throughout the Peace Conference. I know that you will pardon this brief acknowledgement from a very much rushed man.

Cordially and sincerely yours,   Woodrow Wilson

TLS (Letterpress Books, WP, DLC).

To James Cardinal Gibbons

The White House
My dear Cardinal Gibbons: 18 November, 1918.

Thank you for your letter of the 16th. I am not unmindful of the very grave food situation so thoughtfully presented by His Holiness the Pope, and I beg that you will assure His Eminence the Cardinal Secretary of State that it will receive the most considerate attention from us possible in the circumstances.

With sentiments of the most sincere respect and appreciation.

Sincerely yours,   Woodrow Wilson

TLS (Baltimore Cathedral Archives).

To Peter Goelet Gerry

My dear Senator: [The White House] 18 November, 1918.

Thank you for your letter of the 16th, which I value very much. I am going to try my best to get things in course before I get away to the other side, as you suggest, but the dispatches every day make it clearer that I must go, for a time at least. It is very generous of you to give me such lucid counsel and you may be sure I value it.

Cordially and sincerely yours,   Woodrow Wilson

TLS (Letterpress Books, WP, DLC).

To Helen Hamilton Gardener

[The White House]
My dear Mrs. Gardener: 18 November, 1918.

I must frankly say that I do not think it will be practicable to appoint a woman among the delegates to the Peace Conference, much as I should personally like to do so.[1] I would have to go into a great deal of the correspondence that I have been having with the other side to explain to you why this conclusion seems to me necessary, but I am sure that the women of the country will not think that I have turned away from the suggestion through any lack of sympathy with it.

Cordially and sincerely yours, Woodrow Wilson

TLS (Letterpress Books, WP, DLC).
¹ Wilson was replying to Helen H. Gardener to WW, Nov. 13, 1918, TLS (WP, DLC). Mrs. Gardener had recommended that Carrie Clinton Lane Chapman Catt be made a member of the American delegation.

From Gavin McNab

My dear Mr. President: Washington November 18, 1918.

I hope that you will not attend the Peace Conference. Without a league of nations, the sacrifices of this war have been in vain. If the league of nations shall be a fact and not merely a sentiment, it must be because you are its head. You cannot escape this. Would it not be grander that this honor and power should be extended you at the seat of this Government than when present with those who must make the offer?

Besides, you are more than ever required at home to direct and stimulate reconstruction and reorganization.

It is not supposable that soldiers, who offered abroad the supreme sacrifice for the principles you have so spiritually expounded, will be satisfied with less than the broadest, purest and most sympathetic democracy in their own country.

Your power, authority and prestige can, from Washington, accomplish your purposes in Europe. None but you can accomplish the necessary objects here.

There are some things I much desired to tell you concerning the recent campaign, but have felt that with your burdens it would be cruel to seek an interview.

No man was more grieved at results than I and none less surprised.

When the National Committee requested me to again get in harness your services to humanity commanded my duty. In California and Nevada where I directly acted, we gave you an extra Congressman and reelected a Senator.

My dear Mr. President, the causes of our defeat are to my mind perfectly obvious and must be apparent to your advisers. They are subject to remedy, but will continue in an accelerated degree unless removed by your direct action.

Yours very sincerely, Gavin McNab

TLS (WP, DLC).

To Gavin McNab

My dear McNab: [The White House] 18 November, 1918.

There are undoubtedly cogent arguments why I should not go abroad, and the whole matter has caused me a great deal of anxious arguing with myself, but on the whole I do not see how I can escape going, even if I remain only a portion of the time that the conference will be in session.

I wish you would make me a memorandum of the reasons you think were influential in our defeat at the elections. I have come to value your judgments very highly indeed.

In haste, with warmest regard,

Sincerely yours,   Woodrow Wilson

TLS (Letterpress Books, WP, DLC).

Two Letters to Key Pittman

My dear Senator: The White House 18 November, 1918.

It was thoughtful of you to write me your letter of November 15th.

My own opinion chimes with yours. I really think that no personal prestige is worth anything that cannot be exposed to the experience of the worka'day world. If it is so sensitive a plant that it cannot be exhibited in public, it will wither anyhow, and the sooner the better.

Pray do not think I am making fun of the solicitude of my friends, because I know how generous and genuine it is. I am only stating the thing as it looks to me.

Cordially and faithfully yours,   Woodrow Wilson

My dear Senator: The White House 18 November, 1918.

I talked with the Secretary of War about this resolution and find that he approves as heartily as I do.[1]

In haste,

Cordially and sincerely yours,   Woodrow Wilson

TLS (K. Pittman Papers, DLC).
    [1] About this resolution, see WW to NDB, Nov. 14, 1918, n. 1. Pittman introduced it as S.J. Res. 186 on November 18. It was briefly discussed and amended and passed the Senate on November 21, the last day of the session. *Cong. Record*, 65th Cong., 2d sess., pp. 11578, 11606. It was introduced in the House on December 5, was referred to the Committee on Military Affairs, and never emerged. *Ibid.*, 3d sess., p. 168.

To Joseph Eugene Ransdell

My dear Senator: [The White House] 18 November, 1918.

I am afraid I cannot venture to act upon the advice of your letter of November 14th,[1] because it has been my unfortunate experience that the man you mention seeks to take charge of anything he has a part in, and to take charge in a way thoroughly disloyal to his associates. But please believe that I am none the less obliged to you for your thoughtfulness in making the suggestion. I need all the guidance I can get.

Cordially and sincerely yours,   Woodrow Wilson

TLS (Letterpress Books, WP, DLC).
 [1] That Wilson appoint Theodore Roosevelt a member of the American peace commission. J. E. Ransdell to WW, Nov. 14, 1918, TLS (WP, DLC).

From Anna Howard Shaw

My dear Mr. President: Washington November 18th, 1918

The cessation of hostilities is forcing upon our people many problems which must be met in the same broad and humanitarian spirit which you from the beginning of the war have advocated; and since these problems involve the industrial, social and civic interests of women, it is the opinion of the Woman's Committee of the Council of National Defense that women should be appointed upon the Reconstruction Commission.

It was therefore voted at an executive meeting of the Woman's Committee, held in New York November 16th, to ask the President to make such appointments, the consensus of opinion being that this action would serve to allay much of the existing fear that national problems in which women are particularly concerned might be overlooked and perhaps submerged in the interests of commercial and material prosperity, especially with reference to women employed in industry and those engaged in social reforms.

Trusting that our request may appeal to you as just and in the highest interests of the country,

Believe me, Mr. President,

Very sincerely yours   Anna Howard Shaw

TLS (WP, DLC).

To Anna Howard Shaw

My dear Dr. Shaw: [The White House] 18 November, 1918.

Thank you for your letter of today. As a matter of fact, I doubt if I shall appoint a new and separate Reconstruction Commission. I have been trying to get the reconstruction work in hand through existing instrumentalities, altered in their direction and changed a bit in their organization, because I feel that it would take longer to start a new commission than would be wise, and I would value any memorandum that you might send me by way of suggestion, in order that I might see that the necessary counsel of women was tied in with the process.

In haste,

Cordially and sincerely yours,   Woodrow Wilson

TLS (Letterpress Books, WP, DLC).

To William Bauchop Wilson, with Enclosure

My dear Mr. Secretary: The White House 18 November, 1918.

I would very much appreciate a tip from you as to how you think it would be best for me to reply to the enclosed. My own judgment is, of course, that any kind of class representation on the delegation would be a grave mistake and lead to many further complications rather than avoid them.

Cordially and sincerely yours,   Woodrow Wilson

TLS (LDR, RG 174, Office of the Chief Clerk, File No. 163/206, DNA).

E N C L O S U R E

Indianapolis, Ind., November 16, 1918.

The appointment of peace conferees who will meet with the representatives of our allies to negotiate a world-wide and enduring peace translating into a reality the principles of democracy, for which all classes have given their blood and substance, is a matter of grave concern to the toilers of America. Press forecasts uniformly indicate that the personnel of the conferees to be named will not include a direct representative of labor. Speaking for the half million members of the United Mine Workers of America, I respectfully call your attention to the fact that during the war now so triumphantly ended the organized workers of our country have been led to believe that in return for their unstinted loyalty in mine, factory and workshop, and on the battlefield, they would receive direct representation when the time for making peace was at hand. The peace terms to be negotiated will constitute the basis for rebuilding the devastated war areas and will profoundly affect the industrial fabric of all Europe. If the terms agreed to do not safeguard the hopes and raise the standards of living of European workers then American industries cannot compete in foreign markets and American workmen will suffer idleness, resulting in unrest that may bring intensified confusion in our own affairs. Speaking as the authorized spokesman of my union, in my opinion, it is imperative that labor be given direct representation in that at least one of the peace conferees be selected from the ranks of labor. Mere hearings before the peace conference permitting labor to advocate its program will not suffice. The destinies of the nations of the world will be affected by the decisions of this conference and labor proclaims its right to participate in the making of such momentous decisions. I express the confident hope, Mr. President, that no burden of responsibilities will prevent you from giving mature consideration to this request and a proper recognition of its merits.

Frank J. Hayes, President
United Mine Workers of America.

T telegram (WP, DLC).

From Frank Morrison

San Antonio, Texas, November 18, 1918.

The executive council of the American Federation of Labor feels obliged to again address you on the subject of labor having a direct representative on the peace commission. We know that the great masses of the workers feel the necessity of such direct representation as we have communicated to you in our telegram from Laredo, Texas, Saturday.[1] We are also confident that the workers of the United States feel that unless the request is granted the failure to appoint a labor man on the commission will not be considered other than an utter failure to recognize their services and their rights.

By Order of the Executive Council of the American Federation of Labor, Frank Morrison, Secretary.

T telegram (WP, DLC).
[1] It is missing.

From John Hessin Clarke

Washington, D. C.

My dear Mr. President: November 18th, 1918.

Permit me to express the hope that you will not heed the opposition, developing in the newspapers, to your attending in person the peace conference.

Your point of view, which I think I understand, is so different from that of the European statesmen (with the possible exception of Lloyd George), and it is so all important that it should prevail that it seems to me no resource should be spared which can aid in its realization.

Your power of stating the case, the personal prestige you have at home and abroad, and the weight of your great office will give many fold greater influence to your advocacy of any measures than would be given to that of any representatives you may send, however able they may be.

Even though you do not stay through all of the sessions, you can speak to the conference on the great fundamentals involved in such manner as to create, I think, a world-wide public opinion, which will insure their acceptance.

The unfortunate results of the management of international affairs in the past surely justifies your neglecting the protest based on the novelty of the course proposed, and encourages the hope that it is not impossible for the present and the future to improve upon the past.

I believe the League of Nations to Enforce the Peace of the World will fail if you do not go, and this, if obtained, will prove the most important result of the war. If it is not obtained, the sacrifices of the great war will have been, in large measure, made in vain.

Forgive this intrusion—I know your clear vision will not permit you to waver in your resolution.

Very sincerely yours,   John H. Clarke

TLS (WP, DLC).

To John Hessin Clarke

My dear Mr. Justice: The White House 18 November, 1918.

I appreciate sincerely your letter of this morning, and my judgment is your own. I think the reasons for outweigh the arguments against, and it fortifies me in this judgment to have your own valued opinion.

Cordially and sincerely yours,   Woodrow Wilson

TLS (J. H. Clarke Papers, OClW).

From Robert Lansing, with Enclosure

My dear Mr. President: Washington November 18, 1918.

I wish that you would read this memorandum of Mr. Bullitt which has a suggestion that seems to me worthy of consideration because it would strengthen the hands of the enemies of Bolshevism in Germany. It would of course have to be submitted to the Allied Governments for their views as to its wisdom.

Would you be good enough to give me your opinion as to whether I should approach the other Governments on the subject?

Faithfully yours, Robert Lansing.

TLS (WP, DLC).

ENCLOSURE

Washington, D. C., November 18, 1918.

Memorandum for the Secretary:
Subject: The Bolshevist Movement in Europe

My dear Mr. Secretary:

The information which has reached the Department this morning indicates that

1. The general strike which was organized by the Bolsheviki in Switzerland has ended in a complete victory for the Swiss Government.

2. The Bolshevik representatives to Switzerland were refused passage by the new Government of Bavaria and are at present interned in Switzerland.

3. American representatives in Holland are confident that the Dutch Socialists will be unable to overthrow the present Government; but the situation is still serious.

4. The struggle between the moderate Socialists and the Bolshevists of Germany is continuing to center on the question of a Constitutional Assembly. The Spartacus Group opposes bitterly the calling of a Constituent Assembly and favors the establishment instead of a Central General Council of Workmen's and Soldiers' Councils to take over the Government. All other Socialist groups and all bourgeois groups favor the calling of a Constituent Assembly. In anticipation of the election of delegates to such an assembly, the more radical members of the "Delbruck Group" of "moderate liberals,"[1] i.e., the men back of the Max of Baden Government, have formed an anti-Socialist Progressive Republican Party.[2]

If elections to a Constituent Assembly should be held in the latter part of December or the first part of January, there is little doubt that the anti-Bolshevist elements would be in great majority. For not only the mass of the population but also the great majority of the soldiery today is opposed to Bolshevism. But Liebknecht and Mehring are turning a heavy stream of Bolshevik propaganda on the returning soldiers and it is quite possible that, if the calling of a Constituent Assembly is postponed a few months, the Workmen's and Soldiers' Councils will be so radical that they will either prevent the assembly of a Convention altogether or will overthrow it by a coup d'etat.

Because of this possibility it seems important that elections to a Constituent Assembly should be held as soon as the demobilization of the German army has progressed far enough to make a representative election possible. It is respectfully suggested that a statement by the United States and the Allies announcing their determination to sign peace only with the representatives of a Constitutional Assembly might assist greatly the anti-Bolshevist elements.

In view of the complexity of the situation in Germany at present, however, the effect of such a statement cannot be predicted with absolute certainty. And it would seem desirable before taking such a step to discuss it unofficially with Ebert and the other moderate leaders of Prussia and Bavaria. It is respectfully suggested, therefore, that Professor Herron should be asked to go at once to Munich and Berlin to ascertain whether or not the anti-Bolshevist forces would be strengthened if the United States and the Allies should announce that they would sign peace only with representatives of a German Constituent Assembly.

Very respectfully submitted,   William C. Bullitt

TS MS (SDR, RG 59, 840.00 B/4, DNA).
    ¹ That is, the group of university professors, politicians, journalists, high civil servants, businessmen, and industrialists who were associated with the so-called *Mittwochabend*, a political debating society under the leadership of the prominent historian and editor of the *Preussische Jahrbücher*, Hans Gottlieb Leopold Delbrück. Although strongly nationalistic in their political program, Delbrück and his associates had assumed a middle ground between the extremes of annexationism and pacifism and had advocated a moderate war-aims policy. See Annelise Thimme, *Hans Delbrück als Kritiker der Wilhelminischen Epoche* (Düsseldorf, 1955); Klaus Schwabe, *Wissenschaft und Kriegsmoral: Die deutschen Hochschullehrer und die politischen Grundfragen des Ersten Weltkrieges* (Göttingen, 1969); and Paul Rühlmann, "Delbrücks 'Mittwochabend,' " in Emil Daniels and Paul Rühlmann, eds., *Am Webstuhl der Zeit* (Berlin, 1928), pp. 75-81.
    ² In response to efforts by the leaders of the two German liberal parties, the essentially conservative National Liberal party (*Nationalliberale Partei*) and the left-liberal Progressive People's party (*Fortschrittliche Volkspartei*), to form a united liberal party, a group of sixty prominent liberal politicians, journalists, university professors, and businessmen published a proclamation in the *Berliner Tageblatt* on November 16, 1918, calling for the establishment of a "great democratic party for the united Empire." Contrary to the leaders of the established liberal parties, the *Tageblatt* group envisioned this new party not as a party of the liberal center but as a decidedly left-wing democratic party which, in cooperation with the Social Democrats, would form a left-wing bloc in

the national assembly. Although the program of the *Tageblatt* group rejected all "bolshevistic or bureaucratic experiments" in economic policy, it included demands for a republican form of government, the nationalization of monopolistic industries, the confiscation of war profits, and a limitation on the size of landed estates. Subsequent negotiations looking toward a fusion of the three liberal factions failed, since the *Tageblatt* group adamantly opposed a union with the National Liberal party and refused to cooperate with the majority of National Liberal leaders who had advocated an annexationist war aims policy. As a result, on November 20, the *Tageblatt* group and the Progressive People's party, together with the left wing of the National Liberal party, established the left-liberal German Democratic party (*Deutsche Demokratische Partei*), whose final political program was far less radical than the original proclamation of the *Tageblatt* group. Two days later, the remainder of the National Liberal party was transformed into the German People's party (*Deutsche Volkspartei*). For a detailed discussion, see Ernst Rudolf Huber, *Deutsche Verfassungsgeschichte seit 1789* (6 vols., Stuttgart, 1957-1981), V, 973-88, and Werner Stephan, *Aufstieg und Verfall des Linksliberalismus, 1918-1933: Geschichte der Deutschen Demokratischen Partei* (Göttingen, 1973), pp. 13-34.

Two Telegrams from Edward Mandell House

Paris. Nov. 18, 1918.

Number 119. Secret for the President. I believe it is very important that we should do everything possible to establish closer relations with liberal elements here in Paris. Ray Stan[n]ard Baker has been doing work of this character but has now gone to Italy to keep in touch with liberal elements there. I suggest that Miss Ida Tarbell, who has a profound knowledge of French character and institutions and who has written a life (∗) [of] Madam Roland[1] which is exceedingly well thought of by French scholars, be sent at once to Paris to keep in close relations with the liberal elements here and to report on their activities. Miss Tarbell is persona grata with the liberal elements here.   Edward House.

(∗) Omission.

[1] Ida Minerva Tarbell, *Madame Roland: A Biographical Study* (New York and London, 1896).

Paris. Nov. 18, 1918.

Number 120. Secret for the President. Doctor Korosec,[1] President of the Jugo-Slav Provisional Government at Agram,[2] called on me today and expressed apprehension lest owing to the want of sympathy between the Jugo-Slav and the occupying Italian troops, conflicts might ensue. He expressed the fear that political agents might even attempt to provoke such conflicts. He consequently requested the American Government to send American troops to occupy strategic points and points where trouble is feared, in common with the Italians. As Signor Orlando made an identical request of me less than a week ago, asking that American troops be sent to occupy towns and (?) [villages] in former Austro Hungarian territory, where half of the population was Italian and the balance Slav, I feel that the request of Doctor Korosec merits your earnest consideration.

Doctor Korosec said that he ventured to make this request because he and his countrymen regarded the President as a liberator, and the United States as their second fatherland, owing to the large immigration of recent years.

As events are moving rapidly, if any steps are taken they should be taken promptly. I ought to say that even with your approval it will be necessary for me to take matter up with both the British and French Governments as they might have objections.

Edward House.

T telegrams (WP, DLC).
    ¹ The Rev. Anton Korošec, a Roman Catholic priest long active in the Austro-Hungarian Imperial Parliament and as a Yugoslav nationalist leader.
    ² Actually, he was president of the Yugoslav National Council at Zagreb. "Agram" is the German name for Zagreb.

From Bernard Mannes Baruch

My dear Mr. President: Washington November 18, 1918.

As the United States War Industries Board was formed primarily for the purpose of seeing that the war program was carried out with as little dislocation of industry as possible, its work is really over.

I am delighted to have the Secretary of Commerce undertake this and think it an excellent suggestion. We have placed all of our activities at his disposal and have asked him to take over such as he feels would be of use to him, for instance, the conservation and standardization, and planning and statistics.

Very truly yours,   Bernard M. Baruch

TLS (WP, DLC).

From Norman Hapgood

Dear Mr. President: New York, November 18, 1918.

Last night I made a speech to several hundred people in Brooklyn, mostly young men, and largely Jews. Speeches from the floor were permitted afterwards, following the practice of these forums. The whole place was hot with enthusiasm for Lenin and there was very little appreciation of the value and necessity of high-minded compromise. It occurred to me, as I listened to the indignation of these people over political imprisonment, that it might be more effective to pardon our political prisoners rather soon, voluntarily, than to wait until agitation makes the inevitable pardoning seem to be done under compulsion.

With best wishes, always,

Sincerely yours   Norman Hapgood

TLS (WP, DLC).

From Elizabeth Merrill Bass

My dear Mr. President: Washington, D. C. November 18, 1918.

Since I had the pleasure of speaking with you on Friday evening, a number of telegrams have come from all over the United States, either asking me what influence may be brought to bear to secure appointments for women on the Peace Committee or naming some favorite daughter of the state or nation whose claims should be considered.

I would not, of course, make unasked any suggestions to you as to the personnel of women on that Commission. I would, however, venture to suggest again to you that no one, man or woman, should be appointed to any Commission or committee of any sort who is not devoted to you and your policies. In this connection I have a telegram from Mary Foy,[1] a native daughter of California and a real leader of the women there for forty years, who always signs herself "Mary Foy, Democrat." She worships you, and her greatest desire is to be able to tell you so some day. It seems that you have been asked by women of California (and perhaps men) to appoint Mrs. Josiah Evans Cowles[2] on this Peace Committee. She is President of the General Federation of Women's Clubs, because her group of California women praised her extravagantly and worked for the position, although her merit has since been shown to be very slight. Mary Foy called attention to the fact that she is an ardent, partisan Republican and that she was an anti-suffragist until women got the vote. Of my own knowledge I wish to say, Mr. President, that she is one of the most stupid women I ever met. She hasn't an ideal nor a constructive thought and never speaks a sentence of any value whatever. She was put on the Woman's Committee, Council of National Defense because of her official position as President of the General Federation, and was one of those practically retired in their recent reorganization. Dr. Shaw would tell you, should you ask her, that she is a stupid woman of no value. Besides this, I object to her because she is opposed to your Administration. At the late Biennial of Women's Clubs held at Hot Springs, Arkansas, last April, to which I was a delegate, she ignored in her program anything that tended to discuss the war work broadly. She simply claimed some credit for herself as being on the Council of Defense and had a Red Cross report or two, but left out all of the rest of the constructive work which was winning the war, and your name was never mentioned.

I did not speak to you about women on the Peace Commission because it has not seemed to me so important that one or more of them should be there. I have meant to urge upon your consideration the appointment of women on the various commissions or boards to deal with reconstruction problems, and I have hoped to be able to call to your attention later a permanent bureau dealing broadly and constructively with women and their increasing share in the responsibilities and privileges of the new world which is going to be built upon the foundations of the old. We have, however, should you appoint any women to the Peace Commission, many wonderful women of great value in this country. Dr. Shaw and Mrs. Catt, of course, stand for one phase of expression—the Suffrage. Then there are Jane Addams, who though reluctant to have us enter the war, followed you in and then through conscription and into every part of the necessary work, and who, though in ill health, spoke and worked all over the country for the Food Administration, and who stimulated women in the support of the Government everywhere; also Mrs. Glendower Evans, who followed the same course.

May I venture the hope that in the appointment of women you will listen not only to the recommendations of their personal friends or the call of states for their favorite daughters, but that you will, before making appointments, consult some of the women who really know the social work done in this country in the last two decades. I venture to suggest myself as one of those to consult because, in addition to a pretty wide knowledge gained in a long civic experience, I have also the merit of single-minded devotion to you and your aims.   Respectfully yours,   Elizabeth Bass

TLS (WP, DLC).
    [1] Mary Emily Foy, a delegate from California to the Democratic National Convention in 1916.
    [2] Ione Virginia Hill (Mrs. Josiah Evans) Cowles.

From Edward Wright Sheldon

My dear Mr. President: [New York] November 18th 1918.

I cannot let pass the present culmination of epochal changes,—quibus pars magna fuisti,[1]—in world conditions, without a personal message to you of admiration and regard. Through all that you have endured and accomplished, I am deeply gratified to hear that you have held your health unimpaired. At this time of fateful human aspiration, when the soul of man is knocking at the door of opportunity, it is an immense satisfaction to know that all your strength is available to guide the establishment of the spiritual heritage of the race. Everywhere and at all stages of the struggle you will, I hope, find possessors of vision and wise judgment to aid in completing the great readjustment.

Believe me, with warmest greetings,

Yours sincerely,   Edward W. Sheldon

ALS (WP, DLC).
[1] In which you will play a large part.

Robert Lansing to Edward Mandell House

Washington, November 18, 1918.

46. The Swiss Minister,[1] by direction of his Government, has delivered to the Department the following strictly confidential communication: Quote. In view of the revolution which threatens to break out at Vienna under the leadership of the extreme socialist party, the diplomatic representatives of the neutral countries at Vienna, under the presidency of the Papal Nuncio, decided to recommend to their Governments the immediate intervention with the Powers of the Entente with a view to request the occupation, as a strategical point, of the city of Vienna by Entente forces, in accordance with paragraph four of the terms of the armistice. This measure alone could guarantee order. End quote.

Advise Department of action contemplated.   Lansing

TS telegram (SDR, RG 59, 863.00/112, DNA).
[1] That is, Hans Sulzer.

A Memorandum by Robert Lansing

THE PRESIDENT'S GOING TO THE
PEACE CONFERENCE.

November 18, 1918.

The President told me tonight[1] that he had decided to go to Paris and sit at the Peace table. I deeply regret this decision because he will undoubtedly lose the unique position which he now holds in world affairs. He will have to sit there on an equality with the

Premiers of the Allies. That is, he will have to step down from his pedestal, thereby running the risk of weakening his great influence with foreign governments and the popular reverence in which he is held everywhere.

I am convinced that he is making one of the greatest mistakes of his career and imperiling his reputation. Undoubtedly Col. House would disagree with me because he has urged the President to go, as he told me before he left for France. At the time I told him that it was a risky proceeding but he did not think so. I may be wrong, and hope I am, but I prophesy trouble in Paris and worse than trouble here. Congress will resent his leaving and without a guiding hand will act very badly. I believe the President's place is here in America.

T MS (R. Lansing Papers, DLC).
  [1] Wilson saw Lansing in the latter's suite in the Powhatan Hotel during the evening of November 18.

To Robert Lansing

CONFIDENTIAL

My dear Mr. Secretary: The White House 19 November, 1918.

Will you not be kind enough to have the two following messages sent to House?

"Referring to your 119, shall try to get Miss Tarbell to go over."

"Referring to your 120, I entirely approve, and hope that you will in my name urge the acquiescence of the Supreme Command. This seems to me essential to a peaceful settlement."[1]

If you will be kind enough to have these coded and sent as early as possible, I would be very much obliged to you.
                    Cordially and faithfully yours,   Woodrow Wilson

TLS (SDR, RG 59, 763.72119P43/911, DNA).
  [1] Sent as RL to EMH, No. 50, Nov. 19, 1918, T telegram (SDR, RG 59, 763.72119P43/910, DNA).

To Josephus Daniels

My dear Mr. Secretary: The White House 19 November, 1918.

By an Act of Congress of August 8, 1917, as you may remember, authorization is given for a committee composed of the Secretary of War, the Secretary of the Navy, and the Secretary of Commerce to investigate the advisability of the acquisition of the Cape Cod Canal by the government. If they should decide in favor of its

acquisition, the Secretary of War is authorized either to make contracts for its purchase, or, in the event that a satisfactory contract
cannot be arranged, to institute condemnation proceedings through
the Attorney General.

It seems to me from every point of view desirable that we should
acquire the canal and maintain it as a genuine artery, and I would
be very much obliged if the committee thus designated could get
together at an early date and proceed with the business in any way
that they think best.

I am writing to the same effect to the Secretary of War and the
Secretary of Commerce.[1]

　　　　　Cordially and sincerely yours,　Woodrow Wilson

TLS (J. Daniels Papers, DLC).
　[1] WW to NDB, Nov. 19, 1918, and WW to WCR, Nov. 19, 1918, both TLS (Letterpress
Books, WP, DLC).

To Elizabeth Merrill Bass

My dear Mrs. Bass:　　　[The White House] 19 November, 1918.

I am very much disturbed about the desire of the women to be
represented on the Peace Commission, because I had arranged the
whole matter of the commission before I received their petitions,
and have been unable to announce the selections because I have
not yet authoritatively learned from the other side how many delegates would be expected. I am afraid it is too late to consult the
other governments about this matter, and I should feel obliged to
consult them before taking any action of my own, even if I were
free, in view of the circumstances stated above, to take it.

　　　　　Cordially and sincerely yours,　Woodrow Wilson

TLS (Letterpress Books, WP, DLC).

To John Howell Westcott

My dear John:　　　[The White House] 19 November, 1918.

My heart goes out to you in deepest sympathy. I have just learned
of Jack's death.[1] There is everything to be proud of in the thought
that he died in such a service, but I know what a grief it must have
brought you and I want you to know how profoundly and sincerely
I sympathize.　　　Affectionately yours,　Woodrow Wilson

TLS (Letterpress Books, WP, DLC).
　[1] Pvt. John Howell Westcott, Jr., Princeton 1918, had been killed in action on September 29 near Bony, Aisne Département, France.

Two Telegrams from Edward Mandell House

Paris. Nov. 19, 1918.

Number 121. For the President. John Garrett[1] who is here would appreciate *immediately* [an expression of] your opinion regarding the question of the Kaisers remaining in Holland. He believes that the last Dutch Government fell because they permitted him to cross the border.[2] He says he will be asked immediately upon his return on Saturday concerning the views of our Government. Personally he feels that such close proximity to Prussia will inevitably lead to dangerous intrigues. I share this opinion.   Edward House.

T telegram (WP, DLC).
   [1] That is, John Work Garrett, the American Minister to the Netherlands and Luxembourg.
   [2] Although there was much controversy both within and without the Netherlands over William's presence there, the Dutch government had not fallen.

[Paris, Nov. 19, 1918]

[No. 18] I am delighted to receive your telegram No. sixteen. If you recommend [I am] confident that everything will now work [out] satisfactorily. You will probably be made Honorary President of the Congress and the President [French] Prime Minister Acting President.

I am arranging with Pershing to have our army engineers make an approximate estimate of the damage done in Belgium and France.

EBWhw decode (WP, DLC).

From David Lloyd George

London Rec'd. Nov. 19, 1918.

My heartiest thanks for your cordial and kindly message. I am certain that the ideals of our two countries in regard to international reconstruction are fundamentally the same and I feel sure that at the forthcoming peace conference we shall be able to cooperate fruitfully to promote the reign of peace with liberty and true democracy throughout the world.   D. Lloyd George.

T telegram (WP, DLC).

From Bernard Mannes Baruch

My dear Mr. President: Washington November 19, 1918.

The main function of the War Industries Board was to obtain the materials required for carrying out the military program of the United States and the Allies, with as little dislocation of industry as possible. To do this, it was necessary in some instances to restrict non-war production, and to fix maximum prices. With the signing of the Armistice, and the consequent cancellation of contracts, there was no longer a shortage of materials, and the War Industries Board immediately removed its curtailments. In like manner, the necessity for maximum prices is disappearing, except in a few isolated cases which can best be regulated through the War Trade Board.

The facilities of the War Industries Board have been put at the disposal of the various contracting agencies of the Government, such as the War and Navy Departments and the Shipping Board, to aid them whenever they so desire in their consideration of the cancellation of their contracts. This particular function soon will have been completed.

Those activities of the War Industries Board which have lasting value are being transferred to permanent departments of the Government, where they may be carried forward. Thus, the Department of the Interior, Bureau of Mines, in which you have vested authority to enforce the War Minerals Act, has already assumed control over many of the former activities of this Board; the conservation program is about to be undertaken by the Department of Commerce, and the Central Bureau of Planning and Statistics will become a bureau to serve all departments of the Government.

I venture to suggest that the various commodity heads of the War Industries Board, and those who have been associated with them, may in the years that are to come, render much valuable assistance as Trade Advisers to the Department of Commerce and the War Trade Board. I hope that in this, and in other ways, it may be found possible to continue the promotion of a better understanding between the Government and industry, (including in this term employers and employees alike), so that problems affecting all may in times of peace be approached in the same spirit of helpful cooperation that has prevailed during the period of war.

I feel sure that the business men who have been acting as commodity heads will, if requested, be willing to remain here, or be subject to call, if they can be of service to the departments or other Governmental agencies as points of contact between them and industry.

There being no longer a necessity for the continuance of the War Industries Board, which was only a war-making body, and it being your desire, to avoid the incurring of expense for a moment longer than necessary, I am writing to suggest that the United States War Industries Board be discontinued as of January 1st, 1919, and I am now placing my resignation as Chairman in your hands, for whatever action you may desire. Between now and then the industries still under regulations will be called into conference, so as to obtain their views and their help as to the best methods of smoothly adjusting the business life to the changed conditions.

I cannot close without expressing to you my sincere appreciation, and that of my associates, for the opportunity you have given us to work with you in the great task that was set before you, and which has been brought to such a successful termination. As a matter of duty and pride, I should like again to call your attention to the valuable services performed by my associates, and by the War Service Committees of the various industries which co-operated with them. To their untiring efforts and unselfish devotion were largely due whatever results the War Industries Board has been able to attain. Each and every one worked in a spirit that made great personal sacrifices seem a privilege and not a burden. In order that a permanent record may be made of their unselfish service, I shall ask the privilege of forwarding to you a list of the members of the Board, of those associated with them, including Regional Advisors, War Service Committees, and State Councils of National Defense. I should like also to bear witness to the helpful co-operation which the War Industries Board at all times received from all departments and agencies of the Government.

All our efforts, however, would have fallen short had not the entire country responded in a whole-hearted manner. Unlimited credit is due the industries of the country, employers and employees alike, for the way in which they responded to all calls made upon them. Actuated by the desire to serve and not to profit, they pursued the common purpose of bringing the war to a successful conclusion, in a manner in which every American may well take a just pride.

Very sincerely yours,   Bernard M. Baruch

TLS (photostat in Joint Coll., MoU-MoHi).

From Frank William Taussig

My dear Mr. President: Washington November 19, 1918.

The Price-Fixing Committee, for which I am acting as Chairman during Mr. Brookings' absence, regrets extremely that it was unable to reach a more satisfactory outcome as regards the prices of cotton fabrics, to which you refer in your note of the 16th.[1] In justice to the manufacturers it should be said that their attitude was not entirely unreasonable or recalcitrant; they declared themselves ready to accept reductions in maximum prices, if arranged in such way as to give protection against variations in the price of the raw material.

The situation is most perplexing. Not only do cotton fabrics vary widely as regards manufacturing cost, but the price of the raw material affects enormously the price of those fabrics with which we have been most concerned. Had we settled a schedule of prices which could be deemed fair and reasonable in view of the price of raw cotton at the date of our action, that same price would have been distinctly *more* than fair and reasonable in view of the abrupt decline in raw material which took place within a few days. And it was entirely possible that this price should have proved, under the reverse conditions (of rising price of raw cotton) *less* than reasonable. A change of one cent in the price of cotton signifies a change of 10 per cent, or even 20 per cent in manufacturers' profits. The abrupt variations which have taken place since our meeting seem to confirm the wisdom of a policy of maintaining maximum prices, with express statement that they are maxima only, not in any way binding prices.

A further and more serious difficulty confronted us, and confronts us still. It is the necessity of making our action consistent with the policy which the War Industries Board follows in general on readjustment to peace conditions. We cannot well adopt a course of action for one set of commodities, without dealing with others on the same principles; yet no decision has been communicated to us considering the principles on which the War Industries Board proposes to proceed. Pending the settlement of a well-defined policy, we are compelled to make tentative and provisional arrangements, such as those with regard to cotton fabrics.

We would not trouble you with the details of the problem. A memorandum[2] is attached, for your convenience in case you should wish to consider the matter further. Needless to say, we are at your disposal for any desired conference.

I am, with the highest respect.

Very truly yours,   F. W. Taussig

TLS (WP, DLC).
    [1] WW to R. S. Brookings, Nov. 16, 1918, TLS (Letterpress Books, WP, DLC). See also R. S. Brookings to WW, Nov. 11, 1918, TLS, enclosing "Report of the Committee on Cotton," T MS, both in WP, DLC.
    [2] Spencer Turner, "Memorandum To the Price-Fixing Committee . . . ," TS MS (WP, DLC).

From Bainbridge Colby

My dear Mr. President: Washington November 19, 1918.

I am in a position to report to you on the subject of your letter of yesterday, with some specific suggestions, which I think call for prompt action.

It might save valuable time, if I could have a conference of a few minutes with you. The importance of the matter encourages me to suggest this,—and it would be helpful to have Secretary Daniels present.   Faithfully yours,   Bainbridge Colby

TLS (WP, DLC).

From Robert Latham Owen

My dear Mr. President: Washington, D. C. Nov. 19. 1918.

I am rejoiced that you are going to the Peace Conference.

The League of Nations is vital to prevent future wars. It has need of every influence you can personally exert at home and abroad to make it a reality.

You are in a very extraordinarily powerful position to bring about a wise and just conclusion and your failure to attend would hazard the success of this glorious conception.

May the Lord of Hosts, whose servant you are guide and keep you safely.   Yours Faithfully   Robt. L. Owen

Senator Reed is going to make a set speech denouncing a League of Nations and at lunch told me with great emphasis "And I want *you* to listen to me." I said, "I will on one condition." "What is it?" said he. I replied "On condition that here and now you solemnly swear you will listen to me when I reply to you." He promised but I "h'ae me doots."   R.L.O.

ALS (WP, DLC).

From Cleveland Hoadley Dodge

My dear Mr. President: [New York] November 19, 1918.

You will probably remember that when you were at Riverdale a month ago, we spoke about the plans for the rehabilitation and reconstruction of the Christian races in Asia Minor.

Now that the way is open, we find the needs are very great, and the American Committee for relief in the Near East, of which I am Treasurer, formally known as the Committee for Armenian & Syrian

Relief, expect to make an appeal to the American people in January, for a sum which seems very large, but, it will only be a beginning of what we will eventually have to have.

On two former occasions you have issued an appeal to the American people for the work of the Committee in saving, from actual starvation, the poor people of the Near East, and if it is not asking too much of you now, the Committee earnestly hopes that you will be willing to issue another appeal which would help us greatly in securing the large amount of money which we are trying to raise in January.

I enclose a short statement[1] which you may use as the basis for your appeal, which covers all the ground.

Your sympathy and cooperation in the past three years with the work of the Committee has been the largest single factor in enabling us to secure the generous amounts which the American people have given, and if you can see your way to help us again, we will all appreciate it greatly.

Yours cordially and sincerely,   Cleveland H. Dodge

TLS (WP, DLC).
[1] It is missing.

From the Diary of Josephus Daniels

1918 Tuesday 19 November

Cabinet.

Uniform 8 hour law.

Talked to WW about man who came into the service & drew salary from concern that had big contract. Am to see Attorney General. WW st[ate]d Council of Defense in states having Rep Governors had been made political agencies as had the Red Cross. Better dissolve slowly

To A.S.B. Compact organized administration forces in House, elimination of CC & CK.[1] Faithful men who will keep in touch. Same in Senate

League To Enforce Peace. Now purged of Taftism should be encouraged along line of resolution passed.[2]

Greg: Will you appoint C E Hughes No—there is no room big enough for Hughes & me to stay in

As to Chief of Navigation: No man not loyal. Baker imposed upon

[1] That is, Champ Clark and Claude Kitchin.
[2] The executive committee of the League to Enforce Peace, at a meeting held in New York on November 16, had adopted the following resolution:
"Whereas, The President of the United States has proposed as one of the terms of

peace that a League of Nations be organized and this proposal has been adopted as the basis of the armistice:
"Resolved, That the League to Enforce Peace pledges its hearty support to the President in the establishment of such a League of Nations." *New York Times*, Nov. 17, 1918.

To Robert Lansing, with Enclosure

My dear Lansing: The White House 20 November, 1918.

I have read the enclosed, of course, with genuine interest, but is it feasible, in view of the present at least temporary disintegration of Russia into at least five parts, Finland, the Baltic Provinces, European Russia, Siberia, and the Ukraine, to have Russia represented at the peace table, or to admit a part of her by recognizing and receiving delegates from the Omsk government?[1]
                    Cordially and faithfully yours,   Woodrow Wilson

TLS (SDR, RG 59, 763.72119/2752, DNA).
[1] For discussions of the two rival governments functioning at Omsk just prior to this date, see n. 2 to Enclosure I and n. 1 to Enclosure II printed with RL to WW, Sept. 24, 1918 (second letter of that date), Vol. 51. As mentioned in the second of these notes, Admiral Kolchak had just seized dictatorial power in a coup at Omsk on November 18.

E N C L O S U R E

MEMORANDUM.

The Interparty League for the R[e]storation of free Russia has been formed in New York at the beginning of 1918, when it became evident that the Bolsheviki groups in Russia were the tools of the German Government and are leading the country to social and political anarchy and national disintegration. The League is composed of different political groups in America, of Social Democrats, Social Revolutionists, Popular Socialists and Liberals, which means all the political shades of Russia with the exception of the Monarchists and the Bolsheviki. The programme of the League is the establishment of a democratic republic in Russia and the convocation of the Constitutional Assembly on the basis of universal, equal, direct and secret suffrage. The League was active in shaping Russian and American public opinion in this country through different publications, through mass meetings, lectures, conferences in all the greatest cities of America.

The Interparty League considers as its privileges and duty to present to the American Government its wishes and desires in regard to the relations of America and the Allies toward Russia, and the League is fully convinced that it is expressing thereby the will of all those political parties in Russia which are the leading forces in the great work of establishing a free democratic Russia.

It is of great importance for the restoration and liberation of Russia that the American Government should recognize the coalitional Omsk Government which is a settled Government of a part of Russia and the first successful and solid step to the establishment of an orderly free government in all Russia.

It is imperatove [imperative] that Russia shall get a full representation at the Peace Conference, as a free and independent country. America and all the Allies can never forget or ignore the fact that the Russian people and the Russian armies had sacrificed immeasurably in blood and wealth during the first years of the war for the freedom of the world and the safety of civilization.

The repatriation of the Russian prisoners from the Central Powers to Russia must be accomplished under the supervision of a body representing the Russian Democracy.

It is the most solemn will of the Interparty League and undoubtedly of all Russians and Russian-Americans that the Clause of the Armistice according to which the German armies should remain temporarily on Russian soil, as the guardians of order in Russia, should be declared as void and anulled. Russia and the Russian people cannot accept without protest the humiliation that German armies shall become the police force of Russia and the protectors of the population against internal struggles and excesses.

Interparty League for the Restoration of Free Russia.

> The Committee.
> Dr. Sergei Ingerman, Chairman
> Alex. Chernoff, Secretary
> Dr. Nahum Syrkin
> Maurice Kass
> Michael Swariks
> H. Slutzky
> S. Staak.[1]

T MS (SDR, RG 59, 763.72119/2752, DNA).
[1] The only person who can be further identified is Sergius Ingerman, M.D., long-time socialist leader in Russia and the United States and the founder of *Novy Mir*, the Russian daily newspaper published in New York.

To Robert Lansing

CONFIDENTIAL

My dear Mr. Secretary: The White House 20 November, 1918.

If your judgment agrees with mine in the matter, will you not be kind enough to send the following message to Mr. House?

"Referring to your No. 121, it is my own feeling that there are many serious disadvantages in having the Kaiser so near his own former kingdom and so near also to the centers of intrigue. I am at a loss to suggest what course ought to be taken, but I think that Holland will find him an exceedingly inconvenient and even dangerous guest."[1]

Cordially and sincerely yours,   Woodrow Wilson

TLS (SDR, RG 59, 862.001W64/104, DNA).
[1] Sent as WW to EMH, Nov. 21, 1918, T telegram (SDR, RG 59, 862.001W64/104, DNA).

To Robert Lansing, with Enclosure

My dear Mr. Secretary: The White House 20 November, 1918.

I do not like to correspond directly with Sun Yat Sen,[1] much as I have sometimes sympathized with his professed principles and objects. I would therefore be very much obliged to you if you would suggest what answer you think I ought to make to this telegram of his.   Faithfully yours,   Woodrow Wilson

TLS (SDR, RG 59, 893.00/2901, DNA).
[1] At this time Sun was residing in the French concession at Shanghai and devoting himself to writing and party organization.

E N C L O S U R E

Your Excellency: Shanghai Received November 19, 1918.

I congratulate you on the complete victory you have gained over militarism in this world war. You have done the greatest service to civilization and democracy since the world began. When you advised China to join you in the war last year I strongly objected because I knew that the militarists in my country would surely utilize the occasion to strangle democracy in China. My prediction has unfortunately turned out true. In the summer of last year while the question of joining the war was before our national assembly the Boxer Chief Changhsun[1] undertook a coup d'etat under the secret order of the then Premier Tuanchijui,[2] to force the abolition of parliament and to effect the restoration of the Manchu emperor.[3] Thus they intended to crush democracy at one stroke. But this act was not welcomed by all the powers and was bitterly resented by the people of China. Tuanchijui saw that the movement was foredoomed to failure so he changed front at once by joining the christian general, Fengyuhsiang,[4] who was already marching with his brigade on Peking to fight the monarchists. Tuanchijui established himself the chief of this anti-monarchist movement and thus pretended to be the savior of the republic. Immediately after hearing of the restoration of the monarchy and the overthrow of the republic I left Shanghai, on the 5th July, 1917, with a part of the Chinese navy for Canton, with a view to fight the monarchists. But on arrival at my destination all the work I had intended to do had been done already, apparently by Tuanchijui. I congratulated him for his patriotic action and advised him to restore the parliament at once. To my disappointment he ignored my advice and to my surprise I further discovered that he was at the bottom of Changsuns Boxer movement to destroy foreign institutions and to uphold the Manchus. I then took steps upon my own responsibility to reconvene the parliament at Canton. At first I was strongly opposed by the southern militarists also, but realizing that public opinion was with me, they let me have my way. The people of Canton welcomed my proposal and the Kuangtung provincial assembly at once sent out invitations to the members of parliament in all the provinces to come to Canton, and they responded enthusiastically. The southern militarists finding that the constitutional movement being so strongly supported by the people dared not openly come to terms with the north, but they conspired to overthrow democracy in the south as well. Thus, after a year laboring under unutterable difficulties, I finally succeeded in getting the parliament into quorum, which consisted of the majority of both the houses. During that interval the north sent expedition after expedition to crush the south. Thus the southern militarists were compelled to fight for their constitutional cause with my followers purely in self-defense, although they were not working under my direction. This is the real cause of the war forced by the northern militarists upon the south. But it is not a war between the north and south, as commonly supposed to be, for half the number of members of the parliament in Canton now are from the north. It is in fact a war between militarism and democracy pure and simple. The northern militarists knowing well that our cause is just and that we cannot be subjugated by them, created a bogus parliament in order to counteract the one elected by the people to gain public opinion in their territory and thus to throw dust into the eyes of the foreign powers. Since the change of the cabinet in Japan the supply of money and arms to the northern[er]s has been stopped. Being left helpless, the northern militarists now make overtures to the south for a compromise on conditions that both the bogus and true parliament be dissolved and the official posts of the republic redistributed. The southern militarists welcome this idea, as it enables them to divide the nations property among themselves and to crush the peoples rights. It is officially given out from Peking that the United States want[s] China to cease internal war, and if the south does not agree to the terms, the militarists will bring American pressure upon the south. Thus when the world was at war we were accused as anti-war; now, when peace is dawning, we shall likely soon be accused as anti-peace by the militarists. We have fought against overwhelming odds and against Japanese money and arms and yet survive; but if the United States moral and physical forces are to be misused as the Japanese by the Peking militarists against an oppressed people, the hope of democracy in China is gone. Therefore I am compelled to appeal to you personally for the sake of justice democracy and peace in China, and make known to you our peace terms. We insist all along upon one condition only, that is, our parliament must have full liberty to perform its proper functions. If this simple reasonable and moderate condition is denied us we will fight on despite whatever pressure the Peking militarists may bring upon us. For this parliament was won by the blood of the martyrs of our revolution and is the foundation of the republic. We could not suffer to see it so ruthlessly destroyed by the militarists. Moreover, this was the parliament duly authorized to formulate and adopt a permanent constitution for the republic. Until this special duty is fulfilled and the new constitution promulgated, it cannot be dissolved. When Yuanshikai was preparing his way to the imperial throne he abruptly abolished this parliament. Then the people rose and defeated him. This is now the second time that we are fighting for the same parliament. And this very parliament was first recognized by the United States through your own good self.

May I not look upon you now to save democracy in China as you have done in Europe, by saying just a word for the oppressed people of China to the Peking militarists that the parliament which you have recognized must be respected.   Sunyatsen.

T telegram (SDR, RG 59, 893.00/2901, DNA).
    [1] Chang Hsün, former general in the Chinese army, best known for his loyalty to the Manchu dynasty and for his attempt to restore the dynasty to power in June and July 1917.
    [2] That is, Tuan Ch'i-jui.
    [3] P'u-yi, born 1906, the last Manchu Emperor. He had been enthroned on December 2, 1908, and had abdicated on February 2, 1912. His "restoration" in 1917 lasted from July 1 to approximately July 12.
    [4] Feng Yü-hsiang, one of the ablest Chinese generals, at this time defense commissioner of Ch'angte. He had become a Methodist in 1914.

To Henry Lee Myers

PERSONAL AND CONFIDENTIAL

My dear Senator: [The White House] 20 November, 1918.

I think I need not tell you my own cordial feeling towards Mr. Bryan.[1] I should have entire confidence in his principles and in his influence at the conference, but I feel that it is our duty to keep in mind, particularly at this time when all the world is a bit abnormal in its acute sensibilities, the reactions of the public mind of the several countries concerned. Mr. Bryan is soft-hearted, and the world just now is very hard-hearted. It would render a very large and influential body of our public opinion very uneasy if they thought that peace was to be approached in the spirit which they would attribute to Mr. Bryan. I think it highly important to hold opinion steady and calm, and for that reason I do not think that it would be wise to include Mr. Bryan among the commissioners, much as it would personally gratify me to do so.

Cordially and sincerely yours,   [Woodrow Wilson]

CCL (WP, DLC).
[1] Wilson was replying to H. L. Myers to WW, Nov. 18, 1918, TLS (WP, DLC).

To Louis Marshall

My dear Mr. Marshall: [The White House] 20 November, 1918.

My own judgment is that such a public pronouncement as you suggest in your letter of November 16th would be unwise. I think you can hardly realize all the reactions of my attempting leadership in too many ways.

I have no doubt that there will be many opportunities to impress upon the Peace Council the serious aspects of the very great and appealing problem upon which you dwell, and I shall deem it a privilege to exercise such influence as I can.

In unavoidable haste,

Sincerely yours,   Woodrow Wilson

TLS (Letterpress Books, WP, DLC).

To Alexander Mitchell Palmer

My dear Palmer: The White House 20 November, 1918.

I am sorry to differ with you in your judgment about the Busch property,[1] but I really think that we would be in a very indefensible position if we retained it. I have had two full conferences with the Attorney General about it, and he has convinced me on the point of legality. My advice, therefore, is that you release it as soon as possible.

Cordially and sincerely yours,   Woodrow Wilson

TLS (A.M. Palmer Papers, DLC).
    [1] About this case, see WW to A. M. Palmer, Oct. 21, 1918, n. 1, and A. M. Palmer to WW, Oct. 25, 1918, n. 2, both in Vol. 51.

To Grant Squires

My dear Mr. Squires: [The White House] 20 November, 1918.

Thank you for your letter of November 16th.[1] What you send me is indeed interesting, as interesting as it is disturbing.

In unavoidable haste,

Cordially and sincerely yours,   Woodrow Wilson

TLS (Letterpress Books, WP, DLC).
    [1] G. Squires to WW, Nov. 16, 1918, TLS, enclosing Office of Corps of Intelligence Police, New York, to Commanding Officer, Corps of Intelligence Police, Nov. 13, 1918, CCL, both WP, DLC. The enclosure was a lengthy report about a mass meeting at Carnegie Hall on November 12 which had been sponsored by the Socialist party. According to the report, all the speakers had praised the new revolutionary socialist regimes in Russia and Germany and had asserted that it was the socialists of the warring nations who had forced their governments to agree to an armistice. The writer of the report made much of the fact that red flags, red handkerchiefs, red roses, and so on, had been displayed in profusion by the participants in the meeting.

Two Telegrams from Edward Mandell House

Paris. Nov. 20, 1918.

Number 126. Secret for the President and Secretary of State.

Various circumstances are delaying an agreement respecting important points connected with the constitution of the peace conference and the procedure to be followed therein. George and the other members of the English Government are *coterminous* [completely engrossed] in the pending elections and will in all probability be unwilling until the elections are over [on December 14th] to decide definitely how many delegates they will wish to nominate, and who these delegates will be. If George is defeated of course considerable confusion respecting this matter will result. If George wins he will make probably some radical changes in his cabinet which may affect the make up of the English delegation at the Peace Conference. In France, Clemenceau may try to limit the representative[s] to three. He would then head the French delegation and would have with him Pichon and possibly Foch, over both of whom he exercises almost complete control. If it is decided that there shall be more than three delegates Clemenceau would probably have to appoint some man like Briand who would act independently and would have a strong following. In Italy the situation, so far as I am informed concerning it, has not taken any very definite shape. Orlando will of course head the delegation.

In view of the uncertainty in connection with this matter, I suggest that no announcement be made concerning our delegation until England, France and Italy are committed to a definite number of delegates. The French are urging that the French language be used as the official language of the conference. Since the French are to be given the place of meeting and the presidency of the conference, it would seem as if they should meet the convenience of England and ourselves with respect to the language to be used. At the conferences before the Armistice was signed Orlando and Pichon were the only ones that could not understand English. In addition to ourselves and the English, Clemenceau, Sonnino, the Belgian representative, the Servian representative, the Greek representative and the Japanese representative are all able to understand English. I shall take up this question with the English in order to see how they feel [about it].   Edward House.

Paris. Nov. 20, 1918.

Number 130. Secret. For the President and Secretary of State.

Lord Derby has just sent word to me that he has heard from Mr. Balfour that the British Government does not feel that it is bound to consider Versailles as the place finally decided upon for the peace conference. They feel that this is a question which must be finally decided by the inter-Allied Conference. Mr. Balfour points out, however, that after the various delegations have arrived in Paris, and the organizations set up there, it will be most difficult to change the meeting place of the final conference. Lord Derby believes that the British Government has, however, definitely accepted the proposal that the inter-Allied Conference should be held in Paris. Lord Derby states that he is doing his best to hurry the French Government into the taking over of the necessary accommodations for the staff of the British Government. Lord Derby has asked the French Government to take over both the Astoria which has one hundred thirty [230] bed rooms and the Majestic Hotel which has four fifty bed rooms. He says that the rent has not yet been agreed upon.
          Edward House.

T telegrams (WP, DLC).

From Robert Lansing, with Enclosure

My dear Mr. President: Washington November 20, 1918.

Mr. Debuchi[1] of the Japanese Embassy called at the Department this afternoon and left the enclosed document with the statement that the Japanese Ambassador had received instructions from his Government to call upon you and to present the answer of the Japanese Government in the matter which you had up with the Japanese Ambassador recently, but that the Ambassador was just recovering from an attack of influenza and he feared, in view of its contagious nature, to come in personal contact with you and resorted to this means to convey to you the answer of his Government.

If you have any reply to make to the Ambassador I should be glad if you would inform me as to how you would like the reply made.

I am, my dear Mr. President
                    Yours very sincerely,   Robert Lansing.

TLS (WP, DLC).
[1] Katsuji Debuchi, Counselor of Embassy.

E N C L O S U R E

11/20/18
Handed me by Mr.
Debuchi, of the
Jap. Emb. B.L.

The Japanese Government learned with genuine pleasure that the President of the United States was good enough to receive the Japanese Ambassador on the 1st of November and express to him his frank views with regard to certain reported acts of the Japanese military authorities in Siberia.[1]

The Japanese Government always desirous to maintain a perfect understanding and harmony in the relations between the United States and Japan, attach particular importance to such understanding and harmony between the two governments especially at this moment when with practical cessation of hostilities the final object of securing lasting peace remains yet to be settled, the object for the attainment of which the Japanese Government are determined to spare no effort.

Consequently the Japanese Government wish, in the first place, to express to the President their sense of high appreciation of the frankness and candor with which he, in his conversation with Viscount Ishii, passed in review the different incidents in Siberia as reported to him, since such frankness and candor can not fail to contribute, in no small degree, to the better understanding of the two countries.

The Imperial Government did not fail to refer all the points, regarding which the President had been good enough to call their attention, to the most careful investigation of the authorities concerned. They now take the liberty of submitting with equal frankness and candor to the consideration of the President the following facts resulting from the said investigation:

(1) The Japanese forces despatched to the Maritime, Amur, and Za-Baikal provinces in Siberia as well as to North Manchuria attained for a time the strength of 44,700 combatants besides 27,700 non-combatants. Some of them have been since ordered home and the present strength amounts to 42,200 combatants with 16,400   58,600[2] non-combatants. The Japanese forces in the abovementioned regions have to guard the railway lines, extending over a total length of about 3,600 miles, and to secure the rear of the Czecho-Slovaks as well as the Allied contingents and, also, to facilitate the transportation and supply of the war materials. When all these circumstances are considered it will be readily admitted that the Japanese forces in Siberia are far from being excessively large. Such forces are considered absolutely necessary in carrying out the object of the expedition as declared by the Japanese Government at the outset. The Japanese military authorities are reluctant to keep a comparatively larger number of non-combatants engaged in sanitation, transportation, supply and communication. In view, however, of the vast area of the territories actually control[l]ed by the Allied forces and, also, of the extension of the lines of supply in the rear, this was found unavoidable.

(2) It seems to the Japanese Government that there must be some misunderstanding on the part of the American authorities in regard to the alleged refusal by the Japanese authorities to supply the American Army with quarters in Harbin.

Some time ago, the Headquarters of the American forces made an inquiry at the Japanese Army Headquarters in Vladivostok as to the housing accommodation in Harbin and were told that there were no vacant buildings available there. The Japanese military authorities have never refused any request made by the American authorities in that connection, nor were they properly in a position to give any decision on such a matter. It is reported on the other hand that the American authorities were informed by the Russian authorities, to whom they had made a direct inquiry on the subject, of the impossibility of obtaining quarters in Harbin.

The lack of housing accommodation is now most keenly felt everywhere in Eastern Siberia and in North Manchuria, as the winter is setting in. This was why the Japanese expeditionary forces were finally compelled to send back a large portion of their Service Corps to Japan.

(3) The Japanese Army is alleged to be monopolizing the use of the railways to the East of Irkutsk, thus making the westward transportation of the American troops and materials impossible. The Japanese Government can not quite understand the alleged report.

The Russian railways are, as a matter of fact, under the complete control of the Russian authorities themselves. The Japanese troops have never occupied any of them; they have always been within the limit of their duty, i.e. the guarding of the railway zones. The matter of military transportation has been vested in the hands of the Allied Railway Commission in the Maritime and Amur provinces that is as far as the power of the Commander of the Allied forces extends. In the Za-Baikal railway and the Chinese Eastern Railway the military transportation is being carried out upon frequent consultations between the Russian railway authorities on the one hand and the Japanese and Chinese authorities on the other, in view of the fact that the military operations in those regions were at the outset undertaken solely by the forces of Japan and China. Anyway there was no question of railway occupation anywhere and here as elsewhere all possible facilities in regard to the military transportation of the Allied forces have been fully offered. That the westward transportation of the Czecho-Slovaks, British, French and Italian troops have been each time smoothly carried out may serve as a clear proof. The American Commander has never in the past asked for the westward transportation of his contingents or materials. Needless to say that the Japanese military authorities will be fully prepared, so far as they are concerned, to extend every possible facility to the transportation of the American troops or materials whenever requested.

Such is a brief summary of the results of the investigation made. It is perhaps inevitable that some sort of misunderstanding should take place from time to time where troops of various nationalities with their difference in language, in manners and in customs engage in a joint enterprise.

So far as the Imperial Government are concerned they will be ready to take necessary corrective measure[s] whenever they discover any improper step taken by their own authorities and they earnestly request the Government of the United States to frankly express to them whatever doubt action of the Japanese authorities may give rise to. They are of opinion that a perfect understanding and harmony between the two Governments can thus and thus only be firmly established.

T MS (WP, DLC).
  [1] See K. Ishii to the Foreign Office, Nov. 1, 1918, Vol. 51.
  [2] WWhw.

From Henry White

Dear Mr President,   Washington Nov. 20th, 1918

Pray accept the expression of my thanks for the honor you have been pleased to confer upon me.[1]

I sincerely appreciate the confidence in me evinced by your appointing me a member of the Delegation which is to accompany you from this country to the approaching Peace Conference in Europe. I trust that my experience of such international gatherings, which is considerable and my personal friendship with many of those who are to represent other countries, may be of service to you and the members of our delegation, with a view to the attainment of a just and permanent Peace, based in so far as may be possible, upon the fourteen points set forth as the basis of such a Peace, in your address to the Nation and to the World of the 8th of January last.

I am, dear Mr. President,
                    Very Sincerely Yours   Henry White

ALS (WP, DLC).
  [1] White wrote about the circumstances of his appointment as peace commissioner as follows: "I have never been more surprised in my life than when Lansing sent for me last Tuesday (the 19th) toward the dinner hour, and offered me this post on the part of the President. I was not aware that they were even dreaming of me. After asking until yesterday morning to give my decision . . . I accepted; but not until I had insisted that Lansing should explain the significance of the President's points upon the League of Nations, the question of economic barriers, and the freedom of the seas. Nobody appears to have suggested my name, and of course I never dreamed of suggesting it myself. It seems that Lansing and the President hit upon me themselves as the representative of the Republican party." H. White to W. H. Buckler, Nov. 24, 1918, quoted in Allan Nevins, *Henry White: Thirty Years of American Diplomacy* (New York and London, 1930), p. 348.

From Alexander Mitchell Palmer

Sir: Washington, D. C. November 20, 1918.

I am enclosing herewith a Proclamation for execution by you determining certain persons to be enemies under Section 2-C of the "Trading with the Enemy Act."

This Proclamation is necessary to complete our jurisdiction over property already demanded by me.

It is important that the Proclamation should be signed and issued at your earliest convenience.

Yours respectfully,   A Mitchell Palmer

TLS (WP, DLC).

From Herman Henry Kohlsaat

Dear Mr President   Washington, Nov 20 1918

Am sure you will not misunderstand my motive in writing you in regard to taking over the cables *at this time*.

As a war measure it would have been accepted without a murmer, but there is not a paper in this country that will not construe it as an attempt to *control the news* of the Peace Conference.

It is fraught with great danger to *you*, and your administration Mr. Burleson's *explanation*[1] does not *explain*. If there is some good reason for it *you* personally should issue a statement

I am not interested in *any Cable Co.* & only warn you as a sincere well wisher & friend.

Keep the confidence of the world. You have it to a *wonderful* degree This action will breed suspicion

As Ever   Your friend   H. H. Kohlsaat

ALS (WP, DLC).

[1] Wilson, on November 2, had issued a proclamation placing all marine cable systems under the control of the Postmaster General. *Official Bulletin*, II (Nov. 16, 1918), 4. Burleson released his explanatory statement on November 19. Burleson's remarks amounted to an assertion that, because the land telegraph and marine cable systems formed a single continuous communications network in fact, therefore the federal government should control the cable system just as it already controlled the telegraph lines. Burleson buttressed this assertion with the following statement: "There never was a time in the history of this war . . . which called for such a close control of the cable system as today. . . . The absolute necessity of uninterrupted, continuous communication should be apparent to all." He concluded with the remark: "There are many other reasons for taking over the cables which have been suggested by the experience so far in Government control of land lines, but I only think it necessary to state the determining factors." *Ibid.*, Nov. 20, 1918, pp. 1-2, and the *New York Times*, Nov. 20, 1918.

From Philip Albright Small Franklin

Washington, D. C.
November 20th, 1918.

My dear Mr. President:

Your letter of the 18th instant was received this afternoon and it will be placed tomorrow before the Board of Directors of the International Mercantile Marine Company.

I beg to advise you that the action heretofore taken by our Board in this matter was upon our understanding that it met with the approval of our Government and I feel sure that our Board would not wish to take any further steps looking to the completion of the transaction that would be contrary to your wishes.

Sincerely yours,   P. A. S. Franklin.

TLS (WP, DLC).

From Charles Hillyer Brand and Thomas Montgomery Bell[1]

Dear Mr. President: Washington, D. C. November 20, 1918.

For the last two weeks we have been receiving letters and telegrams from constituents in our districts in regard to the cotton situation.

It has been suggested that if the War Trade Board or Mr. Brand's Committee[2] do not give any relief to the cotton grower we appeal to you.

The farmers of our districts as a rule are not selling their cotton. Most of it is stored in warehouses. The warehousemen will not loan a dollar upon this cotton. They claim that they cannot borrow any more money from the banks and for this reason they decline to make any advances no matter how much collateral is offered.

Our people believe if the embargo upon shipments of cotton is lifted or removed that the price thereof will seek its level, which in the judgment of well posted men as well as cotton producers, will be from 35 to 40 cents per pound. This has been a costly crop to make, and to sell it at the present price means a great sacrifice.

We are deeply concerned and interested in this matter. If you do not deem it proper or wise to remove said embargo, we respectfully submit for your serious and immediate consideration the proposition of not only authorizing but ordering the War Trade Board to remove its restrictions upon the shipment of cotton and liberally licensing the same.

This matter is not a question of politics with us or our constituents, but next to the war and the issues growing out of it it is the most serious problem at present confronting our people.

We hope and trust that the matter may receive favorable consideration at your hands.

We beg to remain,

Most respectfully yours,   C. H. Brand
Tho. M. Bell

TLS (WP, DLC).
[1] Democratic congressmen from Georgia.
[2] Banking and Currency.

From William Jennings Bryan

Columbus, Ohio, Nov. 20, 1918.

Permit me to express a double pleasure, first, that you have decided to attend the Peace conference in person, and, second, that to a Democratic President falls the great honor of signing the war prohibition bill that puts an end to the liquor traffic in the United States.[1]   William Jennings Bryan.

T telegram (WP, DLC).
  [1] For a summary of the provisions of the prohibition amendment to H.R. 11945, a supplementary agricultural bill, see JPT to WW, Sept. 7, 1918, n. 1, Vol. 49. The amendment remained essentially unchanged in the final form of the bill which Wilson signed into law on November 21. 40 *Statutes at Large* 1045.

From the Diary of Josephus Daniels

November Wednesday 20 1918

War Cabinet. Baruch McAdoo thought reconstruction would take care of itself. WW wanted to see that there was material for France & Belgium and not gobbled up by those who would boost prices to obtain it. McAdoo feared we were manufacturing munitions we did not need to keep labor employed. It is our business to reduce & protect finances. There is plenty for labor to do. But better to pay labor till adjusted than use it in what is not needed.

To William Gibbs McAdoo[1]

My dear Mr. Secretary: [The White House] 21 November, 1918.

I was not unprepared for your letter of the fourteenth because you had more than once, of course, discussed with me the circumstances which have long made it a serious personal sacrifice for you to remain in office. I know that only your high and exacting sense of duty had kept you here until the immediate tasks of the war should be over. But I am none the less distressed. I shall not allow our intimate personal relation to deprive me of the pleasure of saying that in my judgment the country has never had an abler, a more resourceful and yet prudent, a more uniformly efficient Secretary of the Treasury; and I say this remembering all the able, devoted, and distinguished men who preceded you. I have kept your letter a number of days in order to suggest, if I could, some other solution of your difficulty than the one you have now felt obliged to resort to. But I have not been able to think of any. I cannot ask you to make further sacrifices, serious as the loss of the

Government will be in your retirement. I accept your resignation, therefore, to take effect upon the appointment of a successor, because in justice to you I must.

I also, for the same reasons, accept your resignation as Director General of Railroads, to take effect, as you suggest, on the first of January next. The whole country admires, I am sure, as I do, the skill and executive capacity with which you have handled the great and complex problem of the unified administration of the railways under the stress of war uses, and will regret, as I do, to see you leave that post just as the crest of its difficulty is about to be passed.

For the distinguished, disinterested, and altogether admirable service you have rendered the country in both posts, and especially for the way in which you have guided the Treasury through all the perplexities and problems of transitional financial conditions and of the financing of a war which has been without precedent alike in kind and in scope I thank you with a sense of gratitude that comes from the very bottom of my heart.

Gratefully and affectionately yours,   [Woodrow Wilson]

CCL (WP, DLC).
[1] There is a WWT draft of the following letter in WP, DLC.

From William Gibbs McAdoo

Dear Governor,   [Washington] Nov. 21/18

I am most grateful for your wonderful letter which is a priceless reward for any service I may have rendered to the country. Thank you from the bottom of my heart. I shall make the letters public Friday either for afternoon papers or for Saturday morning papers.

Always your devoted   WGM

ALI (WP, DLC).

From Robert Lansing, with Enclosure

President says
wait till he & Secre-
tary get to Paris.
BM 11/26

My dear Mr. President: Washington [Nov. 21, 1918]

We have recently had a long telegram through the Norwegian Government, giving the text of a note addressed to you by the Bolshevik Commissaire for Foreign Affairs.[1] The note is a specious and upstart arraignment of your policy towards Russia. With characteristic effrontery, the Commissaire states that, in the absence of a reply, the Bolshevik authorities will publish an official statement that their interpretation of the attitude of this Government towards the Russian people is confirmed. Through the same channel, we now have a further note from the Bolshevik Commissaire expressing the desire of the Russian Soviet authorities to terminate hostilities between Russian and American troops.[2]

I think you will agree with me that neither of the notes should be dignified by a formal reply. At the same time, I am reluctant to allow the Russian people to be deceived in any way in regard to our purpose to serve their best interests and assist them to the full extent of our capacity to do so. To me, the situation seems to call for a statement of our position and an illustration of our purpose by some action; it constitutes a definite turning point in our relations with the Bolsheviki.

I have accordingly prepared a statement for publication, based on the replies received to our circular telegram of September 20th which called upon all civilized nations to join in expressing their abhorrence of the reign of terror which exists in parts of Russia.[3] It is true that in the parts of Russia where such terrible conditions still prevail, there is a more complete suppression of the liberty of the press than existed in the days of the autocracy. To reach the masses of the people will be difficult; to convince them of our purpose may be still more difficult. At the same time, I believe we should make the attempt—providing it can be done without involving us in direct communication with the Bolsheviki—through the Norweigian Legation at Petrograd. If for no other reason, I believe the statement should be published in order that our troops at Archangel and Vladivostok should understand the purpose for which their arduous service in North Russia and in Siberia may be prolonged.

I shall be grateful if you will let me know what your views may be.   Faithfully yours,   Robert Lansing

TLS (SDR, RG 59, 861.00/4381, DNA).
    [1] G. V. Chicherin to WW, Oct. 29, 1918, Vol. 51.
    [2] G. V. Chicherin to WW, Nov. 22, 1918, *ibid.*
    [3] See WW to RL, Sept. 20, 1918 (first letter of that date), n. 2, *ibid.*

E N C L O S U R E

PROPOSED STATEMENT REGARDING RUSSIAN SITUATION.

On September 20th the Government of the United States requested its diplomatic representatives abroad to call the attention of the Governments to which they were accredited to the reign of terror existing in parts of Russia and to state its belief that all civilized nations should join in expressing their abhorrence of such barbarism.

The following countries have now expressed their complete agreement with the views of the United States: France, Great Britain, Belgium, Italy, Serbia, Portugal, Greece, Argentina, Colombia, Cuba, Ecuador, Guatemala, Haiti, Honduras, Nicaragua, Panama, Paraguay, Peru, San Domingo, San Salvador, Uruguay, China and Siam.

The neutral countries which, at the time, were still able to maintain representatives at Petrograd, namely: Norway, Sweden, Denmark, Holland, Switzerland, Spain and Persia, had already on September 5th informed the authorities in Russia with whom they were in touch that such acts of violence as were then occurring called for the indignation of the civilized world.

The Government of the United States, in assuming the responsibility of announcing the result of its appeal to all civilized Governments, appreciates fully the grave problems which confront the Russian people and is actuated solely by its frequently expressed purpose to lend its sympathy and support to assist them to restore such orderly government as will enable them to become masters of their own affairs.

In all parts of Russia where the people desire to safeguard the principles of democratic freedom won by their Revolution, the United States purposes to assist by all the means in its power. Exceptional conditions, however, exist in that part of Russia which is dominated by the regime established at Moscow and Petrograd. To judge from the words of its own leaders and from the known practice of its adherents, this regime is as much opposed to democracy as was the autocratic militarism of Germany. Under its control a class war of extermination has been encouraged, the people's money squandered, industry disrupted, the railways demoralized and Russia reduced to economic impotence where formerly she contributed so largely from her bounty to other countries. The United States cannot take part in measures which would tend to prolong the control of such a regime. It cannot, therefore, undertake to render assistance in this part of Russia until the authorities at Moscow and Petrograd definitely abandon government by mass terror and murder and at the same time obligate themselves, openly and in a manner which will leave no opportunity for evasion, to restore order and the due process of the law and set up a government based on the freely expressed will of the whole people.

T MS (SDR, RG 59, 861.00/4381, DNA).

Two Telegrams from Edward Mandell House

Paris. Nov. 21, 1918.

Number 135. Secret for the President.

The French Government have advised me that His Highness, Prince Murat[1] has placed his residence[2] at the disposal of the French Government in order that they may offer it to President Wilson for his use during his stay in Paris. I shall visit this house as soon as possible and cable you fully respecting it. Please make no announcement respecting this matter until I advise you further.

Edward House.

[1] Joachim Napoléon, 5th Prince Murat, Prince of Ponte-Corvo.
[2] At 28 rue de Monceau.

Paris. Nov. 21, 1918.

Number 137. Secret for the President and Secretary of State.

I have just received the following communication from the French Ministry of Foreign Affairs: "You were good enough to communicate to me under date of yesterday telegram of President Wilson expressing desire that the political censorship applied up to the present to press telegrams sent from France to America be completely suppressed. I have the honor to inform you that the French Government is happy to respond to the desire of President Wilson. Dispositions will therefore be taken immediately to suppress all censorship of press telegrams sent from France to the United States. Please accept, et cetera. Signed S. Pichon."

This is of course very satisfactory. I have taken the measures [this matter] up with the British Authorities through Lord Derby, and I expect to have an answer from them before long. I shall advise the press correspondents informally of the action of the French Government, and request them to advise me of any further interference with their press despatches.   Edward House.

T telegrams (WP, DLC).

From William Bauchop Wilson

My dear Mr. President: Washington November 21, 1918.

I am in receipt of your letter of the 18th, inclosing telegram from Frank J. Hayes, urging that a labor representative be named on the peace commission.

There is widespread demand in labor circles in European countries as well as in the United States that some representative of labor be selected from each of the countries as members of the peace commission. I presume you have already been advised of the action of the Executive Council of the American Federation of Labor in urging the appointment of Mr. Samuel Gompers as labor's representative on the American commission. If you determine upon his selection in my judgment it should not be solely because he is representative of labor but because his experience and general attainments qualify him to represent the people of the United States in the consideration of the innumerable and intricate problems that will come before the commission for adjustment.

It has been my lifelong desire to secure the elimination of class distinctions rather than to accentuate them, permitting the various groups that exist in any form of society to associate themselves by the process of congenial selection rather than as a result of inherited status or the possession of wealth. The modern struggle for democracy began with the demand of the nobles for the right to share with the king the privileges and responsibilities of government. That was followed by the middle or commercial classes insisting upon the same privilege. Later the workers demanded a voice in the affairs of state. By the middle of last century the people of the United States had achieved almost universal manhood suffrage. Since then those intrusted with the affairs of government have been responsible to all of the people for their acts rather than to any one group.

Most of the countries of Europe have been in the second stage of this development until the revolutionary forces upset the established order since the beginning of the war. These forces have gone to the opposite extreme. They have in some instances removed the king and barred the nobles and middle classes from participation in the government. In other instances the fear of revolution gives to those who assume to speak for the proletariat a tremendous influence. For that reason some of the countries will no doubt have trade unionists or socialists representing them at the peace table. The effect of these circumstances upon the influence of the United States at the conference is one of the questions that should be taken into consideration in determining the qualifications of the commissioners. The opportunities of working men to secure a broad view of human relations has in the past been limited by the narrow sphere to which their observations and activities have of necessity been confined. The development of the trade union movement has given to large numbers of them the advantages of international observation and a breadth of understanding that would enable them to deal intelligently with international problems. In the selection of representatives to the peace conference these facts should be borne in mind.

My thought therefore is that the commissioners should not be selected simply because they are male or female, white or black, or belong to any particular group, nor should the sex or connection with any group be a bar to their selection. To me there seems to be but two questions to determine: First, is the person selected qualified for the task in hand, all of the political, economic and social circumstances being taken into consideration, and, second, will the majority of the people have faith in his ability to perform the task. The first of these is by far the more important, because the results of the conference will be the measure by which the public and the future historian will determine the wisdom of the selection. I have no hesitancy in saying that in my judgment Mr. Gompers would measure up to the standard.

As to the telegram of Mr. Hayes, I would advise that pending the selection of the commissioners you give the usual formal answer of careful consideration of the suggestion presented.

I am returning Mr. Hayes' telegram herewith.

Faithfully yours,   W B Wilson

TLS (WP, DLC).

From Joseph Patrick Tumulty

Dear Governor: Jersey City, New Jersey 21 November, 1918.

With reference to your trip abroad, I hope you will pardon a personal word at this time. The newspapers carry a story that I am to be one of the party. There is nothing in the world I would rather do, if I consulted my own desires, but I am sure that I can render better service by staying on the job here in this country and keeping you in touch with affairs here, not only with reference to our domestic situation, but to let you have, from this side, American impressions of what you are striving to do on the other.

Sincerely,   J. P. Tumulty

TLS (J. P. Tumulty Papers, DLC).

From John Franklin Fort

My dear Mr. President: Washington November 21, 1918.

At the Commission meeting, day before yesterday, before Mr. Colver left for an address at Cleveland, made I suppose last night, we had about finished Part 2 of the Packers Report, probably the most important single pamphlet of the proposed report of the Commission. It is the statement in detail of the documentary and oral evidence of the proof of the findings of the Commission. It will be in your hands probably tomorrow. Mr. Colver, before going, wrote a little note as Chairman, which will accompany the pamphlet Part 2 for your transmission to Congress at your convenience.

(2) The proposed bill, which we sent you some time ago in the packers' matter,[1] is being anxiously inquired for by Senators and Representatives, but of course, we have done nothing, and will do nothing until we know that you do not disapprove, or if you do disapprove in its present form, whether you have other suggestions for its modification. This bill is framed on suggestions from Judge Glasgow of the Food Administration and Walter L. Fisher of the Chicago Bar, and our own suggestions. We hoped it would at least form a basis for legislative action.

Senator Kendrick earnestly urged me to request that you permit something to be moved on the opening of the session of Congress on December 2, because he fears that if nothing is done between December 2 and the formal opening of the next Congress that legislation may be defeated, because he fears that that Congress will not be as favorable to the legislation as this. In any event, it would give this Congress an opportunity to put itself on record by this legislation, and if its successors should defeat it, the people would know just who is responsible.

If you prefer to see me a minute, and make your suggestions orally, it will give me pleasure to call at any time you designate.

In this connection, may I be permitted to express my appreciation of your action in the case of Captain Luther E. Goble of Camp Dix, and your restoring him to duty.[2] You have done a righteous thing, in my view, and I thank you in his name and on my own behalf for it.

I trust that you will not deem it presuming for the Commission to suggest that in your address at the opening of Congress on December 2, in referring to other matters of importance in the way of future constructive and reconstruction legislation, you may make some reference to the Food Investigation by the Federal Trade Commission, and the importance of legislation looking to the benefits which may be conserved as suggested in its report to Congress. Senator Kendrick and other friends of yours seem to think that such a statement, however guarded, may be most helpful in securing good results.

Your real friends are much pleased that you are going to the Peace Conference. Those who are not your friends are desirous that you should not go for only one reason, in my view,—that you may not be able to fully reap in the Peace Treaty that which you have sown, and thus achieve the greatest success and world commendation that any other statesman of the century has accomplished.

May you be safely taken over and brought back, and receive the praise which the people in this country will be willing to bestow upon your return with this wonderful result accomplished.

Faithfully yours,   John Franklin Fort

TLS (WP, DLC).
¹ See W. B. Colver *et al.* to WW, July 3, 1918, Vol. 48.
² Capt. Goble had been accused of being intoxicated while on duty at Camp Dix, New Jersey, on April 2, 1918. He was tried by general court martial and was found guilty and sentenced to be dismissed from the service. Fort wrote to Wilson on Goble's behalf on September 10 and enclosed a copy of a request from Col. George B. Pond for the transfer of Goble to a new regiment which Pond was then forming, provided that Goble was to be retained in the service. Both Pond and Fort gave strong testimonials to Goble's character and previous service. An inquiry into the exact status of Goble's case revealed that the papers relating to it had been sent to the White House in late May for final action by Wilson but had never been returned to the War Department. Taking advantage of this bureaucratic lapse, Wilson wrote to Newton D. Baker on October 26, saying that he would like to do as Fort requested, provided Baker did not feel that it involved a serious relaxation of discipline. The remainder of the correspondence concerning Goble's case is missing. However, Fort's comment in the above letter makes it clear that Goble was retained in the service and suggests that perhaps the proposed transfer was carried out also. See the correspondence concerning Goble from June 1 to Oct. 26, 1918, in Series 4, Case File No. 398, WP, DLC.

From Gavin McNab

My dear Mr. President: Washington November 21, 1918.

Thank you for the kind invitation to express to you by letter my opinion of the causes of our recent defeat, and the remedy.

I will, but not now.

In the presence of the tragedy of nations, my sense of proportion forbids the thought.

In your going abroad you will carry the prayer and blessing of every worthy soul.

May God's providence aid you in your great work.

Yours sincerely,   Gavin McNab

TLS (WP, DLC).

From Philip Albright Small Franklin

My dear Mr. President: Washington, D. C. November 21, 1918.

Referring to my letter dated November 20th, 1918, I beg leave to advise you that at a meeting of the Board of Directors of the International Mercantile Marine Company, held in New York this morning, it was resolved that, in pursuance to the request contained in your letter of November 18th, 1918, no further action of the Board will be taken in the matter referred to until the views of this Government are fully presented and considered.

Sincerely yours,   P. S. A. Franklin

TLS (WP, DLC).

From the Norman Foster Company

Dear Mr. President,   Trenton, N. J. November 21, 1918.

This office desires to settle satisfactorily with you for the injury to your hand which occurred some months ago.

Our draft in payment under your accident policy was returned as unsatisfactory.[1] Inasmuch as we are at least honor bound not to neglect to pay this, or any other claim, may we ask that you have some one write us as we have no other means of finding out what would constitute a satisfactory settlement. We are more than handicapped in deciding the amount that should be paid.

Very truly yours,   Norman Foster Co

TLS (WP, DLC).
[1] See JPT to Norman Foster Company, Sept. 25, 1918, Vol. 51.

From the Diary of Josephus Daniels

1918 Thursday 21 November

Colby & I went to see the President about the purchase by G.B. of the 85 ships belonging to International Mercantile Co. Very complicated American money is in them but under English laws they are controlled by English directors and if owners attempt to control they are confiscated by England Colby to see Fletcher[1]

[1] Senator Duncan U. Fletcher. See B. Colby to WW, Nov. 23, 1918.

To Frank Lyon Polk

CONFIDENTIAL

My dear Mr. Counselor: The White House 22 November, 1918.

I would be very much obliged if you would have the following cable sent to Mr. House in Paris, in the code which the Department has been using in communicating with him:

"It seems to me that we are justified in insisting on five delegates.

It would be extremely embarrassing to us to have fewer than five. I do not understand that any government can be arbitrarily limited, except by agreement. I think also with you that we are entirely justified in insisting upon the English language being officially sanctioned and used at the conference as well as French. The limitation to French would greatly embarrass us, if only in the matter of constant translation, for which we haven't a suitable confidential force. You will remember that English is the diplomatic language of the Pacific. I would be very much obliged if you would cable whether it would be necessary or wise for us to bring any domestic servants with us. We are exceedingly distressed by the news of your illness[1] and beg that you will take extra good care of yourself. We all unite in affectionate messages."[2]

Faithfully yours,   Woodrow Wilson

TLS (F. L. Polk Papers, CtY).
    [1] House was suffering from influenza.
    [2] This was sent as WW to EMH, Nov. 22, 1918, T telegram (SDR, RG 59, 763.72119/9334b, DNA).

To Robert Lansing

CONFIDENTIAL

My dear Mr. Secretary: [The White House] 22 November, 1918.

I return this memorandum of Bullitt's after giving it very careful consideration. I like it, if there were time to carry it out. You will notice from the dispatches that it is not proposed to assemble the constituent body in Germany until January, or even later. If we made the demands that Bullitt suggests, we would therefore have to wait for German representatives in the conference until after the conference had been for a long time in session. It is for this reason that I think it would hardly be wise to do what he proposes.

Cordially and sincerely yours,   Woodrow Wilson

TLS (Letterpress Books, WP, DLC).

To Rudolph Forster

Dear Forster: The White House. 22 November, 1918

Please say to this gentleman, and to all others who apply for appointments with me, that I find it absolutely necessary from this time until I leave for Europe to reserve all my time for what must be done, and done carefully, by way of preparing for my absence.

I am, of course, willing to consider appointments with public officials when necessary and with members of the House or Senators
who feel that it is imperatively necessary for me to see them, but
I must decline all others unless the conditions are truly exceptional
and such as I cannot now foresee. Even of the case of officials and
members of the Houses, please try to make sure in some courteous
way that the interview is necessary.   The President

TL (WP, DLC).

To William Jennings Bryan

The White House Nov 22 18
Your message of the twentieth is deeply appreciated. May I not
convey to you my most cordial greetings?

Woodrow Wilson

T telegram (W. J. Bryan Papers, DLC).

To Earl Curzon of Kedleston

My dear Lord Curzon: [The White House] 22 November, 1918.

I warmly appreciate your kind letter of November third[1] and feel
like apologizing for the mails that it should have been so long
delayed in reaching me.

I beg you to believe that I am highly honored by the invitation
to deliver the Romanes Lecture and to receive the degree of D.C.L.
from Oxford University. I am going directly to France, and while
I confidently expect to visit England, of course, before returning
to the United States, it seems at present impossible to determine
when and in what circumstances I can do so. I hope that you and
the other authorities of the University will not consider it discour-
teous on my part if at present I merely express my very deep and
sincere appreciation of the honor you have done me in proposing
the degree and in the nomination to the lectureship, and add that
I shall hope to be able when I reach the other side to arrange to
receive the degree.

As for the Romanes Lecture, I have the most unaffected doubt
as to my ability to rise to the standards of the foundation, because
my mind has been so absorbed by practical problems, national and
international, that I doubt my ability to produce a lecture which

would be worthy of the audience I would have. If I may, I will discuss that matter with you when I reach the other side.

Cordially and sincerely yours,   Woodrow Wilson

TLS (Letterpress Books, WP, DLC).
    [1] See EMH to WW, Nov. 10, 1918 (fifth telegram of that date), n. 1.

To Herbert Edward Douglas Blakiston[1]

[The White House]
My dear Dr. Blakiston: 22 November, 1918.

Your kind letter of October 29,[2] which comes to me enclosed in one from Lord Curzon of Kedleston, has brought me a great deal of pleasure. I am highly honored that Oxford should wish me to receive at its hands the degree of D.C.L. and should wish me to accept the appointment as Romanes Lecturer for the year 1919.

I have just written to Lord Curzon that I am embarrassed what answer to make, because although I am going immediately to the other side, it will be my duty to go directly to France and there to give my whole time and attention to the very difficult and delicate questions which will have to be handled at the Peace Conference. I do not now know, and fear that I cannot know until I have been in France for some time, just what my liberty will be. It is my distinct hope that I shall be able to visit Oxford and accept from its hands honors which I shall value most highly, but I cannot be certain, and I hesitate to ask you and the other University authorities to give me the liberty of saying later what I can do. I hope that you will tell me frankly what you prefer and consider consistent with the usages of the University.

As to the Romanes Lecture, I am most unaffectedly doubtful whether I could find the time to prepare such a lecture as I would be willing to offer to such an audience. It is not a question of my desire, for I heartily wish that I could. My mind has been so preoccupied with practical questions for the last few years that I have almost forgotten how to lecture, and my mind has been emptied, I am afraid, of a good deal of its scholarly contents. If you will bear with me, I will be glad to exchange letters with you about this also when I have got into harness on the other side.

With sincere respect and deep appreciation of your kindness.

Sincerely yours,   Woodrow Wilson

TLS (Letterpress Books, WP, DLC).
    [1] Blakiston, not Blackiston, was President of Trinity College, Oxford, and Vice-Chancellor of the University of Oxford.
    [2] H. E. D. Blakiston to WW, Oct. 29, 1918, ALS (WP, DLC).

To Charles Hillyer Brand

My dear Mr. Brand   [The White House] 22 November, 1918.

The letter signed by yourself and Mr. Bell touches a matter to which I have given a great deal of thought and which I sincerely hope is slowly straightening itself out. If it does not do so, it will not be from lack of sympathetic attention, but only from lack of ships and because of the present impossibility of breaking the blockade which is continued by the armistice.

Cordially and sincerely yours,   Woodrow Wilson

TLS (Letterpress Books, WP, DLC).

To Newton Diehl Baker, with Enclosure

My dear Baker: The White House 22 November, 1918.

The Poles certainly need all the disciplined forces they can get to preserve their country from disorder. I therefore send you this to ask you whether what they request is in your opinion practicable or not.   Cordially and faithfully yours,   Woodrow Wilson

TLS (N. D. Baker Papers, DLC).

E N C L O S U R E

Translation from French text.

"Mr. Wilson, President of the United States: In the name of the Polish Army under my Chief Command I beg you, Mr. President, kindly to consent to letting the Polish military formations now under the American flag be sent at the earliest possible date to Poland and incorporated in the Polish Army henceforth united under my command. The Polish Nation which was so long subjected to occupation of the country by foreign troops is now preparing in the greatest enthusiasm to welcome to the native land the sons of the Motherland scattered the world over. It appeals to all the soldiers of Polish birth who have fought under foreign flags. Your consent, Mr. President, whom Poland regards as its foremost protection, will be taken by the whole nation as one more proof of your interest in and good will to the Polish cause.   Pilsudski."[1]

T MS (WP, DLC).

[1] That is, Jósef Klemens Pilsudski, longtime leader of the fight for Polish independence, at this time head of the Polish government in Warsaw.

To Philip Albright Small Franklin

My dear Mr. Franklin: [The White House] 22 November, 1918

Thank you for your letter. I have been in conference with Mr. Bainbridge Colby, who had the advantage of consulting with you and with Mr. Scott,[1] and think I am in full possession now of the facts of the situation.

Very sincerely yours,   Woodrow Wilson

TLS (Letterpress Books, WP, DLC).
    [1] Frederic William Scott, banker of Richmond, Va.; a director and member of the finance committee of the International Mercantile Marine Co.; also at this time a member of the Division of Finance and Purchases of the United States Railroad Administration.

To Herman Henry Kohlsaat

My dear Mr. Kohlsaat: [The White House] 22 November, 1918.

I realize the force of what you say in your kind note of the twentieth about the cables, but it is absolutely necessary for their proper administration that they should be administered as a single system, and I have not the least fear that the misrepresentations you have in mind will do any harm. They are too contemptible to be worthy of notice, and it will presently become evident that what we did was done in the course of business. I am none the less obliged to you for your generous concern in the matter.

Cordially and sincerely yours,   Woodrow Wilson

TLS (Letterpress Books, WP, DLC).

To Vance Criswell McCormick

My dear McCormick: [The White House] 22 November, 1918.

The Southern members of the House and Senate still seem to be under the impression that we are putting restrictions on shipments of cotton, even to neutral countries and even where there is tonnage available, as they say is the case with regard to proposed shipments to Spain. If you have not already done so, would it not be well to make a definite statement in the matter and have it mimeographed and sent personally to every Southern member? I have told all who have spoken to me, repeating what you said the other day, that all restrictions had been removed, so far as shipping was available, but that of course we could not lift the blockade of the central powers.

Always faithfully yours,   Woodrow Wilson

TLS (Letterpress Books, WP, DLC).

To Frank Morrison

My dear Mr. Morrison: [The White House] 22 November, 1918.

I have received a great many messages besides your own very interesting and persuasive message with regard to appointing a representative of labor on the Peace Commission, and have of course given the matter the most serious consideration.

I have at the same time received equally strong appeals to appoint a representative of the agricultural interests of the country, a representative of the socialistic bodies of the country, a representative of the women of the country, and many other similar suggestions. I am not putting all of these upon a par. I am merely illustrating the fact that many special bodies and interests of our complex nation have felt, and felt very naturally, a desire to have special spokesmen among the peace delegates.

I must say, however, that my own feeling is that the peace delegates should represent no portion of our people in particular, but the country as a whole, and that it was unwise to make any selection on the ground that the man selected represented a particular group or interest, for after all each interest is, or should be, related to the whole, and no proper representative of the country could fail to have in mind the great and all-pervasive interest of labor or of any other great body of humanity.

The number of delegates will be small, and I have thought that therefore special representation was out of the question.

Cordially and sincerely yours,   Woodrow Wilson

TLS (Letterpress Books, WP, DLC).

To Alexander Mitchell Palmer

My dear Palmer: The White House 22 November, 1918.

It seems to me that it would not be wise to add just now to the list of alien names, in view of the virtual cessation of hostilities.

I am not now speaking of the merits of any particular case, but of the misapprehensions that would arise if we seemed to be taking advantage of the technical continuation of the war to get hold of this property. The misunderstandings which have arisen in connection with the taking over of the cables will illustrate the misinterpretations which can be put upon actions taken at this time, and I do not want to create the impression on the country that we are eager to get hold of these properties.

I hope that your judgment will coincide with mine, upon a reconsideration of this puzzling matter.

Cordially and faithfully yours,   Woodrow Wilson

TLS (A. M. Palmer Papers, DLC).

To Frank Lyon Polk

CONFIDENTIAL

My dear Mr. Counselor: The White House 22 November, 1918.

I find that our party for Europe will consist, besides myself, of:
Mrs. Wilson
Miss Edith Benham, her Secretary
Rear Admiral Cary T. Grayson
Mr. George Creel
Mr. Gilbert F. Close
Irving [Irwin] H. Hoover,
seven secret service men, namely:
Joseph E. Murphy
Edmund W. Starling
John Q. Slye[1]
William A. Landvoigt[2]
John J. Fitzgerald
Walter G. Ferguson, and
John L. Sullivan;
Arthur Brooks, my personal attendant
Susie Booth, Mrs. Wilson's maid.

Will you not be kind enough to see that the proper arrangements are made for passports? I may have one or two names to add later, but I think not.

Cordially and faithfully yours,   Woodrow Wilson

TLS (SDR, RG 59, 763.72119 P43/2, DNA).
[1] John Queen Slye.
[2] William Arnold Landvoigt.

To Frank William Taussig

My dear Mr. Chairman: [The White House] 22 November, 1918.

I dare say that before now Mr. Baruch has communicated to you the conclusions we reached in our little War Board conference the other afternoon, about the general policy of price fixing.[1] If he has not, I would be obliged if you would have a brief conference with him about it. It takes care of the cotton fabrics matter.

I am warmly obliged to you for your clear letter of November 19th about the cotton fabrics prices. I fully realize the difficulties and the necessities that the Price Fixing Committee felt itself to be under.

Cordially and sincerely yours,   Woodrow Wilson

TLS (Letterpress Books, WP, DLC).
[1] See WW to R. S. Brookings, Nov. 26, 1918, n. 1.

To Henry White

My dear Mr. White: [The White House] 22 November, 1918.

Thank you for your note. You may be sure that it gave me pleasure to show my confidence in you. I shall look forward with pleasure to the association.

Cordially and sincerely yours,   Woodrow Wilson

TLS (Letterpress Books, WP, DLC).

To Edward Wright Sheldon

My dear Sheldon: The White House 22 November, 1918.

Your letter has given me peculiar gratification. I value your approval, and it makes me feel stronger and better to receive it in such generous fashion. It was certainly an act of thoughtful kindness on your part to send me such a message.

Faithfully yours,   Woodrow Wilson

TLS (photostat in RSB Coll., DLC).

From Edward Mandell House

Paris, November 22, 1918.

Number 145. Secret. For the President.

Pursuant to your number 50, November 19, 4 p.m. in answer to our number 120, I communicated with the British Government through Lord Derby respecting this matter and requested him to ascertain the views of his Government. I am now in receipt of the following communication from Lord Derby: "I telegraphed to Mr. Balfour the contents of your letter of yesterday and he has replied asking me to let you know that His Majesty's Government consider that if the Italian troops occupying part of the former empire of Austria-Hungary or which propose to occupy it could be accompanied by American troops it would be of the very greatest value." As soon as I hear from the French Government I will take the matter up with the Supreme Command through General Pershing.

Edward House.

T telegram (WP, DLC).

From Robert Somers Brookings

My dear Mr. President: Washington November 22, 1918.

It is something more than a month since I last heard from you regarding steel prices, and as the PEACE SITUATION has entirely changed our price fixing problem, and as you are soon to sail for France, may I suggest the necessity for your decision regarding the price of steel rails before leaving.

In my opinion, there is now no necessity for fixing the price of rails for either the public or the Railroad Administration, but the manufacturers very properly insist that, as they have been furnishing rails to the Army and Navy for months under an agreement that the Price Fixing Committee should fix the prices they are to receive, the matter should not be allowed to drift indefinitely.

Pardon me for troubling you at this time with such details, but you will recall that we were to take no action in the matter until we received further instructions from you.

Appreciatively and respectfully yours,   Robt S Brookings

TLS (WP, DLC).

From Newton Diehl Baker, with Enclosure

[Washington] Nov 22, 1918

For the President's information

Respectfully   Baker

ALS (WP, DLC).

E N C L O S U R E

Vladivostok November 21st.

Number 78. Secret.

The situation here as I see it merits careful consideration. Conditions in Siberia are growing worse daily. General Horvat, a typical reactionary, supported by the Russian Army Officer class, has been appointed by the Omsk Government representative in eastern Siberia. This crowd if not in favor of a monarchy are certainly in favor of some form of autocratic government. This is well known to and opposed by the great majority of Russians. The opinion just now is that this crowd could not remain in power 24 hours in eastern Siberia after allied troops are removed. As I see the situation they know the poorer class will not attack them as long as allied troops are here and they are utilizing to the fullest extent this time to entrench themselves, get together a military force which they hope will be strong enough to hold them in power when allied troops are removed. I think some blood will be shed when troops move out but the longer we stay the greater will be the bloodshed when allied troops do go, as in effect each day we remain here, now that war with Germany is over, we are by our mere presence helping establish a form of autocratic government which the people of Siberia will not stand for and our stay is creating some feeling against the allied governments because of the effect it has. The classes seem to be growing wider apart and the feeling between them more bitter daily.   Graves.

CC telegram (WP, DLC).

From William Cox Redfield, with Enclosure

My dear Mr. President: Washington November 22, 1918

Our commercial attaché, Dr. W. C. Huntington,[1] has just returned from Russia. He has embodied his views in a memorandum of sixteen pages, which, because of its clarity and poise, I am, after hearing it carefully, sending to you. I do so, realizing the numberless demands upon your thought. Surely, however, Russia is of world interest now and this statement from the inside of Russia, so to speak, is condensed and clear and I believe would be helpful to you.   Sincerely yours,   William C. Redfield

TLS (WP, DLC).
  [1] William Chapin Huntington.

ENCLOSURE

MEMORANDUM ON THE RUSSIAN SITUATION
*Prepared by W. C. Huntington, Commerical Attaché
to the American Embassy in Russia*

It is perhaps not too much to say in referring to the gravity of the Russian situation that it is the most significant factor in the war. My impression is, after a few days in America, that this fact is appreciated to a considerable degree by the American people, but that there is a very general lack of fundamental knowledge and that our people have no back-ground, historical or of personal experience, by which to measure Russia. The strong oriental strain in Russian life and the fact that it is developed along quite different lines from our own or from the life of the countries of Western Europe, and that it is, due to a number of historical causes, two or three centuries behind Western Europe, makes it a problem too complex to be grasped without study and experience by the usually keen shrewdness and practicality of the American mind.

This is the reason why we have had such contradictory and incoherent reports from many Americans returning from a visit to Russia. I am glad to be able to say that the majority of the Americans I have known in Russia have been people who were the country's well-wishers and to whom idealism appealed. Nevertheless we have had a number of inaccurate observers and, worse still, false teachers.

It is the purpose, therefore, of the following carefully weighed experience and thoughts to form a guide for the action which is urgently demanded.

While filled with hope, courage and purpose, let us not underestimate the difficulties of the situation. Russia has been for centuries, is still, and will continue to be for generations, the country of a tragedy, and the shadow of this tragedy is always over it. This fact is evident to all whose interest in life goes deeper than their own personal pleasure and satisfaction. The result of this tragedy is the profound humanity of Russia—its striking social characteristic. Quite without hypocrisy, human nature in all its nakedness is spread out before one. From this spring the chief Russian traits—the tolerance, the pity, the forgiveness, but the passivity, the inertia and the indecision.

The Russian tragedy is one of isolation, of vastness, and, I should like to add, of mediocrity or monotony.

Isolation has always been the fate of Russia. Geographically this nation has been cut off from the western part of Europe which has access to the sea with its indented coast line, and enjoys a convenient variety of mountains and plains. Russia has had only access to inland seas and to the Arctic Ocean in the Far North. In spite of all the splendid river system and the railroad building during the past century, great portions of the empire remain year after year out of close touch with the rest of the world. The religious and intellectual isolation is quite as acute. The Russians were converted to Christianity by missionaries from Constantinople of the Eastern Orthodox Church, and they have ever shown throughout their history a very commendable loyalty to Byzantium, from which their civilization was drawn. However, this cut them off from the Church of Rome. They took no part in the Crusades, they had no share in the Renaissance and were quite untouched by the Protestant Reformation. It is difficult for a man in practical life, without some historical perspective to appreciate the extent of this loss.

There is also the tragedy of the vastness of Russia, of people set on a plain without natural barriers, and for centuries at the mercy of Asiatic raiders, who seemed to tear up life about as fast as it could take root, and ended by dominating the country for two centuries and a half. To throw off this yoke and bring and keep together the various parts of the Russian people whose situation constantly tended to anarchy, an autocracy centered at Moscow was consummated, modeled on the very lines of the Tartar domination. The people endured this autocracy because they preferred it to anarchy and famine. To the autocracy was presently added legalized serfdom, whereby nine-tenths of the population were bound to the land where they were born in slavery. Cruel and harsh as this tyranny seems to us, we cannot forget that in great measure it was the penalty which the Russian people paid for their geographical situation.

With time Russia became, therefore, roughly, a country divided into two classes. Nine-tenths of the people were relatively underfed, poor and illiterate. One tenth lived like Western Europeans. The chasm between these two great classes was so deep that people of the educated class of most excellent christian character have told me that they felt as if the peasants and they belonged to two different races altogether. Such a situation was certainly unwholesome and a tragedy. It explains the lack of patriotism and the eagerness of the upper classes to identify themselves with Western Europe, to speak European languages, and to bring up their children as it seems to us so artificially that sometimes they speak foreign languages better than their own. And yet one cannot judge these people too harshly. Their own country was backward and uncultivated, the great capitals of Western Europe were for them filled with art and refinement. Nevertheless such an attitude and experience did not fit these people for leadership and for governing when the opportunity came.

As we have said, the tragedy produced the fundamental social character of the country, and out of a desire to ameliorate conditions grew the so-called "intelligentsia." These people were a section of the upper tenth of the population with an awakened social consciousness and desire to bridge the chasm between the one-tenth and nine-tenths of the people, and to educate the masses. The very name "intelligentsia" seems strange in an Anglo-Saxon country. We have nothing like it in America, and it would have no place in American life. It is a tacit acknowledgment of the unwholesome state of society which has been described.

In considering political Russia it is not hard to understand how, under the constant tragedy of contrast and tyranny, Radicalism should be most natural. It became, and is, the dominant note in Russian political life. It is not strange that the Russian Radicals, looking to the Western countries for experience, and conceding their superiority, should have imported Socialism, one brand for the industrial workmen in the cities and another for the peasants. Socialism, in the strict sense of the word, demanding as it does a high degree of education and consciousness of one's duty toward the State, and eliminating the spirit of personal initiative so necessary, especially to new countries, seems to me quite unadapted to Russia, but nevertheless the political terminology is full of Socialistic words and phrases. Now that Russia has suffered under Bolshevism for a year most of the Radicals are very chastened and inclined to moderation so that their socialism as a plan of action does not really differ very widely from modern Liberalism.

Beginning with March, and ending in November, 1917, Russia ran the gamut of political, then social, revolution. The upper tenth had not the practicality and force to maintain its leadership, nor the experience in political life, never having been allowed any participation in government by the Bureaucracy. The gulf between it and the lower nine-tenths was too wide to be bridged by the leaders and the lower nine-tenths were too little educated to understand any mean between autocracy and anarchy. The revolution passed through a number of stages, but always in the down direction. It consisted, just as had the revolution of 1905, in an effort by each class to gain power at the expense of the one above it. All the time the so-called "Bolsheviki" were busy.

This leads us to ask just what Bolshevism is. Strictly, Lenin and Trotzky claim that Bolshevism is a logical and literal putting into practice of the principles of Marxian socialism. The theory is, of course, that all the ills of human society, such as war and poverty, are due to its false organization, that if the property owning class were turned out of power and the working proletariat given the reins of government, everything would be well. This contemplates the annihilation of the property owners as a class. The more moderate of the Bolsheviks have hesitated to go further in this process of annihilation than seizing land and industrial property, confiscating houses and "nationalizing" bank accounts. The more violent faction, on the contrary, is quite willing to put large numbers of people to death, and has been doing this for some time.

Bolshevism is really nothing new in the world, being a sort of patchwork of all the most radical theories and a panacea for all the ills mankind is heir to, guaranteed to give satisfaction to any discontented soul. It is only possible where there is anarchy and deep discontent, due to hunger and suffering. Russia in revolution proved a fertile soil for Bolshevik principles. At the time the movement began it offered the crowd everything it wanted and it no doubt enjoyed a great popularity, promising peace, land and bread. The movement is now spent as a popular manifestation and for a long time has continued to exist only as a Terrorism conducted by a few leaders at the head of mercenary soldiers on the body of a prostrate and exhausted country.

The movement, which, due to the bold utterances of its leaders at the beginning, made a considerable appeal to many outside of Russia, has fulfilled none of the early promises and is an utter failure. The cause of its failure is its absolute immorality. Its leaders claim a special code of proletarian morality of their own against all human experience in the past and claim to be able to serve both God and Mammon. The question is so often asked, "Are the Bolsheviks German agents?" Some undoubtedly are direct German agents. Equally dangerous to the cause of democracy, however, and to the Allies are those, who, like Lenin, entertain relations with, and accept money from, and sign binding treaties with, Germany, insisting all the time that they do this in the confident expectation of ruining Germany. The absurdity of this conceit was evident to all observers who saw the superior brain power of the German machine influencing the Bolsheviks far more than the latter were able to influence Germany. As a matter of fact their only principle is "Any means to my end," and they justify all their deeds by the end they seek; namely, the annihilation of the present so-called "bourgeois" society. Their policy is only the policy of expediency and changes from day to day and from hour to hour. One day they ask the French Military Attaché to lend them aid in drilling their troops for a possible future conflict with Germany—this after having signed the Brest-Litovsk peace. Another day they are extremely friendly with the British diplomatic representative. The third day they are affecting great friendliness for America, which, although a very imperfect sort of democracy, is still very near to their hearts. Their constant policy as far as the United States was concerned was to split us off from the other Allies.

And now, what is the present state of the country after a year of Bolshevik rule? It would require more space than is available here to take this subject up in detail. Following are, however, the main features:

To begin with, the whole social and political structure, as we know it, has been turned up side down. The former governing elements are now at the bottom undergoing persecution, and the lowest elements are at the top trying to govern by terror. The Bolshevik government was never very firm, but there was a brief period when it enjoyed a sort of authority in various parts of the country. Now that Bolshevism is no longer recognized by the masses as their movement, the real authority of the central Bolshevik government does not extend beyond Moscow. There is practically entire absence of production, and the country has exhausted its stocks.

The local Soviets go their own way obeying when they please, and opposing the central authority when it suits them. As a matter of fact, the central authority, having founded its power on demagogy, is not able to issue any orders of a constructive or restraining kind.

Many so-called "bourgeois" have been invited by the Bolsheviks to accept positions in their Ministries. One of my friends, who was an engineer of ability, quite neutral in politics, accepted a position as chief of a department in one of the Commissariats, after having consulted with the members of the All-Russian Association of Engineers, to which he belonged. He was well treated by the members of the Bolshevik government, who promised him their full support. Just as soon, however, as he wished to initiate certain reforms in personnel in his office agitators amongst the staff threatened the authorities with a strike and the latter gave in. Finding it impossible to accomplish anything, my engineer friend resigned.

As indicative of the same anarchy, the case may be cited of the official American party leaving Russia. We arrived in Petrograd with our passports properly viséd by the Bolshevik central authority. The "Commune of the North," which is the name of the terroristic government in Petrograd, refused to recognize the visé on our passports, and we were held on the side-track in the Finland Station for four days.

The Bolshevik tyranny is more terrible than anything the Imperial regime ever dreamed of. It is useless to recount instances here, because the activities of the Extraordinary Committee for Combatting the Counter Revolution are too well known through the newspapers.

A representative of the Bolshevik Foreign Office told Ambassador Francis one day in Vologda that the educated classes of Russia were falsely educated, and, therefore, must be annihilated. This policy is being put into effect with an intensity which is only limited by lack of organization and time.

The banking and credit system is smashed. The banks have all become agencies of the People's Bank of The Russian Republic.

Accounts have been confiscated, the books are in a terrible condition, no one has any idea of the solvency of the banks, although they must be in many cases ruined several times over. They are merely agencies for the paying out of paper money, chiefly for the uses of "Government departments," and for paying labor in the factories. This money never returns and there is no circulation.

As for newspapers, there are none, except the Bolshevik organs. They are, of course, purely propaganda sheets, badly run, where every industrial difficulty in America or England is described as a nation-wide strike about to usher in a social revolution in these countries. The front pages of the papers are filled with vitriolic articles urging the people to wipe out the "bourgeois," who continue to exist somehow and cooperate with the Czecho-Slovaks and the Imperialistic Allies against the true will of the people.

The railways continue to run where fighting does not prevent this, and on the line from Moscow to Petrograd there were even International sleeping cars. There is very little movement of freight. The trains are few and conditions grow worse from day to day because of the wearing out of locomotives and cars which cannot be replaced. Side-tracks and round-house yards are filled with locomotives needing comparatively slight repairs to make them useful, but which repairs cannot be executed for lack of material and willing labor. That the railroads run at all is due to the good habits, inertia, and the necessity of earning money of the employees, but beyond all these, to their good-will. The majority of the enginemen, firemen, and trainmen have not been Bolsheviks, and their Central Union fought the Bolshevik authority until it was overcome by superior force, whereupon an artificial union was created in its place, with a safe majority of Bolshevik votes. These train operating men and the station masters and their assistants have kept some sort of traffic going in the face of unbelievable anarchy. Locomotive enginemen and station masters have had pistols pointed at their heads and been forced to run trains out of schedule at the behest of Red Guard detachments. Trains have been held up at station after station by local authorities, so-called, while the passengers were robbed of any food which they might be carrying. Altogether, I think the railway employees, who are virtually running the roads these days, because there is no higher personnel, deserve great credit and should be reckoned with in any scheme to extend aid to and rebuild Russia.

As to town life, this is essentially "bourgeois" life, and every effort has been made to destroy it, but up to September 1 it hung on in the larger centers with a remarkable pertinacity; that is to say, there were still one or two theatres in Moscow; the tramcars running, if very badly; there was a modicum of "Izvozchiks," or cabmen, with rundown horses. Shops were mostly open, but had little to sell. All staple articles had been consumed long since. The shelves were literally empty as soon as one passed the door. From day to day goods would appear in the windows, which had been kept in hiding, in the measure that the proprietor needed money for his personal life. Currency was very scarce and change hard to secure.

Most pitiful was the plight of the "intelligentsia," whose savings had mostly been taken with the confiscation of the banks, and whose incomes were cut off. People of the greatest refinement, and who have been strugglers all their lives for liberal ideals, are living in cramped quarters without sufficient to eat, and with no hope for the future.

The factories are closing down one after another for lack of raw materials to work on. The great textile industry round about Moscow is nearly dead for lack of cotton.

The coming of winter is adding to these horrors. There is an insufficiency of fuel in Petrograd and Moscow. The German scheme cut off Ukraine with its coal and grain, and the Caucasus with its petroleum. Conditions in Turkestan have been so bad that the cotton crop there is very small, even if it could be transported. There is grain enough in Western Siberia to alleviate the starvation in Northern Russia, could it be transported and afterwards properly distributed.

No question is more often asked than, "When will Russia get on her feet?" "When will she have order and decent government?" By this I suppose the average American means, "When will there be democratic equilibrium so that the country may be properly regarded as a selfcontained democracy able to stand alone?" The answer is clear—When the lower nine-tenths have received common school education. This is going to take a generation or more even with the most intensive methods. It must be remembered that Russia is vast and that the processes which we are witnessing are historical processes, of which the unit of time is not months or years, but generations. It should be noted, however, that the war has had a pronounced educative effect on hundreds of thousands of men who had never been away from their villages before, but have now seen something of town life and perhaps even of the enemy countries. These men are undoubtedly having an influence in their villages. Nevertheless, it should not be forgotten that their minds have been filled with an extremely radical hodgepodge of ideas which are by no means yet digested and hardly to be called sound education for life.

Long before real democratic equilibrium is achieved, however, there must be, in the interest of the world, order and progress in Russia. Indeed only in an atmosphere of order can education proceed. Such order can only be brought about by aid from without. Russia cannot save herself.

Another question is, "Why don't the people get together and put down the Bolsheviks?" Like the Insurrectionists, who were described by the driver of Nat Goodwin's jaunting car in Ireland, they are against the tyranny and ready to strike, but unfortunately have not done so because they are afraid of the police![1] The lower nine-tenths are too amorphous, and they are like sheep without a shepherd, because the upper one-tenth are not fitted by history or training to be strong leaders. They lack energy and they lack cohesion. Several thousand officers, for instance, are arrested by the Bolsheviks on a trumped up charge and put into a riding academy, where they are held for days without sufficient water and food, or any bodily conveniences. The building is guarded by a few Red Guards with rifles. A little courage and decision would rush the door, strangle these guards bare-handed and effect liberation of all inside, but it is not done. They would not know what to do after they got out. They will remain on the damp earth floor of the riding academy with a sort of passive courage awaiting whatever the Extraordinary Committee for Combatting the Counter Revolution has in store for them.

Russia cannot get on her feet alone. There will be no crystallization without a nucleus of foreigners from without. She is a problem demanding the highest statesmanship from the League of Nations. The awakened international social consciousness of the world cannot turn its back on Russia, even though it be a white man's burden, and, like forestry in that the full fruits of our work will be

[1] Nathaniel Carll Goodwin (1857-1919), a popular American comic actor. The anecdote referred to above appeared in his autobiography where it reads as follows: " 'Eddie' Sothern, De Wolf Hopper and I were returning to America after a most delightful trip abroad when we suddenly decided to stop off at Queenstown and take a drive through Ireland in a jaunting car. The driver of the vehicle proved a most loquacious fellow who bubbled over with Irish humor. . . . I took a seat beside him and began to question him about the possibilities of Home Rule. He evaded my questions for a time, but presently in a spirit of confidence told me that he was convinced that the time was ripe for the freeing of Ireland. He even gave me a date when they would be relieved from thraldom. He leaned quietly forward and imparted the information, under promise of profound secrecy, that there were ninety thousand men hiding in the County of Kildare, 110,000 in Tipperary and among the hills, rocks and caves of Killarney, 200,000 on the outskirts of Dublin and an equal number distributed through County Cork, combined with several secret organizations throughout Ireland numbering more than 600,000! The hills were well stocked with dynamite and Winchester rifles, sent from America and closely guarded. He further assured me that when the 'head-centre' was satisfied all the forces would be concentrated and Ireland would be free. 'Why don't you do it at once?' I asked. 'Begorra, the police won't let us!' he replied." Nathaniel Carll Goodwin, *Nat Goodwin's Book* (Boston, 1914), pp. 162-63.

for our grandchildren. Humanitarianism and economic interests are both potent reasons for aiding Russia, but a still graver reason is to "make the world safe for democracy." It will not be safe as long as Russia goes on like a volcano, occasionally throwing hot lava on everything round about.

Order must be established in Russia, (1) to stamp out Bolshevism and its attendant tyranny and cruelty, (2) to feed and clothe a miserable people, and (3) to bridge over the long period of education, during which the country is preparing for full self government. To produce such order the League of Nations must furnish active military and economic aid on the grandest scale ever known. In this work America should have the leading role for several reasons. First, because we have not exhausted our resources of idealism, men and materials. In this connection, a prominent British Liberal told me in London that he believed we should have the chief task in helping Russia because the best brains in England have been sacrificed on the battlefield—to such an extent, he thought, that England will be worse governed in the coming years than she has been in the past. From a more practical standpoint, it is my personal experience that the Russian and American temperaments are very compatible. We are free from entangling traditions and we have invested relatively so little money in Russia that we can scarcely be accused of going there to collect our debts, which is the accusation brought, however unfairly, against the British and the French.

In this connection, I cannot forbear to say that Russia holds great economic and business possibilities for the future, but that it would be absolutely a false policy, and putting the cart before the horse, for any country to go into Russia with the prime object of "collecting its debts." Such a course would only end in disaster and the debts would never be collected. If Russia is put on her feet and supported by the League of Nations, and her *productivity* restored and increased, she can pay her debts over a fair period of time without the slightest embarrassment, and while becoming wealthy herself.

Economic, without military, assistance is useless in a country so torn with strife and so completely anarchical as Russia. Russia cannot be conquered, her good will must be won; but, in this, potential force, under tactful leaders as the ultimate appeal in emergency, is vital. Why send an Economic Mission to Russia only to have them arrested or annihilated? Food alone will not produce permanent equilibrium. There was food in Samara, but as soon as the Czecho-Slovak nucleus was removed the backbone went out of the army which had been organized about it. In Archangel there is plenty of food, but now that the question of starvation has been solved the parties are already wrangling about the question of power. It must never be lost from view that Russia is the country of a tragedy, like Poland and Ireland, and that in these countries the *mentality of protest* is developed to a high degree. Mentality of protest is concerned with struggling,—sometimes for generations,—against an evil, and finishes by becoming so used to struggling that it has no plans for the time when its object has been reached.

Liberal men in America will hesitate, perhaps, to enter upon the far-reaching course of military and economic aid which must be furnished to save Russia. They fear the responsibility and the reproaches of Bolsheviks and similar people who will call them tyrants and Imperialists. Modern Liberalism suffers a little from the mentality of protest itself. For years it found it possible to work more or less with Radicalism because they both were directed toward the elimination of certain evils. The conclusion—at least of the first act—of this war has suddenly brought this about in the downfall of autocracy and the freeing of subject peoples. Now what are we going to do about it? If one may be pardoned such an inaccurate term, I think the Liberalism of protest of the past should go—to be replaced by the *executive* Liberalism of the present.

With the example of the Russian Liberal Kerensky before us, let us avoid his historical error—the inability to be consciously sure of his Liberalism, to stand firm and cry "halt." He could not bring himself to make the great decision and oppose the Bolsheviks because he shared with them the mentality of protest and regarded them as fellow strugglers. He spared Bolsheviks' lives and sacrificed his country. The Bolsheviks undermined and engulfed him and his government, and since they have gotten the power have shown no such tenderness toward their opponents.

The restoration of Russia will be the work of years and we must be training the thousands of Americans who will be needed in it. The great lack of Russia is that of brains. There are simply too few brains per square mile to carry on the work which must be done. When several of my Allied colleagues in Moscow praised the objects of the Co-operative Movement to its leader, the moderate Socialist, Berkenheim, in Moscow, he replied, "There is nothing wrong with the plan of our organization, but we haven't the people to run it." "Lyudéi nyetu" (no people). There is everywhere this woeful lack of trained people, not only for the highest positions, but for all positions of responsibility. There are too few foremen, bookkeepers, clerks, office boys, skilled mechanics—the people who do the daily work of life. The men in the military units sent to Russia could,

under proper course of training, learn much of the language and
life of the country, and be ultimately highly useful and indispensable in America's "Russian service."

T MS (WP, DLC).

Edward Mandell House to Robert Lansing

Paris, November 22, 1918.

Number 146. Referring further to our number 137.[1] I am now
advised by the press correspondents that their messages to the
United States are being permitted to pass through without interference by the French censor.   Edward House.

T telegram (WP, DLC).
    [1] EMH to WW and RL, Nov. 21, 1918 (second telegram of that date).

Robert Lansing to Joseph Patrick Tumulty

My dear Mr. Tumulty: Washington November 22, 1918.

I beg to enclose herewith for the President's information, summary of a memorandum signed by Messrs. James L. Barton, Cleveland H. Dodge, and W. W. Peet,[1] members of an American Committee for Armenian Affairs. Copy of the memorandum is also
enclosed.[2]   Very sincerely yours,   Robert Lansing

TLS (WP, DLC).
    [1] William Wheelock Peet, treasurer and business manager of the American Board of Com-
missioners for Foreign Missions in Turkey.
    [2] J. L. Barton *et al.* to RL, n.d., T MS (WP, DLC). The writers called for the
combining of Turkish Armenia and Russian Armenia into an independent "United
Armenia."

Three Telegrams from Edward Mandell House

Paris. Nov. 23, 1918.

Number 150. Secret for the President and Secretary of State.

Referring further to our number 135. Auchincloss visited today
the house placed at the President's disposal by the French Government. This house is number 28 Rumm [Rue] de Monceau, a
couple of blocks above the Boulevard Hausmann and in one of the
highest parts of the city. The house, however, is not far [itself is
set back] from the street, in the center of spacious grounds, which
are surrounded by a high wall. The interior of the house is beautifully furnished and is in first class repair. On the ground floor

there are the following rooms: A, Large dining room capable of seating thirty-five persons; B, large ball room or salon; C, three medium sized drawing rooms. On the second floor there are the following rooms: A, small suit[e] of two rooms; B, small study or library; C, large study or writing-room, which could be used as the President's work-room; D, bed-room and dressing-room and bath which could be used by the President; E, connecting suit of three rooms, bed-room, boulogne [boudoir] and sitting room which could be used by Mrs. Wilson; F, medium size breakfast or dining room. On the third floor there are seven bedrooms and four sitting rooms, all of which are attractively furnished. [There is a private elevator in the house.] There is a private garage on the grounds. I am taking steps to have proper telephonic and wire connections installed in a manner, as near as possible, similar to that at present existing in the White House. (?) [All in all] I believe the house placed at the President's disposal by the French Government is as attractive a residence as there is in Paris, and I have informally advised the Foreign Office that I felt sure the President would be altogether pleased with the arrangements made in his behalf. If there are any particular points that you wish me to attend to with respect to these accommodations, I trust that you will communicate them to me in the near future. The Foreign Office have asked me not to make public the arrangements they are making for the present.

Edward House.

Paris Nov 23, 1918

Number 151. Secret for the President.

Pursuant to your authorization I requested General Pershing to detail such officer in his command as he considered most competent to undertake the work of estimating the damage done by the Germans in Belgium and northern France on account of which reparation should be required from Germany. General Pershing has detailed for this work Brigadier General C. H. McKinistry.[1] I have conferred with General McKinistry and have asked him to advise me after he has considered the problem how he believes this work (should?) [can best] be done.   Edward House.

[1] Brig. Gen. Charles Hedges McKinstry, not McKinistry.

Paris Nov 23, 1918

Number 152. Secret for the President.

Among the important questions which will arise not only at the Peace Conference but probably also at the preliminary inter-allied conferences will be those pertaining particularly to finance, commerce and the use of our raw material and food. The whole world is vitally interested in what manner we propose to use our great strength in finance and in raw material. England, France and Italy *participants* [are] perhaps more interest[ed] in these questions than in almost any others. I suggest the advisability of your taking steps to secure a small body of advisers on these subjects either to come with you or to be ready to come over on short notice.

Edward House.

T telegrams (WP, DLC).

Three Letters from Newton Diehl Baker

My dear Mr. President: Washington. November 23, 1918.

I return herewith the telegram with regard to the Poles. Mr. Padewerski came in to see me a day or two ago, and asked me to release all persons of Polish extraction from the Army of the United States and assign them to the Polish Legion. I asked him why he wanted this done, and he told me: "This war is over for you, but it is just beginning for us. We have to defend our frontiers against the Russians and several other peoples who are menacing it." I told him I did not feel free to take action in any such matter without consulting with you. This telegram brings the same question to the front.

It seems to me that if there is to be continued trouble in mid-Europe some sort of international police agreed upon by the great powers and supplied out of their existing armies ought to undertake the task, rather than helping to organize independent armies for these nations which they might be tempted to use against one another while peace negotiations are going on; so that unless you entertain a different view, my answer to all of these cablegrams would be that the duty of the United States is to demobilize its soldiers and give them an opportunity to return to industrial pursuits, and not to control, or even to stimulate, their accession to any sort of foreign force which would pursue nationalistic objects of any kind pending the determinations of the peace conference which will have to consider all of these matters.

Respectfully yours,   Newton D. Baker

My dear Mr. President: Washington. November 23, 1918.

I am inexpressibly grieved at the resignation of Mr. McAdoo, though I can readily understand that the terrible burdens of his work have made it necessary for him to have more rest than it would be impossible [possible] for him to get here in Washington continuing at the pace he has gone for the past two or three years.

It seems to me that Mac's resignation changes essentially the possibility of my going abroad as a member of the peace commission. Of course, with you in Europe neither I nor anybody else is necessary to the presentation of America's case, but here at home, particularly during your absence, I can perhaps be helpful in conference with the remaining members of the Cabinet. The next two or three months are likely to present situations of uncertainty of opinion and hesitancy on the part of business and labor in process of readjustment, and while no fresh legislative policy perhaps needs to be worked out, I am persuaded that the country would feel more concerned about your own absence if two members of the Cabinet were with you now that the Secretary of the Treasury's post will have to be filled by a man new to those responsibilities.

I trust you will understand the spirit of this suggestion, but I am really deeply concerned not only to have your own stay in Europe made as free from anxiety as possible but to have the situation here kept on the even balance and public feeling and opinion kept in sympathy with both the things you are doing abroad and the policies of the economic and political readjustment here which you desire to have our peace-time establishment take.

May I not suggest for your consideration the possibility of making General Bliss a peace commissioner? And then after the conferences have gone so far that you feel you are able to return here, and leave the details to be reduced to writing for signature, if you then thought it wise I could be sent over to join the commissioners at the windup.   Respectfully yours,   Newton D. Baker

My dear Mr. President: Washington. November 23, 1918.

Mr. Phillips of the State Department has just called to tell me that the Italian Ambassador, having learned from M. Jusserand that he was going to Europe on the ship with you, called upon him (Mr. Phillips) to say that his Government had directed him to accompany the President to Europe if the French Ambassador accompanied him. He further inquired whether it would be possible for him and Madame di Cellere[1] and their three children[2] to be furnished accommodations on the ship. Mr. Phillips told him he was quite sure it would be impossible to make the three children members of the party, and then came to ask me whether I would convey the invitation to Count and Madame di Cellere, doubtless because he thought the War Department was arranging matters about the ship. I have just told him that I frankly could not see how we could avoiding [avoid] asking the Ambassador and his wife on the same terms as the French Ambassador and his wife, but that I did not feel free to take any action in the matter without submitting it to your judgment.

I confess I am terrified to think where this may lead, as there are a large number of diplomatic representatives here and it will be wholly impossible for you to have a comfortable journey if the party is multiplied by many more additions. If you desire it, I will write to the Count and express regret that I did not know of his desire to go to Europe until after the remaining available and suitable accommodations had been placed at the disposal of the French Ambassador; although it may well be that because of the peculiar situation as between Italy and France the invitation ought to be extended to the Italian representative and stop there.

I have made arrangements on the ship which will so far ensure privacy for you and Mrs. Wilson that these additions to the party will not be intrusions upon your privacy.

Respectfully yours,   Newton D. Baker

TLS (WP, DLC).
  [1] Dolores Cabo, Countess Macchi di Cellere.
  [2] The Editors have been unable to find their names.

From Newton Diehl Baker, with Enclosure

My dear Mr. President: Washington. November 23, 1918.
    I enclose an extract from a cablegram just received from General Graves.   Respectfully yours,   Newton D. Baker

TLS (WP, DLC).

ENCLOSURE

"Paragraph 5. General Kalmikof[1] vacancy the Us[s]uri Cossack and on duty in Khabarovsk has been executing quite a number Russians. Probably last three months 100 have been killed. I believe these executions to be a disgrace to civilization and Colonel Styer[2] at Khabarovsk being constantly appealed to for help. Kalmikof stated in his speech to the Usuri Cossacks about a month ago that he had received moral and material aid from the Japanese. I took matter up with Japan about two weeks ago and informed them what Kalmikof had said and protested these executions. They then told me they had helped Kalmikof when we were operating in that section of the country and they would see that he stopped executions. On the 17th he killed at least 10 more and left their bodies quite near where American Troops are quartered and the bodies were being eaten by dogs. Again the people appealed to Colonel Styer to help them give decent burial to their relatives. Colonel Styer took the matter up with Japanese commander and I took the matter up with Japanese here. They have both assured us that such force as necessary will be used in future to prevent executions by Kalmikof. The Russians claim that Kalmikof is being paid by Japanese and is an ally and they can do nothing with him. General Ivanoff[3] stated that he was going to arrest him but I do not think that he will. All factions of the Russians seem to be very bitter against Kalmikof and they freely claim to me that he is a disturbing element in this section of the country and that they cannot understand why our allies will support man of this character. These representations have been made by me to Japanese. It is my belief that excecutions will stop at Khabarovsk but will be carried on in some other part of Cossack Territory under charge of Kalmikof.   Graves.

T telegram (WP, DLC).
   [1] That is, Ivan Pavlovich Kalmykov, hetman of the Ussuri Cossacks.
   [2] Col. Henry Delp Styer, commander of the 27th Infantry Regiment.
   [3] Gen. Pavel Pavlovich Ivanov-Rinov, former czarist army officer, at this time the nominal commander in chief of anti-Bolshevik forces in eastern Siberia.

Two Letters from Josephus Daniels

Dear Mr. President: Washington. Nov. 23. 1918.

If you have not selected the Republican member of the Peace Commission, it has occurred to me that it would be wise to consider Justice Pitney of the Supreme Court. I know him very slightly. You know him well and can judge of his suitability better. My idea is that Mr. Henry White, who in many ways is acceptable, has long worshipped at the shrine of Root and Lodge and is therefore less satisfactory than some man of his own responsibility but who is an orthodox Republican. If Pitney and Brandeis were on the Commission you would have the best legal ability.

Sincerely yours,   Josephus Daniels

Dear Mr. President: Washington. Nov. 23. 1918

To-day I have had independent messages from Senator Swanson suggesting that I urge upon you the importance of emphasizing the need of carrying out the three year programme. Will you permit me to suggest that in your message you refer to the fact that three years ago Congress committed the country to the policy of three year authorizations and that another three year programme is not a new but a continuation of the policy entered upon in 1916.

Sincerely   Josephus Daniels

ALS (WP, DLC).

From Josephus Daniels, with Enclosure

Dear Mr. President: Washington. Nov. 23. 1918

I have talked with Mr. Whipple, counsel of the Shipping Board, about the plan of selling the ships, or the stock, to Great Britain, and asked him to put his views in writing. Enclosed you will find his memorandum, or rather a copy of it. It seems sound. He presents an aspect not touched upon by Mr. Colby.

Sincerely,   Josephus Daniels

ALS (WP, DLC).

E N C L O S U R E

Sherman Leland Whipple to Josephus Daniels

Dear Mr. Secretary: [Washington] November 22, 1918.

Complying with your request that I jot down the substance of what I have just said to you by telephone, let me say that these are my suggestions as to the question of acquiring the stock representing the ships which it is proposed to sell to Great Britain.

We have just expended rising three billions of dollars in order to get ships. Those we have built are costing us from $175. to $200. d.w.t. Some we have purchased have cost us much more. Free ships have been selling in the open market as high as $300 per d.w.t.

But here are 37 ships,—all finer than any that we have built, most of them better than any that we shall build for years, constituting the finest fleet in the world, owned by American citizens, paid for with American money,—it is proposed to sell *for less than $90. per d.w.t.*

How can we justify the expenditure of our billions, with so little present result, while we let this magnificent fleet go out of American ownership, when we could save it by the expenditure of some seventy millions?

The main objective is that the ships, being under the British flag, are under British control; that the American owners cannot use them as they please; that the Government has prior and dominating rights which make their value much less than if they were free ships,—which in its last analysis means merely this, that Great Britain so restricts and heckles American owners by drastic and harsh legislation that she makes ships which are really worth $300 per ton actually worth only $90 per ton, and then buys in what she has made of such little value.

I shall very much doubt whether she would take such an attitude if our Government should make the purchase. But if she did, this course is open to us: The British companies could go into liquidation and offer the ships for sale. If Great Britain purchased them, she would have to pay their fair value; if she waived her option on them we could then purchase and hold them by a title free from restrictive legislation. I do not believe that Great Britain would dare to refuse the request of the American Government that these ships be transferred to our flag after the war emergency is over.

But the most suggestive thing about the situation is this: Our Government is not moving in this matter; England is the one that is disturbing the situation. She is reaching out to get something which she has not now got. She is trying to acquire from American citizens the complete ownership of the finest fleet in the world. We are satisfied with the *status quo*; she is not. Under such circumstances is it not perfectly proper for us to say that we cannot allow our citizens to part with this fleet, which belongs to this country, and that if it is necessary, to save it to its present ownership the Government itself will intervene and acquire it?

I fear that when we are held to account by the American people for the expenditure of the billions which have been put into our shipbuilding program, we shall not find it easy to explain why for such a moderate sum we let slip out of our hands the finest fleet of ships now sailing the ocean anywhere in the world.

Sincerely yours, Sherman L. Whipple

TLS (WP, DLC).

From Bainbridge Colby

My dear Mr. President: Washington November 23, 1918.

Acting upon your suggestion, I have discussed at length the matter of the International Mercantile Marine Corporation with Senator Fletcher. Senator Fletcher called Senator Ransdell into our conference, and I have had the benefit of an expression of his views also. I also consulted Senator Harding. To-day Senator Fletcher discussed the matter at luncheon with Senators Walsh, Owen, Pittman, Pomerene, and Jones of New Mexico. This afternoon I have reviewed the subject quite fully with Judge Hardy,[1] the ranking member of the House Committee on Merchant Marine. Judge Alexander, the chairman of this Committee is not in the city.

Senator Ransdell was quite outspoken that we should not suffer this American ownership to pass into British hands. Senator Fletcher was a little dubious as to spending Government money in the acquisition of an ownership that was in any way qualified. Today, however, when he advised me of the luncheon with his colleagues, he stated that the opinion expressed by all the Senators present was strongly in favor of retaining the ownership, despite the British registry of the vessels in question, and I think Senator Fletcher's opinion has undergone modification since talking with the other Senators, and may be stated to favor the acquisition of this ownership. Judge Hardy went even further, and stated it as his opinion that we should not only acquire the International Company's ownership in the British vessels, but should acquire, if possible at a reasonable price, the stock of the International Mercantile Marine Corporation, carrying with it the ownership of nine ships under the American flag. Senator Harding wished to give the subject further thought, and was non-committal.

I may say that my own view, as the result of the study I have given the subject, inclines strongly to the advisability of not suffering the ownership to depart, but acquiring it on behalf of the Government.

I need not add to the length of my letter by any restatement of the views which you gave me ample opportunity to express at our conference on Thursday. The situation is delicate. The officers of the International Mercantile Marine Corporation are anxious to learn your decision. I am of the opinion that in selling their vessels of British registry to the syndicate, they are acting within their legal rights, and are under no actual restraint beyond the moral effect of your request that final action be delayed. It may be, therefore, that you will feel that the matter is one that should be decided with some promptness.   Yours faithfully,   Bainbridge Colby

TLS (WP, DLC).
 [1] Rufus Hardy, Democratic congressman from Texas.

From Walter Hines Page

St. Luke's Hospital,
New York 23 Nov, 1918.

Dear Mr. President:

The doctors continue to delay their permission for me to travel further, and (I fear) the chance lessens of my having the pleasure to see you and to report to you before you go—on the most momentous journey a man ever took! My formal resignation therefore, is due—or past due, and I have sent it to Mr. Lansing.[1]

I never wrote anything, my dear Mr. President, with such regret. What wd. I not give to be in England when you are there! But my regret is the measure also of my profound appreciation of your giving me the most interesting and (I hope also by far) the most useful experience of my life, an experience that I hope to turn to good use, and to your credit as long as I live.

You will find the heart of England most grateful to us; and the admiration of your extraordinary management of the world's most extraordinary events—beyond bounds. It would be the greatest joy of my life to see them receive you. You have set the moral standard for the world to become a new world.

Great as my disappointment is in this detention here, I am assured that my illness is going well: my detention comes from minor causes. All my great doctors, English, Scotch, and American, assure me of a complete recovery within a reasonable period; and I am now undoubtedly making good progress in that slow process.

How gracious you and Mrs. Wilson were to have had sent to me the other day the beautiful box of roses that still brighten and perfume my prison here! So to be thought of is the happiest experience any prisoner could have.

I am, my dear Mr. President, for your confidence and kindness, always most gratefully yours,   Walter H. Page

This is the first time I have held a pen since I wrote to you—perhaps 3 months ago.[2]

ALS (WP, DLC).
   [1] See WHP to WW, Aug. 1, 1918, Vol. 49.
   [2] The Editors have not found this letter in any repository or collection.

Two Telegrams from Edward Mandell House

Paris, November 24, 1918.

Number 159. Secret for The President. Your number 59, November 22, 5 p.m. It will be unnecessary for you to bring any domestic servants with you except your valet and Mrs. Wilson's maid.

I shall take up the matter of the use of English at the conference with the British and hope to secure their support. I am working to secure a definite agreement from the British and French that England, France, Italy and the United States should each have five places at the table, (?) [in line with my] suggestion contained in my number seven and accepted by you in your number ten.

Thank you so much for your message of sympathy. I am still in bed and very weak but making satisfactory progress.

Edward House.

Paris, November 24, 1918.

Number 161. Secret for The President. In your announcement quoted in your telegram number 16 you state, "The President will sail for France." I understand this to mean that you will go direct from the United States to France and not pass through England. Please confirm this.   Edward House.

T telegrams (WP, DLC).

From William Gibbs McAdoo

Dear Mr. President: Enroute, Nov. 24, 1918.

As a result of my further very earnest thought on the railroad question, I have now arrived at a conclusion which is based upon a thorough conviction as to its soundness.

As you know, I opposed before the committees of the Congress any limitation upon the period of Government control, notwithstanding which the Congress fixed a limitation of twenty-one months after your proclamation of peace, but left unimpaired your power to terminate the control at an earlier date.

With the war at an end and upon the assumption that the proclamation of peace is issued by June 1, 1919, railroad control would automatically terminate March 1, 1921. This would interject the issue into the next Presidential campaign unless the hostile Republican House and Senate should legislate one way or the other in the meantime. If legislation extending the period of Government control is not passed by this Congress, then the next Congress which meets December, 1919, will have to act one way or the other. Otherwise, as I said before, control will expire by limitation March 1, 1921.

I think the Republicans are eager to plague you with this question throughout the remainder of your term. I think they see a political advantage in trying to make it appear that they are opposed to Federal control and that they will do everything in their power to irritate, annoy and hamper the operation of the railroads during the twenty-one months period, and that the constant agitation of the subject will have a most unfortunate effect upon the morale of railroad employees, with serious injury to the efficiency and quality of the service.

We shall play into the hands of our political enemies if we continue the control under the existing law for the twenty-one months period. The Republicans would play skillfully upon the business interests of the country, the shippers, the State Commissions, all jealous of their prerogatives and anxious to exercise them in unrestricted fashion again, upon the corporate officers who are now on the sidelines eager to get into the fray and especially to regain possession of the properties, upon the railway supply men, many of whom do not like Government control for reasons I need not elaborate here, upon discontented security-holders, and upon selfish interests of every character which are eager to make Government operation a failure and to discredit you and your Administration. A nasty fight will be carried on throughout your term, with increasing difficulties in the management and operation of the railroads themselves, but the most serious phase of it all is that it will, in my judgment, be most hurtful to the efficiency of railroad operation and will react detrimentally upon the public welfare.

On the economic side of the problem, we have this serious condition to face if we retain control for the twenty-one months period. Under existing law, it is necessary that every corporation affected by any capital expenditure involving the purchase of equipment, increase of facilities, extensions, or other needed improvements, must agree to such expenditures and finance them with such assistance as the Government can give, or, failing such agreement, the Government can make the capital expenditures and enforce its claims against the corporations in the courts, with the risk that a large part of its investment might be lost or reimbursement might be deferred for many years to come. But this is not all. Many of the essential enlargements and improvements in terminal facilities, track reconstruction and realignments, and extensions which are imperatively needed to improve the railroad machine and provide the adequate and efficient transportation indispensably required by the present and future development of the country, cannot be undertaken except upon comprehensive plans involving intelligent programs of expenditure covering periods of years, certainly not less, in many instances, than five years, which would, of course, outrun the period of Federal control. Such improvements cannot be undertaken with safety to the people's interest, so far as the essential expenditures are concerned, without agreements with the corporations, and, in many instances, essential improvements can never be made by agreement with the corporations because their competitive interests are irreconcilable. But even where agreements could be made with the corporations covering the necessary programs, it would not be safe to undertake the work unless Government control was continued for a five-year period at least. Here again the question of financing these improvements comes in. The corporations will have to agree with the Government upon the financial plans as well. They will have to issue their securities which must be sold in the open market, and the Government will have to stand ready at all times to take up such securities as the public will not buy.

My own judgment is that a very large expenditure, amounting to from $500,000,000 to $1,000,000,000 per annum, will have to be made over a period of at least five years to put the railroad systems of the United States in position to meet the essential demands of the present and of the future.

I am convinced that if we attempt to operate the railroads under the present law for the next twenty-one months, it can only result in failure. The test will be an extremely unfair one for Government control, as the time is insufficient and the law is unsatisfactory. My profound conviction is that you should say in your annual message to the Congress that as the railroads were taken over as a war measure under legislation which is not comprehensive enough, either as to the time of control after the return of peace or as to the provisions which are essential to protect the public welfare and interest, it is your intention by proclamation to relinquish control of the properties and return them to their owners on the 4th day of March, 1919, unless the present Congress shall, in its wisdom, determine to extend the period of Government control for a period of a least five years, with such additional powers, in the event the period is extended, as will enable the Government to carry out the necessary comprehensive plans for improvements in terminal and track facilities and the increases in motive power and equipment which are essential if the railroads are to be made adequate for the service of the people.

The minute you do this, you will put the issue sharply and in its true perspective before the Congress. You will smoke out the Republicans and develop the exact character of opposition to the

Administration and to Federal control. You will get a true and proper alignment of the contending forces in the country, and you will either get the necessary extension of time, or you can relieve yourself of a very unsatisfactory burden, now that peace has returned, by relinquishing the control of the railroads and allowing the owners thereof to resume their operation. I strongly recommend that this course be taken.

I shall be in Washington Friday or Saturday next at the latest.
Affectionately yours,   W G McAdoo

P.S. I enclose a suggestion concerning the railroad question[1] for your consideration in connection with the forthcoming message.

TLS (WP, DLC).
[1] T MS (WP, DLC), a summary of the points in McAdoo's letter.

To Newton Diehl Baker

My dear Baker: The White House 25 November 1918.

Thank you for your letter of November 23rd about the request to release the Poles in our army to serve in their own country. Your judgment is quite sound and right, and I will simply take the memorandum over with me to the other side in order that we may have common counsel as to how the Polish matter is to be worked out. Thank you very much.
Cordially and faithfully yours,   Woodrow Wilson

TLS (N.D. Baker Papers, DLC).

To Edward Mandell House

The White House, November 25, 1918.
Referring to my despatch 16 I shall sail directly for France as you advised.   Wilson.

TC telegram (E. M. House Papers, CtY).

To Robert Lansing, with Enclosure

CONFIDENTIAL

My dear Mr. Secretary   The White House 25 November, 1918.

The suggestion conveyed in the enclosed cablegram from Grant Smith is substantially the same as that made by Bullitt in a memorandum you sent me recently, and it is of course a good one. I suggest this: that you send House a cablegram to the following effect:

"The President is impressed with the wisdom of a suggestion which has recently come to him from more than one quarter, namely that the German authorities be notified that there can be no official dealings with them on the part of the other powers in connection with the final settlements of the peace until a constituent assembly has been brought together and a definite form of government agreed upon and set up. Will you not be kind enough to bring this suggestion to the attention of the other great Powers and ask them if they would be willing to join the President in such a statement to the Germans? It seems to be the judgment of well informed persons that this would bring the uncertainties in Germany to a head and clear the way sooner than any other one influence."[1]

Cordially and faithfully yours,   Woodrow Wilson

TLS (R. Lansing Papers, NjP).
[1] This was sent as RL to EMH, Nov. 25, 1918, TC telegram (RSB Coll., DLC).

E N C L O S U R E

Copenhagen Nov. 21, 1918

Urgent, 3168.

Strictly confidential. The neutral Diplomat mentioned, quoted in the Legation's 1141 Sept. 3, 5 p.m. and 1755 Dec. 31, 6 p.m.[1] writes from Berlin, November 17th as follows: "There is one great danger and that is a Bolshevik movement if the present Cabinet remains in power and there soon comes national assembly. I hope things may still turn out all right, but if there comes disorder and famine, I do not see any end to the terror. The most important thing the Entente can do is of course to send food, because people in the cities are starving and will starve terribly in a few weeks time when the soldiers come back. Another very important thing would be that President Wilson puts it as clearly as possible before the German nation that he wants general elections. I believe this country will do anything the President wants at present."

The last suggestion seems of imperative importance. It is evident from all reports received that the revolutionary movement is fast falling into the hands of the German Bolsheviki and Quasi-Bolsheviki supporters. A demand by the President for some sort of provisional national assembly chosen on democratic lines, to be succeeded by a permanent representation elected after conditions have become settled, would probably result in precipitating crisis which appears unavoidable. The sooner this crisis comes, however, the greater is the chance that it will result favorably for the forces of real democracy, which now probably have the support of the soldiers returning from the front; this may not be the case after the latter have had time to become discontented as the result of the shorter rations, etc., and exposure to the extremists propaganda. Only continued reiteration that an undemocratic Germany can never expect food or raw material from the western democracies would counteract the Bolshevik poison, which is undoubtedly being incessantly injected into the German masses. In this connection a manifest[o] from the American Federation of Labor addressed to the German working classes might be of great effect. The Bolshevik leaders recognize in democracy their most dangerous enemy. Copy to London.   Grant Smith.

T telegram (R. Lansing Papers, NjP).
   [1] These telegrams, cited above only because they both mention the same "neutral Diplomat," are M. F. Egan to RL, Sept. 3, 1917, and U. Grant-Smith to RL, Dec. 31, 1917, both printed in *FR-WWS 1917*, 2, I, 189, 515-16. In the first of these, he is described only as "a neutral diplomat not unfriendly to the Entente and the United States recently returned from a long residence in Germany." In the second, he is identified only by a cross reference to the first. He is not mentioned at all in either Maurice Francis Egan, *Ten Years Near the German Frontier: A Retrospect and a Warning* (New York, 1919), or the same author's *Recollections of a Happy Life* (New York, 1924).

To Josephus Daniels

CONFIDENTIAL

My dear Daniels: The White House 25 November, 1918.
   Thank you for your suggestion about a Republican member of the commission. Confidentially, I had already asked Mr. Henry White.
   In great haste,   Faithfully yours,   Woodrow Wilson

TLS (J. Daniels Papers, DLC).

To Bainbridge Colby

My dear Mr. Colby: [The White House] 25 November, 1918.
   Your letter of the 23rd about your interviews with the Senators and with Judge Hardy of the House brings my balanced mind over to the side of their judgment and your own.
   It is my hope, therefore, that the Shipping Board will at once buy everything there is to be bought in connection with the transactions we have been discussing. I dare say that they can hardly decline

to sell to us rather than to the British. I am inclined to think that perhaps we should better sound them also about the possibility of buying the stock of the International Mercantile Marine Association, carrying with it the ownership of the nine ships under the American flag.

Thank you very warmly for the diligence with which you have pursued this difficult and intricate matter.

Cordially and sincerely yours,   Woodrow Wilson

CCL (WP, DLC).

To Philip Albright Small Franklin

My dear Mr. Franklin: [The White House] 25 November, 1918.

Allow me to acknowledge receipt of your letter of November 21st and to express my appreciation of the action of the Board of Directors of the International Mercantile Marine Company in resolving to take no further action in the matter that has been under discussion until the views of the government are fully presented and considered.

I hope and believe that I can give you the views of the government in a very short time, because I realize that it is not fair to keep the Board of Directors in uncertainty.

With appreciation,   Sincerely yours,   Woodrow Wilson

TLS (Letterpress Books, WP, DLC).

Two Telegrams from Edward Mandell House

Paris. Nov. 25, 1918.

Number 172. Secret for the President. My number 126, your number 59 and my number 159. I have received no definite assurances respecting number of delegates, but I now feel satisfied from informal expression[s of opinion] which I have received from both French and British authorities that there will be no objection to the number being fixed [at five]. Accordingly, I modify my suggestion contained in my number 126 that no announcement be made concerning our delegation until arbitrators [Allies] are committed to a definite number. I now see no reason why you should not make whatever announcement you have in mind respecting our delegates.   Edward House.

Paris. Nov. 25, 1918.

Number 173. Secret for the President. I am in receipt of the following telegram from Lloyd George: "Monsieur Clemenceau is coming to London on the first of December, and I earnestly hope that you will be able to come also as a number of urgent questions require discussion. As I shall not be able to attend any conferences in Paris before the election on the 14th of December, this is specifically [specially] important. I am inviting Senor [Signor] Orlando alone [also]." I have advised Lloyd George that I am still in bed, but that I hope that my Doctor will permit me to go to London on or about December first for the conference in question. I am feeling better but am still weak, and I will not be able to tell before Thursday or Friday of this week whether I can make the journey.

Edward House.

T telegrams (WP, DLC).

From Robert Lansing

My dear Mr. President: Washington November 25, 1918.

In regard to your letter of the 20th containing a copy of a telegram from Sun Yat Sen, I have instructed our Consul General at Shanghai[1] to inform Sun Yat Sen informally that his telegram has been received and will receive due consideration.

I would not go further than this in regard to this man as there are some very ugly stories about him in regard to his acceptance of bribes and his readiness to serve the highest bidder. I believe that the evidence on this subject, as I recall it, is of a very conclusive sort. I doubt if he has any further real influence now in China on account of these reports.

Faithfully yours,   Robert Lansing.

TLS (WP, DLC).
[1] Thomas Sammons.

From Alexander Mitchell Palmer

Dear Mr. President: Washington, D. C. November 25, 1918.

Your letter of the twenty-second instant received. We are not adding to the list of enemy names by the proclamations which were submitted to you. The property of these persons was taken over long ago, and the purpose of the proclamation putting them in the enemy class by name is only to perfect title in case of sale. I have already adjudicated these persons to be enemies because resident within enemy country, but without your proclamation somebody might in the future attempt to go behind this adjudication by alleging that they were not resident in enemy country at the time. The proclamations would make that impossible. In other words, the proclamation is a mere step in a proceeding already begun, and I was under the impression, gained from our last conversation on the subject, that, while we would not seize any new properties, we would proceed with the administration and disposition under the Act of such properties as we had already taken.

I now have some fifty or sixty corporations advertised for sale. They are important industrial and commercial enterprises which the Germans have controlled, and which I very strongly feel should be Americanized. I cannot sell them, however, and give good title unless you sign the proclamations submitted, and also the Executive Order vesting in me the enlarged powers granted to you by the last amendment to the Trading with the Enemy Act. I have these sales advertised for various dates from to-day on, but will, of course, postpone them until I know whether you desire me to stop or to go ahead. That question, it seems to me, depends upon the answer to this: Are we going to return these enemy properties in kind, or simply to account for the proceeds thereof after liquidation? The Congress evidently had in mind that we would not return them in kind, else the power of sale would not have been granted.

Americans who have had property taken by Germany will, in my judgment, neither expect nor desire to have it returned in kind, for they will not want to run the risks involved in continuing their business in Germany under the new conditions. They certainly ought not to be put to the necessity of looking to the German government or German courts for a return of this property. They will prefer to present their claims for such property against this Government, and we ought to take care of them out of the German property here which I have taken over.

I enclose herewith a draft of a proposed plan for disposing of the whole question of enemy property, which I should be glad to have you consider.[1] If the principle of it is approved, we might as well go ahead in the liquidation of these enemy properties, without waiting for the decision of the Peace Conference, because certainly it will be up to the United States alone to determine how its own nationals shall be protected in their claims against German nationals or the German government.

It is very important that before you leave the country I should know your decision in these matters, and I would appreciate it very much if you could spare the time for a conference on the subject before you go.   Respectfully yours,   A Mitchell Palmer

TLS (WP, DLC).
[1] "PLAN FOR DISPOSITION OF ENEMY PROPERTY IN THE UNITED STATES." T MS (WP, DLC).

From Grenville Stanley Macfarland

My dear President Wilson,   Boston, Mass. November 25, 1918.

Thank you very much for your letter of November 20th concerning my suggestion[1] that Governor McCall be appointed on the Peace Commission. I appreciate of course the difficulties of making up this Commission, but I do hope that there is no thought of appointing Elihu Root. I think he and Henry Cabot Lodge are among the worst and most unpatriotic men in America. I do not believe that man ever drew a patriotic breath in his life.

Moreover, his appointment on the Commission would be a slap in the face of the intellectual radicals of the whole world and would put the Commission under suspicion because there is a false notion concerning the man's ability which would make men feel that almost anything our Commissioners did was affected by his great personal influence. I have no such fear at present, for I have studied his career, read all his speeches and public documents, and studied his conduct in such bodies as the late Constitutional Convention in New York, and I am convinced that his reputation for extraordinary ability lies in the extravagant use of language by Roosevelt in his behalf, which he employed when he felt obliged to justify the presence of a reactionary like Root in his Cabinet. The great currency which is given to Mr. Roosevelt's utterances is the foundation for a false popular notion of Root's exceptional ability. But that notion now exists as a fact to be dealt with, and therefore, taking into consideration his notorious reactionary connections, you will not give your Peace Commission fair weather with the progressive thought of the world if you have him as even one member of the Commission.

May I prolong this letter somewhat by calling your attention to the continued propaganda against the Russian Soviet Government and ask you what earthly excuse there exists now for the presence of our soldiers in Russia? I believe that, despite the powerful propaganda in Russia, most of our progressives are doubtful of the consistency of continuing our troops in Russia. It certainly is not consistent with your attitude toward Mexico which I personally heartily supported in opposition to some who were very near to me in business and friendship.

I feel a little discouraged about the prospect of democracy with a large and small "d" in America in the next few years. I see no leadership in our National Democratic Committee or in any of the field forces of Democracy. I have made as thorough a canvas[s] of all the causes of defeat at the Congressional election as our publicity organization would permit, and I am convinced that the defeat was entirely avoidable, and that it does not reflect a popular disapproval of your administration. You will have noticed that wherever the Hearst papers were published we gained in Congress and in all these communities there is a large German vote. This shows what might have been done by proper methods elsewhere.

I wish you a great success and enjoyment on your novel and momentous trip over seas.

Yours sincerely,   G. S. Macfarland

TLS (WP, DLC).
¹ WW to G. S. Macfarland, Nov. 20, 1918, TLS (Letterpress Books, WP, DLC).

A Memorandum by Peyton Conway March

Washington. November 25, 1918.

MEMORANDUM FOR THE PRESIDENT:

The following table gives the troops embarked, including marines, up to December 1, 1917, and during each succeeding month:

To December 1, 1917	145,918
During December	49,589
January, 1918	47,865
February	49,114
March	84,892
April	118,644
May	245,951
June	278,760
July	307,182
August	289,570
September	257,438
October	186,203
November 1-22	35,305
Total embarked to Nov. 22	2,096,431

P. C. March

TS MS (WP, DLC).

From William Cox Redfield

My dear Mr. President: Washington November 25, 1918.

In your letter to Mr. Baruch asking him to accept the Chairmanship of the War Industries Board, you outlined six functions which that Board should have. Two of these were as follows:

(a) The conversion of existing facilities, where necessary, to new uses; and

(b) The studious conservation of resources and facilities by scientific, commercial and industrial economies.

As a result of lengthy and serious discussion, Mr. Baruch and I are both firmly of the opinion that these two functions of the War Industries Board should continue, the former for a limited period and the latter as a permanent institution. We are also both of the opinion that they should become and continue as functions of the Department of Commerce.

Briefly, our reasons for recommending the continuance of these two functions are in the case of the former the need to convert back to normal uses such facilities as have been converted to war uses, and in the case of the latter the generally admitted need of conservation of our resources by constant ascertainment and demonstration of waste prevention measures. Industrial waste has been said to be our greatest shortcoming as a nation.

Obviously, the continuation of these functions under the Department of Commerce will necessitate in addition to your authority the allotment to this Department of sufficient funds to retain or replace the present personnel, space and other facilities of the respective Divisions of the War Industries Board and in this connection it should be noted that we can no longer count on the services of influential business men at nominal salaries.

I need not add that if you approve of this recommendation, prompt action should be taken so as not to lose the benefits of continuity.

It may be said, moreover, that the continuation of this part of the organization of the War Industries Board will provide a clearing house for collective selling on the part of our manufacturers should this prove necessary in view of the policy of collective buying of reconstruction materials already adopted in allied countries. The organization could also serve, if required, in an advisory capacity to the War and Navy Departments in connection with the disposal by those Departments of the vast stores of materials for which they no longer have need. A skilful return to private channels of these materials over a sufficient period of time will prevent, it seems to me, undesirable market disturbances.

Mr. Baruch will be glad to confirm and further elucidate his views on the subject should you so desire.

I am, my dear Mr. President,

Sincerely yours,   William C Redfield

TLS (WP, DLC).

From Vance Criswell McCormick

My dear Mr. President: Washington November 25, 1918.

I have just received your note of November 22nd with relation to our regulations governing the export of cotton.

Copies of the recent War Trade Board Rulings setting out the policy of the Board in regard to the exportation of cotton have already been sent according to our usual procedure to all persons on our mailing list, which comprises some eighteen thousand names and includes all persons known to the War Trade Board to be engaged in, or interested in, the exportation of cotton. Among the latter are a large number of Senators and Representatives. Nevertheless, I heartily approve the suggestion made in your note that the policy in question be specifically brought to the attention of the Southern members of the Senate and House.

I have accordingly directed the Secretary of the Board to send with a personal letter of transmittal to each of these gentlemen copies of the War Trade Board Rulings referred to which govern the exportation of cotton. These letters have already been sent. For your information I enclose a copy of the letter and copies of the Rulings.[1]   Sincerely yours,   Vance C. McCormick

TLS (WP, DLC).
 [1] Printed copies (WP, DLC).

An Appeal

The White House November 26, 1918.

TO THE AMERICAN PEOPLE:

One year ago twenty-two million Americans, by enrolling as members of the Red Cross at Christmas time, sent to the men who were fighting our battles overseas a stimulating message of cheer and good will. They made it clear that our people were of their own free choice united with their government in the determination not only to wage war with the instruments of destruction, but also by every means in their power to repair the ravages of the invader and sustain and renew the spirit of the army and of the homes which they represented. The friends of the American Red Cross in Italy, Belgium and France have told, and will tell again the story of how the Red Cross workers restored morale in the hospitals, in the camps, and at the cantonments, and we ought to be very proud that we have been permitted to be of service to those whose sufferings and whose glory are the heritage of humanity.

Now, by God's grace, the Red Cross Christmas message of 1918 is to be a message of peace as well as a message of good will. But peace does not mean that we can hold our hands. It means further sacrifice. Our membership must hold together and be increased for the great tasks to come. We must prove conclusively to an attentive world that America is permanently aroused to the needs of the new era, our old indifference gone forever.

The exact nature of the future of the Red Cross will depend upon the programme of the associated governments, but there is immediate need today of every heartening word and for every helpful service. We must not forget that our soldiers and our sailors are still under orders and still have duties to perform of the highest consequence, and that the Red Cross Christmas Membership means a great deal to them. The people of the saddened lands, moreover, returning home today where there are no homes must have the assurance that the hearts of our people are with them in the dark and doubtful days ahead. Let us, so far as we can, help them back to faith in mercy and in future happiness.

As President of the Red Cross, conscious in this great hour of the value of such a message from the American people, I should be glad if every American would join the Red Cross for 1919 and thus send forth to the whole human family the Christmas greeting for which it waits and for which it stands in greatest need.

Woodrow Wilson.

TC MS (RSB Coll., DLC).

To Walter Hines Page

My dear Page:　　　　　　[The White House] 26 November, 1918.

It was good to see your handwriting and to see it so steady. It is a very delightful proof to me that you are coming out from under the burden of your illness, and the letter throughout speaks your old spirit, so that I am sure that your health is coming back to its former courses again.

You know with what sentiments and regrets I accept your resignation and how heartily sorry I am that you could not have been an active participant in the present all-important things that are going on on the other side, but undoubtedly you did the wise thing in not attempting to continue. I am only thankful that you did not go on too long.

I hope that the time is not far off when I can see you and catch up with things in a long talk.

With best wishes, and congratulations on your improvement,
Cordially and faithfully yours, Woodrow Wilson

TLS (Letterpress Books, WP, DLC).

Two Letters to Robert Lansing

My dear Mr. Secretary: [The White House] 26 November, 1918.

In his Number 181, House asks what members of my party Mrs. Wilson and I will wish to have stay with us in Prince Murat's house. I would be very much obliged if you would have a cable sent to him, answering his question as follows:

"The President and Mrs. Wilson would be glad to have, besides the President's valet and Mrs. Wilson's maid, the following persons stay in Prince Murat's house with them: Miss Benham, Dr. Grayson, Mr. Close, and Mr. I. H. Hoover."[1]
Cordially and faithfully yours, Woodrow Wilson

TLS (Letterpress Books, WP, DLC).
[1] This was sent as RL to EMH, No. 88, Nov. 29, 1918, TC telegram (E. M. House Papers, CtY).

My dear Mr. Secretary: The White House 26 November, 1918.

I find that it is practically impossible for me to send an individual answer to each one of these messages. May I ask you if you will not be kind enough to have someone in the Department attend to them and ask our representatives, whether diplomatic or consular in the several localities, to extend my warm thanks and an expression of my most sincere and friendly appreciation, and say how much cheer and pleasure the messages have given me?
Faithfully yours, Woodrow Wilson

TLS (SDR, RG 59, 763.72119/2823, DNA).

To the White House Staff

[The White House] 26 November, 1918.

Memo.

Please ask the Federal Trade Commission to what committees in the House and Senate their bill on the taking over of the packing industry by the government *would* go.[1]   The President

T MS (WP, DLC).
[1] Typed at the botton of the page: "Interstate Committee in House Agricultural or Interstate in Senate."

To Robert Somers Brookings

[The White House]

My dear Mr. Brookings: 26 November, 1918.

Rather than reply myself to your letter of November 22nd, I am going to ask if you won't see Mr. Baruch about the subject matter of it, the prices of steel. At the last meeting of the War Board, which meets me on Wednesdays, we settled upon a policy with regard to price-fixing,[1] and I am sure Mr. Baruch can expound it to you orally better than I could expound it in a letter.

Cordially and sincerely yours,   Woodrow Wilson

TLS (Letterpress Books, WP, DLC).
[1] Unfortunately, the extract from the Diary of Josephus Daniels, printed at November 20, 1918, sheds little light upon the nature of the "policy with regard to price-fixing" decided upon at the meeting of the War Cabinet on that date. However, it is clear that the basic decision taken at the meeting was to end all, or virtually all, price controls when the existing price agreements reached their termination dates. Baruch had told Wilson on November 19 that "the necessity for maximum prices" was "disappearing." B. M. Baruch to WW, Nov. 19, 1918. Baruch also issued a public statement on November 20 which said, among other things, that it "was the intention of the War Industries Board to continue all maximum prices thus far established on commodities in operation through the dates orginally set in the price-fixing orders." *Official Bulletin*, II (Nov. 21, 1918), 3. Wilson, in his reply to Baruch's letter of November 19, stated that he agreed "with the conclusions to which you have come." WW to B. M. Baruch, Nov. 30, 1918. See also Robert D. Cuff, *The War Industries Board: Business-Government Relations During World War I* (Baltimore and London, 1973), pp. 256-60.

To the Norman Foster Company

My dear Sirs: The White House 26 November, 1918.

I have your letter of November 21st, but hope that you will forget the matter of the injury to my hand, as I have happily forgotten it. No settlement is necessary.

Sincerely yours,   Woodrow Wilson

TLS (received from Henry B. Cox).

To William Cox Redfield

My dear Mr. Secretary: [The White House] 26 November, 1918.

I have your letter of November 25th concerning the temporary continuation of the activities of the War Industries Board in respect to the conversion of existing facilities, where necessary, to new uses, and the permanent continuation of its activities in regard to the conservation of resources and facilities by scientific, commercial and industrial economies, and I shall be very glad to cooperate in the continuation of these functions in the Department of Commerce, if you will be kind enough to outline the method for me.
Cordially and sincerely yours, Woodrow Wilson

TLS (Letterpress Books, WP, DLC).

To Alfred Emanuel Smith

My dear Mr. Smith: [The White House] 26 November, 1918.

You may be sure I think as highly of Samuel Gompers as you do.[1] He has proved himself a genuine patriot, and if I were taking over representatives of any special group of our fellow-citizens, he would certainly be one of my first choices. It was a pleasure to hear from you and to have this opportunity to send you my most cordial congratulations. Sincerely yours, Woodrow Wilson

TLS (Letterpress Books, WP, DLC).
[1] Wilson was replying to A. E. Smith to WW, Nov. 21, 1918, TLS (WP, DLC).

From Robert Lansing, with Enclosure

My dear Mr. President: Washington November 26, 1918.

Referring to your note of the 22d[1] enclosing some papers which had been sent you by Mr. Scott,[2] I return the correspondence herewith accompanied by a memorandum prepared by Mr. Miller of our Far Eastern Division. Faithfully yours, Robert Lansing.

TLS (WP, DLC).
[1] WW to RL, Nov. 22, 1918, TLS (WP, DLC).
[2] Charles Ernest Scott, "*Confidential Report Asked For By Dr. Brown*," TC MS (WP, DLC), enclosed in C. E. Scott to WW, Oct. 7, 1918, ALS (WP, DLC). Scott asked Wilson to forward his report to the Rev. Arthur Judson Brown, D.D., Secretary of the Board of Foreign Missions of the Presbyterian Church in the United States of America.

ENCLOSURE

Ransford Stevens Miller to Robert Lansing

Mr. Secretary: [Washington] November 26, 1918.

Unfortunately there seems to be a basis of truth to a number of the main charges against the Japanese administration in Shantung mentioned in the confidential report from Mr. Scott to his Mission Board, but I cannot help feeling that much of the harrowing detail is based on hear-say evidence from Chinese sources and should be received with caution. Incidents appear to be stated as general practices, the acts of individuals confused with Government policies and all colored by a strong anti-Japanese prejudice.

The facts as we have them from reliable sources are bad enough. They show that the Japanese, both official and private, have from the outbreak of hostilities against the Germans in Tsingtau acted in a high-handed manner against the Chinese in Shantung. They widened the scope of their operations without apparent military necessity until they were in control of practically the whole Province, and then proceeded, under the screen of military occupation, to "dig themselves in" both commercially and otherwise with apparent confidence in their permanent control of the principal resources and transportation facilities. Complaints have been made of trade discriminations, in practice, and of injustice done to individual Chinese in matters of property rights. Brigandage has been prevalent in the Province and while it might be difficult to establish that the brigands were instigated and led by Japanese, as believed by Mr. Scott, it is stated that the Japanese have done little to discourage these outrages and have interferred with Chinese troops attempting to do so. Questionable practices, such as dealing in opium, establishing brothels, export of copper cash, forced sales of property, and maltreatment of Chinese are reported as not uncommon.

The Japanese Government has recently announced, however, that it is withdrawing its troops along the railway, retaining garrisons at Tsingtau and Tsinan (the terminal points), and will turn over the administration of the territory to the Chinese officals. This may mean much or little according to the way it is carried out.

R.S.M.

TLI (WP, DLC).

From Newton Diehl Baker, with Enclosure

Dear Mr President: [Washington, c. Nov. 26, 1918]

This is the dispatch which had "run together" in my mind. Do you think it better to tell Pershing to withhold action for the present?

Respectfully   Baker

ALS (WP, DLC).

E N C L O S U R E

Versailles November 26th, 1918.

Urgent. Number 287. Confidential. For the Secretary of War and Chief of Staff.

Admiral Benson handed me today two dispatches received by him yesterday from Rear Admiral Bullard[1] the American Naval representative in the Adriatic Sea. First dispatch follows: "Have received report that Italian authorities have ordered two companies American troops to Cettige.[2] This does not seem provided for in the armistice. Army officials apparently have not proper instructions and are dominated by Italians. Italian troops formerly sent there were ordered back by Servians. It is possible there may be clashes if terms of armistice are not rigidly followed."

Second dispatch follows: "Confidential report my representative Fiume indicates Italian authorities have gone much farther than necessary preserving life and property or that demanded by the terms of armistice and Fiume has appearance permanent Italian occupation. It is my judgment that unless Fiume can be placed under real allied control it will be difficult to preserve peace and order. It appears American troops are being used to promote rather than curb Italian activities and our army representative probably has not definite instructions. French support proposition of making Fiume base for French evacuating troops operating Servia which further reason why Fiume should be under allied control and not simply Italian."

It seems to me that there is danger, at this juncture, in leaving small American detachments remote from the control of the American supreme command.   Bliss

CC telegram (WP, DLC).
  [1] William Hannum Grubb Bullard.
  [2] Cetinje, capital of Montenegro.

From Bainbridge Colby

My dear Mr. President: Washington November 26, 1918.

I beg to submit a brief announcement[1] on the matter of the International Corporation which seems to me adequate to the requirements of the moment.

I would be very grateful for any suggestions that occur to you. I had thought of issuing the announcement this afternoon, at 4 o'clock.   Yours faithfully, Bainbridge Colby

TLS (WP, DLC).

[1] The announcement, made on behalf of the United States Shipping Board, stated that the United States Government would not consent to the sale by the International Mercantile Marine Co. of the eighty-five ships being sought by a British syndicate and that the United States Government itself would purchase the vessels on the same terms offered by the British group. The complete statement is printed in the *New York Times*, Nov. 27, 1918.

From Bernard Mannes Baruch

My dear Mr. President: Washington November 26, 1918.

As a citizen, I am writing to express to you as well as I may, and even then inadequately, my appreciation of what you have done for me and mine. God alone, who has given you strength and guidance, knew your task. To me who have seen but a small part, it has seemed humanly impossible. Your wonderful cool judgment, Christian patience and sublime courage, have inspired all; made the faltering steadfast and the weak strong.

In happier days to come, when the world has steadied and composed itself, countless millions will always be thankful to God for having given us Woodrow Wilson, in, perhaps, the greatest crisis of all times. My gratitude is greatly multiplied because of the inestimable privilege given me of serving under you. My admiration for your wonderful achievements is sometimes, I fear, over-shadowed by my affection for you as a man and a friend.

Most sincerely, Bernard M Baruch

TLS (WP, DLC).

From William Emmanuel Rappard

Dear Mr. President,   [Washington] November 26th, 1918.

Emboldened both by the personal kindness and the confidence you are good enough to show me and by the world importance of the subject, I venture to place before you certain views concerning the participation of the neutrals in that part of the peace conference which is to deal with the League of Nations.

In the course of the recent conversation I was privileged to have with you,[1] you outlined as follows, if I rightly understood, the foundation of the Society of Nations.

The League is to be constituted at the peace conference by the belligerent allies alone. It is to secure to all members the advantages of mutual insurance against war and the benefits, not of free trade, but of freer and equal economic intercourse among themselves. The League, once formed, is to remain open to such neutrals as may seek and be granted admittance. A reformed Germany may later on be admitted also. Although neutrals are not to sit at the table around which the constitution of the League is to be discussed, they may ask to be heard on such questions as interest them or be summoned for this purpose before the sub-committees of the conference.

The more I consider this projected method of approach, the more am I impressed with its difficulties and its dangers. May I, Mr. President, be allowed to state my reasons concisely, but in all frankness? I venture to do so not only as a Swiss citizen, but as one of the countless European admirers and supporters of the far-sighted and generous policies outlined in all your past public utterances.

The disadvantages of the proposed method, might, as I see it, be brought under two heads:

I. If the Society of Nations is to be more than a mere consolidation of present alliances, if it is to be based on something better than national interests and forces, the cooperation of all free and stable nations would seem very helpful and indeed indispensable. You have so often and so forcefully emphasized this point that it would be presemptuous to further insist upon it.

But if the free and stable neutral nations of Europe are to cooperate whole-heartedly, it would seem necessary to admit them at the outset as partners, and not later on as adjuncts to, or protectorates of the founders. Their presence at that part of the peace discussion which will deal with the settlement of the rival claims of the belligerents may be improper and uncalled for. But as you have so insistently declared, the conference is to do much more than to settle rival claims. It is to establish "the common standard of right and privilege for all peoples and nations" and to form a League of Nations which will not "merely be a new alliance confined to the nations associated against the common enemy." Does that not, in all democratic fairness imply that all the future members of the family of nations be admitted on equal terms to discuss and determine "the common purposes of all enlightened mankind."

A general statement of the broad underlying principles of the new world order might first be drawn up by one or several of the Allied Governments. But after the publication of such a Declaration of Interdependence, which would flow out of no pen as magnificently as out of your own, the peace conference might broaden out into a constitutional convention, which all prospective constituent nations would be invited to attend.

Would not such a method best avoid jealousy and intrigue at the conference, resentment and open or hidden opposition later on? If the League is to be looked upon without suspicion, if it is to gain and to hold the loyalty of all its members, it seems both just and important that they all be admitted to cooperate in its formation. This plea would seem equitable even if the sufferings innocently endured and the services willingly rendered by most of the free and stable neutral nations of Europe in the course of the war had not established a deeper human solidarity between them and the great belligerent democracies of the world.

II. The plea for the admission of the free and stable European neutrals may, it would seem, be based on grounds of expediency as well as on those of democratic justice. Your policy and your person, Mr. President, have no more warmer friends, no more disinterested advocates, and no more enthusiastic supporters than the common people of Europe. The governments of those countries, who have had no immediate share in the passions of the war, are naturally freest to express the general secret longing for impartial justice which pervades the masses everywhere.

In the abstract, no thoughtful man will deny that impartial justice is the only possible foundation for a lasting peace. But is it to be expected that the belligerent governments of Europe will, or indeed could, in the present temper of the press and of party rivalry, champion the claims of impartial justice against their own immediate interests? Victors in past wars have sometimes been wise and therefore generous. They have never been impartial. Your own exceptional prestige in Europe is due primarily to the exceptional position your political idealism has led you to assume in this respect. For the representatives of neutral governments, on the other hand, impartiality is no rare virtue, but a common necessity. Is it not probable, Mr. President, that, in the course of debate situations may arise where their cooperation and support of your policies may insure the triumph of wisdom over prejudice, of right over violence, and of permanent general stability over momentary special advantages?

I will not venture to further intrude upon your precious time. I repeat it is not primarily as an advocate of Switzerland and a citizen of Geneva, where your name is worshipped with a peculiar democratic fervour, that I write. I write as one who believes that the whole world is on the eve of a new era, that no man in history has ever achieved an opportunity and a responsibility similar to your own. I write as one who would contribute in his small measure to the avoidance of a decision which might possibly imperil the future, by launching the League of Nations in a wrong spiritual direction and thus bring disappointment and dismay to millions who look to you for leadership and light.

To sum up my suggestion in one sentence, it would be to admit to that part of the peace conference where the League of Nations is to be discussed all those free and stable neutral peoples of Europe who may be considered as its probable members. In order to clearly separate the war settlement discussions, which deal with the past and are the special concern of the belligerents, from the debates tending towards the constitution of the League of Nations of the future, which should be the common concern of all free and democratic nations, it might be found advisable to transfer the seat of the latter to some other place, as America or Switzerland.

With the assurance of my highest esteem, profound gratitude for your confidence, and warmest wishes for your complete success, I am, dear Mr. President,

Sincerely yours,   Wm. E. Rappard

TLS (WP, DLC).
    ¹ On November 20, 1918.

From Jessie Woodrow Wilson Sayre

Dearest, dearest Father,   [New York] November 26 [1918]

Your dear, dear, letter made me want to take the very next train and run down to Washington. It would be so *wonderful* to see you, dear Father, and even though New York is much nearer than Boston is, still I feel quite far off, especially when a little trouble I am having with my back makes it very painful to travel. Indeed, I would have gone on down from Phildelphia last week if it had not been for the extreme weariness that sitting up so long in a train causes. Dr. Davis was most reassuring. It is not a permanent ailment he says and indeed by strapping it up with adhesive plaster he has already done wonders with it.

We are all as cozy and happy as can be up here, and are keeping very well. We miss Cousin Helen who has gone down town to be nearer her work. The long rides down town in the mornings were giving her excruciating headaches. I am sorry to say she has no permanent job yet. The orchestra position had to be given up because of hopeless confusion and disorganization in the staff itself, and now she is temporarily in Creel's office while she finds something in her own line.

Frank has not gone yet although Colonel House assured him that he would be needed over there. Indeed four weeks ago Mr. Miller,[1] his immediate superior, told him to be ready to sail at any moment, to come in the next possible boat after him, and Frank had to cancel many important war work campaign speeches in order to comply. But nothing has happened. He was to wait for word from Washington and no word has come. It has been rather trying because plans held in suspension all the time get wearing to say the least. Frank has hesitated to go down and see Lansing about it because he hates to seem to push. Do you think he ought to go down there and see what the matter is?[2]

What a grim Christmas it will be without you all! But with Peace once more on earth we can forget ourselves, can't we? And I am so glad you *are* going over. I should think you would be desperately needed there by now. I shall hope to get a glimpse of you both, anyway, when you pass through. Won't Margaret be happy to have you there!

I shall stay right here, I think. Nell's "family" will all be with her, and anyway it will be an increasingly arduous journey for me to take with the children for so short a time.

But our hearts will be with you in France!

Dearest, dearest love to you both

Ever devotedly,   Jessie.

ALS (WP, DLC).
    [1] That is, David Hunter Miller, at this time a leading figure in The Inquiry and later deeply involved in the drafting of the Covenant of the League of Nations.
    [2] As it turned out, Francis Sayre did not go to Europe with The Inquiry. He later recalled that Wilson had objected to his going on the ground that his political enemies might attack him if a member of his family went to Europe in an official position. Francis Bowes Sayre, *Glad Adventure* (New York, 1957), p. 67.

To Bernard Mannes Baruch

My dear Baruch: The White House 27 November, 1918.

Your letter of yesterday has given me the deepest and keenest pleasure. I hope you have felt how entirely you have won my confidence not only, but my affection, and how I have learned to value your counsel and your assistance. It has been a delightful experience to know you and to work with you, and I have learned to have the highest admiration for your ability and your character.

But your letter sounds too much like a good bye. I do not mean to let you go yet if I can help it, because there is much remaining to be done, and I do not like to feel that I am going away and leaving it to be done by inexperienced hands. We will have a talk about this.   Gratefully and faithfully yours,   Woodrow Wilson

TLS (B. M. Baruch Papers, NjP).

To Albert Sidney Burleson

My dear Burleson: [The White House] 27 November, 1918.
Do you not think that we had better abolish the mail censorship boards? I feel that they are no longer performing a necessary function, and it is clear that everything that is not necessary or that either costs money or interferes with the normal life of the country ought to be cut off. I hope that you agree with me.
In haste,
                      Cordially and sincerely yours,   Woodrow Wilson

TLS (Letterpress Books, WP, DLC).

To Bainbridge Colby

My dear Colby: [The White House] 27 November, 1918.
I entirely approve of the enclosed announcement. I infer from it that a direct offer of purchase has been made by the Shipping Board, and I hope that you will let me know when you know yourself what their attitude is with regard to selling to the government.
                      Cordially and faithfully yours,   Woodrow Wilson

TLS (Letterpress Books, WP, DLC).

To Alexander Mitchell Palmer

My dear Palmer: The White House 27 November, 1918.
I dare say you are right and I was wrong about the method of completing the sales you have already undertaken, and I will sign the proclamation I returned to you the other day, if you will return it to me.[1] Your plan for the disposition of enemy property in the United States meets with my approval in principle, and I dare say will meet with it in detail when I have a chance to compare it with the proposals that will be made on the other side. I am going to take the document over with me as a basis for discussion.

In haste,
           Cordially and sincerely yours,   Woodrow Wilson

TLS (A. M. Palmer Papers, DLC).
  [1] Wilson signed the proclamation on November 29. 40 *Statutes at Large* 1899.

To Ellison DuRant Smith

My dear Senator: [The White House] 27 November, 1918.

You know, I believe, with what solicitude we have been studying the question of the relation of the packing industry to the country. The Federal Trade Commission has now perfected a bill which seems to me to be thoroughly worth our very serious consideration. I am therefore taking the liberty of sending it to you in the hope that you may give it your friendly attention and bring it also to the attention of the Committee on Interstate Commerce, in order that if it is feasible we may have the matter thoroughly debated and, if possible, determined at the approaching session of Congress.
           Cordially and sincerely yours,   Woodrow Wilson

TLS (Letterpress Books, WP, DLC).

To Francis Patrick Walsh

My dear Mr. Walsh: [The White House] November 27, 1918.

It is with real regret that, after carefully considering your letter of November 19th[1] tendering your resignation as Joint Chairman of the National War Labor Board, I am compelled, in justice to the cogent and almost imperative professional reasons you give for this step, to consent to your retirement at this time from the high position whose duties you have administered with such judgment, tact, and robust integrity. For the services you have thus rendered, I thank you not only on my part but on behalf of the Country.

Your personal expressions of good will towards me are reciprocated in the fullest measure, and I think I need not assure you, my dear Mr. Walsh, that you will carry with you into private life and into the practice of your profession, my best wishes for the success you deserve for the high character you have always consistently maintained.
           Cordially and sincerely yours,   Woodrow Wilson

TLS (Letterpress Books, WP, DLC).
  [1] It is missing in WP, DLC. However, it is printed in the *Official Bulletin*, II (Nov. 19, 1918), 5.

To Frank Morrison

My dear Mr. Morrison: [The White House] 27 November, 1918.

Thank you for your letter of yesterday.[1] No one needs to prove to me that Mr. Gompers is one of our leading citizens and that his influence extends beyond the field of labor. You may be sure that I appreciate his unusual qualities to the utmost, but I am sure that his appointment at the present time would be taken as indicating a desire to have the special field of organized labor represented.
          Cordially and sincerely yours,   Woodrow Wilson

TLS (Letterpress Books, WP, DLC).
  [1] F. Morrison to WW, Nov. 26, 1918, TLS (WP, DLC).

To Joseph Patrick Tumulty, with Enclosure

Dear Tumulty: [The White House] 27 November, 1918.

Please say to Mrs. Gardener that I shall hope to make some mention of the amendment in my message.
                              The President

TL (WP, DLC).

E N C L O S U R E

From Helen Hamilton Gardener

My dear Mr. President: Washington, D. C. November 27, 1918.

When I wrote you last, asking that you lead the world toward the light in the recognition of the justice of giving women a place at the Peace and Reconstruction Conference, I did not know that our own and many other organizations of women intended urging upon you the same course.

Your reply took courage out of my heart. Therefore I have *not* given it to even our own officers. I have allowed them to continue to hope, as I cannot help doing, that you will be able to see—and to make the other great international leaders see—that the women of the whole world will feel now and hereafter that when they were sorely needed to help men save man's own idea of civilization, *all* was asked of them and they gave all; only to be denied even a small voice when they asked, in return, to be represented and consulted as to the use to be made of the victory they did so much to secure.

If, as your reply to me seems to indicate, Mr. President, you feel that you cannot venture to lead the world in this step, if you have reason to know that Lloyd George and Clemenceau would not sustain you—as it seems to me, from my study of the two men that they would do, if you took the lead—at least we *all* venture to hope that you will take up, in your forthcoming message to the Congress, our right to the passage of the Federal Amendment in time for us to present our case for ratification in the forty-two legislatures which will convene this winter, thus giving the women of the United States a chance to vote for the next President and to become self-respecting and self-determining factors in the new order of civilization, which, again is to be based, it seems, upon purely male ideals and wholly directed by male insight. Do not, we beg of you, Mr. President, forget to make the Congress, the men and women of America and of the world feel the keen edge of your disapproval of the present humiliating status of American women. We hope that you will urge upon the Congress the passage, *in December*, of the Amendment and take occasion to say how much *you*, personally, wish that history might be able to say that enfranchised American women had a voice in fixing the next great step to be taken toward human freedom and justice and a real civilization at the Peace and Reconstruction Table. We confidently believe that you will assure us of *this* measure of justice in your message even if you are barred in some way, unknown to us, from securing to women the larger and more immediate voice at Versailles. Millions of women await your next message, Mr. President, to see how deeply your heart feels what your head knows—what you as an historian realize—that civilization can no longer hope to travel forward one half at a time, demanding service of all and denying justice to half.

I had hoped that I should not be called upon to write another such appeal to you, but I am urged to send this "lest you forget." Women have been forgotten so often that we are afraid. We await your message.

I have the honor to remain

Yours for a real civilization based on a real democracy,

Helen H. Gardener.

TLS (WP, DLC).

From Samuel Gompers

Sir: Washington November 27, 1918.

There are many matters of importance pressing upon my mind for submission to you, and which I should like to embody in this letter, but realizing how precious are the moments before your departure from our shores to the other side, I must content myself in presenting one particular matter which in my judgment requires your consideration and action before you leave.

I have reference to the fact that after our people have spent terrific energy to the successful prosecution of the war, and after the sacrifice of life and limb, wealth, position, home comfort, they are turning back into normal channels their activities to peace time pursuits,—the problem of readjustment.

These after-war problems are complex and grave. They may be even more difficult of solution unless the same patriotic fervor and enthusiastic response mark our return to normal activities and peace relations, as was manifested in the will of our people to defend the principles of democracy, and safeguard and extend the ideals of our republic.

I confess this problem has given deep concern. With the world seething in unrest, and with the peoples of Europe left to new and untried leadership, there is greater need than ever that our period of readjustment shall not only avoid the pitfalls and dangers of untried experiments of Governments and new relations, but that our Nation's ideals, attitudes and activities in solving these problems shall also prove a source of inspiration and of knowledge and help guide the leadership of distressed nations in the mastering of the inevitable after-the-war situations.

Insofar as the American Federation of Labor is concerned, the need for intelligent, straight-forward, sound and right thinking and action has not been overlooked. The success, or failure, of our plans, however, relate to and in a large degree are dependent upon the attitudes, plans and activities our National Government will adopt, and which will encourage our several States to follow.

No doubt many splendid thoughts have been expressed on this subject, and attractive plans and programs submitted. Men of different schools of thought, prompted by motives pure and unselfish, yet conflicting, inspired by a patriotic zeal to be helpful, are meeting almost every day in conference discussing how best to solve these pressing questions which the ending of the war has forced to our attention, how best to study these inspirations—the hopes and ideals, the plans and program of all our people engaged in different spheres of life and activity, to approve and adopt that which is good and lay aside that which is bad, is a procedure worthy of commendation.

MAY I NOT BE SO BOLD AS TO SUGGEST that the COUNCIL OF NATIONAL DEFENSE, with its advisory Commission and its number of vast organizations, with the co-operation of the American labor movement, is the one agency in our Government that is eminently well qualified and fitted to counsel, advise and coordinate the work of the several departments of Government, and to find an intelligent answer to these problems and indicate approved methods for their solution?

The COUNCIL OF NATIONAL DEFENSE, with its splendid subordinate bodies of similar kind throughout our land, high in the esteem of all our people, surrounded with capable, intelligent, loyal men of different shades of thought and stations of life, political, social and industrial, can undertake this work as can no other single agency in our Government.

Since my return I have received many letters from men who have faithfully, loyally and on every call or emergency, volunteered the best within them to win the war as members of the several committees under my direction, who are willing, aye anxious to continue serving our Government in this great period of readjustment. It would indeed be regretful to lose the services of the organizations of the COUNCIL OF NATIONAL DEFENSE, its Advisory Commission, at a period when all the best minds are needed to deal with the problems of the day. It is perhaps the only agency of the Federal Government which brings the thought of the people to Washington in that it is the only organization which has the machinery to do so.

It is not proposed that the Council of National Defense shall exercise any executive duties, but that it act in an advisory capacity and renew again its invaluable function as a clearing house of problems and actions to the end that the activities of the several departments of the Government may best coordinate their respective functions and avoid confusion and uncertainty. I am fully in accord with your publicly announced attitude that it does not seem necessary that a new agency or commission should be created for this purpose. Then, too, there is no other agency so high in the esteem of all our people and which can so readily, effectively and efficiently maintain that partriotic fervor and enthusiasm, as essential now as in time of war. Indeed it is my best thought that there is a need for the COUNCIL OF NATIONAL DEFENSE, not only to deal with the problems of readjustment but for a time thereafter.

Briefly, some of the leading reasons for urging the suggestion that the COUNCIL OF NATIONAL DEFENSE shall continue and be entrusted with the work herein indicated are as follows:

1. The Council can be made a central point for the examination and clearing of national matters not specifically vested in the executive departments.

2. The Council can be constituted a central point for maintaining closer and more effective relations between the executive departments, particularly with regard to matters of national defense.

3. The Council as a central point will hold together a peace-time organization for mobilizing over again the forces of industry, labor, science and engineering in all future eventualities of whatever kind.

4. The Council is a recognized federated body created by Congress in which organized labor and industry have a voice.

5. The Council can most efficiently function as a clearing house for information and action as to reconstruction problems and measures and act as an advisory body, particularly with regard to labor matters on the same problems.

6. The Council should continue as a distributing point through its Field Division for federal measures and policies. The Field Division, in turn, sending its messages through the Council of Defense system—composed of the state, county, municipal and community defense organizations. The work of the whole being guided by the Field Division.

For these and many other reasons of almost equal importance, I venture to solicit your consideration of the suggestion that the COUNCIL OF NATIONAL DEFENSE be entrusted with this work of readjustment and of counseling, advising and intelligently co-ordinating the activities of the several departments of our Government, of initiating such measures as will prove helpful in this work and of solidifying and unifying our people in thought and action in the solving of these grave, vexing and important problems now demanding our attention.   Respectfully,   Saml. Gompers

TLS (WP, DLC).

To Samuel Gompers

My dear Mr. Gompers: The White House 27 November, 1918.

There is a great deal of meat for thought in your important letter of yesterday,[1] and I thank you warmly for having contributed so much to the consideration of a very difficult and exceedingly important matter. I shall certainly try to think along the lines you suggest.   Cordially and sincerely yours,   Woodrow Wilson

TLS (S. Gompers Corr., AFL-CIO-Ar).
[1] He meant the preceding letter.

To Grenville Stanley Macfarland

[The White House]

My dear Mr. MacFarland: 27 November, 1918.

Just a line to thank you for your letter of November 25th and to assure you that I agree with you in the personal estimates it contains in the matter of the Peace Commission.

My mind is not clear as to what is the immediate proper course in Russia. There are many more elements at work there than I conjecture you are aware of, and it is harder to get out than it was to go in. Cordially and sincerely yours, Woodrow Wilson

TLS (Letterpress Books, WP, DLC).

To May Randolph Petty

My dear Mrs. Petty: [The White House] 27 November, 1918.

Please do not worry about the note.[1] That can be attended to at any time after I get back, and I do not want you to have a disturbed mind about it in any way.

Thank you for your letter. It is good to have such messages from old friends.

Cordially and sincerely yours, Woodrow Wilson

TLS (Letterpress Books, WP, DLC).
[1] Wilson was replying to May Randolph Petty to WW, Nov. 25, 1918, ALS (WP, DLC). About Mrs. Petty, see WW to Helen W. Bones, Feb. 26, 1918, n. 1, Vol. 46.

Four Telegrams from Edward Mandell House

Paris, November 27, 1918.

Number 184. Secret for The President. I have talked the matter over with Admiral Benson and I suggest that you take the southern route and land at Marseilles. At this time of year the chances are very much in favor of your having far milder and more pleasant weather on the southern route than on the northern one. That was our experience last year. Benson tells me that it will only take two days longer and that if you sail on the fourth you would arrive at Marseilles on the fourteenth. This would bring you to Paris in plenty of time for the conference. Will not you please let me know what you decide [to] do. Edward House.

T telegram (WP, DLC).

Paris November 27th, 1918.

Number 188 priority a. Very urgent. Secret for the President. Hoover arrived in Paris Tuesday morning. I am advised of and in agreement with his plans. They are in general as stated in my telegram number 66, which you approved by an exchange of notes,[1] such alterations having been incorporated therein to meet the Allied desire for coordination of action and our policy of maintaining independence of American action. The chief problem presented is the difficulty of devising a plan which will not antagonize the Allies and particularly Great Britain and at the same time permit single American leadership in relief to the civilian population of Europe. I am sure you will agree that American leadership is essential taking into account the fact that we are the most disinterested nation and the other Allies are affected by local political interests. Further, the supplies to be used for this purpose must in the main be obtained in the United States and will *dominate American markets.* As I have previously advised you, George has asked Clemenceau, Orlando and myself to come to London on December first for a meeting of the Supreme War Council. I replied that while I hoped to be able to be present it would depend on my doctor's decision. I think it wise, for reasons other than presented by my physical condition, not to go to London for this conference. The matters which Hoover and I have discussed will not permit of delay in reaching a decision and accordingly I suggest that the views of the United States Government be presented in writing to the three Prime Ministers at their meeting in London. I suggest that you send me a cable instructing me to present to the Supreme War Council the following plan:

"Sirs:

One. I have given much thought to the formulation of the most practicable means of carrying into effect the resolution presented by Colonel House at the last meeting of the Supreme War Council at Versailles to the effect that the Supreme War Council, in a spirit of humanity, desired to cooperate in making available, as far as possible, supplies necessary for the relief of the civilian population of the European countries affected by the war.

[2.] In considering this matter, I have had constantly in mind the urgent necessity of the case and the fact that it is essential in the working out of relief of this character on a large scale, that there be a unity of direction similar in character to that which has proved so successful under French and British chief command in

[1] See EMH to WW, Nov. 8, 1918 (second telegram of that date), Vol. 51, and WW to EMH, Nov. 10, 1918.

the operations of the Allies on the land and on sea, respectively. I suggest that the Supreme War Council proceed along the following lines:

[3.] In order to secure effective administration, there should be created a Director General of Relief whose field of activities will cover not only enemy populations but also the whole of the populations liberated from enemy yoke and the neutrals contiguous to these territories.

[4.] It is obvious that present Inter-Allied administrative arrangements cover the Allied countries themselves, and if the whole of the world food supplies could be made available through sufficient shipping, there appears to be sufficiency over and above Allied necessities to take effective care of these other populations, provided that these supplies are administered with care, with economy, and with single direction.

[5.] The one essential to this plan, in order that all world supplies may be brought into play, is that enemy tonnage shall be brought into service at the earliest possible moment. It would appear to me entirely just that the enemy's shipping, in consideration of relief of enemy territory, should be placed in the general food service of all of the populations released from the enemy yoke as well as enemy territory.

Six. I have carefully considered the suggestion made by Mr. Balfour to the Supreme War Council at the same time the terms of armistice to be offered the enemy were under discussion to the effect that the enemy should be required to place under the operation and control of the Allied Maritime Transport Council the enemy mercantile fleet in enemy and neutral ports. It appears to me that in practice there would be many embarrassments presented by this plan, and that the principle should be maintained that this fleet be used as to its carrying capacity for purposes of relief and be under the direction of the Director General of Relief. In order to secure its adequate operation, the Director General should assign appropriate portions of this tonnage, first, for operation individually by Italy, France and Belgium sufficient to transport the relief to actually liberated nationals of these nations. The administration of relief in the three above instances would then naturally fall entirely under the three Governments mentioned, and would not further interest the Director General of Relief. Second, the remainder of enemy tonnage, or such part of it as is necessary should be placed under the operation of the British Ministry of Shipping and the United States Shipping Board in equal portions. These two would be [institutions] agreeing with the Director General of Relief to deliver in either case [a quantity of] cargo equal to the carrying capacity of these two fleets from such sources to such destinations as the Director General of Relief may direct in supplying the balance of populations to be relieved. Under this plan it does not follow that enemy shipping would be employed directly in the transportation of this cargo but that equivalent cargo should be delivered. This [plan] enables the use of enemy passenger tonnage in the transportation of the United States or British armies homeward, the respective shipping boards giving an equivalent in cargo delivery to the Director General of Relief. This arrangement would in effect end [add] materially to the volume of the world's shipping and release tonnage for the particular purpose of the individual countries.

Seven. In the operation[s] of the Director General of Relief, he will, of course, purchase and sell food stuffs to enemy populations and therefore not require financial assistance in this particular further than working capital. In the relief of newly liberated peoples such as Belgium, Poland, Servia including Jugo-Slavia and Bohemia, it will no doubt be necessary to provide temporary advances from the Associated Governments to these revived [recuperating] nationalities with which they can purchase supplies from the Director General, such arrangements to be worked out by the Associated treaties [Treasuries]. In some cases, public charity may have to be (*made use of?*) [mobilized].

Eight. In the Director General's dealings with neutrals, they of course would provide their own shipping and financial resources and probably some tonnage and food either directly or indirectly for the purpose of the Director General, they acting under his direction and authorization as to supplies and sources thereof. The Director General, of course acting in these matters in cooperation with the blockade authorities of the Allies and the United States.

Nine. It is obvious that it is only the surplus food supply of the world beyond the necessities of the Allies that is (?) [available] to the Director General.

Ten. In order to prevent profiteering the Director General must make his purchases directly from the respective Food Administration of the Associated Governments where his supplies *arise from* their territories, and when purchasing in neutral markets he should act in cooperation with the established Inter-Allied agencies.

Eleven. It is evident that after the Allies have supplied themselves from their own territories at home and abroad and the balance from other sources, the only effective source of surplus supplies available for relief lie to a minor extent in the Argentine but to a vast preponderance in the United States. The Director General will have a large command of American resources and markets and will require the undivided support thereon [of the American people] in saving and productive activities.

Owing to the political necessity of American control over American resources and the greater coordination and efficiency to be obtained thereby, I am sure that you will agree with me that the office of Director General of Relief must be held initially by the United States Food Administrator and in case of necessity by such a successor as may be nominated by me. I would suggest, however, that the policies of the Director General should be determined by the Supreme War Council to whom he should report it being our united policies in these matters not only to save life but also to stabilize Governments."

All these arrangements to be for the period of emergency and it is highly desirable for them to be liquidated as fast as practicable.

It is exceedingly important that I have your advice concerning this matter at the earliest possible moment.

Edward House.[2]

T telegram (SDR, RG 59, 840.48/2598, DNA).
[2] Wilson returned this telegram to Lansing with the following request: "Will you not be kind enough (unless you know some reason to the contrary) to send House word at once that he may propose the plan here set forth (I presume it will not be necessary to repeat the text to him), stating that we understand that Hoover agrees?" WW to RL, Nov. 28, 1918, WWTL (SDR, RG 59, 840.48/2598, DNA). Lansing wrote to House: "On the assumption that Mr. Hoover agrees, the President authorizes you to propose the plan set forth." RL to EMH, Nov. 29, 1918, T telegram (SDR, RG 59, 840.48/2598, DNA). For further discussion about House's proposed letter, see T. F. Logan to E. N. Hurley, Dec. 23, 1918, ns. 3 and 4, printed as an Enclosure with E. N. Hurley to WW, Dec. 23, 1918.

Paris, November 27, 1918.

Number 189, priority A. Secret. For the President. Referring to my cable 188. I have been informed by Davis of the Treasury Department[1] of certain of the financial aspects of this matter. Some of the French officials have expressed a willingness and desire that France should participate with the United States and England in financing the relief *convention* [contemplated]. I understand that the British Treasury has expressed a willingness to participate to the extent of the supplies and services furnished from the British Empire for this relief but nevertheless[2] Davis thinks they would probably be willing to participate equally with France and the United States irrespective of the origin of relief furnished. In view of the fact that we will furnish the major portion of supplies for relief, I had thought it advisable for us to finance such purchases if necessary to the extent of [all] purchases in the United States in order to maintain full directions over our resources so furnished, but if we can obtain this and at the same time a financial subvention from England and France as above indicated, it seems to me that we should do so and I should like to know what your views are in this, and Davis, who is representing our Treasury here in these matters, would like to know McAdoo's views as approved by you for his guidance in operation with the British and French Treasuries. As to France, it is most probable that we would have to advance to them their share of the purchases made in the United States for relief purposes but that as a matter of pride and politics solely want to participate. It seems that any relief to Poland and Jugo-Slavia furnished by us would have to be financed from your funds. I am informed by Hoover that preliminary discussions with French food officials indicate their support of plan outlined in my 188, but that discussion with British authorities indicate possible opposition owing to their desire to effactually dominate by stipulating that all operations shall be carried out through Inter-Allied Food and Maritime Councils which are under effective English control. Discussion between Davis, Hoover and British Treasury officials, however, indicates their full approval of our plan.

Edward House.

[1] Norman Hezekiah Davis, former president of the Trust Company of Cuba, at this time serving as a special agent of the Treasury Department in Paris to assist Herbert Hoover in his negotiations on postwar relief policies.
[2] "nevertheless" not in House's copy.

Paris. Nov. 27, 1918.

Number 191. Priority A. Secret. For the President.

Wiseman, who is here, has received a cable stating that Mr. Balfour agrees: "That [five] delegates on fixed [panel] system would suit us best." I am not entirely certain what this means. It may mean that England might appoint any number of delegates, only five of which could sit at any one time. I shall ask for further explanation of this and will advise you promptly. Wiseman also says that Mr. Balfour believes we will have considerable (∗) [difficulty] in inducing the French to meet our views on the language question. Balfour suggested that Derby and I take up with Clemenceau the question of arranging the use of both English and French as the official languages of the convention [conference]. Shall I act along these lines?"   Edward House.

(∗) apparent omission

T telegrams (WP, DLC).

Two Letters from Newton Diehl Baker

Confidential

My dear Mr. President: Washington. November 27, 1918.

I hope before you go away you can give me a suggestion with regard to the Russian situation and your view of what we should do with regard to Siberia.

I know how fully your own mind is informed and how much you have thought about this subject, but I confess I myself feel it with increasing anxiety. We went into Murmansk and Archangel in order to prevent accumulated military stores from falling into the hands of the Germans. This, it seems to me, we had a right to do, because our Ally Russia was unable to prevent her enemy and ours from using her property against us. We went into Vladivostok to help the Czecho-Slovaks. Neither military expedition was in theory hostile either to Russia or to any faction or party in Russia. The Germans either have withdrawn or are in process of withdrawing both from Russia proper and from Siberia. Such Germans and Austrians as remain in either country are voluntary ex-patriates and have decided to cast their lot with the Russian people. The Czecho-Slovaks in the meantime would not seem to need military aid from us, but undoubtedly could be expedited to their own country, where, of course, they ought to be, and our forces in both places are now, I am afraid, being used for purposes for which we would not have sent them in the first instance. The Northern Russian group is probably now frozen in for the winter and my concern is chiefly about the Siberian end. There we sent about seven thousand men on agreement with the Japaneze that they would send a like number. They immediately notified us that they would increase their expedition up to one division, or about twelve thousand men. From then until now they have increased their force until it is in the neighborhood of seventy thousand men, and they are apparently still dispatching troops into Siberia. In the meantime they have seized the Chinese Eastern Railroad and the report is that they are co-operating with one group of Russians, supplying them money and aiding them in acquiring supremacy over other groups of Russians and thus building up a pro-Japaneze faction among the Russians themselves. The presence of our troops in Siberia is being used by the Japaneze as a cloak for their own presence and operations there and the Czecho-Slovak people are quite lost sight of in any of the operations now taking place. Two reasons are assigned for our remaining in Siberia. One is that having entered we cannot withdraw and leave the Japaneze. If there be any answer to this it lies in the fact that the longer we stay, the more Japaneze there are and the more difficult it will be to induce Japan to withdraw her forces if we set the example. The second reason given is that we must have a military force to act as guardians and police for any civil relief effort we are able to direct toward Siberia. I frankly do not believe this, nor do I believe we have a right to use military force to compel the reception of our relief agencies. Mr. Cyrus McCormick called on me today and argued very earnestly for the sending of additional soldiers, but frankly every argument he advanced could be used in favor of immediate intervention in Mexico, where we have special interests by reason of neighborhood which would justify intervention if it could be justified on such grounds.

I do not know that I rightly understand Bolshevikism. So much of it as I do understand I don't like, but I have a feeling that if the Russians do like it, they are entitled to have it and that it does not lie with us to say that only ten percent of the Russian people are Bolsheviks and that therefore we will assist the other ninety percent in resisting it, which is the case as Mr. Cyrus McCormick states it.

I have always believed that if we compelled the withdrawal of the Germans and Austrians we ought then to let the Russians work out their own problem. Neither the method nor the result may be to our liking, but I am not very sure that the Russians may not be able to work it out better if left to themselves, and more speedily, than if their primitive deliberations are confused by the imposition of ideas from the outside, and I am especially fearful that the Japaneze intervention in Siberia is growing so rapidly and is so obviously beyond any interest Japan could have of a humanitarian or philanthropic character that the difficulty of securing Japaneze withdrawal is growing every hour and I dread to think how we should all feel if we are rudely awakened some day to a realization that Japan has gone in under our wing and so completely mastered the country that she cannot be either induced out or forced out by any action either of the Russians or of the Allies.

It may be that you prefer to discuss this question when you get abroad and seek some concert of action on it with the Great Powers there, but my own judgment is that we ought simply to order our forces home by the first boat and notify the Japaneze that in our judgment our mission is fully accomplished and that nothing more can be done there which will be acceptable to or beneficial to the Russian people by force of arms, and that we propose to limit our assistance to Russia hereafter to an economic aid in view of the fact that our enemies by the armistice have been required to withdraw their armed forces from Russian territory.

I hope you will not object to my re-arguing this point, as you know that I am simply submitting these views to your corrective judgment.   Respectfully,   Newton D. Baker

My dear Mr. President: Washington. November 27, 1918.

I have just talked with Secretary Daniels and he tells me that the Navy Bureau of Operations believe it would be unwise to change the destination from Brest to Marseilles for two reasons:

(1) They have carefully studied out the route to Brest and have arranged to carry you more southerly than the usual Brest route, so that the trip will be in a temperate climate most of the way.

(2) The mine-fields have been specially studies [studied], and much greater safety is felt for the Brest route than through the Mediterranean. The difficulty through the Mediterranean is from floating mines in and about Gibralter where ocean currents both from the Mediterranean and the Atlantic, it is thought, may carry mines against which no safe provision can be made.

I have told Secretary Daniels that I felt on this statement from his Bureau of Operations we ought to adhere to the Brest route, and unless you instruct me to the contrary I will not order the change to Marseilles.

Respectfully yours,   Newton D. Baker

TLS (WP, DLC).

From Bernard Mannes Baruch[1]

My dear Mr. President: Washington November 27, 1918.

The main function of the War Industries Board was to obtain the materials required for carrying out the military programs of the United States and the Allies, with as little dislocation of industry as possible. To do this, it was necessary in some instances to restrict industry and to fix maximum prices. With the signing of the armistice, and the consequent cancellation of contracts, there was no longer a shortage of materials, and the War Industries Board immediately removed its restrictions. In like manner, the necessity for maximum prices disappeared, except in a few isolated cases which can best be regulated through the War Trade Board.

The facilities of the War Industries Board have been put at the disposal of the various contracting agencies of the Government such as the War and Navy Departments, and the Shipping Board, to aid them whenever they so desire in their consideration of the cancellation of their contracts. This function will soon have been performed.

Those activities of the War Industries Board which have lasting value are being transferred to permanent departments of the Government, where they may be carried forward. Thus, the Department of the Interior, Bureau of Mines, in which you have vested authority to enforce the War Minerals Act, has already assumed control over many of the former activities of this Board, and the conservation program is about to be undertaken by the Department of Commerce. I venture to suggest that the various commodity heads of the War Industries Board, and those who have been associated with them, may, in the years that are to come, render much valuable assistance as Trade Advisors to the Department of Commerce and the War Trade Board. I hope that in this and in other ways it may be found possible to continue the promotion of a better understanding between the Government and Industry, (including in this term employers and employees alike), so that problems affecting all may in times of peace be approached in the same spirit of helpful cooperation that has prevailed during the period of war.

There being no longer a necessity for the continuance of the War Industries Board, which was only a war-making body, and it being my desire to avoid the incurring of expense for a moment longer than necessary, I am writing to suggest that the United States War Industries Board be discontinued as of January 1st, 1919.

I cannot do so without expressing to you my sincere appreciation and that of my associates, for the opportunity you have given us to work with you in the great task that was set before you and which has been brought to such a successful termination. As a matter of duty and pride, I should like again to call your attention to the valuable services performed by my associates and by the War Service Committees of the various industries which cooperated with them. To their untiring efforts and unselfish devotion were largely due whatever results the War Industries Board has been able to secure. Each and every one worked in a spirit that made great personal sacrifices seem a privilege and not a burden. In order that a permanent record may be made of their unselfish service, I shall ask the privilege of forwarding to you a list of the members of the Board, of those associated with them, and of the War Service Committees of the Industries.

All our efforts, however, would have fallen short had not the entire country responded in a whole-hearted manner. Unlimited credit is due the industries of the country, employers and employees alike, for the way in which they responded to all calls made upon them.

Actuated by the spirit of service and not of profit, they pursued the common purpose of bringing the war to a successful termination, in a manner in which every American may well take a just pride.

Very sincerely yours,   Bernard M Baruch

TLS (WP, DLC).
   [1] This letter is a slightly revised version of B. M. Baruch to WW, Nov. 19, 1918.

From James Cardinal Gibbons

My dear Mr. President: Baltimore. November the 27th, 1918.

I thank you very much for your courteous reply to my last letter.[1] I have taken the liberty of transmitting your letter to the Holy Father, as I know it will be a consolation to His Holiness.

The Holy Father has, both in letters and in private conversation, so often expressed his great admiration and confidence in you, that I have taken it upon myself to do also what has long been in my mind, which is to make the following request of you. I know that it will give the Holy Father increased confidence and courage to know that you are going to be present at the Peace Conference, for as you will remember in the last message that I had the honor to convey from His Holiness to yourself, the Holy Father expressed to you his conviction that all humanity trusted to your ability and impartiality. I have since learned that while you are abroad you will visit Italy and I take for granted that you will go to Rome, and this brings me to the point of my request.

My dear Mr. President, as an American as well as a Catholic, as one who is bound to you by the bonds of Patriotism as I am bound to the Holy Father in the bonds of religion, I ask you in the strongest and most affectionate manner of which I am capable not to leave Rome without paying a personal visit to the Pope. I ask you to do this not only because it will be a great consolation to the Holy Father who so admires and trusts you, not only because it will bind the hearts of Catholics to you forever, but because it will delight the hearts of all good men, who whether they agree with the Holy Father in religion or not, at least recognize him as the representative of the greatest moral authority left in the world, and because you, Mr. President, in the opinion of all men, are the one who raised the late war from the plane of national jealousies into the plane of idealism and made it a conflict and a struggle for justice, for righteousness, for liberty and for nothing else. I say then that this will give delight to all men of good will to know that you have not disregarded or slighted the representative of the moral order.

I feel sure that I have only asked you to do what you have already determined in your heart to do, but which I felt it was nevertheless my duty to put before you.

I am, my dear Mr. President, with sentiments of the highest esteem,   Very sincerely Yours,   J. Card. Gibbons

TLS (WP, DLC).
    [1] WW to J. Cardinal Gibbons, Nov. 18, 1918.

From Stockton Axson

                                                        Washington, D. C.
My dear Mr. President: November 27th, 1918.

I earnestly hope that the suggestion which this letter contains will commend itself to your judgment, because if it seems wise to you to do what I propose, the result, I am sure, will be to secure a great future to the Red Cross. My suggestion is that you, as President of the American Red Cross, request Mr. Davison to go to Switzerland soon and, in counsel with the Committee of International Red Cross, consider plans for unifying and continuing the work of Red Cross throughout the world, and for drawing into a closer union the Red Cross organizations of all nations.

During the last twelve months Red Cross has absorbed my thoughts and has touched my imagination as perhaps nothing ever has, for it is a wonderful institution in its conception, accomplishments and potentialities, a non-political, non-sectarian institution which has enlisted the hearts and service of millions of men and women who have found in it a means of rendering service to their kind irrespective of differing nationalities. I can think of no other institution which forms so natural a meeting ground for people of all races and different habits of mind. In Palestine, for instance, Christian, Moslem and Jew have been working side by side under the American Red Cross. This Red Cross seems to me to be a very concrete expression of the world community idea which underlies the great purpose of the League of Nations, which under your inspiration is soon to be, I trust and believe, an accomplished fact, for in a remarkable way Red Cross draws all people into one purpose.

The accomplishments of American Red Cross abroad have been extraordinary. The gratitude of European governments, military commanders and the public in general, surpasses in its expression anything I ever saw. The people of our allies are grateful for the concrete aid which they have had from Red Cross, and yet more grateful for the sympathetic spirit of the American people, who have given freely, asking nothing in return. Again and again, while in Europe, I have heard field officers of the American Red Cross say that when they went to their respective localities the people were suspicious, thinking that what was being done for them must have some ulterior motive, and that in each instance these people were won over to Red Cross and a great enthusiasm for the American people because they saw that all that Red Cross wanted to do was to help people who needed help.

What American Red Cross has done has been primarily due to the instinctive generosity of the American people, utilized and made serviceable by a strong organization directed by men of unusual business ability and experience. I have been impressed during my twelve months' association with the Red Cross by the way in which the American business man has found in the Red Cross an opportunity to express his latent idealism. For months I have been wondering if all this must be lost to Red Cross after the war, and at a recent meeting in Paris I was depressed because all the European Commissioners agreed in concert that by March 1st they would be able to conclude the work which they had undertaken, or have it absorbed by some national organization or committee under the government in whose country each had been working. I saw approaching the end of a great enterprise and a beautiful adventure, and I felt that a crisis was at hand, that something ought to be done to conserve the Red Cross spirit, both for the sake of the recipient and of those who administer Red Cross matters.

There is only one way by which the Red Cross of the past eighteen months can be secured for the future, namely, by enlisting permanently the service and the enthusiasm of the able men of affairs who have been expressing their own roused idealism by applying their accumulated business experience to the service of mankind throughout the world. It was the faith of practical men in the thoroughly practical character of Red Cross philanthropy which enlisted their eager co-operation.

On the Executive Committee Mr. Davison and some of his associates should be retained, perhaps a strong chief executive officer should be appointed, possibly a physician, but the great appeal to the country at large should be made in the future, as during the past two years, by a committee of men of affairs in whom other business men have confidence, not only in their integrity, but in their financial and organizing ability.

There is a great welfare work to be done by Red Cross at home. During my sojourn in Texas I became impressed by the need of communities which desired to organize and effectively carry on such work but which were sorely in need of guidance. I did not know then how that could be secured. I know now. It is through the continuance of Red Cross organized as a national institution with its Chapters penetrating the remotest communities of our country and doing for the civil population in times of peace what they did for the army in time of war. During the past year and a half our Home Service Institutes have given more or less technical training to literally thousands of men and women in welfare work. This great host can be utilized in the happiest way by a strong, permanently organized national organization.

But it is of International Red Cross that I am especially speaking in this letter. It is of course impossible for the people of American [America] indefinitely to continue to carry alone the burden of relief and welfare work among the peoples of the world. The people of other nations must be assisted to help themselves. The best way to do this is through a strong International Red Cross. The Central Committee should remain at Geneva. There is every reason, both in sentiment and practicality, for this, but it should be, in reality and not merely in name, an International Committee, a committee on which there will be representatives from all countries, instead of, as at present, a committee consisting of amiable but somewhat ineffective Geneva gentlemen. That which calls itself "international" has grown rather provincial. I am not saying this in criticism, but merely because it states a fact. New blood, new methods, a new and more comprehensive outlook, these things are necessary to utilize the best possibilities of Red Cross. And there is nobody so well equipped by ability and experience and reputation as Mr. Davison to do this work. If he can be persuaded to go to Switzerland and take with him legal and medical advisors, he will be able diplomatically to open up the whole question of the next International Red Cross conference (which in the nature of things would follow this war in any event), and give it scope and effectiveness. There should result a real International Red Cross, penetrating all lands, acting in supplement to all governments in their work of combating communicable diseases, dealing with the results of natural disasters, such as earthquake, famine and plague, promoting physical welfare of children, community hygiene, and many other matters. American Red Cross has learned much that ought to be put at the disposal of the world at large, and I repeat what I have already said that I cannot see how there could be any more concrete expression of the spirit of world community than through the operation of such an International Red Cross. This organization should become more and more the meeting place of all peoples, not merely looking to one country for aid in time of need, but all in association with each other dealing with the needs of the world.

I suggest a letter from you to Mr. Davison, not committing either you or him to any program whatsoever, but merely suggesting that in view of the handsome results which the people of America through their Red Cross have already been able to accomplish, it seems a fitting time that this American Red Cross should take the initiative in considering plans for perfecting the best possible type of world organization. I think it would have a thrilling effect upon millions of people who have been working day and night for Red Cross during the past eighteen months if you should be inclined to say that though the United States was practically the last of the great civilized nations to become signatory to the Geneva Convention (because of our old traditional objection to involve ourselves in European alliances), this same United States has in the Providence of God been able to take a foremost place during this war in carrying out the ideas of the Geneva Convention, and mitigating the sufferings of a world war, and that it should not cease from its good works simply because the war has ended.

Always faithfully yours, Stockton Axson

TLS (WP, DLC); P.S. omitted.

From John Howell Westcott

Dear Woodrow: Princeton New Jersey Nov. 27. 1918.

I am pretty shaky after several days in bed, but I wish to tell you, before you sail, how we appreciate your kind letter about Jack. I was almost surprised that you knew so soon. We are profoundly thankful that he was "not disobedient unto the heavenly vision," but, clearly understanding the cause, was willing to give all that he had. We all understood long ago that compared with its importance all of us, all we had, all we were, were of little account. We had to buy the victory of righteousness, no matter what it cost. So now our thanksgiving is deeper than our sorrow.

Many a time have we thanked God for putting you where you are, with so much power toward realizing in this troubled world, the reign of righteousness which is the only basis for the world's peace. Ever Yours J. H. Westcott

ALS (WP, DLC).

William Edward Burghardt Du Bois[1] to Joseph Patrick Tumulty, with Enclosure

Sir: New York November 27, 1918.

In consultation with Mr. George Foster Peabody, I have been working for some months on the question of the African colonies. The enclosed memoranda has been drawn up and received the assent of numbers of leading colored men, as expressing our ideas.

We want to get this memoranda before the Peace Conference and before the conscience of the world, and we are convinced that the best way to do this is to present the matter formally to the President.

I write to ask if the President would receive before he sails a small delegation of representative colored men, including Dr. R. R. Moton of Tuskegee, and others, to lay this memoranda before him. We would take but a few moments and confine ourselves to a short statement, which could be submitted before hand.

I realize, of course, how very busy the President must be, and I only ask because I understand that this is a matter in which he has great interest, and I am thinking that perhaps it would be helpful for him to have in this form the expressed opinion of Negro America.

I am, Sir,   Very sincerely yours,   W. E. B. Du Bois

TLS (WP, DLC).
[1] At this time Director of Publicity and Research for the National Association for the Advancement of Colored People and editor of *The Crisis*.

ENCLOSURE

MEMORANDA ON THE FUTURE OF AFRICA
By W. E. B. DuBois

1. The barter of colonies without regard to the wishes or welfare of the inhabitants or the welfare of the world in general is a custom to which this war should put an end, since it is a fruitful cause of dissension among nations, a danger to the status of civilized labor, a temptation to unbridled exploitation, and an excuse for unspeakable atrocities committed against natives.

2. It is clear that at least one of Germany's specific objects in the present war was the extension of her African colinies [colonies] at the expense of France and Portugal.

3. As a result of the war, the Germany [German] colonies in Africa have been seized by the Allies, and the question of their disposition must come before the Peace Conference. Responsible English

statesmen have announced that their return to Germany is un-
thinkable.

4. However, to take German Africa from one imperial master,
even though a bad one, and hand it over to another, even though
a better one, would inevitably arouse a suspicion of selfish aims on
the part of the Allies and would leave after the war the grave questions of future colonial possessions and government.

5. While the principle of self-determination which has been recognized as fundamental by the Allies cannot be wholly applied to
semi-civilized peoples, yet as the English Prime Minister has acknowledged, it cannot [can] be partially applied.

6. The public opinion which in the case of the former German
colonies should have the decisive voice is composed of:

    (a) The Chiefs and intelligent Negroes among the twelve and
one-half million natives of German Africa, especially those
trained in the government and mission schools.

    (b) The twelve million civilized Negroes of the United States.

    (c) Educated persons of Negro descent in South America and
West Indies.

    (d) The independent Negro governments of Abyssinia, Liberia
and Hayti.

    (e) The educated classes among the Negroes of French West
Africa and Equatorial Africa and in British Uganda, Ni-
geria, Basutoland, Nyassaland, Swaziland, Sierra Leone,
Gold Coast, Gambia and Bechuanaland, and the four and
one-half millions of colored people in the Union of [South]
Africa.

These classes comprise today the thinking classes of the
future Negro world and their wish should have weight in
the future disposition of the German colonies.

7. It would be a wise step to ascertain by a series of conferences
the desires, aspirations and grievances of these people and to in-
corporate to some extent in the plans for the reconstruction of the
world the desires of these people.

8. The first step toward such conferences might well be the chief
work of the movement to commemorate the three hundredth anniversary of the landing of the Negro in America.

9. If the world after the war decided to reconstruct Africa in
accordance with the wishes of the Negro race and the best interests
of civilization, the process might be carried out as follows: the
former German colonies with one million square miles and twelve
and one-half millions of inhabitants could be internationalized. To
this could be added by negotiation the 800,000 square miles and
nine million inhabitants of Portuguese Africa. It is not impossible

that Belgium could be persuaded to add to such a state the 900,000 square miles and nine million natives of the Congo, making an International Africa with over two and one-half million square miles of land and over twenty million people.

10. This reorganized Africa could be under the guidance of organized civilization. The Governing International Commission should represent not simply governments but modern culture—science, commerce, social reform, and religious philanthropy.

11. With these two principles the practical policies to be followed out in the government of the new states should involve a thorough and complete system of modern education built upon the present government, religion and customary law of the natives. There should be no violent tampering with the curiously efficient African institution of local self-government through the family and the tribe; there should be no attempt at sudden "conversion" by religious propaganda. Obviously deleterious customs and unsanitary usages must gradually be abolished, and careful religious teaching given but the general government set up from without must follow the example of the best colonial administrators and build on recognized established foundations rather than from entirely new and theoretical plans.

12. The chief effort to modernize Africa should be through schools. Within ten years twenty million black children ought to be in school. With[in] a generation young Africa should know the essential outlines of modern culture and groups of bright African students could be going to the world's great universities. From the beginning the actual general government should use both colored and white officials and natives should be gradually worked in. Taxation and industry could follow the newer ideals of industrial democracy, avoiding private land monop[o]ly and poverty, promoting cooperation in production and the socialization of income.

13. Is such a state possible? Those who believe in men; who know what black men have done in human history; who have taken pains to follow even superficially the story of the rise of the Negro in Africa, the West Indies, and the Americans of our day know that the wide-spread modern contempt of Negroes rests upon no scientific foundation worth a moment's attention. It is nothing more than a vicious habit of mind. It could as easily be overthrown as our belief in war, as our international hatreds, as old conception of the status of women; as our fear of education [educating] the masses, and as our belief in the necessity of poverty. We can, if we will, inaugurate on the Dark Continent a last great crusade for humanity. With Africa redeemed, Asia would be safe and Europe indeed triumphant.

T MS (WP, DLC).

Remarks to Members of B'nai B'rith[1]

28 November, 1918.

I cannot, extemporaneously, reply adequately to the very beautiful address you have just read, Sir, but I can reply with great feeling, and with the most genuine gratitude to the order for the distinguished honor they have paid me.

I am sometimes embarrassed by occasions of this sort, because I know the great tasks that lie ahead of us. The past is secure, but the future is doubtful, and there are so many questions intimately associated with justice that are to be solved at the peace table and by the commissions which no doubt will be arranged for at the peace table, that I think in one sense as if our work of justice had just begun. I realize that, for one thing, one of the most difficult problems will be to secure the proper guarantees for the just treatment of the Jewish peoples in the countries where they have not been justly dealt with, and unhappily there are several countries of which that may be said.

And the embarrassment in that connection is this. It is one thing to give a people its right of self-determination, but it is another to enter into its internal affairs and get satisfactory guarantees of the use it will make of its independence and its power, because that, in a way, involves a kind of supervision which is hateful to the people concerned and difficult to those who undertake it.

But I do not care to dwell on the difficulties. I would rather dwell upon the purpose that we all have at heart to see that the nearest possible approach is made to a proper solution of questions of this sort. And I think that this will be evident to everybody who is dealing with the affairs of the world at this time, that if we truly intend peace we must truly intend contentment, because there cannot be any peace with disturbed spirits. There cannot be any peace with a constantly recurring sense of injustice. And therefore we have this challenge to put to the peoples who will be concerned with the settlement. Do you; or do you not, truly desire permanent peace, and are you ready to pay the price—the only price—which will secure it? It will be awkward for them to answer that question except in the affirmative, and impossible for them to answer it genuinely in the affirmative unless they intend that every race shall have justice. So that I think the probability is that the more plainly we speak—I do not mean the more harshly—but the more plainly and candidly we speak, the more probable it will be that we shall arrive at a just settlement. And in the attempt that I shall personally make, I shall be very much encouraged by kindly acts such as your order, as represented by you, performed today, and I hope that you will convey to your associates my very deep sense of the honor and distinction they have conferred upon me. Thank you very much indeed.

CC MS (WP, DLC).
  [1] Adolf Kraus, president of the Independent Order of B'nai B'rith, A. B. Seelenfreund, secretary, Henry Morgenthau, and Simon Wolf called upon Wilson at the White House on November 28 to present him with the organization's gold medal as the person who had rendered the most distinguished service to humanity during the year. Kraus read a formal citation which hailed Wilson as the champion of permanent peace and leader of the fight against militarism, cruelty, and misery. *New York Times*, Nov. 29, 1918.

To Edward Mandell House

The White House [c. Nov. 28, 1918].

Papers indicate that Lloyd George is about to consult Clemenceau about peace proposals and the best way to counter on the German proposals. Do you think there is any danger of their anticipating me. I should be afraid of their formulations.

WWT telegram (WP, DLC).

To Newton Diehl Baker

My dear Baker: The White House 28 November, 1918.

I think you are right about the route of the voyage, and I hasten to confirm the original plans.
                    Cordially and faithfully yours,   Woodrow Wilson

TLS (N. D. Baker Papers, DLC).

To Robert Lansing

My dear Mr. Secretary: [The White House] 28 November, 1918.

You may have noticed the cable which came in yesterday from House advising that we take the Southern route and land at Marseilles. After conference with Daniels and the people of the Navy Department who know the areas of floating mines, etc., I am convinced that it would be wiser to keep to the original plan and land at Brest. Won't you be kind enough to have a cable sent to House to that effect?[1]   Faithfully yours,   [Woodrow Wilson]

CCL (WP, DLC).
  [1] It was sent as RL to EMH, Nov. 29, 1918, T telegram (SDR, RG 59, 033.1140/255b, DNA).

From Edward Mandell House

Paris. Nov. 28, 1918.

Number 195. Priority A. Secret for the President.

Referring to our 137 and 146.[1] I am advised through Wiseman that the British Government have abolished the political censorship of press despatches for the United States from Great Britian.

Edward House.

T telegram (WP, DLC).
[1] That is, EMH to WW, Nov. 21, 1918 (second telegram of that date), and EMH to RL, Nov. 22, 1918.

From Solomon Bulkley Griffin

My dear Mr. President, Springfield, Mass. November 28, 1918.

I have been waiting long to be permitted to tell you how deeply your letter[1] touched and cheered me. One could not escape a sense of guilt that you should have taken time to write in the midst of the profoundly important world problems that crowded for attention, but Mrs Griffin[2] will testify that no better tonic ever entered a sick room.

The kindly attention promoted thought backward and forward. At the Baltimore Convention in 1912, I was oppressed by the need of giving wise leadership to the liberal forces of the country, and for the first time in long years of Convention reporting I felt constrained to employ every ounce of influence I could exert in behalf of your nomination. It is a satisfaction to recall that fact now, in the light of what the years since have brought.

I have remembered, too, your talk to the Gridiron Club when you told us of lining up each forward step with the foundation principles of the Republic.[3] And now it has come about that your job of alignment includes the world!

This letter is hastened by your near departure for Europe, and the consummation of great labors carried on with a breadth of vision that has made acceptance of the American ideal the only way out for the warworn nations. May the blessing of Almighty God go with you to set the seal of His sanction on all you may undertake for the lasting benefit of mankind.

I am your very sincere and grateful friend,

Solomon B Griffin

ALS (WP, DLC).
[1] WW to S. B. Griffin, Oct. 18, 1918, Vol. 51.
[2] Ida M. Southworth Griffin.
[3] See the talk to the Gridiron Club printed at Feb. 26, 1916, Vol. 36.

From Homer Stillé Cummings

Washington, D. C.
My dear Mr. President: Thanksgiving Day 1918

I shall probably not see you before you go to France. Your going is clearly the right thing to do. I have had no other view from the first.

Those who object are either political opponents or friends who have not grasped the full significance of the things that are afoot.

You have undertaken the greatest task of all time.

The hopes of centuries look to the President. I believe you will succeed.

Every earnest wish of which my heart is capable goes with you.
Sincerely yours, Homer S. Cummings

ALS (WP, DLC).

From Thomas Nelson Page

Rome. Nov. 28, 1918.

Urgent. 2423. Very secret. Congressman Carlin[1] of Virginia having been accorded private audience today by the Pope, states that the latter expressed most earnestly his hope that the President will visit Rome during his visit to Europe, declaring that should he come here he would receive most cordial welcome from himself and would be received by him formally or informally in accordance with whatever President's wishes might be. And further, that President would find no embarrassment there touching anything President might wish in visiting others or carrying out any program he might have.

This statement accords with what the head of the American Catholic College[2] had already mentioned to me privately, to the effect that nothing like any conditions such as were proposed when Mr. Roosevelt came to Rome[3] would be suggested now.

The foregoing, taken in connection with the declaration to me by Premier Orlando that the Italian Government will make no difficulties (*) the President's visiting the Pope, I understand to mean that the President will of course be absolutely free to do here as he would at home. Paris informed. Nelson Page.

T telegram (WP, DLC).
[1] That is, Charles Creighton Carlin.
[2] Msgr. Charles Aloysius O'Hern.
[3] Theodore Roosevelt, in the course of his postpresidential European tour, had, in late March 1910, requested an audience with Pope Pius X. Rafael, Cardinal Merry del Val, the papal Secretary of State, had responded indirectly with the intimation that the Pope would be delighted to see Roosevelt provided it was understood in advance that the

latter would have no contact while in Rome with a group of American Methodist missionaries then working in that city. One of the Methodists had publicly referred to the Pope as "the whore of Babylon." Roosevelt had replied through the same indirect channel that, although he still wished to see the Pope and fully recognized the Pope's right to receive or not receive whomever he chose, he in turn had to decline to make any stipulations, or to submit to any conditions which in any way limited his freedom of conduct. When Cardinal del Val refused to modify his previous stand, Roosevelt called off the proposed interview. The incident was widely reported in the newspapers, Roosevelt himself provided the best account of the affair in TR to George O. Trevelyan, Oct. 1, 1911, printed in Elting E. Morison *et al.*, eds., *The Letters of Theodore Roosevelt* (8 vols., Cambridge, Mass., 1951-54), VII, 354-59.

From Edward Parker Davis

My dear Woodrow, [Philadelphia] Nov. 28 1918

I am thankful today that you have been given to our country, for these great events. And I am more than thankful that you are going on the greatest mission ever undertaken for our country by an American. In this, you have our absolute confidence, our abiding faith, our love and prayers.

As ever, Affectionately Yours, E P Davis.

ALS (WP, DLC).

A Press Release

[Nov. 29, 1918]

It was announced at the Executive Offices to-night that the representatives of the United States at the peace conferences would be the President himself, the Secretary of State, the Hon. Henry White, recently Ambassador to France, Mr. Edward M. House, and General Tasker H. Bliss. It was explained that it had not been possible to announce these appointments before because the number of representatives each of the chief belligerents was to send had until a day or two ago been under discussion.

WWT MS (WP, DLC).

To Richard Hooker

PERSONAL

My dear Mr. Hooker: [The White House] 29 November, 1918.

I appreciate both the motive and the advice of your telegraphic message,[1] but must frankly say that I would not dare take Mr. Taft. I have lost all confidence in his character. And the other prominent

Republicans whom one would naturally choose are already committed to do everything possible to prevent the Peace Conference from acting upon the peace terms which they have already agreed to. It is a distressing situation indeed, but one which they themselves have created.

 With warmest regard and appreciation,
Sincerely yours, Woodrow Wilson

TLS (Letterpress Books, WP, DLC).
 [1] R. Hooker to WW, Nov. 27-28, 1918, T telegram (WP, DLC).

To Homer Stillé Cummings

My dear Cummings: The White House 29 November, 1918.

 Thank you warmly for your note. There are so many unfriendly voices in the air just now that the voice of a friend sounds exceedingly cheering, and I value your judgment besides, so that I am particularly grateful.
Cordially and sincerely yours, Woodrow Wilson

TLS (H. S. Cummings Papers, ViU).

To John Sharp Williams

My dear Senator: The White House 29 November, 1918.

 Nothing that concerns our domestic affairs is more on my mind as I turn my face towards the other side of the water than the question of woman suffrage and the impression which is likely to be created that our party is the party that is preventing the adoption of the Federal Amendment. I have found you so frank a friend and always so thorough a sport that I am going to take the liberty of asking you if you think that it is at all possible for you to lend your aid to the passage of the amendment.

 If this is an outrageous or unjustified request, please rebuke me as you will, but if you are willing to consider it at all, I should be very grateful, for the matter is one of great anxiety to me.

 With warmest regards,
Faithfully your friend, Woodrow Wilson

TLS (J. S. Williams Papers, DLC).

To Grenville Stanley Macfarland

[The White House]
My dear Mr. MacFarland: 29 November, 1918

I entertain just the opinion that you do of Governor McCall, but I am afraid it is not going to be practicable to appoint him, as I would like to, to the Peace Commission. You may be sure that this is through no lack of warm appreciation of his splendid qualities. I would trust him entirely.

In haste,   Faithfully yours,   Woodrow Wilson

TLS (Letterpress Books, WP, DLC).

From Robert Lansing

Dear Mr. President: Washington November 29, 1918.

The French Government have expressed a desire to have Mr. Samuel Gompers return to France to be in Paris at the time of peace negotiations. The French Government feels that Mr. Gompers exercises a steadying influence and that it would be very helpful to have him in France at this time. I have also been advised by Sir Charles Ross[1] that many persons in Great Britain are of the opinion that it would be helpful to have Mr. Gompers in Europe at this time.

Will you kindly indicate what action you wish me to take with regard to advising Mr. Gompers?

Faithfully yours,   Robert Lansing.

TLS (WP, DLC).
  [1] Probably Sir Charles Henry Augustus Frederick Lockhart Ross, 9th Baronet, hereditary owner of large estates in Scotland; best known as the manufacturer of a controversial automatic rifle supplied to the Canadian armed forces in France; and sometime adviser to the United States War Department.

From Thomas Watt Gregory

Dear Mr. President: Washington, D. C. November 29, 1918.

I herewith return wire of November 21st, addressed to you by the Socialist Party at San Francisco,[1] and also original letter written to you by Mr. Norman Hapgood on November 18th,[2] both relating to the pardoning of what they term "political prisoners," guilty of sedition, disloyalty, and similar crimes, since we entered the European war.

I discussed the matter with you personally some days ago and we agreed that each application for pardon should be considered on its merits, I return to you these papers, thinking you might wish to reply to Mr. Hapgood's letter.

Permit me again to suggest that these people are in no sense political prisoners, but are criminals who sided against their country; and, while the punishment meted out to some of them was more severe than it should have been, there are many others who are out on bond, have not been in prison for a single day, and who richly deserve substantial punishment.

Faithfully yours,   T. W. Gregory

TLS (WP, DLC).
¹ City Central Committee, Socialist party of San Francisco, to WW, Nov. 21, 1918, T telegram (WP, DLC).
² That is, N. Hapgood to WW, Nov. 18, 1918.

From Antonio Rafael Barceló[1]

San Juan, Received November 29, 1918.

At the inaugural meeting of this special session of the Legislature the Senate of Porto Rico resolves as its first act to express its joy over the victory of the great ideals of peace, liberty and justice gloriously attained by Allied and American arms, thus securing right and justice to mankind over force and tyranny. At this solemn hour, Mr. President, in which we share the universal happiness crowning our own sacrifices, this Senate presents to your excellency its highest esteem and its hearty felicitations and proclaims you humanity's great leader and apostle of right, and affirms its faith and confidence in that full justice will be made to Porto Rico by the United States Congress.   Antonio R. Barcelo

T telegram (WP, DLC).
¹ President of the Senate of Porto Rico.

From Albert Sidney Burleson, with Enclosure

My dear Mr. President: Washington November 29, 1918.

I am enclosing a substitute for the paper I left with you on Tuesday relative to treatment of the telegraph and telephone matter which, while using much of the data contained in the original, is, I think, an improvement upon that statment in that it develops some reasons why the wire service should be owned by the Government.   Faithfully yours,   A. S. Burleson

TLS (WP, DLC).

ENCLOSURE

Under the Joint Resolution of Congress, approved July 16, 1918, I have taken possession and assumed control and supervision of the telegraph, telephone and cable systems and have designated the Postmaster General to exercise supervision, possession, control and operation thereof, during the period covered by said Resolution. This terminates by operation of law upon the Proclamation by the President of the exchange of ratifications of the treaty of peace. Hostilities having ceased, it is now only a question of time as to when this control will end, unless Congress takes immediate steps to provide otherwise.

The Governments of all the principal nations, the United States alone excepted, now operate their telegraph and telephone systems. This practical unanimity among nations gives proof of deep and fundamental reasons for the postal control of electrical as well as the other forms of communication. In fact, the need of communication is a primary need of the individual existing independently of his means or circumstances, and rises higher than those considerations of quid pro quo which must actuate the private investor. Again this service, especially the telephone, is interdependent and complimentary [complementary] in character and cannot be made fully efficient for a single class without extending its use to all classes; that is the service is in its nature reciprocal and must be made approximately universal to give the required or adequate service. This universality has been realized by our Postal System—for it reaches and serves everybody. The electrical means of communication should be added to it, to attain the same sufficiency. Moreover considerations of economy call for this unifying and nationalizing step. In hundreds of thousands of instances throughout the country the citizen must bear the burden of paying for two telephones, while hundreds of thousands paying for the telephone of one company are denied communication with the patrons of another competing company in the same community. This waste of capital and the facilities of communication becomes grotesque when we witness, frequently three and sometimes four of the pole lines of competing telegraph and telephone agencies running together for thousands of miles along the same highway, when but one should better suffice. Economy of operation and cheap communication are not attainable in these circumstances. It has been said "there is a road to every man's house, and there should be a telephone on the inside." I concur in this statement, which is attainable in the United States, and suggest that no part of the reconstruction program could prove of greater service in the employment of industry and labor and the ultimate advantage of society than this needed extension and improvement of electrical communication.

The principle of Government ownership and control of the telegraph and telephone is not only sound but practicable and is sanctioned by that section of the Constitution which provides, through Government control of Post Offices and Post Roads, for Government monopoly of all means of communication known at the time of its adoption. As early as 1844 when the Morse telegraph was in its infancy Congress made an appropriation looking to its absorption by the Postal Service, and the Postmaster General recommended that it be made a part of the Postal monopoly in 1845 and again in 1846. Since 1867 many Postmasters General have urged upon Congress the adoption of similar measures with respect to the telegraph, and President Grant made a like recommendation to Congress in 1871.

The reasons in support of Government ownership of the telegraph apply as well to the telephone. Several Postmasters General have also recommended the purchase of the telephone by the Government.

That the present Congress appreciated the necessity for the protection of users of the telegraph and telephone which the companies have never been able to afford, is shown by the fact that by the Act approved October 29, 1918, providing for the protection of users of the telegraph and telephone service and the properties and funds belonging thereto during Government operation and control. This Act, among other things, protected the public against the tapping of such lines or wilfully interfering with their operation and against divulging the contents of any telephone or telegraph message by any person not authorized or entitled to receive the same, and made other provisions for the protection of the public in the use of the telephone and telegraph systems of the same character as those provided for the United States mails. It is doubtful if these safeguards could be made effective to the operation of these properties under private ownership specially as to intrastate business.

From information now at hand it appears that the physical value of the Western Union Company properties will not exceed $155,000,000., and that of the Postal Telegraph Company will not exceed $28,000,000. The other telegraph companies are very small and their physical value will not exceed in the aggregate $2,000,000.

The physical value of the property of the so-called Bell Telephone System is about $1,200,000,000., and the physical value of the properties of the other telephone companies is roughly estimated at not to exceed $400,000,000.

The question of public ownership of electrical means of communicating intelligence has been so thoroughly discussed for many years that public sentiment should now be more or less crystallized on the subject, and I take it that the principal obstacle in the public mind to the permanent retention by the Government of the properties is the anticipated expense of their purchase at this time when such heavy drains are being made upon the country to pay the expenses of this great war. But this objection is only provisional, for a continuation of the present system of annual compensation or lease of the properties is clearly feasible and may be employed with a sinking fund to retire the capital investment. I am not prepared to recommend at this time any particular method for effecting a purchase of these properties. I may, however, point out that the difference between the cost to the Government for obtaining an amount of money sufficient to purchase these properties and the total cost which the public now has to bear by reason of the higher interest rates on bonds and other obligations of the companies, and the dividends upon the stocks which the public is also now required to pay would establish an amortization fund which would pay for the properties entirely in about twenty-five years.

By act of July 24, 1866, and the acceptance by the telegraph companies of the provisions thereof, the United States obtained an option to purchase the telegraph properties at their appraised value at any time after five years from that date, which option is still in full force and effect. With respect to the telegraph properties I have directed the Postmaster General to proceed under the Act of 1866 and to submit reports showing the result of his action thereunder which will be submitted for your consideration.

I urge upon the Congress immediate action looking to the continuation of Government control of the telegraph and telephone properties and to make provisions for their purchase.[1]

T MS (WP, DLC).
[1] Wilson intended to include this text, or a revised one, in his Annual Message, because under "Special topics" of an outline of that message he listed "The telegraph and telephone" (WWT MS [WP, DLC]), and, attached to what is apparently Burleson's first draft, is a WWhw note saying "Annual address 1918." Burleson's drafts are also with a group of documents which Wilson used in writing his Annual Message. For unknown reasons, he decided not to go into the subject.

To Bernard Mannes Baruch

My dear Mr. Chairman: The White House 30 November, 1918.

Allow me to acknowledge the receipt of your letter of November 19th about concluding the labors of the War Industries Board, and to say that while I agree with the conclusions to which you have come and deem it best, as you do, that the activities of the Board as such should cease with the first of January next, it is with a feeling of very sincere regret that I see this admirable and efficient agency discontinued. I have constantly felt the spirit and quality of the work it has been doing, and it has been a source of great confidence to me in the prosecution of the war that the tasks of the Board were in such hands. I entirely concur in your estimate of the services of your associates, and I want to add my own conviction that the chief cause of the success of the Board and of its happy relations with the departments of the Government has been your own ability, tact, and devotion to duty. It is with the utmost regret that I accept your resignation, and I shall beg that you will not leave Washington but continue to lend us the advice which has been all along so valuable to us.

As I have told you orally, I think that just the right course is being followed in handing over to the proper permanent Departments those activities of the Board with which the Government ought not permanently to dispense.

Cordially and sincerely yours,   Woodrow Wilson

TLS (photostat in Joint Coll., MoU-MoHi).

To James Cardinal Gibbons

The White House

My dear Cardinal Gibbons: 30 November, 1918.

Secretary Lansing has been kind enough to hand me your letter of the 27th, and I turn aside in the midst of a very busy day to say how sincerely I appreciate the personal thought of me and of the interests of the whole world at the present moment, which prompted you to write it. I beg to assure you that it carries the greatest weight.

I have formed no plans at all about what I am to do in Europe except that I am to devote every energy in me to the peace settlement, but it will give me real pleasure to have your suggestion in mind if I should go to Rome.

With very high regard,
Sincerely your friend,   Woodrow Wilson

TLS (Baltimore Cathedral Archives).

To Solomon Bulkley Griffin

My dear Friend: [The White House] 30 November, 1918.

Thank you most warmly for your letter of Thanksgiving Day. You do not say so, but I hope that it means that you are well again, and I am sending you this warm greeting before leaving.

Faithfully yours,   Woodrow Wilson

TLS (Letterpress Books, WP, DLC).

Two Letters to Joseph Patrick Tumulty

Dear Tumulty: [The White House] 30 November, 1918

I am sorry to say that I am not in sympathy with the claims of the District for the suffrage, etc., and therefore naturally cannot do what Mr. Clayton urges.[1]   The President

TL (WP, DLC).
[1] Wilson was responding to William McK. Clayton to JPT, Nov. 26, 1918, TLS (WP, DLC). Clayton, a lawyer of Washington and president of the Young Men's Democratic Club of Washington, urged that Wilson include in his Annual Message a recommendation that Congress enact legislation granting the District of Columbia an elected delegate to Congress. If Wilson could not see his way clear to do this, Clayton went on, then he might at least ask Congress to appoint a joint committee to hear residents of the District on the various suffrage plans which had been proposed. Clayton argued that it would be a considerable coup for the Democratic party if a Democratic President and a Democratic Congress were to take some action in the matter.

Dear Tumulty: [The White House] 30 November, 1918.

Please explain to Fosdick that it would embarrass me very much to do this.[1]   The President

TL (WP, DLC).
[1] Wilson was responding to R. B. Fosdick to WW, Nov. 29, 1918, TLS (WP, DLC). Fosdick reported that Jacob Henry Schiff and other prominent Jewish citizens of New York had asked him to find out whether Wilson would be willing to write a letter to Felix Warburg, chairman of the Joint Distribution Committee of the American Jewish Relief Committee, endorsing a campaign for funds which the committee was to begin on December 8 in connection with their relief work overseas. Fosdick believed that the cause was a worthy one and the organization "one of the few . . . in America that I think should have government endorsement." He enclosed a draft letter for Wilson's consideration.

From Edward Mandell House

Paris. Nov. 30, 1918.

Number 203. Very secret for the President. Clemenceau called on me this afternoon. He said that he had come to give me his solemn word of honor that he would discuss no question of any importance with George in London. He said that the meeting was of no importance whatever and that he thought that George had asked him to come over simply for electioneering purposes. He said that he thought it most inopportune to call a meeting of this sort on the eve of your departure for France. He added that if Great Britain adopted during the conference a grasping attitude, France would oppose it. France, he stated, would be always willing to submit her claims to the judgment of the conference. Our conference lasted only fifteen minutes inasmuch as today has been my first day out of bed. Clemenceau said he would stay in London only two days.   Edward House.

T telegram (WP, DLC).

From Newton Diehl Baker

Dear Mr. President: Washington. November 30, 1918.

The Council of National Defense this morning held a meeting with representatives of the emergency war administrations to discuss the general question of a return to normal conditions. There were present, in addition to the members of the Council of National Defense, Mr. Baruch, Mr. McCormick, Mr. Leffingwell of the Treasury Department, Mr. Rickard of the Food Administration, and Mr. Garfield. Our conference came to the conclusion that the demobilization of the government machinery set up for the war is proceeding rapidly and satisfactorily, and that apart from certain orders needing your signature for the transfer of functions no specific recommendations need be made to you. There were, however, two subjects upon which the conference asked me to lay its view before you.

The first is as to the question of "reconstruction." It was our unanimous feeling that the public opinion of the country has built up expectations about the matter of reconstruction which are based upon an erroneous assumption, and that some word from you, perhaps in your forthcoming address to the Congress, would have a salutary effect. There appears to be a general expectation that you will outline a "policy of reconstruction" which will deal in a broad way with the reestablishment of industry and commercial conditions, and be in the nature of a chart to business. This expectation we think can not be met, because it is formed of the assumption that there is something else to be done than merely remove restrictions and allow business and industry to resume its flow into normal peace-time channels. There is no necessity for governmental action looking toward the building of new lines of commercial and industrial activity in the United States; no great policy of fresh or additional access to raw materials is needed; no word can now be said with regard to the seeking of world markets in international trade; and therefore it was our judgment that some such thought as this might be wholesome.

"Reconstruction" as applied to this country's problems is a misnomer; we did not so convert the industries of the country to war purposes as to require governmental action to reconvert them. The present problem is not one of reconstruction but of readjustment.

The resumption of American industry and commerce is a matter of removing from the enterprise of America those restrictions, temporary in character, which it was found necessary to impose during the period of the war. The absorption of material and labor of the country into the production of war supplies necessarily created shortages so far as domestic consumption was concerned. In order not to allow such shortages to bear unequally or to create unnecessary hardship, restrictions were imposed by the several emergency administrations created under the authority of Congress. Now that the war conditions have abated, all that is necessary for the industries of America to resume is that these restrictions should be relaxed and removed, and this is being done rapidly, with the expected result that American enterprise is taking advantage of its opportunity to reestablish the business of the country.

The restrictions imposed during the war had to do with limitations in the use of raw materials, priorities of access to materials and labor, and restrictions upon import and export trades. The War Industries Board has found it possible to relieve almost entirely the restrictions imposed by it; the War Trade Board in like manner is relaxing the control of imports and exports as rapidly as the terms of the armistice permit, and as shipping is available beyond the necessary needs of the army and the food supplies of countries dependent upon the United States is freeing ocean commerce to profitable opportunity. The Department of Labor is cooperating everywhere throughout the country to restore labor to peaceful industries whose resumption has been made possible by the removal of these restrictions; the War and Navy Departments and the Shipping Board are readjusting their contract relations with the industry of the country and by prompt settlements in accordance with the terms of these contracts are rendering business men certain as to their obligations and their resources for the resumption of former or other production.

In the second place, our conference this morning felt that we ought to call your attention to the situation with regard to the guaranteed price of wheat; whether or not any statement ought to be made by you to the Congress at this time may be debated. The guarantee by the President's proclamation covers crops sold up to June 1, 1920. The present stock of wheat in the country is very large; the Fall planting of this year is four million acres in excess of last year; the Spring planting is likely to be large. We are not yet able to say what the world's need for wheat will be and can not, therefore, with certainty say that there ought to be any discouragement to Spring planting; but it was our thought that a statement of the whole case might be made to the Congress so that there would be no sudden shock should it turn out that the restored activities of the European peoples enable them to supply in large part their own needs in 1920, leaving us with a large surplus production at artificially enhanced prices and a call upon the government to make good the guarantee by a very large disbursement of public money. At present arrangements have been made to take care of the crop now being marketed through the Wheat Corporation; but no machinery of any sort has been set up to deal with the stocks for sale in 1919; nor has any provision been made by financial legislation for the possibility of being obliged to pay the guaranty in money should the stocks prove greatly in excess of our domestic needs. Our only thought in this connection was that a statement of the facts as they are might be made to the Congress so that the appropriate committees could have the matter in mind and either now undertake the construction of machinery to deal with the 1919 crop or at least be saved from any surprises as to the demands which may be made upon them in the matter of financing in 1919 should the world's stocks be so rapidly increased as not to consume the American surplus.

Respectfully yours,   Newton D. Baker

TLS (WP, DLC).

From Newton Diehl Baker, with Enclosure

My dear Mr. President: Washington. November 30, 1918.

I enclose a letter written to you by Mr. Cyrus McCormick as the result of an interview he had with me on the general subject of further military assistance to our forces now in Russia and Siberia. I send it in order that you may add it to your budget of Russia and Siberia papers for a moment's consideration on shipboard.

The principal thing which Mr. McCormick urges is that Mr. John

R. Mott be associated with Mr. Vance McCormick and me in a kind of advisory conference on the Russian situation. I need not assure you how much I value Mr. Mott's knowledge of Russia and his sympathetic judgment about conditions there, so that it will be a great pleasure to me to confer with him and Mr. Vance McCormick if you wish us to confer, but, of course, the solution of this problem really lies in the direction which you pointed out to me verbally yesterday. I think I know your views and wishes and will be able to act understandingly upon any cabled instructions if you find it wise to send any from abroad.

Respectfully yours,   Newton D. Baker

E N C L O S U R E

From Cyrus Hall McCormick, Jr.

My dear Mr. President: Washington, D. C. November 29, 1918.

I am glad that you are going to the Peace Conference. You will be able to exercise a strong and helpful influence in establishing the foundations for a just peace. Our hearts go with you and we pray that your wisdom and courage may solve the difficult problems which will crowd every hour of your sojourn overseas.

My deep and abiding interest in the deplorable condition of Russia is my reason for venturing, even in the pressure incident to your departure, to make some suggestions which seem to me vital, and which are supplemental to my letter to you of 13 September.[1]

Next in importance to making the Peace Treaty, I feel that Russia is the greatest International problem of today. There are two reasons for this:

First: Before the War Russia supplied the largest amount of grain for Europe. England took sixty per cent of her grain from Russia. The cotton crop of Turkestan comes next to that of the United States and Egypt. The beet sugar of Ukraine is an important part of the world's sugar. The dairy products of Siberia—to say nothing of its grain—are a rich possession. Forty thousand tons of its butter are now seeking a market in vain. For this winter and next spring we can help to alleviate the food shortage of Europe, but *next year* Europe must again seek its food from Russia. This requires immediate restoration of order to insure tillage of the soil, resumption of industry and the rehabilitation of transportation.

Second: Left to work out her own destiny, I fear that Russia will, in the end, turn to extreme reaction. After the exultation following the overthrow of autocracy the people find themselves in the grip of an opposite terror. The Czar's regime was bad but it was better than the present condition of unendurable tyranny, disorder and general murder. In the midst of the present turmoil and civil strife, the tendency to reaction—already to be observed—may drive them back to an imperial autocracy. The new autocracy may be created by German brains and German methods and with its vast natural resources, it would face a poverty stricken and divided Europe. It would probably try to repudiate any settlement of its boundaries or its relationships decided upon by the Peace Conference.

This leads me to the following conclusions:

1. The Associated Governments at the Peace Conference must unite upon a plan for Russia which provides for its political and its economic development.

2. You will have the unique opportunity of bringing about such a result. That we should take the lead in this seems to me urgent, for America alone has no self interest in regard to Russia. No one is as well qualified as you to see that Russia and her people are protected for the future and started on a safe road to self development.

3. Petrograd and Moscow are in immediate need of food, clothing, shoes and other economic assistance. Our Quartermaster's Department has millions of dollars worth of supplies not now required by our own soldiers which would be of the greatest usefulness to the Russians during the coming winter. The Siberian Railway must be cleared for the transportation of money, materials, munition and grain and this involves a decision as to Japan's action in blocking the Chinese Eastern Railway.

4. Food can best be supplied and economic help rendered by an increase in the number of Allied soldiers placed, as circumstances may require, to do police duty. At the same time a definite effort should be made to assist further the development of a National Patriotic Russian Army under the command of any one of several capable, efficient, loyal Generals who belong to no party and who enjoy the confidence of the people. Among such are Generals Denikin, Alexeiev, Kornilov, Krasnoff, Dragomiroff and Admiral Kolchak. Denikin and Boldiroff[2] already have considerable armies in the field. Such a Russian Army, if given sufficient aid in money and materials would offer promise of driving out permanently the present influences of destruction, both German inspired and the anarchy brought on by exhaustion and famine. In addition to other efforts, Allied assistance to Russia can be effectively given thru these Russian Generals. The armies they raise and the munitions

they require must be financed for the present by the Allies but they can be expected to play an important and increasingly effective part in bringing order out of chaos.

5. Knowing the excellent organization which you have already arranged, under the Honorable Vance McCormick, for the economic solution of this great problem,[3] I believe you have in him and in the Secretary of War, men who are able to uphold the great responsibilities that will devolve upon them during your absence. May I not suggest that you ask John R. Mott to study the Russian situation from this end and come into conference with the other two in an advisory capacity? The completion of the United War Drive leaves him comparatively free. The military, the economic and the spiritual elements of this great problem would thus be combined in one compact group of three men. I am,

Faithfully yours,   Cyrus H. McCormick.

TLS (WP, DLC).
  [1] C. H. McCormick, Jr., to WW, Sept. 13, 1918, ALS (WP, DLC).
  [2] Persons not hitherto identified in this series were Gen. Anton Ivanovich Denikin, commander of the Volunteer Army; Gen. Petr Nikolaevich Krasnov, ataman of the Cossack Army of the Don; Gen. Abram Mikhailovich Dragomirov, an assistant to Gen. Denikin; and Gen. Vasilii Georgievich Boldyrev, a member of the Ufa Directory and commander of its military forces prior to the Kolchak coup.
  [3] That is, the Russian Bureau of the War Trade Board.

From Samuel Gompers

New York, November 30, 1918.

I have just been authentically informed that the British prime minister has decided that if labor continues to support the coalition government labor will be officially represented at the Peace Conference, the prime minister also declared he could express no opinion as to the holding of an international or concurrent labor conference until he had consulted the other allies. The American Federation of Labor has kept aloof from and refused to meet with the representatives of labor of enemy countries, but has declared that an international labor conference should be called to be held at the time and place where the official peace conference is held. I earnestly trust that you will find it compatible with the interests of our country to support the view that a concurrent international labor conference may be held, and that in accordance with the instructions of the American Federation of Labor I may issue the invitation therefor.   Samuel Gompers.

T telegram (WP, DLC).

From Richard Crane, with Enclosure

My dear Mr. President: Washington November 30, 1918.

I am enclosing herewith a copy of a letter by Mr. Charles R. Crane which was handed to me by Prince Lvoff[1] at the time he saw the Secretary. I thought you would be interested in seeing this letter as it will give you an idea of Prince Lvoff's attitude in taking up questions concerning Russia.

Faithfully yours,   Richard Crane

TLS (WP, DLC).
[1] That is, Georgii Evgen'evich L'vov, the first head of the Russian Provisional Government. He had come to the United States as the unofficial representative of the All-Russian Provisional Government at Omsk, about which see n. 1 to Enclosure II printed with RL to WW, Sept. 24, 1918, Vol. 51 (second letter of that date). He continued as the representative of Admiral Kolchak after the latter seized power in Omsk on November 18. He had seen Wilson at the White House on November 21. The only record of their conversation is the following report in the *New York Times*, November 24, 1918:

"While unable to reveal what President Wilson had said to him regarding his own attitude toward Russia, Prince Lvoff felt privileged to say in an interview today that the President 'would stand by Russia,' and that his mind was open to measures that might be taken by America and the Allies."

E N C L O S U R E

Charles Richard Crane to Prince Georgii Evgen'evich L'vov

Dear Prince Lvoff: Kyoto, October 7, 1918.

I am sorry not to have seen you when our paths so nearly crossed. We are headed in opposite directions and might have exchanged experiences to much advantage. However we must do the best we can by correspondence. I shall begin with America. You must put away your old ideas of America. The new America is as different from the old one as can possibly be. The ideals and interests and aims under Wilson's inspiring leadership are most important for the whole world today. There is no division of public sentiment regarding him, and no monarch ever had so much authority nor over so wide an empire. As his authority is spiritual as well as political—that, the highest statesmanship the world has ever known— it would be well for all of the world to recognize it while it is here and get the most out of it while it lasts. And Wilson is acting for the whole world and not for America alone. The American people understand this and entirely approve. There was never so much sympathy—intelligent sympathy—for Russia as you will find there today from the President down. My son is the private secretary to Secretary Lansing, is well versed in affairs, especially Russian affairs, and I have cabled him of your coming and to arrange for Samuel Harper to be at your disposal. Telegraph "Samuel Harper, University of Chicago" as soon as you arrive in the United States and he will meet you, as you pass through Chicago, and advise with you about newspapers and whom to see and when. You will find our newspaper men very reasonable now and quite content when you say that you will not have any statement to give out until you have been in Washington. Professor Masaryk has made a fine impression and, if he is in America, see him soon. Harper will know how to find him. Harper is the best possible adviser, is most influential in Washington and with the newspapers and of course will be very sympathetic to you and the whole Russian cause. And do not forget my son Richard, at the State Department, nor Mrs. Crane whom you will probably find in Washington. For myself, please sit down soon and write to me as fully about the Russian situation as I am writing to you about the American one. Write, if convenient, in English or French, but, if not, write in Russian and send the letter soon to me at Peking, either through your Embassy or through mine. I should like to know:

I. About the various political groups that are forming in Moscow and Siberia and any possible or promising leaders.

II. A rough estimate of the economic condition, the relations of the peasants to the land, whether they are quieting down, whether they are cultivating, whether they are holding or selling their produce, whether the Germans are getting much of it.

III. What the attitude of the peasants is toward the Germans now.

IV. What hold the Bolsheviki have and where.

V. Whether the Church has regained much of its authority.

And generally anything else you feel that an old and still devoted friend of Russia ought to know to help him in understanding her present problems and doing his best to aid her.

With best wishes to you for your journey in my country,

Yours always sincerely,   Charles R. Crane.

TCL (WP, DLC).

From Simon Wolf

To the President: Washington, D. C. November 30, 1918.

Representing the Union of American Hebrew Congregations and the Independent Order of B'nai B'rith (International), I beg leave to call your special attention to the all important question of se-

curing equal rights, civil and religious for the Jews of those countries where so far they have been denied them.

Poland, Roumania clamorning [clamoring] for Independence must
guarantee justice and not progroms. Settle for all time, the fundamental principal of liberty of thought and action, and you solve
the long endured problem of a Jewish Question. Zionism, Jewish
Nationalism are local—equal rights are universal. Aside from this,
it is a patriotic duty as an American. Unless you secure those rights
for the Jews, immigration will increase, and the burdens of American citizens be increased.

Wishing you the greatest possible success, I am,

Sincerely,   Simon Wolf

TLS (WP, DLC).

From Albert Sidney Burleson

Dear Mr. President: [Washington] November 30, 1918.

I am this moment in receipt of your letter of date November 27th
in which you express the opinion that the mail censorship is no
longer performing a necessary function. I thoroughly concur in the
view expressed and shall accept your letter as a direction to me to
bring same to an end.

On the same day you wrote me I received a letter from Mr. Swagar
Sherley, Chairman of the Committee on Appropriations, advising
me that "it is the purpose of the Committee on Appropriations of
the House of Representatives to begin hearings next Monday with
the view of returning to the Treasury such appropriations and the
cancellation of such authorizations, or parts thereof, granted in
connection with the prosecution of the war, as no longer may be
required under present conditions" and requesting me to take immediate steps to furnish him "the available information" upon which
the Committee could base action looking to the accomplishment of
its purpose. I will make known to the Chairman of the Committee
on Appropriations the action which has been taken in connection
with mail censorship and also advise him that I have reduced the
clerical force used in connection with the enforcement of Espionage
and Trading With the Enemy Acts in so far as they relate to the
Postal Establishment to the lowest possible basis. These are the
only activities carrying appropriations which have been imposed on
the Post Office Department during the progress of the war.

Faithfully yours,   A. S. Burleson

TLS (WP, DLC).

From Bainbridge Colby

My dear Mr. President: Washington November 30, 1918.

Replying to your letter of the 27th, I beg to enclose a copy of the letter which I addressed to the International Mercantile Marine Company on November 26th, announcing, as you will see in the final paragraph "that the Government is prepared to take over the ownership of these vessels upon the terms of the British offer."[1]

I am advised that a letter has been mailed today by the Company to the Shipping Board, acknowledging the receipt of our letter of the 26th, and stating that inasmuch as the British offer was to be net to the Company, and not subject to deduction for British or American income tax, the Company assumes that our offer contemplates the same result to the Company's shareholders. I am told further that the Company expresses its readiness to discuss the details of the transaction and, if it can be worked out on the basis indicated, to make a contract embodying the transaction as finally agreed upon.

I have not received the letter and am informed of its contents by telephone.

This involves a careful examination of the British offer and an accurate interpretation of its meaning and intent on the point above mentioned.

Mr. Whipple and I intend to meet Mr. Franklin and the attorneys of the Company in New York on Monday morning to discuss the subject, in all its bearings. It will take at least a fortnight, I should say, before the matter can be checked up and reduced to clear outlines, and I can then report to you by cable, if you desire. In the meantime, your mind can be at rest, as the matter will be taking the usual course for business of its character and magnitude.

                         Yours faithfully,   Bainbridge Colby

TLS (WP, DLC).
   [1] United States Shipping Board to the International Mercantile Marine Co., Nov. 26, 1918, TCL (WP, DLC). In addition to the statement quoted above, the letter declared that the United States Shipping Board could not give its approval to the proposed sale of the vessels to the British syndicate.

From Georges Roth

Mr. President,   Washington, D. C. November 30, 1918.

You greatly honored me, a few months ago, by authorizing and encouraging me to translate into French your biography of GEORGE WASHINGTON.[1]

Since this permission was granted I have been in communication with your publishers. My recent appointment to the French High Commission in this town has enabled me to call personally on Messrs. Harpers & Brother and reach a final agreement with their representative in New York.

I am therefore pleased to be able to inform you that the French translation of your work will be published, when completed, through the "Editions Bossard" publishing firm.

It was my privilege, as adjudant to the Chief of the French Mission in Bordeaux, to meet and welcome Miss Margeret Wilson on the French soil when she landed in that port. And I have felt both pride and delight when I learned that she had entered Strasbourg with the French Army, the more so as I may consider this town as my native one.

I beg to remain, Mr. President,

Yours very respectfully,   Georges Roth

TLS (WP, DLC).
  [1] See WW to G. Roth, April 25, 1918. Vol. 47.

From Clarence Frederick Lea[1]

Dear Mr. President: Washington, D. C. Nov. 30, 1918.

The revulsion of feeling against the administration that has swept over the country is in my judgment a natural result of the lack of co-operation, sympathy and friendly contact that should exist between the administration and Congress. Specifically in a number of cases members of Congress are at fault, but primarily, in my judgment, it is the fault of the administration.

My record in Congress will justify my claim of loyalty to the administration. I hope it will justify candid speaking. The attitude of a large part of your administration has been one of studied contempt and humiliation to members of Congress. The attitude as I have observed it with deep concern for two years, has been a mistake, grievously and disappointingly so. It has not capitalized the Democratic Party and it has failed to capitalize the administration.

My attention has been called to a rule adopted by the War Department intended to prevent members of Congress from commending men in the military service for promotion or friendly consideration of any kind. It renders our civilian soldiers subject to punishment and humiliation if they do the natural thing of trying to communicate their desires to the military department of our democracy through their chosen representatives. The most wholesome and patriotic interest of a member of Congress whether it be to call attention to the well earned deserts of one of our soldiers or to protest against the petty tyranny, neglect, mistreatment and abuse of our men that has sometimes occur[r]ed, is made an offense against one whose only desire is to fight for and serve our country.

Recently I knew of a case in which one of the most competent and high class surgeons in Northern California volunteered and was received in the Medical Reser[v]re Corps. He was not seeking commissions or army salaries. He was living with his family and pursuing his profession in most happy and prosperous circumstances. He went in the service to help our boys and our country. He left a practice of probably ten or twelve thousand a year to do that. He was a modest man and not a self-seeker. His skill was ignored and he was assigned to the examination of entrants into the camp and to sanitary inspections.

After some time I learned of these facts, and without the knowledge or suggestion of this man, I wrote the Surgeon General a deferential letter calling attention to the skill of this man as a surgeon and suggesting his consideration for that vastly important work so needed by our wounded. Shortly the physician received an insulting and humiliating letter stating in substance that evidently friends were interceding with a member of Congress in his behalf and that a repetition of the matter would render him liable to punishment. This is a characteristic outrage under the Baker administration.

Men without character and standing in their own communities have readily gained admission into the medic[a]l service. Men whom no self-respecting member of Congress would recommend have readily gained promotion. Men of skill, modesty and ability have been humiliated and kept out of the service while charlatans have been promoted and placed in power over their superiors in worth.

Under-ground methods of appointment and promotion prevail. The power of appointment and promotion is used as a personal asset of the appointing officer, a matter of personal pull, a sop "for me and mine." Wholesome and above-board methods are tabooed, members of Congress who know more of local conditions and the merits of appointees than any one else in Washington are treated with suspicion and ostracised from the consideration of the mighty.

As a Democrat and as a member of Congress I claim only the same right to commend or to protest as other ordinary American citizens. I neither desire or claim the right to name appointees in the War Department or elsewhere. I protest against bureaucracy prostituting our departments. I consider the rule above referred to as an unjustifiable insult to every member of Congress and to the great American people and their sons who serve our country and who sent us here to be their advocates and defenders and who love bureaucracy little less than autocracy.

I feel deeply and have spoken candidly on this subject. In the main I have been happy and proud to support your administration and to share even a very humble part of its achievements. It is friendship and hope rather than the disappointment that I feel, that leads me to speak thus candidly. The attitude of the administration toward Congress is leading to dissension, bitterness and defeat for both the administration and the Democratic party. Most of all, the country in the hour of its great need is failing to receive the benefit of that co-operation and friendly contact between Congress and the administration which it deserves.

Most Respectfully Yours   Clarence F. Lea

TLS (WP, DLC).
[1] Democratic congressman from California.

From the Diary of Josephus Daniels

November Saturday 30 1918

Went at 5 to White House to see WW with Gregory to talk about oil reserves. I agreed to bill if all naval reserve agreements are left to the President to decide. He said he had lost interest in the bill and yet would agree on proposition but would not go one step further

Wrote with his own hand nomination of Victor Blue, Chief of Navigation, & Taylor reappointed Chief of C. & R.[1]

[1] That is, Rear Adm. David Watson Taylor, chief of the Navy's Bureau of Construction and Repair. Capt. Blue was being reappointed as chief of the Bureau of Navigation after a tour of duty at sea as commander of U.S.S. *Texas*.

A Memorandum by Frederick Jackson Turner[1]

International Political Parties
in a Durable League of Nations

Nov [30?] 1918

The following is an *abstract* of suggestions, (derived from the study of the history of American sectionalism and the geography

[1] Turner wrote the following document during late November 1918. Wilson took it with him to Paris. It is impossible to know when Wilson read it and what, if any, impact it had upon him. The words in italics were underlined by Wilson. About the background and writing of the memorandum, see Ray Allen Billington, *Frederick Jackson Turner: Historian, Scholar, Teacher* (New York, 1973), pp. 353-55.

of American political parties), upon the bearing of American experience on the problems of a League of Nations. The conclusion is reached that in such a League there should be a Legislative body, with substantial, but at first limited, functions, as well as a Court, or Council of Nations, and particularly that the *operation of international political parties in connection with such a Legislature* would promote the permanence of the League.* Whether the difficulties and social dangers inherent in the suggestion overbalance the other considerations is left undetermined.

The weakness inherent in a League of Nations is that it is exposed to intrigues by one or more of its component nations among the others most amenable to such influences, to produce a situation requiring the application of League force, e[c]onomic or military and naval, as the alternative to submission to intolerable results. But such application of force may well prove to amount to another World War. The danger lies partly in the European habit of diplomacy, the traditions and the training of her statesmen, and the analogy of a Congress of Nations to the historic Congresses of diplomats, and partly in the economic interests and ambitions of the nations under old-time leaders.

On the other hand, American ideals as so nobly set forth by the President, have found a quicker response among the European laboring classes than elsewhere, and in the passion for democratic peace among the masses lies the hope of the peace of the World internationally. What light does American experience cast upon the possibility of so using the masses as to promote international unity?

1. The area of the United States is about that of Europe; its geographic provinces or sections are comparable in area and in resources to Nations of Europe; in some respects these sections have cultural features clearly distinguishing each. Nevertheless, the history of the United States offers a sharp contrast to that of Europe in that *these sections have not become rival nations.*

2. Although *in form the federal aspect* of the United states is that of a union of *States*, in fact such States have acted in *sectional groups*, or have acted with the knowledge that they were backed by a common sectional sympathy. *Actually the federation has been between sections*, concealing their operation for the most part under the form of state action, or under the form of votes in Congress, in National political conventions, or in the distribution of votes in Presidential elections. A rather careful study of such material has shown that such votes are much more often evidences of sectional rather than mere party action than is usually realized. Even when

* p. 4.

a State has included in its borders parts of two sections, the state's representatives have shown a tendency to divide on sectional lines. In the notable case of Virginia there was division into two states, and the attitude of the counties adjacent to the Alleghany mountains in the South during the Civil War is a familiar illustration of how far this phenomenon may go.

3. In short, *the section is the imperfect image of a nation in the European sense, deprived of those attributes of a European nation which have been most productive of war.* Except for the tragedy of the Civil War, there has been a *Pax Americana between these sections stretched across a continent* for a period of over a century and a quarter. This has not been because there was an absence of grounds for sectional antagonisms, or of those antagonisms themselves. Current newspaper discussion in criticism of the alleged domination in Congress by this or the other section made by those out of power, show often a real bitterness. The history of the construction of tariff schedules, transportation problems, the currency, the public lands, etc., is the history of sectional political contests. It is possible to translate American political history into European terms and thereby to make clearer the resemblances between European history and these partly concealed aspects of American history.

Sectional rivalries and combinations in dealing with the growing power of the new Western states, as the nation expanded, are analogous to European contests for "spheres of influence"; rival sections viewed the West as a reservoir for re-adjustment of sectional "balance of power"; their leaders in Congress consciously and avowedly negotiated sectional alliances and *ententes*; sectional contests over the termini of extensive railroad lines, first into the Mississippi Valley from the coast of the Atlantic and later from the Mississippi to the Pacific, were fundamentally like the "Bagdad Railway" contest. We have actually recognized and organized the sectional element in our laws, such as the act for the regional system of reserve banks. Of these facts there is abundant evidence in the utterances of statesmen throughout American history, as well as in the distribution of votes.

4. Granting the powerful influence of economic consolidation, as in business and transportation, the binding force of a common tongue, and institutions, and various other elements which distinguish the American from the European conditions, it is significant that there is so much of likeness between the mild American section and its stronger sister, the European state. So real was the sectional

factor that if sectional governments had replaced state governments, with sectional customs houses (as Calhoun in his *Exposition*[2]
suggested), it may well be doubted whether the influences of interstate commerce and transportation would not have been quite
as much occasions for contention between sections as binding forces.
Even the provision of the federal constitution for action upon individuals rather than upon states in the matters assigned to the
central government might have been too weak for the divisive forces
of sectional controversy.

Had the Union been merely a League of Nations or States, with
provisions even as advanced as those of the Articles of Confederation, it may well be doubted if the nation could have been held
together. This doubt grows when we remember that at various
crises it was to the interest of European nations to foster this division
in the interest of their own policy, and that connection with some
European state was always reckoned with by a remonstrating section. In fact Civil War between sections did finally occur. It would
have come earlier in case of a League.

5. Divergent as are the conditions and the development of Europe
and America, the very freedom of this country from some of the
complexities of Europe, the large lines in which her simpler story
has run, may be helpful, not only as a warning, but as a constructive
contribution to the new order. That Europe is in a receptive mood
appears in the attention which it has given to American ideals of
the worth of the common man, of the hope and faith in democracy
and fair play, and the advantage of self-sacrifice and disinterestedness, which the President has so nobly set forth.

We have given evidence that immigrants from all nations of the
world can live together peacefully under a single government that
does justice. *In our political institutions also are elements worthy
of consideration.*

Parties

Notice has already been taken of the utility of the provision of
the Constitution which assigns to the federal government a direct
relation to the individual in important assigned spheres of jurisdiction. This may not be at first practicable in a League of Nations.
But it is important to call attention to the *significance of the American national political parties, operating upon the whole Union,
not confined to a section. The last tie that snapped before the Civil*

---

[2] John Caldwell Calhoun, "South Carolina Exposition," Richard K. Crallé, ed., *The Works
of John C. Calhoun* (6 vols., New York, 1851-56), VI, 1-57. Calhoun wrote the "Exposition"
in 1828, but his authorship of the document remained a secret until 1831.

War, was the party tie. This has, perhaps, in its working, been *the most effective single political institution for the prevention of sectional disunion.*

In a region as diversified in some respects as Europe itself, and as large, the *national political parties ran across all sections, evoked intersectional or nonsectional party loyalty,* checked the *exclusive* claim of the section to to [*sic*] a vote in the interest of the section, furnished the dissenting minority within the section *an organic connection with party associates in other sections, at the same time that this connection was dependent upon just recognition of the special section* in which the minority lived. It was an *elastic bond, but one that was strong. It ran horizontal cross-sections of party ties across the vertical lines of sectional division.* It *enabled the voter to act continentally,* and it compelled the statesman to act on lines of policy that transcended his section, if he would secure a continental following strong enough to bring success.

6. There is a distinct advantage in utilizing this party system in a League of nations, if it does not carry with it countervailing disadvantages grave enough to lead to its rejection. In essence it means the utilization of that body of internationalism already in evidence not only in such organizations as radical political parties, such as the International, the I.W.W., Socialists generally, etc., but also the opposite tendencies seen in international business combinations, scientific and educational international organizations, and conservative forces generally. The class struggle, so called, is in fact not a national but an international struggle. If party organization of the radical element alone exists, and if this organization is also dominated and shaped by some one or two nations, as Germany or Russia, it will be extended, as it has been, to other countries in the form of secret, or intriguing societies, proceeding by revolutionary methods, with little or no regard for the separate interests of the nation into which it is introduced as an alien, and with its helmsman operating from the outside, and steering a course which almost necessarily involves adhesion to the primary interest of the country in which such a party is recognized as a powerful element in the determination of the policy.

Is it better to try to exclude these international political forces from the organization of the new order, or to utilize their internationalizing tendencies by enabling them to operate upon an international legislative body, responsive to play of parties? Is it worth while to use the fact of class consciousness to diminish the violence of national consciousness?

There can be little doubt that the common people, whether of the extreme radical wing of socialists, or of the conservative party groups, were reluctant to enter the war, and are now in Germany and Austria-Hungary the severest critics of the autocratic group which deceived them and misled them. The labor groups have been more responsive to the policy of internationalism than, as yet, the other groups. At critical junctures their support, in England and France, has been important to the policy of President Wilson. They have a measure of international self-consciousness, partly because they have international organizations. There is no reason why similar organization on an international basis might not be given to conservative parties.

7. One recoils from any suggestion of adding a party loyalty international in its appeal to the loyalty to the individual nation. But the very idea of a League of Nations involves some diminution of the national feeling, some cultivation of international loyalty. If one could keep the Bolsheviki serpent out of the American Eden, he would hesitate to admit any international party organization which permitted such organization.

But in the reconstruction and the ferment which will follow the return of peace, there will be doubts about the existence of Edens anywhere, and the Bolshiviki serpent will creep in under whatever fence be attempted. May it not be safer to give him a job of international legislation rather than to leave him to strike from dark corners, and with no sense of responsibility?

On these questions, I am not sure. Consideration might be given to the probable actual vote possible, considerating [considering] the estimated strength of political parties in the component nations of such a League, before assigning legislative functions in detail. We should have at least a rough estimate of the probable power and probable policies of the various groups. This I have not. So far as the special interests of the United States, however, operate on the decision, she has less to lose by an improvement in the conditions of labor and wages in Europe or Asia than she has to gain. If such a central legislative body, therefore, should gain even the power to standardize labor conditions, it must standardize them upward to avoid revolution, and this result, desirable in itself does not diminish but rather increases the power of the United States to develop international commerce, etc., and makes plain our relatively higher standards

8. For the operation of international parties as a check upon nationalism, there is requisite a Legislative body in the League, with limited but real powers. The evils of combining class struggles with national feeling would be apparent in a mere judicial or ex-

ecutive tribunal with international coercion as its sanction. The League should take to itself a field of legislation.

At first this might be merely certain fiscal subjects, funds for supporting the League activities. Its action might be required precedent to the use of force either by a component state, or by the League as a sanction to its decisions. The kind of economic pressure to be placed upon a delinquent state might be there determine[d]. Principles to apply to the internationally controlled areas might be determined. International tariff legislation might be assigned to it. Legislation upon labor questions as advocated by some of the international labor congresses might even be finally confided to such an organization. Possibly at first its power in such matters might be recommendatory, the formulation of bills or policies to be urged upon national legislatures.

There is an abundant field from which to select. The choice should be made with two ideas prominent: first that progress should be made carefully, without hazarding the system by too sudden a construction, liable to fail by its newness and radical nature; and second that unless some real powers are conferred upon such a legislature, it will fail to call out international parties to affect its action, these parties will be under the domination of special states where their influence will be greatest, and the unifying influence of non-national party organization will not be secured.

I have no doubt that all things considered the international party would tend toward unity in such a league as the intersectional parties did in the United States. But the price to be paid in the loss of national control over important interests of its own, and the danger to the orderly states may be too great. It must also be admitted that the differences between section and nation are many and deep, and that there are some points in which international jealsousy [jealousy] and controversy might be promoted rather than restrained by internationally organized parties operating on a legislature. It might conceivably be used by ultra-conservative majority to restrain reforms in a particular nation. But similar difficulties will exist in the charges of special combinations within a League equipped only with judicial tribunals or consultative congresses, or with administrative organizations. There will be sectional jealousy and suspicion in any League, with whatever form of political organization. It is inherent in its nature. The problem is the introduction of checks and antidotes to this tendency.

T MS (WP, DLC).

To Robert Lansing, with Enclosure

My dear Mr. Secretary,   The White House. 1 December, 1918.

Hurley is quite right in what he says and advises in this message. I am sorry to say that I did not see what was involved with regard to our shipping in the plan House sent us about the food administration and which we approved. Will you not be kind enough to have a message sent to Hurley this evening (so that he may receive it early to-morrow morning) expressing my agreement with him in this particular and asking him to confer with and explain to Mr. House, saying that this was an aspect of the arrangement which I had not taken in?[1]   Faithfully Yours,   W.W.

WWTLI (SDR, RG 59, 763.72119/10067, DNA).
[1] "For Hurley Very Urgent Your No. 2. President agrees with your position and asks that you confer immediately with Colonel House explaining to him that the aspect stated in your telegram was one which the President had not taken into account in assenting to House's suggested communication to Supreme War Council. For Ambassador. Please advise Colonel House of foregoing as soon as possible." RL to E. N. Hurley, Dec. 1, 1918, Hw telegram (SDR, RG, 59, 763.72119/10067, DNA).

E N C L O S U R E

Paris, Nov. 28, 1918

Hurley #2. Very urgent. Secret for the President.

Pending recovery, House who is improving but not yet able to give personal attention to Allied plans for World's food control, feels I should inform you directly that shipping features in plans for Inter-Allied Director General of Relief, cabled yesterday, were not submitted to me and have not received my approval period. My belief is that minor modifications British plans conflicts with your general policy and should be held in abeyance until you have opportunity to outline your program for League of Nations period. Feeling in London is that this emergency plan for food control which is similar to British plan for removing chief incentives for League of Nations period. British are willing to give us title of Directorship but American Director would be under control and report to Inter-Allied War Council period. In line with your instructions I have informed Reading that we cannot enter into agreement to yield control of my ships period. Procedure outlined in cable signed House yesterday amounts to surrender control our ships to foreign bodies to which I believe you are properly and unalterably opposed period. Further, the plans would permit available funds of ships carrying our foodstuffs to be wasted through inefficient Italian and French control and management period. We are rendering as much service in this manner as we have controlled ships for lifting cargoes required to be furnished by us period. We should have unequivocally the temporary use of all enemy passenger steamers for the return of our troops, also cargo ships in enemy ports to lift all relief supplies controlled by us, but plans outlined to you yesterday would divide this tonnage without slightest hope of supplement from British tonnage for this imperative movement of troops period.

Believe present situation which British would like to cure with Committee and Director is complete justification of League of Nations in that it amounts to the disregarding of small nation's rights and yet concedes concerted action is necessary period. For any Director General of Relief to control our shipping under European domination as proposed would tie our hands and would be first step to similar control raw materials period. Matters can certainly wait until you arrive as in any ships in enemy ports will require shipments for repairs and commissioning period. In conference with French and British I will make no concessions without instructions from you.   Hurley

T telegram (SDR, RG 59, 763.72119/10067, DNA).

Two Telegrams from Edward Mandell House

Paris, December 1, 1918.

213. priority A. For the President. Your number 90, November 29, 3 p.m.,[1] which refers to my number 188. After my number 188 had been despatched, it was found that mistake had been made in respect to proposed disposition of enemy passenger ships. Accordingly, Hoover and I, after learning of Hurley's cable to you, had conference with Hurley and explained that feature of food relief plan dividing passenger tonnage with Great Britain was error. This feature has now been eliminated from plan. We feel as he does that enemy passenger tonnage should be available for return of American troops. Hurley asks me to say to you that: "Assuming now that you desire early action without awaiting for announcement of League of Nations program he gives his approval to plan, the error having been corrected." Pursuant to the authorization contained in your number 90, I shall propose the plan, but instead of directing this communication to the Supreme War Council, I shall embody it in a formal communication to Mr. Balfour,[2] Monsieur Pichon and Baron Sonnino requesting them to bring it to the attention of their respective Governments. I believe that in this way rather than by

presentation to the Prime Ministers collectively at their meeting in London, favorable action can be secured.   Edward House.

T telegram (WP, DLC).
¹ That is, RL to EMH, Nov. 29, 1918, quoted in EMH to WW, Nov. 27, 1918 (second telegram of that date), n. 2.
² EMH to A. J. Balfour, Dec. 1, 1918, CCL (WP, DLC).

Paris, December 1, 1918.

214, priority A. For the President from Hoover. "In order to give a working capital to the relief, we consider it will *not* [now] be necessary to set up some agreement of Treasury participation and possibly request Congressional appropriation. In the meantime, that we may proceed in urgent matters, I am anxious to know if you could appropriate to this purpose five million dollars from your Presidential fund. I could later supplement this by dividends to you from Sugar Equalization Board and might avoid appropriations and consequent discussions altogether. Would it be possible to settle this before your departure. Hoover."

Please transmit paraphrase to Food Administration for attention Rickard with the following message: "I have sent foregoing message to the President. Would you follow it up? Hoover."

Edward House.

T telegram (SDR, RG 59, 840.48/2605, DNA).

From Thomas Joseph Mooney

San Francisco, Dec. 1, 1918

I have just read your two communications of March and June nineteen eighteen to Governor Stephens asking him to commute my sentence.¹ This gives me greater pain and grief than if I knew certain death awaited me. Did you not exhort the whole country only a few months ago to fight to the death in the world war against wrong, injustice, and autocracy and to make the world safe for democracy and justice. I have never asked any one to exert any effort in my behalf unless they were positive an injustice was done, and then not to extend me mercy, but plain and simple justice. In light of recent disclosures by J. B. Densmore, Director General of Employment to Honorable William Wilson, Secretary of Labor establishing beyond all doubt that a conspiracy is now and has from the beginning of these cases been going on to rob me of my lawful rights without due process of law as guaranteed every citizen by the constitution of the United States, I ask you in all fairness to your high duty, to myself and in the interest of justice before you leave for the Peace Conference to state exactly what you meant by commutation of my death sentence. I do this because of a desire not to unjustly criticise any one, but if you feel that justice is done me in this case by commuting my death sentence to that of life imprisonment there is no other alternative left me and my defense but to continue our efforts against commutation and injustice and for real democracy and justice.

Very respectfully,

Tom Mooney,   San Quentin Prison, California.

T telegram (WP, DLC)
  [1] WW to W. D. Stephens, March 27, 1918, Vol. 47, and WW to W. D. Stephens, June 4, 1918, Vol. 48. Governor Stephens had commuted Mooney's sentence to life imprisonment on November 28.

From William Cardinal O'Connell

Dear President Wilson,   [Boston] Dec. 1, 1918.

May I wish you God-speed on your sublime and sacred mission.

Every day until you come back to us, my poor prayers and the prayers of millions of faithful hearts, will follow you; that the cause of justice to all, the cause of the persecuted and down-trodden of every land, may find in you their heaven-sent advocate and protector. We know that God will keep you safe, and return you well and strong and triumphant to America, our own land, which by your wise and calm counsel and guidance has become more than ever a beacon to all the earth.

I am, my dear President

Your Devoted Servant   W. Card. O'Connell.

ALS (WP, DLC).

An Annual Message on the State of the Union

Speaking Copy 2 Dec., 1918[1]

Gentlemen of the Congress: The year that has elapsed since I last stood before you to fulfil my constitutional duty to give to the Congress from time to time information on the state of the Union has been so crowded with great events, great processes, and great results that I cannot hope to give you an adequate picture of its transactions or of the far-reaching changes which have been wrought in the life of our nation and of the world. You have yourselves witnessed these things, as I have. It is too soon to assess them;

  [1] WWhw.

and we who stand in the midst of them and are part of them are less qualified than men of another generation will be to say what they mean, or even what they have been. But some great outstanding facts are unmistakable and constitute, in a sense, part of the public business with which it is our duty to deal. To state them is to set the stage for the legislative and executive action which must grow out of them and which we have yet to shape and determine.

A year ago we had sent 145,918 men overseas. Since then we have sent 1,950,513, an average of 162,542 each month, the number in fact rising, in May last to 245,951, in June to 278,760, in July to 307,182, and continuing to reach similar figures in August and September,—in August 289,570 and in September 257,438. No such movement of troops ever took place before, across three thousand miles of sea, followed by adequate equipment and supplies, and carried safely through extraordinary dangers of attack,— dangers which were alike strange and infinitely difficult to guard against. In all this movement only seven hundred and fifty-eight men[2] were lost by enemy attack,—six hundred and thirty of whom were upon a single English transport which was sunk near the Orkney Islands.[3]

I need not tell you what lay back of this great movement of men and material. It is not invidious to say that back of it lay a supporting organization of the industries of the country and of all its productive activities more complete, more thorough in method and effective in result, more spirited and unanimous in purpose and effort than any other great belligerent had been able to effect. We profited greatly by the experience of the nations which had already been engaged for nearly three years in the exigent and exacting business, their every resource and every executive proficiency taxed to the utmost. We were their pupils. But we learned quickly and acted with a promptness and a readiness of cooperation that justify our great pride that we were able to serve the world with unparalleled energy and quick accomplishment.

But it is not the physical scale and executive efficiency of preparation, supply, equipment, and despatch that I would dwell upon, but the mettle and quality of the officers and men we sent over and of the sailors who kept the seas, and the spirit of the nation

---

[2] Actually, the total losses at sea of both army and navy personnel numbered 768. See Leonard P. Ayres, *The War With Germany: A Statistical Summary* (Washington, 1919), p. 123. Of these losses, only 381 were battle deaths, that is, "the direct result of submarine activity."

[3] Wilson was also misinformed here. In only two cases were American troops lost on British vessels on the *eastbound* voyage. Approximately 166 died when S. S. *Tuscania* was torpedoed on February 5, 1918, and fifty-six when S.S. *Moldavia* was torpedoed on May 23, 1918. Neither ship was near the Orkneys.

that stood behind them. No soldiers or sailors ever proved themselves more quickly ready for the test of battle or acquitted themselves with more splendid courage and achievement when put to the test. Those of us who played some part in directing the great processes by which the war was pushed irresistably[4] forward to the final triumph may now forget all that and delight our thoughts with the story of what our men did. Their officers understood the grim and exacting task they had undertaken and performed it with an audacity, efficiency, and unhesitating courage that touch the story of convoy and battle with imperishable distinction at every turn, whether the enterprise were great or small,—from their great chiefs, Pershing and Sims, down to the youngest lieutenant; and their men were worthy of them,—such men as hardly need to be commanded, and go to their terrible adventure blithely and with the quick intelligence of those who know just what it is they would accomplish. I am proud to be the fellow-countryman of men of such stuff and valor. Those of us who stayed at home did our duty; the war could not have been won or the gallant men who fought it given their opportunity to win it otherwise; but for many a long day we shall think ourselves "accurs'd we were not there, and hold our manhoods cheap while any speaks that fought" with them at St. Mihiel or Thierry. The memory of those days of triumphant battle will go with these fortunate men to their graves; and each will have his favorite memory. "Old men forget; yet all shall be forgot, but he'll remember with advantages what feats he did that day!"

What we all thank God for with deepest gratitude is that our men went in force into the line of battle just at the critical moment when the whole fate of the world seemed to hang in the balance and threw their fresh strength into the ranks of freedom in time to turn the whole tide and sweep of the fateful struggle,—turn it once for all, so that thenceforth it was back, back, back for their enemies, always back, never again forward! After that it was only a scant four months before the commanders of the Central Empires knew themselves beaten; and now their very empires are in liquidation!

And throughout it all how fine the spirit of the nation was: what unity of purpose, what untiring zeal! What elevation of purpose ran through all its splendid display of strength, its untiring accomplishment. I have said that those of us who stayed at home to do the work of organization and supply will always wish that we had been with the men whom we sustained by our labour; but we can never be ashamed. It has been an inspiring thing to be here in the midst of fine men who had turned aside from every private interest of

[4] Wilson's spelling.

their own and devoted the whole of their trained capacity to the tasks that supplied the sinews of the whole great undertaking! The patriotism, the unselfishness, the thoroughgoing devotion and distinguished capacity that marked their toilsome labours, day after day, month after month, have made them fit mates and comrades of the men in the trenches and on the sea. And not the men here in Washington only. They have but directed the vast achievement. Throughout innumerable factories, upon innumerable farms, in the depths of coal mines and iron mines and copper mines, wherever the stuffs of industry were to be obtained and prepared, in the shipyards, on the railways, at the docks, on the sea, in every labour that was needed to sustain the battle lines, men have vied with each other to do their part and do it well. They can look any man-at-arms in the face, and say, We also strove to win and gave the best that was in us to make our fleets and armies sure of their triumph!

And what shall we say of the women,—of their instant intelligence, quickening every task that they touched; their capacity for organization and cooperation, which gave their action discipline and enhanced the effectiveness of everything they attempted; their aptitude at tasks to which they had never before set their hands; their utter self-sacrifice alike in what they did and in what they gave? Their contribution to the great result is beyond appraisal. They have added a new lustre to the annals of American womanhood.

The least tribute we can pay them is to make them the equals of men in political rights as they have proved themselves their equals in every field of practical work they have entered, whether for themselves or for their country. These great days of completed achievement would be sadly marred were we to omit that act of justice. Besides the immense practical services they have rendered, the women of the country have been the moving spirits in the systematic economies by which our people have voluntarily assisted to supply the suffering peoples of the world and the armies upon every front with food and everything else that we had that might serve the common cause. The details of such a story can never be fully written, but we carry them at our hearts and thank God that we can say that we are the kinsmen of such.

And now we are sure of the great triumph for which every sacrifice was made. It has come, come in its completeness, and with the pride and inspiration of these days of achievement quick within us we turn to the tasks of peace again,—a peace secure against the violence of irresponsible monarchs and ambitious military coteries and made ready for a new order, for new foundations of justice and fair dealing.

We are about to give order and organization to this peace not only for ourselves but for the other peoples of the world as well, so far as they will suffer us to serve them. It is international justice that we seek, not domestic safety merely. Our thoughts have dwelt of late upon Europe, upon Asia, upon the near and the far East, very little upon the acts of peace and accommodation that wait to be performed at our own doors. While we are adjusting our relations with the rest of the world is it not of capital importance that we should clear away all grounds of misunderstanding with our immediate neighbours and give proof of the friendship we really feel? I hope that the members of the Senate will permit me to speak once more of the unratified treaty of friendship and adjustment with the Republic of Colombia. I very earnestly urge upon them an early and favourable action upon that vital matter. I believe that they will feel, with me, that the stage of affairs is now set for such action as will be not only just but generous and in the spirit of the new age upon which we have so happily entered.

So far as our domestic affairs are concerned the problem of our return to peace is a problem of economic and industrial readjustment. That problem is less serious for us than it may turn out to be for the nations which have suffered the disarrangements and the losses of war longer than we. Our people, moreover, do not wait to be coached and led. They know their own business, are quick and resourceful at every readjustment, definite in purpose, and self-reliant in action. Any leading strings we might seek to put them in would speedily become hopelessly tangled because they would pay no attention to them and go their own way. All that we can do as their legislative and executive servants is to mediate the process of change here, there, and elsewhere as we may. I have heard much counsel as to the plans that should be formed and personally conducted to a happy consummation, but from no quarter have I seen any general scheme of "reconstruction" emerge which I thought it likely we could force our spirited business men and self-reliant labourers to accept with due pliancy and obedience.

While the war lasted we set up many agencies by which to direct the industries of the country in the services it was necessary for them to render, by which to make sure of an abundant supply of the materials needed, by which to check undertakings that could for the time be dispensed with and stimulate those that were most serviceable in war, by which to gain for the purchasing departments of the Government a certain control over the prices of essential articles and materials, by which to restrain trade with alien enemies, make the most of the available shipping, and systematize financial transactions, both public and private, so that there would be no unnecessary conflict or confusion,—by which, in short, to put every material energy of the country in harness to draw the common load and make of us one team in the accomplishment of a great task. But the moment we knew the armistice to have been signed we took the harness off. Raw materials upon which the Government had kept its hand for fear there should not be enough for the industries that supplied the armies have been released, and put into the general market again. Great industrial plants whose whole output and machinery had been taken over for the uses of the Government have been set free to return to the uses to which they were put before the war. It has not been possible to remove so readily or so quickly the control of foodstuffs and of shipping, because the world has still to be fed from our granaries and the ships are still needed to send supplies to our men oversea and to bring the men back as fast as the disturbed conditions on the other side of the water permit; but even there restraints are being relaxed as much as possible and more and more as the weeks go by.

Never before have there been agencies in existence in this country which knew so much of the field of supply, of labour, and of industry as the War Industries Board, the War Trade Board, the Labour Department, the Food Administration, and the Fuel Administration have known since their labours became thoroughly systematized; and they have not been isolated agencies; they have been directed by men which represented the permanent Departments of the Government and so have been the centres of unified and cooperative action. It has been the policy of the Executive, therefore, since the armistice was assured (which is in effect a complete submission of the enemy) to put the knowledge of these bodies at the disposal of the business men of the country and to offer their intelligent mediation at every point and in every matter where it was desired. It is surprising how fast the process of return to a peace footing has moved in the three weeks since the fighting stopped. It promises to outrun any inquiry that may be instituted and any aid that may be offered. It will not be easy to direct it any better than it will direct itself. The American business man is of quick initiative.

The ordinary and normal processes of private initiative will not, however, provide immediate employment for all of the men of our returning armies. Those who are of trained capacity, those who are skilled workmen, those who have acquired familiarity with established businesses, those who are ready and willing to go to the farms, all those whose aptitudes are known or will be sought out by employers will find no difficulty, it is safe to say, in finding place and employment. But there will be others who will be at a loss where to gain a livelihood unless pains are taken to guide them and put them in the way of work. There will be a large floating residuum of labor which should not be left wholly to shift for itself. It seems to me important, therefore, that the development of public works of every sort should be promptly resumed, in order that opportunities should be created for unskilled labor in particular, and that plans should be made for such developments of our unused lands and our natural resources as we have hitherto lacked stimulation to undertake.

I particularly direct your attention to the very practical plans which the Secretary of the Interior has developed in his annual report and before your Committees for the reclamation of arid, swamp, and cut-over lands which might, if the States were willing and able to cooperate, redeem some three hundred million acres of land for cultivation. There are said to be fifteen or twenty million acres of land in the West, at present arid, for whose reclamation water is available, if properly conserved. There are about two hundred and thirty million acres from which the forests have been cut but which have never yet been cleared for the plow and which lie waste and desolate. These lie scattered all over the Union. And there are nearly eighty million acres of land that lie under swamps or subject to periodical overflow or too wet for anything but grazing which it is perfectly feasible to drain and protect and redeem. The Congress can at once direct thousands of the returning soldiers to the reclamation of the arid lands which it has already undertaken, if it will but enlarge the plans and the appropriations which it has entrusted to the Department of the Interior. It is possible in dealing with our unused land to effect a great rural and agricultural development which will afford the best sort of opportunity to men who want to help themselves; and the Secretary of the Interior has thought the possible methods out in a way which is worthy of your most friendly attention.

I have spoken of the control which must yet for a while, perhaps for a long while, be exercised over shipping because of the priority of service to which our forces overseas are entitled and which should also be accorded the shipments which are to save recently liberated peoples from starvation and many devas[ta]ted regions from permanent ruin. May I not say a special word about the needs of Belgium and northern France? No sums of money paid by way of indemnity will serve of themselves to save them from hopeless disadvantage for years to come. Something more must be done than merely find the money. If they had money and raw materials in abundance to-morrow they could not resume their place in the industry of the world to-morrow,—the very important place they held before the flame of war swept across them. Many of their factories are razed to the ground. Much of their machinery is destroyed or has been taken away. Their people are scattered and many of their best workmen are dead. Their markets will be taken by others, if they are not in some special way assisted to rebuild their factories and replace their lost instruments of manufacture. They should not be left to the vicissitudes of the sharp competition for materials and for industrial facilities which is now to set in. I hope, therefore, that the Congress will not be unwilling, if it should become necessary, to grant to some such agency as the War Trade Board the right to establish priorities of export and supply for the benefit of these people whom we have been so happy to assist in saving from the German terror and whom we must not now thoughtlessly leave to shift for themselves in a pitiless competitive market.

For the steadying and facilitation of our own domestic business readjustments nothing is more important than the immediate determination of the taxes that are to be levied for 1918, 1919, and 1920. As much of the burden of taxation must be lifted from business as sound methods of financing the Government will permit, and those who conduct the great essential industries of the country must be told as exactly as possible what obligations to the Government they will be expected to meet in the years immediately ahead of them. It will be of serious consequence to the country to delay removing all uncertainties in this matter a single day longer than the right processes of debate justify. It is idle to talk of successful and confident business reconstruction before those uncertainties are resolved.

If the war had continued it would have been necessary to raise at least eight billion dollars by taxation payable in the year 1919; but the war has ended and I agree with the Secretary of the Treasury that it will be safe to reduce the amount to six billions. An immediate rapid decline in the expenses of the Government is not to be looked for. Contracts made for war supplies will, indeed, be rapidly cancelled and liquidated, but their immediate liquidation will make heavy drains on the Treasury for the months just ahead of us. The maintenance of our forces on the other side of the sea is still necessary. A considerable proportion of those forces must remain in

Europe during the period of occupation, and those which are brought home will be transported and demobilized at heavy expense for months to come. The interest on our war debt must of course be paid and provision made for the retirement of the obligations of the Government which represent it. But these demands will of course fall much below what a continuation of military operations would have entailed and six billions should suffice to supply a sound foundation for the financial operations of the year.

I entirely concur with the Secretary of the Treasury in recommending that the two billions needed in addition to the four billions provided by existing law be obtained from the profits which have accrued and shall accrue from war contracts and distinctively war business, but that these taxes be confined to the war profits accruing in 1918, or in 1919 from business originating in war contracts. I urge your acceptance of his recommendation that provision be made now, not subsequently, that the taxes to be paid in 1920 should be reduced from six to four billions. Any arrangements less definite than these would add elements of doubt and confusion to the critical period of industrial readjustment through which the country must now immediately pass and which no true friend of the nation's essential business interests can afford to be responsible for creating or prolonging. Clearly determined conditions, clearly and simply charted, are indispensable to the economic revival and rapid industrial development which may confidently be expected if we act now and sweep all interrogation points away.

I take it for granted that the Congress will carry out the naval programme which was undertaken before we entered the war. The Secretary of the Navy has submitted to your Committees for authorization that part of the programme which covers the building plans of the next three years. These plans have been prepared along the lines and in accordance with the policy which the Congress established, not under the exceptional conditions of the war, but with the intention of adhering to a definite method of development for the navy. I earnestly recommend the uninterrupted pursuit of that policy. It would clearly be unwise for us to attempt to adjust our programmes to a future world policy as yet undetermined.

The question which causes me the greatest concern is the question of the policy to be adopted towards the railroads. I frankly turn to you for counsel upon it. I have no confident judgment of my own. I do not see how any though[t]ful man can have who knows anything of the complexity of the problem. It is a problem which must be studied, studied immediately, and studied without bias or prejudice. Nothing can be gained by becoming partisans of any particular plan of settlement.

It was necessary that the administration of the railways should be taken over by the Government so long as the war lasted. It would have been impossible otherwise to establish and carry through under a single direction the necessary priorities of shipment. It would have been impossible otherwise to combine maximum production at the factories and mines and farms with the maximum possible car supply to take the products to the ports and markets; impossible to route troop shipments and freight shipments without regard to the advantage or disadvantage of the roads employed; impossible to subordinate, when necessary, all questions of convenience to the public necessity; impossible to give the necessary financial support to the roads from the public treasury. But all these necessities have now been served, and the question is, What is best for the railroads and for the public in the future.

Exceptional circumstances and exceptional methods of administration were not needed to convince us that the railroads were not equal to the immense tasks of transportation imposed upon them by the rapid and continuous development of the industries of the country. We knew that already. And we knew that they were unequal to it partly because their full cooperation was rendered impossible by law and their competition made obligatory; so that it has been impossible to assign to them severally the traffic which could best be carried by their respective lines in the interest of expedition and national economy.

We may hope, I believe, for the formal conclusion of the war by treaty by the time Spring has come. The twenty-one months to which the present control of the railways is limited after formal proclamation of peace shall have been made will run at the farthest, I take it for granted, only to the January of 1921. The full equipment of the railways which the federal administration had planned could not, of course, be completed within any such period. The present law does not permit the use of the revenues of the several roads for the execution of such plans except by formal contract with their directors, some of whom will consent while some will not, and therefore does not afford sufficient authority to undertake improvements upon the scale upon which it would be necessary to undertake them. Every approach to this difficult subject-matter of decision brings us face to face, therefore, with this unanswered question: What is it right that we should do with the railroads, in the interest of the public and in fairness to their owners?

Let me say at once that I have no answer ready. The only thing that is perfectly clear to me is that it is not fair either to the public or to the owners of the railroads to leave the question unanswered and that it will presently become my duty to relinquish control of the roads, even before the expiration of the statutory period, unless there should appear some clear prospect in the mean time of a legislative solution. Their release would at least produce one element of a solution, namely certainty and a quick stimulation of private initiative.

I believe that it will be serviceable for me to set forth as explicitly as possible the alternative courses that lie open to our choice. We can simply release the roads and go back to the old conditions of private management, unrestricted competition, and multiform regulation by both state and federal authorities; or we can go to the opposite extreme and establish complete government control, accompanied, if necessary, by actual government ownership; or we can adopt an intermediate course of modified private control, under a more unified and affirmative public regulation and under such alterations of the law as will permit wasteful competition to be avoided and a considerable degree of unification of administration to be effected, as, for example, by regional corporations under which the railways of definable areas would be in effect combined in single systems.

The one conclusion that I am ready to state with confidence is that it would be a disservice alike to the country and to the owners of the railroads to return to the old conditions unmodified. Those are conditions of restraint without development. There is nothing affirmative or helpful about them. What the country chiefly needs is that all its means of transportation should be developed, its railways, its waterways, its highways, and its countryside roads. Some new element of policy, therefore, is absolutely necessary,—necessary for the service of the public, necessary for the release of credit to those who are administering the railways, necessary for the protection of their security holders. The old policy may be changed much or little, but surely it cannot wisely be left as it was. I hope that the Congress will have a complete and impartial study of the whole problem instituted at once and prosecuted as rapidly as possible. I stand ready and anxious to release the roads from the present control and I must do so at a very early date if by waiting until the statutory limit of time is reached I shall be merely prolonging the period of doubt and uncertainty which is hurtful to every interest concerned.

I welcome this occasion to announce to the Congress my purpose to join in Paris the representatives of the governments with which we have been associated in the war against the Central Empires for the purpose of discussing with them the main features of the treaty of peace. I realize the great inconveniences that will attend my leaving the country, particularly at this time, but the conclusion that it was my paramount duty to go has been forced upon me by considerations which I hope will seem as conclusive to you as they have seemed to me.

The allied governments have accepted the bases of peace which I outlined to the Congress on the eighth of January last, as the Central Empires also have, and very reasonably desire my personal counsel in their interpretation and application; and it is highly desirable that I should give it in order that the sincere desire of our Government to contribute without selfish purpose of any kind to settlements that will be of common benefit to all the nations concerned may be made fully manifest. The peace settlements which are now to be agreed upon are of transcendent importance both to us and to the rest of the world, and I know of no business or interest which should take precedence of them. The gallant men of our armed forces on land and sea have consciously fought for the ideals which they knew to be the ideals of their country; I have sought to express those ideals; they have accepted my statements of them as the substance of their own thought and purpose, as the associated governments have accepted them; I owe it to them to see to it, so far is [as] in me lies, that no false or mistaken interpretation is put upon them, and no possible effort omitted to realize them. It is now my duty to play my full part in making good what they offered their life's blood to obtain. I can think of no call to service which could transcend this.

I shall be in close touch with you and with affairs on this side the water, and you will know all that I do. At my request the French and English governments have absolutely removed the censorship of cable news which until within a fortnight they had maintained, and there is now no censorship whatever exercised at this end except upon attempted trade communications with enemy countries. It has been necessary to keep an open wire constantly available between Paris and the Department of State and another between France and the Department of War. In order that this might be done with the least possible interference with the other uses of the cables, I have temporarily taken over the control of both cables, in order that they may be used as a single system. I did so at the advice of the most experienced cable officials, and I hope that the results will justify my hope that the news of the next few months may pass with the utmost freedom and with the least possible delay from each side of the sea to the other.

May I not hope, Gentlemen of the Congress, that in the delicate tasks I shall have to perform on the other side of the sea, in my efforts truly and faithfully to interpret the principles and purposes of the country we love, I may have the encouragement and the added strength of your united support? I realize the magnitude and difficulty of the duty I am undertaking; I am poignantly aware of its grave responsibilities. I am the servant of the nation. I can have no private thought or purpose of my own in performing such an errand. I go to give the best that is in me to the common settlements which I must now assist in arriving at in conference with the other working heads of the associated governments. I shall count upon your friendly countenance and encouragement. I shall not be inaccessible. The cables and the wireless will render me available for any counsel or service you may desire of me, and I shall be happy in the thought that I am constantly in touch with the weighty matters of domestic policy with which we shall have to deal. I shall make my absence as brief as possible and shall hope to return with the happy assurance that it has been possible to translate into action the great ideals for which America has striven.

Printed reading copy (WP, DLC).

To Antonio Rafael Barceló

[The White House] 2 December, 1918.

Your message sent in the name and on behalf of the Senate of Porto Rico has given me deep pleasure. It is delightful to feel closely associated with the people of Porto Rico in rejoicing over the happy advent of peace and the victory of the armies of freedom over the armies of tyranny. May I not beg that you will extend to the Senate of Porto Rico my most cordial greetings and my congratulations upon the happy associations which have now been so fully established between the islands and the continent of America.

Woodrow Wilson

T telegram (Letterpress Books, WP, DLC).

To Samuel Gompers

[The White House] 2 December, 1918.

Just a line to say that I see no objection to your issuing the invitation referred to in your message,[1] and I know that your personal presence in Paris will be of real service.

Woodrow Wilson

T telegram (Letterpress Books, WP, DLC).
[1] S. Gompers to WW, Nov. 30, 1918.

To Robert Ewing

My dear Friend: [The White House] 2 December, 1918.

You know Senator Gay very well, I believe, and I know that you know the national conditions very well, and I am taking the liberty of writing this to ask if you would not be willing to exert what friendly influence you can upon Senator Gay to induce him to vote for the suffrage amendment. I have this very much at heart, and would be delighted if you could help.

With the best wishes,

Cordially and sincerely yours, Woodrow Wilson

TLS (Letterpress Books, WP, DLC).

To Norman Hapgood

My dear Hapgood: [The White House] 2 December, 1918.

It is always with misgivings that I differ with you upon any matter, but after discussing the cases referred to by you as those of political prisoners again and again with the Attorney General, and after minute inquiries, I must say that I do not think the men you refer to are in any proper sense political prisoners. They have in fact violated criminal statutes of the United States, and while the Attorney General and I are agreed that each case must be taken upon its individual merits and every effort made to hold an even hand of fair treatment, I do not think, and he does not think, that there is any justification for a general "amnesty."

I beg that you will believe that there is a great deal of misrepresentation abroad as to the facts in cases of this sort and as to the temper of the Department of Justice in prosecuting them.

Cordially and faithfully yours, Woodrow Wilson

TLS (Letterpress Books, WP, DLC).

To Newton Diehl Baker

My dear Baker: The White House 2 December, 1918.

I have just read with the greatest interest your letter of November 30th reporting the conclusions of the Council of National Defense in its meeting of that day. I hope that I have done something like what you suggested in my message which I am to deliver today, but I wish that I had gotten the suggestions it contains a little sooner, because I could have done it so much better.

Cordially and sincerely yours, Woodrow Wilson

TLS (N. D. Baker Papers, DLC).

To John Humphrey Small

My dear Mr. Chairman: [The White House] 2 December, 1918.

Presuming, as I do, that the annual River and Harbor Bill will be reported and considered in the present session of Congress, I take the liberty of writing you just a line about it. I hope that you will not think that I am taking an unwarranted privilege in suggesting a line of policy.

Every national circumstance has combined, since we entered the war, to emphasize what was before that very clear in the thoughts of men who were studious of the subject; namely, that the water transportation system of the country should be developed and promoted in every legitimate way and coordinated, wherever possible, with the railroads and other instrumentalities of traffic. The River and Harbor Bill, therefore, scientifically treated and developed, has become of more direct importance to the country than ever before.

May I suggest, therefore, that wherever projects have been completed, they should be by all means adequately maintained, and that improvements which have hitherto been authorized but not completed should be finished? I assume, of course, that appropriations made for maintenance and further improvements will not in any case be in excess of the sums recommended by the Secretary of War and the Chief of Engineers, the War Department through the Corps of Engineers being the agency which has been authorized by Congress to submit estimates. May I suggest also that if new projects are adopted, they should be scrutinized very carefully indeed, in order to make sure that they are in the public interest? Appropriations for the improvements of harbors and rivers can only be justified upon the ground that they promote commerce. If there is not a reasonable certainty that the channels improved will be used when provided, the expenditures of the public moneys cannot be justified.

Local interests, it seems to me, should provide water terminals and the means of interchange of water traffic with connecting lines of railroad, and I take it for granted that we shall have to depend upon private enterprise to provide river boats of a suitable type and size.

While the nation rightly demands economy, particularly at this time, in the expenditures of the Government, I think that it will justify adequate provisions for the improvements of rivers and harbors along the lines I have ventured to suggest.

Cordially and sincerely yours,   Woodrow Wilson

TLS (Letterpress Books, WP, DLC).

To Thomas Watt Gregory

[The White House]
My dear Mr. Attorney General: 2 December, 1918.

Here is an intemperate letter from Oswald Villard.[1] I would not pay any attention to it, except for the specific charges it makes about the treatment of prisoners at Leavenworth. Will you not be kind enough to see whether there is any truth in these charges or not? Cordially and sincerely yours, Woodrow Wilson

TLS (Letterpress Books, WP, DLC).
[1] It is missing in WP, DLC, and there is no copy in the O. G. Villard Papers, MH.

To Bainbridge Colby

My dear Colby: [The White House] 2 December, 1918.

Thank you for your letter of the 30th telling me the stage the business with the International Mercantile Marine has reached and the processes that it is going through? I am entirely satisfied.
Cordially and sincerely yours, Woodrow Wilson

TLS (Letterpress Books, WP, DLC).

To Albert Sidney Burleson

The White House
My dear Mr. Burleson: December 2, 1918.

With reference to the Postal Censorship authorized by sub-Section (d) of Sections 3 of the Trading With the Enemy Act and Sections XIV, XV and XVI of the Executive Order of October 12, 1917, it is suggested that such Postal Censorship be discontinued on the 17th of December 1918, the date of the expiration of the existing term of the armistice.

Please inform the Censorship Board accordingly.
Faithfully yours, Woodrow Wilson.

TCL (Letterpress Books, WP, DLC).

From Prince Georgii Evgen'evich L'vov

My dear Mr. President [Washington] December 2, 18.

I cannot see you again[1] before your departure. I deem it my duty to my country to write you on two questions of paramount importance.

I. I will not describe to you the terrors that confront the Russian prisoners of war after all their sufferings during their detention. You know it well. The conscience of the victors cannot permit it. For the sake of humanity, the defense of Russian prisoners of war should be your first consideration as you are the quardian [guardian] of international morals. It is necessary to render immediate help.

II. You told me that your mind and heart are open on the question of ways in which the Russian people will take part in the Peace Conference. According to the last news General Alexieff[2] is alive. He has the first right to defend the interests of Russia. His name is respected by the majority of the Russian people and he will speak on behalf of the four millions of Russian soldiers who perished in the war for the common cause of the Allies.

I pray that you excuse me for addressing you in writing for the second time.[3] May God speed you.

Yours truly   Prince G. Lvoff

TLS (WP, DLC).
    [1] About L'vov's visit to the White House on November 21, 1918, see R. Crane to WW, Nov. 30, 1918, n. 1.
    [2] That is, Gen. Mikhail Vasil'evich Alekseev, who had, in fact, died of natural causes on October 8, 1918.
    [3] L'vov's earlier letter is missing in WP, DLC.

From Edward Mandell House

Paris. December 2, 1918.

Number 221. Secret for the President. Referring to my telegram number 120 of November 18th and your reply number 50 of November 19th.

I at once took the matter up with the French and British Governments and found that they were in favor of the despatch of American troops to Italy. I thereupon requested General Pershing after conferring with Marshal Foch to inform me whether he approved of despatching American troops for service in Italy. He replied that as far as the military situation was concerned he was opposed to taking this step, but he thought that the troops already in Italy might be used for occupying the disputed territory. He accordingly telegraphed to General Treat[1] to notify him of the disposition which had been made of the American soldiers in Italy. General Treat replied that one battalion was at Cattaro, one at Fiume, and one at Treviso. General Pershing is now in receipt of the following telegram under date of November 28th from the War Department: "Confidential. The use of American troops with the Italian army is a very difficult and complicated matter and the

Secretary of War is of the opinion that our troops there should be withdrawn to your command. Please take this matter up with Marshal Foch and arrange to have American units returned to you. March. Harris."[2] In view of the above telegram General Pershing recommended General Treat to assemble the American troops at an Italian port with a view of returning them to United States direct. Notwithstanding the desire of the War Department to withdraw all American forces from Italy, in view of your one six [105] of November 30th I am still of the opinion that they should be retained there for some little time longer both for the purpose indicated in my telegram above mentioned and also because their withdrawal at this particular time might create an unfortunate impression in Italy. The numbers involved are very small and the Italian Government has made few demands upon the American Expeditionary Force. I suggest that any step which may be taken in this connection be made through the Secretary of War.

Edward House.

T telegram (WP, DLC).
   [1] Maj. Gen. Charles Gould Treat, chief of the American Military Mission to Italy and commander of the A.E.F. in Italy.
   [2] That is, Maj. Gen. Peter Charles Harris, the Adjutant General.

From Robert Lansing, with Enclosure

My dear Mr. President: Washington December 2, 1918.

   The enclosed memorandum was given me by Mr. Polk who stated that the French Ambassador considers it of the greatest importance. I think, myself, that I should get word to him at the earliest possible moment as to your wishes. Will you, therefore, be good enough to telephone me tonight or tomorrow morning whether you approve the plan proposed so that I can advise him and he can telegraph his Government.   Faithfully yours,   Robert Lansing

TLS (WP, DLC).

ENCLOSURE

Frank Lyon Polk to Robert Lansing

My dear Mr. Secretary: [Washington] December 2, 1918.

   The French Ambassador called on me yesterday, Sunday, and said that he had just received a telegram from his Government stating that the Ministers of the French Government who proposed to meet the President are going to Alsace-Lorraine, and that they will arrive at Brest on the 12th. If agreeable to the President, it would be a convenience to the French authorities if the President's ship could arrive at Brest on December 12th at 3:30 p.m. It is then planned to leave Brest at 4:30 the same day and arrive in Paris at 10:30 a.m. on the 13th.

The President of the French Republic and Madame Poincare are anxious for the President and Mrs. Wilson to lunch or dine with them on that day. Could you find out from the President whether these arrangements are satisfactory, and also whether he would lunch or dine on the 13th, so the Ambassador can notify his Government?

The Ambassador also said the French Government are very anxious to have Gompers go over as soon as possible, as they feel that his presence in France would be helpful in holding the French labor party in line. The Ambassador had heard that Gompers was going over shortly as a delegate to the Labor Conference, and it was suggested that he might be able to go over ahead.

FLP

TLI (WP, DLC).

From Frank Lyon Polk, with Enclosures

My dear Mr. President: Washington December 2, 1918.

The French Ambassador brought in on Saturday the enclosed letter and the attached study of the procedure of the Peace Conference. He was very anxious that this should reach you as soon as possible, in order to get your views.

I told him you would probably not have an opportunity to take this up until you were at sea, as you were so rushed, and if you desired to make any observations, they could be then sent to the French Government by wireless.

Yours faithfully,   Frank L. Polk

TLS (WP, DLC).

E N C L O S U R E   I

TRANSLATION

Mr. Secretary of State: Washington, November 29, 1918.

My Government has just informed me that, with a view to expediting the peace preliminaries, which any way can not be actually determined until after the arrival in Paris of the President of the United States, it had taken up a preliminary study of the various problems bearing upon that very important question.

In compliance with the instructions I have received, I have the honor to communicate herewith to Your Excellency a statement of the results of that examination. My Government would be glad to know whether the plan of studies suggested by it, and the principles upon which they rest, meet with the general approval of the American Government. It would be also very desirous of being informed of all the remarks which you might see fit to offer.

Be pleased to accept, etc.,   Jusserand.

E N C L O S U R E   I I

TRANSLATION

The French Government, upon examination of the precedents of the Congresses of Vienna 1814-1815, Paris 1856, and Berlin 1878, has taken up the various problems raised by the determination of the peace preliminaries and the establishment of the general peace treaty by the Congress which is to meet at Versailles.

The arrival of President Wilson in Paris in the middle of December will enable the four Great Powers to agree among themselves upon the conditions of the peace preliminaries to be imposed severally on the enemy without any discussion with him.

The examination will first apply to Germany and Bulgaria, with which it is to our interest to negotiate at once in order to promote on the one hand the disassociation of the countries which compose the first named; and on the other hand, as to the second country, avoid the dangerous Bulgarian intrigues at home and abroad.

The peace preliminaries with Germany will furthermore shape the way for the settlement of the main territorial restorations: Alsace Lorraine, Poland, the Slav countries, Belgium, Luxemburg, the cession of the German colonies, the full recognition of the protectorates of France over Morocco and of England over Egypt, the provisional acceptance of the Constitution of new independent states out of the territories of the former Russian and Austro-Hungarian Empires, as well as the conclusion of the treaties signed among the Allies with Bulgaria; and, about Turkey, the abrogation of the Brest Litovsk and Bucharest treaties, and of all the previous conventions with Russia and Roumania.

The speedy establishment of peace preliminaries with Germany raises the question of a future regime. Even now one may notice the antagonism of the Centralist tendency, which was that of the Hohenzollern Prussian Administration, the National Liberals and the Socialists, to the Federalist tendency (represented by the dynasty and administration of the secondary states and by the deputies to the Reichstag). We are interested in favoring Federalism and furnishing it with a basis by elections held under universal suffrage by promoting the manifestation of variances through the clauses of the treaty. Indeed, we can not negotiate except with a Constituent Assembly freely elected by universal, secret, and direct suffrage.

The peace preliminaries with Bulgaria will likewise define the main lines of the respective territorial status of the Bulgarian [Balkan?] countries.

The question of peace preliminaries with the other two enemy powers presents itself in a different aspect. With respect to Austria Hungary it is not even existent, since that Power has disappeared; it will then be within the province of Congress to admit *de plano* the two new states that have already been recognized: the Czecho-Slovaks and Poland, and to listen to the claims of the Jugo-Slav state now forming. As for the country of the Magyars (formerly Hungary stripped of the Slovaks, Roumanians of Transylvania, and Croatians), and Austria (German), the objections of (blank in the text) growing out of their interpretations suggest exclusion.

The same, of course, applies *a fortiori* to Turkey whose complete reorganization, accompanied by intervention in her internal regime, (which on principle is barred with respect to other states) is worthy of consideration. It seems preferable to leave to the Congress the discussion of the fate of those nationalities, for if peace preliminaries were signed with them, it would be tantamount to pledging ourselves at once to maintain the Ottoman Empire, that is to say, a rule which for a century has perpetrated its abuses, crimes, and causes of discussion among the great civilized states. Furthermore, where could the power authorized to ratify in the name of Turkey be found? Is it not better that the Allies should determine the fate of the territories lying within the former Ottoman Empire without the encumbrance of negotiations with that Empire?

After reaching an agreement as to the peace preliminaries, the representatives of the Great Powers will have to come to an agreement on the principles of the representation of the several belligerent, neutral, and enemy states at the Peace Congress. They will take up *seriatim* the cases of the actual and theoretical belligerents, the newly recognized states, and the states in formation, the former Allies who have concluded treaties with the enemy but whose treaties have not been recognized by us (Russia and Roumania), the neutrals and the enemies. Among the belligerents it will be proper to distinguish in respect of the number of plenipotentiaries and of admission to the sessions as between the small and the great powers. The great victorious powers alone will attend all its sessions, the small powers being called only to sessions designated for their special affairs. As for the neutrals and states in formation, they may be called when their own interests are at stake.

The number of plenipotentiaries will be limited to avoid congestion and confusion in the debates; the Great Powers may designate from three to five plenipotentiaries, the small powers from one to two, the neutral and forming states only one. As the decisions are to be taken by a majority vote, and as the representation of a state is but one unit, it is not necessary that any state should have as many representatives as a power of the same category, as provided by the precedents of the Congresses of the nineteenth century: each state may freely choose the number of its delegates within the limits above cited.

It seems that the labors of the Congress should be divided into two main series: the settlement of the war properly so-called, and the organization of the Society of Nations. The examination of the second question no doubt calls for the settlement of the first. Furthermore, the settlement of the concrete questions should not be confounded with the enforcement of the stipulation of general public law. Besides, that distinction is made necessary by the fact that the enemy has no right to discuss the terms that will be imposed upon him by the victors, and that the neutrals will only be called in exceptional cases to attend the sessions where the belligerents will fix the peace terms, while all the peoples, whether belligerents, neutrals or enemies, will be called to discuss and take part in the principle of the Society of Nations.

On the contrary those principles of President Woodrow Wilson's which are not sufficiently defined in their character to be taken as a basis for a concrete settlement of the war, even if appealed to as they have been admitted by the Allies, will resume their full strength in the matter of the future settlement of public law, and this will remove one of the difficulties that might obstruct the Allies.

The procedure of the Congress will also be determined at the preliminary meetings in the second half of December: Election of the President, appointment of the secretarial forces (charged with the duties of drawing the protocols, filing the archives, preparing daily communiqués, provide for the administrative organization of the Congress and the regular operation of the services) motions in writing read at the previous session discussed jointly (so as to bring about an agreement on the principle and afterwards work out the details) printing of the protocols, organization of a drafting committee, etc.

The program of the labors will then be determined, for in all the previous Congresses the stipulations of a treaty (the Paris treaty of May 30, 1814 at the Vienna Congress; the protocol signed at Vienna on February 1, 1854 at the Paris Congress; the treaty of San Stefano signed March 3, 1878 at the Berlin Congress), had served as a basis while the Congress of 1919 has no fixed basis before it: indeed neither the four armistices signed with Bulgaria, Austria-Hungary, Turkey and Germany, nor the answer of the Allies of January 10, 1917, jointly making known their war aims to President Wilson, nor the President's fourteen propositions which are principles of public law can furnish a concrete basis for the labors of the Congress.

That basis can only be a methodical statement of the questions to be taken up which may be classified as follows:

First—Settlement of the War

A. Political stipulations.
   1. New states: -a- already recognized (Bohemia)
      b. Being informed [formed] (Yugo-Slavia, Russian States, etc.)
   2. *Territorial questions*: restitution of territories.
      Neutralization for protection purposes.
         -a- Alsace-Lorraine (8th Wilson proposition)
         -b- Belgium (7th Wilson proposition)
         -c- Italy (9th Wilson proposition)
         -d- Boundary lines (France, Belgium, Serbia, Roumania etc.)
         -e- International regime of means of transportation, rivers, railways, canals, harbors.
   3. *Eastern questions*. (12th Wilson proposition)
   4. *Colonies*. (5th Wilson proposition)
   5. *Far East*.
B. Military and naval stipulations.
   Military guarantees on land and at sea. Number of effectives, dismantling of fortifications, reduction of war manufactures, territorial occupation.
C. Indemnities stipulations: Reparation for war damage on land and at sea, restitution, reconstruction, compensation in kind, reimbursement of expenses unlawfully imposed. "(C.R.B.)"[1]

---

[1] That is, the Commission for the Relief of Belgium.

D. Economic and financial stipulations: raw materials, economic systems, settlement of accounts.

E. Stipulations of private law: settlement of private debts, liquidation of sequestrated property.

F. Punishments to be inflicted on account of acts of violence and crimes committed during the war in violation of public law.

G. Stipulations of a moral character: Recognition by Germany of the responsibility and premeditation of her rulers justifying the measures of penalization and precaution taken against her. Solemn disavowal of the breaches of international law and of the crimes against humanity.

H. Restoration of the conventional regime broken by the war.

Second.—Organization of the Society of Nations.

A. Stipulations of general public law.

B. Guarantees and penalties.

C. Freedom of the seas (2nd Wilson proposition).

D. International economic regime (3rd Wilson proposition).

E. Publication of the treaties (1st Wilson proposition)

F. Limitation of armaments (4th Wilson proposition)

G. International arbitral organization of the Hague.

H. Society of Nations.

The program of labors being thus defined, there would be left only to make a logical distribution determining their order and the conditions under which *commissions* should study them as to territorial and political affairs and *committees* as to general international questions.

A. *Commissions*
1. Polish affairs.
2. Russian affairs.
3. Baltic nationalities.
4. States sprung from former Austria-Hungary.
5. Balkan affairs.
6. Eastern affairs.
7. Affairs of the Far East and the Pacific.

B. *Committees.*
1. Committee on Jewish affairs.
2. Committee on the international river navigation (Rhine, Danube, Scheldt, Elbe) practice of the society of nations.
3. Committee on international railways (railways of the 45th parallel from the Adriatic to the Baltic, Bagdad trans-African railways from Capetown to Cairo and from Capetown to Algiers.[)]
4. Committee on public law (free determination of the peoples

combined with the rights of the ethnical and religious minorities.[)]
5. Committee on international labor legislation. (A very important question, the initiative, management and settlement of which must not be left to the Socialists.[)]
6. Committee on law relative to patents and trade marks.
7. Committee on punishment for crimes committed during the war.

It may be remarked that a certain number of the questions that are raised have to be settled directly amongst the great powers without calling upon any committee to discuss them. This also applies to colonial affairs which essentially concern England and France. It also applies to indemnities, for outside of the torpedoing from which the British fleet mainly suffered, Belgium and France alone are entitled to indemnities on account of the systematic devastation suffered by them. (The states which have become independent and those which have secured considerable territorial enlargement would have but a slight claim to indemnities.) It also applies to economic and financial stipulations, the amount of which will be determined by the great powers but the mode of payment of which alone will be discussed by the peace treaty.

The Congress finally could place itself as has sometimes been done in the past under the invocation of some of the great principles leading to justice, morals and liberty, which would be proclaimed at its very opening and even before fixing the procedure (concerning which an unofficial agreement only would have been reached): right of self-determination of the peoples, right[s] of the minorities, suspension of all previous special agreements arrived at by some of the Allies only, with a view to the fullest freedom of the examination by the Congress; declaration that the metropolitan and colonial territory held by the Allies on August 1, 1914, shall not be touched; solemn repudiation of all the violations of international law and of humane principles and disqualification of enemy delegates who have signed violated instruments or are personally guilty of violations of the law of nations or of the crimes against humanity.

The foregoing sums up the plan of study and the principles suggested by the French Government.

T MSS (WP, DLC).

From Thomas James Walsh

Mr. President: Washington December 2, 1918.

I am sure you will not overlook the opportunity in the intimate conferences you are sure to have with the British statesmen to impress upon them the necessity of a speedy solution of the question of self-government for Ireland. We shall not escape the harsh judgment of posterity if we do not insist on the same measure of justice for the people of Ireland in the matter of their government that we have declared our purpose to exact, and are now in a position to exact, for the peoples heretofore held unwilling subjects of the Central Powers and the governments allied with them. The luster of our achievement in insisting successfully on the re-establishment of Poland, the return of Schleswig-Holstein, and the creation of the Slav republics will be measurably dimmed if we close our eyes to the equally commendable national aspirations of the Irish.

Those whom you will address on the subject may be more amenable to another line of argument. You are going abroad to labor to make war a remote possibility only, instead of a condition to be expected and sure to come. You know how earnestly I hope and pray that your mission may be successful, and that the League of Nations may be launched under the most favorable auspices. I must confess that the general approval given by the English press to Churchill's utterances that the naval supremacy of Great Britain must be preserved[1] has filled me with misgivings. I need not dwell on the possibility of differences with our English brethren, should that view prevail, and of the dangers that will inhere in the new order even under the League. A vast multitude of people in this country, not alone those of Irish descent, regard the continuance of English rule in Ireland as unjustifiable, and the exasperating course that has been pursued in relation to Home Rule as highly discreditable. England has precipitated the troubles that now confront her by her weak submission to the threats of an Ulster uprising against the very moderate measure of Home Rule that was conceded after an agitation of nearly half a century, indeed that has been conducted in one form or another since the Act of Union.

If the Peace Congress dissolves without a reasonably satisfactory settlement there will not be a controversy between this country and Great Britain, however trivial, that will not be fanned into what may some day be a consuming flame.

Sentimentally the Irish question is the only one that any longer remains as a barrier to the entire friendship of English-speaking peoples. You may, and I think should, be able to induce Lloyd-

George to reconsider his recent declaration that Ireland shall not be allowed to separate herself from the Empire and that Ulster will not be coerced.[2]

There is no answer to the suggestion that the principle of self-determination is as applicable to the case of Ireland as it is to Czecho-Slovakia or Poland. Within the territory which will be organized into new states, as a result of the war, there will, in each case, be found some people not of the dominant race. Doubtless in some instances a minority will find itself leagued with a hated race. Germans are not rare in Bohemia and Turks will doubtless abound in Armenia and Mesopotamia. Under whatever new form of government Ireland is to live, if anything new is to be tried, it ought to extend over the whole island. Historically the recalcitrants of Ulster have, as you are aware, little justification for the claim that the island should be partitioned in their interest.

Assuring you of my very high regard, I remain,

Faithfully yours,   T. J. Walsh

TLS (WP, DLC).
    [1] During a speech in Dundee on November 26, 1918, Winston S. Churchill, Minister of Munitions, had declared that, although he would do everything in his power to make a league of nations a "practical and powerful reality," the league would be no substitute for the supremacy of the British fleet. *New York Times*, Nov. 27, 1918.
    [2] In their pre-election address to the country, Lloyd George and Bonar Law, on November 21, 1918, had insisted that "all practical paths" toward a settlement of the Irish question had to be explored. "There are two paths, however," they had added, "which are closed, namely, one leading to the complete severance of Ireland from the Empire and the other the forcible subjection of the six Ulster counties to a Home Rule Parliament against their will." *New York Times*, Nov. 23, 1918.

From Newton Diehl Baker, with Enclosure

[Washington, Dec. 2, 1918]

For the President's information   Respectfully   Baker

ALS (WP, DLC).

ENCLOSURE

Versailles. December 2d.

Number 291. For the Secretary of War and the Chief of Staff.

I received yesterday your Number 110 stating that the President has appointed me one of the Peace Commissioners to represent the United States at the Peace Conference. Please convey to the President my deep appreciation of the honor which he has done me of the heavy responsibility which is imposed on me.   Bliss.

T telegram (WP, DLC).

From the Diary of Josephus Daniels

1918 Monday 2 December

Went with Addie to capital to hear address of President to Congress. Republicans had said they would give him an ice bath and they were sullen and quiet, not even applauding his reference to brave soldiers and sailors. It was the most unhandsome performance—churlish. Later the President referred to it & said he was interested in remarks made to him by the special committee. "Mann is a bitter partisan but he is a sport" he said. "He wished me a good voyage and success," but Lodge put emphasis upon his wish for a good voyage—nothing else. When I get out of this office, I will tell them what I think of them.

A Memorandum by Stockton Axson

December 2, 1918.

Mr. Davison and Mr. Axson met the President by appointment at 6:30 at the White House. After a word of congratulation from Mr. Davison to the President, Mr. Davison proceeded to the topic in hand. He said, "Knowing how valuable is your time, I wish to come at once to the point, which is this,—that the work of the War Council of the American Red Cross is drawing to a close, and we feel that it is time to take thought for the future. Only a strong word from you can direct this future. The War Council, which you appointed for a definite task, has accomplished that task now to its satisfaction." Here Mr. Davison smiled and said, "Perhaps I should not use just that expression."

The President said, "You have a right to a feeling of satisfaction, for you have performed a beautiful work."

Mr. Davison, after thanking the President, proceeded: "Probably by March 1st the War Council shall be able to withdraw. Mr. Axson tells me that you are satisfied that we shall postpone the annual meeting appointed for December 11th, until some time after your own return from Europe."

The President assented, saying: "I should think such a postponement desirable, as such a meeting should occur after you have formulated some designs for the future."

"Yes," said Mr. Davison, "that is just what we have come to talk about. It is our feeling that, when the War Council resigns, there should be some reorganization of the Executive Committee; that at its head there should be a strong executive officer who will give his whole time to Red Cross. Mr. Taft is at present the Chairman, and Mr. DeForest Vice-Chairman.[1] I would suggest, if it meets with your approval, that Mr. Taft and Mr. DeForest both be appointed Vice-Presidents, and that the Chairmanship be held by the Executive officer of whom I am speaking."

The President asked: "Are these appointments or elections?"

As no one present was quite clear on the point, the President said, "I hope it is by election," and smilingly added, "I should not like to reduce the rank of my honored predecessor."* * *[2]

This technical point was passed over and Mr. Davison proceeded to say: "It is our desire to have a very strong permanent organization. It is our hope that Mr. Axson will remain as permanent National Secretary of the organization, and we now have in mind for the executive head of the organization a certain man whose name I want to suggest to you. We have just thought of him within the past twenty-four hours, but we are all agreed that if the nomination meets with your approval, and if we can secure his services, he will be just the man for the place. I refer to Dr. George E. Vincent."[3]

The President nodded and smiled, and said, "He is certainly a human dynamo."

Mr. Davison said, "Would his nomination be acceptable to you?"

The President, turning to Mr. Axson, said, "I should think, don't you, that he would be an admirable man for the position?" And Mr. Axson assented.

Mr. Davison then said, "As I have intimated, we do not know whether we can get him. The matter has not been suggested to him at all. We did nothing until we could consult with you. Supposing we do not get him, and in view of your own absence from the country, would it be according to your pleasure that a committee of three, consisting of Secretary Lane, now a member of the Executive Committee, Mr. Cleveland Dodge, and Dr. Ireland,[4] be appointed to select an executive head.

The President asked: "You mean the new Surgeon General?"

"Yes," said Mr. Davison.

[1] That is, Robert Weeks De Forest, lawyer and philanthropist of New York, who was involved with numerous charitable organizations. He was, in fact, Vice-President of the American Red Cross and a member of its executive committee.

[2] The deleted paragraph reads as follows: "(I think there was some little confusion about the whole matter. Mr. De Forest appears as Vice-President of the general organization, Mr. Taft is Chairman of the Central Committee, of which Mr. Eliot Wadsworth is Vice-Chairman, and Mr. Taft is Chairman ex-officio of the Executive Committee, which in turn is elected by the Central Committee.) S.A."

[3] That is, George Edgar Vincent, former President of the University of Minnesota, at this time President of the Rockefeller Foundation.

[4] That is, Maj. Gen. Merritte Weber Ireland, who had been appointed Surgeon General of the United States Army on October 4, 1918.

The President smiled and said, "I consider that an eminently safe committee."

"Then," said Mr. Davison, "you would be willing to have this committee make the selection?"

"Entirely so," said the President.

"But," said the President, "is it impossible for you yourself, Mr. Davison, to be this executive officer?"

"Oh, yes, Mr. President, entirely impossible," said Mr. Davison.

"I feared that was so," said the President.

Mr. Davison said a few words in developing his idea that there should be a very strong permanent Red Cross.

The President then said: "I have been trying to visualize Red Cross internationally. I read Axson's letter,[5] and I liked the suggestion which it contained. But I have been wondering just how the American Red Cross can function under a strong world organization. I foresee that, with the conclusion of the work undertaken by the War Council, there will necessarily be a contraction of American Red Cross, and I do not want to see it contract. Probably there will be a tendency towards some jealousy in foreign nations if the American Red Cross is too obviously occupying the foreign fields. The question of adjustment between the strong American Red Cross, and the less strong Red Cross organizations of other countries, is a very important question. As Axson said in his letter, the present international committee consists of rather amiable gentlemen of Geneva. It seems to me that the entirely proper thing would be for you, Mr. Davison, to proceed to Geneva as quickly as possible and take counsel as to how the Red Cross organization[s] of the world can be brought together into a common understanding, and with something approximating a common standard under the not too obtrusive leadership of the American Red Cross. When, after you have looked over the field, it should be possible to call an international conference of Red Cross in which a program for the future could be worked out, a program which would be suggested by what the American Red Cross has already accomplished and which could be expanded throughout all the countries of the world—such a plan of action as this would react back upon the American people with something of the same sort of stimulation that they received from the work which they did for actual war. And I should think it would be better to postpone all questions of reorganization until some such program can be worked out. While it is very desirable to maintain the American Red Cross, it should be maintained for a

---

[5] S. Axson to WW, Nov. 27, 1918.

more or less definite object, and I should think this object could scarcely be defined until after negotiations, which I am now suggesting to you, at Geneva."

Mr. Davison said: "However, Mr. President, the difficulty about that is that it would take many months to bring about the conference and the program resulting from the conference, and, meanwhile, our great active American organization will have begun to disintegrate. That disintegration we are very anxious to avoid."

Mr. Axson then interpolated: "You see, Mr. President, we are not entirely dependent upon this fascinating international and worldwide program, in order to carry on an active American Red Cross. There is a great work to be done here at home through the extension to our civilian population in general of the idea of home service. As I told you in my letter, I have been very much impressed, during my residence in Texas, by the earnest, but by no means always intelligent, endeavors of people in some of the more remote communities, to organize and conduct public welfare work. Our Red Cross Chapters, Home Institutes, and Chapter courses in social service, form just the machinery and provide just the personnel for carrying on this welfare work everywhere."

"But," said the President, "there would not be enough of this to occupy the chapters in anything like the intensity of work with which they have been occupied during the course of the war."

"No," said Mr. Axson, "this would differ in different localities. I think I express the opinion of Mr. Davison as well as of myself, when I say that there is no expectation that National Headquarters will govern this kind of work in any arbitrary way. The government would indeed be a decentralized government, a government by localities, the energy and initiative proceeding from the locality, and National Headquarters acting as the directing agent."

The President nodded and Mr. Davison assented to the point.

"Then," said the President, "I am agreeable to the plan which you gentlemen suggest, and I repeat my suggestion that you, Mr. Davison, proceed to Geneva as quickly as possible."

"Of course, Mr. President, I cannot commit myself to that action until I have had opportunity to consult with my business associates in New York. But if I cannot go, we can certainly find someone who is competent for the task."

To this the President demurred, saying, in effect, that it was clear that the man who had been most responsible for and most conspicuous in the development of the American Red Cross, should be the man who should undertake the international task.

The President then said, "And if you will permit me, I, hoping that you are yourself going to Geneva, will prepare, in Paris, a letter in which I shall request you to take up this work at Geneva."

Said Mr. Davison, "Would you be so good as to give me, before you leave, just a note of three or four lines, stating your general request that I undertake this work?"

The President replied, "Certainly, I shall write that tomorrow."

This practically closed the interview, Mr. Davison rising to make a motion to go and expressing his sympathy for the obviously heavy cold under which the President was suffering, and begging him to take the best care of himself on his foreign voyage.

T MS (War Council File, DARC).

From the Diary of Henry Fountain Ashurst

December 2, 1918.

Vast crowds assembled in the corridors, attempting to secure admission to hear W.W. address the joint session. The disgruntled Senators trooped over to the House. When the President appeared the applause was meagre; his message was long, and surely he must have felt the chilliness of his reception. Two or three times his friends attempted to incubate an ovation for him but it was impossible. Talk of questioning him from the floor of the House evaporated when he appeared.

T MS (AzU).

From the Diary of Dr. Grayson[1]

Tuesday, December 3, 1918.

The trip to Europe began on Tuesday, December 3rd, when the President left Washington at midnight. A special train made the run to Hoboken without incident. Secretary Tumulty accompanied the President as far as Hoboken but returned immediately afterward to the White House in order to remain there, to represent the President, and to keep him advised at all times of the progress of home affairs.

T MS (received from James Gordon Grayson and Cary T. Grayson, Jr.).
    [1] This manuscript was typed from what was probably a handwritten version. Dr. Grayson, probably in 1920 or 1921, seems to have had the typed version prepared with a view to its publication. He edited the typed copy occasionally by adding retrospective and prospective comments and observations. These additions will not be included in the entries printed in this series. The Editors are grateful to James Gordon Grayson and Cary Travers Grayson, Jr., for permission to reproduce their father's diary. Readers should note that James Gordon Grayson and Cary Travers Grayson, Jr., retain ownership of the copyright of the Grayson Diary.

To Henry Pomeroy Davison

My dear Mr. Davison: The White House 3 December, 1918.

Pursuant to our conference of yesterday, I am writing to ask if you will not be kind enough to make arrangements, if possible, to come to France at an early date for the purpose of conferring with me and others there as to the international relations and cooperations of the Red Cross. I sincerely hope that you will give the most serious consideration to this and that you will arrange to come, if it is at all possible.

Cordially and sincerely yours,   Woodrow Wilson

TLS (War Council File, DARC).

To Thomas James Walsh

My dear Senator: [The White House] 3 December, 1918.

I appreciate the importance of a proper solution of the Irish question and thank you for the suggestions of your letter of yesterday. Until I get on the other side and find my footing in delicate matters of this sort I cannot forecast with any degree of confidence what influence I can exercise, but you may be sure that I shall keep this important interest in mind and shall use my influence at every opportunity to bring about a just and satisfactory solution.

I greatly value the expressions of your confidence and feel very much strengthened by them.

With the best wishes,

Cordially and sincerely yours,   Woodrow Wilson

TLS (Letterpress Books, WP, DLC).

To Richard Crane

My dear Mr. Crane: The White House 3 December, 1918.

Thank you for your kindness in sending me your father's letter to Prince Lvoff.[1] I am going to take it with me as one of the documents by which I hope to understand things.

Cordially and sincerely yours,   Woodrow Wilson

TLS (R. Crane Papers, DGU).
[1] The Enclosure printed with R. Crane to WW, Nov. 30, 1918.

To John Nevin Sayre

My dear Nevin: [The White House] 3 December, 1918.

Almost immediately after your visit yesterday, I went over in person to see the Secretary of War and found him much more sympathetic than I had expected, in view of the interviews you reported to me.[1] He has promised me to follow the matter up personally, has ordered a new and thorough investigation, and assures me that I can count at least upon this; that nothing barbarous or mediaeval will be permitted to continue in any form.[2]

In haste, With warm regard,

Faithfully yours,   Woodrow Wilson

P.S. I am returning the papers you left with me.

TLS (Letterpress Books, WP, DLC).
[1] Wilson had seen Sayre over lunch at the White House on December 2, 1918. Sayre had come to talk to Wilson on behalf of the Fellowship of Reconciliation, a group of Christian radicals and pacifists, about the mistreatment of conscientious objectors in the disciplinary barracks of army camps.
[2] As a result of Sayre's interview and Wilson's intervention, Baker, on December 6, 1918, announced that the War Department had ordered the abolition of the practice of tying military prisoners to the bars of cells and of all other methods of severe corporal punishment. In addition, on December 21, 1918, the War Department announced the dismissal from the army of two officers for "negligence in connection with unduly severe disciplinary measures against conscientious objectors" at Camp Funston, Kansas. See the *New York Times*, Dec. 7 and 22, 1918, and "Behind Prison Walls," *The World Tomorrow*, II (Jan. 1919), 20-21.

To Harry Augustus Garfield

My dear Garfield: The White House 3 December, 1918.

Of course I understand why you must be more often at Williams, and I accept the decision of your letter of December first[1] with great reluctance but with the clear consciousness that it is inevitable. You have done a splendid piece of work. My judgment and my approval have been with you constantly and I am sure that it will be more and more appreciated, now that your control is in some degree to be relaxed.

I entirely approve of the suggestion you make as to the continuance of the work until the first of April, and thank you sincerely for your thoughtful setting forth of the whole matter.

With cordial best wishes and the most affectionate good bye,

Sincerely yours,   Woodrow Wilson

TLS (H. A. Garfield Papers, DLC).
[1] Wilson was replying to H. A. Garfield to WW, Dec. 1, 1918, TLS (WP, DLC). Garfield had offered his resignation to take effect at Wilson's convenience.

To James Robert Mann

My dear Mr. Mann,   The White House 3 Dec., 1918.

May I not, just before leaving, say how much I appreciate and admire the patriotic and thoroughly fair and sportsmanlike position you have taken?[1]

Cordially and sincerely Yours,   Woodrow Wilson

ALS (J. R. Mann Scrapbook, DLC).
[1] During a debate in the Senate on December 3, Republican senators had sharply attacked Wilson for leaving the country to attend the peace conference. For example, Senator Sherman had introduced a resolution (S. Con. Res. 26) which called upon the Senate to declare that, during Wilson's absence, the office of President was vacant and that its powers and duties would have to be assumed by Vice-President Marshall. In addition, Senator Knox had submitted a resolution (S. Res. 361) for a declaration by the Senate to the effect that the purposes of the American government at the peace conference would be strictly confined to matters germane to the reasons which had caused the United States to enter the war; that all questions concerning the formation of a league of nations and changes in the laws of the sea would be postponed until after the peace conference; and that the President would be relieved of the extraordinary war powers which Congress had conferred upon him. In response to these attempts to tie Wilson's hands, Representative Mann, in his capacity as the Republican floor leader in the House, had issued the following statement:
"There will be no concerted effort on the part of the Republicans of the House to embarrass the President in any way while he is abroad. I am of the opinion that the American people would not be in sympathy with any attempt to pin-prick the President while he is abroad on so important a mission. Personally I am not at all in sympathy with any of the resolutions which have appeared in the Senate or House regarding the President's absence from Washington or his visit abroad.
"I cannot help what individuals may do in the House, but the Republican members of the House as a body will certainly make no concerted move to embarrass or hamper the President in any way while he is engaged abroad on a mission that affects so vitally the interests of the American people. I believe he should have the support of Congress in so far as those interests are involved and that factional strife ought not to be permitted to interfere with his mission, or to give the rest of the world the impression that the American people are divided on issues involving the peace of the world. . . .
"The President is engaged in a highly important mission. I am opposed to any attempt to throw rocks in his way. I do not think he should be hampered, but should be given the fullest opportunity to carry out his mission successfully." See *Cong. Record*, 65th Cong., 3d sess., pp. 23, 24-31, and the *New York Times*, Dec. 4, 1918.

To Joseph Patrick Tumulty

Dear Tumulty: The White House. 3 December, 1918.

Will you not be kind enough to give out the letters[1] that accompany these warrants, accompanying them with this statement:

"It was announced at the Executive Office today that the President had pardoned Colonel George W. Mixter and Colonel J. G. Vincent, whom the recent report on Aircraft Production showed to be technically guilty of a breach of statutes, because he entirely concurs in the views of the Attorney General with regard to these two cases. He believes that the two gentlemen concerned were entirely innocent of any improper or selfish intention, that their guilt was only technical, and that their services to the Government, which have been of the highest value and of a most disinterested sort, deserve the most cordial recognition."[2]

The President

TL (WP, DLC).
[1] They are missing in WP, DLC. However, they were TWG to WW, Nov. 23, 1918, two letters, CCL (JDR, RG 60, Straight Numerical Files, No. 192136, DNA), and were published, under the date of December 3, 1918, in the *Official Bulletin*, II (Dec. 4, 1918), 1-2. Gregory recommended that Wilson pardon Lt. Col. George Webber Mixter, the production manager of the Bureau of Aircraft Production, and Lt. Col. Jesse G. Vincent, the head of its Airplane Engineering Division. Mixter, a former vice-president of Deere & Company of Moline, Illinois, and Vincent, a former vice-president in charge of engineering of the Packard Motor Car Company and one of the designers of the Liberty engine, had been accused in Hughes' report on the investigation of aircraft production of violating Section 41 of the Criminal Code. It prohibited any person who was directly or indirectly interested in the pecuniary profits or contracts of a corporation from acting as an officer or agent of the United States for the transaction of business with such corporation. For a detailed account of the two cases, see also United States Department of Justice, *Report of the Aircraft Industry* (Washington, 1918), pp. 60-66.
[2] This statement was published, *inter alia*, in the *Official Bulletin*, II (Dec. 4, 1918), 1.

To Robert Lansing

My dear Mr. Secretary: The White House 3 December, 1918.

Will you not be kind enough to make the following reply to this message from House:[1]

"Please let Mr. Hoover know that, very much to my regret, I fear that the terms of the appropriation for National Security and Defence would not justify my making the allotment to which he refers."[2]   Faithfully yours,   Woodrow Wilson

TLS (SDR, RG 59, 840.48/2608, DNA).
[1] EMH to WW, Dec. 1, 1918 (second telegram of that date).
[2] This was conveyed in FLP to EMH, No. 127, Dec. 5, 1918, TC telegram (RSB Coll., DLC).

From Bernard Mannes Baruch

Washington, D.C.

My dear Mr President,   Tuesday [Dec. 3, 1918]

I would have called to say Good bye and God speed to you and Mrs Wilson but I knew how precious was your time.

Here I shall wait for your return for whatever purpose I can serve you and the great cause, and here will I see you acclaimed again as the greatest of all leaders by the very men whose jealousies blind them to your high purpose.

With you go the hearts and prayers of the people worth while[.]
We are all so proud of you and in that confidence born of experience
await in happy mood your triumph there and here.

With best wishes for a safe voyage

Most sincerely   Bernard M Baruch

ALS (WP, DLC).

From Jesse Holman Jones

Dear Mr. President: Washington, D. C., December 3, 1918.

Your message yesterday was in all respects splendid. To repeat
an expression of a fellow Democrat, you "stopped the Republicans
at the Marne." You passed two very serious and knotty problems
to Congress.

Your reference to your trip to the Peace Conference was certainly
all that you could afford to say under the circumstances, and they
all know it. There has seemed no doubt in my mind but that you
should go.

Our fighting forces have done their full share, and it is now clearly
your duty to finish the job. I feel sure that you need have no fear
from the Congress during your absence. They are answerable for
their acts, and time will prove the wisdom of your going.

Bon voyage to both you and Mrs. Wilson,

Very sincerely yours,   Jesse H Jones

TLS (WP, DLC).

From Harry Augustus Garfield

Dear Mr. President: Washington, D. C. December 3, 1918

The more I study the coal situation, the more difficulty there
appears in carrying out the cancelation of prices by the middle of
this month, a plan which I advised you on Wednesday might be
put into effect.

The price regulations are so bound up, as it seems to me, with
other regulations, especially those of the zoning system, that in
order to do justice by both the public and the industry, they must
be removed at substantially the same time.

Moreover, I find that a removal of the maximum price at this
time would probably result in reduced prices of steam sizes and an
increase of prices to domestic consumers.

Also there seems to be an inconsistency in canceling prices at this time, while saying to labor that its agreement as to wages holds until peace is promulgated. At any rate, labor has been quick to take this view on the strength of even the intimation that maximum prices might be discontinued after the 15th of December, and strikes have been called in several of the Districts.

I have had a long session with Mr. Hines this afternoon, as well as with my own staff, including my transportation and labor advisors, and shall continue careful investigation of the question, but in view of my statement of last Wednesday I did not wish you to leave the country without knowing that further consideration of the question makes me doubtful of the course to pursue.

My present impression is that substantially all the Fuel Administration regulations which have interfered with the normal activities of the coal industry, should be removed at the same time, that the date of such removal should be fixed as promptly as possible and full notice of that date be made public. The date for such removal which at present appears to me as the most suitable, is April first, the end of the coal year and at the end of the period in which transportation difficulties are most likely to occur, as well as being the date at which negotiations of wage contracts in the coal business are ordinarily taken up.

I am called to New York tonight by the death of a very dear friend, but can be reached tomorrow morning at University Club if you wish to get any word to me.

Cordially and faithfully yours,   H. A. Garfield

TLS (WP, DLC).

Two Letters from Josephus Daniels

My Dear Mr. President:			Washington. Dec. 3. 1918.

No cabinet officer ought to wish his chief a happy voyage and in the same letter enclose a copy of his report.[1] If he expects the President to read the report, the voyage cannot be happy. I am not handing you this report expecting you to read it, but I thought you might like to look over the scope of the work in the Navy's greatest year. I have tried to give as full a story of the Navy's achievements as possible in so short a time. Your approval of the three year programme will help mightily, and I will press it the best I know how.

With confidence in the success of your great endeavor, I am,

Sincerely your friend,   Josephus Daniels

[1] United States Navy Department, *Annual Report of the Secretary of the Navy for the Fiscal Year . . . 1918* (Washington, 1918).

Dear Mr. President: Washington. Dec. 3. 1918.

Admiral Badger, Chairman of the Executive Committee of the General Board, furnished me this paper prepared by the Board.[1] He thought you would like to read it before you reached Paris as it touches upon questions that will come up for consideration.

Sincerely yours,   Josephus Daniels

ALS (WP, DLC).

[1] Charles Johnston Badger, "Memorandum for Chief of Naval Operations," Dec. 2, 1918, CCS MS (WP, DLC). This memorandum discussed at length a number of questions concerning the rules of warfare and the future naval activities of the United States which, according to the General Board of the Navy, should be taken into consideration during the peace negotiations. The board argued that, ideally, the use of submarines, bomb-dropping airplanes, and mines should be prohibited, since it had led to flagrant violations of accepted international rules. However, the board realized that those weapons had proved to be very effective and that it was unlikely that all nations would agree to abandon them. Thus, new rules governing their use had to be formulated which would not only reestablish the prewar conduct among nations but would give additional force to the principles of international law laid down by the Hague Conferences of 1899 and 1907 and codified in the Declaration of London of 1909. The memorandum then reviewed the question of the disposition of the German colonies in the Pacific. It discussed in great detail the reasons why the United States, for strategic purposes, should acquire the Mariana Islands, the Caroline Islands, and the Marshall Islands. As to the future of the United States Navy, the Board recommended that its size be increased rather than decreased in the aftermath of the war, since the sea power of a nation had to be considered from an international point of view, not from the perspective of internal or domestic safety. Navies would have to be the principal supports of a league of nations, and the United States would be called upon to contribute a substantial share of any international police force. In conclusion, the board suggested that the United States seek compensation from the Central Powers for all shipping lost due to submarine attacks, as well as reparation for the lives of private American citizens lost on the high seas through illegal acts of the enemy, both during the period of neutrality and during the war.

From Robert Lansing

My dear Mr. President: Washington December 3, 1918.

I have been very much exercised as to what we can do for Consul Roger C. Tredwell who is reported to have been imprisoned by the Bolsheviki at Tashkend, Turkestan[1] and hope Mrs. Buxton, his mother,[2] realizes that everything possible is being done.

I have conferred with the military authorities and I am told that a military expedition is impracticable. I do not think anything can be done through civilians which would not entail danger to the lives of other civilian officers in addition to Mr. Tredwell.

I think you may already know that as soon as we learned of the Consul's reported arrest we not only telegraphed the American Minister at Teheran[3] and also the Norwegian Government, which is representing our interests in Russia,[4] but also obtained the cooperation of the British Government to do everything possible resulting from the presence of British forces in North Persia and on the borders of the Caspian Sea. So far our efforts have brought no tangible result. At the same time I am very confident that we have left no stone unturned. So far as we are advised the Consul has experienced no violence or ill treatment other than the fact of his arrest.

Mrs. Buxton has conferred at length with officers of this Department who have appreciated her anxiety and sympathize with her feeling that she, too, must not leave any effort untried.

Faithfully yours,   Robert Lansing

TLS (WP, DLC).
[1] Roger Culver Tredwell, former United States Consul at Petrograd and Vologda, had proceeded to Tashkent in May 1918. According to the *New York Times*, he was put under house arrest in late October under orders from Moscow which instructed officials in Tashkent, among other things, to imprison all subjects of "enemy powers" and to arrest all foreign representatives. As it turned out, Tredwell was not released until April 1919. See the *New York Times*, Nov. 13, Dec. 26 and 27, 1918, and April 27, May 4 and 14, 1919; and FR *1919, Russia*, pp. 167-90.
[2] Frances Vail Culver Tredwell (Mrs. Arthur Kennard) Buxton.
[3] That is, John Lawrence Caldwell.
[4] The Norwegian government was negotiating with the Bolshevik authorities for the release of American and British prisoners in Russia.

From the Diary of Henry Fountain Ashurst

December 3, 1918.

I called upon W.W. After greetings the following conversation occurred:

Pres. Wilson. "What are those **** on the hill doing today?"

Sen. HFA. "Mr. President, the House of Representatives would impeach you and the Senate convict you if they had the courage. Their lack of nerve is all that saves your removal from office; Congress opposes your going to Europe."

Pres. Wilson (with percussion on each word). "Congress has a brain-storm but as soon as I am on the high seas they will recover."

The mercury of the President's manners fell and I detected in him such frigidity and symptoms of uncivility that in ordinary circumstances I would have delayed asking him to reverse the action of one of his Cabinet ministers, but I refused to be taken aback and presented my item for his attention.

From the Diary of Dr. Grayson

Wednesday, December 4, 1918.

The train arrived at Hoboken at seven o'clock. It backed through the streets to the Army wharves, the tracks being lined with men and women enroute to work who had stopped to cheer the President and to wish him God-speed on his momentous voyage.

At the entrance to the large Army pier, formerly the home of the North German Lloyd Line, the president was greeted by a guard of honor of marines, blue-jackets and regular troops. Following the arrival of the train General McManus,[1] Commandant of the Port, entered the President's car and presenting his compliments notified him that the Army Transport GEORGE WASHINGTON was in readiness and that he (McManus) was prepared to escort the President and Mrs. Wilson on board at their convenience. The President told the General that he would have breakfast first in the car, and the train waited outside of the dock until shortly after 7:45, when the President and Mrs. Wilson left the car and passed between lines of soldiers with their rifles at the "present" into the dock area. The approach to the dock and the upper story of the dock building was wonderfully festooned in flags and bunting. Escorted by the Army chiefs and by Captain McCauley[2] of the GEORGE WASHINGTON, the President and Mrs. Wilson and myself passed through and went immediately on board the steamer.

The President went at once to his office, where he gave an interview to R. J. Bender, of the United Press; J. E. Nevin, of the International News Service; and R. C. Probert, of the Associated Press,[3]—the three correspondents whom he had invited to accompany him to Europe. The President's voice was husky and it was suggested that he was suffering from a cold. He replied: "Yes, I have a cold in my throat. Grayson says he will get rid of it for me by the time we get over there. You know I will have to do some plain talking when we get on the other side. I will need my voice there. I was surprised at Colonel Roosevelt's statement in this morning's papers.[4] He virtually says that England won the war and should have everything she wants. I don't believe our boys who fought over there will be inclined to feel just that way about it. We won the war at Chateau Thierry. A single half-hour's delay there in our coming up that day would have made a vast difference. We have the Allies' admission of this fact. We have it in affidavits. We took no chances.

"Militarism is equally as dangerous when applied to sea forces as to land forces. This move just suggested, to have the American and British navies act as the sea patrol of the world is only a new kind of militaristic propaganda. No one power, no two powers, should be supreme. The whole world must be in on all measures designed to end wars for all time."

In reply to a question on the subject, the President expressed the belief that if it came to a point of England refusing to reduce naval armaments, "the United States should show her how to build a navy." "We would be in a position to meet any program England or any other power might set forth." He pointed out "we have now greater navy yards, thousands more shipbuilders than we ever had before, and an abundance of raw materials such as would make it possible for us to have the greatest navy in the world."

It was just 10:15 when the GEORGE WASHINGTON backed out of her pier. As her stern swung north, pandemonium broke loose. Every whistle valve in New York City and on every craft in the harbor was tied down and the din was terrific. Tug boats and launches of every description were about the big liner as she steamed majestically down the harbor, passed the Statue of Liberty and out through the Ambrose Channel. Above in the air circled army aeroplanes and naval sea-planes. South of the Statue of Liberty a number of destroyers were waiting, and after we got into the lower bay the Battleship PENNSYLVANIA, flying the four-starred flag of Admiral Mayo, was sighted. As we passed down the lower bay a big naval dirigible swung out and sailed directly over the top of the GEORGE WASHINGTON. One or two of the more venturesome of the army aviators endeavored to see how close they could come to the President's ship with the result that they caused a little nervousness to Mrs. Wilson and some of the others in the party. The weather was perfect, clear and cold, as we left New York Harbor. The sun shone brightly and altogether the elements were in our favor. In fact, no person could have wished for a more auspicious commencement of an eventful trip.

[1] Brig. Gen. George H. McManus.
[2] Capt. Edward McCauley, Jr., commander of U.S.S. *George Washington.*
[3] Robert Jacob Bender, John Edwin Nevin, and Lionel Charles Probert.
[4] In response to Wilson's address to Congress of December 2, 1918, Roosevelt, on the following day, had issued a lengthy statement in which he sharply attacked Wilson for his alleged failure to give "the slightest explanation" of his views or of the reasons for his participation in the peace conference. In fact, Roosevelt charged, Wilson had never permitted the American people to pass judgment on his peace proposals, nor had he ever defined or clarified them. As to the Fourteen Points, Roosevelt maintained that, while the Central Powers had welcomed them enthusiastically, neither the Allies nor the United States had ever accepted them. To be sure, certain individuals in the United States, including Wilson and William Randolph Hearst, along with a number of German sympathizers, pacifists, and international socialists, had advocated the Fourteen Points as a basis for peace. However, the American people, as far as they had expressed any opinion on them at all, had effectively rejected them in the elections in November. "The simple truth is," Roosevelt stated, "that some of the fourteen points are thoroughly mischievous under any interpretation and that most of the others are so vague and ambiguous that it is nonsense to do anything with them until they have been defined and made definite." With regard to the role of the United States at the peace conference, Roosevelt continued: "Inasmuch as Mr. Wilson is going over, it is earnestly to be hoped that it is his business not to try to be an umpire between our allies and our enemies, but act loyally as one of the Allies. We have not suffered as much and we have not rendered as much service as the leading Allies. It is the British Navy and the French, British, and Italian armies that have done the most to bring about the downfall of Germany, and, therefore, the safety of the United States. It is our business to stand by our allies.

"The British Empire imperatively needs the greatest navy in the world, and this we should instantly concede. Our need for a great navy comes next to hers, and we should have the second navy in the world. Similarly, France needs greater military strength than we do, but we should have all our young men trained to arms on the general lines of the Swiss system.

"The 'freedom of the seas' is a phrase that may mean anything or nothing. If it is to be

interpreted as Germany interprets it, it is thoroughly mischievous. There must be no interpretation of the phrase that would prevent the English Navy, in the event of any future war,
from repeating the tremendous service it has rendered in this war. The British must, of course,
keep the colonies they have conquered. . . . As for Mr. Wilson at the Peace Conference, it is
his business to stand by France, England, and our other allies and to present with them a
solid front to Germany." *New York Times*, Dec. 4, 1918.

From Edward Mandell House

London 4 December 1918

Number 228 Priority

SECRET FOR THE PRESIDENT

I have just heard from Mr. Balfour that December 16th would
be perfectly convenient so far as the British Government are concerned for the holding of the first meeting of the Interallied Conference. STOP. Balfour adds that Clemenceau expressed the view
that December 16th might prove too early. STOP. Balfour suggested
that it may be wise to allow a few days for informal discussions
before the actual meeting of the Conference.

Edward House.

T telegram (E. M. House Papers, CtY).

To Juan Luis Sanfuentes Andonaegui[1]

Washington. December 4, 1918.

You are instructed to hand the following statement to the President of Chile: "The President of the United States desires to inform
your Excellency that the various incidents leading up to the severance of consular relations between the Republics of Chile and
Peru[2] have been viewed by the Government of the United States
with the gravest apprehension. Any agitation tending to lessen the
prospect for permanent peace throughout the world, particularly
on the eve of the convoking of the Peace Conference in Paris, in
which it is confidently expected that steps will be taken to provide
for an era of lasting peace among all peoples, would be disastrous,
and those persons who had caused this condition would be charged
with grave responsibility before the world for their actions.

The President of the United States feels it his duty to draw to
the attention of the Governments of Chile and Peru the gravity of
the present situation and to point out to these Governments the
duty which they owe to the rest of the world and to mankind in
general to take immediate steps to restrain popular agitation and
to re-establish their peaceful relations.

That a satisfactory and peaceful solution of the matter in dispute between the two countries may be arrived at there can be no doubt and the Government of the United States stands ready to tender alone, or in conjunction with the other countries of this hemisphere, all possible assistance to bring about an equitable solution of the matter."

⟨The President of the United States, however, before leaving for the Conference in France, desires to make it clear that the Government of the United States is prepared to seek every means in its power to avert the outbreak of war in the Western Hemisphere and in the event of hostilities would feel obliged to withdraw its moral and material aid from that nation which may be responsible for hostilities." End quote.⟩[3]

The foregoing has been handed to the President of Peru.[4]

Polk, Acting

T telegram (SDR, RG 59, 723.2515/345a, DNA).
    [1] President of Chile. The following message was sent as FLP to Joseph Hooker Shea, United States Ambassador at Santiago.
    [2] An incident in the continuing dispute over the two former Peruvian coastal provinces of Tacna and Arica, which Chile had occupied since its victory in the War of the Pacific of 1879-1884. In the Treaty of Ancón of October 20, 1883, the two countries had agreed that, following ten years of occupation by Chile, the permanent ownership of Tacna and Arica was to be decided by a plebiscite of their inhabitants. However, for various reasons, the plebiscite was never held, and the question of the final disposition of the two provinces continued to strain relations between Chile and Peru for more than forty years. The recent crisis had been precipitated in late November 1918 by riots and mob violence in Tacna and Arica and several cities in northern Chile against Peruvians who had supported their government's intention to seek a settlement of the controversy at the Paris Peace Conference in accordance with the principle of self-determination. See the *New York Times*, Nov. 23, 26, and 30, 1918, and the documents printed in *FR 1919*, I, 123-26. For a detailed discussion of the entire controversy, see William Jefferson Dennis, *Tacna and Arica: An Account of the Chile-Peru Boundary Dispute and of the Arbitrations by the United States* (New Haven and London, 1931).
    [3] Words in angle brackets stricken out by Wilson or Polk, or by both of them.
    [4] José Pardo y Barreda. It was conveyed in FLP to Benton McMillin, United States Minister at Lima, Dec. 4, 1918, T telegram (SDR, RG 59, 723.2515/345b, DNA).

Colville Adrian de Rune Barclay to the Foreign Office

Washington. December 4th, 1918

No. 5417 In reply to my enquiry a few days ago as to dispute between Chile and Peru, Assistant Secretary of State informed me that their official reports did not appear to be so serious as press reports. Mindful of your despatch No. 500, I said the time appeared to have come when a solution of the longstanding questions between them should be found and that H.M.G. was ready to give any assistance the U.S.G. might think desirable to the accomplishment of this end. Mr. Phillips thanked me for this kind offer.

Yesterday he told me that matters were becoming more serious

and that S. of S. had unofficially given counsels of moderation to respective Representatives here.
Confidential.

This morning Mr. Polk told me confidentially that a personal appeal from the President was being sent today to the Presidents of Chile and Peru giving them a friendly warning that the U. S. would regard any hostile action with much concern and would hold the aggressor responsible.

He added that the U. S. would not tolerate any breach of the peace and hinted that they were prepared to take action to prevent it if necessary.

Mr. Polk said the U.S.G. considered it would be most inopportune if any of the Powers were to sell any naval or military supplies to Chile or Peru at this time and he hoped that H.M.G. would concur. They were approaching French and Italian Governments in this sense also.

T telegram (FO 115/2362, pp. 205-206, PRO).

From the Diary of Dr. Grayson

Thursday, December 5, 1918.

Owing to a cold, the President remained in his rooms and made of the day a period of rest.

The President is accompanied on his trip by the following:

Mrs. Wilson
Secretary of State
Mrs. Lansing
Hon. Henry White, ex-Ambassador to France
Hon. John W. Davis, Ambassador to Great Britain
The French Ambassador
Madame Jusserand
The Italian Ambassador
Countess Macchi di Cellere
Admiral Harry S. Knapp, U.S.N.[1]
Rear Admiral Cary T. Grayson,
Captain Pratt, U.S.N.
Brigadier General Churchill
R. B. Fosdick,
George Creel,
R. J. Bender, United Press.
J. E. Nevin, International Press Service.
L. C. Probert, Associated Press.

Gilbert F. Close,
Charles L. Swem,
Charles C. Wagner[2] } Of the White House Staff.
I. H. Hoover,
Joseph E. Murphy,
Miss Edith Benham,
John Queen Slye,
E. W. Starling,
W. A. Landvoight,
J. J. Fitzgerald,
W. G. Ferguson,
J. L. Sullivan,
Arthur Brooks,
Susie Booth

[1] That is, Harry Shepard Knapp, who had been promoted to the rank of rear admiral in August 1916.
[2] White House stenographer.

From the Diary of Edith Benham[1]

December 5, 1918

I begin to think that I am a great person for Mr. Wilson certainly does away with the idea that great men don't sleep a lot. He was dead tired yesterday, as we all were, and slept two hours in the afternoon and went to bed at nine. He and Close, his stenographer, were going over and opening mail for over an hour yesterday in the office across from their suite, and he said it was all the trashy kind of stuff which is always opened in the office in Washington and which he never sees.

I discovered yesterday more dinner cards, a sample of which I have kept for the President and Mrs. Wilson, to invite people to dinner on board ship. I told Mrs. Wilson and we agreed to keep it from him. No use! At luncheon he said with a stricken look: "I found a most extraordinary thing—some dinner cards all engraved ready for us to give dinners. Can they expect us to do that?" You have never seen a more pathetic face, and Mrs. Wilson laughed heartily at him and said we would. I am going to talk over plans with Dr. Grayson. The night we left Mr. Phillips called me up and told me a Mr. Harrison is aboard who is going as one of the State Department representatives and is excellent and to consult with him, if I wanted, about foreign procedure. Mr. Phillips was good enough to say though I had an awfully hard job ahead he knew I could do it.

At dinner tonight Mr. Wilson seemed much better and he talked at more length, about more interesting things than usual. The conversation began in regard to people who simply reflected the views of those with whom they were thrown and he said in as nearly these words as I can remember: "If I find any of the people who are over there in this Commission who are anything but Americans and put anything but America first, I shall send them home." I remember now how it started. It was apropos of the membership of the Peace Commission. Mrs. Wilson said she couldn't remember the fifth member and in enumerating them Bliss' name was mentioned and Mr. Wilson said he was the only one of the men over there who had not shown violence and he considered him a real statesman, all of his judgments being mature. This seems odd when one considers the very general Army opinion of him—that he is only a fluent talker and his head is "solid ivory."

Then Mr. Wilson spoke of Sims, "As for Sims, he has only become an adjunct of the British Navy and is constantly making speeches to the effect that the British fleet saved us and that all our dependence was in it. It is disgusting. Not that Sims isn't a good officer." He then went on to speak of Pershing as we had been speaking of the casualty lists which he said were so much larger than they should have been and so much larger because Pershing had gone "glory mad" and contrary to Foch's advice—not orders— had insisted on attacking around Metz simply to make more of a name. Foch had advised him that the German demoralization was complete and that their surrender was inevitable and that it was not necessary to push the attack. Concentrated before Pershing for the defense of Germany was what remained of the flower of the Army and the slaughter of the Americans was correspondingly higher, but Pershing persisted all to make more of a name for himself.

I give this as I remember it. Some one, Dr. Grayson possibly, asked if it were presidential born, but Mr. Wilson said it probably never will come out. He also added, "Think of the bitterness and hatred of the American mothers to think their boys had been sacrificed so needlessly—what would they have to say."

He said that when two Congressmen who had been with Pershing recently came to him at different times and reiterated this "glory mad" idea, they said he had become so imbued with the idea of vengeance and had said the Americans and allies should bring home in the same way to the German people by war in their own territory the sufferings of France and Belgium. "Think of such a feeling, to wish for our clean boys to repeat the outrages of the Germans, though I don't think Pershing meant those against women. I thank God devoutly for our fine boys and their cleanness and they come home unstained by all this."

This point of view of his, of course, most of us had guessed. I cannot help but feel that the United States in the recent elections repudiated his ideals. Not that they are not fine but that they are not representative of the American people. We have sent over serious minded men who have gone into this as a crusade. But the kind of crusade is not a Y.M.C.A. ideal, but the ideal of men who perhaps work in the Lord's way of retribution and visit the sins of the guilty on their accomplices.

I can't help but feel that he is beaten out in America, that he has been deluded by the people around him and he has been carried away by his ideals. It is to be the final test of his strength—this coming Congress—and if he can force his ideals on the allies. They may be too poor to dare to refuse.

Later in the evening when the wireless came Winston Churchill's speech was quoted,[2] being in substance that England would not give up her freedom of the seas by limiting her armament. He [Wilson] said that if they would not we would build the biggest Navy in the world, matching theirs and exceeding it for we have the money, the men and resources to do it, and then if they would not limit it, there would come another and more terrible and bloody war and England would be wiped off the face of the map.

I can begin to see now why he felt he must go—with his ideals to uphold. If he forces them with the Congress I wonder how long he can make them hold. They are so lucid to me and I love them (Mrs. Wilson and he) so that I cannot help but feel sorry for the defeat he may have. Earlier in the evening in speaking of Sims he said: He was so exasperated by the people who said the Allies had saved America whereas it was our troops who had turned the tide.

T MS (Edith Benham Helm Papers, DLC).
[1] Miss Benham, whom Wilson appointed Social Secretary of the White House on October 27, 1915, stayed with the Wilsons until her marriage to Rear Adm. James Meredith Helm in April 1920. She began her diary as also occasional letters to Helm. She later published portions of her diary in Edith Benham Helm, *The Captains and the Kings* (New York, 1954). However, she left out any passages which she thought might throw an unfavorable light upon Wilson.
[2] About which, see T. J. Walsh to WW, Dec. 2, 1918, n. 1

From the Diary of Raymond Blaine Fosdick

Thursday, December 5th, 1918.

Walked the deck with Colonel Jordon[1] with a half-gale blowing. The destroyers—now eleven in number—are all about us with the "Pennsylvania" in the lead. Talked with Henry White and read some history. The President and his wife, walking the deck, stopped to chat with me for a few moments. He looks well in spite of his weariness. They introduced me to Miss Benham, Mrs. Wilson's secretary, who was with them. The President wears a cap and walks with a quick, eager step that matches his wife's. He seems to listen interestedly to her conversation. I am writing this as they pass back and forth in front of my steamer chair. Every time he goes by he nods or waves his hand to me. They are followed by four Secret Service men and an Officer of the Marines—quite a procession. In fact, Secret Service men are everywhere on the boat. Most of them I know, as they constitute the White House outfit. Armed Guards of the Marines with guns parade the decks and corridors and stand on duty at the head and foot of the stairs. There is a continual saluting. I think it bothers the President a bit. Just now a small eight year old boy—the son of Ambassador Jusserand[2]—got out of his steamer chair for about the fifteenth time and took his hat off as the President went by. Every time he did so he dropped something—an apple core, a book, or his steamer rug. Just now, the President stopped and told him it wasn't necessary—once was enough.

Boat drill was this afternoon at three o'clock. My boat station is next to the President's. We all wore life preservers. The President seemed to enjoy it and listened eagerly to the instructions of the naval officers. . . .

The President strolled around the deck this evening with Mrs. Wilson on his arm. "Stroll" is the wrong word; they always seem to walk with a quick, brisk step, followed, as usual, by the Secret Service men. The boat is rolling so badly, however, that they soon gave up their walk. Two or three times I saw the Secret Service men dart forward to catch the President as he slid along the deck.

T MS (R. B. Fosdick Papers, NjP).
    [1] Col. Richard H. Jordan.
    [2] It must have been the son of the Italian Ambassador, Count Macchi di Cellere. The Jusserands had no children.

From Newton Diehl Baker

My dear Mr. President: Washington. December 5, 1918.

After I saw your good ship started on its way yesterday an incident took place which seemed so striking that I thought I had better write it to you, as it seems to indicate a total disappointment of Mr. Lloyd-George's hope that contact between American soldiers and British soldiers was likely to cement friendly ties between the two peoples. This is a view which I feel sure Mr. Lloyd-George will bring up in some conversation with you and whether or not the incident should be repeated to him I tell it to you so that your own knowledge of the situation may be complete.

I went over to Pier 60 to see the "Laplander," a Red Star steamer under a British Captain and crew, discharge some two thousand American soldiers who were returning after having spent various periods of residence in England ranging from two weeks to several months. As I stood on the bridge looking forward I saw perhaps four or five hundred American soldiers with their overcoats on and packs made up ready to leave by the gangplank. One of the soldiers recognized me, and called out some pleasantry about Cleveland which was probably his home. I waved my hand to them and said, "Are you glad to be back home boys?," at which one clear voice sang out, "You bet—we are glad to get away from England anyhow." I started to turn away, when another voice called out, "You know what we are going back for the next time we go, don't you?," at which there was considerable applause among the assembled soldiers. I confess I was shocked and embarrassed by the whole incident, but it is a rather striking confirmation of the judgment expressed to me repeatedly by American men and women working in the Y.M.C.A. huts in London, to the effect that American soldiers get along with the Canadians, fairly well with the Australians, but not at all with the British.

Now that you have actually gone the press of the country has taken generally a settled and sensible view of your going. Mr. Taft had a lucid interval this morning, and wrote a very sensible article on the subject which I enclose,[1] although you probably will have seen it elsewhere by the time this reaches you.

Respectfully yours,   Newton D. Baker

TLS (WP, DLC).
    [1] William Howard Taft, "Taft Defends Wilson's Trip; Says Advantages Are Clear; Constitution Confers the Right," Philadelphia Public Ledger, [c. Dec. 5, 1918], clipping, WP, DLC. In his comment on some of the criticisms of Wilson's trip, Taft stated that the President's participation in the peace conference would "stamp upon it a democratic character in the eyes of all but the wild bolsheviki." Wilson's presence would help considerably to allay the unrest among the peoples of the Allied countries. There could be no doubt that it was legitimate for Wilson to take part in the negotiations. Unlike the Allied heads of state, Wilson was not only the titular head of a nation, but his powers were analogous to those of the Allied Prime Ministers. The personal contact of the "real leaders," Taft continued, their informal conversations, and "the human touch of it all" could only contribute to a better understanding between the United States and the Allies. Taft then addressed the widespread belief that Wilson aspired to be president of the league of nations. If this was the case, Taft maintained, it was a proper aspiration, since the disinterestedness of the United States in most issues which would have to be decided by the league made the American President "a most fitting head." As to the constitutionality of Wilson's trip abroad, Taft concluded that there was no constitutional inhibition, explicit or implied, which prevented the President from leaving the country in the discharge of a function which was clearly granted to him by the Constitution. Moreover, Taft continued, Wilson could easily perform all his executive tasks by cable from Paris. At present, his duty abroad was far more important than any of his duties at home in connection with a session of Congress, and Congress could well be expected to wait until his return. Although Wilson's persistence in ignoring the Senate and the entire Congress by failing to appoint a senator to accompany him and by giving no real exposition of his present view of the peace terms had created a "resentful feeling," Taft believed that it did not warrant retaliatory action by senators and congressmen. In particular, the disposition of some members of Congress to "nag the President" by calling for the appointment of Vice-President Marshall

as Acting President during Wilson's absence did not meet with popular approval. Taft concluded: "If the fact or the manner of the President's going is a mistake, and it is unpopular with the American people, that may be made a legitimate ground for criticism in a political campaign. But those who would now seek to create an embarrassment out of the present situation will not commend themselves as engaged in a patriotic purpose. If it be true that the President has acted without due consideration to the Senate or to Congress, the people will not justify the Senate or Congress in a retaliatory action. For the Republicans it is the poorest kind of politics. . . . Mr. Mann's position in this respect is a wise one and all Republicans should approve it."

From Edward Mandell House

Paris Dec. 6 [5][1], 1918

233. Secret for the President. Sonnino, Lord Derby and Clemenceau have each given me a separate account of the proceedings of December second and third at the conferences held in London between Lloyd George, Clemenceau, and Orlando. The following is a summary of these proceedings.

One. Meeting held December second at eleven a.m.

Resolution (A). Regret expressed my absence on account of illness and Mr. Balfour directed to transmit conclusions of conference to me.

Resolution (B). Establishment of Inter-Allied Commission Belgium, France, Great Britain, Italy and the United States, each to have three delegates thereon and Japan one delegate, to examine and report on amount enemy countries are able to pay for reparation and indemnity. Form of payment also to be considered. The commission to meet in Paris provided the United States Government agrees. Each Government to compile its claims for reparation which will be referred for examination by Inter-Allied Commission to be nominated when claims are prepared.

Resolution (C) is, British, France [French], and Italian Governments agree that Kaiser and principal accomplices should be brought to trial before international court. Telegram respecting this was sent to Washington on December second.[2] (I assume that you have

[1] The date on the copy in the House Papers.
[2] "It is very important that the following communication shall reach the President and Mr. Lansing before departure.

"At a Conference of the Governments of France, Great Britain and Italy held in London this morning the three Governments agreed to recommend that a demand ought to be presented to Holland for the surrender of the person of the Kaiser for trial, by an International Court to be appointed by the Allies, on the charge of being the criminal mainly responsible for the war and breaches of International Law by the forces of Germany by land, sea and air.

"During its deliberations the Conference had before it the opinion of a Committee of nine of the most eminent Jurists of the British Isles, who recommended unanimously that the Kaiser and his principal accomplices should be brought to trial before a Court consisting of nominees of the principal nations victorious in the war.

"In coming to the conclusion set forth above the Conference were influenced by the following principal considerations.

already seen it, and therefore do not quote it.) Immediate action to be taken in this matter provided President Wilson agrees, otherwise matter to be left for discussion after President Wilson arrives.

(D). British, France and Italian Governments agree that before preliminaries of peace shall be signed an Inter-Allied conference be held in Paris or Versailles the date thereof to be set after the arrival of the President. France, Great Britain, Italy, Japan, and the United States should each be represented by five delegates. British Colonial representatives to attend as additional members when questions directly affecting them are considered. Smaller Allied powers not to be represented except when question[s] concerning them are discussed. Nations attaining their independence since the war to be heard by Inter-Allied conference.

Two. Meeting December second, four p.m.

Resolution (A). British, France and Italian Governments authorize Foch to renew armistice on December tenth for one month.

Resolution (B). British, France, and Italian Governments empowered Admiral Wemyss, on condition that forts at entrance to Baltic are demolished to satisfaction of Allied naval commission to waive military occupation of said forts.

Resolution (C). British, France, and Italian Governments approve requirements of Admiral Beatty that while interned in British ports German flag shall be hauled down on board German men of war.

Resolution (D). British, France and Italian Governments agree to formation of Inter-Allied Commission of four Admirals (Ameri-

"A. That justice requires that the Kaiser and his principal accomplices who designed and caused the war with its malignant purpose or, who were responsible for incalculable sufferings inflicted on the human race during the war, should be brought to trial and punished for their crimes.

"B. That certain inevitable personal punishment for crimes against humanity and international right will be a very important security against future attempts to make war wrongfully or to violate International Law and is a necessary stage in the development of the authority of a League of Nations.

"C. That it will be impossible to bring to justice lesser criminals, such as those who have oppressed the French and Belgians and other peoples, committed murder on the high seas, and maltreated prisoners of war, if the arch-criminal, who for 30 years has proclaimed himself the sole arbiter of German policy and has been so in fact, escapes condign punishment.

"D. That the Court, by which the question of responsibility for the war and its grosser barbarities should be determined, ought to be appointed by those nations who have played a principal part in winning the war and have thereby shown their understanding of what freedom means and their readiness to make unlimited sacrifices in its behalf. This clause is intended to relate only to the composition of the Court which will deal with the crimes committed in connection with the late war and is not intended to prejudice the question of the composition of the International Courts under a League of Nations.

"The Conference hopes that the Government of the United States will share its views and cooperate with the Allies in the presentation to Holland of a demand for the surrender of the persons of the ex-Kaiser and of the Crown Prince for trial before an International Court to be appointed by the Allies." British embassy to Department of State, received Dec. 3, 1918, quoting A. J. Balfour to C. A. de R. Barclay, Dec. 2, 1918, FR 1919, II, 653-54.

can, British, France, Italian) to inquire and report on existing situation and advise as to future activities to eliminate trouble in Adriatic territories occupied or to be occupied by Allied forces not including those mentioned in article three of Austrian armistice terms such as Corfu, Spalato, Fiume, et cetera.

Three. Meeting December 3rd. 11:15 a.m.

Resolution (A). Proposed conference between Foch and Chief of British Staff[3] respecting arrangements of British portion of army of occupation agreed to by British Government.

Resolution (B). Expenses of occupation of Austria to be arranged for by Italian Commander in Chief[4] and General Franchet D'Esperey. When military proposals are formulated, they are to be submitted to Governments concerned through Foch.

Resolution (C) British, French, and Italian Governments agreed theoretically not to object to international relief, labor or any other conference in relation to peace conference being held provided that until peace is signed it is held in a neutral country.

Four. Meeting December third. 4 p.m.

Resolution (A) Exact question of victualing and supplying enemy, Allied and neutral countries in all its aspects including the use of enemy merchant vessels is referred to the following for examination and report. Clementel and Bouisson[5] (representing the French) Reading and Maclay (representing the British) Crespi and Villa[6] (representing the Italian) Hoover and Hurley if available (representing the United States).

Resolution (B) British troops in any part European Turkey to remain under command of General Franchet D'Esperey. Rest of British army under General Milne[7] may be transferred to Caucasus or elsewhere upon agreement being reached between countries concerned. If so transferred, British army will cease to be under command of D'Esper[e]y.

Resolution (C) British, French and Italian Governments agree that conclusions of conference should be regarded as provisional only and subject to the United States *accepting* [excepting?] those which require immediate action or do not concern United States.

With respect to resolution[s] taken at meeting December 2nd at 12 [11] a.m. I am advising the Governments concerned. One. That

---

[3] That is, Gen. Sir Henry Hughes Wilson.

[4] That is, Gen. Armando Diaz.

[5] Etienne Clémentel, Minister of Commerce, Industry, Posts and Telegraph, Maritime Transport, and the Merchant Marine; and Ferdinand Emile Honoré Bouisson, Commissioner for Maritime Transport and the Merchant Marine.

[6] Silvio Benigno Crespi, Minister of Supply, and Giovanni Villa, Minister of Transport.

[7] That is, Lt. Gen. Sir George Francis Milne, commander of the British Salonika Force and the Army of the Black Sea.

eliminating the word "indemnity" from resolution (B) the United States agrees. Two. That resolution (C) should be discussed after your arrival. With these exceptions I suggest that the United States agree to these resolutions.

With respect to resolutions taken at meeting December 2nd 4 p.m. I have discussed the naval and military features with General Bliss and Admiral Benson and am stating to the Governments concerned that the United States agrees to these resolutions.

With respect to resolutions taken at meeting December 3rd 11 a.m. I suggest that you authorize me to state that the United States agrees to these resolutions.

With respect to resolutions taken at meeting December 3rd, 4 p.m. I have suggested to Lord Derby that instead of following the procedure outlined in resolution (A) that a food section of the Supreme War Council serve with representatives of the United States, Great Britain, France and Italy thereon and that substantially to [the] plan suggested in my number 188[8] as substantially [subsequently] amended be adopted. With this exception, I suggest that you authorize me to state that the United States agrees to these resolutions.

I would appreciate an expression of your views as soon as possible.   Edward House

T telegram (SDR, RG 59, 763.72119/3221½, DNA).
[8] EMH to WW, Nov. 27, 1918 (second telegram of that date).

From the Diary of Dr. Grayson

Friday, December 6, 1918.

The President remained in his room during the most of the day. I had been working hard on his cold with the result that it was now beginning to show signs of clearing up. In fact, so noticeable was the improvement that during the afternoon I suggested to the President that it was necessary for him to take some exercise, so he and Mrs. Wilson came on deck and we took a two-mile walk around the glass-enclosed deck. The President enjoyed the exercise very much and as a result when he returned to his quarters he was able to eat a very hearty dinner. He asked me what the program was for the evening, and I told him that they had a moving-picture show which would be put on at eight o'clock in the main dining salon. He decided that he would go, and he and Mrs. Wilson and myself went upstairs and enjoyed the pictures. Afterwards the President retired and slept fine.

From Edward Prentiss Costigan

Dear Mr. President: Washington December 6, 1918.

On the morning of December 4th, I arrived in New York from England after approximately two and one-half months in France and England. Delay in reaching here, due to war conditions, precludes me from seeking a brief interview with you before your European trip. Under the circumstances, (though at the risk of repeating commonplaces and other information which may reach you through your immediate advisers) may I venture to outline certain possibly suggestive deductions, based both on independent observation and on frequent conversations with distinguished men on both sides of the English Channel?

Bearing in mind that the foreign panorama in these critical times is constantly shifting, before leaving France and England I had drawn the following conclusions:

1. In France, England, and, so far as their spokesmen represented them, among the "suppressed nationalities" of Europe, there is extraordinary and unmatched faith among the masses of the people in you, your insight and leadership.

2. The governing influences in London are more liberal and less bitter than in Paris,—in part because

(a) The British Islands have not been the theater of the recent actual conflicts;

(b) Great Britain indirectly, and even without intention, has become the chief world beneficiary of allied military prestige in the near east, and of the collapse of Great Britain's most conspicuous European competitor;

(c) Among the majority of British statesmen there is keen comprehension of the nature of the bonds uniting English speaking peoples, and of the value of drawing such bonds closer.

In this connection, it should perhaps be said that it is believed the feeling of the French people as a whole is more temperate than that of French Government leaders toward France's recent enemies, the peoples of Central Europe.

3. Notwithstanding these cooperating tendencies toward American fellowship, much pressure continues to be exerted by certain influential Englishmen in support of aggressive French efforts to impose conditions of future economic servitude on the defeated enemy; and Mr. Hughes of Australia (though seemingly with scant backing from the British Government) is lending his colonial endorsement to this policy.

4. Perhaps in consequence, there has been, for the past several weeks, a steady effort in certain circles and in much of the public press both of France and England to emphasize the military and

naval services of Great Britain and France and to minimize America's war contribution, which, it is privately stated, turned the tide last summer from threatening defeat to triumph. To an onlooker, there is possibility of misunderstanding in the reiterations on both sides of the Channel of the statement, "our country won the war," in lieu of the generous and fairer assertion "the common efforts and sacrifices of all of us have been victorious."

5. For these and other reasons there are indications that the Peace Conference at Versailles may develop strongly conflicting currents, in which dissatisfaction with American simplicity and democracy, and strong tendencies towards the disingenuous and discredited practices of the old diplomacy, will immediately underlie the surface.

6. Certain foreign influences are apparently merely awaiting opportunity to voice their skepticism toward America's "idealistic" advocacy of reasonable peace conditions for a fallen foe; open diplomacy; freedom of the seas; the rejection of economic war; some phases of self-determination; and an effective League of Nations; and, in case of serious division at Versailles, many illiberal plans toward future commerce and international politics will come into the open and strive for war-reviving peace conditions.

7. Your own powerful and outspoken leadership is the most hopeful and least dispensable factor of the situation, and, in so far as you may secure the aid—for which, as indicated, prevailing conditions are favorable—of the real leadership of Great Britain, you will be strengthened in avoiding the loss, either by frontal attack or by technical quibbling, of the real significance of the peace conditions, drawn and best interpreted by you.

8. In the economic field, imperial preferences, even in the case of dependent colonies, appear to be taken for granted both in France and Great Britain. Some dissatisfaction with the dependent colony phases of such preferences is being privately voiced in London, occasion for it being afforded by Mr. Lloyd-George's letter to Mr. Bonar Law of November 2, 1918,[1] indicating sanction of such preferences by the government with respect to articles such as tea, already subject to custom duties. Regret over this declaration was expressed to me by persons of weight in London, who sense in it such economic discrimination as you have opposed. Although at the same time the Prime Minister, who was then launching his political campaign, indicated that like preferences will be favored in the case of other articles hereafter subjected to tariff charges, it was, when I left London, generally considered improbable that the number of articles affected by the tariff will be much increased.

[1] It was published, e.g., in the London *Times*, Nov. 18, 1918.

9. Far reaching economic importance attaches to the inaugura-
tion by the British Government of a definite system of loans and
grants in aid of investment, investigation and expansion of production in the dye industry. It is asserted that domestic production
and development are to be stimulated throughout the somewhat
undetermined field of "key industries" by the same means, under
government licenses, safeguarding prices and distribution of products. The machinery for the distribution of such aid is described
in a recently issued official publication ("State Assistance to the
Dye Industry. Memorandum by the Board of Trade, ∗ ∗ ∗," November 1918 Cd. 9194).

10. Keeping in view that what was said to me in France about
the tariff was spoken before the acceptance of general peace terms,
there was general expectation in Paris in the middle of last October
that in addition to social ostracism, stringent immigrant prohibition,
and strong tariff discrimination against Germany would follow the
war. I was advised in Paris from a responsible and authoritative
source that a multiple after-war tariff system would prevail—maximum rates applying to the products of Germany and other enemy
countries, an intermediate and general set of customs duties affecting the articles of the Allies, the United States and neutral
countries, and a group of minimum rates applying to French colonial products. This assertion was made in the same breath in which
it was affirmed that France subscribes to your opposition to economic war.

11. In the middle of last October—and therefore to what extent
modified by the subsequent peace basis, I am unable to say—France
was preparing to use hereafter the most-favored-nation clause in
commercial treaties conditionally and for such bargaining purposes
as may be considered most appropriate. In England, on the other
hand, after the signing of the armistice, I was advised that the
British strongly prefer to adhere to the unconditional use of the
most-favored-nation clause.

12. When I left London, doubt was being cast on the possibility
of agreement in the peace era on the precise construction to be
given such ph[r]ases as "equality of trade conditions" and "the
removal so far as possible of all economic barriers." Certain influential men were therefore inclined to believe that an advisory international commission should be empowered to define and recommend for international sanction standards by which economic
discrimination may hereafter be tested.

13. The proposed League of Nations, as you know, is exciting
much attention abroad and while a strong group of thinkers in
England—notable among whom are Professor Gilbert Murray and

Mr. H. G. Wells—are preparing to make detailed recommendations of a thorough-going organization, dominant British governmental opinion appears at present to be disposed to adopt a cautious and experimental attitude. The well-known author, Mr. A. L. Zimmern[2] (who is associated with the British Foreign Office) sent me as I was leaving the advance sheets of a critical exposition of some problems of the League from the latter standpoint.[3] As you know, the thorough-going plan contemplates the organization of some sort of international congress, police force and judicial body. The other (Zimmern) tentative recommendations look rather toward inter-state treaties requiring renewal approximately every ten years, thereby emphasizing rather than minimizing state sovereignty; annual conferences of various foreign ministers and secretaries for the more or less private discussion of international problems, quadrennial conferences or congresses, apparently without voting authority, meeting for the discussion and disclosure of the "organized opinion of mankind"; the reference of judiciable disputes to suitable international inquiry; the administration of international regions by separate states under defined conditions of international trusteeship; and the appointment of numerous commissions to solve and administer equitably such problems as the extension of international transportation, and to inquire into and make recommendations on perplexing questions calling for agreement and ratification by the separate states.

14. Considerable British sentiment favors adjournment of the Paris Conference to a subsequent date, following the opening sessions, in order to enable committees, the designation of which is desired, to investigate and later report in detail on problems of the Conference.

15. There is general and earnest hope that the war powers of such governmental bodies as the Shipping and War Trade Boards may continue international cooperation at least through the period of transition to peace, and longer if possible.

16. Leading Russians abroad are profoundly anxious that you be further advised on the appalling gravity of the situation confronting their country. One of their most authoritative spokesmen in Paris wished particularly to say to you that Russia may yet be saved, but Russia unless assisted—and under American guidance—may also perish. In brief, these representatives of a stricken people ask:

(a) That in the interests of permanent peace, men whom their

[2] Alfred Eckhard Zimmern, former lecturer and tutor in ancient history at New College, Oxford; at this time, associated with the Political Intelligence Department of the Foreign Office.

[3] About this cabinet paper, see George W. Egerton, *Great Britain and the Creation of the League of Nations* (Chapel Hill, N. C., 1978), pp. 95-97.

people in happier days to come will necessarily consider representative—whatever the insufficiencies of their immediate credentials—shall be constantly advised with during the progress of the Peace Conference, whenever problems affecting Russia call for determination;

(b) That there shall be strong and consistent international adherence to policies of economic and industrial help, and of temporary military aid, to avert starvation, and to assist the Russian people in establishing their own responsible and representative government.

I must believe you will pardon the nature and length of this communication to which I have been led by a sense of public obligation. Under the circumstances I know no better way to bring its fresh impressions to your attention. I regret that lack of opportunity has prevented me from stating to you in person the elements contributing to its more important intimations.

With much respect,   Very sincerely,   E. P. Costigan

TLS (WP, DLC).

From the Diary of Dr. Grayson

Saturday, December 7, 1918.

The President slept late but early in the afternoon went on deck for another exercise walk. We were now in the Gulf Stream, and the weather was almost summery. Enroute about the deck the President encountered M. Jusserand, the French Ambassador to the United States, and the latter shook hands with him and chatted briefly. Jusserand, who is probably the most wily of all of the French diplomats, made it very plain that he did not desire at this time to interfere with the President's rest, and his conversation was for the most part of an informal nature. After leaving Jusserand the President encountered Count Cellere, the Italian Ambassador. The latter was far less wise than his colleague and endeavored to get the President into a discussion of the merits of Italy's peace claims. The President did not rise to the occasion and turned the matter off with a few pleasant remarks dealing with the weather and the pleasant voyage generally.

Passing around the deck the President asked the three newspaper men how they were faring and chatted with them for some time.

He told them a number of amusing stories, one of which dealt with the late Russell Sage, whose saving, sometimes called miserly, habits were a by-word. The President said that he had been told of a dream dealing with Russell Sage's death, which had some amusing characteristics. According to it when Sage died his soul proceeded to heaven and knocked on the gates. When St. Peter appeared he asked: "Who is there?" The reply was: "Russell Sage." "What do you want?" "To come into heaven." "On what do you base your demand for entrance," demanded St. Peter. Russell in reply declared: that he had contributed to numerous charities. St. Peter then called upon the Guardian Angel to look up the records and to find out whether Sage actually had ever contributed personally of his own volition. The record brought out the fact that Russell had contributed three pennies on three separate occasions to three distinct charities. St. Peter than slammed the gate in Russell's face, turning to the Guardian Angel and saying: "Give him back his three cents and tell him to go to hell."

Among other matters that the President touched on was a discussion of the characteristics of various men. In that connection the President told me that he had discovered that usually when a man was lacking in humor he was also lacking in tact. However, in the opinion of the President this feeling in a great many men has been overcome by the possession of strong feelings of sympathy. The President expressed the opinion that sympathy and understanding very frequently will assist in accomplishing things which tact and diplomacy cannot.

To Harry Augustus Garfield

U.S.S. George Washington,
My dear Garfield: 7 December, 1918.

I opened your letter of December 3rd after I reached the steamer. I fully understand the situation and shall gladly trust you to work it out according to your own judgment.

You have been of great comfort as well as of most invaluable assistance to me, and I want you to know how truly and sincerely grateful I am. We are having a favorable voyage as I write, and are hoping to get in within something less than a week now.

Please give my warmest regards to Mrs. Garfield and your daughter[1] and believe me,   Your grateful friend,   Woodrow Wilson

TLS (H. A. Garfield Papers, DLC).
[1] That is, Belle Hartford Mason Garfield and Lucretia Garfield.

To Bernard Mannes Baruch

U.S.S. George Washington,
My dear Baruch: 7 December, 1918.

Your little note of Tuesday reached me on the steamer. I am warmly obliged to you for it. I am looking forward with the greatest pleasure to seeing you on the other side, because I am sure we shall need you within a very short time. I dare say Tumulty conveyed my message to you. I tried to reach you by telephone on Tuesday, but unfortunately could not get you.

Please give my warmest regards to Mrs. Baruch[1] and make my apologies to her for planning to take you away from her again. Unfortunately, you have made yourself indispensable.

With affectionate regard,
Sincerely yours,   Woodrow Wilson

TLS (B. M. Baruch Papers, NjP).
[1] That is, Annie Griffen Baruch.

To Josephus Daniels

U.S.S. George Washington,
My dear Daniels: 7 December, 1918.

No apology was needed for sending me your Annual Report. I was mighty glad to get it, and gladder still to get your greeting along with it. I know that you and all my colleagues will keep your eyes skinned against anybody getting the better of us while I am on the other side of the water.

In haste,   Affectionately yours,   Woodrow Wilson

TLS (J. Daniels Papers, DLC).

To Robert Lansing

[U.S.S. *George Washington*]
My dear Mr. Secretary: 7 December 1918.

I have been thinking over this telegram[1] since we spoke together about it, and I am wondering whether it might not be wise to send a wireless to House, suggesting that all arrangements for the meeting of an inter-allied conference be postponed until the preliminary informal discussions have shown just what would be best in all the circumstances.   Faithfully yours,   [Woodrow Wilson]

CCL (WP, DLC).
[1] That is, EMH to WW, No. 228, Dec. 4, 1918.

From James Viscount Bryce

My dear Mr. President   Forest Row, Sussex. Dec. 7th, 1918

It is very pleasant to know that you are on your way to Europe to join in settling the greatest and most difficult mass of problems statesmanship has ever had to deal with. We look forward to having you for a little with us in England where you will have the warmest possible welcome.

With this I am venturing to send to you a little volume[1] of things I have written during the last four years. You will not have time to read the first six among them, but in the last but one[2] there is a list of the questions relating to nationalities affected by the war, with some remarks interspersed, which may perhaps be of some use to your Secretaries, while the last contains an enumeration of the chief points which have arisen in our English discussions of the subject of a League of Nations for the preservation of peace.[3] It is a great source of hope to us that you have taken so warm an interest in this supremely important and difficult subject

Believe me   Very sincerely yours   James Bryce

ALS (WP, DLC).
[1] James Bryce, *Essays and Addresses in War Time* (New York, 1918).
[2] "The Principle of Nationality and Its Applications," *ibid.*, pp. 141-75.
[3] "Concerning a Peace League," *ibid.*, pp. 176-204.

Frank Lyon Polk to Robert Lansing

Washington, December 7, 1918.

8. The following received from Archangel: "634, December 3, 6 p.m. The Department may be interested in the following outline of British policy in Russia which Lindley[1] tells me he has just received from the Foreign Office: To continue as at present at Archangel and Murmansk; to continue present operations in Siberia; to hold Baku-Batum Railway for the present; to resist [assist] Demonken [Denikin] with money, munitions and advice; to send squadron to Reval[2] which would be helping anti-Bolshevik elements maintain order. Troops will not land in Baltic provinces but munitions may be furnished anti-Bolsheviks. It is understood that the French will take the lead in the Ukraine and the British in the Caucasus in accordance with the arrangement made in November or December, 1917, and reported by me from Rostoff. Lindley says he has no intimation of British policy in Central Asia but understands that the British control Trans-Caspian Railway eastward from Krasno-vodsk for a distance not known to him. Sent to Paris also."

Polk, Acting.

T telegram (WP, DLC).

¹ That is, Francis Oswald Lindley, British Commissioner in Russia.
² That is, Tallinn, the capital of Estonia.

From the Diary of Dr. Grayson

Sunday, December 8, 1918.

The President attended church in the enlisted men's quarter at ten o'clock. This service was held in what was called the "Old Salt Theatre"—on D deck, well below the water line. There was a conglomeration of smells from the cook's galleys and the Chaplain,¹ who conducted the services, was noticeably nervous. However, he essayed his best, and the President was not inclined to be in any way critical.

During the afternoon the President sat for a while on deck with Mrs. Wilson, and later he and I walked two miles around the deck. Afterward the President had an informal conference with Secretary of State Lansing, and another with former Ambassador White, at which they discussed the latest wireless reports received from Colonel House, who was in Paris attending to the preliminaries dealing with the peace conditions.

After dinner the President invited the three newspaper correspondents to come to his office, and he talked with them quite freely. The President in part said:

"The plot is thickening! I think it now is necessary that we get a clear comprehension of exactly my position in this situation. As you know, Clemenceau, Lloyd George, and Orlando have held a meeting in London. Colonel House was unable to be there. He has not yet been able to throw off his attack of the influenza as rapidly as he expected. The men apparently got together on a programme which I have just received. It was badly garbled in cable; hence the delay in my getting it. It is very obvious in reading between the lines of Colonel House's report to me that these representatives of France, Great Britain and Italy are determined to get everything out of Germany that they can. They know Germany is down and out. Instead of going about the thing in the fair way, namely, determine what they think they are justly entitled to demand of Germany and then seek the means of securing it through learning how Germany may be expected to meet the demands—if she can meet them at all—and arranging their claims accordingly, they favor the appointment of a commission to study exactly what Germany has got today and the naming of another commission to apportion what Germany has among the governments that have fought her in this

¹ Lieut. Paul Frederick Bloomhardt.

war. I am absolutely opposed to this. A statement that I once made that this should be a 'peace without victory' holds more strongly today than ever. The peace that we make must be one in which justice alone is the determining factor.

"Upon the first occasion that I have after meeting these gentlemen and letting them know what sort of a fellow I am and giving myself the opportunity of determining what sort of chaps they are, I will say to them, if necessary, that we are gathered together, not as the masters of anyone, but that we are the representatives of a new world met together to determine the greatest peace of all time. It must not be a peace of loot or spoliation. If it were such we would be an historical scourge. I for one shall, if necessary, tell them that if that is the kind of peace they demand, I will withdraw personally and with my commissioners return home and in due course take up the details of a separate peace. Of course, I do not believe that that will come to pass. I think once we get together they will know that we stand for no bargaining but will hold firmly by the principles we have set forth; and once they learn that that is my purpose, I think that we can come to an agreement promptly."

The President explained that he favored having himself and the premiers of England, France and Italy get together, much as the Foreign Relations Committee of the Senate get together, and go over the details of the proposed peace treaty, and later submit these as propositions to the conference of all the belligerent nations. He did not favor having all of the allotted commissioners of Great Britain, France, the United States and Japan get together and formulate the treaty and then call in the balance of the belligerents merely to approve it. He recognized the difficulties of 25 or 30 belligerents attempting to mull over the details of a treaty at the same time, and thought the same purposes could be accomplished more quickly and just as satisfactorily by having the tentative proposals prepared in advance of the full meeting by a selected few. This would embody secret conferences, even as confidential matter is mulled over in the Foreign Relations Committee of the Senate, but so far as the final gathering of the peace commissioners is concerned, he believed the debate should be open to the public.

In agreeing to the fourteen principles, the President pointed out, England was in the peculiar position of submitting to the principle of disarmament while simultaneously announcing through her statesmen that she meant to retain naval supremacy. On this point he said he had talked with Andrew Tardieu, the French High Commissioner, saying laughingly but pointedly, that if England hoped to retain a naval dominance, the United States could and would build the greatest navy in the world.

"If England holds to this course," the President said, "it means that she does not want peace, and I will so tell Lloyd-George. I can do it with a smile, but it will carry its point."

The President definitely set forth his views on the freedom of the seas. The war had brought the necessity for material and specific changes in present international law, and he mentioned the need now for increasing the limits of territorial waters about any nation, owing to the greater carrying power of naval guns. Also, there was the need to accurately define regulations of blockade, in peace as in war times. England, the President pointed out, very seriously infringed on America's rights before we became a belligerent through the improper use of her blockade,—in fact did the same thing on the seas as Germany did to Belgium, and on the same grounds— necessity. He declared that at one time if it had not been for his realization that Germany was the scourge of the world, he would have been ready to have it out with England.

It must be definitely set forth, the President explained, that no one nation or group of nations can say what shall or shall not be done on the high seas. A league of all nations could declare a blockade or override international laws for purposes of punishing a country which threatened the peace of the world, but this power could not be vested in any single nation. He said it was going to be very difficult to give everybody everything they wanted out of this war. Italy, for instance, the President declared, had an entirely different idea of what she was entitled to under his principles than his advisers felt she had any right to expect, but he expressed a desire to be very generous in the matter of Italy's demands.

On the Polish question there also were problems to be solved in holding to his determination to give Poland an outlet to the sea, the President explained. If this plan were followed literally, he said, it would mean that part of East Prussia would have to be turned over to Poland, leaving another part of Prussia between two sections of Poland, which would be very confusing. These problems, he indicated, would have to be worked out deliberately.

On the question of the league of nations, he said that Germany's present chaotic state would make it necessary to put her on probation, as it were, until she showed herself fit for reception into the League. He indicated that a similar policy probably would be necessary toward the other "war babies" which have come out of the war, such as Jugo-Slavia, etc. As for Russia, he said his policy toward her must now naturally be altered, "owing to the fact that Russia has broken up into several different states." It will be necessary to follow the principle of self-determination in ascertaining under what sovereignty these various states desire to come, he explained.

An interesting problem, the President said, has arisen under this same principle of self-determination in the purported decision of German Austria to become affiliated with the original German empire. Such affiliation, he pointed out, would mean that the new Germany would be one of the most powerful countries in Europe. Also, it would constitute a great Roman Catholic power. While he said he had no objection to the strength of the Roman Catholic Church, there was danger of its becoming a powerful political entity should such a situation as this develop. Applying the principle of self-determination, however, he said that the problem was certainly vexatious, but might be handled by the associated powers demanding that Austria and Germany act separately until they had proved their sincerity and worth.

Discussing the general programme of the league of nations, he declared emphatically that it must constitute part and parcel of the peace treaty itself and not be left to any later consideration. The President thought it might be advisable to turn over the captured German war vessels to France and Italy, thus bringing about a situation whereby the navy of one power would be as great as the combined navies of the other powers associated in the league. The nucleus of the league, he said, could readily be formed of Great Britain, France, Italy, the United States, and Japan; the others would of necessity come in to preserve their own interests.

The President regretted the apparent acquiescence of the American people in the idea that England won the war and therefore should get what she wanted out of it. He mentioned also with regret that some of our own representatives abroad have shown marked signs of becoming pro-British, mentioning specifically Admiral Sims, who, he said, might as well be a British Admiral.

The President said that Premier Borden of Canada, on a recent trip back from England with Representative Swagar Sherley of Kentucky, declared that Canada did not want the mother country to attain any more colonies, and indicated a desire that the German colonies if turned over to anybody be turned over to the United States. "But," said the President, laughing, "we don't want them and won't have them." He regarded as very interesting and rather significant the premier's attitude on this point.

Asked how Premier Clemenceau lined up with him on general issues of peace, he said that he did not know. The only indication he had of Clemenceau's personal attitude toward him, he added laughingly, was that once Clemenceau said that "General Pershing is the stubbornest man I know and I am saying that knowing Mr. Wilson, the President of the United States." He added, however, that he felt that on most points any one of the associated governments would rather be lined up with the United States than with any other nation. In other words, he said, Italy would far prefer to be on the American side than the French or British side on most points, and the same held with the other governments. In view of this, he said, in the preliminary conferences it probably would be a question of standing pat on his own interpretation of the fourteen principles and trying to accommodate the others one by one in an effort to prevent any combinations in which this country would not figure.

The President indicated that he would have to be back before the close of the present Congress to take care of bills. He intimated that it might be necessary for him to return to Europe later. He assumed also that after the present peace conference is concluded, there will be a later conference of the nations of the world to formulate a new international code.

He designated as absurd London press accounts that England would demand indemnities amounting to $40,000,000[,000] from Germany, and that France's demands would probably exceed that. He declared it would be impossible to get that much money out of Germany within a generation, unless she repudiated her entire public debt.

From the Diary of Raymond Blaine Fosdick

Sunday, December 8th, 1918.

Went to church and heard a poor little sermon by a poor little Navy Chaplain who was so scared at the presence of the President that he could hardly talk. . . .

I was reading in the Conference Room when the President came in to look at some maps. He is much interested in getting exact statistics of population by nationality in the border lands between the disputed territories, as, for example, between Italy and Austria, and he showed in his conversation a broader grasp of ethnological detail than one would expect of an administrator. His years of study as a college professor are standing him in excellent stead. I happened to be reading Henry Jones Ford's "Washington and his Colleagues"[1]—a discussion of the work of construction in building the national government 1789-1795. In describing the formation of the Secretary of State's office, Ford quotes from the Congressional debates of 1789 in which the hope was expressed that the office would be temporary on the grounds that the time would undoubtedly come when the United States would not have any foreign relations whatever. I showed this to the President, who was vastly amused and made a note of it. Later he asked for the book. The President sat on the table and we swapped negro stories, his easily out-rivaling mine. He had just started to tell of a darky's comment on the Episcopalian service when Mrs. Wilson came in to take him for a walk around the decks. I suggested that it might be well to suspend temporarily anything that could be considered an attack on the Episcopal Church, but Mrs. Wilson told us to go to it, remarking that if necessary she could tell some things about Scotch Presbyterianism that would make interesting reading. The President laughed, put his arm around her for a second, and went on with his story in which a darky says of the Episcopalian service: "Dey spend too much time readin' de minutes of de las' meetin.' "

[1] Henry Jones Ford, *Washington and His Colleagues: A Chronicle of the Rise and Fall of Federalism* (New Haven, Conn., 1918).

From the Diary of Edith Benham

December 8, 1918

When I have something interesting I suppose the best plan is to write it down right away. At luncheon today Mr. Wilson, who is very bitter always against the English and their demands, and in fact about England and her part in the war generally, was reading the wireless news. He read in one place that Lloyd George had said that England would demand an indemnity of eight billions.[1] Mr. Wilson said, "Not if I can prevent it." I judge he is going over to see that England's demands are not too exorbitant as well as to bring about his freedom of the seas.

[1] That is £8,000,000,000.

Robert Lansing to Edward Mandell House

U.S.S. George Washington. Dec. 8, 1918.

For Colonel House.[1] The President requests that final conclusions with regard to all the resolutions taken at the conference (?) on the second of December, eleven A.M., be withheld until his arrival in Paris and regards this as imperative to prevent misunderstandings.

He is satisfied with your position with regard to the resolutions adopted at the subsequent meetings of the conference except that he reserves judgement as to restricting Labor Conference to a neutral country where hostile influences are more likely to have free access.   Lansing.

T telegram (SDR, RG 59, 763.72119/2929, DNA).
[1] This was a reply to EMH to WW, No. 233, Dec. 5, 1918.

Frank Lyon Polk to Robert Lansing

Washington, December 8, 1918.

Argentina: Department in receipt of cable from American Ambassador, Buenos Aires,[1] stating that the President of Argentina[2] had asked him on December sixth to call to see him. The President appeared very favorably impressed with the action of the United States in regard to its statement sent to Chile and Peru re. Tacna and Arica dispute and that he stated that he desired to follow the lead of the United States in this as well as in all other matters tending to the permanent peace and welfare of the Americas and asked that this reponse be transmitted to the President of the United States by wireless. He informed the Ambassador that he would send messages through the representatives of Argentina at Santiago and Lima to the presidents of Chile and Peru similar or substantially identical to that of the United States. Ambassador reports that the manners of the President were most cordial and seemed to be overjoyed at taking action in connection with the United States in what he termed "such an epochal moment in history for the Western Hemisphere."

Brazil: Ambassador Rio de Janeiro[3] reports December sixth that Government Brazil in response to public opinion has invited Ruybarbosa[4] to attend Peace Conference as its representative; that Da Gama (will not go?) [also that it is improbable that da Gama will go][5] as he has been in office such a short time.

Costa Rica: American Legation has been closed and Charge d'Affaires[6] is enroute to United States in United States war vessel.

Peru: American Minister reports on December sixth[7] that President of Peru received statement President Wilson with evident pleasure and satisfaction and asked if there was any objection to its publication. Department has instructed Minister to inform him that there is no objection and it is so informing Government of Chile.[8]   Polk, Acting.

T telegram (WP, DLC).
[1] Frederic Jesup Stimson to FLP, Dec. 7, 1918, T telegram (SDR, RG 59, 723.2515/355, DNA).
[2] Hipólito Irigoyen.
[3] That is, Edwin Vernon Morgan.
[4] Ruy Barbosa, eminent Brazilian jurist, a future member of the Permanent Court of International Justice.
[5] Correction from the copy in SDR, RG 59, 723.2515/355, DNA. Domicio da Gama, the former Brazilian Ambassador to the United States, had recently become the Brazilian Foreign Minister.
[6] Stewart Johnson. Lansing had ordered the closing of the legation in San José on November 26, 1918, after a popular demonstration of friendship for the United States and President Wilson at the legation in the wake of the signing of the Armistice had been brutally disbanded by the police, and the Costa Rican authorities had made explicit threats against the lives of American citizens and United States officials in Costa Rica. For a detailed account, see the documents printed in FR 1918, pp. 271-75.

⁷ B. McMillin to FLP, Dec. 6, 1918, T telegram (SDR, RG 59, 723.2515/349, DNA).
⁸ FLP to B. McMillin, Dec. 8, 1918, and FLP to J. H. Shea, Dec. 8, 1918, T telegrams, both in SDR, RG 59, 723.2515/349, DNA.

From the Diary of Dr. Grayson

Monday, December 9, 1918.

The President worked in his study during the morning cleaning up a batch of papers that he had brought with him and which up to the present time had not been touched. He had fully recovered from his cold and was in splendid shape. The general treatment and course of action which I had recommended had been followed rigorously and I was proud of the fact that the President seemed physically able to cope with any task that he might encounter when our voyage was ended.

In the afternoon he went for a long walk about the deck with Mrs. Wilson, and in the evening we all attended the moving picture display in the dining salon.

At dinner the President told me what he characterized as one of his favorite stories. It was of two Irishmen who met on the evening of election day. The first asked the other what ticket he had voted. Pat replied that he had voted the Socialist ticket because, he explained, Socialism meant common ownership, and he went into some detail to explain to his colleague just what the Socialist party stood for. The latter listened in amazement and said: "Do you mean to say that if you had two houses you would give me one of them?" Pat replied: "Of course, I would." "Yes, and if you had two automobiles would you give me one of them?" "Sure," was Pat's reply. "Well, then, if you had two hogs would you give me one of them?" "You go to hell," said Pat; "you know damn well I have two hogs."

Continuing the conversation, the President said that Roland S. Morris, the American Ambassador to Japan, had sent him the clearest and most concise despatches of any of the Americans in the diplomatic service. I asked the President whether he thought Mr. Morris had had any special training in this line. "Oh, yes," the President replied to me, "you know, he was a student of mine at Princeton."

From the Diary of Edith Benham

December 9, 1918

Last night we went down to the "Old Salt Theatre." The crew had a "sing" to which all the rest of us were invited and the first to arrive was the President for he is always on the minute of time. At home the only thing that can get Margaret on time is when she has to go out with her father. The place was packed and the words of the songs were thrown on the screen, and we all sang, the President with great gusto, for he has a good voice, and Mrs. Wilson and I piping along merrily. Some poet laureate had composed a verse lauding the President and the crew all took kindly to that and whooped it out with great glee. A fearsome movie followed with ladies losing their clothes and gentlemen likewise—but not in unison as it were. Mr. Wilson made a ten-strike with the crew asking Captain McCauley if he might shake hands with the men. Murphy stood as usual just ahead of him on the little stage, Starling behind and Mr. Irving Hoover bossed the job from in front, admonishing the laggards and encouraging the timid. You never saw such a lot of happy faces as those waiting to be greeted. (I will remark here I had suggested this idea to him in casual conversation at table, as I have suggested a few other things; this, however, for ourselves.) I told Mrs. Wilson that there were probably a lot of men on watch and all who hadn't been able to shake hands, and so she asked Captain McCauley if they could be located and Mrs. Wilson would greet them, so I think everybody ought to be happy. Mr. Wilson said in shaking hands with one man, "How are you?" "Ganz gut," said this Anglo-Saxon.

Mr. Henry White drew a depressing word picture for Mrs. Wilson's Virginia ears about the reception of Miss Susie Booth in England. Miss Booth is of great width and blackness and has not yet the grand manners of Major Brooks, the President's man, who came to the White House with Mr. Taft and who has seen the life. He is also an Episcopalian which is a distinct social rise, Miss Booth belonging to Shiloh Baptist. Mr. White says that at Buckingham Palace Miss Booth will be led in to dinner on the arm of the Major Domo of the palace to her seat beside him in the servant's hall. I wish you could have seen Mrs. Wilson. She promptly said, "I will let her have a sandwich in her room and lock her in."

From Edward Mandell House

[Paris] December 9, 1918.

Number 19. For the President. According to present plans I understand that you will arrive in Paris at ten a.m. on Saturday December 14. Upon your arrival you will be taken at once to your residence. At twelve thirty a large formal lunch will be given in your honor at the Elysse Palace by the President. A committee of laboring men and socialists headed by Albert Thomas, Renaud Geer

[Renaudel], and Cabrain [Cachin][1], wishes to present you with an address at three thirty p.m. on Saturday the fourteenth and to hold a monster parade in your favor at that time. This is not definite but will probably take place. On Monday December 16, a formal reception will be tended you and Mrs. Wilson by the city of Paris at the Hotel de Ville at two thirty p.m. and I have accepted for you.

I have told Wiseman to tell Balfour and George that you will (*) [keep] Tuesday December 17, Wednesday December 18, and possibly the 19th free for conferences with them and I expect that both Balfour and George will be in Paris on the 17th. December 19 and 20th the King of Italy, the Italian Prime Minister and Baron Sonnino will be in Paris. The French and Belgian Governments are most insistent that you should make a trip to the devastated regions of France and Belgium. Accordingly the French Government are making arrangements for you to take a trip beginning December 26 which will occupy approximately three days through northern France and Belgium. At the same time it is planned that you should visit our army. Your trip to Italy, which I believe is necessary, might be begun on December 29 or 30th in order that you may return to Paris by January 3 or 4th for the first formal conference of the Allies. Clemenceau has told me that the English elections, the French celebrations, and the official visits to Paris have made it absolutely impossible to begin these formal conferences before January 3 or 4th.

Will you please let me know if you wish me to take any particular action with reference to the foregoing.   Edward House.

*Apparent omission.

T telegram (WP, DLC).
[1] Marcel Cachin, Socialist member of the Chamber of Deputies and editor of *L'Humanité*.

Frank Lyon Polk to Robert Lansing

Washington. December 9, 1918

For Ambassador Jusserand: "Mr. Pichon instructs me to send to you by wireless the two following telegrams bearing the dates of December fourth and sixth: 'First telegram text. University of Paris has expressed the desire to bestow on President Wilson, during a solemn session which would take place at the Sorbonne, the degree of Doctor Honoris Causa which, as you know, is conferred for the first time. The dean of the law school[1] would remit on the same occasion to the President an address signed by several law professors from the allied nations which you have referred to.

You would oblige me in transmitting this invitation to President

Wilson and also in asking the President to place you in a position to let us know the day which would be the most convenient to him for a visit to the American army.

I remind you that the sojourn of the King of Italy in Paris is scheduled for the nineteenth and the twentieth, the sojourn of the Prince Regent of Servia[2] for the twenty-sixth and the twenty-seventh. Signed Pichon.'

Second telegram answering your telegram just received. 'With great pleasure we shall expect President Wilson in Brest on the thirteenth instead of on the twelfth. The municipality of Paris would prefer under the circumstances to receive him on Monday the sixteenth at half past two-o'clock. The tour to the devastated regions might take place the seventeenth and eighteenth. You would oblige me in letting me know with the utmost haste whether these dates prove convenient. According to the President's wishes a luncheon instead of a dinner shall be tendered to him and to Mrs. Wilson on the day of their arrival at half past twelve o'clock. Signed Pichon.'

The French Government wish to know as soon as possible whether these arrangements are agreeable to the President. They expect a prompt answer if possible via Washington. Respectfully Chambrun."[3]   Polk, Acting.

T telegram (WP, DLC).
    [1] Fernand Larnaude.
    [2] Alexander, Crown Prince of Serbia, who had been appointed Regent in 1914.
    [3] Count Louis Charles de Chambrun, Counselor of the French embassy in Washington; at this time, Chargé d'Affaires ad interim.

From Juan Luis Sanfuentes Andonaegui

Santiago December 9, 1918.

Important. Following reply of President of Chile to telegram of President Wilson December 4, 6 pm. "The President of Chile has received the most friendly declaration of His Excellency President Wilson which informs him of the apprehension with which the United States Government has viewed the various incidents which have resulted in the suspension of consular relations between the Republics of Chile and Peru. It is his duty to state in reply that said incidents have not altered for one moment the serenity with which the Government of Chile has considered these events which in some form or other might produce inquietude in its international relations.

His Excellency the President of the United States judiciously considers that any agitation which might disturb the prospects of world peace would be disastrous; in that the Peace Conference soon to be convoked in Paris will take under consideration the establishment of an era of the permanent peace among all people, and points out the grave responsibility that would be incurred before the world by those who caused such agitation.

The President of Chile takes the opportunity to state on this occasion that the Chilean people, for the past thirty five years happily at peace with all nations have devoted all their energies to the establishment of their prosperity and well being and have justly settled all differences with their neighbors, and now most fervently desire to work for a definite peace among all peoples, a peace such as will be established by the Peace Conference of Paris.

His Excellency President Wilson calls the attention of the governments of Chile and Peru to the obligation which they have to the rest of the world, and to humanity relative to the maintenance of their peaceful relations.

The President of Chile is in accord with such an elevated concept, and can say that his Government has always done its best to disregard any event that might alter without reason the good relations which it has maintained and cultivated with all peoples, and more especially with the different countries of the American continent.

The message of His Excellency the President of the United States terminates by affirming his belief in the peaceful solution of the existing differences and manifests at the same time his readiness to offer alone or conjointly with other countries of this hemisphere every possible assistance to secure an equitable solution of the question.

The President of Chile is thankful for and is pleased with the most friendly sentiments of the Government of the United States, and trusts that the misunderstandings which Chile has with Peru, and which it has always tried to settle, will be definitely solved in conformity with the precepts of the treaty of Ancon which governs the relations between the two countries, and to the fulfillment of which the faith of the nation is bound. . . ."   Shea[1]

T telegram (SDR, RG 59, 723.2515/359, DNA).
   [1] In the remainder of the telegram, Shea reported that the Argentine Ambassador at Santiago, Carlos F. Gomez, had been directed by his government to offer mediation of the dispute in conjunction with the United States. However, President Sanfuentes had argued that the United States had not offered mediation but only assistance, and the Chilean Foreign Minister, Alamiro Huidobro Valdes, insisted that there was a distinct difference between assistance and mediation.

From the Diary of Dr. Grayson

Tuesday, December 10, 1918.

We sighted the Azores this morning. We ran close enough in so that we could discern the hills of the islands and the harbor mouth. The President came on deck as soon as we were fairly abreast of the land and remained there watching the picturesque scenery. Just before we passed the harbor of Ponte Delgada a Portugese gunboat, about the size of an ordinary harbor tug, steamed out and when she came abreast of us began firing a Presidential salute from a small brass gun mounted well forward. The GEORGE WASHINGTON's saluting battery responded. A number of camouflaged marine vessels that were anchored off the shore dipped their colors as we steamed by.

After we had passed the islands the President went to his study where he held conferences with the various members of the Peace Commission's experts staff, who reported to him upon the data which they had worked up for the commission. Afterward, the President sent for Ambassador Jusserand and they were together for more than a hour, the Ambassador presenting certain facts to the President which had been sent to him for that purpose by his own government.

Following luncheon the President, Mrs. Wilson and myself went to the bridge of the GEORGE WASHINGTON to witness an exhibition on the part of the anti-aircraft gun crews of the PENNSYLVANIA. They sent up a number of hot-air balloons and the gun crews essayed to shoot them down. The targets were none too distinct and more got away than were reached with the shrapnel.

Before returning to his cabin, the President, Mrs. Wilson and myself posed for some pictures with the three newspaper correspondents.

Clive Day[1] to Elizabeth Dike Day[2]

[U.S.S. *George Washington*] Dec. 10, 1918

After writing the above, last night, I dropped in at the movie show in the upper saloon, and took part in a very cordial demonstration that occurred when the President, making a speech, appeared on the screen while the President was in the audience.

We had proposed to continue our exploration of the boat today by a trip thru the engine-room, but Seymour[3] and I were told that the President might want some light on Austria-Hungary, so hung about the map room in readiness. Just after twelve we were asked to go to the President's office, where about a dozen of the principals in the Inquiry gathered, were introduced, and sat about while he talked to us for three-quarters of an hour.

Even men in the State department have not been kept informed of the President's ideas about the Conference and the part to be played by the U. S. Even Mr. George Creel, who is supposed to know as much as anybody, complained that he "did not know a God-dam thing about what the President was thinking." One of the younger men in the Department suggested yesterday to the President that it would be wise, before the party landed, to make clear his position to some of the men who are to be at the Conference; and apparently this gathering was the result.

After some discussion Charlie[4] and Westerman[5] and I are agreed that it would be improper to keep even memoranda of the points covered, and I shall not of course describe them here.

The President was genial and charming, with a fund of humor and of happy literary allusions. He impressed me as both sincere and earnest, and if he desired to get our most loyal contribution to the end that he has in view, he went about it the right way; the attitude that he outlined has my whole-hearted support—indeed, my admiration. Perhaps he is idealistic; only time can show; but his ideals are worth fighting for.

The outlook for the Inquiry has changed vastly for the better, in the opinion of all of us who were at these conferences; and if they are a fair indication of the temper of the men at the top it will be our own fault if we do not make good—so far as other conditions do not prevent.

The President said that he wanted to talk with some of us individually, on problems in different parts of the field, and probably those of us who have worked in Austria-Hungary will have a chance to answer some questions.

ALS (C. Day Papers, CtY).

[1] Professor of Economic History at Yale University; at this time, chief of the Balkan Division of The Inquiry and expert on Balkan questions on the advisory staff of the American Commission to Negotiate Peace (A.C.N.P.).

[2] Mrs. Clive Day.

[3] Charles Seymour, Professor of History at Yale University; at this time, chief of the Austro-Hungarian Division of The Inquiry and expert on Austria-Hungary on the advisory staff of the A.C.N.P.

[4] That is, Charles Seymour.

[5] William Linn Westermann, Professor of Ancient History at the University of Wisconsin; at this time, chief of the Western Asian Division of The Inquiry and expert on western Asia on the advisory staff of the A.C.N.P.

From the Diary of William Christian Bullitt

On Board the George Washington:
Tuesday, December 9 [10], 1918.

Last night just before the moving picture began, I sat down beside the President and said to him that he ought to call together the members of the Inquiry and other important people on board and explain to them the spirit in which he was approaching the conference and so far as possible the policies he intended to pursue, particularly in regard to a League of Nations. I explained that everyone on board was in a thoroughly sceptical and cynical mood and that it would have a fatal effect if when we reached Paris and met our British and French friends we were ignorant of or cynical concerning his intentions and policy. He said that he did not quite understand, and I explained further that most of the men with brains on board had been treated like immigrants and felt entirely left out of the game. The President at once replied that he would call together the party this morning and that he was greatly obliged for the suggestion and that it simply had not occurred to him that such a conference would be necessary.

At twelve this morning we received a summons to meet the President in his office, and he explained his entire program in some detail to a group of about ten including, Mezes, Bowman, Lunt, Seymour, Day, Westerman, Haskins, Beer and Humbolt.[1] I have never seen the President in a franker or more engaging mood. He was overflowing with warmth and good nature. He sat at his desk and we grouped about in chairs. The President talked for an hour, an occasional word being thrown in by one or another of us. As we rose to go he asked us to consider the conversation entirely confidential.

In the course of the talk the President made his position fairly clear in regard to the following points:

1. League of Nations. The President does not believe that any hard and fast constitution of the "League to Enforce Peace" variety can be established at the present time. He hopes that a Council of a League of Nations may be established by regular meetings of the Ministers of the powers accredited to some designated neutral state such as The Netherlands or Switzerland. It would be the business of this council to report to the Governments composing the League, if it considered that war was likely to break out in any quarter of the globe and the business of the Governments to step in and stop it. "War," said the Presi[d]ent, "must no longer be considered an exclusive business. Any war must be considered as affecting the whole world. If any nation refuses to listen to the powers composing the league it is my idea that they should be boycotted absolutely

by the other powers, cut off not only from goods, but all train, telephone, telegraph, mail and other forms of communication cut off absolutely. Their frontiers would be hermetically sealed."

The Presi[d]ent then repeated what he said at Jusserand's the other evening at the Alsace-Lorraine celebration to wit: "My idea is that we should make sure that the world will combine against an outlaw in the future just as it has combined in the present war against Germany."

The President also said that he thought the League of Nations should be given power to readjust frontiers on appeal of the population in any territory. He prefaced this remark by saying that the League would guarantee the sovereignty and territorial integrity of the component states.

2. Indemnities. The President said that certain of the Allies were conspiring to appoint a commission first to determine how much Germany possibly could be made to pay, and another commission later to determine their damages. The President said that he would oppose any indemnity except for the damage actually done by Germany, that this damage should first be determined scientifically and then an attempt should be made to have it paid; but that under no conditions would he assent to the imposition of indemnities beyond the damage actually suffered.

3. In regard to colonies the President said that he believed the German colonies in Africa should become the common property of the League of Nations and that they should be given to one of the smaller states to administer as the mandatory of the League of Nations. Trade rights to be equal for members of the League, exclusively. The colonies to be administered primarily in the interest of the natives. He also said that the [he] believed that Constantinople should be owned jointly by the League of Nations and administered by some small state as mandatory for the League.

4. The President indicated that he believed that Posen should go to Poland but that east Prussia should not be detached from the rest of Germany and that Poland should get access to the sea merely by making Danzig a free port and guaranteeing Poland transit on the railroads and water ways leading thereto.

5. The President talked at some length on the general spirit in which he was approaching the conference, saying that the United States was the only nation which was absolutely disinterested, that he felt that the leaders of the allies did not really represent their peoples,[2] that there was much hostility between Italy and France and some between France and England but that all were anxious to cooperate with us. He emphasized the fact that our only question throughout would be—is it just—and said he thought that question would be embarrassing to some of the allies.

6. The President said that he considered it necessary for Germany to pass through a probationary period before being admitted to the League of Nations. He considered this necessary because it must still be proved that the German people have a responsible, decent government.

7. The President did not mention Russia directly but said: "The only way I can explain susceptibility of the people of Europe to the poison of bolshevism, is that their Governments have been run for wrong purposes, and I am convinced that if this peace is not made on the highest principles of justice it will be swept away by the peoples of the world in less than a generation. If it is any other sort of a peace then I shall want to run away and hide on the Island of Guam or somewhere else remote, for there will follow not mere conflict but cataclysm."

8. The President also expressed very strongly several times the conviction that it was the right of each nation to have the sort of Government it desired, and indicated, I thought, that he was not considering a further advance against the Bolsheviki.

9. Several times the President said that all he wanted was to be convinced of the justice of a position and that he would fight for it to the end "politely if possible, rudely if necessary."[3]

10. In conclusion he asked us individually and collectively to come to him for frank discussion if there were any points on which we desired further information as to his opinion.

The conference broke up with the decentest sort of feeling and all the soreness and cynicism of the past week are now gone. The President really has great charm.

He told a story which I had not heard before to the effect that at Chateau Thierry, there was a gap in the French line thirty miles wide, that the American troops were ordered to retreat with the retreating French, that the American commander tore up the orders and commanded his divisions to advance, that this advance saved Paris and the war. "It is not too much to say that at Chateau Thierry we saved the world," said the President, "and I do not intend to let those Europeans forget it. They were beaten when we came in and they know it. Pershing has it all down in black and white from their own hands. They all acknowledged that our men at Chateau Thierry saved them. Now they are trying to forget it."

Two remarks of the President: "Tell me what is right and I'll fight for it." "I want a guaranteed position."

T MS (W. C. Bullitt Papers, CtY).
[1] Persons not heretofore identified in this series were Isaiah Bowman, director of the American Geographical Society and one of the leaders of The Inquiry, chief of territorial questions and expert on Russia and Poland on the advisory staff of the A.C.N.P.; William Edward Lunt, Professor of English History at Cornell University, expert on

Italy in The Inquiry and on the advisory staff of the A.C.N.P.; Charles Homer Haskins, Professor of History and Political Science and Dean of the Graduate School of Arts and Sciences of Harvard University, chief of the Division of Northwest Europe in The Inquiry and expert on western Europe on the advisory staff of the A.C.N.P.; George Louis Beer, specialist on Africa in The Inquiry and expert on colonial questions on the advisory staff of the A.C.N.P.; and Capt. Stanley Kuhl Hornbeck (not "Humbolt"), Professor of Political Science at the University of Wisconsin and a special expert attached to the United States Tariff Commission, chief of the Far Eastern Division of The Inquiry, and expert on the Far East on the advisory staff of the A.C.N.P.

[2] In his notes of the meeting, Charles Seymour summarized this part of Wilson's remarks as follows: "Official representatives did not really represent. If ominous poison of Bolshevism to be avoided necessary to get in touch with real masses of people. Existing statesmen too weatherwise to see the weather. If coming peace based on anything but justice and comprehension of opinion of masses next catastrophe would not be a war but a cataclysm." Charles Seymour, "Conference on George Washington with Woodrow Wilson, Dec. 10, 1918," Hw MS (C. Seymour Papers, CtY).

[3] In his diary, George Louis Beer commented on Wilson's statement as follows: "While he is in a fighting mood and is prepared to fight for a just peace, he virtually said that absolute justice in any specific instance was not attainable." The Diary of George Louis Beer, Dec. 10, 1918, T MS (G. L. Beer Papers, NNC).

A Memorandum by Isaiah Bowman

Memorandum on Remarks by the President
to Members of the Inquiry on December 10, 1918.

After a few introductory remarks to the effect that he was glad to meet us, and that he welcomed the suggestion of a conference to give his views on the impending peace conference, the President remarked that we would be the only disinterested people at the peace conference, and that the men whom we were about to deal with did not represent their own people.

He next mentioned the advisability of not leaving in purely political hands the question of the German indemnity, and went on to say that the matter should be studied by a commission to determine the just claims of the Allies against Germany, and that after such determination Germany should be made to pay. The President illustrated the difficulties of Allied action in imposing an indemnity by a reference to the Boxer question of a few years ago, and contrasted the attitude of the United States with that of Germany and the other European powers.

As for the form of Poland's government and questions like that of the disposition of Danzig, he would only say that he was in favor of their having any government they damned pleased, and that he was for imposing upon them no other provision than those which applied to individuals—the important thing is what a person ought to have, not what he wants.

The President pointed out that this was the first conference in which decisions depended upon the opinion of mankind, not upon the previous determinations and diplomatic schemes of the assembled representatives. With great earnestness he re-emphasised the point that unless the conference was prepared to follow the opinions of mankind and to express the will of the people rather than that of their leaders at the conference, we should soon be involved in another breakup of the world, and when such a breakup came it would not be a war but a cataclysm.

He spoke of the League to Enforce Peace, of the possibility of an international court with international police, etc., but added that such a plan could hardly be worked out in view of the fact that there was to be only one conference and it would be difficult to reach agreements respecting such matters; and he placed in opposition to this view of the work of the conference and of the project of a League to Enforce Peace the idea of covenants, that is, agreements, pledges, etc., such as could be worked out in general form and agreed to and set in motion, and he particularly emphasised the importance of succeeding experience to guide subsequent action.

As for the League of Nations, it implied political independence and territorial integrity plus alteration of terms and alteration of boundaries if it could be shown that injustice had been done or that conditions had changed. And such alteration would be the easier to make in time as passion subsided and matters could be viewed in the light of justice rather than in the light of a peace conference at the close of a protracted war. He illustrated his point by the workings of the Monroe Doctrine, saying that what it had done for the western world the League of Nations would do for the rest of the world; and just as the Monroe Doctrine had developed in time to meet changing conditions, so would the League of Nations develop. In fact, he could not see how a treaty of peace could be drawn up or how both *elasticity* and *security* could be obtained save under a League of Nations; the opposite of such a course was to maintain the idea of the Great Powers and of balance of power, and such an idea had always produced only aggression and selfishness and war; the people are heartily sick of such a course and want the peace conference and the powers to take an entirely new course of action.

He then turned to some specific questions and mentioned the fact that England herself was against further extension of the British Empire.

He thought that some capital, as The Hague or Berne, would be selected for the League of Nations, and that there would be organised in the place chosen a Council of the League whose members should be the best men that could be found. Whenever trouble arose it could be called to the attention of the Council and would be given thereby the widest publicity. In cases involving discipline there was the alternative to war, namely, the boycott; trade, including postal and cable facilities, could be denied a state that had been guilty of wrong-doing. Under this plan no nation would be permitted to be an outlaw, free to work out its evil designs against a neighbor or the world.

He thought that the German colonies should be declared the common property of the League of Nations and administered by small nations. The resources of each colony should be available to all members of the League, and in this and other matters involving international relations or German colonies or resources or territorial arrangements, the world would be intolerable if only *arrangement* ensues; that this is a peace conference in which arrangements cannot be made in the old style. Anticipating the difficulties of the conference in view of the suggestion he had made respecting the desires of the people of the world for a new order, he remarked, "If it won't work, it must be made to work," because the world was faced by a task of terrible proportions and only the adoption of a cleansing process would recreate or regenerate the world. The poison of Bolshevism was accepted readily by the world because "it is a protest against the way in which the world has worked." It was to be our business at the peace conference to fight for a new order, "agreeably if we can, disagreeably if necessary."

We must tell the United States the truth about diplomacy, the peace conference, the world. He here referred to the censorship, saying that he had arranged in the face of opposition from Europe for the free flow of news to the United States, though he doubted if there would be a similarly free flow to the peoples of other European countries; after a considerable effort he had secured the removal of French and English restrictions on political news. Thereupon he finished his reference to the frank conditions under which the conference had to work and the necessity for getting the truth to the people by saying that if the conference did not settle things on such a basis the peace treaty would not work, and "if it doesn't work right the world will raise Hell."

He stated that we should only go so far in backing the claims of a given power as justice required, "and not an inch farther," and referred to a remodeled quotation from Burke: "Only that government is free whose people regard themselves as free."

The European nations reminded one of the episode in Philippopolis—for the space of two hours they cried, "Great is Diana of the Ephesians"—to which the President appended in an aside, "in the interest of the silversmiths."

The President concluded the conference by saying that he hoped to see us frequently, and while he expected us to work through the

Commissioners according to the organization plans of the conference, he wanted us in case of emergency not to hesitate to bring
directly to his attention any matter whose decision was in any way
critical; and concluded with a sentence that deserves immortality:
"Tell me what's right and I'll fight for it; give me a guaranteed
position."

T MS (I. Bowman Papers, MdBJ).

Charles Seymour to His Family

December 10, '18.

. . . I was stopped writing this morning by a call to a conference
with the president. He explained that the particular subject he
wanted to discuss with me he was going to leave until later, but
that he wanted to go over the whole situation with the Inquiry
specialists. The others came in,—Clive, and Westermann, Haskins,
Lord,[1] Bowman, Beer, Mezes, and Bullitt, who is acting as the only
liaison officer between us & the State Department. The president
said that he wanted to go over the situation with us and make
absolutely clear his position and his policy. He talked for an hour
and a quarter and at the end of that time asked and answered
questions. I can't put on paper what he said—he asked us to keep
it confidential and I should be afraid of the letters being opened. I
shan't even put it in a memorandum book. Much of it will doubtless
come out anyway during the next month. Much I can probably
remember. I can say this that he is on what seems to me the right
track exactly as regards general policy and you know pretty well
how I feel. You will remember how your father[2] felt in the matter
of a probationary period for Germany before she enters the league
of nations. He will be interested to know that the president agrees
with him, although I did not and do not.

The whole talk was very intimate and in one respect it was really
a historic occasion because it is absolutely the first time the President has let anyone know what his ideas are and what his policy
is. His manner was very friendly. He explained that he could not
know the details of all the questions that were coming up, but would
be forced to rely on the information we gave him, that he wanted
us to come to him freely and that we must expect him to call on
us. One phrase sticks in my head—"You tell me what's right and
I'll fight for it."

His talk was impromptu and colloquial, but very fluent, with a
literary flavor & constant allusions or quotations; what interested
me and surprised me most was the constant humor running through

everything. Equally interesting was his unconscious use of phrases—epigrams; it has become second nature: such as, "When certain men applaud me, I know I am wrong." And others with regard to the current situation which I don't dare quote. Everyone agreed that the personal impression made was very favorable. There was no touch of egotism—he spoke with extreme modesty and twice laughlingly apologized for his ideas saying that they werent very good but he thought them better than anything else that he had heard. At times he showed great vigor—saying in regard to a certain point that "his back was up and very stiff"; another time he was semi-humorous in regard to a point which he considered vital saying that if it were not secured "the conference wouldn't be worth either your or my attendance, and I wouldn't come home, but would go to Guam."

I sat about three feet from him and in talking he fixed each [of] us with a very direct look of several seconds. Standing, he is short, as you know, but sitting he looked very large. His personal magnetism is very strong—I realized it as I had years ago in college. Several points he made seemed better then than afterwards. But I am enormously relieved; I think tremendous difficulties and dangers are ahead of us, and complete success impossible; but I do think that he has a policy and that in its broad lines it is the right policy. Naturally we are pleased that he is going to use us, for we have been worried by the feeling that Lippmann's connection with the Inquiry had discredited the whole organization.

I wish your father would have sat in at the conference. I thought of him several times and his interest in things.

AL (C. Seymour Papers, CtY).
    [1] Robert Howard Lord, Assistant Professor of Modern European History at Harvard University, head of the Eastern European Division of The Inquiry, and expert on Russia and Poland on the advisory staff of the A.C.N.P.
    [2] Thomas Hamer Watkins, father of Seymour's wife, Gladys Marion Watkins Seymour. Watkins was a coal operator of Scranton, Pa.

From the Diary of Edith Benham

December 10, 1918

The more I am with the Wilsons the more I am struck with their unrivaled home life. I have never dreamed such sweetness and love could be. One never hears anything between them but just love and understanding, and it is very beautiful to see his face light up and brighten at the very sight of her and to see her turn to him for everything, though she is a woman of a lot of spirit. Then they are so lovely to me I hate to be away from them, for they are so nice, and always make me feel they want me around. I told Mrs. Wilson my only regret was I hadn't a nice, thick setter's tail to thump on the deck to show how happy I am.

The President has become a movie fan. He was so tired out at first that he slept nearly all the time, but now he is rested and from despising the movies he clamored to go last night.

He is suffering terribly under the elaborate French cooking. Everything, of course, comes with a sauce and he says he can't "see any sense in wrapping up food in pajamas." He loves ice cream and can't get even that without a sauce. Mrs. Wilson and I love it, of course, all women do. He is having growing forebodings of the food to be served at the Murat palace, but blackest of all is the thought of the cold in that princely residence. . . .

Mr. Creel and Dr. Grayson came in to luncheon today. The former is a very amusing person. Mrs. Wilson said he had been talking to her before luncheon and said he had hated during the war to bring anything more in to distress the President, for he said, "As I brought those weighty things to him I could see his eye begin to twitch." Her eyes, poor dear, filled with tears as he said this as I know she is anxious about this little twitching of his left eyelid (lower) and a little throbbing which comes in his cheek. Mr. Creel spoke of the President's great modesty and said hearing him talk you would think all he expected in Paris was to receive a few letters and have a few circulars sent him from the Bon Marche! Mr. White had spoken of the same thing this morning saying that the governments and press were trying to stir up feeling against him, but the peoples of Europe looked on him as a god and savior. This from a Roosevelt Republican! He thinks that the President is very different from the popular idea of him. I spoke of his sweetness and lovableness, and he said he thought the impression of him as an austere person had grown up on account of his innate shyness, and the fact that he didn't surround himself with people and have them dropping in to meals.

At luncheon they spoke of Admiral Sims who has cooked his goose very effectively with Mr. Wilson by making his speech about the British Navy having won the war. The President said it seemed impossible to send anyone over there who didn't get the English viewpoint, and he had told Mr. Davis jokingly he would recall him if he ceased to represent America. Conversation shifted to James Hazen Hyde,[1] whom Creel said had improved greatly, but Mr. Wilson said he did not believe in mingling with the branches of a tree whose roots were rotten. Creel spoke of Whitney Warren[2] who has been making anti-Wilson speeches in Italy, and said they were so anti-American he felt he should have been sent home. In fact, one of his men in Italy had said he ought to have his passports taken away.

¹ See G. Creel to WW, Aug. 2, 1918, Vol. 49.
² See EMH to WW, May 14, 1916, n. 1, Vol. 37.

To Edward Mandell House

U.S.S. George Washington,
Memorandum for the Secretary of State: 10 December, 1918.

The President asks if you will be kind enough to have for [the] following message sent in code to Mr. House in France:

"Referring to your No. 19, December 9th, the President asks me to say that while he greatly regrets the necessity for postponing the beginning of the formal business of conference until the third or fourth of January, he is of course willing to acquiesce in the programme as outlined, subject of course to such changes as may be mutually agreeable upon conference after his arrival. But he wishes me to ask if it would not be possible, in some tactful way that would not give offence or be misunderstood, to avoid the demonstration of laboring men and socialists which you say is being planned for the afternoon of Saturday. The President fears embarrassment from any seeming identification with any single element, and recalls the criticisms already made by those interested in opposing his principles with regard to the source of the popular support which he is receiving."   The President

CC MS (WP, DLC).

From Edward Mandell House

Paris, December 10, 7 p.m. [1918]

Secret for the President. After sending you my number 233,¹ I concluded that it would be best simply to advise Lord Derby that I had communicated summary of these proceedings to you. I have not committed you to any of the resolutions.

Edward House.

T telegram (WP, DLC).
¹ That is, EMH to WW, Dec. 5, 1918.

A Memorandum and a Statement by Herbert Clark Hoover and John William Davis

[Dec. 10, 1918]

Memorandum of a Conference held in London on December 10th, at which were present Lord Reading, Sir Joseph McClay,[1] M. Clementel, M. Boret,[2] and M. Crespi, being a Committee appointed by the Allied Premiers to discuss with Messrs. Hoover and Hurley the proposals of the President relative to European Relief. Mr. Hurley being absent, was represented by Mr. Norman Davis, who also represented the U. S. Treasury, and Mr. J. P. Cotton[3] was present, at the invitation of Mr. Hoover.

After several previous meetings for discussion of the President's proposals, this final meeting took place on December 10th, at which were present the above-mentioned gentlemen.

After considerable discussion, and after Messrs. Reading, Clementel, and Crespi had presented the views of their respective Governments, Mr. Hoover, on behalf of the American members, stated that according to their understanding, the views were not far apart and that the President's plan was accepted in principle, with the exception that a Council with ministerial powers should be set up to perform the functions suggested in the President's plan, for the Supreme War Council, to determine broad policies in connection with the Relief Problem in Europe. Mr. Hoover also explained that it had never been the contention of the United States that the Relief should be solely an undertaking by the American Government, as evidenced by the President's proposal.

The Allied Representatives assented to this interpretation, but as nothing specific had been stated regarding that portion of the proposal relating to the use of German tonnage (although, as above indicated, it was indirectly accepted) Mr. Hoover, in order to avoid any misunderstanding, called attention to the President's proposal regarding the handling of shipping, and specifically mentioned that it was the understanding of the American Representatives that the whole of the President's views regarding Shipping were accepted, and that the only question in relation thereto was the method of approaching the Germans on the problem. It was agreed that such approach should be made through the Armistice Authorities, with the object, if necessary, of embodying this in a renewal of the Armistice.

[1] That is, Sir Joseph Patton Maclay (not "McClay"), British shipping controller and head of the Ministry of Shipping.

[2] Victor Boret, French Minister of Agriculture and Supply.

[3] That is, Joseph Potter Cotton, the representative of the United States Food Administration in Europe.

Lord Reading specifically abandoned the notion, which he had advanced at previous meetings, that an Allied administrative Board should be created around the Director General of Relief, and it was finally proposed by the American Representatives that the Allied Representatives should draw up a memorandum, for submission to the War Council, expressing agreement with the President's plan in principle, and embodying the exception above mentioned, they stating that, although they had no authority to accept any alteration in the President's plan, yet they believed there would be no objection to the proposals as above indicated.

A discussion took place as to the details of administration which the Director General of Relief would erect, and Mr. Hoover outlined the method of determination of need, taking up existing bodies, plus other bodies which he would create for the purpose of advising the newly erected Council, and that through this expression of need sufficient co-ordination could be obtained as between Allied and Relief supplies.

At previous meetings, M. Clementel had proposed the erection of a complete economic Council controlling all raw material, finance, transportation, and food, and in the discussion at the meeting above referred to, in answer to a specific question, he stated that he moderated his proposals entirely to the problem of dealing with Food as an emergency measure for the period of the Armistice. M. Clementel emphasized the necessity for consolidation of Relief with other European Food problems, and the necessity of this newly erected body supervising all European food, including that of the Allies, to which Mr. Hoover represented that it was, from an American point of view, wholly impossible, and submitted a memorandum indicating the domestic reasons in the United States why this was not feasible. Mr. Hoover also submitted a memorandum embracing the views of the American Representatives as to the internal organization of the Directorate General of Relief, embodying the views expressed at the meeting.

STATEMENT FURNISHED BY MESSRS. HOOVER AND DAVIS TO THE COMMITTEE APPOINTED BY THE ALLIED PREMIERS TO CONSIDER RELIEF MATTERS, LONDON, DECEMBER 10, 1918.

In consideration of suggestions made by the U.S. in connection with relief, it may be helpful to state and understand some of the difficulties in the relation of the U. S. to the task in hand.

The Armistice and the sequent liberation of considerable shipping will open to the Allies the Chief food markets of the southern hemisphere and thus automatically create a larger surplus during the next eight months from the U. S. than would have been the case with continued war. This surplus, however, will be entirely deficient in providing for the larger number of mouths now proposed to feed unless rationing can be continued by the American people on a voluntary basis and any other basis than voluntary action could not be forced upon the American people under Armistice or Peace conditions except under an appeal for high humanitarian service. It must be obvious that the continued provision of such services through voluntary action can only be obtained by American officials and in the belief that these savings are being devoted to purely humanitarian purposes through the administration of their own agents.

The American people, far removed as they are from the seat of action, necessarily believe that the trade restrictions which have been imposed by the Government will be quickly removed and control of price of export foodstuffs which exists today will be felt more and more onerous as time goes on. The pressure of various trades for freedom of action is already being felt to a marked degree and any indication that the price control and distribution of American food stuffs was carried out by agencies over which their government did not have absolute control would break down the whole basis of American systems under these policies. The Allied Buying Agencies in the U. S. are already subject to suspicion, not because of any failure of proper action but simply because of the large volume of their transactions and to extend these Buying Agencies to a practical purchasing of the entire surplus of the U. S. would raise an amount of opposition that would break all hope of price restraint. Furthermore, any attempt to use these agencies to control the direct trading between the U. S. and neutrals (with agreed restrictions regarding re-export) would be the death-knell of such associations.

It should be possible on the background of the necessities of starving people to maintain through the agency of solely American Government Officials who are responsible to their own people, a background of high sentiment upon which a reasonable and proper control can be built. The American people have given ample evidence of their repugnance against profiteering but any action on their part must be voluntary and not compulsory by virtue of the control of foreign buying agencies.

A third matter of great importance lies in the fact that there is a strong tendency on the part of the American people to return to their instinctive desire for separation from European entanglements beyond cooperation with their associates in winding up the war. It is manifest that the American people must be impressed constantly with their national duty in participation in the helping of the Allied and other countries of Europe from the effects of the war. There is no way through which the national conscience can be so awakened and retained constantly upon this problem as through their participation in a matter which so strikes national imagination and that is that by self-denial on their part that they should be providing food stuffs for millions of people in Europe.

The logical development of the organization of relief to liberated neutrals and enemy populations, as proposed by the President, would be as follows:

The Director General of Relief would departmentalize his organization into Purchase, Transportation, Finance, Statistics, Alimentation, etc.

Purchases in countries of Associated Governments would be made from or through the Governmental agencies in such countries and in neutral countries through or in cooperation with established interallied agencies.

Transportation would likewise be secured from the Associated Governments or, in the case of the chartering of neutral shipping, it would be through established Allied Agencies, or in the case of enemy shipping, operated by various governments in accord with the President's proposal.

In finance, Neutral countries and Germany must pay in acceptable exchange, some sections of Austria and certain liberated populations probably likewise. This portion of the problem becomes one of working capital which the Director General can probably solve without call upon the European Allies. Certain liberated populations must be financed by advances contributed, presumably by the Associated Governments. Necessarily, accountability for all operations would be organized under the Finance Department.

Statistics on world supplies and world needs must be organized in close cooperation with agencies of the Associated Governments in determination of available resources.

A Department of Alimentation with competent investigators into the needs of populations relieved would need to be maintained.

In order to maintain intimate contact with the various Food Ministries, Foreign Offices, Blockade, Munitions, and Military Controls of the Associated Governments, and the Inter-Allied Committees on Food, Transport, Purchase, Blockade, etc., a series of liaison officers would need to be set up by the Director General between himself and staff and these agencies.

It may be found advisable to maintain a Director of Relief in some of the countries relieved, to attend to Administrative matters, acting in accord with the representatives in those countries of the Associated Governments, in the same manner as the Director General accords with the Supreme War Council or with such delegated body as may be agreed in the broad policies as suggested by the President.

As distribution must be carried out through Governments or Municipalities the Administrative staffs in various countries would be very small.

All Staff and personnel would be chosen and retained on the grounds of personal fitness and loyalty to the organization, without regard to nationality.

CC MSS (WP, DLC).

From the Diary of Dr. Grayson

Wednesday, December 11, 1918.

The President again talked with the newspaper men on deck. He was asked his personal views on the guilt of the Kaiser. He had just stated that in New Jersey the corporation laws made it very definite that guilt was personal. Wasn't it a fair analogy that the same ratio of personal guilt would prevail in the case of the Kaiser, the President was asked by Nevin. "Exactly," he replied, "but this also would prevail. You can't always find out actually who is the guilty party. I am not wholly convinced that the Kaiser himself was entirely responsible for the war and the results of it. There were a good many evidences from time to time that he was coerced, and there also exist plenty of evidence that the war in reality was the product of the system of the great German General Staff that surrounded and dominated the Kaiser. Within the year before the war started Germany, after a really great attempt to conquer the world commercially, was on the verge of realizing her object. Although, about to do so, the German military party thought they saw a short cut by employing military power instead of the peaceful means theretofore used. They thus showed that they were very stupid. They figured that they could dispose of their opponents one by one, and they plainly did not dream that England would come into the war. They should have known, if they had any sense at all, that England was the very nation that must come in."

Speaking about government and about our own system of government in particular, the President classed it as really a government of committees rather than a government of party leadership. He said he believed sooner or later we would come to a cabinet form of government. Great Britain now has such a government. He believed it would be a process of evolution. The President pointed out that in this cabinet form of government a man rises to his position of leadership upon his proven ability, by what he does. In the English parliament he proves his ability to put through measures for the government, and his ability in debate, and he goes through this period of probation, as it were, at the end of which he has proved his worth and established his own level among other men. He naturally winds up as a party leader and takes charge of party measures. The President said that that form of government has a greater responsibility to the people than our own government. He added however that he thought our present form of government was the best in time of war. This was indicated by the fluidity of the situations developing and overturning the cabinets on the other side; whereas, ours was compact all the time.

Talking about whether it was fair to assume that the average Congressman was fairly representative of his constituency, the President thought on the whole he was, but there were some very startling examples. He did not believe that Senator Sherman of Illinois was fairly representative of the sentiments of the people of Illinois; nor was Medill McCormick.[1]

[1] That is, Lawrence Yates Sherman and Joseph Medill McCormick, Republican senator and congressman, respectively, from Illinois.

From the Diary of Raymond Blaine Fosdick

Wednesday, December 11th, 1918.

I had an hour's conference alone with the President in his rooms this afternoon on matters of which I may not write. He looks much better than when he came on board and talks with his old-time succinctness and lucidity of statement. I think his mental processes function more easily and logically than in any other man I have ever met, and the compelling power of his personality is tremendous. Yet he is simple and modest, giving an impression of eagerness to learn and a desire to profit by any new fact or thought he can get hold of. "Tell me what America wants in the War," he told his economic advisers yesterday afternoon, "and I'll go into the Peace Conference and fight for it." He talked to me with the utmost frankness—indeed, with an amazing frankness—and his characterizations of Lloyd George, Clemenceau, Lord Milner, Pershing and others were keen, almost dramatic, and would have been interesting coming from any man. To my great delight he called B.,[1] an American college president, a "crook." He discussed the spread of Bolshevism—"a poison," he called it—and speculated on its future, not only in Russia but around the world. In assisting to bring about a "liberal" peace, I think he feels that he is up against the hardest fight of his life. "The Peace terms must have the support of the progressive elements in the world, or they won't last for a generation," he told me.

The outstanding impression that one gets of the President is that he is a pronounced Liberal. Conservatism he defined as the policy of "Make no changes and consult your Grandmother when in doubt." He is a Liberal not only from conviction, but as a matter of expediency. The Conservatives do not realize what forces are loose in the world at the present time. Liberalism is the only thing that can save civilization from chaos—from a flood of ultra-radicalism that will swamp the world. (I am paraphrasing the President's argument.) Those who argue for the *status quo ante bellum*, or for any other *status quo*, or for the maintenance of things as they were, are like so many vain kings sitting by the sea and commanding the tide not to rise. Liberalism must be more liberal than ever before; it must even be radical, if civilization is to escape the typhoon.

The President's wit has not suffered in the years since he left Princeton. He punctuates his remarks with anecdotes and does not hesitate to use slang. He loves funny stories and cannot resist going out of his way to tell one. He recited a limerick which I had not heard before:

> "Behold the marvelous Pelican,
> His bill holds more than his belly can.
> He takes in his beak
> Enough food for a week:
> I don't understand how the hell he can."

Mrs. Wilson came into the room just as we were finishing. I noticed he called her "sweetheart." They seem to be greatly attached to each other.

The crew to-night put on for our benefit a musical comedy which was good stuff. The President laughed his head off at it. I walked the deck with Creel and others until midnight. Wish I could be sure that the men around the President were capable of giving him the best advice obtainable. He is so extraordinary a figure: Why should he lean on frail reeds?

¹ Nicholas Murray Butler?

From the Diary of William Christian Bullitt

Wednesday: [Dec. 11, 1918]

Raymond Fosdick came to my room and awakened me last night to tell me the following story and ask me what he should do about it: When he reached the 23rd street ferry on his way to the boat at 6 A.M. December 4, he noticed hundreds of young men and women and old men and women hurrying off the ferry boat and away into the darkness. He asked his taxi driver who they were and was told that they were sweat shop workers. He happened to meet one of them buying a morning paper and asked the man how long he worked a day. The man replied: "Fourteen hours. But do you see that boat (pointing across the river towards the George Washington) there's a man aboard her that is going to Europe to change all that."

I advised Fosdick to tell the story to the President and to advise him that he must see to it that a bill of industrial human rights was written into the treaty of peace—a bill providing for world wide maximum hours of labor (at least in civilized countries) minimum wages, unemployment insurance, etc.

Fosdick did this today. The President replied that it frightened him to think how much the common people of the world expect of him. That he did not consider it possible to take up any such matters at the peace conference. That he hoped the international labor conference on which he looked with much favo[r] would press for these matters. Helms[1] talked with the President today. The President said that the proposition for a conference with Borah and Hughes had not reached him, though I had both McCormick's and Polk's explicit assurance that the[y] would put it up to him.

In the course of his talk with Fosdick, the President called Lloyd George "a man without principle," Milner "a Prussian," Clemenceau "an old man, too old to comprehend new ideas," Orlando, "a damned reactionary."

[1] Maj. Birch Helms, a lawyer of New York and treasurer of the Republican National Committee. A graduate of the Officers Training Camp at Plattsburg, he was at this time a member of the Army General Staff and a special military aide on the staff of the A.C.N.P.

Clive Day to Elizabeth Dike Day

[U.S.S. *George Washington*] Dec. 11, 1918

. . . Last night I had further talk with Mr. White, about the Balkans, and this morning was reading on that subject when word came that the President wanted to see Young,[1] Seymour, Lord and me. Lord was undressed in his berth, getting over the effect of a typhoid inoculation, the rest of us went at once to the Presidential office, where we were greeted very cordially and chatted informally for half an hour on the specific problems in the field of Austria-Hungary and thereabouts. The President showed good general information, asked good questions, and showed what seem to me to be in general sound ideas. He suggested a plan of procedure, which might shorten the period of deliberation, and which we are going to study with regard to our particular fields; I have as yet no matured opinion on its practicability.

Mrs. Wilson entered the office twice, to get the text of the address which Pres. Poincaré will make tomorrow when we land. (Last night I read the text of the President's reply; Mrs. Wilson had called in Shotwell,[2] on Creel's nomination, as Shotwell had lent Creel a French manual, and thereby established his reputation for scholarship; and Shotwell was at her request translating it into French. M. Jusserand, I'm told, has since then revised the translation.) She apologized very sweetly, and the President introduced us to her. Hanged if I can remember what she wore. Charlie insists that she reminds him of somebody and can't remember who it is.

I can illustrate the tone of the discussion by a remark of the President when we were discussing Montenegro. He said that the King[3] had written him a number of letters to which he had sent replies in the spirit of the Irishman: "Not that I care a dam—but how's your mother?"

This afternoon I have been in a heated discussion with Charlie, Bullitt, Raymond Fosdick and for a brief period Mr. White, over the President's plan regarding a League of Nations. The importance and the difficulty of doing things right grow on me as we approach France.

One impressive thing is the way in which young men like Bullitt and Fosdick go to the President and tell him what they think he ought to do. They have real influence, for they have ideas for which they are willing to stand—and many in the party are not of that class. I hope that the Inquiry may be in that class, and may exercise its influence within its somewhat narrow field. It has made a promising start. One danger which it runs is that academic specialists may not be able to get away from details, so as to block out questions in bold outlines. I distrust some of my colleagues. If we had some measure of Charlie's gift of exposition it would be a great advantage.

. . .

ALS (C. Day Papers, CtY).
　[1] That is, Allyn Abbott Young, Professor of Economics and Finance at Cornell University, head of the Division of Economics in The Inquiry, and chief of the Division of Economics and Statistics of the A.C.N.P.
　[2] James Thomson Shotwell, Professor of History at Columbia University, director of research in The Inquiry, and chief of the Historical Division of the A.C.N.P.
　[3] Nicholas I.

From the Diary of Edith Benham

December 11, 1918.

I have taken in a detective story Mrs. Knight[1] gave me before leaving for the President to read. He is very fond of them and I hope this will prove to be a good one. He has another trait peculiar to great thinkers. He likes to play solitaire and plays nearly every night before going to bed. At the White House he is very apt to come in at noon when he has no appointments, and play for an hour before luncheon. I think Mrs. Wilson taught him to play, and that he never did it much until lately. He does away with the theory that great people do not sleep much for he always sleeps a lot. Mrs. Wilson is a night hawk and he says they are going on the vaudeville stage as "Midnight Mary" and "Dopey Dick."

. . . Yesterday afternoon I asked Mrs. Wilson what our plans are and she says they are very indefinite yet. Saturday is the luncheon President Poincare gives to the President, and Monday at the Hotel de Ville (town hall) in Paris, he is to be given the freedom of the city or something. President Poincare has sent a copy of his address and the query came if Mr. Wilson would reply in French or English, to his great amusement. He has been asking at meals about different French expressions and what they mean, but he didn't feel his holdings in the tongue sufficient to warrant a reply in French. He sent this reply to Mr. Creel—to be translated. Creel gave it to an American, an excellent French scholar, to translate but the latter said it was too hard for him and he thought it would be better to give it to one of the French. Creel said it was a good idea, for the French had had an awful time in putting Mr. Wilson's English into French, particularly one sentence in which he used the expression "uneasy struts."

He is very much perturbed over the fact that the formal beginning of the conference will not be until January, on account of the general election in England. He called the three press representatives into conference the other night on receiving this news and asked them to make a statement to their papers putting this in the best light, for he didn't want our country to think that he came over on a junketing trip, and the conferences were to be so much delayed. He feels that the informal conferences which will precede the formal ones are really more important than the regular sessions. I suppose it is a species of trying out. . . .

Last night we had some incident in the shape of a vaudeville by the bluejackets in the "Old Salt Theatre." It was a very good show, with some abandoned looking soubrettes in blond wigs and tattooed arms. The President enjoyed it hugely and two of the chorus came down from the stage and shook him warmly by the hand. He has been so dear and human, doing everything asked of him, and seeming to enjoy it all immensely. Today at luncheon Captain McCauley came to ask if he would go down to be photographed forward with the crew, and he went at once and a lot of views and movies were made. The Army photographers are busy taking for official archives, and today Major Griffin,[2] my old friend of the pigeons, asked Mrs. Lansing and me if we would go. So up we went and made fools of ourselves talking animatedly for the movie man and posing for the cameras. Secretary Lansing came up and we chatted with him in the movies. Major Griffin says he is going to make up an album of all the photographs and present one to every one on the trip, so I shall be assured of mine.

[1] Unidentified.
[2] Frank J. Griffin, with the Signal Corps.

From Joseph Patrick Tumulty

The White House, December 11, 1918.

Am sending for your information and comment following, quoted from Echo de Paris in American newspapers, quote.

The President is quoted as having made this reply, colon, inner quote.

Only by years of long years [sic] of repentance can Germany atone for her crimes and show sincerity. No true American could think of visiting Germany unless forced to do so by strict official obligations. That is to say, I decline in advance to consider any suggestion of the kind. unquote.   Tumulty.

T telegram (WP, DLC).

From the Diary of Dr. Grayson

Thursday, December 12, 1918.

This was our last night on shipboard. The President had cleaned up all of his work early in the day and had spent a very considerable part of the afternoon on deck. We went to the movies tonight. At the conclusion of the pictures the entire choir of the GEORGE WASHINGTON, led by the orchestra, sang the hymn: "God be with you till we meet again." All of the officers and guests stood on their feet and participated in the singing. The farewell was inspiring and touching to all of us.

During his stay on the ship the President had made himself very popular with every member of the personnel, from Captain Mc-Cauley to the last enlisted apprentice boy. He had visited all parts of the ship, had his picture taken with the "black gang" up from the engine and boiler rooms, and with the remainder of the personnel on the forward deck. Whenever the President appeared on deck the crew would gather where they could watch him, and he never failed to wave his hand to them, and when they were close enough to give them a friendly greeting. It was this very democratic spirit that brought about the strongest feeling of admiration and love for the President from the ship's personnel.

From the Diary of Raymond Blaine Fosdick

Thursday, December 12th, 1918.

This has been a perfect day,—clear and crisp but not cold. We are now far north of the Azores and are heading toward Brest. The President spent most of the day in his rooms, working on the Peace business. He goes to face the lions, if ever a man did. "It frightens me," he told me yesterday, "when I think of what the people of the civilized world are expecting as a result of the Peace Conference."
. . .

We had our last "movie" to-night—Geraldine Farrar in an excellent film. At the end, just before the lights went up, a group of fifty bluejackets who had gathered unseen in a corner of the dining room, sang: "God be with you till we meet again." They sang it softly, in splendidly modulated voices, while we all stood. The President was visibly affected. His head was bowed and I could see the tears on his cheeks. At the end we all joined in "Auld Lang Syne."

From Joseph Patrick Tumulty

The White House, 12 December 1918.

Insinuations that for improper reasons Hog Island report[1] suppressed. Advise its immediate release. Colby suggests statement accompany it explaining delay. Do not think this wise. I can handle unofficially reasons for delay in giving it out. Everything fine here. Our political situation improving very much. No disquieting developments. Better understanding of your mission. I am sure it will be a triumph.   Tumulty

T telegram (WP, DLC).
[1] About which, see TWG to WW, Sept. 13, 1918, n. 2, printed as Enclosure I with WW to E. N. Hurley, Sept. 16, 1918, Vol. 51.

From Edward Mandell House

Dear Governor: Paris. December 12, 1918.

The doctor thinks it will not be prudent for me to go to Brest, therefore I am awaiting your arrival here.

There will be an official déjeuner of some two hundred and fifty people at the Elysee Palace at 12.30 on Saturday. President Poincaré will make a short speech to which you will be expected to reply. These speeches are usually limited to from ten to forty lines. If I were you I would confine my remarks to a statement indicating that the United States understands and sympathizes with the heavy trials and suffering which the Allies have undergone for the past four years, and that we are deeply sensible and sympathetic of the problems with which they are now confronted.

There has been an effort here to make it appear that we are not only ignorant of the situation but are not in sympathy with it. Such a statement from you would clear the atmosphere and make easier the work which awaits you.

You will probably not reach Prince Murat's residence before 11.15, but you will be expected to immediately return the President's call in the state carriage which will be held at your residence for this purpose. It seems absurd to make a call at 11.30 when you are to lunch at the Elysee Palace at 12.30 but such are the ways of official Europe.   Affectionately yours,   E. M. House

If you desire Gordon can put you in touch with the situation up to date.

TLS (WP, DLC).

From Edward Nash Hurley

My dear Mr. President: Paris, December 12, 1918.

I went into the various conferences with Mr. Hoover and the British, French and Italian representatives with reference to the shipping phases of the program for emergency control and distribution of food, but I found that it was not necessary to disclose my own anxiety for a postponement until your arrival. The British themselves felt that the plan proposed would create the impression among the peoples to be relieved that the Allies were holding aloof from relief work; that the American Food Administrator alone was feeding the liberated peoples and the enemy countries. Lord Reading argued that while Hoover should be at the head of the organization, the work should be carried on in the name of all the associated governments. Minister Clementel, of France, felt that the whole question should be held in abeyance until your arrival. Both the British and the French will submit their proposed modifications in writing.

In line with my cablegram to you,[1] I have been convinced that no great harm will come from this relatively slight delay. Hoover has informed me that there is already in existence an agreement under which the neutrals are being supplied with food. There are some urgent services to be performed, but in working out the plan for general relief I felt that it would be a tactical error for any concessions to be made to the British and French except by you personally. In shipping as well as in food I have believed that concessions can and probably should be made, but that if these concessions were made before your arrival the larger solutions you have in mind would be more difficult.

In all the conferences I have had on this side, I have been impressed with the fact that it is not the League of Nations, nor an International Court, nor even the Freedom of the Seas that is feared by Lloyd-George, Clemenceau, Orlando or their associates. What they are thinking about, as you are probably already aware, is the increased power of our shipping, commerce and finance. In every conversation the commercial question has come to the front. France fears that she will not be able to get the raw materials she needs at the same price as other nations; Great Britain fears that we will have a bigger merchant marine than she will be able to build, and that our government will operate it, regardless of cost, so that we can capture the best markets in the world.

Sir Joseph Maclay, Shipping Comptroller of Great Britain; Lord Reading, and their chief shipping expert, Mr. Salter,[2] all have told me with considerable feeling that they are planning to turn their ships back to private operation at the earliest possible date. They indicated, in feeling me out, that they presumed we would do the same thing. I gave them no reassurances whatever. I felt that it might be well for them to entertain their fears until you find it advantageous to state your position.

In the same manner, Clementel, Minister of Commerce and Transportation of France, formally proposed to me that we provide France with 800,000 tons of shipping in the next three years. Fearing that Great Britain and the United States will dominate the shipping in the world, the French are frantically anxious to have a merchant marine of 6,000,000 tons by the end of 1921. They had 2,000,000 tons before the war. They want to treble their pre-war tonnage. They point out that Great Britain has charged them exorbitant freight rates. They have placed an order for 500,000 tons of ships with England. It would be to our advantage to build them 800,000 tons, but they would regard it as a distant concession. I have indicated to them my doubt about the feasibility of the project. My reason for this was that I felt that this, as well as all other concessions, should be reserved for you to make yourself.

The French want to be sure they will obtain their raw materials at the same price other nations receive theirs. They feel that domination of shipping by the United States and Great Britain means domination of freight rates and, consequently, control of raw materials. The Italians are already trying to protect themselves by passing bills to establish govenment monopolies over various commodities. Both the British and the French are talking of nationalizing their oil, and other commodities, in order to make their markets as exclusive as possible.

Somewhere, in your larger plans, it may be possible for you to deal with these tendencies in such a way as to provide the reassurance of fair-play. Equalization of conditions on the seas, commercially, may be possible. Certainly I am convinced that it will be helpful if you can get what is in the back of the minds of the men who express any fear of the League of Nations. None of the European nations want another war. They are aware that if another conflict should come more thrones, and more governments would crash to the ground. They know, moreover, that their peoples will rally to the support of any proposal that you make with a view to preventing future wars.

If there is any way in which the general principles you have in mind could be applied immediately to the relief problem in Europe, it would go a long way towards getting the League of Nations into practical operation and would shorten the period of abstract discussion. To a certain extent the various councils of the associated governments have illustrated the practicability of a League of Nations, but these councils have been exclusive. It may be possible to make some adaptation or extension of the idea immediately. If this could be done, it would be at once reported to the world that the League of Nations is already under way. It would be possible then to build around the nucleus thus provided.

Our shipbuilding capacity, which had not been exhausted by any means when the war ended, makes it possible for us to build ships for any nation in the world, and I think that you will find it advantageous, in your conferences, to recall that our present law prevents foreigners from placing orders with our yards without the government's consent.

I am convinced that the principles you have applied to American business are adaptable to the international situation. The European nations are really suffering from an attack of "nerves." They have had a bad night, and the morning finds them depressed and worried. The British Navy was built largely to protect its merchant marine. The British are fearful that under a League of Nations the United States, with its present wealth and commercial power, may get the jump on the markets of the world.

If it can be made clear to them that the essense of the League of Nations is international fair-play, that membership in the League is dependent upon square-dealing, and that a nation becoming a member of it would not be able to put into effect retroactive and confiscatory legislation against foreign interests, as Mexico did to England's disadvantage and our own, I am convinced that whatever opposition there may be will be swept aside.

I realize that your plans may contemplate only the discussion of the larger principles, but I am convinced that whatever commercial concessions or assurances are to be made should come directly from you, with a clear understanding that they do come from you, so that your larger task may be made easier. If either I or any of your lieutenants should make these concessions, the British and French and Italians would be quick to think that it is easier to deal with us than to deal with you. Your own influence, which has been the greatest asset of the whole world in this war of humanity, should not be frittered away by segregated groups.

At the first convenient opportunity I would like to present the shipping phases of the matter to you in greater detail. At any moment now I can arrange for sufficient tonnage for the return of our army, but Pershing tells me the effort to retain our troops here is very strong. Personally, I feel that we should get the larger portion of the troops back as soon as possible.

Faithfully yours,   Edward N. Hurley

TLS (WP, DLC).
   [1] That is, E. N. Hurley to WW, Nov. 28, 1918, printed as an Enclosure with WW to RL, Dec. 1, 1918.
   [2] That is, James Arthur Salter, British director of ship requisitioning, secretary of the Allied Maritime Transport Council, and chairman of the Allied Maritime Transport Executive.

Cary Travers Grayson to Joseph Patrick Tumulty

On Board U.S.S.

Dear Tumulty: George Washington, December 12, 1918

Everything going fine so far.

You will be interested to know that the President gave the newspaper men a second interview about the fourth day out which extended over a period of an hour and in which, as he expressed it to me afterward, he told them everything he knew about his proposed peace plans. The newspapermen are simply carried away with enthusiasm for his ideas and plans. He has shown them on this trip more friendship and good feeling than he has for some time.

The State Department tried to hog all the best accommodations on shipboard, and have dominated things generally, putting most of our party in the second and third cabin, but I got hold of Harrison,[1] who seems to be the major domo of the State Department, and explained to him that we were under the impression that the trip was for the benefit of the President, not the State Department. I told the President about it, and had things changed somewhat. I don't know where all these boll weevils come from that are on ship, but I am told they are indispensables. I am not criticising, of course; only they are here in great numbers, and the President is much displeased at the sight of them. They have adopted a very ultra-superiod [ultrasuperior] attitude toward our humble party.

The President went to Church Sunday with all the sailors. The crew numbers about a thousand. He frequently goes to the movies at night. One night he shook hands with the crew, and they are wild about him.

It would do your heart good to see what an old salt one C. Swem is. He is on deck for every meal. He is such a sailorman these days that hairs are growing on his chest.

Creel had a hearty lunch the first day out and thanked God for it, and bid us all good-bye. He was sighted with the Azores on the sixth day out. Creel, by the way, is very much disturbed as to what his duties with the President are to be when he arrives. He has tackled the President several times to let him handle and digest his paper work, or to serve him in any way that he possibly can, but the President is standing pat.

The President has entirely thrown off his cold and the trip has already done him a world of good physically.

With warmest regards,

Cordially yours,   Cary T. Grayson

TLS (J. P. Tumulty Papers, DLC).
[1] That is, Leland Harrison, at this time diplomatic secretary of the A.C.N.P.

Charles Seymour to His Family

Thursday, December 12, '18

Clive and I were called into conference with the president about ten o'clock and were with him for the rest of the morning. He is going to Italy next week and wants to have certain general points established. It was extremely interesting both as giving us further information on the points toward which we should work and as indicative of his attitude which is that he wants to know the facts and wants to have our opinion on the policy which he ought to adopt. This means that if we know how we can exercise far greater influence then seemed possible. He said several times—"Tell me what I ought to do in this connection," or "What means, Mr. Seymour, can be utilized to bring pressure upon these people in the interests of justice?" He finally asked me to write a memorandum upon policy to be adopted in a certain case. Moral factors appeal to him strongly, but he shows himself distinctly a practical politician— a distinct idealist, but thoroughly aware of the foibles of human nature and willing to utilize them.

He puts one distinctly at one's ease. I found myself arguing and opposing some of his points freely, quite as I would in talking with your father, and saying "If you do this, it is absolutely vital that this other should be done." His whole attitude is the reverse of omniscience. He began for example by saying "Am I right in these assumptions, which I suppose are true but which you gentlemen are capable of judging." And always a strain of humor, which, strangely enough reminded me of Mr. Taft. Talking about the union of Montenegro and Serbia he said that he had been receiving various congratulatory and polite letters from the King of Montenegro which had rather mystified him, but to which he had replied courteously in the spirit of the Irishmen who wrote: "Not that I give a damn, but how's your mother?" He also showed much dry humor in talking of the extreme demands of the Poles. Mrs. Wilson came in twice while we were talking and chatted briefly. She had mislaid the copy of the President's reply to the greeting which Poincaré is going to make to him on Saturday. The president said: "This business of writing the answer to a speech which has never been delivered is rather complicated." (Poincarés address came in by wireless yesterday).

In conversation Mrs. W. is simple—quite unaffected—making a pleasant, but not a striking impression. She is of the type of Clara's Wallingford friends.

The points covered in our talk with Mr. Wilson were of such

importance that I spent two hours with Bowman, Young, and Haskins in talking them over and discussing the means by which we can present our facts to him most satisfactorily. He wants matters put at first in certain broad lines, and does not wish to be bothered by details. He is interested in simplifying everything so far as possible. . . .

AL (C. Seymour Papers, CtY).

From the Diary of Dr. Grayson

Friday, December 13, 1918.

It was three o'clock in the afternoon when the GEORGE WASHINGTON swung into her anchorage outside of the breakwater in the harbor of Brest. The lucky 13, which has figured so much in the President's career, was still in evidence. For weeks it had been raining hard in Brest. The town was a veritable mud-hole. Yet today when the GEORGE WASHINGTON steamed into the harbor, the sun was shining brightly, and the sea was as tranquil as the proverbial mill-pond. A tender from ashore steamed alongside the GEORGE WASHINGTON as soon as she anchored, and M. Pichon, the French Minister, accompanied by an escort of French Admirals and Generals, General John J. Pershing, Admiral Sims, Admiral Benson, and numerous others came on board to greet the President. The greetings on the GEORGE WASHINGTON were entirely informal, as a program had been prepared which was to be carried out as soon as the President stepped on French soil. A converted channel steamer had been fixed up by the American port authorities as a tender and the President and party were escorted on board and the vessel steamed to the main dock, which had been wonderfully decorated in honor of the occasion, French and American colors blending and garlands of flowers being festooned about the pier and the structures thereon.

The President was greeted as he stepped from the tender by the Mayor of Brest,[1] who delivered an address of welcome. The speech was a tribute to the President and expressed the great satisfaction of the people of France that he had seen fit to personally aid in restoring peace to the world.[2] The President responded briefly, after which M. Pichon said to the President: "We are so thankful that you have come over to give us the right kind of a peace." The President declined to be led into any trap, and in reply he simply said: "I think you mean that we all will cooperate to bring about a just peace,"—which seemed to please the French Minister.

Motor cars which had been sent down from Paris were in waiting
to convey the President and the majority of the members of his
party from the dock to the railroad station. Double lines of American
soldiers in field uniform were along the street, and behind them
the people of Brest were gathered to cheer the President on his
way. The crowd admittedly was the largest that had ever assembled
in the picturesque old Brittany city, and its enthusiasm was characteristic of the Gallic history. Men, women and children cheered
the President, wished him God-speed, and threw bouquets of flowers in front of his automobile. Brest is the chief city of Brittany,
and it was remarkable the number of its inhabitants who came to
greet the President in their gorgeous native costumes. Many of
these costumes actually were priceless; of hand-worked lace, some
of them even centuries old. They are handed down from mother to
daughter and are guarded with the greatest of care at all times.
That they were donned in honor of the President was a remarkable
tribute to the individual and the head of the world's greatest Republic. The colors of some of the costumes were most bizarre, but
all were picturesque, and the flowing headgear added a touch to
the ruddy faces of the women folk that lent itself very much to the
picture. Many of the older men were playing musical instruments,
apparently a modification of the Scottish bag-pipe. If they were a
modification in appearance, they were none the less shrill, and the
music was hardly of a kind to soothe a musical ear. "Vive l'America"
was the cry of all.

A special train had been prepared for the President's use, and it
was one of the best of its kind in France. Scenes along the road
were duplications of what was experienced in Brest. Men, women
and children had gathered to see the train go by, although they
could only hope to catch the briefest of glimpses of the Presidential
figure in the special car. As a matter of fact, the demonstrations
continued all through the night. Even at three o'clock in the morning when I looked through the window of my drawing-room, I saw
not only men and women but little children standing with uncov-
ered head to cheer the passage of the specal train.

[1] Ernest Amélie Hervagault, who was, in fact, the Deputy Mayor of Brest and Acting
Mayor from 1914 to 1919.
[2] It is printed in *Le Temps* of Paris, Dec. 14, 1918.

A Translation of an Exchange of Greetings with the French Foreign Minister

[[December 13, 1918]]

[Pichon] We, my colleagues and I, have the distinguished honor to bring you the greetings of welcome of the government of the Republic upon your arrival in France.

We salute in your person the illustrious head of the great American nation which, during the war, has rendered decisive services which we sustained in common and which, we are sure, will render the same services in the making of the peace.

All of France is ready to acclaim you in enthusiastic demonstrations. As delegates of the government and of the National Assembly, we are proud to have been appointed to express, upon your arrival, the sentiments of confidence and of gratitude which are unanimously those of our country.

[Wilson] I am deeply moved by the words of welcome which have been addressed to me. As I approach the shores of France, I feel that I can bring nothing to this noble nation which it does not already possess in abundance.

It will be a privilege for me to contribute in France to a peace which will again allow movement toward the progress of the entire world.

It gives me pleasure to remember the long-standing friendship which unites our countries at the moment when I am about to set foot on the soil of France. These bonds of friendship designate for me your country as the natural point of my landing in Europe. We will examine in common what you have done, what we have done, and we will consecrate the results of our common victory.

I repeat to the government of the Republic and to the National Assembly my sincere and deeply felt thanks for their welcome which has touched me profoundly.

Printed in *Le Temps* of Paris, Dec. 15, 1918.

A Reply to the Mayor of Brest

[Dec. 13, 1918]

Your generous greeting is very delightful. I feel honored that the City of Brest should have granted me the distinction of being associated with it. Since the United States entered the war, we have felt in some particular way identified with Brest. It has attracted to itself some of the intimate interest and affection we feel for our own home cities. Its hospitality to our men, its welcome to those who came to fight alongside of France in the common cause against an outlaw, have given it a peculiar association with our own people and our own action in the great struggle. That the citizens and the Municipal Council of Brest should have been so thoughtful of my pleasure and should have honored me as they have, will remain with me as one of the most acceptable and pleasurable memories of my errand. It is delightful for me to realize that I have come to join my counsel with that of your own public men in bringing about a peace settlement which shall be consistent alike with the ideals of France and the ideals of the United States.

Will you not be kind enough to convey to your colleagues of the Municipal Council my very own warm appreciation of their generous resolutions, along with my most cordial greetings on my own behalf and on behalf of the great people whom I represent, and to whom the citizens of Brest have offered such hospitable service.

T MS (WP, DLC).

From Edward Mandell House

Dear Governor: Paris, December 13, 1918.

Just a hurried line to tell you that I was mistaken in informing you that your official call on the President of the French Republic should take place after your arrival at the house, and before the luncheon to be tendered you at the Elysee.

I find that you are not expected to pay this visit until some time on Sunday, the 15th. The hour for this visit will be set by the Foreign Office, and you will be notified in due course through the Embassy.

Affectionately yours,   E. M. House

I shall call just as soon as the parade is over & I can get through.

TLS (WP, DLC).

From Allyn Abbott Young

My dear Mr. President: [Paris] Dec. 13, 1918.

Supplementing our conference of yesterday, I have ventured to ask Professor Lunt, our specialist on Italian boundaries (who was not present at the conference) for a short memorandum and sketch map on the boundaries in the Southern Tyrol (Trentino).[1]

Very truly yours,   Allyn A. Young

ALS (WP, DLC).

[1] W. E. Lunt to A. A. Young, Dec. 12, 1918, TLS, enclosing "Memorandum for the President," c. Dec. 12, 1918, T MS, both in WP, DLC.

Alfred Lucking[1] to Joseph Patrick Tumulty

Personal & Confidential.

Dear Mr. Tumulty: Detroit, Michigan December 13, 1918.

I happened to be in the same train with former President Taft yesterday, and had quite a visit with him. We got to talking about the League of Nations, which, of course, is a subject of great interest to him, as you know.

I said to him "it looks to me as if Mr. Roosevelt is commencing to hedge on that question, notwithstanding his former bitter enmity to it, and that before long he will be on the other side of the question." Mr. Taft laughed very heartily and said that he had noticed his change of sentiments as shown in the newspapers, and then went on to tell how bitterly Mr. Roosevelt had scorned the project and the projectors in a magazine article a little over a year ago. He then told me that Mr. Roosevelt had signified recently in a conversation with him that Roosevelt would be with him (Taft) on the question, but that he must give him a little time to turn the corner.

This communication is wholly confidential, and I send it to you in the hopes that Mr. Wilson may learn of it, because I have personally been convinced for two or three weeks past that Roosevelt would land on that side of the question, and probably, as usual, so maneuver as to claim credit for a *practical* application of the principle and that he would be in a position to attack Mr. Wilson should Mr. Wilson fail, for any reason, to uphold his pronouncement in favor of League of Peace. In fact, I would expect that in case of any mishap, that Mr. Roosevelt will be carrying the flag of the League of Peace in the front line in the campaign of 1920.

In my opinion, it is the most popular portion of the President's program, because the most far reaching and most useful.

With kindest regards, I remain,

Yours truly,   Alfred Lucking.

TLS (WP, DLC).

[1] Lawyer of Detroit, former congressman from Michigan (1903-1905), and long active in Michigan Democratic politics; at this time, a member of Lucking, Helfman, Lucking & Hanlon and general counsel to the Ford Motor Co. and the Henry Ford interests.

From the Diary of Dr. Grayson

Saturday, December 14, 1918.

The President's special train arrived in Paris at ten o'clock. It was run into the special station which was reserved for the accommodation and reception of visiting dignitaries of royal blood. The President of the United States was accorded all of the honors which a European country pays to a reigning monarch. The station itself was gorgeous. Bunting and flags of varied hues were festooned about the walls and around the pillars, while from the top of the station on twin staffs floated the starry banner of the United States and the tri-color of France. Great masses of green ferns were ranged along the sides of the station platform, on the steps and in the reception room of the station. In the reception room great clusters of roses and carnations and other flowers had been arranged, and the high-ceilinged room was heavy with their perfume.

The President was met as he alighted from the train by President Poincaré of France, Premier Clemenceau, and all of the other members of the French Government who had not proceeded to Brest to welcome him there. As the President walked down the station platform, escorted by President Poincaré, he was wildly cheered by thousands upon thousands of people who occupied points of vantage on the roadway above the station, on the roofs of houses, and in every window that overlooked the point of arrival. Half a dozen French state carriages drawn by two horses, and in charge of coachmen and footmen resplendent in the national livery were in waiting to convey the President and the official party from the station to the Hotel Murat, where the President was to remain during his stay in Paris. It was another beautiful, sunshiny day. The streets were lined with troops who had been brought in from the front to aid in holding back the crowds. Behind them on either side was massed practically the entire population of Paris and the surrounding country. It was one of the largest crowds that I have ever seen. Men, women and children had turned out to greet the President of the United States and to welcome him to France; and they performed their task with an enthusiasm that was gratifying to say the least. From the time the procession started from the station until it drew up in the yard of the Murat Palace, the enthusiasm was sustained. The cheering had a note of welcome in it, and it required the best efforts of the troops to prevent some of the overenthusiastic breaking through and overwhelming the Presidential party. Summing it up, President Poincaré himself declared that the reception accorded to President Wilson stood alone among the welcome given any previous visitor to Paris.

Arriving at the Hotel Murat, the President and Mrs. Wilson were shown to their rooms. I looked the place over before I went to my own apartment.

The Murat Palace was loaned to the French Government for the use of the President by Prince Murat. The mansion is 300 years old and a feature of historic Paris. One of the ancestors of the owner married Napoleon I's sister, while the paintings and photogravures with which the house is adorned are reminiscent of Napoleon himself.

President Poincaré had arranged a luncheon in honor of the President and Mrs. Wilson, and they went there shortly after their arrival at the Murat Palace. I accompanied them to the luncheon. Among the guests were Field Marshal Joffre, Premier Clemenceau, former Prime Minister Viviani and others. The President made his first extended speech at this luncheon. It was delivered impromptu.

Returning to the house the President held his initial conference with Colonel E. M. House, who had been in Paris for some months arranging for the participation of the American Peace Commissioners in the Peace Conference.

This evening the President dined with Mrs. Wilson, Miss Margaret Wilson, Miss Benham and myself. Although he was tired, the President was extremely well-pleased with the cordiality of his reception. He had carefully watched the attitude of the crowd and he was satisfied that they were most friendly.

From the Diary of Raymond Blaine Fosdick

Saturday, December 14th, 1918.

The memory of this day will live in my mind for ever. We arrived in Paris at six o'clock in the morning, and established ourselves at the Hotel Crillon, facing the Place de la Concorde. This is the headquarters of the American representatives to the Peace Conference. The President's train came in at ten o'clock—at the Bois de Boulogne station, where he was met by Poincaré and Clemenceau. The parade from the station to the Murat house in Rue de Monceau, which is to be his official residence, was accompanied by the most remarkable demonstration of enthusiasm and affection on the part of the Parisians that I have ever heard of, let alone seen. Henry White, who has witnessed every important coronation or official greeting in Europe for fifty years, told me that there never had been anything like it. The reporters said that the greeting given to King George V and to the King and Queen of Belgium some weeks ago was about one-tenth that accorded to Wilson.

The parade over a four-mile drive consisted merely of eight carriages, preceded by a handful of hussars of the guard. In the first carriage rode the President and Poincaré. Mrs. Wilson with Madame Poincaré and Margaret Wilson came in the second. Clemenceau was in the third carriage with Ambassador Sharp; Lansing

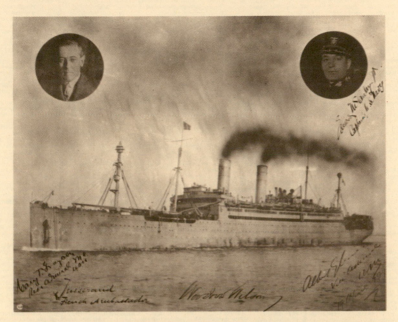

U.S.S. *George Washington*

On the bridge with Captain McCauley

Talking with reporters on the U.S.S. *George Washington*. From Wilson's left:
John E. Nevin, Robert J. Bender (hidden), Lionel C. Probert

Murat Palace

Paris greets Wilson

With Raymond Poincaré

Reviewing and meeting troops with General Pershing on Christmas Day 1918

Arriving at Dover. The Duke of Connaught is on Wilson's left

With George V

In serious conversation with the King

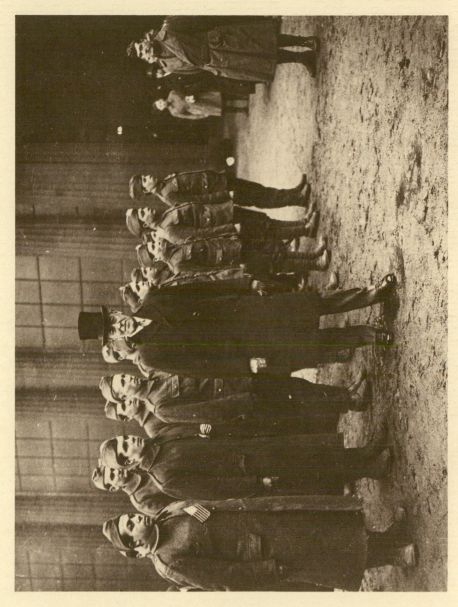

In the courtyard of Buckingham Palace with a group of American soldiers just returned from German prison camps

Arriving in Milan

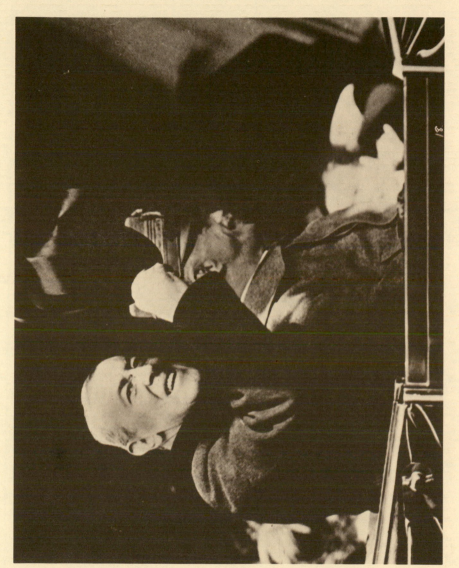

With Vittorio Emanuele III

The American Peace Commissioners: Edward M. House, Robert Lansing, Wilson, Henry White, Tasker H. Bliss

1549/3

and the French Minister of Foreign Affairs in the fourth; while in the other carriages were Henry White, General Bliss, General Pershing, Jusserand, and other notables. Troops, cavalry and infantry, lined the entire route and tens of thousands of persons fought for a glimpse. The streets were decorated with flags and banners, Wilson's name was everywhere, and huge *"Welcome Wilson"* and *"Honour to Wilson, the Just"* signs stretched across the streets from house to house.

I was in a window in a building taken over by the American Army at the corner of the Rue Royale and Place de la Concorde. It is estimated that 100,000 people filled the Place. Certainly I never saw a larger crowd. The route of march lay by way of Avenue du Bois de Boulogne, through the Arc de Triomphe, the Champs-Elysées, across the Seine by the Alexandre III bridge to the Quai d'Orsay, back again by the Concorde bridge, across the Place de la Concorde, through the Rue Royale to the Boulevard and thence to Rue Monceau. The carriages approached at a trot. We could hear the cheers across the Seine. Wilson was smiling and waving his hat. Mrs. Wilson, almost buried in a huge bouquet, looked radiant. The noise was deafening. It was all over in a minute, and we could hear the cheers rolling up Rue Royale to the Madeleine. The troops started to march, but the crowds broke through and for an hour Place de la Concorde was a riot of colour and fun. I noticed twenty or thirty British soldiers marching with this sign: "The British—vos Alliés de *1914*-1918." I hope this is not symbolic of any trouble at the Peace table.

To-night the Boulevards of Paris are still celebrating. I dined at Café de Paris with Major Marston[1] and Major Helms and afterward we saw the sights. It was like our Armistice celebration at home without quite so much rough house and a little more love-making. An American can have anything he wants in Paris to-day,—he owns the city. The girls even try to kiss him on the streets. I wonder—and the thought keeps coming back to me—what will be the greeting of the French when the Peace is finished and Wilson comes to go home. I wish it could be guaranteed that their affection for America and the Americans would be as real and as enthusiastic as it is to-day. Poor Wilson! A man with his responsibilities is to be pitied. The French think that with almost a magic touch he will bring about the day of political and industrial justice. Will he? Can he?

[1] Hunter Sylvester Marston, a banker of New York; at this time, a major in the Army Intelligence Corps and a member of the Army General Staff.

A Reply to President Poincaré[1]

[Dec. 14, 1918]

Mr. President: I am deeply indebted to you for your gracious greeting. It is very delightful to find myself in France and to feel the quick contact of sympathy and unaffected friendship between the representatives of the United States and the representatives of France. You have been very generous in what you were pleased to say about myself, but I feel that what I have said and what I have tried to do has been said and done only in an attempt to speak the thought of the people of the United States truly and to carry that thought out in action. From the first the thought of the people of the United States turned toward something more than the mere winning of this war. It turned to the establishment of eternal principles of right and justice. It realized that merely to win the war was not enough; that it must be won in such a way and the questions raised by it settled in such a way as to insure the future peace of the world and lay the foundation for the freedom and happiness of its many peoples and nations.

Never before has war worn so terrible a visage or exhibited more grossly the debasing influence of illicit ambitions. I am sure that I shall look upon the ruin wrought by the armies of the Central Empires with the same repulsion and deep indignation that it stirs in the hearts of the men of France and Belgium, and I appreciate, as you do, Sir, the necessity of such action in the final settlement of the issues of the war as will not only rebuke such acts of terror and spoliation, but make men everywhere aware that they cannot be ventured upon without the certainty of just punishment.

I know with what ardor and enthusiasm the soldiers and sailors of the United States have given the best that was in them to this war of redemption. They have expressed the true spirit of America. They believe their ideals to be acceptable to free peoples everywhere and are rejoiced to have played the part they have played in giving reality to those ideals in cooperation with the armies of the Allies. We are proud of the part they have played and we are happy that they should have been associated with such comrades in a common cause.

It is with peculiar feelings, Mr. President, that I find myself in France joining with you in rejoicing over the victory that has been won. The ties that bind France and the United States are peculiarly close. I do not know in what other comradeship we could have fought with more zest or enthusiasm. It will daily be a matter of pleasure with me to be brought into consultation with the statesman of France and her Allies in concerting the measures by which we may secure permanence for these happy relations of friendship and cooperation, and secure for the world at large such safety and freedom in its life as can be secured only by the constant association and cooperation of friends.

I greet you, Sir, not only with deep personal respect but as the representative of the great people of France, and beg to bring you the greetings of another great people to whom the fortunes of France are of profound and lasting interest.

I raise my glass to the health of the President of the French Republic and to Madame Poincaré,[2] and to the prosperity of France.

[1] At the luncheon in Wilson's honor at the Elysée Palace. The guests included the members of the French cabinet; former French Presidents, Prime Ministers, and Foreign Ministers; the Presidents and Vice-Presidents of the Senate and the Chamber of Deputies; French high commissioners; the Marshals of France; the Allied Ambassadors and Ministers; the American plenipotentiaries to the peace conference; and American military and naval leaders. In his address, Poincaré stated that Paris and France had awaited Wilson's arrival with impatience, eager to acclaim "the illustrious democrat whose words and deeds were inspired by exalted thought, the philosopher delighting in the solution of universal laws from particular events, the eminent statesman who had found a way to express the highest political and moral truths in formulas which bear the stamp of immortality." France, Poincaré continued, had a "passionate desire" to offer thanks, through Wilson personally, to the United States for its invaluable assistance to the defenders of right and liberty. After a brief review of the humanitarian efforts and the military contributions of the United States, Poincaré went on to recount in detail the atrocities of the German army, its "deliberate savagery," and its cynical "program of pillage and industrial annihilation." Wilson would soon have the opportunity to see for himself the extent of these disasters, and he would be able to judge and pronounce a verdict on the enormity of the crimes. "Should this guilt remain unpunished, could it be renewed," Poincaré declared, "the most splendid victories would be in vain." France had not struggled, endured, and suffered for four long years only to see those responsible go unpunished and only to face the possibility of being some day again exposed to aggression. All that the country was yearning for now was a "peace of justice and security." Together, the United States and France had to build a peace which would prohibit the "deliberate and hypocritical renewing of an organism aiming at conquest and oppression." Poincaré concluded: "Peace must make amends for the misery and sadness of yesterday, and it must be a guarantee against the dangers of tomorrow. The association which has been formed for the purpose of war, between the United States and the Allies, and which contains the seed of the permanent institutions of which you have spoken so eloquently, will find from this day forward a clear and profitable employment in the concerted search for equitable decisions and in the mutual support which we need if we are to make our rights prevail. . . . We must introduce into the peace we are going to build all the conditions of justice and all the safeguards of civilization that we can embody in it. To such a vast and magnificent task, Mr. President, you have chosen to come and apply yourself in concert with France. France offers you her thanks. She knows the friendship of America. She knows your rectitude and elevation of spirit. It is in the fullest confidence that she is ready to work with you." *New York Times*, Dec. 15, 1918.

[2] Henriette Benucci Poincaré.

Remarks to a Delegation of French Socialists[1]

[Dec. 14, 1918]

Gentlemen: I receive with great interest the address which you have just read to me. The war through which we have just passed has illustrated in a way which never can be forgotten the extraordinary wrongs which can be perpetrated by arbitrary and irresponsible power. It is not possible to secure the happiness and prosperity of the peoples of the world or to establish an enduring peace unless the repetition of such wrongs is rendered impossible. This has indeed been a people's war. It has been waged against absolutism and militarism, and these enemies of liberty must from this time forth be shut out from the possibility of working their cruel will upon mankind.

In my judgment it is not sufficient to establish this principle. It is necessary that it should be supported by a cooperation of the nations which shall be based upon fixed and definite covenants and which shall be made certain of effective action through the instrumentality of a league of nations. I believe this to be the conviction of all thoughtful and liberal men. I am confident that this is the thought of those who lead your own great nation, and I am looking forward with peculiar pleasure to cooperating with them in securing guarantees of a lasting peace of justice and right dealing which shall justify the sacrifices of this war and cause men to look back upon those sacrifices as upon the dramatic and final processes of their emancipation.

T MSS (WP, DLC).
    [1] Wilson received Thomas, Renaudel, Cachin, Longuet, and other leaders of the French Socialist party at his residence in the afternoon of December 14. Renaudel read a lengthy statement, signed jointly by the General Labor Confederation (C.G.T.) and the Socialist party of France, which emphasized the "deep understanding in spirit between the French workers and the President of the United States on the idea of war and peace." There is an Hw MS of their statement, dated Dec. 14, 1918, in WP, DLC.

From the Most Reverend Randall Thomas Davidson[1]

Dear Sir,   Lambeth Palace, S.E.1. 14th December 1918.

In the name of the promoters of our Christian Churches' organisation on behalf of the League of Nations I venture to approach you in order to ascertain whether it would be by any means possible that you should when in England address those who are responsible for the organisation of our joint effort to promote the League of Nations as an essentially Christian mode of policy and action. The position and character of our particular effort will be best seen by reference to the printed appeal which I herewith enclose.[2] The names appended to that appeal give evidence that, with the exception of the Roman Catholics, who have desired to act independently, if at all, we speak in the name of practially all Christian communions in this country.

It occurred therefore to us that you might possibly be willing, and even desirous, to take an opportunity of saying something on the subject from the distinctly and definitely Christian standpoint. It is of course obvious that you may have good reasons for not desiring to avail yourself of such an opportunity; but you will I am sure understand our wish to approach you with the suggestion in case you should desire to follow it. The gain would I believe be very great.

I ventured to send on behalf of our Christian communities a telegraphic message while you were still upon the high seas. I enclose a copy of it herewith.[3]

May I take the opportunity which this letter offers of expressing my own sense of the supreme value and importance of your visit to Europe and to England at this great juncture in the history of the world, and of giving you the assurance of my earnest prayers for a blessing upon all your endeavours.

I have the honour to be, with much respect,

Your faithful and obedient servant,   Randall Cantuar:

TLS (WP, DLC).
[1] Archbishop of Canterbury.
[2] Randall Cantuar et al., *The Church and the League of Nations. An Appeal to Christians*, press release dated Dec. 5, 1918 (WP, DLC).
[3] Randall Cantuar to WW, n.d., TC telegram (WP, DLC).

From the Diary of Colonel House

December 14, 1918.

This has been a glorious day in many ways. The day itself is the best we have had since we have been here, and the reception which the President received is said to be beyond anything in the history of Paris. I did not go to the station to meet him but remained at the Crillon until after he arrived and then went to the Hotel Murat.

I gave the President a brief summary of the situation, particularly the relations between France, England and ourselves, relations which seem to grow steadily better. Our relations with Italy have always been good.

I found him in an ugly mood toward Lansing. He did not know until he was on the ship that Leland Harrison and Philip Patchin[1] had been picked by Lansing for Secretaries under Grew,[2] nor did he know that Grew himself had been selected. He thought I was building up an organization and that when they got here we would determine together who should officer it. He declared he intended to put them all out; send Patchin and Harrisom [Harrison] back home, and do the thing as it should have been done in the first instance. He wanted to know if I had anyone in mind for the places.

I told him I had not. That when the cable came notifying Grew to take charge, and naming Harrison and Patchin as his assistants, I had let the matter drop and had given it little thought except to advise with Grew when my advice was asked. I told him that Grew while not the man for the place, was a gentleman, was honest and trustworthy, and I hoped he would not remove him.

Sometime ago I determined to let Lansing carry his own fortunes without help or hindrance from me. He has not been entirely considerate, after what I have done for him. On the other hand, I always appreciate the fact that I have been what Gerard once terms [termed] "Super-Secretary of State," and Lansing has played a minor part and has done it without complaint.

We went to the Elysee Palace for déjeuner. There were some two hundred or more guests. I thought Poincaré's speech was more apropos and more eloquent than the President's. Poincaré had memorized his and did not use manuscript. The President read his. Of course, the President is a much more impressive figure and his performance was creditable though not up to my expectations because he excels in that kind of thing. It was an occasion when I particularly desired him to be at his best.

He was visibly nervous. I suppose it was on account of acting a new role and on a new stage and he was not sure of himself. I think the fact that Poincaré spoke extemporaneously and that he read his speech shook his nerves a little.

The President and I had a two hour conference in the afternoon. We went over all matters of importance. I arranged that he should see Clemenceau tomorrow afternoon at six, and that he should dine with Lord Derby on the 21st, 22nd or 23rd as might later be arranged. We also settled upon a meeting with the King of Italy. The King is to call upon the President. At first, I thought to ask the Italian Ambassador[3] to have them together at dinner, but upon reflection, I knew this was impossible because of the festivities that had already been arranged in honor of the King. I suggested to the President the protocol he should follow while here should include acceptance of dinners at the homes of Ambassadors, but not of Ministers, and that he should accept invitations if offered by high functionaries like the President of France, the President of the Council and the Foreign Minister. He accepted this without discussion.

We went hastily over the different methods of procedure for the Conference he is to hold. I advised making the League of Nations the centure [center] of the whole program and letting everything revolve around that. Once that is a *fait accompli*, nearly all the very serious difficulties will disappear.

The President and Mrs. Wilson urged me to remain to dinner but I declined because I knew the President was tired and I wanted him to rest, which he would not do if I were there to talk to him.

I have seen many other people today like Lansing, White and other members of the Commission. It was a great joy to greet Janet who came on the President's ship. She had a delightful experience and said the President and Mrs. Wilson were kindness itself.

All of the Specialists spoke in the highest terms of the President, of his courtesy and his generous praise of their work. They were equally critical of Lansing whom they said was austere, and treated them with scant politeness. I am sure Lansing does not mean to be brusque and impolite, but he has an unfortunate manner.

I arranged with the President this afternoon to have his work done by Gordon, Frazier, George Creel and the staff I have built up here. The code clerks and the typists I have also offered to turn over to him. It leaves me practically without a staff but I can readily build up another. I think he promised Tumulty that he would not have a regular secretary because of Tumulty's hurt feelings at not being brought over. I shall give his matters my personal attention so he may lack for nothing that I can supply. He has never cabled me that he was relying upon me to look out for him while here, therefore, while I offered to do so in a cable, not having heard from him I presumed he was bringing some sort of organized help himself. In this he is like my brother T. W.[4] who always expected me to know by intuition what he was thinking.

T MS (E. M. House Papers, CtY).
    [1] That is, Philip Halsey Patchin, who had been appointed Executive Secretary of the A.C.N.P. on November 30, 1918.
    [2] That is, Joseph Clark Grew, at this time Secretary General of the A.C.N.P. with the rank of Envoy Extraordinary and Minister Plenipotentiary.
    [3] Count Lelio Bonin Longare.
    [4] Thomas William House, Jr., prominent businessman and banker of Houston.

From the Diary of Dr. Grayson

Sunday, December 15, 1918.

Following breakfast the President, Mrs. Wilson and myself attended church in the Rue de Berri.[1] On leaving the church we drove to the tomb of Lafayette, where the President deposited a wreath which he had arranged for. On the wreath the President attached his personal card, on the back of which he had written in his own handwriting: "In memory of the great Lafayette, from a fellow-servant of liberty."

After luncheon Premier Clemenceau called, and the President and he conferred for a little while. The President told Clemenceau several stories, the French Premier being the first to hear one of the President's stories on the European side of the Atlantic. The story which seemed to please Clemenceau was that which dealt with a yachting adventure of the late King Edward VII of England. The King with his retinue were on a yacht in the Mediterranean, when it was caught by a sudden squall. The storm was severe and for a time the small craft was in serious danger of foundering. Finally, however, the wind died down, the sun came out, and then speculation began among the ship's company as to the procedure which should have been followed had the vessel actually been wrecked. Whether the ladies on board should have been first rescued or the King—was the point that caused the discussion. "Should we have saved the ladies before the King?"—one of the crew asked. "Most assuredly," was the reply; "we would have saved the ladies; let God save the King!"

At 4:30 in the afternoon we attended the American Church of the Holy Trinity, where a military service was held with Bishop Gerry[2] of South Carolina presiding. We had our first experience at this service of the European method of watching the distinguished visitor through opera-glasses. On the right hand side of the church a man sat in a pew and he kept his opera-glasses levelled on the President during the entire service, not even taking them off once in a while to have a look at the Presiding Bishop.

At dinner that night the President told me that the reception he had received in France was so spontaneous and hearty that it made him feel thoroughly at home.

[1] The American Presbyterian Church in Paris. The Rev. Chauncey William Goodrich, the pastor of the church, officiated at the service.
[2] The Rt. Rev. William Alexander Guerry, Protestant Episcopal Bishop of South Carolina and President of the Synod of the Fourth Province of the Protestant Episcopal Church.

To Edward Mandell House, with Enclosure

My dear House: [Paris] 15 December, 1918.

The enclosed is the result of my conference with Hoover this evening. Would you be willing to communicate this paper to the Allied Governments, as you conveyed the original note[1] about the relief administration to which this refers?

Affectionately yours,   Woodrow Wilson

TLS (E. M. House Papers, CtY).
[1] See EMH to WW, No. 188, Nov. 27, 1918 (second telegram of that date), and No. 213, Dec. 1, 1918 (first telegram of that date).

ENCLOSURE E[1]

The President requests me to say that The discussions of <my>*his* proposal of December 1st, submitted through <Colonel House,> *me* for the creation of a European Relief Administration and the appointment of a Director General of Relief, <has> *have* been reported to <me> *him.* <No doubt I shall> *He entertains no doubt that he will* receive in due course <a reply> from the Allied Governments <to my note above mentioned,> *a reply to that note* but it appears <to me> *from the discussions* that some time will be required to reconcile the differences of view involved in the undertaking.

The objects of the United States Government in connection with food supply—<during> *which concern only* the Armistice emergency,—are <the saving of> *to save* life, <and the preservation of,> *to preserve* order throughout the liberated, neutral, and enemy territories, and to create an efficient organization to accomplish these <objectives> *purposes.* <With this> *In these* purposes <I feel sure> *he feels assured* of your entire sympathy and co-operation.

Pending further discussions of the entire problem, *however,* the situation in certain areas is of so critical a nature, and requires such immediate emergency action, that <I am> *he wishes me to inform you that he is* instructing the United States Food Administration to take <at once> measures <for furnishing immediate> *at once to furnish* food supplies and to establish an organization to this end in <those> *certain* places outside of Germany.

<I feel sure> *Taking it for granted* that you will also be anxious to undertake immediate action in these matters through your various food departments, *and* In order that there shall be *full* co-ordination in this task, <I have> *he has* asked Mr. Hoover to indicate to you these situations and the points <on> *at* which he proposes to establish representatives for the administration of relief measures, so that if you see fit, you may also send your representatives to these points, and these gentlemen <can> *may* mutually co-ordinate their various efforts.

T MS (WP, DLC).

[1] In the following document, words in angle brackets deleted by Wilson; words in italics added by him. Wilson was undoubtedly revising a draft by Hoover. There is a CC of the version as revised by Wilson in WP, DLC.

From Theodore Wright[1]

Long Beach California
My Dear Friend: Sunday Dec 15, 1918

Harking back to Sunday, Dec. 28, 1856, something happened.

And I wish to tell you how glad I am that you still live.

I trust God will bear you up and strengthen you in body, mind and soul, for your great task as peacemaker for the nations, and that you may live long to enjoy the grateful regard of your fellow-men.   Faithfully Yours,   Theodore Wright

ALS (WP, DLC).
    [1] President of the Record Publishing Co. of Philadelphia and former editor in chief of the *Philadelphia Record* (1877-1912), now living in retirement in California.

Sir William Wiseman to the Foreign Office

MEMORANDUM.

SECRET.   PARIS. December 15, 1918.

I had a long interview today with Colonel House. He is quite recovered from the influenza, and very satisfied with the result of his talks with the President. As soon as he arrived the President seems to have turned to House for advice, and asked him to arrange his Secretariat and map out his programme of work.

The President's Secretariat will consist of Gordon Auchincloss, Hugh Frazier, and George Creel. Creel, however, will be well controlled by the other two.

The President came over with the intention of sitting at the Peace Conference as chief American delegate, but House has persuaded him to abandon this idea, and he will remain in Paris in close touch with his own representatives and the Allies for informal conferences. The President does not expect to stay much more than a month.

I do not think he has any specially cut-and-dried proposals to make regarding any of the important questions at issue, but will rather re-affirm his general principles and expect the Allies to make their definite proposals.

On the question of the LEAGUE OF NATIONS, he is, however, very strongly of opinion that the formation of a League—at any rate a definite agreement as to its form among the great Powers—should be the first work of the Peace Conference. He considers that almost all the difficult questions—Colonies, Freedom of the Seas, the Balkan difficulty, Russia, and Reduction of Armaments—and, in fact, all the important problems that will arise, can only be satisfactorily settled on the basis of a LEAGUE OF NATIONS. He has a very open mind as to the form of the League, the extent to which it should go, and the machinery by which it should be operated. He is even willing to agree to the French proposal that the Germans should be excluded from the League for a time.

The question of Indemnities may raise some difficulty, as the American view is that the Allies are bound by their Armistice formula. But the President is not disturbed by the Election speeches, and quite understands the strong demand in Allied countries that Germany be made to pay the cost of the war.

The Food and Relief situation is not very satisfactory. HOOVER returned from London in a very angry frame of mind, and is to have a conference with the President tonight. This is a sort of situation where we should use the good offices of House, as he takes a much more reasonable view of our case than Hoover.

I spoke to House quite frankly about the bad impression created in England by certain recent statements and newspaper articles in America—particularly on the Freedom of the Seas. He said that he doubted whether Daniels and Admiral Badger had been correctly quoted; or, at any rate, the sentences were taken too much out of their context.[1] He admitted, however, that there were grounds for our complaint, and that there are mischief-makers in the States who are very busy at the moment. He emphatically repudiates the suggestion that these sentiments in any way reflect the President's mind. I pointed out the need for reassuring in some way the public in England, and suggested to him that the President should give an interview to the Paris correspondent of the "Times" apropos of his forthcoming visit to England, and that the President should take occasion to pay a generous tribute to England's effort and express his sympathy and friendly feeling. House likes the idea very much, and thinks he may be able to get the President to adopt the suggestion.[2] He said the President would only hesitate on account of other newspapers and of [the] possible feeling of the French Government. Some of the mischief-makers in Paris (among them those who should know better) have been busy telling House that there is a growing feeling in England of jealousy against the United States; but, of course, it does not make any difference what such people say to House.

Generally, Colonel House is most optimistic about the coming Conferences. He says there is no real difference that he can see between the British and American point of view; and that the President has come over with no intention of laying down the law, or insisting on his own solutions of difficulties. He will only reaffirm the American principles and offer his counsel to the Allies for the common good.

I also spoke to House about the danger of any American Press campaign in Paris during the Conferences. He is entirely opposed to anything of the sort.

T MS (W. Wiseman Papers, CtY).
¹ Wiseman was probably referring to statements by Daniels and Badger before the House Committee on Naval Affairs during its hearings on the naval appropriations bill on November 20 and December 12, respectively. Both Daniels and Badger strongly supported a large increase in the size of the United States Navy, and they argued in favor of an appropriation of $600,000,000 for a new three-year naval building program. While Daniels believed that the size of the United States Navy should be close to that of the British navy, Badger contended that, by 1925, the United States Navy had to be as large as Great Britain's and equal to the most powerful navy maintained by any nation in the world. See the *New York Times*, Nov. 21 and Dec. 13, 1918.
² Wilson gave the interview. It is printed at December 18, 1918.

Edith Bolling Galt Wilson to Her Family

Dearest Ones: [Paris] Sunday, Dec. 15, 1918

I have a half hour before dinner, & as it is the 1st unclaimed time since we landed, I will begin a line to you all.

Wilmer¹ has just gone after spending the day with us & going to the American church to a military service with us where Bishop Gary of South Carolina preached an excellent sermon.

This morning we went to the other American church, & afterwards to the tomb of Lafayette to put a wreath or, as they say over here, "a crown" on it. This was an interesting journey to a very old part of Paris—& the cem[e]tary is in the grounds of an old convent where there are still some old nuns—all very old women dressed in white with capes & funny old white hoods this shape [here she draws a picture]—and on their breasts 2 bleeding hearts with tongues of fire. We drove down a long avenue of trees whoes [whose] trunks & limbs were green & old, to a quiet corner, where are only a few tombs of the old, old, families of France—the inscriptions of the names are like turning a page of history.

From there we came back to the main part of Paris where the streets were thronged with people all shouting as we passed, "Vivi Wilson." At 3 we went to call on the President & Madame Pontcaret, and had a very nice call. Then home where Wilmer & Miss Benham joined us & we again went to church.

It seems strange I have begun this with a description of today instead of our arrival at Brest & then at Paris—but I think the reason of this is that today is simple and easy to describe, and the other was so tremendous and overwhelming that it seems impossible to picture for you. So many emotions crowded into a small space of time that my mind is tired. To begin with the weather was perfect, clear with pale sunshine even at Brest where, they say, it rains 99 days out of every 100. We docked at 3—but of course things were happening on the George Washington & all around it long before that.

We were on deck by 9 a.m. to see the Fleet which came out to meet us, 9 Battleships, 40 Destroyers, 2 French Cruisers beside the Convoy we had with us. This was a wonderful sight. Then French Air planes appeared & a huge Dirigible. We had early lunch & were ready to receive the 5 Admirals who came aboard as soon as we dropped anchor—Adms. Sims[,] Wilson, Mayo, Benson & Rodman[2] there. A delegation of Frenchmen <Petain> Pichon,[3] Tardieu[,] de Blanpre,[4] etc. with whom came Margaret[5]—looking splendidly well. We had to anchor outside & came in on a tender & I never saw a more picturesque place than Brest. The streets were arched with Wreaths of Laurel & flags waving every where, & dense crowds of people crowding every inch of space, all over the fortifications, which surrounde the road leading to the station, on the roofs of houses, in the trees, hanging to Lamp posts—everywhere

Brest is in Brittany & many of the people were in their lovely native costumes.

We were laden with flowers, & from every window or elevation they threw flowers as we passed.

Finally we reached the station where a crimson carpet was stretched clear out the length of the platform. The train was the one which the Govrment gives its President—all furnished in old rose Brocade, with delightful easy chairs, footstools & cushions where you could luxuriate and see the entire lovely country through great broad windows, low and unobstructed. On tiny tables were numerous baskets of flowers, tied with ribbons, & bearing welcoms from many, many societies & people of France. In addition to this car, there was a sleeping car—2 bedrooms, each with Bathrooms, servants rooms etc. & smoking room. Besides an elaborate Dinnery car, which seated 18 people at a long table for a formal dinner. The train left Brest at 4, & stopped at 7 for 3 hours while dinner was served. We all got out after dinner & took a walk before retiring. Here I have written nearly a letter without telling Bert that her dear Gen. Harts[6] arrived with Gen. Pershing with the French Delegation on the George Washington, & has been with us pretty much ever since. He seems so glad to see us, & is as nice as of old. He looks older & quite thin, but has the same enthusiasm for everything & seemed most appreciative of B's message.

Now to resume my story—after a very comfortable night we reached Paris at 10 exactly Saturday Dec. 14.

Here the *world* seemed to be waiting to welcome and acclaim my wonderful husband.

The streets were one unbroken wall of people over miles of streets which we rode through. It was touching and bewildering the many ways in which they tried to express their feeling.

The President & Madame Poincaré met us at the station where a crimson carpet covered the Platform & Palms etc with flags outlined a bower effect. There were bands playing everywhere & Madame presented me with wonderful orchids. We then got into low hung carriages drawn by splendid horses & started on our triumphal way—which I cannot describe.

At last we arrived at 28 Rue de Monceau, which is charming. The Guard of Paris,[7] (with the gold helmets & horse tails down their backs) were our immediate Escort—all mounted on Black Horses.

The Prince Murat was here to welcome us & show us over his splendid house. One of his sons has been killed in the war & the Princess has just lost a sister, so we have not met her, but he seemed very nice. The house is truly Napoleanic—& the little Emperer is pictured everywhere.

There are wonderful tapestries and paintings, and the most beautiful furniture. Every room is either panelled Wood, or hung with rich old Brocades. I have Drawing room, Bed Room, Boudoir & Bath & Woodrow the same on the opposite, save in place of Boudoir there is a study or Library. There are closets & Armuers [armoires] & Cabinets galore each lined with blue satin in which to put every thing you ever owned. All the servants (17) are in Livery—knee breetches crimson coats etc. & we have delicious food.

Down stairs are 3 drawing rooms, Ball Room & Large Dining room—all filled with beautiful things—but I will have to tell you of these when I come.

We had time to get baths & dress before going to Lunch at the Elyseé Palais to lunch.

I wore my new black dress with the fur, my black Hat with the gray feathers & some of the orchids which were blue-gray. There were 250 guests at the lunch & the Elyseé is much larger than the White House. The table decorations were violets, the French flower, all outlining large Set pieces, the one right in front of us being the Ship of State. Then there were air planes etc. & in between garlands of Similax coupled with Red White & blue flowers.

We met all of the officials & wives Ambassadors, etc. & got home about 3:30. W. had to see a number of people so Margaret[,] Ben-hem & I took a drive, getting back to find Wilmer here. We kept him to dinner.

Tuesday Dec. 17.

Yesterday was another wonderful day, when we went to the Hotel de Ville for W. to be welcomed as a citizen of Paris & tendered a magnificent Reception.

I am keeping all the papers which describe these public func-tions, but I won't have time to write about them

Woodrow was presented with a gold medal most artistic & I with a huge jeweled piece which is more interesting than beautiful as it has Doves of Peace on it as large as this [here a picture]

We bearly saw them in the moment of Presentation but they said they would send them to us & they have not yet come.

I wore my violet velvet & violet hat, & it looked so pretty. I made Wilmer come to lunch & go with us, as it was such an historic occasion. We had the Nelson-Pages to lunch with us yesterday, as they came all the way from Italy to welcome us. We have promised Gen. Pershing to come to his Headquarters for Xmas dinner with the troops beyond that we have no plans, as Woodrow is busy here every moment & feels he must put through the big thing he came to do first. His cold is about gone, & the house is so warm & comfortable he is in good shape. Yesterday he called on M. Cle-menceau & when he left M. C. gave him a piece of the German flag of truce—to give to me. It looks like an old piece of table cloth, but it is such an interesting thing to have. I must stop now & write him a note to thank him.

I find I will have so little time to write I have decided to keep my journal in this way. Will you show this to each one of the dear ones, & Annie Fendall[8] and then keep it for me as a record of our trip.

At 5 we have the Sharps & Italian Ambassador to Tea, & we go at 8 to a big dinner at the Sharpes with a reception afterward of 700. This will reach you too late for Xmas but not too late to bring again our warm love & every happy wish to each one from us both

Fondly   Edith.

ALS (EBWP, DLC).

[1] Richard Wilmer Bolling, brother of Mrs. Wilson, who was in Paris as an agent of the United States Shipping Board.

[2] That is, Rear Adm. Hugh Rodman, who had been appointed commander of United States battleships in April 1918. Wilson wrote in Rodman's name for Mrs. Wilson. Adm. Wilson, just mentioned, was Henry Braid Wilson, commander of United States naval forces in France.

[3] WWhw.

[4] Comdr. de Blanpré, former French Naval Attaché in Washington.

[5] Margaret Woodrow Wilson had gone to Europe in early November 1918 to sing to American soldiers in France, England, and Italy. She had joined President and Mrs. Wilson upon their arrival at Brest on December 13.

[6] William Wright Harts, at this time, commander of the American troops in the District of Paris and, again, a military aide to Wilson.

[7] That is, the Garde Républicaine.

[8] Annie A. Galt (Mrs. Reginald) Fendall, a sister of Mrs. Wilson's first husband.

From the Diary of Colonel House

December 15, 1918.

I was to have gone to Picpus Cemetery with the President today to lay a wreath on the grave of LaFayette, but I missed him at church where we were to meet. He sent his car for me and that too I missed.

I have had an infinite amount of work to do. The President cheerfully unloads matters upon me. I am having worked out the boundary lines between the Jugoslavs and the Italians and a number of matters of that sort. I have no time for my correspondence and but little time for this diary.

I arranged yesterday for the President's trip to the Front on December 24th so he might spend Christmas with the troops. I also arranged, tentatively, his trip to Italy, and one to the devastated regions of France and Belgium.

Sir William Wiseman is back from London and gives me the latest news from the British Cabinet. When he is with me I often wonder how I got along while he was away. My letters to Balfour and others, cables which have come in for me form [from] McAdoo and others are all attached.

I called on Clemenceau at 5.30 in order to coach him before he saw the President, and to take him to the Hotel Murat. I had already suggested to the President what he should say to Clemenceau.

Clemenceau, the President and I were together for an hour. I did little or nothing to guide the conversation for it was felicitous from start to finish. I have never seen an initial meeting a greater success. The President was perfect in the matter and manner of his conversation and Clemenceau was not far behind. Neither said anything that was particularly misleading. They simply did not touch upon topics which would breed discussion. I saw to that in advance. I took Clemenceau down stairs afterward and he expressed keen delight over the interview and of the President personally. The President was equally happy when I returned upstairs and discussed the matter with him. It was a pleasant augury for success.

When I was with Clemenceau at the Ministre de Guerre, he told me he had changed his mind about the President sitting in at the Peace Conference. After thinking it over he had concluded it would be a good idea. It immediately flashed through my mind that the reception the President received from the French people was the thing that made him change, or it might be that he believes it will pull Wilson down from his high pedestal and put him on a level with George, Orlando and himself.

When speaking to me about it first he said, "According to the Protocol, it is not right, but damn the Protocol. Let's do what we please. Poincaré will want to sit in and I will have a fight with him, but I do not mind that. I rather enjoy it. I will also have a fight with Lloyd George but that, too, I do not mind. If you think Italy will be with us, France, Italy and the United States will be three out of four and we will do it whether the English like it or not."

I had previously told Clemenceau that I had talked the President out of sitting in. I did this in less than ten minutes. It is a question now whether the President will want to sit in since I so thoroughly convinced him it was not the right thing to do. However, after the three of us had finished talking it was decided to leave the matter for final decision later.

Grayson tells me that McAdoo really resigned because he thought the President would bring Baker over as a Peace Commissioner. He said he understood that Gregory was to resign and that Tumulty was thinking of doing so. When I asked Grayson who was responsible for the President's pre-election address, asking for a democratic Congress, he declared he did not know. He said everyone believed it was the cause of democratic defeat.

December 16, 1918.

I had a long talk with Henry White this morning. He is very happy over his appointment as a Peace Commissioner. He told me of his conversations with Roosevelt, Root, Lodge and other republicans and of their views of the Peace Conference. White knows next to nothing about the work we have in hand. I gave him a brief outline of what should be done with the League of Nations. Up to the time of my talk, he was of the opinion the League should not be formed until after the Peace Conference. He readily saw the necessity of pressing it to the fore.

He is a well meaning, accomplished old gentleman and may be of some service later on. I had a talk with Lansing and found him completely ignorant of most of the things with which he should be cognizant. He did not even know that Sharp had resigned, neither did he know why Baker was not brought after he had been notified of his appointment. Lansing is a man that one cannot grow enthusiastic over, but I do think the President should treat him with more consideration. As the matter stands today the President and I are doing everything, the balance are marking time as far as I can see, except General Bliss who is busy gathering information about military matters, and preparing to be useful at the Peace Conference. He is a scholarly, statesmanlike, soldier. He has not the army point of view at all. His work will be of service as far as actual work is concerned, but of no value whatever from a political standpoint. In fact, he is so little known and understood that he will be a liability to the President when, indeed, he could have appointed someone who would have been a political asset.

I went with the President to call on Clemenceau and going and coming we settled many matters of passing interest. It has been a busy day with him and I have tried not to disturb him. His public receptions etc. have taken the larger part of his time.

I told him that a "head-on collison" was about to occur with Creel on the one side and with Lansing and the State Department on the other. I advised him to see Lansing and not allow the thing to get into an impossible condition. He said he would do so. I told him that Lansing's dislike for Creel was only equalled by Creel's dislike for Lansing. I urged him not to disrupt the organization which Lansing had suggested to Grew because while Harrison and Patchin were perhaps not the best selections, yet their removal at this time would be unfortunate.

I forgot to say the other day that Clemenceau asked me whether I thought it necessary to appoint Marechal Foch one of the French Peace Plenipotentiaries. I did not think so. He wanted to know then if Foch could be brought into the conferences from time to time when necessity for his advice was apparent. I said this could be arranged. I explained to the President what I had said to Clemenceau and why.

The President and I are contemplating with much concern the general lack of understanding of the world situation which we find amongst the Allied Governments. He and I realize how necessary for the future well-being and orderly conduct of all governments a liberal program is. I was glad to have the President ask me whether I thought something could be done or said at the Peace Conference which would bring the hours of labor, throughout the world, to a maximum of eight out of the twenty-four. He said it was entirely irrelevant to a Peace Conference, but he wondered if it could not be brought in. I thought it could be. I do not know just how, but we will try and find a way. It can be done by resolution, but that would not be binding, and would merely indicate a sentiment.

From the Diary of Dr. Grayson

Monday, December 16, 1919 [1918].

The President and Mrs. Wilson today had their first sight of Versailles. They motored out and rode around through the grounds, inspecting the golf links. The officer in command invited them to enter and be shown through the palace, but the President did not have the time and returned to Paris.

In the afternoon at 2:30 the President and Madame Poincaré called for the President and Mrs. Wilson and escorted them to the Hotel de Ville. Here the formal ceremony of making the President a citizen of Paris took place. The reception was most elaborate. A double guard of French soldiers surrounded the entire building, and invitation to the ceremony was by card. All officers of the Army and Navy were in uniform, while the diplomats wore court dress. The spectacle was very impressive and picturesque. So great was the demand for tickets to this ceremony, which marked an epoch in the history of the municipality of Paris, that a number of smaller diplomatic representatives were unable to secure cards. The President was presented with a gold medal, while Mrs. Wilson was given a jeweled dress ornament. Responding to the address extending him the formal freedom of the city of Paris, the President made a speech which was the subject of very warm newspaper approval. The procession to and from the Hotel de Ville was in every respect a duplicate of that which marked the formal entry of the President into the city of Paris. The same formal equipment in the line of carriages and escort was utilized.

Following the return to the Hotel de Ville, the President returned the formal call of Premier Clemenceau. The President's call on Clemenceau was made at the latter's office in the War Office. Clemenceau met him at the door and held out both hands to greet him, saying: "I am so glad to see you, Mr. President; it is so good of you to come to see me, and I want to say right here that I am going to swear eternal friendship to you." The President and the Premier sat down in the office and di[s]cussed a few plans leading up to the formation of the Peace Conference, Clemenceau making reference to the fact that the people of France had their heart in the tribute which they had paid the President this afternoon and on the day of the President's arrival. The President introduced me to Clemenceau. It was my first meeting with him.

The President returned to the Villa Murat in time to receive General Pershing, who had come to Paris to pay his respects. General Pershing told the President that the great desire of the A.E.F.

was to get home as rapidly as possible. The President explained to the Commanding General that this was the one thing which he had been [insisting on] and would insist on. Everything was to be done to send the men home with the same expedition that marked their being brought overseas. General Pershing invited the President to spend Christmas with the A.E.F. and to be his guest at G.H.Q. at Chaumont on Christmas Day. The President said that that was what he wanted to do, but he emphasized to General Pershing that he did not want to become a guest at a formal function confined to officers of the Army. Instead, the President explained, he wanted to have his dinner with the American soldiers in the field, to be served from the field kitchen in the manner that they were served and to eat from their regular mess kit. General Pershing promised that this would be done.

An Address at the Hôtel de Ville in Paris[1]

December 16th, 1918.

Your greeting has raised many emotions within me. It is with no ordinary sympathy that the people of the United States, for whom I have the privilege of speaking, have viewed the sufferings of the people of France. Many of our own people have been themselves witnesses of those sufferings. We were the more deeply moved by the wrongs of the war because we knew the manner in which they were perpetrated. I beg that you will not suppose that because a wide ocean separated us in space, we were not in effect eye-witnesses of the shameful ruin that was wrought and the cruel and unnecessary sufferings that were brought upon you. Those sufferings have filled our hearts with indignation. We knew what they were not only, but we knew what they signified, and our hearts were touched to the quick by them, our imaginations filled with the whole picture of what France and Belgium in particular had experienced. When the United States entered the war, therefore, they entered it not only because they were moved by a conviction that the purposes of the Central Empires were wrong and must be resisted by men everywhere who loved liberty and the right, but also because the illicit ambitions which they were entertaining and attempting to realize had led to practices which shocked our hearts as much as they offended our principles. Our resolution was formed because we knew how profoundly great principles of right were affected, but our hearts moved also with our resolution.

You have been exceedingly generous in what you have been

gracious enough to say about me, generous far beyond my personal deserts, but you have interpreted with real insight the motives and resolution of the people of the United States. Whatever influence I exercise, whatever authority I speak with, I derive from them. I know what they have thought, I know what they have desired, and when I have spoken what I knew was in their minds, it has been delightful to see how the consciences and purposes of free men everywhere responded. We have merely established our right to the full fellowship of those peoples here and throughout the world who reverence the right and whose purpose is inflexibly fixed upon the establishment of genuine liberty and justice.

You have made me feel very much at home here, not merely by the delightful warmth of your welcome, but also by the manner in which you have made me realize to the utmost the intimate community of thought and ideal which characterizes your people and the great nation which I have the honor for the time to represent. Your welcome to Paris I shall always remember as one of the unique and inspiring experiences of my life, and, while I feel that you are honoring the people of the United States in my person, I shall nevertheless carry away with me a very keen personal gratification in looking back upon these memorable days. Permit me to thank you from a full heart.

T MS (WP, DLC).
¹ Wilson was responding to a speech of welcome by Adrien Mithouard, President of the Municipal Council of Paris. Mithouard had hailed Wilson as the great expounder of the meaning of the vast conflict which had been waged on French soil. Wilson's distance from the war, Mithouard said, had given him an almost historical perspective on the significance of events in Europe. Wilson's words, as well as the entrance of the United States into the conflict and the coming of American troops to Europe, had inspired the French nation to new efforts. A French text and an English translation of Mithouard's remarks, both T MS, are in WP, DLC.

Two Telegrams to Joseph Patrick Tumulty

Paris (Received Dec. 16, 1918, 9 32 am)

Hog Island matter will be taken up at once with Hurley. Reception here of the most extraordinary character. Everybody says that nothing approaching it has ever been known in Paris. Confidentially it has had a most happy effect upon the prospects of common counsel. All join in affectionate messages.

Woodrow Wilson.

T telegram (J. P. Tumulty Papers, DLC).

Paris (Received Dec. 16, 1918, 3 58 pm)

Number four. Hog Island report should be released at once as you suggest without any accompanying statement except in case the Department of Justice desires to issue a supplementary statement.[1]   Woodrow Wilson.

T telegram (WP, DLC).
[1] It was printed in the *Official Bulletin*, II (Dec. 23, 1918), 9-14.

From Herbert Bruce Brougham

Dear Mr. President: Paris, 16th December 1918

It is nine years since you wrote on *Hide-and-Seek Politics* for the North American Review.[1] I remember it vividly because it was the first year of my acquaintance with you and with your example.

In that article you analyzed the qualities of privilege and their utter dependence upon secrecy; insomuch that even a politician like Mr. Roosevelt would hold the exponents of privilege at his mercy by his refusal, when so minded, to respect the confidences of their councils and by his readiness to blazon them to the world, watching them shrivel under the public gaze.

In London and Paris during the last month I have heard high and low—but chiefly "higher up"—and in apparently unrelated quarters expressions like this: "Yes, Mr. Wilson will get a League of Nations, but not, perhaps, the League of Nations pictured by his lofty ideals." What sort of thing it is to be seems already determined beforehand. Who or what influences have predetermined it are not revealed. What it is has not been published. The plan of it, and the pledges for it, have been arrived at in secrecy. The exponents of privilege intend that it shall be an arrangement which shall favor them, which shall permit them to continue exploiting the peoples of the world. They fear the "unprecedented things" to which you have committed your advocacy. In the tumult and the shouting, in this overwhelming adulation to which you are treated they hope you will forget about the unprecedented things or surrender, for their acclaim, your American birthright to aid in creating a United States of the World with representation, with powers to judge, to administer and control.

They say national pride will not permit forming a real League of Nations. Behind the words "national pride" they shelter their own designs to shut off from growing populations raw materials indispensable to their growth; to get for themselves purchases of material and access to markets denied to their neighbors, and concessions for investment in the backward countries without public and international control, besides exclusive or preferential power over seaports and over transport along international rivers, canals, straits and railroads. Their appeal to national pride covers up purposes of which they are deeply conscious but which they dare not avow.

With your advocacy of democratic principles and of representation for the world's commonwealths you seem to stand alone. You have united against you the opposition of the great governments of Europe and of individuals—many of them worthy according to their lights, which are the lights of a narrow nationalism—who have talent and adroitness to keep the old and trodden road, to love rest, conservatism, appropriation, inertia, to accept the actual for the necessary. But they lack character. And the actual has become so terrible that the peoples of the world were never so determined as now to dispose of it at the expense, if need be, of the governments super[im]posed upon the actual.

The instrumentalities controlled by Mr. Creel, I think, can be brought into play to overcome the odds which seem to be against you. I recall your words to the recalcitrant members of the New Jersey legislature: that you wished to put upon them no arbitrary coercion, but to establish a free field of debate—before their constituents. A legislature at first hostile finally voted your measures. Now as the spokesman of a great nation drawn into this conflict and sharing its terrible risks you have the right, Mr. President, to speak on equal terms with the leaders before the constituencies of the world. I know that you will not flinch from that high duty. Your life as I have studied it shows that you are willing to submit naked and unsparing the purposes of your mission as before your God, and to ask that those who present themselves as bearing the sacred trust of their peoples shall submit themselves with like rigor. May God prosper you in this design.

I am here in Paris charged by the Secretary of Labor to "study cooperation with special reference to industrial reconstruction after the war." Your theme of cooperation, reported in yesterday's papers,[2] nearly concerns this mission.

Cordially and sincerely yours,   Herbert Bruce Brougham

TLS (WP, DLC).
[1] It is printed at March 2, 1910, Vol. 20.
[2] In Wilson's reply to Poincaré, printed at Dec. 14, 1918.

Frank Lyon Polk to Robert Lansing

Washington, December 16, 1918.

33. For the Secretary of State. For your information. Had talk with Gompers and found him a little disturbed because labor was not represented on Peace Mission. Feeling on his part not very deep. He said he would not go to Paris however unless he had some reason for being there as he could not be in a position of waiting around. Feels strongly that Labor Conference,[1] if held, should be held in Paris at the same time Peace Conference, in which case he would go.   Polk, Acting.

T telegram (SDR, RG 59, 185.161/3, DNA).
[1] That is, an international labor and socialist conference to consider problems of the coming peace settlement of particular interest to the working classes of all countries. An active movement for such a meeting had been under way since the Armistice. However, the various socialist and labor parties in the nations of the Entente were badly divided, as were the governments of those countries, on the questions of whether the proposed conference should be in Paris or in a neutral country such as Switzerland, and whether representatives of labor and socialist groups in former enemy countries should be allowed to participate. Gompers strongly favored a conference in Paris limited to delegations from the Allied and Associated nations. For a detailed discussion of the proposed conference, see Arno J. Mayer, *Politics and Diplomacy of Peacemaking: Containment and Counterrevolution at Versailles 1918-1919* (New York, 1967), pp. 373-80.

Edward Mandell House to Frank Irving Cobb

My dear Friend: Paris, December 16, 1918.

The President was keenly disappointed when he found you were not here. He had accepted as literal that letter I wrote on the Northern Pacific in which I outlined the organization and program which seemed to me wise to carry out here.[1] But, unfortunately, he took it for granted that I could read his mind and that it was not necessary to make any confirmation.

He expected you to direct the whole editorial policy of the American case at the Conference. We are now at sea for there is no one capable of doing this great work.

You will never know how much help you were to me during the trying days before the Armistice, and what a gratification it was to have you interpret England in the way you did.

Things have speeded up since the President's arrival so that the days are as full of interest as they were when we first came, and I miss your advice beyond measure. I feel, though, that you will do a great work for our country at home, and I shall rest content with that. We have cabled Frank Polk to give you all the news that we send over whenever you telephone for it.

Sincerely yours,   E. M. House

TLS (WP, DLC).
[1] EMH to WW, Oct. 22, 1918, with Enclosure, Vol. 51.

Sir William Wiseman to Sir Eric Drummond

[Paris] December 16, 1918.

The PRESIDENT is not anxious to sit at the Peace Conference. On the contrary, he thinks it would not be wise. At yesterday's interview CLEMENCEAU told the PRESIDENT that, although he had been opposed to the idea, he had changed his mind after meeting him, and urged him to attend as the chief American delegate.

T telegram (W. Wiseman Papers, CtY).

Lord Derby to Arthur James Balfour

Strictly personal & Secret

Dear Arthur   Paris. 16 December 1918.

I want you to read and then burn this letter for reasons I will give you.

I was not very satisfied with Clemenceau's account of his interview with President Wilson with reference to the latter attending the Conference so I went round to see House and I showed him a paraphrase of the telegram[1] I had sent you this morning giving Clemenceau's account of the interview. As I thought it was not a true account. The initiative for the proposal came, not from the President but from Clemenceau. House had seen the President and had convinced the latter that it would be wrong for him to attend. He (House) believed at that moment that this was in entire accord with Clemenceau's views. He was present at the interview which on the whole was very satisfactory and at the end he thought he would bring up a subject on which they were both in entire accord so he mentioned the point as to whether the President should attend. Judge of his surprise when Clemenceau admitted that he had turned completely round and begged the President to attend. The President gave no answer and said he would consider the circumstances. After the meeting House saw Clemenceau who gave him various reasons why he had changed his mind, including the one that I gave you. House has since seen the President and he feels practically certain that the President will not ask to attend but he cannot make out any more than I can why Clemenceau is playing this game. House and I are both agreed that I should let you know the former's version as well as Clemenceau's of this meeting but we are equally agreed that it must be for your eye and your eye only. We both know that if it once got to the P.M's knowledge he would undoubtedly blurt out something which would let Clemenceau know that I had suspected the accuracy of his statements and had consulted House on the subject. What House therefore recommends is that you should give no answer to the telegram whatever. You should leave matters just as they are and he thinks you will find they will come out in accordance with his view. May I suggest therefore that without mentioning this letter you should advise the P.M. and the War Cabinet to take this line of action. Meanwhile if I get any telegram from you giving an expression of your views on the subject I shall not send it on until I hear further. On the other hand I will call this letter "A" and if you telegraph to me to say "Letter 'A' received. Am acting on your suggestion" I shall know what you mean. I think after reading it you will understand why I want the letter destroyed.   Yours ever   D

TLI (A. J. Balfour Papers, Add. MSS 49744, British Library).
  ¹ It was probably destroyed.

From the Diary of Dr. Grayson

Tuesday, December 17, 1918.

Marshal Foch made a formal call upon the President this morning. He does not talk English nor understand it, and the conversation was through an interpreter. Naturally it was somewhat stilted as a result, but the President's impression of the French Field Marshal coincided exactly with what he had previously pictured him in his mind to be—plain, strong, calm and forceful, the "embodiment of sense and sensibility." Marshal Foch explained to the President his own impressions of the general situation so far as Germany was concerned. Among other things he said that the German people knew absolutely nothing about the conditions of their government, neither did they know that the acceptance of the armistice terms was due entirely to the collapse of the German army. The people had been kept in complete ignorance of all that had been going on, especially of the fact that the offensive had been a complete failure. The German people could not understand why it was that their soldiers were returning home, Marshal Foch told the President. The Marshal seemed somewhat nervous on his arrival and apparently his meeting the President was more or less of an ordeal to him, he being far more the soldier than the diplomat.

In the evening the President dined at the American Embassy, the guests including President and Madame Poincaré, General Pershing, Marshal Foch, General Bliss and others.

To Edward Mandell House

My dear House: Paris, 17 December, 1918.

I have been thinking a great deal lately about the contact of the Commission with the public through the press and particularly about the way in which the Commission should deal with the newspaper men who have come over from the United States. I have come to the conclusion that much the best way to handle this matter is for you and the other Commissioners to hold a brief meeting each day and invite the representatives of the press to come in at each meeting for such interchange of information or suggestions as may be thought necessary. This I am sure is more preferable to any formal plan or to any less definite arrangement.

I am also convinced that the preparation of all the press matter that is to be issued from the Commission is a task calling for a particular sort of experienced ability. I beg, therefore, that you and your fellow Commissioners will agree to the appointment of Mr. Ray Stannard Baker as your representative in the performance of this duty. Mr. Baker enjoys my confidence in a very high degree and I have no hesitation in commending him to you as a man of ability, vision and ideals. He has been over here for the better part of a year, has established relationships which will be of the highest value, and is particularly esteemed by the very class of persons to whom it will be most advantageous to us to be properly interpreted in the news that we have to issue. If you see no conclusive objection to this, I would suggest that you request Mr. Baker to do us the very great service of acting in this capacity.

I am writing in the same terms to the other members of the Commission.[1]   Sincerely yours,   [Woodrow Wilson]

CCL (WP, DLC).
[1] Wilson wrote the same letter, *mutatis mutandis*: WW to RL, Dec. 17, 1918, TLS (R. Lansing Papers, DLC); WW to H. White, Dec. 17, 1918, TLS (H. White Papers, DLC); and WW to T. H. Bliss, Dec. 17, 1918, TLS (T. H. Bliss Papers, DLC).

To James Viscount Bryce

My dear Lord Bryce: [Paris] 17 December, 1918.

It was a real pleasure to see your handwriting again,[1] and I am warmly obliged to you for sending me the little volume of "Essays and Addresses in War Time," which you were thoughtful enough to let me see. I am sure that I shall derive help and instruction not only from the papers to which you specially call my attention, but from others.

I believe that with perfect frankness and sincerity of dealing, the perplexities of our present problems will be greatly simplified, and I am hoping that we may soon see our way to making the foundations of peace as secure as fallible judgment can make them.

With warm appreciation of your thoughtful friendship,

Cordially and sincerely yours,　Woodrow Wilson

TLS (J. Bryce Papers, Bodleian Library).
¹ James Viscount Bryce to WW, Dec. 7, 1918.

To the Most Reverend Randall Thomas Davidson

Paris, December 17, 1918.

Your gracious message sent me on behalf of the responsible leaders of Christian churches in Great Britain and Ireland who have issued an appeal to all Christians respecting the church and the League of Nations in which you are kind enough to invite me to speak at a public meeting in London on Christianity and the League of Nations has given me the most sincere pleasure. I wish that I could accept the invitation but I really dare not. The claims upon me of the important business upon which I came are so great and so constant that I feel I must devote my whole thought and attention to them and I am afraid to undertake any important engagements outside this immediate line of duty. Paragraph. I am sure that you will understand this scruple and I hope will approve it though I deeply regret being obliged to send this reply.

Woodrow Wilson.

CC telegram (WP, DLC).

To Herbert Bruce Brougham

My dear Mr. Brougham:　　　　　[Paris] 17 December, 1918.

I value your letter of the 16th. I have been aware of the forces which you tell me are at work, and I beg you to believe that I have not been deceived by the acclaim with which I have been received, or rather it would be more correct for me to say that I have been instructed by it, because I know upon what it is based. It is based upon the trust that I will stand fast to the principles and purposes which I have avowed. I must, and, so far as I have the power, will.

Cordially and sincerely yours,　[Woodrow Wilson]

CCL (WP, DLC).

From Joseph Patrick Tumulty

The White House, 17 December 1918.

Labor leaders urgently ask modification of order issued by you September 16, 1918, prohibiting use of grain in manufacture of soft drinks. Baruch and Garfield in favor but other members of Board oppose. Since you left this office has received numerous telegrams from leading citizens, bankers, and others, resolutions passed by chambers of commerce and other business organizations, requesting order prohibiting manufacture of non-intoxicating soft beverages be removed. Manufacturers have on hand ample supply of coal and raw materials for their purposes; therefore granting this request will not affect food or coal supply. Understand materials used in manufacture of these beverages are now exported to Canada, France and England. Unless order is rescinded, approximately six thousand men will be thrown out of employment during winter months in St. Louis alone, and just at this time men formerly engaged in munition factories there are without employment. Urgency of appeal from all sources is directed solely to need of continuing employment of men in winter time, and not throwing them out of employment in competition with returning soldiers and discharged munition workers. Labor leaders and organizations have materially supplemented this appeal of business men.

Tumulty

T telegram (J. P. Tumulty Papers, DLC).

From Robert Somers Brookings and Others

To the President: Washington December 17, 1918.

The members of the Price Fixing Committee hereby beg to tender their resignations, to take effect at the earliest moment compatible with the public interest. The War Industries Board, of which the Price Fixing Committee is a branch, is happily no longer needed for the mobilization and regulation of the country's industries, and the occasion for the functions of the Price Fixing Committee has also ceased. No new price regulations seem to be called for, and those which have been made will be allowed by the Committee to expire at the dates severally set.

The latest date for the expiration of a price-fixing agreement is March 1, 1919. Until that time, questions may arise concerning the interpretation and administration of the agreements still pending. The Committee stands ready to continue in service for the disposition of any such questions. Although some members of the Committee may withdraw from government service before March 1, others will remain, and will be able to serve if needed. The Committee accordingly requests that it be finally released from its duties on that date.

The Committee begs to express to yourself its appreciation of the confidence you have shown in the assignment to it of a difficult task, and for the careful attention and favorable judgment with which you have considered its recommendations.

Robt. S Brookings   Chairman

B M Baruch	Hugh Frayne
Robt H Montgomery[1]	F. W. Taussig
Lt Col. USA	
William B. Colver.	H. C. Stuart
John M Hancock[2]	H. A. Garfield.
Commander (P.C.)	
U.S.N.	

TLS (WP, DLC).

[1] Robert Hiester Montgomery, a lawyer of New York and Assistant Professor of Economics at Columbia University; at this time, chief of the price-fixing section of the Division of Purchase, Storage, and Traffic of the War Department and the representative of the War Department on the Price Fixing Committee.

[2] John Milton Hancock, commander of the Supply Corps of the United States Navy.

Sir Eric Drummond to Sir William Wiseman

London. 17.12.18.

Your telegram of yesterday:

502. URGENT. LORD DERBY telegraphs that CLEMENCEAU told him that the PRESIDENT would like to attend Conference, that he felt it desirable that the President's wish should be met, that he therefore intended to support proposal but that he would like the Prime Minister's and Mr. Balfour's views.

We are replying that if the President desires to attend we should, of course, be delighted that he should do so.

Please explain exact position to Col. House.

T telegram (W. Wiseman Papers, CtY).

A Memorandum by Lord Robert Cecil[1]

[Dec. 17, 1918]

LEAGUE OF NATIONS
I.
Organization.

The General Treaty setting up the League of Nations will explicitly provide for regular conferences between the responsible representatives of the contracting Powers.

These conferences would review the general condition of international relations and would naturally pay special attention to any difficulty which might seem to threaten the peace of the world. They would also receive and as occasion demanded discuss reports as to the work of any international administrative or investigating bodies working under the League.

These conferences would constitute the pivot of the League. They would be meetings of statesmen responsible to their own sovereign Parliaments, and any decisions taken would therefore, as in the case of the various Allied Conferences during the War, have to be unanimous.

The following form of organization is suggested:

1. *The Conference.*

    Annual Meeting of Prime Ministers and Foreign Secretaries of British Empire, United States, France, Italy, Japan and any other States recognized by them as great Powers.

    Quadrennial Meeting of representatives of all States included in the League.

    There should also be provision for the summoning of *special conferences* on the demand of any one of the great Powers or, if there were danger of an outbreak of war, of any member of the League (The composition of the League will be determined at the Peace Conference. Definitely untrustworthy and hostile states, e.g., Russia, should the Bolshevist Government remain in power, should be excluded. Otherwise it is desirable not to be too rigid in scrutinizing qualifications, since the smaller Powers will in any case not exercise any considerable influence.)

2. For the conduct of its work the Inter-State Conference will require a *Permanent Secretariat*. The General Secretary should be appointed by the Great Powers, if possible choosing a national of some other country.

3. *International Bodies.*

    The Secretariat would be the responsible channel of communication between the Inter-State Conference and all International bodies functioning under treaties guaranteed by the League. These would fall into three classes:

(a) *Judicial*; i.e., the existing Hague organization with any additions or modifications made by the League.

(b) *International Administrative Bodies,* such as the suggested Transit Commission. To these would be added bodies already formed under existing treaties, (which are very numerous and deal with very important interests e.g. Postal Union, International Labour Office, etc.)

(c.) *International Commissions of Enquiry*: e.g. Commission on Industrial Conditions (Labour Legislation), African Commission, Armaments Commission.

4. In addition to the above arrangements guaranteed by or arising out of the General Treaty, there would probably be a *periodical congress* of delegates of the Parliaments of the States belonging to the League, as a development out of the existing inter-Parliamentary Union. A regular staple of discussion for this body would be afforded by the reports of the Inter-State Conference and of the different International bodies. The Congress would thus cover the ground that is at present occupied by the periodical Hague Conference and also the ground claimed by the Socialist International.

For the efficient conduct of all these activities it is essential that there should be a permanent central meeting-place, where the officials and officers of the League would enjoy the privileges of extra-territoriality. Geneva is suggested as the most suitable place.

II.
Prevention of War.

The covenants for the prevention of war which would be embodied in the general treaty would be as follows:

(1) The members of the League would bind themselves not to go to war until they had submitted the questions at issue to an international conference or an arbitral court, and until the conference or court had issued a report or handed down an award.

(2) The members of the League would bind themselves not to go to war with any member of the League complying with the award of a court or with the report of a conference. For the purpose of this clause, the report of the conference must be unanimous, excluding the litigants.

(3) The members of the League would undertake to regard themselves, as, ipso facto, at war with any one of them acting con-

trary to the above covenants, and to take, jointly and severally, appropriate military, economic and other measures against the recalcitrant State.

(4) The members of the League would bind themselves to take similar action, in the sense of the above clause, against any State not being a member of the League which is involved in a dispute with a member of the League and which does not agree to adopt the procedure obligatory on members of the League. (This is a stronger provision than that proposed in the Phillimore Report.[2])

The above covenants mark an advance upon the practice of international relations previous to the war in two respects:

(1) In ensuring a necessary period of delay before war can break out (except between two States which are neither of them members of the League);

(2) In securing public discussion and probably a public report upon matters in dispute.

It should be observed that even in cases where the conference report is not unanimous, and therefore in no sense binding, a majority report may be issued and that this would be likely to carry weight with the public opinion of the States in the League.

T MS (WP, DLC).
[1] About Wilson's receipt of this document, see n. 1 to the memorandum printed at Dec. 26, 1918. Cecil submitted this memorandum to the War Cabinet, the King, and the Imperial War Cabinet on December 17, 1918.
[2] About which, see Lord Reading to WW, July 3, 1918, n. 1 (second letter of that date), Vol. 48.

From the Diary of Colonel House

December 17, 1918.

It is difficult to chronicle except meagerly the happenings of the past few days. I did something today which has pleased me more than anything I have done since signing the Armistice with Germany. I took Lord Northcliffe for a ride and a walk of an hour. I succeeded in committing him not only to a League of Nations, but to its immediate formation at the Peace Conference and making it a part of the Treaty itself. I did more than that. I made him admit that the Entente Governments as now constituted could not interpret the aspirations of the peoples of their respective countries and that Wilson was the only statesman who could do so. He agreed that the phenominal greeting which the President has received in Paris was an expression of the great body of the people. That in Wilson they had found an exponent of their hopes for a better world and for a lasting peace. I urged Northcliffe to take the lead in England and become there the voice of the people, and it is within the range of possibility that he may do this. I told him the Entente statesmen were idling the days away while the world was in agony, and that he ought to use his great press to stir them to action. He promised to do this.

Sir William Wiseman, I approved, and Gordon largely wrote an interview which we hope the President will give to the London Times. I saw the President and told him my reasons for wishing this and he consetned [consented] to do it. My argument was that Lloyd George had been telling the English people things about him which were not true, and I wanted him in this interview indirectly to brand them as untrue.

Northcliffe and I agreed that the President should visit England at once and reveive [receive] the reception there which we knew awaited him. The reception he received in Paris has changed the political sentiment, even in governmental circles, for the better, and we believe if he goes to England and gets such an endorsement from the English people, Lloyd George and his colleagues would not dare oppose his policies at the Peace Conference.

I asked the President to do this and he consented without argument. I then sent for the British Ambassador and told him if the English desired the President to come, he would be able to come at the end of this month or the first of January. I thought if he did not go to England at once, he would probably go to Italy, and I preferred him to go to England first because there was always the possibility of his being suddenly called home without giving him further opportunity. Lord Derby sent an urgent cable to his Government asking if it would be convenient for the President to come at the time indicated. He hoped to receive a reply tomorrow. It will upset the plans of Lloyd George and Balfour who have in mind to go to the South of France for the holidays.

I called upon the President in the afternoon and we settled a good many pending matters.

Among the many people that called on me were, M. Aubert,[1] who is to be liaison officer between the French Plenipotentiaries and those of the United States, Ellis Loring Dresel,[2] who is to be attached to our Embassy in Berlin. He is going into Germany again to report on what measures of relief are necessary. I sent by him direct word to Walter Rathenau,[3] who has addressed me an open letter in the *Vorwarts*.[4] It is a pathetic appeal and all too true. I will do Rathenau the justice to say that from the very inception of the war he held these views and they seem never to have changed during my visits to Berlin. I desired Rathenau to know that I had brought his open letter to me to the attention of the President, and that I was conscious that his attitude at the beginning of the war was the same as now.

I asked Dresel to see Solf, Secretary of Foreign Affairs, who had also sent me messages. I suggested that he meet Max[i]milian Harden and say to him from me that his articles had been the only vocal note of sanity to come from Germany during the war.

Mark Sullivan came to inform me as to the newspaper situation.

The Spanish Ambassador[5] called to tell me that Romanones,[6] Prime Minister of Spain, would come to Paris on the 19th or 20th if he could see the President and me at that time. I told the Ambassador if the Prime Minister arrived here before the 23rd the President would be able to see him.

I am in constant touch with Sir William Wiseman who is working earnestly and intelligently for the best interests of all.

Ambassador and Mrs. Sharp gave a dinner and reception to the President and Mrs. Wilson tonight. I went to the dinner and remained for a half hour afterward and then quietly slipped away. There was an enormous crush before I left, and it was difficult for me to get from one end of the drawing room to the door as I knew practically everyone in the house—foreigners and Americans. I had to speak to each one as I passed by.

I had a talk with the Japanese Ambassador[7] and rather disturbed his usual equilibrium by asking whether he thought the President should sit in the Peace Conference. I was amused at his efforts to give a non-compromising reply. I had talks with many Americans, Madame Poincaré and other foreigners.

At my request, Dr. Mezes brought the Specialists, twelve or fourteen, to call in a body. I stood for a half hour talking with them. They are as intellectual, and scholarly lot of men as one could find. I believe that our expert organization will excel in material if not in quantity, and as an American citizen, I am proud of them.

[1] Louis Aubert, distinguished French publicist, expert on ethnographic questions in the French delegation at the peace conference, and director of the service of research and information in the Commission on Franco-American Affairs of War.

[2] Chief of the Division of Political and Diplomatic Questions of the A.C.N.P.

[3] Walther (not Walter) Rathenau was president of the Allgemeine Elektrizitäts-Gesellschaft, former head of the department of raw materials in the Prussian Ministry of War, and one of the foremost conservative liberal writers and critics of Imperial Germany; at this time, a founding member of the German Democratic party.

[4] It is reprinted in Walther Rathenau, *Gesammelte Schriften* (6 vols., Berlin, 1925-29), VI, 268-73. See also the *New York Times*, Dec. 11, 1918.

[5] José María Quiñones de Leon.

[6] Álvaro Figueroa y Torres, Count de Romanones.

[7] Keishiro Matsui.

From the Diary of Dr. Grayson

Wednesday, December 18, 1918.

The President spent the morning in his study going over important matters requiring his attention. At 12:30 o'clock he had a conference with M. Hanotaux.[1] At five o'clock he went to the Crillon Hotel for a conference with the American Peace Delegation. Upon his return to the Murat Palace he saw Mr. Adam,[2] of the London Times, and at 6:30 o'clock he had an audience with Monsignor Cerretti,[3] of Rome.

[1] Gabriel Albert Auguste Hanotaux, former French Foreign Minister (1894-1895, 1896-1898), president of the Franco-American Committee, and a member of the Académie Française. He called on Wilson to discuss the arrangements for the induction of Marshal Joffre as a member of the Académie Française on December 19. Hanotaux was Joffre's sponsor before the Académie, and Wilson, as an honorary member, was planning to attend the ceremonies. After his interview, Hanotaux issued the following statement: "We talked no politics. I do not meddle with politics any more. President Wilson is exactly as we had anticipated and hoped he would be. He has conquered the heart of Paris by his affability. His charming smile has something so familiar that we immediately feel upon mutual democratic ground. He is thoroughly master of himself. Mrs. Wilson is also very winning." *New York Times*, Dec. 19, 1918.
[2] George Jefferys Adam, the Paris correspondent of the London *Times* since 1914. His interview with Wilson is printed below.
[3] That is, the Most Rev. Bonaventura Cerretti, the titular Archbishop of Corinth and Papal Secretary for Extraordinary Affairs; at this time on his way to the United States as a special envoy to the celebration of the golden jubilee of Cardinal Gibbons. Cerretti presented to Wilson a letter from Benedict XV. It pleaded for Wilson's assistance on behalf of small oppressed nationalities, especially Armenia and Poland; expressed the hope that a just and durable peace would be achieved through enlightened action; and asked Wilson to help the new countries arising from the dissolution of the Hapsburg Empire to realize their ambitions, regardless of race and religion. The letter is missing in WP, DLC. However, see the *New York Times*, Dec. 19, 1918.

A Statement

December 18, 1918.

The statement contained in the Paris edition of the Chicago Tribune this morning in a dispatch, accredited to its correspondent in Washington, declares that before leaving for France I gave[1] assurance that I approved of the plan formulated by the League to Enforce Peace. This statement is[2] entirely false. I am, as every one knows, not only in favor of a League of Nations, but believe the formation of such a League absolutely indispensable to the maintenance of peace, but the particular plan of the League to Enforce Peace[3] I have never, directly or indirectly, endorsed.

T MS (D. H. Miller Papers, DLC).
[1] At this point "Mr. Taft" is in an earlier version: T MS (WP, DLC).
[2] At this point "absolutely and" were deleted.
[3] Here the earlier draft reads "has always seemed to me impracticable."

Remarks to Representatives of the American Press in Paris

[*Dec. 18, 1918*]

I have been asked to say a few words in regard to my reception here. The reception was so tremendous that I do not know what to say. I was delighted with it, but I was delighted for a special reason which is not personal.

I was saying to several of our French friends that I understood it because I saw in the eyes of the crowd just the feeling that I had for them and was aware it was but a sort of reciprocal feeling. But that moved me very much because that, of course, meant more than mere generous cordiality on the part of these delightful people.

It meant a thoughtful background to the thing which was very welcome, and to come into that sort of feeling in this wonderfully beautiful city made a combination of emotions that one would not have more than once in a life-time. That is as well as I can put it offhand.

Printed in the *New York Herald*, Dec. 19, 1918.

From Joseph Patrick Tumulty

The White House, Received Dec. 18th [1918].

Before finally declining invitation to visit Vatican, hope you will consider influence Pope can wield in favor of your ideals among free peoples of all countries in case an appeal to world necessary to sustain your principles. His influence of incalculable advantage. Misstep in this matter may be most hurtful. While there is political danger in visit, the larger aspects must be considered. The great issue which you are pushing forward in Europe and throughout the world will depend upon the popular sentiment behind you throughout Europe. The Vatican can help in this. We should use every instrument that can help you in this great hour. If you succeed—which is certain—visits to Vatican will be forgotten in realization of larger result. Tumulty.

T telegram (WP, DLC).

A News Report of An Interview

From Our Paris Correspondent, December 18, 1918.

President Wilson honoured *The Times* to-day by receiving its Paris correspondent and by outlining to him in words,[1] the meaning of which is clear to any thinking man, his attitude towards the whole vast series of problems which will come up for discussion next month.

It used to be a tradition of journalism that the President of the United States might make statements, but did not grant interviews. President Wilson has shown already in the course of his term of office that he was no slave to tradition, that he had his own way of working and his own way of thinking—his very arrival in Europe is a proof of this. An additional proof is to be found in his departure from precedent by receiving me this afternoon. The interview which he was good enough to accord me will show how sincere is his desire to speak with downright frankness, not through the formal channels of diplomacy, but through the democratic megaphone of the Press to the peoples whose fate he, as one of those concerned in the building of the New World, will have to mould.

I first met President Wilson at Brest on his arrival. I have seen him receiving the tremendous welcome of a whole people in the streets of Paris. I saw him again this afternoon at the Hôtel Crillon, the great Peace Arsenal of America, where he was passing from floor to floor inspecting the various departments of this branch office of the American Government. The President has a punctuality which Kings, who are credited by popular saying with possessing a monopoly of this form of politeness, might well envy. He had fixed an hour at which to receive me, and rather than depart from his rule of punctuality he curtailed his inspection at the Crillon, and the fourth floor will have to wait for another day.

I followed the President up to the charming residence that has been placed at his disposal by Prince Murat in the rue de Monceau. For days the street has been blocked by crowds of people, and a considerable service of police and of troops has been necessary to keep the road clear for the comings and goings of the President and those with him. This evening, however, heavily falling rain had driven away those dense crowds, and the electric lights which outline the great porte-cocher and the wall of the outer courtyard were reflected without hindrance upon the wet pavement. A word

[1] The T MS (allegedly by Auchincloss) containing the direct discourse in this interview is in WP, DLC. Wilson emended it, and we have indicated his emendations in the footnotes below. Wilson then made a few additional changes on a draft which was sent to Adam and is missing in WP, DLC. However, there is a TC of this second draft in WP, DLC.

to the Secret Service opened the main doorway for our car, and we entered the wide inner courtyard, also glowing with lights, which picked out the architectural features of the Paris "White House." A couple of sentries came to the salute with that rather jerky smartness which characterises the American soldier.

I was conducted to the first floor, where I found Mr. Hoover[2] and Admiral Grayson, and had not had more than time to shake hands with them when a door opened behind me and President Wilson came straight up to me, without waiting for any formal introduction, welcomed me, and conducted me to the room in which at present he does most of his work. He has not yet installed his study in the magnificent Empire salon which is next door, where the full glory of Empire furniture, with its ormolu,[3] can be appreciated better than in any place I know, with the exception of Malmaison, where also the great artist of the Empire, David, is worthily represented.

The room he is at present using is large, lofty, and square, and is adorned, as is indeed the whole of the house, with admirable works of art. On the writing-table stands a low, well-shaded electric light, giving a little warmth to the colder light falling from the ceiling. It may be rude to scrutinize too closely your host, but I will perhaps be pardoned for having examined with the very keenest interest the features and the play of thought across the face of a man who, without question, will play an extremely important part in the history that will be made in Paris and Versailles during the next few months.

President Wilson is not the lean, long-faced, somewhat cadaverous-looking man that the camera seems to have found—the camera is a notorious libeller. He is tall, well set up, an athletic figure of a man to whom it would be very difficult to give even an approximate age. Casually he might be placed among the numbers of well-educated, healthy Americans of middle-age who were to be seen on nearly every golf course of Great Britain before the war. You would know at once, even if you were only looking at his back, that this man in his grey lounge suit, well cut into his body, was a gentleman in the best sense of the word; that he was an American; and also in some way which I cannot define that he was Somebody. As he sat under the table-light upon his study desk I examined his features with what care courtesy permitted. His features are those of a man who has sought to combine spirit and body to the best advantage. Our talk led us over many topics, some grave and some gay. President Wilson has been surprised by the warmth of his

---

[2] That is, Irwin Hood Hoover.

[3] A variety of brass or bronze made to imitate gold in appearance.

welcome in France, but he is even more surprised by the devastating effect of his smile. He is amazed to find that people imagined that he was some curious kind of dour-faced Covenanter who was unable to taste and enjoy what sort of humour life has in it. He jokingly remarked that in spite of his somewhat Lowland-Scottish-Irish ancestry—his mother came from Carlisle and his father's people from the neighbourhood of Londonderry—he had something of the imagination and the sense of fun of the Celt. He admitted that he had no genealogical tree by which to prove his Celtic tendency, but claimed the touch of Celtic blood entirely by what he had inside of him, namely, a capacity for cheerful optimism and an innate tendency always to try and use humour in meeting the buffets of existence.

He is by far the best teller of an anecdote—and they are good anecdotes—to whom I have ever listened. He told me in particular a story about the way in which the Americans have solved the problem of governing their Irish population by letting the Irish police them, and told it with a gusto which I have never found in any other teller of stories. While he was talking in a better Irish brogue than I have yet heard, I had a very good opportunity—although I felt rather like a dissector—of analysing the smile which he has made famous. There seems to be some kind of competition between the upper and the lower halves of his features. His eyes and forehead remain serious, whereas his mouth can express every kind of gaiety, from the quiet smile of a man who enjoys within himself some deep feeling of satisfaction to the broad laugh of the man who is frankly enjoying a tickling joke.

When our conversation touched upon the great questions of Peace, the smile remained in abeyance, the lower half of the face became switched off, and it was mainly in the eye, shaded a little by glasses, that Mr. Wilson expressed himself. He has that automatic habit, which comes from natural causes, of making his eyes look, as it were, inwards with a deep and penetrating glance when he is weighing his words or reflecting, and the change between that look and the humorous human twinkle, when lighter subjects are being talked about, is marked and curious.

I know that President Wilson will be pleased if I say that he impressed me as a man who before every other thing, leaving aside his culture—he was a leader of university life—regards himself as a very ordinary mortal who, by his personality and by the wishes of the American people, has been called to the highest office of his country and is fully conscious of the tremendous responsibility which lies upon his shoulders, and is also fully aware that he shares that responsibility with the leaders of European peoples.

It is not as a master that he has come to Europe. He drew, indeed, a very interesting contrast between the Congress of Vienna, which was responsible for so much evil in the world, and the Congress of Versailles, which the world hopes will right the old wrongs as permanently as frail humanity can expect to do.

The Congress of Vienna, he pointed out (and here his eyes turned inwards), was a Congress of "bosses." The delegates were concerned more with their own interests, and of those of the classes they represented, than with the wishes of their peoples. Versailles, as Mr. Wilson said, must be a meeting of the servants of the peoples represented by the delegates. And, he added, "There is no master mind who can settle the problems of to-day. If there is anybody who thinks that he knows what is in the mind of all the peoples, that man is a fool. We've all got to put our heads together and pool everything we've got for the benefit of the ideals which are common to us all."

Mr. Wilson visited France on a very brief journey some 14 years ago. He knows England better, in fact he is probably better acquainted with the splendid scenery of our English Lake Country than are many Britons. He stayed at Rydal some years ago for some four or five months, and has cycled and walked all through the Lake district. He regards some of the views to be had down those valleys as the finest scenery of the world. And, as he told me, in an amusing anecdote, he has only once known the loveliness of one particular view to fail in silencing a bore.

But he knows that he could not in America become sufficiently acquainted with the various men in Europe with whom he has to collaborate. He quoted to me a little anecdote about Charles Lamb. Lamb, with his stutter, announced that he hated a certain Mr. L., and when one of the company pointed out that Lamb didn't even know the Mr. L. in question, Lamb stuttered back, "But how do you expect me to hate a man I know?" Mr. Wilson is going to meet and to know everybody, and if the impression of an interview which lasted half an hour and a close study of the President's various declarations count for anything at all he is going to know everybody very well.

I told him, in the blunt manner of the interviewer, that some people were asking why the President of the United States should come to Europe at this time. Mr. Wilson replied, "To me the answer seems very obvious.4 The issues which must be determined at the forthcoming Conferences will be of such overwhelming importance that the United States cannot refuse to share with the Allies their

4 "clear" in the unemended draft.

great responsibility to civilization, and it is only by the frankest personal counsel with the statesmen of the Allied countries that I can in some measure assist in the solution of these problems."

The words "some measure" are not a vain or camouflaged expression of President Wilson's real desire to help, together with the delegates of all the nations, at the meetings which are about to take place in Paris, in laying the real foundations of the Society of Nations and in safeguarding the future peace of the world.

When I asked the President what, in his mind, was the great purpose of the Conference and the great goal towards which its delegates should strive, he replied: "I think the plain man on the street could answer that question as well as I can. The plain people of all nations are now looking with anxious expectation towards Versailles, and I am sure that they are asking themselves this one question,[5] 'Will there be found enough of wisdom and purpose among the statesmen[6] there assembled to create a safeguard against future wars?' The difficulties and responsibilities, some of them very urgent and pressing, which are presented by the successful termination of the great war must of course be shared by the great nations of the world as comrades of the less powerful."[7]

That Mr. Wilson is approaching those very great responsibilities in the right spirit is shown very clearly by his reply to my question as to his plans for the immediate future.

"It will be my privilege," he said, "I hope, in the near future, not only to confer with the Allied statesmen in France, but also to visit the Allied countries and there learn by personal contact, as much as I can, of the general sentiments with regard to the chief problems involved. My first wish, of course, is to visit the American Army. They were the special object of my thought during the progress of the hostilities, for it was they we were obliged to sustain and support in every possible way, and, of course, my heart has become greatly involved in their fortunes. I want to see as many of them as I can consistently with my present duties. If I should not have an opportunity of visiting the Allied armies, I shall hope at least to see something of our comrades in arms in their own country. I am anxious to visit Italy, the country from which so many of my fellow-citizens have come, and I am interested and gratified to learn that there is in the Italian Army so large a number of men who have spent at least a part of their lives in the United States. I shall look

[5] In the unemended draft: "As a sailor in a storm looks through the darkness for a guiding light, so the plain peoples of all nations are looking towards Versailles and I think they are asking themselves one question:"

[6] "great statesmen" in the unemended draft.

[7] "of course" and "as comrades of the less powerful" added by Wilson in the first draft.

forward also with peculiar interest and satisfaction to visiting Brussels, now happily delivered from the hands of her enemies and restored to her own people and king. In the United States we have felt, and tried to express, the very poignant sympathy with the people of Belgium for the stedfast faith which they have maintained throughout their terrible trial, as well as for the peoples of Northern France and Northern Italy, upon whom the burden of the war has fallen so tragically."

It was perhaps natural that, as a Briton, I should have perhaps interrupted the President in his recital of the Allied forces whom he hopes to visit to inquire whether he would have the leisure to visit the Grand Fleet.

Mr. Wilson replied, and his tribute cannot but please us: "I am afraid that I shall not have time to do that now. I have so fully realized from the beginning that behind the great armies there was the strong, silent, and watchful support of the British Navy, securing the communications of the Allies, that it would give me a great deal of pleasure to visit the Grand Fleet if it were possible for me to do so. There has been a very happy comradeship and loyal cooperation between the Navy of Great Britain and the Navy of the United States, and I am sure that all of our people at home are keenly appreciative of it and know its full significance in the winning of the war."[8]

President Wilson, in discussing the *rôle* of the British Fleet in maintaining what, at any rate during the war, has been the "Freedom of the Seas" for the free people of the world, spoke with a sincerity which no amount of writing can convey. His accents convinced me that he is a believer in the decency and honesty of the Anglo-Saxon race; and when I asked him if he would have time on his present visit to go to England his reply confirmed my feelings.

He said: "I am glad to say that I am hoping to visit England very shortly. I am the more anxious to go because I have reason to know with what unanimity and with what passionate conviction the people of Great Britain and America have entertained the same conception of liberty and justice. It is essential to the future peace of the world that there should be the frankest possible cooperation, and the most generous understanding between the two English-speaking Democracies. We comprehend and appreciate, I believe, the grave problems which the war has brought to the British people, and fully understand the special international questions which arise from the fact of your peculiar position as an Island Empire."[9]

[8] The foregoing paragraph greatly expanded in the second draft.
[9] This paragraph slightly expanded in the second draft.

This verbatim text of the President's remarks cannot convey the real solid tone of sincerity with which this particular point of the "Freedom of the Seas" was dealt with by Mr. Wilson. He discussed in the freest manner the outstanding features of this problem, and is convinced that nothing can possibly prevent the approaching Conference from producing what all the world wants: a really solid guarantee of peace in the future.

I asked him whether he felt any anxiety as to the outcome of the meetings we are going to have. There are people who declare that the horrors of peace will be almost worse than the horrors of war. Mr. Wilson is not among them, and replied to my question that he felt no anxiety at all, and continued: "On the contrary, I am confident that by common counsel the statesmen of the world will be able to reach a just and reasonable solution of the problems which will be presented to them, and thus earn the gratitude of the world for the most critical and necessary service which has ever been rendered it."

I have seen, and met, and conversed with a great many leaders of public opinion, but there is none who has given me a greater feeling than did Mr. Wilson that I was in the presence of a man who without any *arrière pensée* was seeking in the great machinery of International Conferences to find the particular lever which will make the wheels go round smoothly. He is going to meet men of his own class from various countries, men who in their own way have just as much character, just as much, and perhaps even more, knowledge of European conditions. He will meet them and talk with them with but one idea, that he in common counsel with them, as he said to me in the course of our talk this evening, is serving the common cause of all the freedom-loving world. He will have but one idea before him, that of the weal, not only of his own nation, but of that greater nation of the world which this war and our victory have brought into being.

I left the President with assurance ringing in my ears—an assurance that was not required—that he desired to cooperate with the British, and with all the Allies, in ordering with their counsel a new state of affairs throughout the world.

I took the opportunity of visiting this temporary Washington. I had viewed it from the outside.

It is impossible to help wondering, as one approaches the Hotel Murat, what impression the house and its contents must make upon a native of the Southern States. Virginia and Kentucky first copied the debased Grecian style of architecture which the early Georgian era had spread over the English countryside. Then, under the influence of new land, new conditions, new country, new skies, they simplified their houses till they conformed, as did the Greek houses, to the combined necessities of domestic life, and outward decoration submitted to the influences of local climate. From the white pillared houses of the South States to the formality, the minimized grandiosity of the big Paris mansion, is a far cry.

The Hotel Murat is a little palace. It conforms in every aspect of architectural etiquette to the accepted traditions of Royal residences. It is formal, symmetrical, and while it is uniformly eighteenth century in exterior, it is also a "period house" within. The furniture is very largely First Empire, almost too fully encrusted with metal work, but the metal-work is such as cannot be reproduced to-day. The lines are severe, the detail elaborate. In the working room which President Wilson is to use from to-day on the gracious lines of David's "Amour et Psyche" appear rather unexpectedly above the wings of a bronze eagle which surmounts the ornate Empire desk. The combination strikes the eye at first as incongruous, but the symbolism is unmistakable. The tradition of the Old World is here in all its historical severity, in all its restrained voluptuousness; and into this atmosphere of a past formed by the successive efforts of ancient peoples is introduced the new element, the vital, straining element of the eagle with widening wings.

When I saw President Wilson he had not yet installed himself in this room; he was working in a smaller one, and one less formal, and it seemed better to conform to his character than the ranged beauties of the larger chamber. However, he is henceforward to confront the Eagle and the David picture as he works, and the touch of the Celt in him will enable him to see in the conjunction an epitome of the dramatic situation he is to help in solving.

His bedroom is strictly First Empire. Most people, save those who neglect their morning papers, are now aware that the Prince Murat's bed is too short for the inches of the American. Apart from this detail, the room is worthy of attention as being thoroughly correct. There is a Récamier couch, upholstered in Empire brocade, long enough for the longest President; there is an Aubusson carpet with the prized circular decoration, which the richest American might covet; there are lovely prints and delicate paintings on the walls, and there is a discreet amount of marble on the side-tables. A slight crowding of bronze on the mantelpiece is balanced by a great space in the middle of the room, where a man may walk or halt as his thoughts dictate.

Mrs. Wilson's rooms, on the contrary, are meant for leisure. While the furniture is as fine in its way as that in the more austere apartments, it is more relaxed in its lines, more soft in its upholstery, more abundant and more scattered in its arrangement.

Apart from its physical aspect this house abounds in interest for its guests. It is full of souvenirs of Ney and Murat. It recalls the glories and the miseries of the days when, for services rendered to an Emperor now fallen, the Murats were banished from France, and one of them married in Washington an American girl. It is a house with an atmosphere and a pride of its own; it belongs to Paris in every stone, but reaches out into history with every picture and every piece of furniture. It backs on to that curious product of civilization, the Parc Monceau, a garden where, although all may come, the poor by tacit consent leave the rich to enjoy themselves in privacy. President Wilson, a man who likes to go into his garden to think, will not overlook this aspect of the public garden on which his windows give. When he remembers the long, low, stately white houses of Virginia with their outward columns rigid and beautiful, their furniture of plain mahogany, their heavy plain silver, their many-branched candelabra, he can hardly escape the realization that nearly all the effective history of mankind is reflected in its homes.

In this stately and historic frame it will be Mr. Wilson's duty to work for the building of a larger, a more lasting home in which the history of Peace will have a durable chapter graven not upon stone, nor yet limned upon canvas, but founded upon the inner aspirations of the whole world.

Printed in the London *Times*, Dec. 21, 1918.

Gordon Auchincloss to Gilbert Fairchild Close, with Enclosure

My dear Mr. Close: Paris, 18 December 1918.

If you will be good enough to ask to [the] President whether he is in agreement with the views expressed by Mr. McCormick and Mr. Polk in this telegram, and advise me to that effect, I will see that the proper steps are taken to carry out the President's views.

This is a pretty important matter and one which we have already heard from the Department of State on several times.

                    Faithfully yours,   Gordon Auchincloss

TLS (WP, DLC).

ENCLOSURE

[Washington] Dec. 13 [1918]

No. 25 From McCormick.

For the President of the United States. There is on foot here a serious movement to abolish forthwith all censorship insofar as the United States is concerned. While in full appreciation of the fact that there should be a material and progressive relaxation in censorship administration, it is equally clear to me that prior to the abolition of censorship as a war measure, this whole problem should be made the subject of Inter-Allied discussion, presumably at Paris. One of the effective means for weakening Germany economically has been the censorship. It would have been and would now be impracticable, without censorship, to prevent the strong commercial and financial groups in Germany from undertaking any profitable operations through their branches rewarding neutral countries at the expense of the Allies and weaker neutral nations. By abolishing censorship there would be removed a most potent influence for paralizing German efforts at economic rehabilitation through financial and commercial operation abroad before the conclusion of peace. Thus the censorship is one of the recognized measures of blockade which have been demonstrated by all of the Associated Governments, and which constitutes still an influence most important, particularly on the wealthier classes in Germany, the foreign connections of which are unimpaired, and in large part still maintained. The elimination of Censorship might lessen appreciably the importance, particularly to those classes in Germany, of the speedy conclusion of a definite peace.

That blockade conditions shall remain unchanged is provided in the terms of the Armistice, and it certainly was not contemplated that any one of the Associated Governments should, during the Armistice, abruptly and by independent action, totally abandon a blockade measure as important as censorship. If we do so, it would be impossible, however, to place us in an unintentional light before our associates, and we would lay ourselves open to the charge of hastening to secure a trade advantage through the permitting of a revival of enemy trade in our interests, and further, we can be charged with desiring to shift to our associates the odium of maintaining an unpopular measure.

If it meets with your concurrence that the view that the abolition of censorship should be made, first of all, the subject of Inter-Allied discussion, from you, a common understanding may possibly be arrived at. It would be appreciated if you cable me to this effect, as there is considerable doubt as to your views hereon. I should like an expression thereof to show if it does not seem that Navy, Congressmen and other officials would welcome an expression of your opinion. The foregoing view is fully concurred with by Mr. Polk, as to the unfortunate effect which independent action on our part, would have on our International negotiations at this time.

Whereas, in my judgment, the most important, according to our proposed abolition of censorship, is the effect which it would have on the International negotiations from a domestic standpoint, it may be noted that the Trading With The Enemy Act, which remains law, cannot with[out] the aid of the censorship, be enforced and that the Alien Property custodian is daily obtaining, through censorship, important information as to property owned by the enemy and not heretofore reported to him.

TC telegram (WP, DLC).

Gilbert Fairchild Close to Gordon Auchincloss

My dear Mr. Auchincloss: [Paris] 18 December 1918.

With reference to the attached cable from Mr. McCormick, serial No. 25, the President directs me to ask if you will not please say to Mr. Polk, that the President is quite in accord with Mr. McCormick in the judgment that the censorship should be carefully maintained so far as it constitutes a trade blockade against the central empires and their areas.

This is what the President understood would be done, and he takes it for granted that Mr. McCormick will find the authorities in Washington ready to acquiesce in this judgment.

Sincerely yours,   [Gilbert F. Close]

CCL (WP, DLC).

From John Joseph Pershing

My Dear Mr. President   [Chaumont] Dec. 18, 1918

I hope that you and Mrs. Wilson will look upon my quarters as your home while you are in France, to which you can come at any time. It would give me very great pleasure to have you so regard the chateau which I occupy as living quarters. It is in a quiet place on the Marne where you could be absolutely free to do as you please. Of course, the horses and autos would be entirely at your disposal, so when the cares become too great and you wish to escape for a few days or weeks, please come out here. You will have a chance to see the place on Christmas, and I am sure it will appeal to you both.

Believe me, Mr. President, with the highest personal regard
Yours Very Sincerely,   John J. Pershing.

ALS (WP, DLC).

From Ray Stannard Baker

Paris. 18 December, 1918.

MEMORANDUM FOR THE PRESIDENT

Marked changes have taken place in Italy since the great offensive. There was much talk in September and October of the impossibility of making any offensive at all, of the need of 200,000 American troops before anything could be done. A thoughtful movement headed by Professor Salvemini[1] and others and backed by the most influential newspaper in Italy, the Corriere della Sera, was then working for broad justice and even generosity in dealing with the Jugo-Slavs—not because there was any love lost upon the Slavs—but because it was to the selfish best interests of Italy to have a friendly neighbor on her east who would buy her wares. The excellent feeling generated by the Rome Conference in July[2] still persisted; and Bisollati, the man in the cabinet with the most vision and nearest to President Wilson in his real convictions, had brought over the uncertain Orlando to his side in their controversy with the Bismarckian Sonnino.

But the great Italian victory, which astonished the Italians as much as anyone, gave a tremendous impetus to the extreme nationalistic and imperialistic point of view. One hears much bitter talk of the brutality of the Jugo-Slavs; of the impossibility on the one hand of getting any real unity between the Serbs, Croats and Slovenes, and at the same time of the danger to Italy of a strong Jugo-Slav State; and that the Allies are bound to favour Italy because it has the higher and more precious civilization.

Italian opinion regarding territorial settlements may be divided roughly into four groups:

[1] Gaetano Salvemini, Professor of Medieval and Modern History at the University of Florence. A strong opponent of fascism, he emigrated to the United States in 1932, became a naturalized American citizen in 1940, and held the Lauro de Bosis Lectureship in the History of Italian Civilization at Harvard University from 1933 until his retirement in 1948.

[2] About which, see T. N. Page to the American Commissioners, Jan. 18, 1919, n. 3.

1. Extreme imperialists who want everything in sight, who would like, as Signor Treves,[3] the Socialist Deputy said, to "make the Adriatic an Italian lake," and to claim parts of Asia Minor, etc. In the upper classes and among many newspapers this view is common.

2. Nationalists who would adopt the pact of London as the minimum of Italy's claims, and would insist upon Fiume in addition. This is generally thought to be Sonnino's position and it will command great support among all the upper classes.

3. The view held by Professor Salvemini and his group, and supported formerly by the Corriere della Sera. This group has now only a small following.

4. The great masses of the people, peasants, the working class, and the socialists, have little or no interest in territorial demands of any kind. Where they are articulate, as in socialist strongholds like Turin, they declare that they are glad that Italy will have the Trentino and Trieste, for these are really Italian, but they could not now be persuaded to go to war for any other territorial ambitions whatsoever—in my opinion. They are real believers in self-determinism, and bitterly against the Government in its imperialistic policy.

There exists a wide-spread feeling among all the upper groups in Italy that the war is going to end in a game of grab—with notable exceptions, they think the League of Nations moonshine—and that if England and France grab, Italy must also protect herself. They have sent 150,000 soldiers into Istria and 200,000 to the east coast of the Adriatic—18,000 of which are at Fiume—where actual clashes have been avoided, probably, only because of Colonel House's urgent pressure on both sides, and because there have been contingents of American, British and French troops in several places, tending to give the people the impression that the occupation was in the interests of the four Allies. The unwillingness of the Italians to liberate 30,000 Jugo-Slavs confined in concentration camps and to denounce the pact of London are the two most serious obstacles to a harmonious understanding between the Italians and the Jugo-Slavs.

It is generally believed that Italy's policy will be governed largely by the example of England and France.

The feeling toward France is steadily growing more bitter, for the leaders, and many newspapers, say that France is opposed to any expansion of Italy. One even hears now and then among the extremists talk about "Irredentist Italy in France," and the reclaim-

[3] Claudio Trèves, a journalist, founder of *Tempo*, and former editor of *Avanti!*

ing at some future time of Corsica and Savoia. On the other hand the French press and leaders give the Italians some cause for their hostility. Above all, one should be careful not to pass upon the justice of Italian claims in the court of French opinion alone.

The labor and socialist groups are solidly and sincerely behind Mr. Wilson and his program. The radicals are certainly increasing in power and it seems clear that the soldiers, when they return, having had exaggerated promises made to them, will swell these forces. The split in the socialist ranks, which was never serious when judged in numbers, is undoubtedly healing. The present government is very unpopular with the working classes; they feel that it has no policy regarding the great issues of reconstruction and demobilization. The government itself seems to fear to demobilize only less than it fears not to demobilize. A food stringency is likely this winter, unless America comes to the rescue, for the government is faced with the immense task of feeding not only its own population, but the people of the repatriated provinces, the Italian prisoners who are being returned, and several hundred thousand Austrian prisoners still held by the Italians.

The American control of food supply might be made a very powerful instrument in modifying excessive demands.

One cannot visit Italy without feeling that the situation is exceedingly tremulous, and will have to have very wise handling. Though the government has concealed the facts, there have been recent serious demonstrations and strikes at Turin, Milan, Terni and other places. The old parliament is stale and does not rise to the situation. Italy is of all the European states the one most in slavery to a central bureauc[r]acy. It has developed its centralizing government into a monstrous power, to the point of creating a state more or less separated from the Nation. This bureaucracy is as inefficient as it is powerful. As one of the able leaders of young Italy has said: "The country was obliged to rebel against the Government in order to make the war, to take the place of its ministers and generals in order to save itself after Caporetto, and for everything it must rebel and fight against its central powers."

Mr. Wilson's popularity in Italy is undoubtedly greater at the present time than in either France or England. The visit by him to Italy will have the effect of greatly strengthening the devotion to his program, especially if he can impress upon the Italian people the need of the adoption of a positive reconstructive program in order to avert the dangers of an old fashioned get-and-grab peace.

Unofficial agents of the Italian government and prominent Jugo-Slav representatives are endeavoring to draw a line between Jugo-Slavia and Italy which will inflict as little hardship as possible upon the populations of the disputed territory. There is some hope that their efforts will be successful and that a mutually satisfactory frontier may be traced. There can be no doubt, however, that a more generous attitude on the part of the Italian political authorities and a less provocative attitude upon the part of the Italian military and naval commanders will increase the chances of a satisfactory agreement. Ray Stannard Baker

TS MS (WP, DLC).

Robert Lansing to Frank Lyon Polk

Paris, December 18, 1918.

Confidential for Polk. Your 33, December 16, to Ammission.

You will say very confidentially to Mr. Gompers that the President's views were that a labor conference might very properly be held in Paris or in any other place at any time that the leaders of labor deemed it wise; that is, he believed that they should feel entirely free to do what they conceived best. Please inform Gompers that this, of course, is for his own information and not for general use. Lansing

T telegram (SDR, RG 59, 185.161/3, DNA).

Jessie Woodrow Wilson Sayre to Woodrow Wilson and Edith Bolling Galt Wilson

Dearest Father and Edith, New York Dec. 18, 1918

Many, many, happy returns of today![1] It is wonderful to read all about your doings in detail every day, three or four columns of it. The papers make it all seem a real love feast. I hope all goes as smoothly underneath as appears on the surface.

Some of the places you have been and all the familiar names of streets and churches remind me of our own wedding trip five years ago. To think that this whole war has crashed its way between our trip and yours. I am always amused when I think how serenely unconscious Frank and I were of what was to come so soon!

We are moving in February back to Cambridge. Frank is to teach Constitutional Law and International Law at an extra session of the Law School[2] from Feb. 1st to Aug. 15. He undertakes to move the family up there after I have gone to Philadelphia.[3] I believe he can do it, he is the most efficient hustler I know. Of course this is in case we can sublet here and find what we want there, but if it is at all possible, Frank can do it.

We are very much pleased about it and Frank is keen to begin work, and we love Cambridge. I don't think we shall ever consider returning to Williamstown, for Frank isn't happy unless he has almost more work to do than the length of the day will compass.

We are to have a cozy little Christmas here, Helen, and Nevin and one or two cousins of Frank's. But you both will be in our circle and our hearts will go out to you with unending love and prayers for your happiness and success in this most wonderful of undertakings. Dear dear Father, how I love you and how I wish I could help you some how, some way.

With all our hearts' love and wishes for a joyous Christmas

Devotedly, Jessie

ALS (WP, DLC).
    [1] Their wedding anniversary.
    [2] That is, the Harvard Law School.
    [3] She was expecting her third child in February and planned to go to Philadelphia to be under the care of Dr. E. P. Davis.

Gordon Auchincloss to Frank Lyon Polk

[Paris, Dec. 18, 1918]

No. [blank]. Very secret for Polk only from Auchincloss. A conference between Clemenceau and President Sunday night was exceedingly satisfactory. Clemenceau was most favorably impressed and is willing to stand for various proposals of the President which previously he has been strongly opposed to. Size of demonstration here in Paris may account for this in part but not entirely. A newspaper man told me the other day that when asked whether he wanted the President to come to France Clemenceau said "Yes, the land imperialists in France are pursuing me. The sea imperialists in Britain are pursuing Lloyd George. Lloyd George is pursuing me. Yes, I am very glad the President came to France." Now Clemenceau is even in favor of the President sitting in the conferences. Official entertainment of the President was concluded on Monday night.

From the Diary of Gordon Auchincloss, T MS (G. Auchincloss Papers, CtY), Dec. 18, 1918.

From the Diary of Colonel House

December 18, 1918.

The four United States Plenipotentiaries held a meeting this morning. The other three were pretty much at sea as to what the President desired regarding the press arrangements, publicity etc.

etc. I therefore suggested that I ask the President to meet with us. I did this and he came to the Crillon at five o'clock. We held a session of nearly three quarters of an hour and had our pictures taken together.

The President then met the newspaper men. Before attending the meeting, I brought him up to my personal quarters on the third floor of the Crillon in order to show him where his work was being done in conjunction with mine. It was agreed to meet the newspaper people at 10.30 every morning.

When the President got home he remembered it had been agreed for the two of us to meet M. Clemenceau at his home at ten o'clock I told him it made no difference my attending the meeting of newspaper men, but he insisted that I should do so and, since we could not put Clemenceau off, I am arranging for the newspaper men to come at half past twelve.

This morning the President telephoned asking if I did not think we ought to have a serious conversation with Clemenceau. I thought so. He desired to know if we had not better take up the most important subject—the League of Nations. I agreed to this. He asked if I would not make an appointment for tonight at eight or tomorrow morning at ten. I had Frazier arrangement [arrange] the engagement with Clemenceau at ten at the President's house. The President particularly wished me to be present.

The President gave the interview to the London Times. Northcliffe is the happiest man in Paris, so I am told. He writes me a letter expressing his warm appreciation, which I attach. Northcliffe, himself, gave Grasty[1] of the New York Times an interview which has greatly pleased me. There is nothing that could be better from our viewpoint. It will make opposition to the League of Nations sick at heart, and it will help make the American people understand the need for it. The President was immensely pleased when I told him of this.

Northcliffe told Wiseman, when he first let him know that the President was willing to give an interview to the London Times, that he, Northcliffe, would go up and take the interview himself. Wiseman knew this would create a sensation that was not desirable and pointed out to Northcliffe the reasons why it was better not to do so.

It has been another great day and everything so far goes well. I have not yet heard from Derby concerning the President's proposal to make an early trip to England. Letters, cables and what not are attached.

At my suggestion, the President has asked Ray Stannard Baker to interpret for the newspapers of the world the American viewpoint regarding matters which will come up from time to time at the Peace Conference. Lansing wanted Patchin, but the President would have none of him.

[1] Charles Henry Grasty.

From the Diary of Dr. Grayson

Thursday, December 19, 1918.

The King of Italy, accompanied by his son, the Prince of Piedmont,[1] arrived in Paris this morning. The same arrangements had been made for his reception which marked the arrival of the President, but there was a distinct and decided contrast in the entire affair. The streets were more or less deserted excepting at the principal squares, and the guard of soliders which lined the thoroughfares had no work to do to control the crowd. The King was dressed in the field-gray uniform of a general in the Italian Army, and his reception was far from being either spontaneous or warm. After he had paid the formal calls necessitated by custom to the French officials, the King came to the Villa Murat and called on the President. The President met him at the front door, and the contrast between the two men—the one small and swarthy, and the other tall and pale—was very marked. The President shook hands with the King and told him that he was very glad to see him. He then drew him in through the door into the main reception room, where they sat down and conversed at some length. The Italian King speaks perfect English, and the meeting was far less formal than anything of the kind to date. As the King looked around the room and scrutinized the almost priceless tapestries, pictures and very expensive furniture, he shook his head, and turning to the President said: in a most impressive tone: "My God, Mr. President, I can't provide any such palace as this for you in Italy." This ejaculation made a decided hit with the President, who assured the King that whatever arrangements he made for his comfort during his stay in Italy would be appreciated. The President was very much impressed by the plain, matter-of-fact, democratic manner of the King. I asked the President, after the King had left, what were his impressions of his caller, and he responded: "He is a simple, sincere and straightforward little fellow." It was remarked by the President and myself that the King wore very high heels on his boots in an apparent effort to increase his height. When something was said that seemed to amuse the King instead of laughing like an ordinary mortal, he chuckled almost in the nature of snuffles.

[1] Umberto (or Humbert) Nicola Tommaso Giovanni Maria, Prince of Piedmont, heir to the throne of Italy.

To Joseph Patrick Tumulty

Paris, undated, received Dec. 19 [1918].

Please transmit following to Tumulty from the President.

The following arrangements have been made by the President with respect to the handling of our newspaper publicity while he is in Europe. The liaison officer between the newspaper men and the President will be Maximilian Foster.[1] All announcements regarding plans of the President and the Commission and all special news items and routine stuff will be given out by Foster. At ten thirty each morning the four members of the Commission, other than the President will meet the press in one room and be questioned by them at that time. Ray Stannard Baker has been designated by the President to act with the newspaper men as the interpreter of the American position at the conference, to look after the publicity of the Commission and to reflect the general spirit and purposes of the American Commission to negotiate peace. Dissemination and spreading broadcast through the world and the United States of all publicity given out by the Commission will be in charge of Creel. The policy of the Commissioners is to be very frank and give as much information as possible to the newspaper men, trusting that they will not publish any information that would in any way cause trouble or be indiscreet. We are not able to tell over here whether or not the newspaper men have respect for our confidence or not. We are not able to tell whether or not they publish information which is not for publication and which was given to them as "a steer." The President wants you to watch the press and cable him exactly the tone of the press and whether or not any particular papers are acting in an indiscreet way. He also wishes you to make any suggestions that may occur to you from time to time and which would assist with our work in regard to the newspaper men.

T telegram (J. P. Tumulty Papers, DLC).
[1] Novelist and journalist, most recently a roving war correspondent for the Committee on Public Information with the A.E.F. in France.

From Joseph Patrick Tumulty

The White House, 19 December 1918.

A mutual friend saw Cobb in New York. Cobb suggested that I get in touch with you and say it is his opinion that Clemenceau and Lloyd George are in strict agreement and that the cards are stacked against you. He says Blythe and Grasty[1] know all the facts and that they would be able to enlighten you. He suggests you send for Blythe who is your friend and anxious to serve. He further suggests that you see Northcliffe who has powerful influence he could throw your way in case of critical situation. Everything fine here. Newspapers speak flatteringly of your reception.

Tumulty.

T telegram (J. P. Tumulty Papers, DLC).
 [1] That is, Samuel George Blythe and Charles Henry Grasty.

From Carter Glass

Washington [Dec. 19, 1918]

For the President. From Glass. First. On assuming my duties as Secretary of the Treasury,[1] situation regarding our foreign loans gives me grave concern. Second. Our loans to foreign governments now aggregate nearly eight billions of dollars and will probably approximate eight billion five hundred millions of dollars before declaration of Peace, an account sufficient to pay all our governmental expenses for about eight years on the basis existing immediately preceeding our entry into the war. Congress believes these loans are good and should be collected, and the possibility that the debts may be forgiven or exchanged for debts not as good is fomenting opposition to extending the authority of Treasury within the limits of the existing ten billions of dollars appropriation to make loans after the war to Allied Governments previously participating in the War against the enemies of the United States, for purchases in the United States for reconstruction purposes. Third. I judge from the recent semi-official inquiries that European Allies may attempt to bring up at Peace Conference query concerning our foreign loans. You will recall speeches which Wickersham and Beck[2] have made advocating our cancelling foreign obligations. An Associated Press Despatch from Paris published December 17th, announces probable presentation by French Government to Chamber of Deputies a bill to establish an International Union to distribute the expenses of war already incurred and to be incurred between Nations on basis of populations and power to contribute. Same despatch states similar plan under consideration by British Government, but no definite steps taken by it.

(Fourth) While British loans to the Foreign Governments exceed seven billion dollars including British loans to Russia of about two billion seven hundred million dollars, it might be that Great Britain would not be averse to canceling war loans which it has made, in consideration of cancelation of perfectly good debt of British to United States, now about four billion dollars.

(Fifth) French Finance Minister[3] has indicated that he does not think it desirable to discuss at this time converting French demand obligations held by United States into long time obligations as the maturities which French Government would consider as desirable and fair will depend upon moneys made available to them from Germany as a result of peace terms. As a few months ago Finance Minister strongly urged settlement of maturity dates. He had in mind the proposal of some plan permitting France to settle her debt to us by transferring a part of her claim for reparation against Germany.

(Sixth) From Treasury standpoint it would be distinctly advisable to keep all questions regarding our foreign loans out of discussions at peace conference in which event I can undertake definite settlement of these matters in Washington in such manner as to fully preserve the value of our foreign loans. If, however, Allied Governments are able to force discussion of these matters as a preliminary to or as part of peace agreement I recommend that Treasury be officially represented so that it may keep you advised of my views concerning these and any other financial questions arising, and be prepared to participate in such discussions as may be necessary. I feel that these financial questions are different in character from those with which existing Treasury representatives in Europe have been dealing and I agree with my predecessor's instruction to them, not to participate in the pending peace discussions. If you should determine to have Treasury represented, trust you will notify me as far in advance as circumstances permit, so I may select and personally instruct my representatives and send them to Paris for this express purpose.   Polk, Acting.

CC telegram (WP, DLC).
  [1] Wilson had nominated Glass to succeed McAdoo on December 5. The Senate confirmed the appointment on December 6, and Glass assumed office on December 16, 1918.
  [2] That is, George Woodward Wickersham and James Montgomery Beck.
  [3] That is, Louis Lucien Klotz.

From William Graves Sharp

My dear Mr. President: Paris, December 19, 1918
Referring to my letter written to you in November,[1] soon after the signing of the armistice, in which I asked you to accept my resignation as Ambassador to France, to take effect at some date early in the coming year, I wish now to renew in a more formal manner that request. A long absence from my business affairs seemed to make such action wise, but, as I then wrote you, only the ending of the war finally prompted me to tender my resignation.

It has always been my consistent purpose to serve at my post until the coming of that long hoped-for event. Subject to your own desires in the matter, however, it will be agreeable to me to remain in charge of this mission until my successor is appointed and ready to assume his duties. All through a period of unusually trying conditions, into which the events of a century seem to have been crowded, I have deeply appreciated the constant support of our Government at Washington. Your own great part in shaping the destiny of those far-reaching events has given a new importance—one already decreed to be permanent—to American diplomacy abroad, and I must express to you my grateful recognition of the aid which it has brought to me in meeting the problems of the work of this Embassy. It has been such as to make Americans hold higher their heads in just pride of their country.

While a rest from such exacting labors will have its compensation for me, yet it is with feelings of sincere regret that I sever my relations with a country whose Government has been so helpful and generous to me—and this quite as much before our entrance into the war as afterwards. For the masses of its people I came long ago to have a warm affection born of an understanding of their real qualities of mind and heart. As such traits of character made France so heroic in her time of stress and sacrifice, so now in the hour of victory and the peace to follow they will serve to knit together all the more closely the common interests of our two peoples.

Will you please accept, Mr. President, my earnest thanks for the confidence which you have reposed in me, and my best wishes for the success of your administration in the important work with which it is charged.　　　　　Very sincerely yours,　Wm. G. Sharp

TLS (WP, DLC).
¹ W. G. Sharp to WW, Nov. 14, 1918.

From Herbert Clark Hoover

Dear Mr. President:　　　　　　　　[Paris] December 19, 1918.

I am in receipt of a cable from Mr. Tumulty with regard to the re-opening of brewing in the United States, and have also received direct cables from our own office to the same effect.

It appears to me that the matter has several phases: The first is that as quickly as shipping becomes more available for exports from the United States, which is not likely to be more than 30 days hence, the real situation with regard to feeding stuffs for animals will quickly develop. The world is entirely short of these grains, and from a point of view of food conservation, there can be no question as to the desirability of the cessation of brewing.

The matter, however, is one that has many internal moral and economic complexities which I do not pretend to judge at this distance. I may mention, however, that in addition to the very difficult internal problems involved, there is a tendency to expand brewing in Europe, under the same types of pressure.

You will of course realize that under the new Congressional Act, brewing would in any event cease on the first of July, and that the labor difficulties cannot be so great now as they will be at that time when there is a larger demobilization.

It would generally appear to me that, if you do not wish yourself to make a decision on a matter so difficult to determine from this end, it is a matter which should be settled by the Cabinet as a whole.   Yours faithfully,   Herbert Hoover

TLS (WP, DLC).

A Memorandum by Henry Wickham Steed[1]

[Dec. 19, 1918]

THE ADRIATIC DIFFICULTY.[2]

All proposed solutions of the Adriatic question should take into account three main considerations,

  a) The right of Italy to security;
  b) The right of the Jugoslavs and Serbia to national union and free economic development;
  c) The expediency of reaching a settlement of which the justice will commend itself to future generations of Italians and Jugoslavs so that their relations may be friendly.

Two main difficulties have to be overcome. The first is that the majority of Italians are convinced that Dalmatia, Istria, and their islands are mainly, if not entirely, Italian in racial character. A few Italians, including Signor Orlando, the Premier, know and admit that Dalmatia is overwhelmingly, and the interior of Istria preponderatingly Slav, but they dare not tell their own people the truth lest they be accused of a lack of patriotism or, at least, of fouling their own nest.

The Southern Slavs, on the other hand, know the truth, but are apt to be uncompromising and to under-estimate the great value to themselves both of good relations with Italy and of the spread of Italian language and culture among them.

The Italians are entitled to be sure that no Southern Slav fleet will ever revive, either singly or in alliance with other peoples, the menacing situation which existed as long as Austria-Hungary was in being. In other words, if the Jugoslavs insist upon maintaining a naval force, Italy will be entitled to demand strategic guarantees against it.

In the same way the Southern Slavs are entitled to demand that, if all possibility of Southern Slav naval action against Italy be eliminated, no large tract of Southern Slav territory shall, for strategic reasons, be assigned to Italy.

This can be done if the Southern Slavs renounce their right to possess a naval force, agree to the neutralisation of their coast, islands and territorial waters, and to the policing of those waters by a supernational maritime authority, acting on behalf of the League of Nations.

Thus freed from any naval danger under a guarantee from the League of Nations, Italy would no longer require strategic safeguards, but would be able, without any dereliction of national duty, to settle the territorial dispute, as nearly as practicable, in accordance with the principles of nationality and of government by the consent of the governed.

It will be found technically impossible to fix a line of demarcation strictly in accordance with the principle of nationality. Starting from the Isonzo, it will probably be found necessary to assign the city and much of the district of Gorizia to Italy, though the city is partly, and the district wholly Slovene. Similarly, the coast of the Gulf of Trieste up to the watershed of the Carso (including, of course, the city of Trieste itself) and the Western coast of Istria with Capodistria, Parenzo, Rovigno, Pola and a sufficient belt of territory to ensure communication by land between Pola and Trieste, would have to be alotted to Italy. This arrangement would inevitably include within the Italian frontier several hundred thousand Southern Slavs, among whom would be comprised the Slovene minority of the inhabitants of Trieste and the Slovene majority of the immediate hinterland of Trieste. To these Southern Slavs, freedom to use their own language should be assured. Trieste should be a free port under Italian administration. The tariffs of the two main railways serving it should be internationally fixed so as to prevent discrimination for or against any of the peoples using them.

Fiume should be a free port under Southern Slav administration with full municipal and linguistic rights for the Italian-speaking population of the city. The tariff of the Fiume-Agram-Budapest railway should be internationally fixed. Were the present city and territory of Fiume to be assigned to Italy, the Southern Slavs would inevitably create a better port at Buccari, a few miles away, connect

it with the Agram railway and divert all their trade to it. The prosperity of Fiume would thus be jeopardised.

A similar consideration applies to Zara, the capital of Dalmatia,
the only other city in which there is a considerable Italian population. Zara ought not to be assigned to Italy without full consultation of its inhabitants. Otherwise they might be ruined by being
cut off from intercourse with the hinterland. They should be given
full protection for their language and culture and might, if they
desired it, be given a statute as a free city in the Southern Slav
State.

No Italian demand for the possession of any other point in the
Eastern Adriatic can be justified except on the grounds of strategic
necessity. The only possibility of reaching a settlement that will not
embitter the future relations of the two peoples, lies in the removal
of all strategic necessity by neutralisation. Otherwise friction will
inevitably lead, sooner or later, to armed conflict, and the development of commercial intercourse between the two shores of the
Adriatic will be seriously impeded.

It is a question whether the principle of neutralisation should not
be applied to the whole of the Eastern Adriatic coast from Pola to
Cape Stylos, except in so far as coercive action under the authority
of the League of Nations may at any time be found necessary.

Wickham Steed

TS MS (WP, DLC).
  [1] Foreign editor of the London *Times*, author of books and articles on Italy and Austria-
Hungary.
  [2] A covering note, dated Dec. 19, 1918 (T MS, WP, DLC) reads as follows: "For the
perusal of the President before he sees the King of Italy. Sent at the request of Colonel
House."

A Translation of a News Report of a Press Conference
Held by Dr. Grayson

[Dec. 19, 1918]

Mr. Wilson is two men, he told us:[1] the President of the United
States, who is grave, punctual, conscientious in the extreme, and
leaving nothing to chance; and the private man, who is good, simple, of great sensitivity, and of a rather cheerful disposition.

As President, Mr. Woodrow Wilson arises every morning at seven
o'clock. At 7:45 he takes his breakfast and then goes to his office,
where he remains until 1 p.m. He tends to do everything himself.
From one to two o'clock, luncheon *en famille*. From two until four,
he receives persons who come to discuss affairs of state: cabinet

ministers, members of Congress, military leaders, and the like. From four to six-thirty, he continues working. At 6:30, he goes down for a walk in the White House gardens or in the streets near the presidential palace. He returns at seven for dinner and spends evening *en famille*. Nevertheless, he often has occasion to work again for part of the evening.

When Mr. Wilson gives a speech to Congress or at a public ceremony, he generally improvises, but if a "message" is involved, he types it himself on his machine—a first class typewriter—and reads the text at the session, in order not to risk involuntarily changing a word.

As a private person, Mr. Wilson adores sports, the theater, literature, music. He is even endowed with a rather good tenor voice, and in earlier days enjoyed singing, but, as President, he has few opportunities to exercise these talents. He also adores children, and they respond well to him. There are always those who recognize him in the street when he strolls incognito; they go to him, through those mysterious intuitions which draw children to those who love them.

Earlier, Mr. Wilson practiced all sports, notably football and baseball. Today, he hardly has the leisure for them. He limits himself to golf and riding. When he plays golf, he devotes himself to it just as seriously as to work and will not accept a partner who plays halfheartedly or without spirit. He allows himself this pleasure or that of horsemanship about three times a week, from eight to ten-thirty in the morning. Still, he has agreed to this only on the formal recommendation of his physician, and he makes up for hours thus devoted to his health by work after dinner. With the family, he plays only solitaire, ignoring other games, especially card games.

Mr. Wilson passes for a cold man, but, on the contrary, he is sentimental, very faithful to friends, loves to laugh with his old college companions, whom he receives intimately with the greatest cordiality, and he takes pleasure in evoking with them joyous memories of their youth. Apart from his political responsibilities, he has a horror of protocol and etiquette, and observes the greatest simplicity in all things.

Mr. Wilson does not smoke, but he does not stop others from smoking around him. He is frugal in his meals, drinks neither wine nor liquor, and drinks herb tea instead of coffee.

Mr. Wilson does not speak French—out of timidity—but he understands it very well and reads our classics in the originals.

Mr. Wilson dearly loves France, where he has come but once before, fifteen years ago. At that time, he traveled almost entirely by bicycle, and he declares that he would very much like to do so again.

Printed in *Le Gaulois* of Paris, Dec. 20, 1918.
    ¹ Grayson spoke to a group of reporters for Paris newspapers on December 19, 1918. Other reports of the interview or conference appeared in the Paris *Journal*, Dec. 20, 1918, and the Paris *Oeuvre*, Dec. 20, 1918. We have translated and print what we think is the fullest and best report.

From the Diary of Colonel House

December 19, 1918.

I went to the President's house fifteen minutes before Clemenceau arrived. I wanted to suggest a method by which the conversation could be easily brought around to the League of Nations. The freedom of the seas was the topic I thought best suited to this subject.

During the hour and a half we were together, the President did nearly all the talking. Clemenceau said very little. I thought the President indiscreet when he told Clemenceau, among other things, that the American people were anti-British and that the easiest thing in the world would be to get them to build a navy larger than the British Navy. Clemenceau expressed himself, in a mild way, in agreement with the President. He thought a League of Nations should be attempted, but he was not confident of success, either of forming it or of its being workable after it was formed. The truth is, he believes in war. He has something of the Roosevelt idea that war enables [ennobles].

The President talked well, but he did not put the plan for a league of nations as I thought it should be put, neither did he argue as to the freedom of the seas in a way which I thought was most effective. He seems to have forgotten a good deal of what we agreed upon at Magnolia regarding the Covenant for a League of Nations, and I shall take occasion sometime to have this out with him again. It seems necessary for him to get his mind refreshed.

Clemenceau said Lord Derby had told him the President was going to England next week and that Lloyd George and Mrs. [Mr.] Balfour would not come over on Saturday as planned. This disturbed the President as he had counted upon George and Balfour being here. Clemenceau said that Derby had ab [an] engagement with him at 11.30 and suggested that I drive with him to the War Office and have it out there.

I did this and Derby gave me the cable from his Government which is attached. They have asked me to come with the President. In a telephone message which Wiseman had with the Foreign

Office today, they almost insisted that I should come. I have no notion, at the moment, of doing so. Lansing wants to go and I have promised to ask the President to take him.

We have agreed that the President shall go on the 26th and remain in England the 27th, 28th, 29th and 30th. Derby thought if I would authorize him to insist upon Lloyd George and Balfour coming over to keep their Sunday and Monday appointment with the President, they would do so. I did not believe they would because all their plans for a Christmas holiday had been interrupted and I was quite sure this visit of the President next week was looked upon by them as something little short of a calamity.

I returned to the President's house and gave him the story. He hoped I would insist upon George and Balfour coming. He asked how I thought he had gotten along with Clemenceau. My reply was, "better than I expected, for you at least got Clemenceau to admit it was necessary to try to form a league of nations." I thought that he, the President, had successfully jumped the first hurdle.

I returned to the Crillon to meet the newspaper men with the other Commissioners. Later I saw Admiral Benson to go over with him matters relating to the Navy, and to discuss with him what may be done as to the sea laws of the future.

Tardieu called to ask several questions about which the Prime Minister and himself desired information. They were of minor importance.

I had a long talk with Hoover. I asked him the direct question whether he was a democrat or republican. He replied, "neither." "I would be a democrat if it were not for the reactionary element in the South. I would be a republican if it were not for the reactionary element in the East. I shall give support to either one of the parties which has a progressive program." He declared that he did not desire the Presidency; that he intended to buy a newspaper in the United States and see what good he could do with it. In my opinion, he is mistaken in believing he would not like to be President.

From the Diary of Dr. Grayson

Friday, December 20, 1918.

The President had a number of engagements today. He had conferences in the morning with Orlando and Sonnino; he received the Ambassadors and Ministers from foreign countries to France as well as the President and the committee of the French Senate and he made a call on the King of Italy.

His first caller was the Spanish Premier who had made a special trip from Madrid in order to ask the President what the attitude of the Peace Conference would be towards the neutrals, and especially to assure the President that charges that Spain had unduly favored Germany during the war were unfounded. The President took no positive position regarding the question of the neutrals, explaining to his caller that inasmuch as a League of Nations was to be organized it would be impossible to determine what participation any nation would be given in that League until a constitution actually had been framed. The Spanish Premier told the President that Spain's economic position was none too good and said that it had suffered very much in the war because of its remaining and continuing neutral to the end.

In the afternoon the President and Mrs. Wilson were the guests of honor at the meeting of the Academy of Sciences, the occasion being the conferring of membership on Marshal Joffre.[1] The veteran French soldier made a very remarkable speech, which greatly impressed the President.[2] Joffre paid the highest tribute to the French Army and declared that it was the soldier of France that had saved France rather than the leaders of the soldiers. The Field Marshal had prepared his speech in advance and read it very carefully, sticking closely to his manuscript. The President in commenting on Joffre's speech afterwards told me that in addition to being a soldier he had given evidences of being a good scholar.

[1] Grayson was confused. The ceremony honoring Joffre at the French Academy took place in the early afternoon of December 19, not December 20.
[2] Wilson had an English-language abstract (T MS, WP, DLC) in hand while Joffre spoke. Wilson wrote out in longhand (WWhw MS, WP, DLC) the following sentence from the abstract: "Let her [France] never forget that the weak and the small cannot live free in the world if the strong and the great are not ever ready to place their strength and power at the disposal of right." Brackets WW's.

To Joseph Patrick Tumulty

Paris, (Received Dec. 20, 1918)

Have conferred with Hoover about the suggestion of allowing breweries to use grain for the manufacture of soft drinks. It appears that as quickly as shipping becomes more available for exports from the United States which is not likely to be more than thirty days hence, the real situation with regard to foodstuffs for animals will quickly develop but that it cannot develop sooner. In the circumstances I think it would be very unwise until the whole situation is disclosed to relax the prohibition which now exists.

Woodrow Wilson.

T telegram (J. P. Tumulty Papers, DLC).

To the Most Reverend Randall Thomas Davidson[1]

Your Grace: Paris, 20 December 1918.

I am very much obliged to Your Grace for your letter of December 14th, which I have read with the greatest interest.

I foresee that my visit to England must, of necessity, be brief and hurried and that I must probably confine myself while there to the official courtesies which I should wish fully to observe, and, therefore, it is only too plain to me that I cannot have the pleasure which you offer me.

It would be a pleasure. I believe that the solid foundation of the League of Nations is to be found in Christian principles and in the sustaining sentiment of Christian peoples everywhere, and it would be extremely stimulating to me to be privileged to address the representatives of the body of churches of whom you speak.

I hope that, however brief my visit may be, I shall at least, sooner or later, have the pleasure of expressing to you in person, my appreciation of your kindness.

Cordially and sincerely yours, [Woodrow Wilson]

CCL (WP, DLC).
[1] Wilson had obviously forgotten that he had answered the Archbishop's letter on December 17, 1918.

From Newton Diehl Baker

My dear Mr. President: Washington. December 20, 1918.

I enclose two orders for your signature with a request that they be signed and returned to me as immediately as your convenience will permit. Explanatory letters drawn up by the Judge Advocate General[1] are also enclosed which you need not read, unless you so desire, in view of the fact that in this letter I am stating the case fully enough to justify your action.

These two orders affect trials by court martial involving nineteen negro soldiers who, while at Camp Grant, Rockford, Illinois, were arrested and charged with the crime of rape, and were convicted of that crime by court martial assembled for the purpose of the trial.

The fact of the crime is certain; it is doubtful whether a more brutal, degenerate and revolting crime was ever committed, as some nineteen or more negroes successively, in daylight, one after another ravished a white woman, while the members of the party by force and threats restrained her white escort in whose company the ravishing mob found her. The crime not unnaturally aroused the deepest resentment in the community of Rockford. In all of its details it is the worst rape case of which I have any knowledge.

Unhappily the Division of which these men were members was on the point of embarking for France. As a consequence the trial was conducted with such haste and with so little regard to the usual rights of the defendants that a review of the record convinces us all of its gross and prejudicial errors, to such an extent that no member of the Judge Advocate General's Office is able to escape the conviction that a fair trial was not had, and that these men were deprived of practically every safeguard which either law or practice ordinarily throws around defendants. I have myself examined the record and am obliged to agree with the lawyers and with the Judge Advocate General himself. I could not advise you to confirm these sentences. There is a possible question as to the right of the military authorities to re-try these men. The Judge Advocate General makes a strong case in favor of the right, and I have already directed preparations to be made for an immediate re-trial under conditions which will assure a vigorous prosecution attended by an orderly regard for the rights of both the Government and the accused. Whatever the outcome of this new trial, the fact remains that there is not in this record a basis upon which men could, in good conscience or in law, be ordered hanged by an officer upon whom the law places the burden of confirming, after a review, sentences imposed.

The longer of the two orders enclosed deals comprehensively with all the trials except one. The second order deals with the case of Edward Champ, who was tried separately, and in whose trial no prejudicial errors arose. The order in his case is, therefore, merely a stay of execution in order that he may be used as a witness in the re-trial of the other cases, his testimony being important to the Government. When a re-trial has been had and sentences come to be dealt with by you as the result of it, final action can be taken at the same time in the Champ case, either in the way of directing execution at a fixed day or by such modification as may then seem just.

The cases have been long studied in the Judge Advocate General's Office because of their gravity, and it is of the greatest importance that the re-trial should proceed at the earliest possible day. For that reason I recommend and request the immediate signature of these orders and their return to me by the earliest boat.[2]

Respectfully yours,   Newton D. Baker

TLS (WP, DLC).
    [1] They are missing.
    [2] Wilson, on March 5, 1919, ordered a retrial of the nineteen soldiers. The Editors have been unable to find any information about the outcome.

From Herbert Clark Hoover

Dear Mr. President, Paris, 20th December, 1918.

Soon after the Armistice, you took one or two occasions to make clear that the maintenance of order in Germany by the German people was a prime requisite to food-stuffs and to peace, and that the necessity of feeding Germany arose not only out of humanity but out of its fundamental necessity to prevent anarchy.

It would seem that these warnings have a little worn off and I have a feeling that it would be desirable, if some joint and very pointed statement could be made by the four associated governments on the positive subject of Bolshevism in Germany.

As you are aware, there is incipient or practical Bolshevist control in many of the large centres; there is also a Separatist movement in progress amongst the German States, arising somewhat from fear of Bolshevism; there is also—apparently largely supported—a movement towards the election of a constitutional assembly of some kind.

Viewing the German Empire from a food point of view, there will be no hope of saving these people from starvation if Bolshevist activities extend over the Empire in a similar manner to Russia, with its sequent break-down in commercial distribution and in the control and distribution of existing food. The extremes to which such a situation can extend are well exemplified by the already practical depopulation of the cities of Moscow and Petrograd, and such a situation would not be confined to two cities as in Russia, but to thirty cities in Germany, and the saving of the German people would be absolutely hopeless if the normal commercial and distributive functions and food control should cease, as it certainly would under a Bolshevist regime.

Again, a political Separatist movement amongst the German States would produce the same situation that we have in the old Austrian Empire, where some sections of the Empire have a surplus of food and by practical embargoes are creating food debacles in other centres. We must maintain a liquidity of the existing food stocks in Germany over the whole Empire, or again the situation will become almost unsolvable.

In order to visualize to you somewhat the problem, if we say that the normal consumption of the German people, without restraint, is 100, the German Empire within its old boundaries must possess to-day somewhere about 60% of this quantity. If there is distribution and control, the population can probably go through without starvation on something like 80% of normal, and therefore the problem is to find 20% by way of imports. If there is an extension of the Bolshevist movement or extension of the Separatist movement, so far as food is concerned, we shall have some localities consuming 100 out of their local supplies and feeding any surplus to animals. The problem will be unsolvable by way of the available supplies in the world for import because the total consumption under such conditions would run a great deal more than 80% and all this aside from the almost impossible completion of dealing with distribution in the hands of such highly incompetent agencies as Bolshevist Committees.

It would appear to me therefore that some announcement with regard to the food policies in Germany is critically necessary, and at once. If that announcement could be made something on the line that the United States and Allies could only hope to solve the food difficulties in Germany until next harvest through the hands of a stable and experienced government based on an expressed popular will, and a hint be given that the Allies cannot anticipate furnishing the food assistance to Germany through the hands of Bolshevist elements, it would at once strengthen the whole situation in Germany and probably entirely eliminate the incipient Bolshevism in progress, and make possible the hope of saving their food situation. I realize that this is a suggestion of some delicacy but I feel that I should present it to you.

Yours faithfully,   Herbert Hoover

TLS (WP, DLC).

From Edward Nash Hurley

My dear Mr. President: Paris, December 20, 1918.

I have just been informed, from my office in Washington, that the Senate on Wednesday passed a resolution calling upon the Shipping Board for information as to "whether or not war time restrictions as to construction of steel ships in American shipyards have been removed." The Senate wants to know why the restrictions have not been removed, if they have not been, and, if the Shipping Board is under instructions not to remove the restrictions, the Senate asks who issued the instructions. The resolution apparently is quite detailed, asking what applications have been received by American shipyards to build for foreign account, what policy foreign governments are pursuing, and a great many other pointed questions.

It is evident that the pressure from the shipyards is growing greater every day. Private interests unquestionably are forcing the issue, charging that they are being prevented from taking profitable business that would replace cancelled contracts and keep their labor intact. I would advocate a firm adherence to our present policy, considering the larger questions at issue, but it has occurred to me that the ultimate goal may be served better by reaching an understanding with the French and Italians immediately.

You understand, of course, that the French have formally asked me to enter into an agreement whereby we will supply them with 800,000 tons of shipping over a period of three years. The whole question is one of time—whether we should say "yes" now or later. I am inclined to think it would be helpful to agree to the French proposal immediately, as this would be the best assurance of our good faith. If we keep our fist closed until they open theirs, the result may be a delay in the settlement of the larger issues.

I have likewise been in touch with the Italians. They want us to provide them out of our existing tonnage or by contract for new tonnage a total of 500,000 tons of shipping. The question here, as in the case of the French, is whether we should act now or later.

If our answer to the Senate should not be satisfactory, that body might, of course repeal the section of the law which now requires the approval of the President, through the Shipping Board, before any contracts with foreign nations are accepted by an American shipyard. It would be far better, naturally, for us to keep a position in which we can regulate the matter ourselves. If the arrangements I have suggested can be utilized to bring about the results you have in mind, it will enable us to include in the tonnage we allow to the French and Italians certain of the smaller coal burning ships which were built solely for the emergency and which, frankly, it would be better to sell.

If when you leave for England you could feel that you had made satisfactory arrangements with the French and the Italians, I think that it might facilitate your mission in London.

You will understand, of course, that if we let down the bars now, we cannot very well keep them up against anybody. The British have made no formal proposition, but it has been intimated to me by some of their big ship operators that they would like to place orders, probably aggregating 2,000,000 tons over a period of years.

The advantage that the French will have if we negotiate with them immediately is that their orders, placed early, will naturally have priority. I am not at all sure that they will be so desirous of placing large orders later. If we give affirmative replies to the French and Italians now we probably can get assurances from them that will smooth the way for what you have in mind. So that this matter can be correlated with the larger program, I feel that it is important that you personally should tell them what America is willing to do. If you think well of the suggestion, I will arrange to bring

M. Clementel, Minister of Transportation and Commerce, to see you, and later I would bring the Italian representative. All you would need to do is indicate to them your willingness to help them in the way I have indicated.

In this way we could end the pressure in the United States, which may even result in legislation taking the ban off, and at the same time further the larger project. The matter requires, as you will understand, an early decision. I may be able to work out something to hold the Senate off if you would prefer a course different from the one I have outlined.

Faithfully yours,   Edward N. Hurley

TLS (WP, DLC).

Three Letters from Lord Derby to Arthur James Balfour

Confidential

My dear Arthur   Paris. 20 December 1918.

. . . I asked Clemenceau whether he was satisfied with his talk with President Wilson. He said Yes and No and Poincaré told me very much the same thing. They said that he was very amiable but shockingly ignorant of the European situation. They however thought on the whole he will not give much trouble.

Now with regard to President Wilson. I have not had any conversation with him. I am going to see him this evening and he is dining with me tomorrow night but I gather that the reason for his suddenly wishing to go to England is that he is rather disturbed at the effect he hears that has been produced in England by the American Naval programme and he wants to reassure England on the subject. I cannot quite make out what his idea is but apparently he is afraid of the strength of the English Navy now that the German Navy has disappeared, as he feels at the present moment in case of any row between England and America—though why he should anticipate such a row I cannot conceive—American Seaport towns would be entirely at the mercy of the English Fleet. He therefore wants to come to some arrangement by which apparently England and America shall have the only two navies of the world and shall undertake what I may call Naval policing of the whole Universe.

I think his visit to England should do good and I am perfectly certain that the more I hear, from conversations I have had with House, his one desire is to work with England; that he is somewhat aghast at the demands for territorial aggrandisement of France and more especially Italy and he feels that in resisting these demands he must have England's backing. . . .

Since dictating the above I have had the opportunity of a short conversation with House. It is now perfectly all right about you and the Prime Minister not coming and the friction of yesterday has completely disappeared. I spoke to him on the subject of the delay in the meeting of the formal sitting of the Conference to enable Clemenceau to get his holiday and he is in entire agreement, and I think what President Wilson will suggest to you, or at all events what if you suggest to him he would accept, is that the various members of the principal countries involved should come to Paris on say the Monday, engage in conversations amongst themselves (at which perhaps it would be advantage that Clemenceau should not be present) and the formal opening of the Conference take place on the Thursday. He is entirely in agreement with Clemenceau's suggestion that President Poincare should open the ball by welcoming the delegates.   Yours ever,   Derby

Confidential

My dear Arthur   Paris. 20 December 1918.

I hope I may never again have to do with arrangements for a Presidential visit to England. The President is treated so like a God that one only gets his views second hand and it was only when I saw him personally this afternoon that I really found out what his views are and I am sending a long telegram which I am afraid will materially modify the arrangements which have been made for him.

No discourtesy was intended on his part with regard to the King's invitation but he did not like to answer accepting until the date was definitely fixed and he believed that the right way to do it was through me, hence his instructions to me this afternoon. I think that this ought to be conveyed to His Majesty. Will you kindly see to that.

Now with regard to the arrangements. He is very much averse to banquets and entertainments as far as they can be avoided and he wishes to limit them to the King's Banquet and to one at the Guildhall. He says that America sent him over for business and they will not understand it if he goes to these so-called festivities.

With regard to his other visits the one to Carlisle is purely sentimental but I think you will understand his feeling in this matter.

With regard to Manchester he is particularly anxious to go there. I a little tried to choke him off but he would not be choked off. He says Manchester is probably more like American towns than any other town in England and he is particularly anxious to pay it a visit and I think that must be included in the programme.

Oxford he would like to have visited if it had been possible but it was quite evident to him that it is not possible and it was a question of cutting out that or Manchester and there was no doubt in his mind which should go.

He would like to have returned on Monday but under pressure I think he would remain till Tuesday morning. His journey would have to be made as speedy as possible and under the circumstances he would not mind leaving between 8 and 9.

Yours ever   D

Private

My dear Arthur   [c. Dec. 20, 1918]

I had seen House this afternoon and he told me that it was all right and he quite understood the Prime Minister not coming over here but I found very much the opposite when I talked to the President himself. He said of course he would not wish to criticise Lloyd George for not coming but at the same time he could not understand his not doing so. He had kept these two days purposely for conversations and altogether he seemed very vexed about it. However no good crying over spilt milk but I still regret L.G. not having come because there really is a gathering of the clans. Orlando, the Spanish Prime Minister, the Belgian Prime Minister[1] have all arrived here today in the hopes that they would be able to have some conversations and I gather from what the Americans tell me they are a little outspoken at being disappointed.

Yours ever   D.

TLS and TLI (A. J. Balfour Papers, Add. MSS 49744, British Library).
[1] That is, Léon Delacroix.

From the Diary of Dr. Grayson

Saturday, December 21, 1918.

In the afternoon the President was given a degree by the University of Paris. This was made a gala occasion in French educational circles, all of the students of the various schools being gathered about the grounds to cheer the President and bid him welcome as he drove in. The ceremonies themselves were very formal in character, and the President made a speech in response which dealt almost entirely with the value of education.

After the degree was conferred Mrs. Wilson went for a walk through the shopping district of Paris. She was not recognized to any extent.

Following the services at the Sorbonne, the President returned to the Villa Murat, where he conferred with Premier Orlando and

Foreign Minister Sonnino. They discussed with him Italy's aspirations in the Adriatic, and also questions at issue between Italy and the proposed Jugo-Slavia Republic.

That evening the President smashed another precedent by being the guest of honor at a dinner at the British Embassy at which the Earl of Derby presided.

Returning from the British Embassy, the President remarked to General Leorat,[1] who had been detailed by the French Government to act as one of his honorary aides, that there was no light burning in the Eiffel Tower, although he had noticed it last night. The General explained that it had burned the night before as a tribute to the visit of the King of Italy. The President playfully remarked: "You mean to infer by that that the King is so small that you have to turn the light on in the Eiffel Tower in order to see him when he is in Paris." This remark pleased the General immensely.

[1] Gen. Anne Henri Joseph Leorat.

From the Diary of Edith Benham

December 21, 1918

This afternoon I went to the most impressive ceremony I have seen yet.[1] Mrs. Wilson, Colonel Lobez[2] and I drove over a little ahead of the President to the Sorbonne, where he was to have the new degree "honoris in causa," I think it is called, conferred on him. We were taken in a side door and up to a room where Mme. Poincare,[3] Mme. Jusserand and some other French ladies were. The only ones I knew anything about were another Mme. Poincare,[4] wife of the brother of the President of France, and Mme. Hovelaque,[5] whose husband[6] had come over with Viviani and Joffre, and whom I think I told you spoke such beautiful English and such wonderful French. He is a professor at the Sorbonne.

The great hall of the Sorbonne is bowlshaped. We came in the back door on a slightly raised gallery directly facing the tribune, where the two Presidents—France and United States, sat.

For color and beauty the sight was wonderful. The Sorbonne comes from [the] Middle Ages. Its head was responsible to none of the civil authorities, only to the King, and its scholars were a turbulent lot, and the brawls were constant between the authorities in Paris and the students. A stone's throw away is the old palace of the Abbots of Cluny, built beside the baths of the Emporer [Emperor] Julian. It is the very oldest part of Paris. The roots of the tree of learning and culture of the Christian world centered here, and it is the oldest seat of learning in France, which made today a new degree, for a man whom it wishes to honor, and reads, "honoris in causa."

When we stepped out to the front seats of the gallery we faced one of the most beautiful paintings of Puvis de Chavannes, the great mural decorator of France, all done in soft tones and a marvellous background for the sea of color made by the red hoods of the professors from all the French colleges, grouped behind the President. To his left were the doctors who had taken various degrees, all with colored capes, reds of different shades, some with bands of fur, almost all wore pleated white cravats. The papers will have to tell me tommorrow just who was there. I can only think of the impressions of it, the beauty of color, and the packed galleries and floor and that very quiet, very dignified and majestic figure of our President, sitting between his colleague of France and the rector of the Sorbonne in his black robes.

The three addresses were in the most beautiful French and, as Colonel Lobez said, the name which Poincare, the Sorbonne head,[7] gave him in that place, "Wilson the Just," will go down with him through the ages. They said the most wonderful things to him and worked through parallel and panegyric to the crowning point of the presentation. There was applause and applause at times, but none greater than when they hailed him as "Wilson the Just." Then he got up to reply and they went crazy and he stood very quiet, but his every pose is compelling. Just as he stood and put his hand on the stand in front of him was compelling.

His speech was short, delivered as he likes best without notes, and one of his best, for he has been deeply moved by all this.

After the applause ended, the stately little procession started, headed by some imposing ushers in black with curious looking maces, evidently relics of the Middle Ages ceremonial, then the two Presidents and the heads of the Universities, leaving the flags of America and France to watch over the great hall, under the Chavannes painting.

From there we went to an upper room to watch the procession of all the students of the colleges, universities and public schools of Paris, passing under the window to do him hon[o]r. France has suffered so much, most of her men have gone and it gripped the heart to watch these eager young things cheering and cheering this scholar from the new world overseas, as he faced the old grey world of the Cluny across the street, all this young France of the new order below in the streets. It seemed as though they would never end with their banners. They are the young things who are taking the places of those others who went out so quietly in 1914, surprising all the world by their silent determination to do—and they did. The women in their black dresses tell that.

A few delegations came up to shake hands with him, and he stooped to shake a tiny little boy by the hand with his usual kindliness for children. Then we went down and I drove back behind them with General Harts and Colonel Lobez. The Streets were filled with students and they almost mobbed the car, but we finally got out following a different route from that we had taken, as one President could not follow another—as per Protocol.

[1] The University of Paris, on December 21, 1918, awarded Wilson the degree of Doctor, Honoris Causa, the first honorary degree ever given by the University of Paris. Raymond Poincaré attended in his capacity as President of the French Republic, along with many other high French civil and military officials and members of the diplomatic corps. Alfred Croiset, Dean of the Faculty of Letters, and Fernand Larnaude, Dean of the Faculty of Law, participated in the ceremony. Lucien Antoine Poincaré, Vice-Rector of the University and brother of Raymond Poincaré, made the principal address in which he praised both Wilson and the many Americans who had either sympathized with France or fought on her soil during the war. *New York Times,* Dec. 22, 1918.
[2] The Editors have been unable further to identify him.
[3] That is, Henriette Benucci Poincaré, wife of the President of the French Republic.
[4] The Editors have been unable to discover her full name.
[5] The Editors have been unable to discover her full name.
[6] That is, Émile Lucien Hovelaque.
[7] That is, Lucien Antoine Poincaré.

An Address at the University of Paris

December 21, 1918.

Mr. President, Mr. Recteur: I feel very keenly the distinguished honor which has been conferred upon me by the great University of Paris, and it is very delightful to me also to have the honor of being inducted into the great company of scholars whose life and fame have made the history of the University of Paris a thing admired among men of cultivation in all parts of the world.

By what you have said, Sir, of the theory of education which has been followed in France, and which I have tried to promote in the United States, I am tempted to venture upon a favorite theme. I have always thought, Sir, that the chief object of education was to awaken the spirit, and that inasmuch as literature, whenever it touched its great and higher notes, was an expression of the spirit of mankind, the best induction into education was to feel the pulses of humanity which had beaten from age to age through the utterances of men who had penetrated to the secrets of the human spirit. And I agree with the intimation which has been conveyed today, that the terrible war through which we have just passed has not been only a war between nations, but that it has been also a war between systems of culture—the one system, the aggressive system, using science without conscience, stripping learning of its moral restraints, and using every faculty of the human mind to do wrong to the whole race; the other system reminiscent of the high traditions of men, reminiscent of all those struggles, some of them obscure but others clearly revealed to the historian, of men of indomitable spirit everywhere struggling toward the right and seeking above all things else to be free. The triumph of freedom in this war means that spirits of that sort now dominate the world. There is a great wind of moral force moving through the world, and every man who opposes himself to that wind will go down in disgrace. The task of those who are gathered here, or will presently be gathered here, to make the settlements of this peace is greatly simplified by the fact that they are masters of no one; they are the servants of mankind, and if we do not heed the mandates of mankind we shall make ourselves the most conspicuous and deserved failures in the history of the world.

My conception of the league of nations is just this, that it shall operate as the organized moral force of men throughout the world, and that whenever or wherever wrong and aggression are planned or contemplated, this searching light of conscience will be turned upon them and men everywhere will ask, "What are the purposes that you hold in your heart against the fortunes of the world?" Just a little exposure will settle most questions. If the Central Powers had dared to discuss the purposes of this war for a single fortnight, it never would have happened, and if, as should be, they were forced to discuss it for a year, war would have been inconceivable.

So I feel that this war is, as has been said more than once today, intimately related with the university spirit. The university spirit is intolerant of all the things that put the human mind under restraint. It is intolerant of everything that seeks to retard the advancement of ideals, the acceptance of the truth, the purification of life. And every university man can ally himself with the forces of the present time with the feeling that now at last the spirit of truth, the spirit to which universities have devoted themselves, has prevailed and is triumphant. If there is one point of pride that I venture to entertain, it is that it has been my privilege in some measure to interpret the university spirit in the public life of a great nation, and I feel that in honoring me today in this unusual and conspicuous manner you have first of all honored the people whom I represent. The spirit that I try to express I know to be their spirit, and in proportion as I serve them I believe that I advance the cause of freedom.

I, therefore, wish to thank you, Sir, from the bottom of my heart for a distinction which has in a singular way crowned my academic career.

Printed in *Addresses of President Wilson on First Trip to Europe December 3, 1918 to February 24, 1919* (Washington, 1919).

To William Graves Sharp

My dear Mr. Ambassador: [Paris] 21 December, 1918.

In view of what you have so fully explained to me with regard to the circumstances which make you feel it your duty to retire from your present post and give your close personal attention to business affairs which depend upon you, I cannot in conscience refuse to accept your resignation as Ambassador of the United States to the Government of France, and I do so with the understanding that the resignation is to take effect when your successor qualifies.

I am sincerely obliged to you that you are willing to make this arrangement and to remain in France until your successor can actually take your place. It is an arrangement which relieves me of a good deal of anxiety, because I should not wish the highly important post at Paris to be vacant for even a short time.

Let me tell you again how highly I have valued the unusual services which you have rendered our government. They have at every turn of the critical events of recent years been of the highest value, and it has been a source of confidence and of strength to feel that we had such a representative here. I am expressing not only my personal feeling but the feeling of all those who have been familiar with your services here. You are certainly entitled to your release, and I assure you that you carry with you the affectionate regard and confidence of those who have had the pleasure of being your co-laborers in our Government.

Cordially and sincerely yours   [Woodrow Wilson]

CCL (WP, DLC).

Two Telegrams from
Frank Lyon Polk to Robert Lansing

Washington, December 21, 1918.

92. For the Secretary of State.

In a cable dispatch from Tokyo dated December 18, on the Siberian railway situation,[1] Morris reports that his British Colleague,[2] failing to receive instructions from his Government, has relapsed into his former unsympathetic indifference. Morris then asks: "Would it be expedient at this time to point out to the British Ambassador reasons affecting the entire situation in the Far East, and particularly China, which call for closest cooperation of our two Governments in establishing a policy which shall limit pecuniary, exclusive commercial or political control?"

In raising this question Morris has evidently in mind Japan's demands on China in 1915, her subsequent loan policy, the secret military agreements of this spring intended to give Japan control of Chinese military establishment, equipment and related industries, Japan's extensive military activities in Siberia, and in general the tendency of Japan's policy to so combine her commercial and political activities that they become one and inseparable, and in practice to make both as far as possible exclusive of the interests of all others wherever she obtained sufficient foothold. Mister Reinsch is even more emphatic in his statements as to the tendency and probable results of Japan's policies in China and the Far East.

I am very anxious, as you know, about the whole Far Eastern situation, feeling that if matters are left to their course, the doctrines of equal opportunity for all will disappear as the Japanese political and commercial program extends and that herein lies an actual danger of future complications between the powers concerned in the Far East.

Morris is evidently impressed with the feeling that in order to meet the situation the American and British Governments should reach a frank understanding of each others purposes and act at least on parallel lines in order to avoid needless misunderstandings and possible antagonisms.

It occurred to me that with the approaching visit of the President and yourself to London, the opportunity will come as perhaps never again, to reach some broad and comprehensive understanding with the British Government on the whole question of relations of the United States and Great Britain in the Far East, particularly as to whether the interests and ideals of the two nations and those of France and even Italy are not identical; and if so, whether this is not the moment to agree upon a reasonable policy and to have our respective representatives clearly so instructed.

In another telegram from Morris just received,[3] he states that the general staff controls the Siberian situation and that popular opinion in Japan favors a strong policy in all Asiatic questions. He believes that the Hara[4] Ministry are sincerely convinced that Japan's interests will best be served by policy of cordial cooperation with the United States, but that without popular support they are too weak to take issue with the general staff. It would seem, therefore, that a complete understanding between the United States and the European Governments might strengthen the hands of the liberal element in Japan as against the ambitious political program which is now being conducted by the military party.

I sincerely hope that this question and the opportunity for its solution will appeal to the President and to yourself as it does to me.   Polk

T telegram (WP, DLC).
  ¹ From the outset of the dispatch of American troops to Siberia, the United States had been engaged in a protracted struggle with the Japanese government to prevent Japan from gaining exclusive control of the Trans-Siberian and the Chinese Eastern railways. American officials, concerned about the large size of the Japanese expeditionary force and about the close cooperation between Japanese military authorities and Japanese merchants in the promotion of Japan's commercial interests in the region, feared that Japan was preparing for a permanent occupation and an exclusive economic penetration of Siberia and Manchuria. As early as August 1918, John F. Stevens, whose Russian Railway Service Corps had returned to Siberia from Japan in the spring of 1918, complained to the State Department about the constant interference of the Japanese military authorities with his work and about their apparent effort to take over the railways. He recommended that the lines be put under joint military control and that the Railway Service Corps be authorized to operate them. As a result, Lansing, on August 30, 1918, instructed Ambassador Morris to propose to the Japanese government that Stevens be given "general direction of the Trans-Siberian and the Chinese Eastern Railways and their several branches." See RL to WW, Aug. 30, 1918, n. 1, Vol. 49. Although the French and Italian governments were willing to support the American proposal, Great Britain refused to take sides on the question and merely promised to endorse any agreement which could be reached between the United States and Japan. However, the Japanese government flatly rejected the plan as "constituting intervention in Russia's domestic administration," which the Associated Powers had always denounced.
  While the State Department continued through regular diplomatic channels to try to secure Japan's consent to the American proposal, Morris proceeded to Vladivostok in an attempt to negotiate an agreement with Allied, Russian, and Japanese representatives in Siberia. On October 13, 1918, he succeeded in gaining the approval of the local representatives of a plan which placed the Trans-Siberian and the Chinese Eastern railways under joint military protection and effectively entrusted Stevens with their management and operation. Despite the approval of the Japanese representative at Vladivostok, the Japanese government was reluctant to endorse the agreement. Anxious to avoid any American influence over the Chinese Eastern Railway, the Foreign Office presented an alternative scheme which called for sole Japanese operation of the Chinese Eastern Railway and for the joint management and operation of the Siberian railways by Stevens and a Japanese railway expert. However, not only was Stevens adamantly opposed to sharing authority over the Siberian railways, but the State Department also absolutely refused to sanction a Japanese monopoly on the Chinese Eastern Railway.
  As the informal negotiations between Morris and Japanese officials dragged on, it became obvious by late October that the Japanese General Staff had quietly proceeded to take over the operation of the Chinese Eastern Railway, leaving it to the Foreign Office to explain the accomplished fact. See B. Miles to RL, Oct. 28, 1918, and its Enclosure, Vol. 51. Moreover, the Japanese Foreign Minister, Viscount Yasuya Uchida, confidentially informed Morris that the General Staff would not consent to Stevens' operation of the railways. Finally, after a bitter struggle between the General Staff and the Foreign Office, the Japanese government, on December 3, 1918, submitted a counterproposal which advocated the creation of a technical board composed of representatives of the Associated Powers in Siberia. This board, with Stevens as its president, would act in an advisory capacity to the Russian railway administration.
  Although Morris and the State Department were willing to accept the latest Japanese proposition, Stevens still objected. He believed that, in a mere advisory capacity with no means to enforce his decisions, he would be unable to accomplish anything. Morris'

telegram of December 18, 1918, which is printed in *FR 1918, Russia*, III, 296-99, conveyed, among other things, Stevens' objections and an amended plan by Morris which gave Stevens full authority to operate the railways. For the significant correspondence about this matter, see *ibid.*, pp. 239-307. A brief summary of the complex negotiations may be found in Betty Miller Unterberger, *America's Siberian Expedition, 1918-1920: A Study of National Policy* (Durham, N. C., 1956), pp. 103-17.

² That is, Sir William Conyngham Greene.
³ It is missing in the files of the Department of State.
⁴ Takashi Hara, Prime Minister since September 29, 1918.

Washington, December 21, 1918.

86. For the Secretary of State. Your 24, December 18.

Please tell the President that Gompers is disposed to call a labor conference to be held in Paris and put the burden on the foreign Governments of refusing to let it take place. I gave him the President's message and suggested to him that it would be better to wait and try to arrange matter with the foreign governments as they might now see the advisability of holding this conference in Paris.

It seems to me that it would be very dangerous to hold conference in neutral country as there would be a chance of its being captured by the extremists and Bolsheviks. Please let me know if any progress is being made in these negotiations so I can keep Gompers quiet.

As soon as he issues call for a conference he and his associates will go to Paris. Am forwarding for him today a message to the President.   Polk, Acting.

T telegram (SDR, RG 59, 185.161/5, DNA).

From the Diary of Colonel House

December 21, 1918.

The President, Orlando, Sonnino and I were together from ten until twelve o'clock. The President talked well but he did not convince the Italians that they should lessen their hold on the Pact of London. On the contrary, Sonnino convinced the President that from a military point of view, Italy was pretty much at the mercy of the nations holding the Dalmatian Coast.

The President afterward said in talking with me that the next time they had a conversation he thought he would suggest some way by which their argument could be met. This might be done by insisting that the forts along the Dalmatian Coast should be demolished, and that the Jugoslavs should agree to have no navy and but a small standing army. I thought this would not meet the Italian objections, for the reason that they were not candid in their contention that it was for protection they desired this territory.

From the Diary of Dr. Grayson

Sunday, December 22, 1918.

The President and Mrs. Wilson today came into personal contact with a large number of American wounded soldiers for the first time in the war. They went to the American Hospital at Neuilly, where there were more than 1200 wounded Americans, a majority of whom had participated in the great battle at Chateau Thierry, which turned the tide of the entire war. The President and Mrs. Wilson were met at the entrance by the Commanding Officer of the Hospital, Colonel James F. Hutchinson,[1] of Philadelphia. They spent more than four hours passing through the various wards shaking hands with the wounded men and commenting with them on the great task they had assisted in accomplishing. "The country is proud of you and of your work," he told these men. And as he would go out of the door from each ward, he would stop and wave his hand and say: "Good-bye, I wish you as pleasant a Christmas as you can have in the circumstances." In shaking hands with one patient, he asked his name, and the soldier smiled and said: "My name is Wilson." The President replied: "That's not a common name but a usual one; I am proud of what you have done for the name." He saw another big husky fellow at the foot of his bed and said: "Haven't I seen you before"; and the soldier replied: "Yes, sir; I am the traffic cop at the Grand Central Station, New York City." The President asked one soldier: "I am struck with so many men being wounded in their thighs and legs"; and the fellow sobbingly replied: "Most of those who are wounded above are not here."

In one ward in which the French wounded were being cared for the President found a husky negro American dough-boy ensconced in his bed. The humor of being the sole American among the French apparently had struck this negro because he had printed a sign which proudly hung above the bed, reading: "Only English spoken in this bed." Naturally this amused the President.

After lunch the President and Mrs. Wilson visited the large French Hospital—DE GRACE. Word had been telephoned that he was coming to the hospital and a large crowd had gathered at the entrance to greet him. He went through all the wards. When he entered one ward a Frenchman who had been blinded insisted upon being allowed to stand and sing "The Marseilles," which he did in a most touching manner.

After a very tiresome but very human day the President returned home.

[1] Actually, James Pemberton Hutchinson, M.D.

From the Diary of Edith Benham

December 22, 1918

At dinner tonight the President was very amusing about the French language. He happened to look, he said, at his laundry list, saw the item "16 chemises," felt compromised and went indignantly to my dictionary, and found it was all right. He was speaking about the price of fruit and Dr. Grayson said some one told him grapes were a half franc a grape, and we all began to chatter about the extravagance of eating any, and he smiled quizzically and said, "Well, we will make France another loan and they will get even." You see, the French Government is paying for everything here at the house. . . .

We had an amusing time at tea this afternoon. Mrs. Wilson said to ask Mrs. Lansing, her sisters-in-law[1] who have been doing canteen work over here and were decorated by the French Government for helping care for wounded during a Boche bombardment, and Mme. Jusserand. She had talked of asking Mrs. House but decided not, and who should appear but that lady. She had met Mrs. Lansing, inquired where she was going, and just came along. She had been giving several very broad hints about going to London, and I think is quite grieved because the old Colonel, who is an old dear, didn't feel well and just wouldn't go for he felt there was no necessity for him to be there. The President told quite a good story about her on one of these trips to London. An invitation to dine came via the American Embassy for both him and her to dine at Buckingham Palace. When they arrived there was some commotion. He thought something was wrong and it turned out it was a men's dinner and the Embassy had made a mistake. While the officials were fussing around he turned to her and said: "Lulie, scoot" and "Lulie" scooted. Mrs. Wilson told me very confidentially a story about the McAdoos. It seems he worked Heaven and earth to get on this Commission. The President said he didn't belong on it and he couldn't be put on it on account of family relationship. He said he felt better qualified than anyone to be on it. Then he said he wanted to put in his resignation before the Commission was announced so that people wouldn't think he had been discriminated against. Then both he and she came at Mr. Wilson. He said he had resigned and had expected to take two months rest but as a servant of the public he felt he owed it as a national duty to serve. Mr. Wilson in his usual graceful way put it off. He said, "but the relationship still exists." He said that was all very well in social affairs but should not be considered in public matters. His father-in-law remained firm, but since we have been over here Colonel

House has received a fifty word cable urging his appointment on the Commission and wishing him to suggest it to the President. Mrs. Wilson agrees with me that he is out of politics for a time only to get the public used to the idea of his being poor, and then he will come back for the presidency. We will see.

¹ Emma Sterling Lansing and Katherine Ten Eyck Lansing of Watertown, N. Y. They had been engaged in canteen work for the American Red Cross in France since September 1917. The French government had decorated both sisters with the Croix de Guerre in August 1918 for their heroism under German bombardment at Epernay.

A Statement

Paris, 22 December, 1918.

I went through the American Hospital at Neuilly with the greatest interest and with the greatest gratification. I found the men admirably taken care of and almost without exception in excellent spirits. Only a very few of them looked really ill, and I think that their mothers and friends would have been entirely pleased by their surroundings and by the alert look in their eyes and the keen interest they took in everything about them. I am sure that they will go back to their loved ones at home with a new feeling of joy, alike in their recovery and in the fine service they have been able to render.

T MS (WP, DLC).

To Joseph Patrick Tumulty

[Paris, Dec. 22, 1918]

It is certainly not my intention to back the Allies up in the matter of sinking German ships.¹ I am utterly opposed to such silly extremes. Please say to the Attorney General that I approve his proposals with regard to the removal of restrictions on alien enemies.² Shall hope to send Christmas greetings to our people.³ Warmest greetings.   Woodrow Wilson

T telegram (WP, DLC).
    ¹ Wilson was replying to JPT to WW, Dec. 21, 1918, T telegram (WP, DLC). Tumulty wrote on this subject as follows: "If it is America's intention to back up Allies in sinking German ships, the idea is so vague in this country that there ought to be a great deal of elucidation if the President intends to take this stand."
    The *New York Times*, November 26, 1918, had carried a brief news report which stated that the German battleships and cruisers held by the Entente Powers would "probably . . . be sunk, as apparently there is no disposition on the part of the Entente to risk the controversies which would be likely in case of an attempted division of them." The editors of the *New York Times* considered this report significant enough to comment on it in an editorial on November 27 entitled "Enough Ships Already Have Sunk." They

suggested that a better disposition of the German warships would be to give them to the League of Nations to serve as its navy. The editors discussed the subject at greater length in editorials on December 2 and 12. The *Times* reported on December 19 that "the American delegates" to the peace conference had "resolved to advocate the sinking of the surrendered enemy warships and resist any proposition to distribute them on the basis of naval losses." In a lengthy article on December 20, the *Times* reported that there seemed to be no authoritative source for the reports about the sinking of the German fleet. Josephus Daniels, for example, had denied any official knowledge of the proposal. Republican senators such as Lodge, Borah, and Harding expressed indignation at the idea. Lodge, on December 19, had introduced S. Res. 390, which called on the Secretary of State "to inform the Senate whether the report that the peace delegates of the United States at Paris are advocating the destruction of the ships of war surrendered to the allies and to the United States is correct; and, if so, by what authority the delegates to the peace conference are demanding the destruction of enemy property in part surrendered to the United States." *Cong. Record*, 65th Cong., 3d sess., p. 648.

Tumulty gave out the following statement on the subject on December 23: "It may be stated authoritatively that President Wilson will oppose in the most direct fashion proposals from any source to sink the warships surrendered by Germany under the terms of the armistice." *New York Times*, Dec. 24, 1918.

² Wilson was here replying to TWG (via JPT) to WW, Dec. 21, 1918, T telegram (WP, DLC). The telegram read as follows: "Request authority to announce certain restrictions of German alien enemies will soon be rescinded. Further, that on and after Christmas day enforcement will be discontinued of all such regulations except those relating to internment and foreign travel. Secretary Daniels and military intelligence concur in recommendation. Immediate reply by cable requested. Letter follows." The "letter" mentioned in the last sentence is missing. However, the significance of the relaxation of the regulations is discussed briefly in "Alien Enemy Regulations Modified by the President," *Official Bulletin*, II (Dec. 26, 1918), 5.

³ Wilson was here responding to JPT to WW, Dec. 21, 1918 (fourth telegram of that date), T telegram (WP, DLC). Among other subjects mentioned briefly, Tumulty stated that "Christmas greetings" from Wilson to the American people would have a "happy effect."

Lord Derby to Arthur James Balfour

Confidential

My dear Arthur   Paris. 22 December 1918.

The President and Mrs. Wilson dined here last night. I of course took her into Dinner and liked her very much.

After Dinner I had a talk to him. Nobody can help liking him but at the same time his views seem to me to be of the most visionary character. He began by saying that he hoped there would be no difference between him and England. I said that there seemed to be only two things on which we could have differences. That was the question of the Colonies and the Freedom of the Seas.

With reference to the Colonies he said that never for one minute would he recommend that they should be returned to Germany but he thought that they ought to be neutralised and worked in the common interests of humanity by some small nation acting under the control of the League of Nations. I pointed out to him that past experience had not shown that small nations made the best Colonists and why should not these Colonies be put under us with perfect freedom to other nations to help in their development. He agreed that it was true that small nations had made bad colonists but he said if these colonies were to remain under us it would probably eventually mean that we should eventually take possession of them. I asked him why should we take possession if we are to be under a League of Nations and subject to the control of that League of Nations. Why should we have any more power to take possession than a small Nation would have? To that he seemed to have no reply except to say that of course it would be so much easier for a big nation than for a small nation to take possession, which seems to me rather illogical if the League of Nations is to have the power that he thinks it ought to have.

On the Freedom of the Seas he was equally vague. He agrees that England must have a large Navy on account of its widely distributed Dominions and he considers that the only other nation which would be entitled to a big Navy should be America on account of its extensive seaboard. That we should between us do the whole of the marine policing of the world and that the size of our navies should be determined by agreement between ourselves, but that together we should have vastly preponderating navies over any forces that could be possibly brought against us.

I asked him whether the whole of his schemes did not stand or fall by a working scheme of the League of Nations and he said most certainly it did. I asked him a few questions with regard to this League of Nations and again it seems to me his views are of the haziest description.

It is apparently to be a sort of general Parliament of Ambassadors who are to be the Ambassadors to some small State. I think he took Switzerland as being the State. The Ambassadors to Switzerland, because they are to be Ambassadors and not Ministers, should not be only Ambassadors to that Country but shall be Ambassadors to the League of Nations Conference, or whatever else you like to call it. Every nation great or small shall have one vote and however small the Nation it is therefore to have exactly the same power in the Conference as any of the Great Powers of the world; on this point he was very definite. He told me however perfectly frankly that he had not got any very clearly defined idea as to how it could work, but he said if you can once start the machinery of a Conference their work would gradually develop but that there were two things which would have to be decided immediately. One was that if what he described as "a sore between two nations began showing signs of running" that the two nations concerned should at once be ordered to lay their cases before this Conference and no action of a military or naval character should be taken by either of them before say two months, during which time the question could be thoroughly discussed. If action was taken during that time by either of the Nations concerned it would be the duty of the rest of the League of Nations to combine against that Nation.

I am afraid you won't think this letter very clear but honestly I am not clear myself as to what he meant and though he is evidently very much in earnest I do not think he has any very definite ideas.

He is very anti-Italian. I asked if there were any people he wished to talk to after dinner. He said he was sick to death of Orlando and Sonnino and all their ways and he particularly did not want to have any conversation with them.

I have seen House this morning about the President's visit. He does not like the scheme as well as the one proposed from here but at the same time he feels it would not be right for him to offer any objection on the Presidents behalf except in regard to the Dinner at Lancaster House about which I am going to try and talk to George Curzon on the telephone.

House himself is I think very seedy again. He got a chill at the Italian Embassy and at the present moment he is undecided whether he will go over or not. If he is all right he will go but unless quite well he will not do so.   Yours ever,   Derby

TLS (A. J. Balfour Papers, Add. MSS 49744, British Library).

From the Diary of Dr. Grayson

Monday, December 23, 1918.

The President disposed of a number of matters which had accumulated and required his attention. His entire morning was spent in his study. In the afternoon he had conferences with Mr. Herbert Hoover of the Food Administration and Ambassador Sharp.

To Carter Glass

Message for Glass: Paris, Dec. 23, 1918.

Quote: Hearty welcome to your new duties. I am trying to keep a close watch on the verdicts [various][1] plans and maneuvers about the loans to which you refer and shall continue to do so with the distinct determination that none of the things to which you refer shall be accomplished. I am confident it will be possible to prevent them. Many such things have once or twice [only] to be exposed to be disposed of. There can be no proper basis for a discussion of our foreign loans in connection with the Peace Conference. At the same time it will be very serviceable to have some one in whom you have the utmost confidence sent over here to represent you in these important matters. When I left, Leffingwell seemed to be the best posted but perhaps you need him at home. End quotation.

Woodrow Wilson.

T telegram (TDR, RG 56, Office of the Secretary, General Corr., 1917-1932, DNA).
[1] Corrections from a T transcript in WP, DLC.

To John Joseph Pershing

My dear General: Paris, 23 December 1918.

Your generous letter asking Mrs. Wilson and me to look upon your quarters as our home while we are in France is greatly appreciated by both of us. I am afraid we cannot avail ourselves of your kindness but it is none the less delightful to receive such an offer of hospitality from you.

We are looking forward with the keenest pleasure to being with you on Christmas Day.

Cordially and Sincerely yours,   Woodrow Wilson

TLS (J. J. Pershing Papers, DLC).

A Memorandum from Edward Mandell House, with a Reply

Paris, 23 December 1918.

MEMORANDUM FOR THE PRESIDENT.

The Commanding General, S.O.S.[1] has received a telegram from General Rhodes[2] at Spa substantially to the following effect:

"The French financial representative has recommended that a specially qualified commissioner from each of the Allied Governments be appointed immediately to take up with the commission representing the German Treasury and the Imperial Bank consideration of the general financial conditions in Germany with special reference to retiring German marks and controlling the exportation of German securities. The financial committee of the Armistice Commission recommends that our Government get in touch with the French Government (in view of the fact as they state that in a short time the United States will probably be a heavy creditor of Germany in the furnishing of food supplies) and that one of our most prominent and best qualified financiers be selected to sit with the eminent representatives already chosen by the French, German and Belgian Governments, and that the British Government is about to take action in the matter also."

The above was submitted by General Dawes[3] to Mr. Norman Davis, of the Treasury, who has taken the matter up with me.

General Rhodes and General McAndrews[4] have asked for instructions in this metter [matter], and I should like to know what your wishes are.   E. M. House

I think this desirable, and take it for granted that the representative of the Treasury whom we are hoping Glass will send over at once, may himself represent us in these important conferences.
Woodrow Wilson

TS MS (E. M. House Papers, CtY).
    [1] Maj. Gen. James Guthrie Harbord, commander of the Service of Supply of the American Expeditionary Force.
    [2] Maj. Gen. Charles Dudley Rhodes, chief of the American section of the Permanent Interallied Armistice Commission at Spa, Belgium.
    [3] Brig. Gen. Charles Gates Dawes, president of the Central Trust Company of Chicago, at this time the General Purchasing Agent of the A.E.F.
    [4] Maj. Gen. James William McAndrew, Chief of Staff of the A.E.F.

From Robert Lansing, with Enclosure

SECRET AND URGENT:

My dear Mr. President: Paris, December 23, 1918.

The plan of guaranty proposed for the League of Nations, which has been the subject of discussion, will find considerable objection from other Governments because, even when the principle is agreed to, there will be a wide divergence of views as to the terms of the obligation. This difference of opinion will be seized upon by those who are openly or secretly opposed to the League to create controversy and discord.

In addition to this there will be opposition in Congress to assuming obligations to take affirmative action along either military or economic lines. On constitutional grounds, on its effect upon the Monroe Doctrine, on jealousy as to congressional powers, &c., there will be severe criticism which will materially weaken our position with other nations and may, in view of senatorial hostility, defeat a treaty as to the League of Nations or at least render it impotent.

With these thoughts in mind and with an opposition known to exist among certain European statesmen and already manifest in Washington I take the liberty of laying before you a tentative draft of articles of guaranty which I do not believe can be successfully opposed either at home or abroad.

I do not see how any nation can refuse to subscribe to them. I do not see how any question of constitutionality can be raised as they are based essentially on powers which are confided to the Executive. They in no way raise a question as to the Monroe Doctrine. At the same time I believe that the result would be as efficacious as if there was an undertaking to take positive action against an offending nation, which is the present cause of controversy.

I am so earnestly in favor of the guaranty, which is the heart of the League of Nations, that I have endeavored to find a way to accomplish this and to remove the objections raised, which seem to me today to jeopardize the whole plan.

I shall be glad, if you desire it, to confer with you in regard to the enclosed paper or to receive your opinion as to the suggestions made. In any event it is my hope that you will give the paper consideration.   Faithfully yours,   Robert Lansing.

TLS (WP, DLC).

E N C L O S U R E

SUGGESTED DRAFT OF ARTICLES
FOR DISCUSSION.

VERY SECRET   December 20, 1918.

The parties to this convention, for the purpose of maintaining international peace and preventing future wars between one another, hereby constitute themselves into a League of Nations and solemnly undertake jointly and severally to fulfill the obligations imposed upon them in the following articles:

A

Each power signatory or adherent hereto severally covenants and guarantees that it will not violate the territorial integrity or impair the political independence of any other power signatory or adherent to this convention except when authorized so to do by the decree of the arbitral tribunal hereinafter referred to or by a three-fourths vote of the International Council of the League of Nations created by this convention.

B

In the event that any power, signatory or adherent hereto, shall fail to observe the covenant and guaranty set forth in the preceeding article, such breach of covenant and guaranty shall *ipso facto* operate as an abrogation of this convention in so far as it applies to the offending power and furthermore as an abrogation of all treaties, conventions and agreements heretofore or hereafter entered into between the offending power and all other powers signatory and adherent to this convention.

C

A breach of the convenant and guaranty declared in Article A shall constitute an act unfriendly to all other powers signatory and adherent hereto, and they shall forthwith sever all diplomatic, consular and official relations with the offending power, and shall through the International Council, hereinafter provided for, exchange views as to the measures necessary to restore the power, whose sovereignty has been invaded, to the rights and liberties which it possessed prior to such invasion, and to prevent further violation thereof.

D

Any interference with a vessel on the high seas or with aircraft proceeding over the high seas, which interference is not affirmatively sanctioned by the law of nations shall be for the purposes of this convention considered an impairment of political independence.

T MS (WP, DLC).

From Herbert Clark Hoover

Dear Mr. President: Paris, 23rd December 1918.

In order to adequately handle the problem of European food relief, it is necessary that we should establish stocks of food, particularly cereals and fats, at certain strategic ports, these stocks to be drawn upon for the supply of different countries from time to time. Such an arrangement enables us to maintain constant transport and a regular drain of our food supplies from the United States. This arrangement, together with many political considerations involved, require that the foodstuffs in transit and in storage at these bases of supplies should remain in the name and possession of the United States Government. The War Department, with your approval, is now performing this function in respect to certain stocks in the Adriatic, but I assume that their action is only for the emergency, and beyond this it is necessary for us to establish further such stocks at points like Rotterdam, possibly at Gutenberg [Goteborg?], and even at German ports.

The United States Food Administration has the right to buy and sell foodstuffs as may be required in the common defense. The appropriations to the Food Administration for these purposes lie entirely in the Food Administration Grain Corporation, of which you are the sole stockholder. The Directors of the Grain Corporation feel that, as a corporation, they should have your approval to this extension of their operations outside of United States territory. There is no reason either in law or in the purposes of the United States to maintain the common defense that does not warrant such action, and there is abundant actual reason why this action should be taken as a part of the necessity of the United States to maintain tranquility in Europe while its armies are entangled here.

It is not proposed to part with any of the foodstuffs thus belonging to the Grain Corporation without prior payment. There is, of course, some commercial risk in the matter, also there might be further outbreak of hostilities in Europe that some of our bases of supplies might be involved. This, however, I regard as a risk of war that cannot be avoided.

I would, therefore, be glad to know if you authorize the Grain Corporation to extend its operations to the extent of establishing these stocks and carrying them on the capital and credit which it possesses.   Yours faithfully,   Herbert Hoover

Approved, 23 December, 1918.
Woodrow Wilson

TLS (Hoover Archives, CSt-H).

From Oscar Terry Crosby, with Enclosure

Dear Mr. President: Paris, le 23d December, 1918

Deeming it probable that during your stay in Europe the Secretary of the Treasury may desire to submit for your approval propositions for loans to Allied Governments, I have prepared the enclosed memorandum. Perhaps it will be useful as a reference in respect to any such propositions.
                    Cordially yours,   Oscar T. Crosby

TLS (WP, DLC).

ENCLOSURE

LOANS

The Secretary of the Treasury has indicated to the Allied Governments the following generalizations respecting loans to them by the United States:

1. That he is not disposed to establish further credits for purchases outside of the United States.

2. That he looks for an early curtailment in advances for purchases in the United States, which are expected, as a general rule, to be limited to foodstuffs. Existing commitments for other materials, if originally approved by the Treasury and if they cannot be canceled, will also be covered by loans. He expressed the desire that the borrowing governments should endeavor to cover their United States purchases through private operations.

3. He has notified the various Governments concerned that he considers the loans made after September 24, 1917, as demand obligations, not only technically, but in fact. Whether these shall be funded at all, and if so in what maturities, are matters within the Secretary's discretion. But he advises them that demand for payment will not be made if they are unable to meet such demand.

The Finance Ministers of France and Great Britain have indicated that they consider all of their obligations held by us as, of right, transferable into time obligations.

LOANS TO GREAT BRITAIN

By the United States Treasury (as of November 18, 1918)
Total credits established $3,945,000,000
By the American Public   967,477,584 (approximately)
The majority of these loans mature previous to Nov. 1, 1921.

The amount desired by the British Treasury in future loans was estimated by them at $600,000,000. This amount is presumed to cover chiefly existing commitments and foodstuffs, and was estimated after taking into account the Two or Three hundred million dollars which the War Department will owe to the British Government in settlement of accounts for materials delivered to the A.E.F.

The Secretary of the Treasury has notified the British Government that he proposes advances to Great Britain should cease with the exhaustion of the existing credits, plus a further advance of $250,000,000 against an equivalent amount of sterling, providing this sum is necessary to cover our commitments in Great Britain.

LOANS TO FRANCE

By the U. S. Treasury (as of Nov. 18, 1918)

General credits established	$2,445,000,000
Special credit securing note	
issues of the Bank of France	200,000,000
Loans from the American Public	536,000,000

(Last maturity date of these loans, Oct. 31, 1921)

No estimate has yet been made by the French as to the amount which they are likely to need in the way of future advances. It is probable that they cannot, within the next two years, receive from us goods greater in value than the amount which will be expended by the United States in liquidating its war indebtedness in France and in support of the United States troops until their complete withdrawal.

No account is taken in the above statement of any possible sale of shipping to France.

LOANS TO ITALY

By the U. S. Treasury (as of Nov. 18, 1918)

Total credits	$1,210,000,000
Loans from the American public	none

No specific estimate has yet been made by the Italians as to the amount of loans they would like to receive in future, but they indicate that their needs will be large.

Italy owns $91,000,000 worth of wheat (or about 40,000,000 bushels) available for delivery after February, 1919.

LOANS TO GREECE

Under an agreement made in Paris in December, 1917, the Secretary of the Treasury joined with the British and French Treasuries in advances of $50,000,000 each, made available as a basis for the issue of 750,000,000 drachmas to Greek national banks, which were used to defray certain expenses of their army. This credit has been used up nearly to the total amount provided for, but in any case, according to recent determination by the Secretary of the Treasury, will terminate on the 31st of December, 1918, whether or not the full $50,000,000 shall have been drawn on that date.

The British and French Treasuries have proposed to continue the support of the Greek Army, provided the United States Government assumes one-third of the burden.

LOANS TO RUMANIA

From the United States Treasury
    Special credit $5,000,000
    It is understood that Rumania has drawn drafts for approximately
$2,500,000 against this credit, but none have yet been presented
for payment at the Treasury.
    It is contemplated that no further drafts will be drawn, as Ru-
mania's ability to use the credit ceased with the signing of peace
between the Central Powers and Rumania early in 1918.

LOANS TO BELGIUM

From the United States Treasury (as of Nov. 18, 1918)
    Credits $192,520,000
    The Secretary of the Treasury has indicated that he is prepared
to continue in part the advances made in the past for the support
of the Belgian Army and to continue in full the advances for relief,
and possibly to increase these latter, but has indicated that he would
await the recommendation of Mr. Hoover on this score.

T MS (WP, DLC).

From Edward Nash Hurley, with Enclosure

My dear Mr. President: Paris, December 23, 1918.
    I am enclosing a letter handed me by Mr. Logan,[1] summarizing
his observations with reference to the League of Nations as requested by me. You will remember that I told you I was having
him do this, and that I would send you his letter. I think that the
information contained in it will prove very interesting to you.
                            Faithfully yours,   Edward N. Hurley

TLS (WP, DLC).
    [1] At this time, a special commissioner of the United States Shipping Board.

E N C L O S U R E

Thomas Francis Logan to Edward Nash Hurley

My dear Mr. Hurley: Paris, December 23, 1918.
    You asked me to note in our various conferences with the French,
British and Italians all the threads of discussion that led to the
League of Nations and the Freedom of the Seas. I have followed
your suggestion with care.
    The chief result of my observations is the conviction that there

never has been so favorable an opportunity for the establishment of a League of Nations, but that if an agreement upon the League is not reached as the very first step in the peace conference the issue will be confused by bickerings over boundaries.

I am quite confident that the President realizes this better than any of us. The proposal made by Senator Knox[1] in the Senate several days ago for the settlement of all other issues before a League of Nations is set up must impress everyone either as pernicious or stupid.

Clementel, of the French government, Crespi of the Italian government, and Northcliffe, have expressed to us the same thought on this subject. Each has said that the League of Nations must come first. Each has said that the peoples of Europe have given to President Wilson the greatest reception ever given to any man because they believe that he has come to Europe to stop wars. Lord Northcliffe summed it up this way:

"European statesmen dare not oppose any proposal made by President Wilson that gives promise of stopping future wars. If he succeeds in reaching an immediate agreement with reference to the League of Nations, he will prove himself the greatest man since [the] Nazarine. The way is clear now; I am not so sure it will be clear when each nation begins to tell what it wants out of the war. But if the President forces the issue now, neither Lloyd-George nor anyone else dare stand against him on the larger principles of a program to prevent wars. Lloyd-George's government would fall if he were found in conflict with the President on these larger issues."

You will remember that M. Monet,[2] the French representative on the Allied Maritime Transport Council, made practically the same statement with reference to Clemenceau. The latter is the most popular man in France. The people will follow him so long as they believe he is working with the President to prevent future wars and to reduce the financial burden of heavy armaments in peace. Politically, however, there are other elements in France which must be reckoned with. One political group is led by Briand, who

[1] Knox, on December 3, had introduced a resolution (S. Res. 361) which declared that the "purposes" of the United States in the coming peace conference should be confined to "restitution, reparation, and guarantees against the German menace," and that "any project for any general league of nations or for any sweeping change in the ancient laws of the sea . . . should be postponed for separate consideration not alone by the victorious belligerents but by all the nations if and when at some future time general conferences on those subjects might be deemed useful." This resolution was referred to the Committee on Foreign Relations and was not acted upon, but it did provide a basis for discussion in the Senate later in December and in early January 1919. Knox explained and defended his resolution in the Senate on December 18. *Cong. Record*, 65th Cong., 3d sess., pp. 23, 602-606.

[2] Jean Omer Marie Gabriel Monnet (1888-1979).

wants to succeed Clemenceau. Another is led by Albert Thomas, who was the Minister of Munitions of France when Lloyd-George was Minister of Munitions of Great Britain. Thomas is the socialist leader. Lloyd-George works rather closely with him.

You have probably observed, as I have, the close cooperation between the British and the French. The cooperation is not an arrangement that springs from public sentiment. The British every day are endeavoring to increase the obligations of France to Great Britain. You will recollect how we ascertained the existence of the contract whereby England has agreed to provide the French with 500,000 tons of shipping in the next two years. I have learned that they have further intimated to the French that there need be no concern on their part as to a future supply; that if America won't do business with them, the British will. The British are making gifts which involve no sacrifice on their part. Sir Joseph Maclay told us that their figures indicated a world surplus of tonnage when conditions become normal. They are beginning to cut rates already.

I am inclined to think that Lord Reading, with his usual cunning, is utilizing our position with reference to food relief in the same manner. Our position was wholly justifiable. A council wherein all the associated governments are equally represented, unless under a League of Nations, might lead to confusion of administration. Since we supply the food and most of the finances, the American Food Administrator should be left unrestricted, as Mr. Hoover bluntly told them.

This has been used as an indication that we want to retain for ourselves all the credit for feeding Europe; that we want to keep France and England and Italy out of it so that it will appear that they have held aloof from the aid given to the enemy countries and the liberated peoples. You will remember the shrewd way in which Reading put forward this idea in the conferences which we attended with the French, British and Italians.[3] He repeated, until it became rather tiresome, that "the hand that feeds Europe will control its destinies." I have no doubt that he indicates to the French and Italians that we want to hold all the advantages we have, and gather in new advantages as well.

The British have argued that the various inter-allied councils are, to all intents and purposes, a League of Nations. The French, who first opposed, and now favor these councils, say they cannot understand why we are opposed to them. As at present constituted

[3] About these conferences, held on or before December 12, see E. N. Hurley to WW, Dec. 12, 1918. See also the Report of the Committee Appointed by the Allied Premiers to Consider Victualling and Supply of Allied, Neutral, and Enemy Countries, Dec. 12, 1918, *PPC*, II, 654-58.

and operating I believe they are doing more harm than good, but the British have convinced the French that the nations will fall apart and that the establishment of a League of Nations will be difficult if the cooperative arrangements are discontinued during the armistice. The French believe that the councils should be broadened with other nations represented upon them as the first step in a League of Nations. At least this is what Clementel suggests.

I am recalling these attempts to create misunderstandings merely with a view to showing the manner in which some of the British statesmen are trying to line France on their side if conflict should develop. The working arrangement which has developed as a result of the contract to build 500,000 tons of shipping for France, and other concessions of like size, including raw material promises, was demonstrated several days ago when the French, before sending their reply to President Wilson on the food relief situation,[4] sent it over to the British for approval.

So far as the British are concerned, their chief fear is that we will have government operation of ships. They know that under government operation the ships can be run at a loss if necessary to capture the best markets in the world. This is one club that should not be dropped until peace is actually signed. Other concessions might be made to show our good faith, and to dissipate any suspicion of selfishness, but we should continue to remain in a position where we can give them a dose of their own medicine if they want the competition in merchant ships and armament to continue.

The closest friends of Lloyd-George seem to agree that he has not given any close study to the proposed League of Nations. Lord Robert Cecil, who is slated to represent Great Britain on the League of Nations Committee, is an ardent advocate of a League. Reginald McKenna, Asquith's strongest supporter, believes in a League and advocates further that there should be international inspection of armament to insure the keeping of faith.

I was glad to see that President Wilson had denied the report that he had committed himself to the program of the League to Enforce Peace because, as a matter of fact, the program of the

<hr/>

[4] S. J. M. Pichon to EMH, Dec. 23, 1918, *ibid.*, pp. 684-85. This letter was sent in response to the "cable" proposed by House in EMH to WW, Nov. 27, 1918 (second telegram of that date). Wilson approved the draft. See WW to RL, Nov. 28, 1918, printed in n. 2 to EMH to RL, Nov. 28, 1918, second telegram of that date. House then sent the cablegram as letters, in the name of the President, to Balfour, Pichon, and Sonnino on December 1, 1918, *PPC*, II, 646-48. In his reply, Pichon agreed in general to the principles set forth by House and Wilson but stressed that all measures for food relief should be carried out in the name of and under the supervision of all the Allied and Associated powers. S. J. M. Pichon to EMH, Dec. 23, 1918, *ibid.*, pp. 684-85.

followers of Lord Bryce goes further and is more practicable. Dwight Morrow, who, despite his partnership with J. P. Morgan, is an enlightened radical, has given close study to the historical records of the movement for a League of Nations. One thought that I have obtained from him seems really worth while. Representation on the International Court of Arbitral Justice has always been one of the stumbling blocks. If the smaller nations are equally represented, their votes would dominate the larger nations. Shall the smaller nations be given a fraction of a vote, or shall they form themselves into geographical groups, each group having a vote? Morrow suggests rotation, one small nation being represented this year, and another being represented the following year. The larger nations would, of course, have permanent representation.

The Council of Conciliation, which accompanies every plan that has been put forward, naturally does not require such care on the question of representation, because its work would be conciliatory and not judicial.

The President himself, in the address published this morning,[5] hit the keynote of progressive thought everywhere when he said that, "Just a little exposure will settle most questions." That is the basis of the law in Canada providing for the handling of railroad strikes, and there have been no strikes since the law, which requires a published report before action is taken, was written on the statute books.

The President also said: "If the Central Powers had dared to discuss the purposes of this war for a single fortnight, it never would have happened, and if, as should be, they were forced to discuss it for a year, war would have been inconceivable." This is the central thought in the Bryce proposals—a year's delay in the course of which time there shall be a published report, with no hostile preparations on either side until the report is published. The nations involved might then go to war if they wished to do so, but infractions of the rules of the League of Nations would be followed by concerted action.

My impression, from the conferences we had at the British Ministry of Munitions, is that the British, when President Wilson outlines his plans to them, will agree to the Freedom of the Seas, as the pivotal principle in the program for a League of Nations. The sentiment throughout Great Britain naturally is strong for a large Navy, but ultimately they will withdraw from any insistance upon preponderance of armament.

They will agree to it because they know that President Wilson

---

[5] Wilson's speech at the University of Paris on December 21.

with one address in London or Manchester can oust the present British government. The people of Europe want no more wars, and on this issue no man in Europe dares challenge the President.

Sincerely yours,   Thomas F Logan

P.S. I have stated the facts without drawing unnecessary deductions. I have tried to be impartial. The conclusion is inevitable, however, that the British are dealing cards from the bottom of the deck.

TLS (WP, DLC).

From Raymond Poincaré

Dear Mr President,   [Paris] 23 12 18

Mr Léon Bourgeois, a Senator, whose name you know, who was Prime Minister and who represented France at the Conference of the Hague, has studied all the questions concerning The League of Nations with several French statesmen and scholars, especially with Mr Lavisse,[1] one of our great historians.

He would be very glad if you could receive him a few minutes and allow him to hand his interesting works to you.

He lives at 3 rue Palatine in Paris; but if you prefer it, I can myself inform him of the day you appoint for the desired interview.

Believe me, dear Mr President,

faithfully yours,   R Poincaré

ALS (WP, DLC).
[1] Ernest Lavisse (1842-1922), at this time retired, for many years Professor of Modern History and director of historical studies at the University of Paris, author and editor of many textbooks and general studies of French, German, and European history.

From Tasker Howard Bliss

My dear Mr. President: Paris, December 23, 1918.

At the request of the American Peace Commission, I submit the following for your consideration:

The Commission held a meeting today at 12:30 o'clock, in the apartments of Admiral Benson, for the purpose of hearing a statement presented by Captain Gherardi,[1] United States Navy, of the present conditions on the east coast of the Adriatic. Captain Gherardi has just returned from that quarter, having been sent there to investigate these conditions.

I do not now refer to these conditions in general, but only to those which concern, and which to some extent have been brought about by, the use of the small force of American troops serving with the Italian Army.

It is the unanimous opinion of the American Peace Commission that Captain Gherardi's statement of facts as observed by him indicates that the American troops are being used to further a policy of occupation and penetration which, if not contrary to the terms of the armistice with Austria-Hungary, is at least unnecessary under that armistice. In one case, an attempt was made to use a small American force to effect, without any apparent justifiable reason, a penetration into Montenegro.

In general, it seems that the policy governing the use of this regiment has been to ensure the scattering of it so that at no time does it come, as a unit, under the control of its commander[2] who is the only experienced officer with it. The result appears to be that the regiment is being employed not for legitimate military purposes but to further political aims. And this, almost of necessity ensues from having a small force entirely separated from the control of its Supreme Command.

I have already stated to you my reasons for thinking that it would not be well, at this late stage in the operations under the armistice to entirely withdraw this American regiment. But the American Peace Commission thinks that you may find it desirable to authorize it to draw up certain general rules to govern the use of this regiment (without, of course, the slightest interference with its command or administration), to be submitted to the Commander-in-Chief of the American Expeditionary Forces in France and transmitted by him to the Commander of the American regiment in Italy for his general guidance during the armistice. These rules would be transmitted to the regimental commander through the American general who is our Liaison Officer in Italy[3] and who would effect a general understanding on the subject with the Italian authorities.

Very respectfully,   Tasker H. Bliss

CCL (H. White Papers, DLC).
    [1] That is, Walter Rockwell Gherardi.
    [2] Col. William Wallace, U.S.A., commander of the 332nd Infantry Regiment.
    [3] That is, Maj. Gen. Charles Gould Treat, chief of the American Military Mission to Italy.

From the Right Reverend Charles Gore

Dear President Wilson,   Wheatley, Oxon. Decr. 23 18

I do not know whether this letter is likely to reach you while you are in England. Perhaps it is impertinent of me to write it. But since I returned from America I have become more and more conscious how much there is, among the "educated" classes in Europe, which is set to resist the ideas of international justice, & the principles of peace-settlements for which you stand. But I am also conscious that the heart and mind of the common people are with you: and that, though they wish the Kaiser punished, they do not desire Germany to lose its chances of moral or commercial or political recovery: and they do desire war to be made (as near as may be) impossible in the future by the curbing of ambitious designs by international control. And there are very many who are not what is called "working" people who share these desires. I heartily wish you had Lord Grey of Fallodon with you at the Peace Conference. I am only writing because my desires & my prayers go with you to France & the Conference—that you may have the wisdom and the courage to stand against many adversaries.

Forgive me if I am impertinent in writing this.
Believe me to be
your faithful disciple   Charles Gore Bishop of Oxford.

ALS (WP, DLC).

Grenville Stanley Macfarland to Joseph Patrick Tumulty

Boston, Mass., Dec. 23 1918

Will you please send the following cable to the President at my expense. (Quote) How can you permit the invasion of Russia for capitalistic exploitation without violation of your several messages to Congress and number six of your fourteen conditions of peace. Will you permit the formation of another holy alliance to destroy self determination and democracy in Russia, one sixth of the earth. Do not let the reactionary forces trade with you a paper league of nations for the right to de[s]troy democracy and self determination in Russia. We are with you for a League of Nations. It means real self determination whether we like the kind of determination exercised or not but if it is to be another holy alliance protecting the kind of determination that we like and using our united power to crush what we do not like, such a League will be a pitiful failure receiving at best only the applause of the passing hour. (Unquote.)

Greenville S. MacFarland.

T telegram (WP, DLC).

Lord Derby to Edward Mandell House

Dear Colonel House: Paris. December 23rd, 1918.

I have this morning received a telegram from Mr. Balfour stating that Their Majesties hope that the President and Mrs. Wilson will return to Buckingham Palace as Their Majesties' guests on arriving from Manchester on Monday evening next. May I have the favor of an immediate communication as to the reply I may send.

Yours sincerely,   Derby.

If you will let me know I will send word to Derby.   E.M.H.

Accepted with great appreciation.   W.W.

TCL (E. M. House Papers, CtY).

From the Diary of Dr. Grayson

Tuesday, December 24, 1918.

The President conferred at great length with Premier Clemenceau today outlining to him various matters of interest to the coming Peace Conference. The plans had been completed for the President's visit to G.H.Q. for Christmas, and he was then to proceed to England. The fact that the President had accepted the invitation to visit England at this time was none too pleasing to Clemenceau, who had opposed it, explaining to the President that he thought it would be better for him to remain in Paris, at least until the formal sessions of the Peace Conference had been begun. The actual conference between the President and Clemenceau, however, was very interesting, inasmuch as it was plain that Clemenceau was hopeful of lining the President up for the French peace plans, which included a great many things neither England nor Italy were expected unqualifiedly to approve.

After Clemenceau left a delegation of Italians from the redeemed provinces of Italy visited the President and presented him with a memorial address.[1]

At midnight the President and Mrs. Wilson, accompanied by a select party, left in a special train to pay the promised visit to General Pershing at G.H.Q. at Chaumont. The trip was made in the French official train, which was extremely cold. The bed clothing had apparently been sent directly from the laundry and put on the beds without having been thoroughly dried and was damp. I felt impelled to persuade the President to remain up for an hour in his car while we had all of the heat possible turned on and the sheets aired. I threw my sheets out of the bed and slept between blankets, while others of the party did the same thing.

¹ The Editors have been unable to find this document.

To Benedict XV

Your Holiness: Paris, 24 December, 1918.

The letter¹ which Your Holiness sent me by the hand of Archbishop Cerretti has given me real pleasure and I must avail myself of this opportunity in replying to assure you that I am speaking not only for myself but also I am sure for the whole body of the American people when I say that the sufferings of no other people have appealed to them more deeply than those of the Armenians. It will certainly be one of my most cherished desires to play any part that I can in securing for that wronged and distressed people the protection of right and the complete deliverance from unjust subjection.

May I not thank Your Holiness for the whole message of your letter and beg you to accept my sincere personal regards?

Respectfully,   [Woodrow Wilson]

CCL (WP, DLC).
¹ It is summarized in n. 3 to the extract from the Grayson Diary, Dec. 18, 1918.

To Raymond Poincaré

My dear Mr. President: [Paris] 24 December, 1918.

I very much appreciate your kind letter of introduction of Mr. Leon Bourgeois. I regret exceedingly that I have not been able to make an appointment with Mr. Bourgeois before leaving for England, but I have sent him word that I shall hope to have a conversation with him after my return. I shall look forward to it with the greatest interest, knowing how much serious attention he has put to questions in regard to which my thought is deeply engaged.

Cordially and sincerely yours,   [Woodrow Wilson]

CCL (WP, DLC).

To Robert Lansing, with Enclosure

My dear Mr. Secretary: Paris, 24 December, 1918.

I entirely agree, and I believe you do, with the judgment expressed by Mr. Gompers in the enclosed letter. Would it not be

possible for you to have frank conversation with the French authorities and representatives of the English Government in order
to straighten this matter out? The only wise and prudent course,
indeed the only expedient course, is to allow these people to hold
their sessions when and where they will and I am clear in the
judgment that if they are forced to sit in a neutral country their
discussions and conclusions will certainly be dominated by dangerous radical elements.

Faithfully yours,   Woodrow Wilson

TLS (SDR, RG 59, 185.161/7, DNA).

E N C L O S U R E

Washington, Dec. 22, 1918.

No. 87."A" For the President from Gompers QUOTE. "The attitude
of those Governments which interpose objections or place obstacles
in the way of my issuing for American Federation of Labor, invitation to labor for concurrent international conference at the same
time and placed where the official Peace Commissioners are to
meet, is not only unjust but most unwise and calculated to react
most injuriously. If the Labor Conference is not permitted to take
place at Paris, the Italian British French and our own so called
Radicals will be given the seeming justification to demonstrate that
freedom of assemblage and speech is denied by the governments
claiming to be democratic; they will charge the American Labor
movement with having deceived labor of the world into the belief
that an opportunity would be afforded to discuss world labor problems and to aid in their rational solution. Persistence in this course
by Allied Governments may make impossible American labor coming to Paris and there rendering assistance. Indeed the American
Federation of Labor will be humiliated and made the laughing stock
of the world. If objection is removed American labor delegation
myself included can leave United States soon and remain in Paris
until official Peace Conference convenes and be of some service
and thereafter meet with the labor conference and help to guide
the conference aright."   Polk, Acting.

T telegram (SDR, RG 59, 185.161/6, DNA).

To Joseph Patrick Tumulty

Paris, 24 December, 1918.

URGENT!! RUSH!!

We all unite in sending the most affectionate Christmas messages to you and the family. I hope that you will give the following out as my message to the folks at home: QUOTE

"I hope that it will cheer the people at home to know that I find their boys over here in fine form and in fine spirits, esteemed by all those with whom they have been associated in the war and trusted wherever they go, and they will also I am sure be cheered by the knowledge of the fact that throughout the great nations with which we have been associated in this war public opinion strongly sustains all proposals for a just and lasting peace and for a close cooperation of the self-governing peoples of the world in making that peace secure after its present settlements are formulated. Nothing could constitute a more acceptable Christmas reassurance than the sentiments which I find everywhere prevalent." UNQUOTE

Woodrow Wilson.

T telegram (WP, DLC).

To Alice Wilson Page

Paris, 24 December, 1918.

Our hearts go out to you in deepest sympathy for the loss of your distinguished husband[1] whose services to the country will long be remembered.   Woodrow Wilson.

T telegram (WP, DLC).
  [1] Walter Hines Page had died on December 22.

From George V

London [c. Dec. 24, 1918]

Having just heard from My Ministers that you propose to come to London on the 27th instant I hasten to say that the Queen and I hope that we may have the pleasure of receiving you and Mrs. Wilson as our guests at Buckingham Palace during your stay in this country.   George R.I.

T telegram (WP, DLC).

From Maksim Maksimovich Litvinov

Mr. President: Stockholm, December 24, 1918

In addition to general peace offer recently addressed by Soviet Government to the Allies,[1] I formally informed today the Stockholm Ministers of the United States and of Allied Countries that I am authorized to enter into negotiations for a peaceful settlement of all questions making for hostilities against Russia. The principles proclaimed by you as possible basis for settling European questions, your avowed efforts and intentions of making settlement conform to demands of justice and humanity, induce and justify me to send you this statement, inasmuch as most points of your peace program are included into the more extensive aspirations of the Russian workers and peasants, now rulers of their country. It was they who first proclaimed and actually granted to nations right of self determination, who suffered most sacrifices in fighting Imperialism and Militarism, both at home and abroad, who dealt severest blow to secret diplomacy and inaugurated open diplomacy. And it was partly for these innovations in politics that they have been fiercely attacked by the former ruling classes of Russia and their counterparts in other countries. To justify this attack a network of lies and calumnies has been woven round the activities of the Soviets and forged documents put into circulation.[2] Unfortunately Allied statesmen accept all monstrous accusations against Soviets at face value without taking trouble to check them. While agents of anti-Soviet parties are allowed and encouraged to move freely in Allied countries and disseminate untruth, representatives of the accused side have never been allowed to put fully their case and to answer charges made against them. In fact the chief aim of the Soviets is to secure for the toiling majority of Russian people economic liberty without which political liberty is of no avail to them. For eight months the Soviets endeavoured to realize their aims by peaceful methods without resorting to violence, adhering to the abolition of capital punishment, which abolition had been part of their program. It was only when their adversaries, the minority of the Russian people, took to terroristic acts against popular members of the Government and invoked the help of foreign troops that the labouring masses were driven to acts of exasperation and gave vent to their wrath and bitter feelings against their former oppressors. For Allied invasion of Russian territory not only compelled the Soviets, against their will, to militarize the country anew and to divert their energies and resources so necessary to the economic reconstruction of Russia, exhausted by four years of war, to the defence of the country, but also cut off the vital sources of foodstuffs and raw materials, exposing the population to most terrible privations bordering on starvation. I wish to emphasise that the so-called Red Terror, which is grossly exaggerated and misrepresented abroad, was not the cause but the direct outcome and result of Allied intervention. The Russian workers and peasants fail to understand how foreign countries, which never dreamt of interfering with Russian affairs when Tzarist barbarism and militarism ruled supreme and even supported that regime, can feel justified in intervening in Russia now when the working people itself after decades of strenuous struggling and countless sacrifices succeeded in taking power and the destiny of their country into their own hands, aiming at nothing but their own happiness and international brotherhood, constituting no menace to other nations. The Russian workers and peasants are determined to defend their dearly won power and liberties against invaders with all means their vast country puts at their disposal, but mindful of the inevitable wanton loss of life and treasure on both sides and wishing to avert the further ruining of Russia, which must result from the continuation of internal and external fighting, they are prepared to go to any length of concessions as far as real interests of other countries are, if they can secure thereby conditions enabling them to work out peacefully their social schemes.

I understand that the question of relations with Russia is now engaging the attention of Allied statesmen. I venture then to submit to you, Mr. President, that there are only two courses open to them. One is continued open or disguised intervention on the present or on a still larger scale which means prolongation of war, further embitterment of the Russian masses, intensification of internal strife, unexampled bloodshed, and perhaps total extermination of the Russian Bourgeoisie by the exasperated masses, final devastation of the country, and in case of the interventionists, after a long struggle, obtaining their ends, White Terror eclipsing the atrocities of the Finnish White Guardists, inevitable introduction of military dictatorship and restoration of Monarchy, leading to interminable revolutions and upheavals and paralysing the economic development of the country for long decades. The other alternative, which I trust may commend itself to you, is impartially to weigh and investigate into the onesided accusations against Soviet Russia, to come to an understanding with the Soviet Government, to withdraw the foreign troops from Russian territory and to raise the economic blockade, soothing thereby the excited passions of the masses, to help Russia to regain her own sources of supply and to give her technical advice how to exploit her natural riches in most effective way for the benefit of all countries badly in need of foodstuffs and raw materials. The dictatorship of toilers and producers is not an aim in itself, but the means of building up a new social system under which useful work and equal rights would be provided for all citizens irrespective of classes to which they had formerly belonged. One may believe in this social ideal or not, but it surely gives no justification for sending foreign troops to fight against it or for arming and supporting classes interested in the restoration of the old system of exploitation of man by man. I hope and trust above all that before deciding on any course of action you will give justice to the demand of audiature et altera pars.[3]

MAXIM LITVINOFF,

Late Representative for Great Britain
of the Russian Federative Republic.

T telegram (WP, DLC).
    [1] The Soviet government had sent Litvinov to Stockholm in early December to establish contact with the United States and the Allies. He sent a letter on December 23 to the Ministers of the United States, Great Britain, France, and Italy. The significant portion of the letter read as follows: "I am told to inform you that I have been authorized by the Soviet Government to enter into preliminary peace negotiations with representative[s] of the Allied countries should their Governments reciprocate the desire of the Russian Republic of a peaceful settlement of all the outstanding questions which may give rise to a continuation of hostilities between the countries concerned. I shall be glad if you will kindly bring the above declaration to the notice of your Government and also of the President of the United States now in France," I. N. Morris to F. L. Polk, Dec. 24, 1918, *FR 1919, Russia*, pp. 1-2. For a discussion of the Soviet policy which led to this and other similar diplomatic initiatives at this time, see John M. Thompson, *Russia, Bolshevism, and the Versailles Peace* (Princeton, N. J., 1966), pp. 82-90.
    [2] A reference to the Sisson Documents, about which see D. R. Francis to RL, Feb. 13, 1918, n. 1, Vol. 46.
    [3] That is, "to hear even the other side."

From Thomas Nelson Page

Personal & Confidential

My dear Mr. President: Rome December 24, 1918.

    I was unable to say to you the other evening all that I wanted to say, so I am writing you this personal letter.

    I do not believe anyone in the world has a fuller comprehension of the great principles of Liberty which you have put forward before the nations as those for which America stands than myself, and I know that no one is in more complete sympathy with them. The thoughts which you have suggested to me are so majestic that I have felt myself drawn to do my modest part towards putting them into practical operation with a sort of—I might almost say—elevation which has taken away the sense of labor however arduous this labor has been. I could never tell you what a profound feeling I have had about your work and about the privilege of serving under and with you in trying within my own sphere here in Italy to implant

in the heart of this people the idea of what you are trying to accomplish for the Freedom of mankind. That I have fallen far short
of what I wished to do goes without saying, but I think that at least
something has been done which will remain.

I have felt that the chief thing that was necessary was to interpret
the American people to the Italian people, that is, to interpret to
them what America, under your guidance, has stood for in this war
as the result of generations of devotion to Liberty, a devotion which
has in this great and definitive struggle been moulded by you into
the most vast and unselfish force which the world has ever known
in its history. Next to this motive of interpreting America to the
Italian people, I have had in my work a great desire to interpret to
America the spirit of freedom which lies deep in the heart of the
Italian people, and which is essentially different from the spirit
which is often observable on the surface and is so often expressed
by some of their public men. I might almost term this second motive
a part of the first because I have felt that if our people could come
to know the Italian people—I mean that element which is the element for which you so often speak at home—the sympathy which
they would have with the Italian people would evoke from them
an appreciation of our people whose result would be such a friendship that no arts nor wiles of Diplomacy could impair it. They are,
next to our people, perhaps the greatest lovers of Liberty among
the nations. My appreciation of them came from my study of the
great struggle of the Risorgimento in which, if the leaders like
Mazzini and Garibaldi and Cavour, have eclipsed those who worked
and fought and suffered with them, it was only because they caught
the light and not because there were not in every little town and
village of Italy heroes who labored and struggled and died for Liberty.

Italy has felt herself greatly isolated during this war and she has
suffered from the feeling that through the action of some of her
public men she has been misunderstood and misjudged by the
outside world as to her action at the beginning of the war. It has
been my aim, and I think I may say I have had some success in
it, to make Italy feel that you and America understood her. It has
been not only a grateful but a joyous task for me because I have
felt that instead of an indifferent or lukewarm people who neither
knew nor cared much about the United States, we were awaking
here a knowledge and a feeling for us which has turned that people
into one of the most sympathetic nations with America in all the
world. It has not been difficult; for they were pining—the People
of Italy—to find some great people who would appreciate them
without trying to exploit them for selfish purposes, and you, through

your utterances and your actions, have inspired them with a confidence which no one but you yourself can now take away.

You will remember from your boyhood how we in the South felt when some important man at the North in the years after the war spoke words of sympathy with us. The Italian people, whatever their faults, are singularly idealistic and every word that you have uttered has found its way to their heart. You have become to them something which I scarcely know how to express. A man of high standing said to me to-day that they regard you now as a sort of Messiah sent to save them from all the ills that the war has brought on the world. It is because of this feeling for you and for America that I have been so urgent for you to come to Italy. Your visit will, I believe, not only prove to you the devotion which they feel towards you as the leading champion of the people in their struggle for liberty and peace but will give you one of the strongest backers of your policies which the world affords. You have just been elected a citizen of Rome and Don Prospero Colonna, the Mayor of Rome, representative of perhaps the oldest noble family in Italy or for that matter almost the oldest in Europe, spoke of you in terms which only his knowledge of the sincerity of the people of Rome with himself at the head could have inspired.

I hope you will let me know at the earliest possible moment when you think you may be in Italy and also approximately who will come with you besides those who were mentioned in the list which you gave me. If I might suggest again as I did when I saw you the other evening, I feel that it would have a strong political effect if the Secretary of State and also if the Peace Commissioners from America could come with you. Italy would feel not only that the great honor of your coming personally to her had been done her; but there would be a further effect which I hardly know how to define. I only know that there would be a further feeling that the United States desired to testify by every possible means appreciation of what she has done and is.

I cannot close this personal letter without wishing you and Mrs. Wilson all the good wishes of this Christmas Season which you have done so much to make happy for the world. I feel at this moment almost like the old Italian woman who said she had heard there was "a great Saint over in America who was making peace for us all."

Always, my dear Mr. President,

     Your most sincere friend, Thos Nelson Page

TLS (WP, DLC).

André Tardieu to Edward Mandell House, with Enclosure

My dear Colonel House,   Paris, December 24th, 1918.

The Cabinet this morning have agreed on the terms of the following memorandum, which they asked me to forward to you to be submitted to the President before he leaves for London.

Believe me, my dear Colonel House, With High regards,

Very truly yours,   André Tardieu

Tardieu was anxious for you to get this before you reached London. He said Clemenceau was very interested in it.   E.M.H.

TL (WP, DLC).

ENCLOSURE

MEMORANDUM

The French Government is considering how to deal, in consultation with the associated Governments, with the economic problems during the transitional period after the war.

The French Government's aim is to avoid too deep a perturbation in the social life of nations and to prevent some of them having suddenly to face a disadvantageous situation, solely caused by the war.

Up to the present, the supplies for the Allies are mostly guaranteed through interallied organizations that are connected with either the Allied Food Council or the Interallied Maritime Transport Council or the Program Committees.

The French Government realizes that these organizations must be modified so as to be adapted to the new conditions deriving from the cessation of hostilities; however, they want to expose to President WILSON that, in their opinion, these councils cannot be suppressed without all the Allies incurring a great danger before they could discuss of new steps that would be found opportune.

Therefore the French Government expresses the earnest wish that American Representatives be maintained until further notice in these councils, at least as consulting members.

T MS (WP, DLC).

Lord Derby to Arthur James Balfour

Confidential

My dear Arthur   Paris. 24 December 1918.

I do not know whether there have been any letters or any messages from you with reference to the President's visit but there has been such a storm that apparently no boats crossed yesterday and rumor says they are prevented also today, so I am afraid Henry Wilson will not have been able to give you certain messages which I had sent by him.

I saw House this afternoon. I think he is very far from well and the fact of the crossing now being so bad is I think the determining factor in making him decide not to start tomorrow night. I have endeavoured to persuade him to go and I think I have a little shaken him in his resolve not to and I will have another try tomorrow morning. He however does not seem to think he would be any good and he anticipates you will have no trouble with the President.

I spoke to him about the various weird creatures that the President was supposed to want to see and he told me the whole of that was dropped and that the only man that he did wish to see was Grey and I do not suppose there is any objection to his going to Buckingham Palace to see him. I told him if he did want to see Ramsay Macdonald & Co—though I hoped he would not, but if he did, that he must see them at his own Embassy and nowhere else.

I told House that I had had a conversation with the President who had rather horrified me with his ideas with reference to the Colonies and the League of Nations. House says that I need not be alarmed and that he (House) can talk him out of his view with regard to the Colonies whenever it is necessary to do so. He recognises that it is quite impossible even if we wanted to, to give back S. W. Africa, East Africa or the Pacific Islands, in view of the opposition we should meet with from our own Colonies. He says that we need anticipate no real difficulty on this score.

With reference to the League of Nations he also says that I need pay no attention to what the President said to me about each of the Nations having the same representation. It is quite ridiculous and he is sure the President will not adhere to it. I told him I was very glad to hear it but at the same time it rather frightened me that the President should express such views, especially if he did not really mean them and that if he went to England and told the Ministers that he held those views they would put him down as a visionary incapable of grasping the problems of Europe. House said he had talked to him and he did not think anything of this character would be said whilst in London.

I spoke to him about the meeting of the Conference. He told me that he thinks the actual first formal meeting of the Conference is really a very little matter as compared with the necessity of getting everybody together, with perhaps the exception of Clemenceau, by the 4th or 5th of January. He looks upon that as vital. He is endeavouring to persuade the President as soon as ever he returns from England to pay his visits to Italy and Brussels but the President does not seem very anxious to do this and he cannot at the present moment get a decision.

Every possible good wish to you for Christmas and the New Year.

Yours ever   D

TLI (A. J. Balfour Papers, Add. MSS 49744, British Library).

Edith Bolling Galt Wilson to Sallie White Bolling and Others

Dearest Mother & each one: Paris, Xmas Eve. 9.10 P.M.

We are leaving in an hour for Gen. Pershings headquarters but before we go I must send a word of loving greetings & Merry Xmas to each of you dear ones.

I have just given Hoover a cablegram to send to you which I hope will be delivered tomorrow.

I do hope you will all be together & have a happy day. We will be with you in spirit every moment.

It is a week today since I sent you a letter, & I thought I would be able to keep a "line a day" on a letter at least, but every moment has been claimed. However I feel sure the papers keep you informed of what we are doing & I am keeping the published record as a diary of each days events.

I wrote you just before we started to the "Hotel de Ville" last Tuesday, where Woodrow was made an honorary Citizen of Paris, & it was one of the most beautiful scenes I ever witnessed. They presented him with a large gold medal, & me with a jeweled piece— (which is interesting, but ugly) but is in a wonderful box. We drove miles through the city in open carriages amidst the same cheering throngs of people as upon the day of our arrival.

Flowers were put in the carriage at every corner & one girl presented me with a charming doll in Alsacian costume. That night we went to the American Embassy to dinner. There were 50 at dinner, & 500 came afterwards to the Reception. The Sharpes have a charming house & nearly every one but the French officials were Americans. The President & his wife & most of the Cabinet were

there & all the Ambassadors & their wives. I wore my blue & silver,
& every one liked it. Wilmer came to the Reception, & he went out
with Miss Benham & me to do some shopping this A.M. & came
back to lunch with us. He looks so much better & seems to have
made many friends.

On Wednesday we went to the Academy of France to see Mar-
rushall Joffre made a member. This was a most interesting ceremony, & very picturesque as all the members of the Academy wear
a stunning green uniform with a crimson decoration.

Both Joffre & the President of the Academy made a tribute to W.
in their speeches & every one rose & cheered. W. was on the floor,
but I was in a box with Madame Pointcaré.

There was a Reception afterwards. On Thursday we went to the
Franco American Club, where they gave an afternoon Reception
in our honor & where most of the people were French. On Saturday
W. was given a Degree at the Sorbonne, & we will never forget the
beauty & impressiveness of the entire afternoon All the noted scholars were gathered from every corner of France—hundreds of them—
and their Academic gowns are either crimson, or gold, with many
colored Hoods, & the effect of them as they sat was brilliant beyond
description. The addresses made to him were fine, & his reply was
a gem, & people were wild about it. I sat in a box with Madame
P.[,] her sister in law, whose husband is the Head of the Sorbonne
now, & several other ladies. After the addresses etc. we went into
a beautiful salon, where a table was spread & where the members
all came in their gowns, preceeded by 8 solemn mace bearers in
black gowns which made another beautiful picture. In the centre
of the room by a broad window was a platform carpeted, & after a
moment for refreshments they asked W. & the President of France[,]
Madame P. & me to go up there. The window was opened & we
looked out to see all the students in caps & gowns carrying banners
& lanterns march by—hundreds & hundreds of them. Although it
was about 5.30 it was dusk & just enough light in the sky upon
which to see the outline of the Museé de Cluny, & many towers &
old buildings of Paris, & the contrast of this old old city, with its
streets crowded with youth & vigor was striking—for all the *men*
are in the army & the students are mainly boys. We went to the
British Embassy that night to another lovely dinner & Reception
afterwards.

On Sunday we gave the day to the American & French Hospitals.
The former is at Nuilly, & I know Gertrude[1] will be particularly

[1] Gertrude Bolling (Mrs. Alexander Hunter) Galt, Edith Wilson's oldest sister.

interested in this as she has done so much for that work. I will have to wait & tell her about it, but I wish she could see what a splendid work they are doing. They say their work is getting light now as they have only *1180* patients, & most all of them rapidly recovering except the amputations which will be slow. We got there at 10.30 & left at 2, & while it was interesting & what we wanted to do, it was an awful trial to see some of the badly wounded, but there was the same splendid spirit among them that makes all those boys the admiration of the world. In the afternoon we went to "Val de Grace" the French Hospital here in Paris—an old convent of the time of Louis 14th converted into a hospital. Dreadful place to be sick in, but charming as a place of interest in architecture, with an old church in the midst. They are all so grateful & appreciative & it breaks your heart that personally you can do so little for them.

Then one afternoon, Dr. G. Miss B. & I went to the "Light House" you know Miss Holt's[2] place for the Blind, where she has them treated by skilled Drs. & taught to *see* with their *fingers* when the eyes are beyond help.

This place too leaves you speechless with yearning pity, but with it comes a thankfulness that some light is left in their awful darkness & they can be taught a trade, and given new inspiration.

Then 2 afternoons I had people to tea—among them the "Lansing girls"[3] with their "Choir de Gare." From Gen. Pershings we go on Thursday to London to stay until Saturday. We are to be the guests of the King & Queen at Buckingham Palace which I rather dread. We hope to get back here on the 31st a week from today, when we will go almost immediately to Italy. Margaret stayed just a week with us & then went off on another tour. She is loved by every one who meets her.

Please let each one see this & tell Ann F. & Sterling I wrote Sterling Jr. a few days after getting here & I hope to have him come to see us as soon as we are settled back again.

Now I must put on my hat. Woodrow joins me in warm & tender love to each one. I wish for you all every day. We hope soon to have letters from home. Love & merry Xmas.   Yours   Edith.

ALS (EBWP, DLC).
  [2] Winifred Holt, for many years a leader in the rehabilitation of the blind, founder and secretary of the New York Association for the Blind. She had helped to establish "Lighthouses," that is, educational, employment, and recreational centers for the blind, in many American cities. At the request of the French government, she had recently organized Lighthouses in Bordeaux and Paris to aid French soldiers blinded in battle.
  [3] That is Emma S. Lansing and Katharine T. E. Lansing.

From the Diary of Dr. Grayson

Wednesday, December 25, 1918.

The train pulled on a siding a few miles outside of Chaumont shortly after daylight and remained there until nearly eight o'clock while the party had breakfast in the dining car. A detachment of soldiers from the 77th Division and from the 26th were on guard duty alongside the train. The President on looking out of the window of his car was saluted by a husky young New York City doughboy. The President wished him a Merry Christmas, which plainly delighted the infantryman, who again saluted and smiled very happily. Following breakfast the train proceeded to the Chaumont station, where was gathered General Pershing, surrounded by members of his staff and a number of other Generals, who had been invited to be present at the review. Leaving the train the party were escorted to waiting motor cars and driven to the Hotel de Ville, where the city authorities had arranged to formally welcome the President to the city of the American Army government in France. Passing through the courtyard between lines of soldiers standing stiffly at salute, the President and Mrs. Wilson passed upstairs into the main council chamber of the Hotel de Ville. There were four addresses delivered—all in French. The first was by the Mayor of Chaumont; second, by one of the chief councilmen, and the other two by French officers.[1] The President listened very gravely to the speeches[2] and afterward made a very pleasant little speech expressing his gratification over the welcome.

Leaving the Hotel the motor cars were re-entered and the trip was resumed to a field midway between Humes and Langres, which had been selected as the scene for a Presidential review of units representing the American Expeditionary Forces. A stand had been erected to the side of this field with a plank walk leading across a muddy course directly to it. The weather was extremely cold. All along the route American infantrymen had been standing stiffly at salute, while gathered about the field were several thousand who had not been chosen to participate in the review, and who were interested spectators. There was also present a large gathering of French people from the countryside. The scene was most inspiring. As far as the eye could reach American soldiers in campaign uniform stood in unbroken ranks, lined up facing the stand. General Pershing escorted the President and Mrs. Wilson to the seats that had been reserved for them directly in front of the stand. Seated behind the President were Generals of Divisions—American and French—the French Ambassador and Madame Jusserand and a number of invited guests. General Pershing personally introduced the President to the troops in a brief speech.[3] The President then addressed the men. The first half of his speech naturally was designed for continental consumption, but the latter half was a wonderful tribute to the valor and patriotism of the men who stood before him and no one who listened to the President's speech ever will forget what it all meant.

Immediately after the speech was ended, the troops passed in review. The mud was very deep. Directly in front of the stand there was a small hummock with a little stream of water in such position that as the regiments came down in company front formation, the men were forced to waver and break, just sufficient to spoil the alignment. Instead, however, of detracting from the spectacle, this presented a very human touch that added to the impressiveness of the review. All branches of the service were represented in this review, but the chief hit was made by the tanks, which lumbered away from far across the field, and swinging around, passed directly in front of the stand. A couple of humorists in one of the tanks got a real laugh when they swung the turret of their tank to "Eyes Right," as they moved past in front of the President.

Following the review General Alexander,[4] commanding the 77th Division, which was made up entirely of New York City draft men, and trained at Camp Upton, Long Island, presented Mrs. Wilson with a small replica statue of the Statue of Liberty, the statue having been adopted by the Division as its shoulder designation.

The President and Mrs. Wilson shook hands with a large number of soldiers and officers. The motor cars were then re-entered and a trip made to Montigny le Roi, where the headquarters of the 26th Division had been established. The 26th Division was the first National Guard Division to arrive in France. It was made up entirely of New England troops, and formerly was under the command of Major General Clarence Edwards, who was relieved shortly before the armistice. The President on arriving at the Division was chagrined and very much surprised to find that his request made personally to General Pershing in Paris—that he be allowed to have dinner in the field with the soldiers themselves—had been ignored, and that instead he was slated to eat as the guest at the mess of the officers of the 26th Division Staff. For a little while the President seriously considered whether it would not be well to decline to mess with the Division Staff, not that he did not appreciate the fact that these men had a fighting record, but because it had been his dearest wish to spend the day with the doughboys themselves. However, after considering the matter he decided that as the plans could not be changed at that late hour, it would be just as well to let the program be carried out as arranged. Dinner was served in a room in one of the oldest chateaus in this section. The divisional staff had done the best they could to get the customary "turkey and trimmings," but had found it impossible, so they served chicken with celery and other food more or less American in character. However, they demonstrated their Yankeeism in the dessert, the cooks having prepared wonderful pumpkin pie—the typical New England kind, sweetened with molasses. Everyone enjoyed the dinner.

Leaving the chateau the President made it very plain to General Pershing that he wanted to see how the men were cared for. He spent the entire afternoon visiting soldiers of the Expeditionary Forces billeted in barns and houses. At one place he climbed up a ladder and entered a hay-mow, where half a company was quartered. The men were very comfortable, and the President chatted with them asking them as to their daily routine. Later on he visited a constructed cantonment where the beds were designed so that two men slept on a square-piece with a board between. The President remarked, in this connection, that if he had his choice he would rather sleep in the barns than in the houses themselves, as the barns seemed more comfortable. At one place on the route the President was held up by a number of boys who gave him a small memento that they had made themselves and expressed in French their love and affection for him. Ambassador Jusserand interpreted their remarks and the President was touched by the unaffected tribute. All along the road American soldiers had been lined at attention. Passing through a village in which was located a French interpreters school, the President's automobile was halted by a score of French soldiers and young girls, who simply lined up shoulder to shoulder across the road and refused to give way when the chauffeur blew his horn. The soldiers opened the door of the President's car, and a young girl pushed her way through the crowd, climbed on the step, and handed the President a bouquet, at the same time leaning over and kissing General Pershing. This caused quite a little amusement to the President.

Late in the afternoon the party proceeded to a French chateau, where General Pershing maintained his headquarters. This chateau was a most magnificent structure. It dated back beyond French revolutionary times and was furnished with antique furniture, almost priceless in character. General Pershing had assembled to greet the President all of the members of his personal staff and the divisional staffs from the several divisions quartered in the neighborhood of G.H.Q. He also had invited in a number of men and women, French residents of that vicinity. General Pershing's headquarters were extremely palatial in their character. They were a revelation to the President, who had been used to simplicity so far as Army Officers were concerned. The General had a very elaborate luncheon and a display of vintage champagnes for his guests, but owing to the lateness of the hour few of the members of the party were able to partake of the proffered hospitality.

Leaving Pershing's headquarters a quick run was made to the Chaumont station, where the train was [a]gain boarded, and at seven o'clock that night we left for Calais.

¹ The Mayor of Chaumont was Léon Georges Maxime Lévy-Alphandéry. One of the officers was Gen. Henri Wirbel, commander of the 21st military region of France. The names of neither of the other two persons mentioned by Grayson appear in newspaper accounts of the event. However, one M. Fossien, identified by the newspapers as Prefect of the Department of the Marne, was present to greet Wilson at the railroad station, and one of the speeches cited in n. 2 below was that of the "Prefect of the Haute-Marne, one M. Jossier."
² T MSS copies of the speeches, in both French and English, are in WP, DLC.
³ It is printed in *Addresses of President Wilson on First Trip . . .*
⁴ Maj. Gen. Robert Alexander.

Remarks at Humes to American Soldiers

December 25, 1918.

General Pershing and fellow countrymen: I wish that I could give to each one of you the message that I know you are longing to receive from those at home who love you. I cannot do that, but I can tell you how everybody at home is proud of you; how everybody at home has followed every movement of this great army with confidence and affection; and how the whole people of the United States are now waiting to welcome you home with an acclaim which probably has never greeted any other army. Because this is a war into which our country, like these countries we have been so proud to stand by, has put its whole heart, and the reason that we are proud of you is that you have put your heart into it; you have done your duty, and something more. You have done your duty and done it with a spirit which gave it distinction and glory.

And now we are to have the fruits of victory. You knew when you came over what you came over for, and you have done what it was appointed you to do. I know what you expect of me. Some time ago a gentlemen from one of the countries with which we are associated was discussing with me the moral aspects of this war, and I said that if we did not insist upon the high purposes for which this war was entered by the United States I could never look those gallant fellows across the seas in the face again. You knew what we expected of you and you did it. I know what you and the people at home expect of me; and I am happy to say, my fellow countrymen, that I do not find in the hearts of the great leaders with whom it is my privilege now to cooperate any difference of principle or of fundamental purpose. It happened that it was the privilege of America to present the chart[er] for peace, and now the process of settlement has been rendered comparatively simple by the fact that all the nations concerned have accepted that chart[er] and that the application of those principles laid down there will be their explication. The world will now know that the nations that fought this war, as well as the soldiers who represented them, are ready to make good—make good not merely in the assertion of their own interests, but make good in the establishment of peace upon the permanent foundations of right and of justice. Because this is not a war in which the soldiers of the free nations have obeyed masters. You have commanders, but you have no masters. Your very commanders represent you in representing the nation of which you constitute so distinguished a part, and this being a people's war, everybody concerned in the settlement knows that it must be a people's peace, that nothing must be done in the settlement of the issues of the war which is not as handsome as the great achievements of the armies of the United States and the Allies.

It is difficult, very difficult, men, in a formal speech like this to show you my real heart. You men probably do not realize with what anxious attention and care we have followed every step you have advanced, and how proud we are that every step was in advance and not in retreat; that every time you set your faces in any direction, you kept your faces in that direction. A thrill has gone through my heart, as it has gone through the heart of every American, with almost every gun that was fired and every stroke that was struck in the gallant fighting that you have done. And there has been only one regret in America, and that was the regret that every man there felt that he was not here in France, too. It has been a hard thing to perform civil tasks in the United States. It has been a hard thing to take part in directing what you did without coming over and helping you do it. It has taken a lot of moral courage to stay at home, but we were proud to back you up in every way that was possible to back you up, and now I am happy to find what splendid names you have made for yourselves among the civilian population of France as well as among your comrades in arms of the French army. It is a fine testimony to you men that these people like you and love you and trust you, and the finest part of it all is that you deserve their trust.

I feel a comradeship with you today which is delightful as I look about upon these undisturbed fields and think of the terrible scenes through which you have gone and realize now that the quiet peace, the tranquillity of settled hope, has descended upon us all; and while it is hard so far away from home confidently to bid you a Merry Christmas, I can, I think, confidently promise you a Happy New Year, and I can from the bottom of my heart say, God bless you.[1]

Printed in *Addresses of President Wilson on First Trip . . .*
  [1] There is a WWsh outline of these remarks in WP, DLC.

From Edward Mandell House, with Enclosure

Dear Governor: Paris, December 25, 1918.

Gordon telephoned from London this morning saying that he had information that the British Cabinet had been sitting for several days, and the concensus of their opinion was that they would back you in your League of Nations project almost to the extent of letting you write the covenants of it yourself. He said, however, they were still much disturbed concerning the freedom of the seas, and upon that they were like a majority of the British public, unwilling to accept any radical change.

He also said that the naval officer who has been delegated to meet you at Dover, and will be attached to your party—a certain Lord Herschel,[1] is of the ultra "blue water school" and he advised caution in discussing naval matters with him.

I am enclosing a letter from Lord Derby which explains itself. I told Gordon to remain in London at the Ritz Hotel to do anything that you desired, and to look after your wants in every way possible. He is of course, working in close touch with Sir William[2] and the Foreign Office. I shall send through him anything of pressing importance that happens here that I think you should know.

Di Cellere tells me that you intend leaving for Italy almost immediately upon your return from London. We have tentatively arranged, therefore, for your leaving on the night of January 2nd. I have also made out with di Cellere a tentative itinerary.

I noticed that in discussing your trip, Orlando and Sonnino did not urge you to go to Milan and Turin. As a matter of fact, they are the two essential places for you to visit. They are the only reasons why you should go to Italy at all. They are the big manufacturing centers and the greatest strength you have is there.

Affectionately yours,   E. M. House

TLS (WP, DLC).
  [1] Richard Farrer Herschell, 2nd Baron Herschell, Lord in Waiting in Ordinary to George V.
  [2] Sir William Wiseman.

Lord Derby to Edward Mandell House

Dear Colonel House: Paris, December 25, 1918.

According to a telegram which I have just received from Mr. Balfour, the dinner at Lancaster House on Saturday has been cancelled in deference to the President's wishes. Instead, the Prime Minister will give a small dinner in the President's honour at No. 10 Downing Street, to which the members of the Imperial War Cabinet will be invited.

The President will leave Buckingham Palace at 9 a.m. on December 31st, and Victoria Station at 9.15 a.m.

Will you let the President know that the occasion for his most important speech will be Saturday at the Guildhall. At the Lord Mayor's luncheon afterwards the toasts will be quite informal.

Your sincere,   Derby.

TCL (WP, DLC).

From the Diary of Dr. Grayson

Thursday, December 26, 1918.

The President's special train halted thirty minutes outside of Calais for breakfast. While it lay on the side-track the regular passenger train went by and French soldiers and a number of American newspaper correspondents who were on board cheered the President. Calais was reached at 9:00 o'clock and the train ran directly to the dock where the British Hospital Ship BRIGHTON was in waiting to transfer the party across the Channel.

Outside of Calais, just before the city was reached, the President had his first sight of German prisoners of war. A score of them were working on the railroad and unloading supply cars stored on side tracks. It was very plain from their attitude that they had been warned to expect the President and they stopped work to watch as the train went by. There was no demonstration of any kind until the Calais dock was reached. Here a guard of French troops was in waiting, lined up at attention. The President inspected the guard as usual, and then met the British officers who had been sent over to escort him across the Channel. Among these was Sir Charles Cust,[1] A.D.C., and Personal Equerry to King George, who had been especially detailed by the King to act as an Aide to the President. The BRIGHTON was preceded all the way across the Channel by a British Cruiser Destroyer, which had been used as the flag-ship of the British monitor squadron that kept guard off the Belgian Coast during the war. Pulling out of Calais harbor a flotilla of eight French destroyers took positions to port and starboard of the BRIGHTON. From their signal mast they displayed the code signal of AU REVOIR; SAFE PASSAGE; SPEEDY RETURN. Above the heads of the party whizzed a squadron of British aeroplanes in battle formation, who maneuvered above the Channel all the way across to Dover. Two French dirigibles and half a dozen French aeroplanes accompanied the flotilla well into the Channel. Arriving at exact "mid-channel" the French destroyers circled out, dipped their flag in salute, and headed back towards the shores of France, while a flotilla of eight British destroyers took up the work of escorting from that point to land. It was just noon as the BRIGHTON headed in through the entrance to Dover Channel. The chalk cliffs shown white in a beautiful sun that had dissipated the mists that earlier in the day had over-shadowed the Channel. As the bow of the BRIGHTON came abreast the Channel entrance the guns in Dover Castle—the same guns which had welcomed Drake—boomed out a Presidential salute.

As the President came down the gang-plank he was greeted the moment he set foot on British soil by the Duke of Connaught,[2] who had been sent down as the personal representative of the King. The Earl of Reading, British Ambassador to the United States, and John W. Davis, American Ambassador to Great Britain, were in the welcoming party, which included a large number of officials of the British Government. The President inspected the guard, which was lined up along the docks, and then passed into the railway station, where the Lord Mayor of Dover, the High Sheriff of Dover and the Town Clerk,[3] garbed in the scarlet robes of their office, wearing side arms and powdered wigs, were waiting. The Lord Mayor delivered an address of welcome, to which the President responded in a fitting manner.[4]

In the station there was waiting King George's own special train, which had been sent down to bring the President and his party to London. This train was exactly the same which the King used in all of his trips about Great Britain, with the exception of one car—a salon and drawing room equipage that had not been needed. The run to London was made in record time. Aeroplanes accompanied the train, soaring over the tracks, while occasionally some of the very adventurous of the birdmen essayed "hedge-hopping," the latest sport of the British aviator, and which consisted of seeing how close one could get without touching the hedges that separated the various fields. It was a lively sport, inasmuch as a single miscue would have meant death to the bold aviator.

Charing Cross Station was reached at 2:30. The President was met as he alighted from the train by King George, Queen Mary and the Princess Mary, Premier Lloyd-George, and all of the members of the British Government. There was a brief exchange of greetings, the King formally welcoming the President to British soil, and the President explaining that he was very pleased to be there.

Outside in the station courtyard were waiting the semi-state equipages used by the King on the occasions when he formally opened Parliament. These were open carriages of the landau type, hung by leather straps from elliptical springs, with a box in front for the coachman and an assistant, and one behind for two grooms. Magnificent horses were used to pull these vehicles. They were of solid color and the harness was tipped with gold, glistening in the sunlight.

From the railway station to Buckingham Palace the entire route was lined with soldiers. Behind them the sidewalks were literally jammed with men, women and children. The roof tops were covered, while every window held its complement. Massed about the Victoria Statue, which we passed enroute, were wounded veterans of the Great War. The enthusiasm was really surprising. We had been told by Britishers we met in Paris that the average Briton was phlegmatic and loathe to show his emotions. That warning, however, was not borne out by the facts. A rather peculiar feature of it was that at two places along the route, and again just in front of Buckingham Palace, the crowd yelled in unison—"We want Wilson!"

In the first carriage was the King and President Wilson; in the second, Queen Mary, Princess Mary and Mrs. Wilson. Passing through Pall Mall the Dowager Queen Alexandra, the widow of the the late King Edward, and her sister, Queen Maude of Norway, came down to the sidewalk and waved a greeting, to which the President responded by rising to his feet in the carriage and waving his hat.

Entering the main entrance of Buckingham Palace the President was escorted through the various corridors up to the second floor and out on a balcony that looked down on the square below. Gathered in this square were soldiers and sailors, veterans of the war, many of whom had been wounded, a large number of children orphaned as a result of the struggle, and many people not in uniform. The wounded men were seated in the front ranks, and they cheered the President until he finally was forced to make a short speech. "I honor you men who have been wounded in this fight for freedom," he declared, and then warmly thanked them for their friendly welcome. Mrs. Wilson first waved a small American flag at the crowd below, which simply rose to her, waving back small American flags. She then paid a very graceful tribute to her welcomers by taking from the corner of the balcony a small Union Jack and waving it to the people below. This started a fusilade of cheering, which lasted until the President and Mrs. Wilson finally withdrew into the palace proper.

King George and Queen Mary escorted the President and Mrs. Wilson to that section of the palace that had been set apart for their use, and then retired, leaving them to rest for a very short time. About thirty minutes after he arrived at the palace, the President accompanied by myself entered a carriage and was driven to the home of Queen Alexandra, the Queen Mother, to pay his respects. She met him at the doorway, shook hands with him in a very democratic manner, and asked him for his photograph. Although quite old, the Dowager Queen had lost none of her vivacity and charm and retained that grasp on domestic affairs which made her conspicuous during the lifetime of King Edward. She chatted with the President for some few moments and asked him to send her an autographed photograph of himself, which he promised to do.

Returning to the palace, the President and Mrs. Wilson dined informally with King George and Queen Mary. The dinner was entirely without stiffness, and the President and King got along very nicely together. After dinner the President and King discussed men and events and told stories touching upon their own experiences. One story which the President told the King seemed to please His Majesty very much. It was to the effect that he had received a letter a short time before from a woman who was anxious to raise money through holding a charity bazaar. One of the booths in the bazaar was to sell aprons and in order to secure unique ones that would bring good money she had decided that they would be made of the shirt-tails of famous men. So she wrote the President asking him to send one of his shirt-tails to her, with a history of the state functions, etc., which he had attended while wearing it. The President did not say what action he took on the request. The King also had a number of amusing stories. One that plainly had made a decided impression on him dealt with his inspection of a regiment of American soldiers, waiting in England to be transferred across the channel to the front. As he drove up to the regiment he heard one soldier say to another—"Who's that bug over there?" His comrade replied: "You darn fool, don't you know that's the King? " The first soldier looked at him for a minute in disgust, and then said: "Where do you get that stuff; if that is the King where in the hell is his crown?" The King laughingly told the President that as far as he was concerned he did not mind being called a bug but he did think it was at least ridiculous that any one should expect that he would inspect a regiment with a crown attached to his head.

[1] Sir Charles Leopold Cust.
[2] Arthur William Patrick Albert, Duke of Connaught and Strathearn, uncle of George V and father of Prince Arthur of Connaught.
[3] Edwin Wood Thorp Farley was Mayor of Dover; Lt. Col. John Middleton Rogers was High Sheriff of Kent; and R. E. Knocker was Town Clerk of Dover.
[4] It is printed in *Addresses of President Wilson on First Trip . . .*

From William Sowden Sims

My dear Mr. President: London December 26, 1918

As I have during the past 20 months been continuously and quite intimately associated with the naval people of Great Britain and her allies, and also with many of the civil authorities on terms of considerable intimacy, I think it possible that the knowledge I have thus acquired, not only of their point of view but, particularly, of their *real attitude* and *feeling* regarding the United States, might be of interest to you.

If you think this likely, I would be glad if you could give me a few minutes at any time.

The Naval Headquarters telephone number is *Victoria 9110*, and a call from one of your aides would bring me at short notice at any time.

I am, Sir, very respectfully   Wm S Sims

ALS (WP, DLC).

From John Joseph Pershing

My dear Mr. President: Chaumont, December 26, 1918.

In my conversation with you on Christmas day, when discussing the work of the A.E.F. in France, I did not perhaps bring out the splendid work of our General Staff and of our Staff Departments during the period of our Field Operations. May I call this to your attention now, because of the persistency of adverse criticism of this subject, spread, perhaps, for ulterior motives by those who profess a deep friendship for our Country. There is not the least foundation in fact for such adverse criticism. The officers who are best competent to judge—not only in our own Army, but in that of our Allies—know that the exact contrary is the case, that our Staff is entitled to the highest praise for its splendid work.

Since the success of an Army in the Field depends primarily on the efficient functioning of the Staff, it was necessary from the very beginning that we should organize and train a Staff that would meet our every requirement. To this I have given my personal attention.

A year ago last November there was instituted at Langres—the center of our Army Schools in France—a General Staff College for the training in General Staff duties of properly qualified and carefully selected officers. This College has since that time turned out several hundred bright, intelligent men who have taken a three months' course therein under the very best instructors available in our own, in the British and in the French Armies. The instructors from our own Army were for the most part graduates of our Staff College at Fort Leavenworth or of the War College, and these instructors proved more satisfactory than the Foreign Officers. The officers who met all tests during their course at the Staff College and who showed themselves of good staff materials were assigned, upon graduation, to duty as understudies with the best staffs of units in all armies on the Western front. After this they were assigned to duty on the staffs of our own Armies, Corps and Divisions. In practically every instance, even among Reserve Officers, we found that they brought to their duties a knowledge of which few officers of our Allied Armies could boast.

No Army can be successful without an efficient Staff, and the measure of the success of an Army in the field is usually that of the efficiency of its staff. Ours have met every demand upon them. In the Meuse-Argonne operation, the American Army was given as difficult a problem as ever faced any army in the world. It was known at the very beginning what determined opposition we would encounter at this vital part of the Western front. It was so important that German defeat there meant the loss of the Mesieres-Sedan railway and the German line of communication. A more difficult country to campaign in could scarcely be found. Probably there was in September no other army but the American that could have undertaken such a difficult operation with any promise of success. To ensure that success required wonderfully efficient staff work. That the operation was successful proves that the staff knew how to do its work well. Their problems were such as seldom ever faced the staff of any army. For that reason we cannot give too great praise to the staffs of our units engaged.

The officers of our divisions that served under the French and British assert unhesitatingly that the Staff work of the A.E.F. is and has been throughout our campaign superior to that of corresponding units in other armies. Our troops suffered hardships and endured losses due to inefficient staff work while serving in the other armies that might have been avoided had their staffs proven more efficient. American Army officers who know by personal experience whereof they speak, do not hesitate to place our General Staff and our Staff Department on a higher plane of efficiency than they place any of the other armies.

I ask your indulgence for dealing with this matter at such length, but I feel it is due in justice to the splendid men composing the Staff of the A.E.F. that you should know what remarkably efficient work they have done, and know how largely they have contributed to the success in the field of our Army.

With every assurance of my highest respect, and with every good wish,   Respectfully and sincerely,   John J. Pershing.

TLS (WP, DLC).

From Sir George Paish[1]

Dear President Wilson,   Pall Mall S.W. Dec. 26. 1918

Your visit to Europe has filled me with pleasure and with hope as I know it has everyone I have met and I cannot refrain from letting you know how much your visit means to us who are fighting as privates in the cause of which you are the leader and champion.

You will be glad to know that practically the whole of the British people look to the creation of a League of Nations to prevent war in future. This is evident not only from our newspapers but from public meetings of a non party character held in all parts of the country at which resolutions have been supported by Conservatives Liberal and Labour candidates alike demanding and supporting the principle of cooperation between the nations for mutual defence and mutual assistance.

The loss of Dr. Page is a matter of deep regret to me and I would ask you to accept my sincere sympathy. I have no doubt that all he sought to attain will be accomplished for never have the hearts of the British people beat in closer harmony and sympathy with their kinsmen overseas than they do to day.

In sending you my heartfelt wishes for your happiness in the New Year I feel as if the Sun of the new day, the beginning of a new time had arisen and that with your happiness the happiness and well being of mankind will be preserved and will become infinitely greater   Yours sincerely   George Paish.

ALS (WP, DLC).
[1] Paish, former adviser to the Chancellor of the Exchequer, seems not to have held a public or private position since 1916. He had just published *A Permanent League of Nations* (London, 1918).

A Memorandum[1]

[Dec. 26, 1918?]

LEAGUE OF NATIONS

A.

1. That in the vast multiplicity of territorial, economic and other problems with which the Conference will find itself confronted, it should look upon the setting-up of a League of Nations as its primary and basic task, and as supplying the necessary organ by means of which most of those problems can find their only stable solution. Indeed, the Conference should look upon itself as the first or preliminary meeting of the League, intended to work out its organization, functions, and programme.

2. That, so far at any rate as the peoples and territories formerly belonging to Russia, Austria-Hungary, and Turkey are concerned, the League of Nations should be considered as the reversionary in the most general sense, and as clothed with the right of ultimate disposal in accordance with certain fundamental principles. The reversion to the League of Nations should be substituted for any policy of national annexation.

3. These principles are: Firstly, that there shall be no annexation of any of these territories to any of the victorious States, and secondly, that in the future government of these territories and peoples the rule of self-determination, or the consent of the governed to their form of government, shall be fairly and reasonably applied.

4. That any authority, control, or administration which may be necessary in respect of these territories and peoples, other than their own self-determined autonomy, shall be the exclusive function of and shall be vested in the League of Nations and exercised by or on behalf of it.

5. That it shall be lawful for the League of Nations to delegate

[1] The following document is a copy of the specific proposals set forth in Jan C. Smuts, *The League of Nations. A Programme for the Peace Conference. . . . 16 December 1918* (London, 1918), which Wilson had typed for ready reference. Wilson made check marks before the number of each proposal. A copy of Smuts' pamphlet is in WP, DLC.

It is not known when Wilson had Smuts' proposals typed. However, Wilson received a copy of Smuts' *The League of Nations* in London on December 26, 1918. At the same time, Wilson was also given a copy of the memorandum by Lord Robert Cecil printed at Dec. 17, 1918. Auchincloss Diary, Dec. 26, 1918. Wilson took Smuts' memorandum with him for study on his trip to Italy and began to read it during the evening of January 1, 1919. See the extract from the Benham Diary printed at January 2, 1919. The impact of Smuts' plan and proposals on Wilson's own thinking about the constitution of a league of nations will also become fully evident in the following documents. Meanwhile, see Egerton, *Great Britain and the Creation of the League of Nations*, pp. 101-106; George Curry, "Woodrow Wilson, Jan Smuts, and the Versailles Settlement," *American Historical Review*, LXVI (July 1961), 975; and Peter Raffo, "The Anglo-American Preliminary Negotiations for a League of Nations," *Journal of Contemporary History*, IX (Oct. 1974), 153-76.

its authority, control or administration in respect of any people or territory to some other State whom it may appoint as its agent or mandatary, but that, wherever possible, the agent or mandatary so appointed shall be nominated or approved by the autonomous people or territory.

6. That the degree of authority, control, or administration exercised by the mandatary State shall in each case be laid down by the League in a special Act or Charter which shall reserve to it complete power of ultimate control and supervision as well as the right to appeal to it from the territory or people affected against any gross breach of the mandate by the mandatary State.

7. That the mandatary State shall in each case be bound to maintain the policy of the open door or equal economic opportunity for all, and shall form no military forces beyond the standard laid down by the League for purposes of internal police.

8. That no new State arising from the old Empires be recognized or admitted into the League unless on condition that its military forces and armaments shall conform to a standard laid down by the League in respect of it from time to time.

9. That, as the successor to the Empires, the League of Nations will directly and without power of delegation watch over the relations *inter se* of the new independent States arising from the breakup of those Empires, and will regard as a very special task the duty of conciliating and composing differences between them with a view to the maintenance of good order and general peace.

B.

10. The constitution of the League will be that of a permanent Conference between the Governments of the constituent States for the purpose of joint international action in certain defined respects, and will not derogate from the independence of those States. It will consist of a General Conference, a Council, and Courts of arbitration and conciliation.

11. The General Conference, in which all constituent States will have equal voting power, will meet periodically to discuss matters submitted to it by the Council. These matters will be general measures of international law or arrangements or general proposals for limitation of armaments or securing world-peace, or any other general resolutions, the discussion of which by the Conference is desired by the Council before they are forwarded for the approval of the constituent Governments. Any resolutions passed by the Conference will have the effect of recommendations to the national Governments and Parliaments.

12. The Council will be the executive committee of the League, and will consist of the Prime Ministers or Foreign Secretaries or other authoritative representatives of the Great Powers, together with representatives drawn in rotation from two panels of the middle powers and the minor States respectively, in such a way that the Great Powers have a bare majority. A minority of three or more can veto any action or resolution in the Council.

13. The Council will meet periodically and will, in addition, hold an annual meeting of Prime Ministers or Foreign Secretaries for a general interchange of views and for a review of the general policies of the League. It will appoint a permanent secretariat and staff, and will appoint joint committees for the study and co-ordination of the international questions with which the Council deals, or questions likely to lead to international disputes. It will also take the necessary steps for keeping up proper liaison, not only with the Foreign Offices of the constituent Governments, but also with the mandataries acting on behalf of the League in various parts of the world.

14. Its functions will be—

(a) to take executive action or control in regard to the matters set forth in Section A or under any international arrangements or conventions;

(b) to formulate for the approval of the Governments general measures of international law or arrangement or for limitation of armaments or promotion of world peace.

(Its remaining functions in regard to world-peace are dealt with in the following Section C[)].

C.

15. That all the States represented at the Peace Conference shall agree to the abolition of conscription or compulsory military service; and that their future defence forces shall consist of militia or volunteers, whose numbers and training shall after expert inquiry be fixed by the Council of the League.

16. That while the limitation of armaments in the general sense is impracticable, the Council of the League shall determine what direct military equipment and armament is fair and reasonable in respect of the scale of forces laid down under (15); and that the limits fixed by the Council shall not be exceeded without its permission.

17. That all factories for the production of direct weapons of war shall be nationalized and their production shall be subject to the inspection of the officers of the Council; and that the Council shall

be furnished periodically with returns of imports and exports of munitions of war into or from the territories of its members, and as far as possible into or from other countries.

18. That the Peace Treaty shall provide that the members of the League bind themselves jointly and severally not to go to war with one another—

(a) without previously submitting the matter in dispute to arbitration or inquiry by the Council of the League; and

(b) until there has been an award or a report by the Council; and

(c) not even then, as against a member which complies with the award or recommendation (if any) made by the Council in its report.

19. That the Peace Treaty shall provide that if any member of the League breaks its covenant under paragraph (18), it shall *ipso facto* become at war with all the other members of the League, which shall subject it to complete economic and financial boycott, including the severance of all trade and financial relations and the prohibition of all intercourse between their subjects and the subjects of the covenant-breaking State, and the prevention, as far as possible, of the subjects of the covenant-breaking State from having any commercial or financial intercourse with the subjects of any other State, whether a member of the League or not.

While all members of the League are obliged to take the above measures, it is left to the Council to decide what effective naval or military force the members shall contribute, and, if advisable, to absolve the smaller members of the League from making such contribution.

The covenant-breaking State shall, after the restoration of peace, be subject to perpetual disarmament and to the peaceful regime established for new States under paragraph (8).

20. That the Peace Treaty shall further provide that if a dispute should arise between any members of the League as to the interpretation of a treaty, or as to any question of international law, or as to any fact which if established would constitute a breach of any international obligation, or as to any damage alleged and the nature and measure of the reparation to be made thereto, and if such dispute cannot be settled by negotiation, the members bind themselves to submit the dispute to arbitration and to carry out any award or decision which may be rendered.

21. That if on any ground it proves impracticable to refer such dispute to arbitration, either party to the dispute may apply to the Council to take the matter of the dispute into consideration. The

Council shall give notice of the application to the other party and make the necessary arrangements for the hearing of the dispute. The Council shall ascertain the facts with regard to the dispute and make recommendations based on the merits and calculated to secure a just and lasting settlement. Other members of the League shall place at the disposal of the League all information in their possession which bears on the dispute. The Council shall do its utmost by mediation and conciliation to induce the disputants to agree to a peaceful settlement. The recommendations shall be addressed to the disputants and shall not have the force of decisions. If either party threatens to go to war in spite of the recommendations, the Council shall publish its recommendations. If the Council fails to arrive at recommendations, both the majority and the minority on the Council may publish statements of the respective recommendations they favour, and such publication shall not be regarded as an unfriendly act by either of the disputants.

T MS (WP, DLC).

From the Diary of Dr. Grayson

Friday, December 27, 1918.

The President had his first meeting this morning with Premier Lloyd-George and Arthur James Balfour. They called upon him at the palace. The President had been somewhat in doubt as to the attitude that the British would assume in connection with the Peace Conference. One reason for this was that Lloyd-George, after having promised to meet him in Paris prior to Christmas, had failed to come and had let it be known that he would not be able to leave England until the complete results of the Parliament election had been announced. The inference had been drawn in certain quarters that in reality the British Premier was playing for delay and was not anxious to be entirely frank in his dealings with the President. This impression, it developed as a result of today's meeting, was entirely unfounded. It was true that Lloyd-George had done his best to gain time before meeting the President but this was due to his wish to ascertain definitely exactly what endorsement his government had received at the hands of the people in the Parliament election.[1]

---

[1] The British general election, the first since December 1910, had taken place on December 14, but the votes were not counted until December 28. Lloyd George and his political allies had at first proposed to stress the problems of postwar domestic reconstruction but, as the brief campaign progressed in early December, they turned

The President met his two visitors in the main reception hall and escorted them into the study that had been set aside for him. There was an open fire burning in the grate on one side of this room, which was furnished in a most magnificent manner; a small table stood just to the left of the center of the room, and beside it the President had drawn up two comfortable arm-chairs, with another directly facing them. They sat in this manner—Lloyd-George on the President's right, Balfour slightly to his left. From 10:30 until 1:25 the three men in whose hands reposed a good part of the destiny of the world talked freely and frankly. It was a meeting of strong minds and the entire gamut of all of the subjects that must come up at the Peace Conference was touched upon: the League of Nations, the question of the freedom of the seas, as it was affected by the League of Nations, the necessity for an international labor policy, the necessity of curbing Italy's extravagant ambitions, the grave menace of the Irish problem—all were touched upon. The conference itself made a real impression on the President, and after his visitors left he told me that he believed it had been generally satisfactory. No positive agreement was reached; in fact, none was striven for. What the President had desired, and what apparently his visitors also were anxious to attain, was a general measuring-up of aims and hopes. The President found Lloyd-George and Mr. Balfour pleasant and seemingly willing to aid him in bringing about a program for the Peace Conference that would make for a minimum of friction.

Following the conference the President was driven to *10 Downing Street* (?) where Premier Lloyd-George had invited to meet him and other members of the British Cabinet. They had a very interesting discussion during and immediately following the lunch. Balfour, Henderson, Bonar Law & others were present. In connection with the lunch there was unveiled a portrait of George Washington, which had been purchased and donated to the British Government

---

more and more to demands for a Carthaginian peace settlement against Germany and attacks upon the alleged "Bolshevism" of the British Labour party. This was the first election in which nearly universal manhood suffrage and widespread woman suffrage existed in the British Isles. The Lloyd George coalition polled 5,091,528 votes and elected 484 members of Parliament, of whom 338 were Conservatives, 136 were Lloyd George Liberals, and ten were Labour and other supporters of the Coalition. The Labour party, which had withdrawn from the coalition in November, won 2,374,385 votes and elected fifty-nine members of Parliament. However, most of its well-known leaders, such as Ramsay MacDonald and Arthur Henderson, were defeated. The Asquith Liberals polled 1,298,803 votes and elected twenty-six members of Parliament, but most of their leaders, including Asquith himself, lost. The new Parliament also included forty-eight noncoalition Conservatives, nine independents, seven Irish nationalists or home-rulers, and seventy-three members of Sinn Fein. The Sinn Feiners never took their seats. For a concise analysis of the election and its results, see Charles Loch Mowat, *Britain Between the Wars, 1918-1940* (Chicago, 1955), pp. 2-8.

by members of the American Pilgrim Society. Lloyd-George called attention to the fact that it was in this very building that the British Cabinet had met and declared the American Revolutionary leaders outlaws and directed that they should be exterminated by force of arms. Lloyd-George took the President down to the Cabinet Room, in which the then British Premier had directed that Washington and his associates of revolutionary days be proscribed as rebels and a price put upon their heads. The conference at Downing Street lasted until 5:30. The President had an opportunity on this occasion to meet with the British labor leaders and to discuss rather briefly with them their intentions and aspirations dealing with the proposed international labor agreement.

Returning to Buckingham Palace the President that night was the guest of honor at a state dinner, which was the first really elaborate function of the British Government since that nation entered the war. The great court dining-room, feudal in its magnificence, was utilized. This dining-room is one of the most remarkable in the world. On the walls are hundreds of pieces of solid gold decorations, plaques, shields and the like. In one end, directly facing the throne, which is at the other end, is a magnificent organ. The arrangement of the tables in the dining-hall is in the form of a hollow-square, and all of the table service is of solid gold, bearing the royal arms. The value of the gold dishes is said to be approximately $15,000,000. Representatives of the diplomatic corps, Sir Douglas Haig, Commander-in-Chief of the British Army, and Admiral Beatty, Commander of the British Grand Fleet, were included among the guests.

The attendance at the dinner was declared to have been the most representative present at any British function in the memory of the officials. The leaders of the various political factions who had been at each other's throats for many years were guests of the King, as were the noted financiers, merchants, and literary leaders. Included in the latter were Rudyard Kipling and Conan Doyle. It was freely commented upon that in welcoming the President, the Crown had invited to greet him the representatives of every faction in Britain. This was designed partly as a compliment to the President and partly to strengthen King George's own position before the British people.

The arrangement of the guests at the dinner table was entirely along the English plan—the King and Queen sitting side by side, and the President and Mrs. Wilson likewise.

Following the dinner all of the guests were ushered into the Royal Reception Room, where coffee and liquors were served. This was the first occasion in which wines and liquors had been served in the Royal Palace since the outbreak of the war. Queen Mary and the Princess Mary, with their ladies-in-waiting, remained in the ante-chamber of the Royal Reception Room and held a private levee. They invited in to meet them a number of guests, including myself, and briefly converse with them. Meanwhile, in the main reception room King George and the President stood surrounded by the dinner guests, and each was afforded the opportunity individually to meet both the President and the King and to chat with them briefly.

On the afternoon of my arrival I was threatened with a cold and sore-throat as the result of the ride in the cold French train the night before. Upon being shown to my suite in Buckingham Palace, I was assigned by the Lord of the House a royal attendant, whose dress was of colonial style. He wore a white wig, a red coat, black velvet knee trousers, white stockings, and large silver buckles on his shoes. He was of fine physique, had small side-burns, and spoke a pronounced Cockney English. It was very difficult for me to understand him, almost as much so as the Frenchman I had left the day before. My pronunciation seemed to be difficult for him to understand. It is the English custom to serve tea in the afternoon, and they are as systematic about this custom as they are about their meals. While sitting before the open-fire in my sitting room, the attendant came in in a very royal manner and asked: "Will you have your tea now, sir?" I told him that I didn't care for any tea; whereupon he looked not only amazed but shocked, and said: "I beg pardon sir; I did not understand you to say you would not have tea, sir!" I replied: "No, I do not care for any tea." He said: "You will have something though, won't you, sir? " And not wanting to disappoint him, and at the same time feeling in need of a little help for my cold, I asked if I might have some whiskey. But he did not seem to understand me. I then said: "I would like to have some Haig & Haig, if you please." He seemed to understand the order, made a stately bow, and departed. In a short while he returned, bearing a tray on which reposed two soft boiled eggs. Not wishing to embarrass or offend my picturesque attendant, I ate one of the eggs.

After-Dinner Remarks at Buckingham Palace

Dec. 27, 1918.

Your Majesty: I am deeply complimented by the gracious words which you have uttered.[1] The welcome which you have given me and Mrs. Wilson has been so warm, so natural, so evidently from the heart that we have been more than pleased; we have been touched by it, and I believe that I correctly interpret that welcome as embodying not only your own generous spirit toward us personally, but also as expressing for yourself and the great nation over which you preside that same feeling for my people, for the people of the United States. For you and I, Sir—I temporarily—embody the spirit of two great nations; and whatever strength I have, and whatever authority, I possess only so long and so far as I express the spirit and purpose of the American people.

Any influence that the American people have over the affairs of the world is measured by their sympathy with the aspirations of free men everywhere. America does love freedom, and I believe that she loves freedom unselfishly. But if she does not, she will not and cannot have the influence to which she justly aspires. I have had the privilege, Sir, of conferring with the leaders of your own government and with the spokesmen of the governments of France and of Italy, and I am glad to say that I have the same conception that they have of the significance and scope of the duty upon which we have met. We have used great words, all of us, we have used the great words "right" and "justice," and now we are to prove whether or not we understand those words and how they are to be applied to the particular settlements which must conclude this war. And we must not only understand them, but we must have the courage to act upon our understanding.

Yet, after I have uttered the word "courage," it comes into my mind that it would take more courage to resist the great moral tide now running in the world than to yield to it, than to obey it. There is a great tide running in the hearts of men. The hearts of men have never beaten so singularly in unison before. Men have never before been so conscious of their brotherhood. Men have never before realized how little difference there was between right and justice in one latitude and in another, under one sovereignty and under another. And it will be our high privilege, I believe, Sir, not only to apply the moral judgments of the world to the particular settlements which we shall attempt, but also to organize the moral force of the world to preserve those settlements, to steady the forces of mankind, and to make the right and the justice to which great nations like our own have devoted themselves the predominant and controlling force of the world.

There is something inspiriting in knowing that this is the errand that we have come on. Nothing less than this would have justified me in leaving the important tasks which fall upon me upon the other side of the sea, nothing but the consciousness that nothing else compares with this in dignity and importance. Therefore it is the more delightful to find myself in the company of a body of men united in ideal and in purpose, to feel that I am privileged to unite my thought with yours in carrying forward those standards which we are so proud to hold high and to defend.

May I not, Sir, with a feeling of profound sincerity and friendship and sympathy propose your own health and the health of the Queen, and the prosperity of Great Britain?[2]

Printed in *Addresses of President Wilson on First Trip* . . .
[1] There is a T copy of the King's remarks in WP, DLC.
[2] A WWsh outline of these remarks is in WP, DLC.

To William Sowden Sims

My dear Admiral Sims: London, 27 December, 1918.

My inclination jumps with yours. I should be very glad indeed to have a conference with you, but it is already painfully evident that it is going to be all that I can do to carry out the programme already set for me, without additions, and I know of no time which will be really my own.

I hope that you will not consider it a hardship if I should a little later ask you to come over to Paris for a conversation.

Cordially and sincerely yours,   [Woodrow Wilson]

CCL (WP, DLC).

To Edward Booth[1]

My dear Mr. Booth: London, 27 December, 1918.

I am promising myself the privilege of attending service in the Lowther Street Congregational Church on next Sunday, but I am sorry to say that it will not be possible for me to deliver an address. I wish that it would. The truth is that I am anxious not to appear in Carlisle as President of the United States, but as the grandson of the Rev. Thomas Woodrow making a pilgrimage of the heart. I consequently want to be just as informal and unofficial as possible.

Cordially and sincerely yours,   [Woodrow Wilson]

CCL (WP, DLC).
[1] Pastor of the Lowther Street Congregational Church, Carlisle, England.

From Newton Diehl Baker

Dear Mr. President: Washington. December 27, 1918.

It is suggested that in view of the armistice, it would be advisable to modify the Executive Order of September 26, 1918, concerning the censorship of submarine cables, telegraph and telephone lines so far as it affects the telegraphic and telephonic censorship.

The pressure of military necessity is removed, and the activities of German agents in Mexico are no longer of a sort to require so elaborate and expensive an organization for their observation or control.

A draft of a new Executive Order is attached.[1]

Very sincerely,   Newton D. Baker

TLS (WP, DLC).
[1] T MS (WP, DLC). Wilson signed this Executive Order on January 25, 1919, and it was sent to the State Department on February 10.

From the Diary of Colonel House

December 27, 1918.

I had a long conversation with Gordon from London. He had a talk yesterday with Lloyd George which lasted three quarters of an hour. George went over the different matters he had in mind to discuss with the President. Gordon saw the President later and gave him some idea of what was in George's mind.

Balfour and George went to Buckingham Palace at 10.30 yesterday morning and up to 1.20 they had not finished, although they all had to go to a lunch at No. 10 Downing Street. Gordon is to give me the details of the conference in the morning. He is to get the British version from Wiseman and the President's view from himself. Gordon is to go to the banquet which the King is giving tonight at the Palace. It is a great opportunity for him and if I had gone to London, he would have missed most of it.

He said the President wished to know what I would advise saying to George and Balfour when they came. I suggested that he take up the League of Nations and to make that the keystone of his talk, and if the British yielded to our views on that part of the Treaty, not to contend for anything else at present. If they brought up the question of the freedom of the seas, colonies and other subjects, my advice was to listen sympathetically, but not to commit himself and not to antagonize them. The main thing is to get the League of Nations. With that accomplished, everything else follows or becomes minor considerations.

Gordon gave the President this advice and he said he would follow it. Melville Stone took lunch with me. We had a very interesting time. He seems better than when I last saw him and he talked in a way which made me understand his past great influence.

Lord Derby, Hoover and I conferred together, the substance of which is embodied in a telegram Derby is sending Mr. Balfour. He never gets his facts quite accurate, and this dispatch is no exception to the rule. Derby told me before Hoover came in that there would be no difficulty about the food administration except for Hoover himself; that what he wanted was to be food dictator and that the French and British Governments were willing to let us have what we liked, short of that. I take it there is some reason in his assertion, for that is Hoover's besetting fault.

Dr. Robert Moton of Tuskegee and Dr. Jones of Washington[1] were other callers. Moton came to Europe at the request of the Secretary of War to talk to the negro troops and to urge them to live up to the high ideals of the American Army after they returned to the United States. Moton made an interesting statement, which was to the effect that the American Negro was treated better and had greater opportunities than his brothers anywhere in the world. I had not realized this, but it is so patent after one thinks of it that it is a wonder it is not oftener stated.

We hold a meeting of the Commission every morning and see the newspaper men afterward. I shall not give any details as to what we do because I take it the minutes of our meetings will be written by Mr. Grew and become parts of the record.

[1] Thomas Jesse Jones, B.D., PhD., specialist in Negro education in the United States Bureau of Education and director of research for the Phelps Stokes Fund. Moton later recalled that he, Moton, had gone to France at the request of President Wilson as well as of Baker "to look into conditions affecting Negro soldiers, many of whom were undergoing hardships of one kind or another." "Secretary Baker said," Moton continued, "that he and President Wilson felt that my going to France would be encouraging to the men, and that the presence and words of a member of their own race would be particularly helpful, in view of all the circumstances under which they were serving the nation, at the same time inviting me to make any suggestions that might in my judgment help the situation." While in France, Moton visited "nearly every point where Negro soldiers were stationed." He had, he remembered, "authority to go anywhere and get any information from any source, so far as the American Expeditionary Force was concerned." Aside from making many speeches of encouragement to American black soldiers, Moton devoted most of his time to investigations of the frequently made charges that they were especially prone to commit rape and that they were poor fighters, especially when commanded by black officers. He found both charges to be essentially baseless. See Robert Russa Moton, *Finding a Way Out: An Autobiography* (London, 1920), pp. 250-65.

From the Diary of Dr. Grayson

Saturday, December 28, 1918.

This was President Wilson's 62nd birthday. He received a number of gifts. The President characterized the day as "the greatest of my life"; but he also added that "birthdays are coming too fast."

At ten o'clock King George, accompanied by the Duke of Connaught, visited the President's apartments personally to extend his congratulations. He also presented the President with a set of books containing the history and description of WINDSOR CASTLE. After the King left I accompanied the President to the American Embassy, where he had agreed to meet a number of American delegations, some of whom called to pay their respects, and others who desired to present him with resolutions endorsing the League of Nations plan. The President was escorted to the office of the Ambassador on the second floor of the Embassy building. On the wall of this office were the pictures of former Ambassadors Choate and Reid.[1] Ambassador John W. Davis, who had just taken over the post, acted as master of ceremonies and introduced the visitors to the President. Among the delegations that arrived was one representing the British League of Nations Society, and included in its membership was Viscount John [James] Bryce (Author of the American Commonwealth), and the Archbishop of Canterbury. Another member of the party was Earl Grey,[2] whom the President met for the first time. Earl Grey was the head of the Government which brought Great Britain into the war, that is, he was Minister of State for Foreign Affairs and responsible for the foreign policy. They greeted the President warmly and expressed the hope that he would succeed in his mission. After meeting the delegations Ambassador Davis presented personally to the President all of the attachés of the Embassy from the Counselor down to the latest arrived office boy. The President shook hands with all of them.

The President went back to Buckingham Palace immediately after the reception in order to prepare for his visit to historic Guild Hall. The Guild Hall ceremony was a very notable function, the President not only being made a citizen of London, but he also being accorded special privileges in connection therewith, which are usually given only to reigning sovereigns. The occasion had been made a semi-state one. The entire route from Buckingham Palace was lined with troops. The trip to and from Guild Hall and the Lord Mayor's Mansion was made in the state carriages. However, there were no representatives of royalty in the procession, and the carriages today, instead of being drawn by four horses, were drawn only by two. This was designed to differentiate between the city function and the state function. The Procession to Guild Hall was preceded by a troop of the King's household cavalry, who presented a very picturesque appearance, mounted on magnificently selected horses. The make-up of this troop is rather unique, membership in it being by election and being confined almost exclusively to scions of the nobility.

The President and Mrs. Wilson rode in the first carriage directly behind the cavalry escort. They were accompanied by a personal representative of the Lord Mayor of London.[3] En route to Guild

Hall, which is in the old quarter of London City, the President passed through streets that were literally jammed with cheering crowds. The buildings along the route were festooned with flags and the national ensigns of the United States and Great Britain were entwined everywhere. The great chimes of Westminster caroled the American and British national anthems as the procession moved on to Guild Hall. Every available inch of space in ancient Guild Hall was filled before the President arrived. The ancient costumes of the guards had been brought out and the whole affair was picturesque in the extreme.

The President was met at the entrance to Guild Hall by the Lord Mayor, and the High Sheriff,[4] in their robes and chains of office. In the robing ante-room, just previous to ascending the platform, the Lord Mayor presented to the President the Aldermen of the City of London. The arrangements for the function had been carried out to the most minute detail, even the dress which the spectators wore having been prescribed in the invitation which was sent out. Officers of the Army and Navy wore their uniforms and decorations, while civilians were restricted to afternoon dress with top hats and the ribbons of any orders which may have been conferred upon them.

The President's reception in Guild Hall was extremely friendly. The clerk of the Corporation of London[5] formally read the decree conferring upon him the freedom of and citizenship of the City, and he was afterwards given a copy beautifully embossed on parchment. The President made a feeling response in which he indicated for the first time that the friendliest of relations existed between Great Britain and the United States. The custom in Guild Hall is never to applaud an address but a precedent was established in this case. The Lord Mayor attempted to quiet the audience but it was impossible to hush the applause called forth by the President's speech. The address was praised by everyone.

On the left of President Wilson and the Lord Mayor were seated all the living former Lord Mayors, garbed in their robes of office. Under the British system they were not characterized as ex-Lord Mayors, but rather as "those who have passed the chair."

From Guild Hall the party proceeded to the home of the Lord Mayor of London, where a select company had been invited to be luncheon guests of the Lord Mayor and Lady Mayoress.[6] This luncheon also was extremely formal. The grand dining room in "Mansion House," the home of the Lord Mayor, was utilized for the function. Previous to the luncheon we had stopped for a few moments at the Lord Mayor's private residence. The President made another speech at the Mansion House function, in which he covered somewhat similar lines to that of his earlier effort.

In this speech the President gave the British an interesting light upon his personality. He called himself a Scot, but said he suspected that he had in his veins some of the Celt, for the reasons that at times he enjoyed certain "delightful periods of irresponsibility" that he could only attribute to Celtic origin. This made a hit with Lloyd George, who is himself Celtic.

Following the President's speech at the luncheon Viscount Morley said to me: "History will accord only two figures in this war— Wilson, the Statesman, and Foch, the Soldier." Former Premier Asquith, the Bishop of London,[7] and the Archbishop of Canterbury acquiesced in this declaration.

From Mansion House the President returned directly to Buckingham Palace, the same order of procession being observed as on the trip to Guild Hall.

This afternoon Lord Herschel said that the King wished to see me. I was escorted over to his suite, and he presented me with a handsome pair of diamond and platinum cuff links, bearing the royal coat of arms. On one link was a raised "G" in diamonds, and on the other a raised "M" also in diamonds—meaning Georges Majesty. Around the letters was inscribed the Garter motto: "Evil to him who evil thinketh." As we walked out into the hall-way, the King said: "I hope that you are comfortable and are receiving every attention." I assured him that I was not only most comfortable but was the recipient of excellent attention. I further said: "The servant who had been especially detailed to look after my comfort is not only very attentive but accompanies me whenever I walk around Buckingham Palace; in fact, he is so attentive that I am beginning to wonder if he is not watching me." The King laughed.

That evening the President attended a formal stag dinner given by Lloyd George, leaving at 11:00 o'clock in the royal train for Carlisle and the North, accompanied by the King's representatives, Sir Charles Cust and Lord Herschel. The King and Queen accompanied the President to the train.

[1] That is, Joseph Hodges Choate and Whitelaw Reid.
[2] Actually, Viscount Grey of Fallodon.
[3] Sir Horace Brooks Marshall was the Lord Mayor of London.
[4] He meant either Banister Flight Fletcher or Col. William Robert Smith, M.D., both of whom held the title of Sheriff of the City of London and were mentioned in newspaper accounts of the affair as being present. The High Sheriff of the County of London was Frederick Huth Jackson.
[5] Sir James Bell, Town Clerk of London.
[6] Laura Siggs Marshall.
[7] The Rt. Rev. Arthur Foley Winnington-Ingram.

Remarks in London to Free Church Leaders[1]

December 28, 1918.

Gentlemen: I am very much honored, and might say, touched, by this beautiful address that you have just read, and it is very delightful to feel the comradeship of spirit which is indicated by a gathering like this.

You are quite right, Sir, in saying that I do recognize the sanctions of religion in these times of perplexity with matters so large to settle that no man can feel that his mind can compass them. I think one would go crazy if he did not believe in Providence. It would be a maze without a clue. Unless there were some supreme guidance we would despair of the results of human counsel. So that it is with genuine sympathy that I acknowledge the spirit and thank you for the generosity of your address.

[1] Sir Robert William Perks, lawyer, former M.P., and a well-known Methodist lay leader, introduced a delegation from the National Council of the Evangelical Free Churches to Wilson at the American embassy. The Rev. Dr. Frederick Brotherton Meyer, pastor of Christ Church (Baptist), Westminster Bridge Road, London, and a leader in many international evangelical movements, read an address of welcome. The London *Times*, December 30, 1918, did not indicate the nature of Perk's and Meyer's remarks, but R. W. Perks to WW, December 28, 1918, ALS (WP, DLC), indicates that they expressed strong support for a league of nations and were also especially concerned about "the rescue of the Armenian Christians."

Remarks to the League of Nations Union[1]

December 28, 1918.

Gentlemen: I am very much complimented that you should come in person to present this address, and I have been delighted and stimulated to find the growing and prevailing interest in the subject of the league of nations, not only a growing interest merely, but a growing purpose which I am sure will prevail. And it is very delightful that members of the government which brought this nation into the war because of the moral obligations based upon treaty should be among those who have brought me this paper, because on the other side of the water we have greatly admired the motives and subscribed to the principles which actuated the government of Great Britain. In obeying that moral dictate you have shown what we must organize, namely, that same force and sense of obligation, and unless we organize it the thing that we do now will not stand. I feel that so strongly that it is particularly cheering to know just how strong and imperative the idea has become.

I thank you very much indeed. It has been a privilege to see you personally.

I was just saying to Lord Grey that we had indirect knowledge of each other and that I am glad to identify him. I feel as if I met him long ago; and I had the pleasure of matching minds with Mr. Asquith yesterday.

[1] The deputation from the League of Nations Union which called upon Wilson at the American embassy consisted of Viscount Grey of Fallodon; the Archbishop of Canterbury; Viscount Bryce; Thomas Shaw, Baron Shaw of Dunfermline, a Lord of Appeal; Herbert Asquith; Sir Willoughby Hyett Dickinson; and George Gilbert Aimé Murray, Regius Professor of Greek at Oxford. Lord Grey, the Archbishop, and Asquith spoke briefly. Their remarks are printed in the London *Times*, Dec. 30, 1918.

An Address at Guildhall

December 28, 1918.

Mr. Lord Mayor: We have come upon times when ceremonies like this have a new significance, and it is that signficance which most impresses me as I stand here. The address which I have just heard[1] is most generously and graciously conceived and the delightful accent of sincerity in it seems like a part of that voice of counsel which is now everywhere to be heard.

I feel that a distinguished honor has been conferred upon me by this reception, and I beg to assure you, Sir, and your associates of my very profound appreciation, but I know that I am only part of what I may call a great body of circumstances. I do not believe that it was fancy on my part that I heard in the voice of welcome uttered in the streets of this great city and in the streets of Paris something more than a personal welcome. It seemed to me that I heard the voice of one people speaking to another people, and it was a voice in which one could distinguish a singular combination of emotions. There was surely there the deep gratefulness that the fighting was over. There was the pride that the fighting had had such a culmination. There was that sort of gratitude that the nations engaged had produced such men as the soldiers of Great Britain and of the United States and of France and of Italy—men whose prowess and achievements they had witnessed with rising admiration as they moved from culmination to culmination. But there was something more in it—the consciousness that the business is not yet done, the consciousness that it now rests upon others to see that those lives were not lost in vain.

I have not yet been to the actual battlefields, but I have been with many of the men who have fought the battles, and the other day I had the pleasure of being present at a session of the French Academy when they admitted Marshal Joffre to their membership. That sturdy, serene soldier stood and uttered, not the words of triumph, but the simple words of affection for his soldiers, and the conviction which he summed up, in a sentence which I will not try accurately to quote but reproduce in its spirit, was that France must always remember that the small and the weak could never live free in the world unless the strong and the great always put their power and strength in the service of right. That is the after-thought—the thought that something must be done now not only to make the just settlements, that of course, but to see that the settlements remained and were observed and that honor and justice prevailed in the world. And as I have conversed with the soldiers, I have been more and more aware that they fought for something that not all of them had defined, but which all of them recognized the moment you stated it to them. They fought to do away with an old order and to establish a new one, and the center and charac-teristic of the old order was that unstable thing which we used to call the "balance of power"—a thing in which the balance was determined by the sword which was thrown in the one side or the other; a balance which was determined by the unstable equilibrium of competitive interests; a balance which was maintained by jealous watchfulness and an antagonism of interests which, though it was generally latent, was always deep-seated. The men who have fought in this war have been the men from free nations who were deter-mined that that sort of thing should end now and forever.

It is very interesting to me to observe how from every quarter, from every sort of mind, from every concert of counsel, there comes the suggestion that there must now be, not a balance of power, not one powerful group of nations set off against another, but a single overwhelming, powerful group of nations who shall be the trustee of the peace of the world. It has been delightful in my conferences with the leaders of your government to find how our minds moved along exactly the same line, and how our thought was always that the key to the peace was the guarantee of the peace, not the items of it; that the items would be worthless unless there stood back of them a permanent concert of power for their maintenance. That is the most reassuring thing that has ever happened in the world. When this war began, the thought of a league of nations was in-dulgently considered as the interesting thought of closeted stu-dents. It was thought of as one of those things that it was right to characterize by a name which as a university man I have always resented; it was said to be academic, as if that in itself were a condemnation, something that men could think about but never get. Now we find the practical leading minds of the world deter-mined to get it. No such sudden and potent union of purpose has ever been witnessed in the world before. Do you wonder, therefore, gentlemen, that in common with those who represent you I am eager to get at the business and write the sentences down; and that I am particularly happy that the ground is cleared and the foundations laid—for we have already accepted the same body of principles? Those principles are clearly and definitely enough stated to make their application a matter which should afford no fundamental difficulty. And back of us is that imperative yearning of the world to have all disturbing questions quieted, to have all threats against peace silenced, to have just men everywhere come together for a common object. The peoples of the world want peace and they want it now, not merely by conquest of arms but by agreement of mind.

It was this incomparably great object that brought me overseas. It has never before been deemed excusable for a President of the United States to leave the territory of the United States; but I know that I have the support of the judgment of my colleagues in the Government of the United States in saying that it was my paramount duty to turn away even from the imperative tasks at home to lend such counsel and aid as I could to this great, may I not say, final enterprise of humanity.[2]

[1] The address of greeting read by Sir Forrest Fulton, the Recorder of the City of London. A TC of these remarks is in WP, DLC.
[2] There is a WWsh outline and a typed "analysis" of this speech in WP, DLC.

An Address at Mansion House

December 28, 1918.

Mr. Lord Mayor, Your Royal Highness,[1] Your Grace,[2] ladies and gentlemen: You have again made me feel, Sir, the very wonderful and generous welcome of this great city, and you have reminded me of what has perhaps become one of the habits of my life. You have said that I have broken all precedents in coming across the ocean to join in the counsels of the peace conference, but I think those who have been associated with me in Washington will testify that that is nothing surprising. I said to members of the press in Washington one evening that one of the things that had interested me most since I lived in Washington was that every time I did anything perfectly natural it was said to be unprecedented. It was perfectly natural to break this precedent, natural because the demand for intimate conference took precedence over every other duty. And, after all, breaking of precedents, though this may sound strange doctrine in England, is the most sensible thing to do. The

harness of precedent is sometimes a very sad and harassing trammel. In this case, the breaking of precedent is sensible for a reason
that is very prettily illustrated in a remark attributed to Charles
Lamb. One evening in a company of his friends they were discussing a person who was not present, and Lamb said, in his hes-
itating manner, "I h-hate that fellow." "Why, Charles," one of his
friends said, "I didn't know that you knew him." "Oh," he said, "I-
I-I-d-don't; I c-can't h-hate a man I-I-I know." And perhaps that
simple and attractive remark may furnish a secret for cordial international relationship. When we know one another we can not
hate one another.

I have been very much interested before coming here to see what
sort of person I was expected to be. So far as I can make it out, I
was expected to be a perfectly bloodless thinking machine; whereas,
I am perfectly aware that I have in me all the insurgent elements
of the human race. I am sometimes by reason of long Scotch tradition able to keep those instincts in restraint. The stern Covenanter
tradition that is behind me sends many an echo down the years.

It is not only diligently to pursue business but also to seek this
sort of comradeship that I feel it a privilege to have come across
the seas, and in the welcome that you have accorded Mrs. Wilson
and me you have made us feel that that companionship was accessible to us in the most delightful and enjoyable form. I thank
you sincerely for this welcome, Sir, and am very happy to join in
a love feast which is all the more enjoyable because there is behind
it a background of tragical suffering. Our spirits are released from
the darkness of clouds that at one time seemed to have settled upon
the world in a way that could not be dispersed—the suffering of
your own people, the suffering of the people of France, the infinite
suffering of the people of Belgium. The whisper of grief that has
blown all through the world is now silent, and the sun of hope
seems to spread its rays and to change the earth with a new prospect
of happiness. So our joy is all the more elevated because we know
that our spirits are lifted out of that valley.

Printed in *Addresses of President Wilson on First Trip* . . .
   [1] The Duke of Connaught.
   [2] The Archbishop of Canterbury.

From the Trades Union Congress Parliamentary Committee and the Executive Committee of the Labour Party

Sir,   [London, Dec. 28, 1918]

In the name of the British Trades Union Congress and the British Labour Party, representing nearly five million organised workers, we wish to join in the general welcome offered to you on your arrival in Europe. As the elected leader of the American people, bred in the same democratic traditions as ourselves, and sharing the same ideals of freedom and peace, you have spoken in the greatest of wars in the name of the silent masses of humanity, and have guided the mighty energies of your Republic in the effort to win for these masses a safer and a happier future. By your courageous and far-sighted statesmanship you have drawn to your side the forces of organised democracy in the countries which, in the war against militarist Imperialism, have been associated with your own. Your utterances have given to the world conflict the character of a war of liberation, not only for Belgium, but also for the oppressed and driven peoples of Central and Eastern Europe. In speeches and messages elucidating your policy during the war you have formulated principles to which we have given our whole-hearted assent, and to which we sought to give effect in the decisions of the Inter-Allied Labour and Socialist Conferences, as embodied in our own Memorandum on War Aims.

You have clarified the vision and fortified the will of the organised democracy of Europe by interpreting and applying with consummate mastery the principles of democratic diplomacy in which we believe. Secret diplomacy has brought European nations near to ruin. By the adoption of methods of candour and open dealing in your relations with both the Allied and enemy Governments, you have shown to Governments and peoples a more excellent way.

Your own resolute advocacy has brought the great project of the League of Nations to the point of realisation.

Organised democracy now turns with renewed hope and energy to building upon the ruins of European Imperialism a real fellowship of peoples. We share with you the belief that only within the League of Nations can the sundered peoples be reconciled.

We desire to assure you that your efforts at the Peace Congress to give effect to the principles you have formulated will receive the support of the organised men and women for whom we speak.

In the deliberations of the Peace Congress we are assured that all nations which seek freedom, and which desire to tread the path of peace, will find in you a firm and wise friend and counsellor, and that the final settlement of the war in which they have all poured out their blood and treasure will be determined by an even-handed justice.

Printed in The Trades Union Parliamentary Committee, *Thirty-Second Quarterly Report, March 1919* (London, 1919), p. 46.

From Robert Lansing

My dear Mr. President:　　　　　　　Paris. 28th December, 1918.

The Tacna-Arica controversy between Chile and Peru is bound to be a vexatious one, and the enclosed telegram[1] setting forth a Bolivian solution makes it even more complex because there is a measure of justice and reason in the Bolivian desire for a seaport and for territory separating the rivals, Chile and Peru. I doubt very much, however, whether any influential or considerable number of public men in either country would favor the Bolivian suggestion. Bolivia would have to rely upon the United States to obtain such a cession. The general principle for such settlement is one which we have declared, but to obtain it I fear we would gain the dislike of both Chile and Peru.

Meanwhile we are being asked about an arbitration, what sort we prefer and whether the tribunal should have an American on it. The decision of the tribunal, however just, will be resented by one party at least. The whole situation is charged with trouble which it will be hard to avoid.

My own opinion in regard to this telegram is that, because of your absence from Washington, it would appear to be an inopportune time to send a delegation from Bolivia to the United States, but that, in view of the possibility of questions arising as to the general organization of the world in connection with the Peace Conference, it might be well to send two or three delegates to Paris, who could, while watching the course of events, informally discuss the Arica matter with you. I do not think the question should come before the Peace Conference.

Will you be good enough to tell me your wishes in the matter so that I can advise Mr. Polk?[2]

Faithfully yours,　　Robert Lansing

TLS (SDR, RG 59, 723.2515/2, DNA).
[1] FLP to RL, Dec. 13, 1918, T telegram (SDR, RG 59, 723.2515/2, DNA). Polk informed Lansing that the Bolivian government intended to send a special delegation to Washington to present Bolivia's case for the acquisition of a port on the Pacific Coast. According to the Bolivian Foreign Minister, a considerable body of opinion in both Chile and Peru was in favor of the cession of the province of Arica to Bolivia. Moreover, with

Bolivian territory placed between Chile and Peru, the vexatious Tacna-Arica question would be solved, and peace in South America would be made more secure. The Bolivian Foreign Minister stated that his government was eager to have the United States take the initiative in the settlement of the problem by making specific suggestions to Chile, Peru, and Bolivia, by calling and presiding over a conference of the countries involved, or by any other appropriate method. In the event that nations which had not actually participated in the war were admitted to the Paris Peace Conference, Bolivia intended to present its case at the conference, unless the United States, in the meantime, had taken steps toward a settlement. Polk requested Wilson's opinion as to whether the United States should signify a willingness to receive a special Bolivian delegation at Washington and whether the question of Bolivia's desire for a port would be taken up at the peace conference.

[2] See WW to RL, Jan. 9, 1919 (second letter of that date).

From the Diary of Dr. Grayson

Sunday, December 29, 1919 [1918].

The President woke up while the train was lying on a siding in the outskirts of Carlisle. It had been raining very hard through the night and it was a very dark, damp morning. The President's trip to Carlisle was entirely unofficial—simply that of a son paying a visit to the girlhood home of his mother, and to the place where his grandfather, the Reverend Thomas Woodrow, had served as a minister of the gospel. Because of this fact the President had emphasized to the British authorities that he desired to make his visit as democratic as possible, although he had consented to the town authorities arranging a general program for him, which was designed to receive him entirely as a private citizen instead of as the chief of a great nation.

Following breakfast on the train, the journey into Carlisle City was resumed. At the Carlisle station the President was greeted by the Lord Mayor of Carlisle[1] and all of the city officials. There were happy introductions and Mrs. Wilson was presented with a magnificent bouquet of flowers. Carriages were then entered and the party proceeded to the Crown and Mitre Hotel, where a public reception had been arranged. Here the President met and shook hands with all of the leading citizens of the town, the town councilmen and others, and he also met a number of distant relatives. The President was shown several old documents concerning his grandfather and his mother, and several letters written by the Reverend Thomas Woodrow himself.

One very interesting episode was his introduction to the oldest inhabitant, Thomas Watson, ninety years of age, who had been a member of the Sunday School class which the Reverend Thomas Woodrow taught in his life-time. The President asked the old man

[1] Bertram Carr.

whether he remembered his (the President's) grandfather. The old gentleman said that he did very dimly, but did not take advantage of the opportunity offered to indulge in reminiscences of his boyhood. The President posed for a picture with the old man, which brought about a little amusing incident. The photographer set off a flash light, which startled him, and he turned and clutched the President by the arm. Then apparently realizing what it had meant, he whispered in the President's ear and the President nodded, and then told the Photographers to take another flash. It developed later that the old man had said to the President: "Can't we take another; I am sure I blinked that time, and the picture won't be good, and I want a good picture in your honor."

Despite the fact that it was pouring rain outside, the President and Mrs. Wilson, accompanied by myself and other members of the party, entered the carriages and drove through the city to the house in which the President's mother was born. It was a little brick house, of solid construction, in the very heart of a solid block, and distinguishable from those on either side only because of the presence there of crossed American and British flags. The President alighted at the house and entered only to find that two or three of the people living there were ill with a touch of influenza. He passed into the room, however, in which his mother was born, and after stopping a few moments, and shaking hands with the occupants, returned to the carriage and proceeded to the church from the pulpit of which his grandfather had formerly preached. The entire church was crowded, and at the conclusion of the regular service, the President was invited to make a brief address, which he did, paying a wonderful tribute to his mother and to the mothers of men generally. The President was reminded that when he visited Carlisle before, he did so incognito on a bicycle. He walked into the church and being unknown and dressed in bicycle costume, he was regarded with some suspicion and notwithstanding the fact that he himself was a Presbyterian elder, he was given a seat in some far-off corner of the church. The President said the contrast between the two visits was "quite noticeable." . . .

Leaving Carlisle we proceeded to Manchester, which we reached after dark that afternoon. The President was given a great reception in Manchester. Large crowds had gathered along the sides of the streets but were held back behind ropes by troops that had been sent into Manchester for that purpose from a big British camp nearby. The President was driven directly to the Manchester Town Hall, where he was the guest over-night of the Mayor.[2] This build-

[2] The Lord Mayor of Manchester was John Makeague, not McTeague.

ing was a typical old English structure. There were no elevators and the Lord Mayor's living quarters were on the top floor, which was reached after a rather trying climb up various flights of stairs.

Mrs. Wilson said to the Lady Mayoress:[3] "I did not catch your name." The Lady Mayoress replied: "*Me* name is McTeague, but now they call me the Lady Mayoress." And then she said: "We came into office just three weeks ago."

The first caller to see the President was Mr. Scott,[4] Editor of the Manchester GUARDIAN. He had a conference with the President which lasted nearly an hour. Mr. Scott was the successor of Gladstone as the leader of British Liberalism, and his editorials were considered the most trenchant of any printed in a British publication. He was very proud of the fact that his individuality marked his paper, and although the Liberal Party has been exterminated in the recent Parliament elections, Scott showed no sign of downheartedness; in fact, he declared that Liberalism would be re-born before very long. Mr. Scott and the President measured each other up, and both enjoyed the meeting very much. As Scott, who is a very elderly man and had been associated with all of the great British leaders for many years, was leaving the room he turned to me and said: "This has been a particularly pleasing meeting for me; I think the President is the greatest man in the world; he is the greatest man I have ever met."

Mr. [Robert] Peacock, the Chief Constable of Manchester, arrived after Mr. Scott to confer with me regarding the arrangements for the morrow. Mr. Peacock, although his title was only that of Chief Constable, was fearfully and wonderfully attired. He wore black trousers, with a two-inch wide stripe of silver braid down each leg, a blue coat trimmed with gold and silver lace, and carried a Napoleonic cocked hat, adorned with a long white ostrich plume. Mr. Peacock apparently loved to dine well, being extremely rotund, with a very red face and nose. His clothes apparently had been made when he first assumed office, before he commenced his round of wining and dining, and it looked as though a lively sneeze from him might have resulted in a tragedy. Incidentally, however, Peacock proved one of the most efficient officials that we met anywhere on our tour. He had charge of the arrangements for the parade and in the halls, and he carried out all of these arrangements in a systematic manner, which saved us any inconvenience whatever.

After Mr. Scott and Mr. Peacock left we were entertained at dinner in the family apartments of the Lord Mayor and the Lady

---

[3] The Editors have been unable to discover her names.
[4] That is, Charles Prestwich Scott.

Mayoress. The dinner was rather a unique affair. It was held in what in normal times is the state dining-room of Manchester City. The large table had room for more than sixty guests. At the head of the table the Lord Mayor sat in his state chair. The President was on his right; then came the Lady Mayoress, with her gold chain of office hanging around her neck; I sat to the right of the Lady Mayoress; to the left of the Lord Mayor, Mrs. Wilson was placed, and adjoining her was the Town Clerk of Manchester[5]—another picturesque character—and then came Miss Benham and Sir Charles Cust. The Town Clerk was the real Major Domo of the Manchester government. He had held office for many years and was familiar with all customs, while Lord Mayors came and went annually. The result was that whenever the President addressed a question to the Lord Mayor the latter would turn to the Town Clerk, repeat it, and then say: "How about that, Mr. Town Clerk?" And the response would always be immediate and illuminating. The Town Clerk was an undersized man, rather thin, but his robes of state were elaborate in the extreme, while he wore a closely curled gray wig, with a long cue tied with ribbon—the whole well-powdered. He had a short cropped gray beard, which he would pull whenever a question was directly addressed to him. Although much smaller in stature than Chief Constable Peacock, it was apparent that the Clerk, like the Constable, enjoyed good living. . . .

During the dinner and afterward conversation was general and the President related a number of good stories, which were appreciated by the company. When the conversation veered to the general policies of the governments at war, the President said that he had been much impressed by what Marshal Foch had told him regarding conditions in Germany, and especially the manner in which the German Government had kept the German people from any knowledge as to the barbarous acts of the Army. The German people, Foch told the President, as a whole, knew practically nothing of the general atrocities. This was due to the fact that the German control of the press was absolute. The President said that Foch told him when he got into Germany he had found that there was no real feeling of enmity or bitterness on the part of the German people toward the French soldiers. The conversation then veered over to Mexico and the situation that had been encountered by the United States there. The President explained his Mexican policy as a general policy of allowing nations to be the judges of their own internal affairs, and to settle their internal affairs in a way that would be satisfactory to the great majority. We then left the dining room,

[5] Thomas Hudson.

and as we passed out the Lord Mayor, who had proven a most attentive listener, said to me: "This is a great man. The people of England and of France are for him. But the politicians—No! No!"— and he shook his head—"but they are afraid of him."

Remarks in His Grandfather's Church in Carlisle

December 29, 1918

It is with unaffected reluctance that I project myself into this solemn service. I remember my grandfather very well, and, re- membering him as I do, I am confident that he would not approve of it. I remember how much he required. I remember the stern lessons of duty he spoke to me. I remember also, painfully, the things which he expected me to know which I did not know. I know there has come a change of times when a layman like myself is permitted to speak in a congregation. But I was reluctant because the feelings that have been excited in me are too intimate and too deep to permit of public expression. The memories that have come to me today of the mother who was born here are very affecting, and her quiet character, her sense of duty and dislike of ostentation, have come back to me with increasing force as those years of duty have accumulated. Yet perhaps it is appropriate that in a place of worship I should acknowledge my indebtedness to her and to her remarkable father, because, after all, what the world is now seeking to do is to return to the paths of duty, to turn away from the savagery of interest to the dignity of the performance of right. And I believe that as this war has drawn the nations temporarily together in a combination of physical force we shall now be drawn together in a combination of moral force that will be irresistible.

It is moral force that is irresistible. It is moral force as much as physical that has defeated the effort to subdue the world. Words have cut as deep as the sword. The knowledge that wrong was being attempted has aroused the nations. They have gone out like men upon a crusade. No other cause could have drawn so many nations together. They knew that an outlaw was abroad who pur- posed unspeakable things. It is from quiet places like this all over the world that the forces accumulate which presently will overbear any attempt to accomplish evil on a large scale. Like the rivulets gathering into the river and the river into the seas, there come from communities like this streams that fertilize the consciences of men, and it is the conscience of the world that we are trying to place upon the throne which others would usurp.

T MS (WP, DLC).

From Joseph Patrick Tumulty

[The White House] December 29, 1918

New York World in article by Seibold intimates you discussed Home Rule with Lloyd George.[1] If this is so, could not tip be diplomatically passed out to [other] correspondents? Country deeply interested in the matter. Vitally important from many standpoints. Am advised Postmaster General and Kitchin intend fighting zone provision revenue bill[2] which passed Senate last week. Can't you intimate to Burleson that opposition to zone provision has not your approval? It will be most salutary to let country know that you are fighting in stating (?) [Kitchin][3] on some big thing like this.

Have you heard from Williams on suffrage? Important to know. Everything fine here. Nothing to worry about.   Tumulty

T MS (WP, DLC).

[1] Louis Seibold, "British Plans Revealed to the President . . . ," New York World, Dec. 28, 1918. Seibold's single sentence on the subject of Ireland reads as follows: "There is reason to believe, but no positive information, that the President at the first conference with Minister Balfour and Premier Lloyd George voiced the widespread American sentiment in favor of a satisfactory solution to the Irish question."

[2] As approved by the Senate on December 23, the revenue bill (H.R. 12863) contained a provision which repealed the zone rates on second-class mail included in the Revenue Act of 1917 (about the zone rates see WGM to WW, Sept. 25, 1917, n. 1, Vol. 44) and substituted a flat rate of 1 cent a pound for distances less than 150 miles and 1½ cents a pound for any distance over 150 miles. This substitution had the effect of lowering the rates for second-class mail substantially to what they had been before the passage of the Act of 1917 and thus would have considerably increased the annual deficit of the Post Office Department. Neither Burleson nor Kitchin seems ever to have made public their position on the proposed revision of the second-class rates. However, since Burleson had been the chief instigator of the zone system of 1917, it seems likely that he opposed the revision and wished to preserve the scheme established in 1917. The revision of rates for second-class mail was deleted from the new revenue bill before its final passage in February 1919, thus leaving intact the provisions included in the Act of 1917. For an extensive discussion of second-class mail rates and the significance of the proposed revision, see the Senate debate of December 19, 1918, Cong. Record, 65th Cong., 3d sess., pp. 648-67.

[3] As has been said before, corrections, additions, etc., in square brackets in telegrams between Wilson and Tumulty from the "telegrams sent" in the Wilson and Tumulty Papers.

From Herbert Henry Asquith

Dear Mr President   Sutton Courtney, Berks. 29 Dec 1918

Like yourself, I have always been a University man, and I venture to ask your acceptance before you leave England of a few purely 'academic' discourses which I have recently collected into a volume.[1]   Very sincerely yours   H. H. Asquith

ALS (WP, DLC).

[1] Herbert Henry Asquith, Occasional Addresses, 1893-1916 (London, 1918). This volume is in the Wilson Library, DLC.

From Lord Rothschild[1]

Mr President   Tring Park Dec. 29th 1918

In the name of the English Zionists I wish to offer you our most grateful thanks for the very benevolent attitude you have shown towards Zionist aspirations. The great majority of the Jews of the World must be forever grateful to you, Sir, & the great American people for your sympathy and promises of help.

If the great desire of the Jews to reestablish a home in the land of our ancestors is attained after two thousand years of exile & suffering we shall largely owe it to the good will & help of yourself & the American nation.

We can never feel sufficiently grateful for the liberal treatment accorded to the Jews by America & Great Britain which contrasts so strongly with the oppression & ill treatment suffered by them in most other countries. The endorsement by you Sir & the great American people of the proposed resettlement in Palestine will increase our debt of gratitude a hundred fold. In thanking you, Sir, for what you have already done for the Zionist cause, may we hope that this cause, which is the ardent desire of some ten million Jews, will continue to receive your powerful support at the Peace Conference.

I venture also in my own name & that of all the Jews of the World to ask you, Sir to use your powerful influence to put an end to the terrible oppression & massacre being inflicted on the Jews in most countries of Eastern Europe. These awful outrages have been steadily increasing during the war & since the Armistice have been spreading far & wide.

I have the honour to be, Mr President
                    Your obedient servant   Rothschild

ALS (WP, DLC).
    [1] Lionel Walter Rothschild, 2nd Baron Rothschild.

From the Diary of Dr. Grayson

Monday, December 30, 1918.

The President was the guest of Manchester most of the day. Leaving the Town Hall at nine o'clock he was driven through the streets to the Manchester Ship Canal. En route the President had a first-hand view of the effects of child labor. Hundreds of stunted children, boys and girls, illy clad and under-nourished, lined the streets to see him. The route took in a good bit of the poorer section of Manchester and the entire people thus seen were for the most

part plainly suffering from under-nourishment. It was a rather piti-
able sight.

The President boarded a White Star tender and was taken several
miles down the Manchester Ship Canal in order to witness this
great triumph of engineering. The canal is deep enough to allow
ocean ships to proceed directly to the docks in Manchester. It connects Liverpool with Manchester and has reduced costs very materially, inasmuch as cotton-laden vessels can load directly from
Galveston and other American ports and discharge into the mills
here without transfer at Liverpool. Passing down the Canal the
President had a view of a captured German submarine, on which
the American and British flags flew above that of the Imperial
German Navy. He also saw the Hydrebad, a decoy vessel which
had been used with great success to combat the submarine. Out-
wardly the ship presented the appearance of an ordinary ocean
tramp, dingy and dirty, and with no distinguishing characteristics.
When the tender came directly abreast a whistle sounded on the
vessel; her sides dropped down, revealing gun crews at their posts,
with guns ready to sink any submarine that might be seen. Officials
of the port explained that until the Germans finally learned of this
method a large number of their best submarines had been destroyed
by decoy ships of this character.

Returning to Manchester the President was escorted through the
streets back to the Town Hall, where he changed his attire, and
then proceeded to the Free Trade Hall where he delivered his chief
address of the day. It was a remarkable coincidence that the President declared in this speech that "America is not interested in
European politics but is interested in the partnership of right between America and Europe." He also declared against any combination of powers which was not a combination of all nations. This
was accepted as a direct reply to the previous day's address of
Premier Clemenceau,[1] although the President had not previously
been apprised of what Clemenceau had said.

---

[1] Clemenceau had addressed the Chamber of Deputies in the late evening of December
29 in response to criticism from the Socialists that he had not divulged his program for
the peace conference. Clemenceau began by saying that he saw no reason to rush to
the rostrum to make a speech about peace plans merely because Lloyd George had
recently done so and because Wilson had arrived from America with "magnificent ideas."
He explained the basic principle of his foreign policy in the following paragraph: "Do
not forget that France is in a peculiarly difficult situation. She is the nearest country
to Germany. America is far off, and naturally took some time to come to us. Great Britain
came at once at the call of Mr. Asquith. . . . During all this time it is we who have
suffered; it was our men who were mown down; our towns and villages that were
devastated. It has been said, 'This must not occur again.' Quite so; but how? There is
an old system which appears to be discredited today, but to which I am not afraid of
saying I am still faithful. Countries have organized solidly defended frontiers with the
necessary armaments and the balance of Powers. . . . Here in this system of alliance,

When the President entered Free [Trade] Hall every inch of space in the buiding was filled. As he settled back in his seat the Lord Mayor arose to call the assemblage to order. Simultaneously and apparently without any pre-arrangement the audience struck up— "For he is a jolly good fellow." Everyone in the building joined in the singing, while the President smiled, plainly very happy, at the unexpected and spontaneous tribute. It developed afterwards that this was in no way a part of the program. It was as much a surprise to the Lord Mayor and the committee in charge as it was to the President and ourselves.

From Free Trade Hall the party passed, escorted by soldiers and police, to the Royal Exchange, where the President entered the visitors gallery and looked down upon the Stock Exchange in operation. From the Exchange he proceeded to the Midland Hotel, where he was the guest of honor at a public luncheon given by the

---

which I do not give up, is the thought which will guide me in the conference, if your confidence allows me to be present at it. There must be nothing which can separate in the period after the war the four Great Powers whom the war has united. I shall make every sacrifice to maintain that Entente."

Clemenceau then made an indirect reference to proposals for international organization: "As to international guarantees, I say that if France is left free to organize her own military defence—for she does not wish to be invaded again—if she is mistress of her own military organizations, I shall accept any supplementary guarantees which may be given to me. I go further, and say that if those guarantees are such as will demand sacrifices in the way of military preparation, I shall accept those sacrifices with joy, because I do not wish to see my country suffer without necessity."

Clemenceau refused to give any specific details of his peace program: "Big and little peoples will come to the conference demanding justice, and if I were to sketch out the decision which may be expected from our debates, I should be the worst head of a Government in Europe. My chief concern has been to refrain from giving room for too much hope in order not to arouse the reaction of too much disappointment."

Finally, Clemenceau commented upon his relations with Wilson. "People," he said, "have spoken of the visit President Wilson paid me. He did do me the honour of calling upon me. I made it a principle not to question him, and let him talk to me. He did so. He explained his views, his reasons, and his means of supporting them. It would be a lie if I said that I was in agreement with him upon all points. America is far away from Germany; France is quite close to it, and I have concerns which do not affect him so much as they do a man who has seen the Germans in his own country during four years. There are old wrongs to be righted. So you believe that we can right all those wrongs? I do not think so, because we are only human. . . . President Wilson, whom certain people with party interests credit with thoughts which are not his, has a wide, open, and lofty mind, and is a man who inspires respect by the frankness of his speech and by the high candour of his mind." As many commentators noted, both at the time and later, Clemenceau's phrase, "noble candeur," can be interpreted either as "noble candidness," "well-intentioned simplicity," or "noble naiveté." Clemenceau's use of the phrase evoked a storm of protests from the Socialist deputies. Charles Seymour, *Letters from the Paris Peace Conference*, ed., Harold B. Whiteman, Jr. (New Haven, Conn., 1965), p. 85.

All of the above quotations are from the lengthy extracts of Clemenceau's speech in English translation printed in the London *Times*, Dec. 31, 1918. A full text of the speech in French appears in *Journal Officiel de la République Française, Chambre des Députés, Débats Parlementaires, Session Ordinaire, 1918*, pp. 3732-34. For the background and context of the speech, see Mayer, *Politics and Diplomacy of Peacemaking*, pp. 170-87; also Arthur Walworth, *America's Moment: 1918; American Diplomacy at the End of World War I* (New York, 1977), pp. 153-55.

Manchester business men. The President's reception in Manchester was a very hearty one. Probably nowhere on his trip up to date had the personal element entered as largely into the welcome as it did here. This was commented on because of the century-old saying that "as Manchester thinks today, so all England will think a month from now." This quotation had been repeated to the President by Editor Scott of the Manchester GUARDIAN the night before, and it was again emphasized several times by the speakers at the luncheon and other public men who met the President.

The President had not expected to make any address whatever at the luncheon. When he was told that he would be expected to respond to the sentiments expressed thereat, he became somewhat nervous, as he always does before speaking. Finally, he leaned over to the Lord Mayor, who was sitting on his left, and asked him what he (the President) would speak about. The Lord Mayor in reply said to him: "As you are responsible for the unity of command of the military forces that won the war, it might be well to tell us something about that."

Manchester was left in the late afternoon and a speedy run made to London, which was reached at 7:15. The King and Queen again met us at the station and accompanied us to Buckingham Palace, where we dined informally with the King and Queen and about thirty guests, and spent the night.

Upon my arrival in the Palace I found my trusty retainer attired in his wonderful palace livery, waiting to look out for my comfort. And his attentions were fully as assiduous as on my previous visit.

Our entry into Buckingham Palace this night was as formal as only a British function can be. The King and Queen and the President and Mrs. Wilson preceded us, escorted by liveried wand-bearers and other palace attachés—lords and ladies-in-waiting, etc. As we passed through the public reception room and on up the steps, I was amazed to see over to the right of the entrance seated in front of a fire-place, in his stocking-feet, calmly toasting his toes at the open grate, my friend, Jesse H. Jones, of Houston, Texas. He had arrived in London that day and finding that we were expected back at the palace, he had come directly there and demanded to see me. He was told to take a seat and wait after he had "worked" his way into the building through a dozen guards of various character, all of whom subjected him to a severe interrogation as to who and what he was, and what his mission actually was. Jones, however, is a very plausible talker and he accomplished a task that very few had been able to do. Finding when he at last got inside that his feet were a trifle damp, he had removed his shoes and was drying his socks when the royal party escorting the President put in their appearance. He jumped to his feet, pushing his shoes behind him, and pulled his trousers down as far as possible in a frantic effort to hide the stockings. Meanwhile, he stood at attention facing the King and Queen and the President and Mrs. Wilson. It was rather fortunate for Mr. Jones that the attention of the President and Mrs. Wilson and the King and Queen was attracted elsewhere, and he was able to prevent any one noticing the fact that he was not in strict court attire. I went over and chatted with him and found that he was as much embarrassed as a Texan could be under the circumstances. I asked him what he was doing in his stocking-feet with the royal party about to put in an appearance, and he replied: "Well, it was the first fire I had been able to see in four or five days, and my feet were very cold, and I did not think these folks hereabouts would object to a man warming his feet when they were cold"—a typical Texas explanation. Jones accompanied me to my room after putting his shoes back on and inspected the quarters assigned to me very closely. Discovering some Buckingham Palace stationery with the King's crest on the envelope on a desk, he sat down and wrote a letter to a friend in Texas, which read as follows:

"Dear Fred:
Here I am.
Yours,
Jesse H. Jones."

At the dinner that night I had a place between Mrs. Waldorf Astor[2] and Lady Acheson.[3] Mrs. Waldorf Astor was a Miss Langhorne of Virginia. Lady Acheson was a Miss Mildred Carter of Virginia—a rather remarkable coincidence that three natives of the Old Dominion State should be found seated together at a dinner in a royal palace. Mrs. Astor did not know anything about my antecedents, although I knew all about her. After she had criticised to some extent certain American and British customs, I turned to her and quietly asked: "Don't you think this is rather a long jump from Albemarle County, Virginia, to Buckingham Palace; I realize it is a long jump from Culpeper here." She looked at me for a moment in apparent utter-amazement and then said: "Do you mean to say that you also are poor white trash from Albemarle?" Smilingly I replied: "Well, if you leave out the trash; I am poor all right." From that moment we were very good friends and enjoyed a delightful chat about people whom we knew in our native Virginia.

[2] That is, Nancy Witcher Langhorne Shaw (Mrs. Waldorf) Astor.
[3] Mildred Carter Acheson, Lady Acheson. Her husband was Archibald Charles Montagu Brabazon, Viscount Acheson.

A Luncheon Address in Manchester

December 30, 1918.

My Lord Mayor, ladies and gentlemen: You have again made me feel the cordiality of your friendship, and I want to tell you how much I appreciate it, not only on my own behalf but on behalf of my partner.

It is very interesting that the Lord Mayor should have referred in his address to a vital circumstance in our friendship. He referred to the fact that our men and your men had fought side by side in the great battles in France, but there was more than that in it. For the first time, upon such a scale at any rate, they fought under a common commander. That is the advance which we have made over previous times, and what I have been particularly interested in has been the generosity of spirit with which that unity of command has been assented to. I not only had the pleasure of meeting Marshal Foch, who confirmed my admiration of him by the direct and simple manner in which he dealt with every subject that we talked about, but I have also had the pleasure of meeting your own commanders, and I understand how they cooperated, because I saw that they were real men. It takes a real man to subordinate himself. It takes a real soldier to know that unity of command is the secret of success, and that unity of command did swing the power of the nations into a mighty force. I think we all must have felt the new momentum which got into all the armies so soon as they became a single army, and we felt that we had overcome one of the most serious obstacles in the strength of the enemy, that he had unity of command and could strike where he would with a common plan and we could not.

And with that unity of command there rose the unity of spirit. The minute we consented to cooperate our hearts were drawn together in the cooperation. So, from the military side we have given ourselves an example for the years to come; not that in the years to come we must submit to a unity of command, but it does seem to me that in the years to come we must plan a unity of purpose, and in that unity of purpose we shall find that great recompense, the strengthening of our spirits in everything that we do. There is nothing so hampering and nothing so demeaning as jealousy. It is a canker. It is a canker in the heart not only, but it is a canker in the counting room; it is a canker throughout all the processes of civilization. Having now seen that we can fight shoulder to shoulder, we will continue to advance shoulder to shoulder, and I think that you will find that the people of the United States are not the least eager of the parties.

I remember hearing a story of a warning which one of your Australian soldiers gave to one of ours. Our soldiers were considered by the older men a bit rash when they went in. I understand that even the Australians said that our men were a "bit rough," and on one occasion a friendly Australian said to one of our men, "Man, a barrage is not a thing meant to lean up against." They were a little bit inclined to lean up against the barrage, and yet I must confide to you that I was a bit proud of them for it. They had come over to get at the enemy, and they did not know why they should delay.

And now that there is no common enemy except distrust and marring of plans, we can all feel the same eagerness in the new comradeship, and can feel that there is a common enterprise for it. For, after all, though we boast of the material sides of our civilization, they are merely meant to support the spiritual side. We are not men because we have skill of hand, but we are men because we have elevation of spirit. It is in the spirit that we live and not in the task of the day. If it is not, why is it that you hang the lad's musket or his sword up above the mantlepiece and never hang his yardstick up? There is nothing discreditable in the yardstick. It is altogether honorable, but he is using it for his own sake. When he takes the musket or the sword, he is giving everything he has and getting nothing. It is honorable, not as an instrument of force, but as a symbol of self-sacrifice. A friend of mine said very truly that when peace is conducted in the spirit of war, there will be no war; when business is done with the point of view of the soldier, that he is serving his country, then business will be as histrionic as war. And I believe that from generation to generation conceptions of that sort are getting more and more currency and that men are beginning to see, not perhaps a golden age, but at any rate an age which is brightening from decade to decade and may lead us some time to an elevation from which we can see the things for which the heart of mankind has longed.

Printed in *Addresses of President Wilson on First Trip* . . .

An Address in Free Trade Hall

December 30, 1918.

My Lord Mayor, ladies and gentlemen—perhaps I may be permitted to add fellow citizens: You have made me feel in a way that is deeply delightful the generous welcome which you have accorded me. Back of it I know there lies the same sort of feeling for the great people whom I have the privilege of representing. There is a feeling of cordial fraternity and friendship between these two great nations, and as I have gone from place to place and been made everywhere to feel the pulse of sympathy that is now beating between us, I have been led to some very serious thoughts as to what the basis of it all is. For I think you will agree with me that friendship is not a mere sentiment. Patriotism is not a mere sentiment. It is based upon a principle—upon a principle that leads a man to give more than he demands. And, similarly, friendship is based not merely upon affection, but upon common service. A man is not your friend who is not willing to serve you, and you are not his friend unless you are willing to serve him, and out of that impulse of common interest and a desire of common service rises that noble feeling which we have consecrated as friendship.

So it has seemed to me that the theme that we must have in our minds now in this great day of settlement is the theme of common interest and the determination of what it is that is our common interest. You know that heretofore the world has been governed, or at any rate an attempt has been made to govern it, by partnerships of interest, and they have broken down. Interest does not bind men together. Interest separates men, for the moment there is the slightest departure from the nice adjustment of interests jealousies begin to spring up. There is only one thing that can bind peoples together, and that is a common devotion to right. Ever since the history of liberty began, men have talked about their rights, and it has taken several hundred years to make them perceive that the principal part of right is duty, and that unless a man performs his full duty he is entitled to no right. This fine correlation of the two things of duty and of right is the equipoise and balance of society. So when we analyze the present situation and the future that we now have to mold and control, it seems to me that there is no other thought than that that can guide us.

You know that the United States has always felt from the very beginning of her history that she must keep herself separate from any kind of connection with European politics, and I want to say very frankly to you that she is not now interested in European politics. But she is interested in the partnership of right between America and Europe. If the future had nothing for us but a new attempt to keep the world at a right poise by a balance of power, the United States would take no interest, because she will join no combination of power which is not the combination of all of us. She is not interested merely in the peace of Europe, but in the peace of the world. Therefore it seems to me that in the settlement that is just ahead of us something more delicate and difficult than was ever attempted before is to be accomplished–a genuine concert of mind and of purpose. But while it is difficult, there is an element present that makes it easy. Never before in the history of the world, I believe, has there been such a keen international consciousness as there is now. Men all over the world know that they have been embarrassed by national antagonisms and that the interest of each is the interest of all, and that men as men are the objects of government and international arrangements. There is a great voice of humanity abroad in the world just now which he who cannot hear is deaf. There is a great compulsion of the common conscience now in existence which if any statesman resist he has gained the most unenviable eminence in history. We are not obeying the mandates of parties or of politics. We are obeying the mandates of humanity. That is the reason why it seems to me that the things that are most often in our minds are the least significant. I am not hopeful that the individual items of the settlements which we are about to attempt will be altogether satisfactory. One has but to apply his mind to any one of the questions of boundary and of altered sovereignty and of racial aspiration to do something more than conjecture that there is no man and no body of men who know just how it ought to be settled. Yet if we are to make unsatisfactory settlements, we must see to it that they are rendered more and more satisfactory by the subsequent adjustments which are made possible.

So that we must provide a machinery of readjustment in order that we may have a machinery of good will and of friendship. Friendship must have a machinery. If I cannot correspond with you, if I cannot learn your mind, if I cannot cooperate with you, I cannot be your friend, and if the world is to remain a body of friends it must have the means of friendship, the means of constant friendly intercourse, the means of constant watchfulness over the common interest—not making it necessary to make a great effort upon some great occasion and confer with one another, but have an easy and constant method of conference, so that troubles may be taken when they are little and not allowed to grow until they are big. I never thought that I had a big difference with a man that I did not find when I came into conference with him that, after all, it was rather a little difference and that if we were frank with one another, and did not too much stand upon that great enemy of mankind which is called pride, we could come together. It is the wish to come together that is more than half of the process. This is a doctrine which ought to be easy of comprehension in a great commercial center like this. You cannot trade with men who suspect you. You cannot estabish commercial and industrial relations with those who do not trust you. Good will is the forerunner of trade, and trade is the great amicable instrument of the world on that account.

I feel—I felt before I came here—at home in Manchester, because Manchester has so many of the characteristics of our great American cities. I was reminded of the anecdote of a humorous fellow countryman who was sitting at lunch in his club one day and a man whom he did not like particularly came by and slapped him on the shoulder. "Hello, Ollie, old fellow, how are you?" he said. Ollie looked at him coldly and said, "I don't know your face; I don't know your name; but your manners are very familiar." I don't know your names, but your manners are very familiar. So that I feel that in the community of interest and of understanding which is established in great currents of trade, we are enabled to see international processes perhaps better than they can be seen by others. I take it that I am not far from right in supposing that that is the reason why Manchester has been a center of the great forward-looking sentiments of men who had the instinct of large planning, not merely for the city itself, but for the Kingdom and the Empire and the world, and with that outlook we can be sure that we can go shoulder and shoulder together.

I wish that it were possible for us to do something like some of my very stern ancestors did, for among my ancestors are those very determined persons who were known as the Covenanters. I wish we could, not only for Great Britain and the United States, but for France and Italy and the world, enter into a great league and covenant, declaring ourselves, first of all, friends of mankind and uniting ourselves together for the maintenance and the triumph of right.

Printed in *Addresses of President Wilson on First Trip . . .*

From Brand Whitlock

Dear Mr. President: Brussels. 30 December 1918

I should like to feel that somewhere in the mighty chorus that welcomes you to these shores you have detected the accent of our own pride in you, of our personal affections, and of our joy in your coming. Our joy is the deeper because we are to have the distinguished honour of receiving you in Brussels, where we are so happy to be again. The King sent for me the other afternoon and retained me for an hour telling me of the pleasure he was anticipating in your visit and of his gratitude for the moral benefit that will result to the Belgian people from your very presence among them. He is very simple, and quite democratic, and you have no greater admirer—excepting myself. He is eager, as he told me, to have Belgium profit by American experience, eager to have his land brought under this influence of Anglo-Saxon culture and ideals. And he repeated, what he has so often said to me, that it was a source of pride and consolation to him that he could find in you a great and good and disinterested friend for his country.

I must not burden you with a long letter, for I realise how precious your moments are, but the opinion of the King is shared by the whole people. Your portrait is in all the shop windows and in humble homes all over Belgium. The other afternoon when the two chambers did me the signal honour to receive me in joint session to express the gratitude of the nation for what they were pleased to call my services to the nation, there was as I addressed the assembly, a mighty demonstration in your honour; at the mention of your name the senators and deputies spontaneously sprang to their feet, and cheered as I have never heard men cheer. And this was repeated every time reference was made to your extraordinary services to humanity. Thus in love and gratitude the whole nation awaits your coming.

I have witnessed many pageants in the Grand Place here; I have seen Kings and envoys go there in state, and I saw the city humiliated then by the presence of invading German hordes. But when in the traditional historic ceremony by which the city receives its distinguished guests, you are acclaimed there, it will be a moment which in its historic implications, will surpass all that the old guild houses have ever looked down upon. I can not think of it without a quicker heart beat, or without emotion reflecting [?] that it is our President who brings to the people of this poor, weary, cynical and disillusioned old Europe a hope they had almost feared any more to cherish.

We shall try to spare you all the fatigue possible, and, Sir, if you desire, there is a golf links to which perhaps, we might steal away for a round!

My wife[1] unites her compliments to my own, and we send you our fervent wishes for a Happy New Year in your household. Permit me to present my hommage to Mrs. Wilson, and to beg you to believe me, dear Mr. President,

Your most devoted and obedient servant

Brand Whitlock

ALS (WP, DLC).
[1] Ella Brainerd Whitlock.

From Grant Squires

My dear Mr. President   New York. December 30 1918

It seems strange to be addressing you elsewhere than at the White House, but you know how I felt about your going and I am only confirmed in my assurances to you of October last[1] in the success which seems to be attending your mission since your arrival on the other side of the Atlantic.

I am not unduly concerned about the activities of the elements of disorder in this city, but since you have gone I have been as watchful as my position would permit to observe what so-called advanced radicals are thinking and doing and saying; and I have taken the liberty of going to one dinner and meeting that they gave a fortnight ago suitably disguised in name and appearance and have had the result of that meeting written out and am enclosing to you herewith a copy of the report.[2] It was at this dinner that I heard Scott Nearing declare in the leading speech of the evening his hope that he would have the good fortune to address the same audience within the next five years with Bolshevik government replacing the present incompetent one at Washington as prevails to-day in Russia and as he hoped would prevail before many days longer in Germany. I am also enclosing a copy of some articles which appeared both as news and as editorial comment in the Novy Mir, the radical Russian daily paper published here in New York on December 18, and in the radical Hungarian paper on December 20 and in the ultra-socialist paper Neu Yorker Volkszeitung on December 21, in the Russian, Hungarian and German languages respectively.[3]

I am continuing to "cover" all these activities personally or by deputy as has been done during the past six months and will keep you advised if it seems important to do so.

Please let me know if this letter reaches you without delay or intervention.   Faithfully yours   Grant Squires

TLS (WP, DLC).
[1] See G. Squires to WW, Nov. 9, 1918, n. 2.
[2] Capt. John B. Trevor, U.S.A., to Director of Military Intelligence, Dec. 16, 1918, CCL (WP, DLC).
[3] CC MS (WP, DLC). All of the materials are translations from Novy Mir, Dec. 19 (not 18), 1918. With one minor exception, all are concerned about G. V. Chicherin to WW, Oct. 29 and Nov. 2, 1918, printed in Vol. 51. The full text of that telegram was included among the materials which Squires sent to Wilson.

Frank Lyon Polk to Robert Lansing

Washington, December 30, 1918.

Urgent. 37. Confidential. For Ammission and to repeat to London.

In connection with negotiations regarding Siberian Railways, the Japanese Ambassador has just handed me the following memorandum: "In their declaration of August 2, 1918,[1] the Japanese Government made it clear the primary object which they had in view in undertaking military expedition to Siberia was to relieve the critical situation of the Czecho-Slovak troops in that region, due to the pressure of the German and Austro-Hungarian armed prisoners, and of the Bolshevic forces under Teutonic influence and command. Soon after the advance of Japanese detachments to Trans Baikalia, coupled with the operations conducted by the Allied forces in the Ussuri and Amur districts, the Czecho-Slovaks who had been isolated in the interior of Siberia succeeded in reestablishing communication with their comrades and the Allies in Vladivostok and elsewhere. The grave danger that had once threatened their existence has thus been averted and the primary object of the military activities undertaken by Japanese in Siberia in cooperation with the powers Associated against Germany has now been successfully achieved. At the same time the Japanese Government fully realize that the immediate and complete withdrawal of the Japanese or the Allied troops from Siberia at the present moment would be calculated to produce serious consequences, more especially as regards the maintenance of order and security in the localities in which those troops are now operating. Nor do they feel that the number of the Japanese troops so far maintained in the north of Manchuria and eastern Siberia is wholly unwarranted by any necessity, as was remarked by Mr. Lansing, in his conversation with Viscount Ishii on November 16th. They are, however, quite ready to re-examine the Siberian situation in the light of the changed circumstances and having regard to the expressed views of the American Government they have decided to effect as much reduction in number of the Japanese troops in Siberia as an absolute requirement for the preservation of public order in the localities will permit. Already thirteen thousand men of those troops had been withdrawn up to the end of November and it is now intended to proceed to a further withdrawal of thirty four thousand men in due course."

This memorandum should be considered also in connection with the following confidential telegrams received from Ambassador Morris, Tokyo, dated December 29, 4 PM.

"The formal announcement of the intended withdrawal of thirty four thousand troops from Siberia and Manchuria as report[ed][2] in my December 28th, 1 PM [a.m.],[3] and the concession made by the Japanese Government in regard to the proposed operation of the Siberian Railways as reported in my December 27th, 10 PM,[4] materially modified [marked the] conclusion of a month's period of discussion and controversy in Government circles here. As I view it, the results are far more satisfactory than I had dared to hope and indicate that Hara has not only succeeded in modifying Japan's Siberian policy, so that it seems to more nearly accord with the expressed views of our Government, but to have also won an initial victory over the reactionary forces on the General Staff. During the last three weeks Hara has kept me advised through Hishko [Kaneko][5] of the progress he was making, and a few days ago Hishko [Kaneko] felt justified in confidentially telling me that Hara's policy would prevail. This policy had four main objects: (First) to withdraw as many troops as possible and thus correct Terauduhi [Terauchi] 'blunder.' (Second) to abolish the independent military commands in Manchuria and Siberia, which had resulted in [friction] confiscation [and conflict] of authority, and to confer on Otani[6] full jurisdiction over the entire Japanese Military expedition. (Third) An agreement satisfactory to our Government for the operation of the Chinese Eastern and Trans Siberian Railways. (Fourth) To discontinue the subsidizing of Semenoff and Kalmikoff.[7] He greatly feared the effect of withdrawal on public opinion, but the formal announcement which appeared yesterday is an amazingly clever statement and appears to have been well received. The consolidation of Military authority has already been completed. Speaks of still [The Ministry still] having trouble with the General Staff on the question of Semenoff.

Your December 11, 6 PM[8] and December 6, [16][9] 6 PM,[10] have been of the greatest value.

Opportunities largely unsought have [been] offered, and during the past two weeks I have frankly and informally discussed the entire situation with Hara, ? [Gotō,] Uchida and Shiande Hara [Shidehara],[11] and also with several men not in office but who are influential in Government circles. I will summarize the impressions gathered from these discussions in a subsequent telegram. Makino[12] might speak unreservedly if given an opportunity during his stay in Washington. Recent advices from Harbin indicate that Stevens is not well and greatly impatient at the slow progress of the negotiations. The following telegram to me exhibits his state of mind, which is not surprising when one considers his experiences during the past year. 'I have returned to Harbin much disappointed in not meeting you. My position in the Shimoneck [personally unchanged] as to conditions [In] no way could I submit even to semblance of Japanese control. Japanese newspaper Harbin publishing most bitter attacks upon American motives in general.'

Trust he will not permit his quite justifiable irritation to influence his judgement aid [on the] new proposals of Japanese Government.["]

Under date of December 29, General Graves telegraphs as follows "General Romanoffski[13] has just informed me that he thinks the Russians will have to abandon to Family [Japanese], Siberia east of Baikal, as it is impossible for them to do anything against the Family [Japanese] powers now here: that Family [Japanese] will not permit them to use any force against Semenoff to arrest government railroad men and interfere with all their plans; that Russia will have to trust the United States to force Family [Japanese] to carry out honestly their agreements or the matter will have to be settled when Russia is under a stable government; that there is no use talking to Family [Japanese] as the Russians can put no dependence in what they tell him; that General Horvat, the other influential Russian in the East is vacillating and will take no decisive stand against the Family [Japanese].

Following from intelligence officer Verk[h]neudin[s]k this date: 'Representative of Semenoff arrived here last night with soldiers and machine guns, put all public officials under arrest and his own men in their places. Family [Japanese] withdrew guards which had been promised.' This supports Romanoffsky statement that Semenoff allowed to do as he pleases without interference."

Department believes that these three telegrams when read together summarize the present situation and that it only remains to be seen as to how far in practice the Hara Ministry will continue to prevail over the General Staff.   Polk.

T telegram (WP, DLC).
[1] About which, see FLP to WW, Aug. 3, 1918, n. 1 (first letter of that date), Vol. 49.
[2] Corrections in Morris' telegram from R. S. Morris to RL, Dec. 29, 1918, T telegram (SDR, RG 59, 861.00/3545, DNA).
[3] That is, the telegram just quoted by Polk.
[4] Printed in FR 1918, Russia, III, 301-303. It transmitted a modified plan for the supervision of the Trans-Siberian and the Chinese Eastern railways which Morris had been able to work out with Japanese officials in order to meet Stevens' objections to earlier proposals. This so-called Japanese plan placed the railways under the joint military protection of the Associated Powers in Siberia. The general supervision of the railways was entrusted to a committee composed of one representative each of the Associated Powers and headed by a Russian representative. In addition, the plan created a technical board, composed of railway experts of the Associated Powers, to administer the technical and economic management of the railways, and a military transportation board to coordinate the movement of troops and supplies. The technical board would elect a president, who would be in charge of the technical operation of the railways and select his staff from among the nationals of the Associated Powers. Although a Russian manager

was to remain at the head of each railway, in matters of technical operation the president was empowered to issue instructions to the Russian managers. According to an understanding between Morris and Japanese officials, Stevens was to be elected president of the technical board. The arrangement would cease upon the withdrawal of the troops of the Associated Powers from Siberia, and all foreign railway experts appointed under the agreement would be recalled at that time. Stevens agreed to the plan on January 9, 1919, and Ishii submitted it to the State Department on January 15, 1919. The United States formally accepted the Japanese railway plan on February 10, 1919. See also Unterberger, *America's Siberian Expedition*, pp. 113-17 and the documents relating to this subject in Vol. 54.

[5] Viscount Kentarō Kaneko, distinguished statesman, diplomat, constitutional scholar, and one of the drafters of the Meiji Constitution (1884); at this time, a member of the Privy Council, a senior consultative body to the Emperor on important matters of state.

[6] That is, Gen. Kikuzo Otani, commander of the Japanese troops in Siberia.

[7] That is, Ivan Pavlovich Kalmykov, ataman of the Ussuri Cossacks and anti-Bolshevik military leader.

[8] Printed in *FR 1918, Russia*, III, 293-94.

[9] Our correction.

[10] Printed in *FR 1918, Russia*, II, 462-63.

[11] Kijūrō Shidehara, Vice-Minister of Foreign Affairs.

[12] That is, Baron Nobuaki Makino, former Foreign Minister (1913-1914) and a member of the Advisory Council on Foreign Relations, which had largely replaced the Foreign Office in the formulation and execution of Japanese foreign policy. About the establishment of the Advisory Council on Foreign Relations, see R. S. Morris to RL, March 12, 1918, n. 1, Vol. 46. A plenipotentiary delegate at the peace conference, Makino was at this time in the United States on his way to Paris.

[13] Gen. I. P. Romanovskii, Chief of Staff to Gen. Denikin.

A Memorandum

[Dec. 30, 1918]

S E C R E T.   IMPERIAL WAR CABINET 47.

DRAFT MINUTES of a Meeting held at 10 Downing Street, S.W., on MONDAY, DECEMBER 30, 1918, at 3-30 p.m.

PRESIDENT WILSON'S VISIT.

Statement by the Prime Minister.

(1). Mr. Lloyd George reported the substance of the conversations which he and Mr. Balfour had had with President Wilson. No notes or *proces-verbal* had been kept, and there had been no attempt to arrive at anything in the nature of an agreement. There had simply been an informal interchange of views in order to feel what the relative positions of the two parties were.

The President had opened at once with the question of the League of Nations, and had given the impression that that was the only thing that he really cared much about. There was nothing in what he said which would in the least make it difficult for us to come to some arrangement with him. His mind was apparently travelling in very much the direction of the proposals advocated by Lord Robert Cecil and General Smuts. He had no definite formal scheme in his mind, and was certainly not contemplating anything in the nature of giving executive powers to the League of Nations. The question of Germany's inclusion had not been raised, but was not apparently contemplated by him as a matter for the immediate future. What he was anxious about was that the League of Nations should be the first subject discussed at the Peace Conference. Both Mr. Lloyd George and Mr. Balfour were inclined to agree, on the ground that this would ease other matters, such as the questions of the "Freedom of the Seas," the disposal of the colonies, economic issues, etc. The President having attained his object, could then say that these matters could be left to be worked out by the League of Nations. There was also the consideration that the President might have to go back to America before the Conference concluded, and would wish to be able to say that he had achieved his purpose of creating the League of Nations.

Lord Curzon added that the President had, on another occasion, given to him as a reason for beginning with the League of Nations, that the question of giving a mandate to certain Powers in certain territories could not be settled unless there was a League of Nations to give it.

Mr. Lloyd George said that as regards the Freedom of the Seas the President was very vague. He did not oppose his suggestion that the matter could be left for further consideration after the League of Nations had been established and proved its capacity in actual working. The impression he gave was that he might not resist that proposal, provided the League of Nations had been actually agreed to before the question of the Freedom of the Seas was raised.

As regards disarmament, the President had urged that a definite decision should be arrived at before the Conference separated and before the League of Nations was actually constituted. He admitted, however, that the intricate problems involved in relative disarmament all round could not be settled during the Conference. Eventually they agreed that the Conference should not separate before a definite provisional limitation of armaments had been imposed on Germany and her allies, a limitation which would enable them to maintain order in the troubled conditions of their territories, but no more. Subsequently Germany might raise at the League of Nations the question of revising this provisional limitation. They felt, if that was done, that France would have to follow suit, and that she could hardly maintain an immense army under those conditions. In discussing this matter they had not overlooked the question of reserves and system of training, and he himself had reminded the President of what Prussia had done when her forces were limited to a fixed figure by Napoleon. He had suggested that Germany should not be allowed to impose conscription in any shape or form until she had entirely failed by voluntary means to raise the army provisionally assigned to her, after which she might be allowed to make good the deficit by ballot. In answer to a question by Sir J. Cook,[1] Mr. Lloyd George said that what he contemplated would prevent Germany from enforcing even the compulsory training of the young, such as they had in Australia.

Lord Robert Cecil raised the question of whether conscription was to be forbidden to the friendly new States created in the territories of Austria-Hungary, e.g., the Czechs, and the Yugo-Slavs. He was inclined, with regard to them, to hold General Smuts' view, that they should not be allowed to build up large armies.

Mr. Lloyd George concurred, and considered that this was one of the questions which the Chief of the Imperial General Staff might consider.

The Imperial War Cabinet instructed—

The Chief of the Imperial General Staff[2] to make a provisional recommendation as to the strength to which the military forces of the various enemy countries should be limited, taking into consideration the need for maintaining internal order, and as to the manner in which they should be raised.

The Imperial War Cabinet similarly instructed—

The Deputy First Sea Lord,[3] in the light of the same considerations, to revise the estimate which the Board of Admiralty had already made with regard to the strength to which the enemy fleets should be reduced.

Reports on the above subjects to be available early next week.

With regard to RUSSIA, Mr. Lloyd George explained that President Wilson, though not pro-Bolshevik, was very much opposed to armed intervention. He disliked the Archangel and Murmansk expeditions, and would, no doubt, withdraw his troops from there. He was not very much in favour of the Siberian expedition, though as regards that his principal anxiety was as to the conduct of the Japanese, who were apparently taking the whole of Eastern Siberia into their own hands, sending sealed wagons into the interior, and generally behaving as if they owned the country. His whole attitude, in fact, was strongly anti-Japanese.

Lord Robert Cecil reminded the Imperial War Cabinet that the

[1] Sir Joseph Cook, Minister for the Navy of Australia and a member of the Imperial War Cabinet.
[2] That is, Gen. Sir Henry Hughes Wilson.
[3] Rear Adm. George Price Webley Hope.

Japanese had just informed us that they were removing 30,000 out of the 60,000 Japanese troops now in Siberia.

With regard to the Western frontiers of Russia, Mr. Lloyd George said that they had discussed the question but had come to no sort of conclusion, as they felt the information was too defective. It was not clear, for instance, how far the so-called invasion of Esthonia or Poland was a direct invasion by Bolshevik forces, from outside, or an internal Bolshevik rising in those countries. The President had not shown any keenness on the idea that Russia should be represented at the Conference. On the other hand, he had suggested that we should ask M. Litvinoff formally and definitely what his proposals were. Mr. Lloyd George suggested that it might be possible to take more formal steps to ascertain exactly what the Bolshevik Government might be prepared to do.

A short discussion followed with regard to the informal negotiations which had already taken place, arising out of the telegram from M. Litvinoff, transmitted by Mr. Clive[4] (Stockholm, No. 3759, dated 24/12/18).[5] It was pointed out by Lord Robert Cecil that we could not definitely act on President Wilson's suggestion without communicating with our Allies, some of whom took a very strong line against the Bolsheviks. We ourselves had in fact asked our Allies and some neutral Powers to keep out the Bolsheviks. The discussion on this question, however, was postponed pending the production of M. Litvinoff's answer to our request for definite proposals.

With regard to the NEAR EAST, Mr. Lloyd George informed the Imperial War Cabinet that President Wilson expressed himself in favour of the Turks being cleared out of Europe altogether, but of their place at Constantinople being taken by some small Power, acting as a mandatory of the League of Nations. Mr. Balfour had told the President that the eastern Committee had been in favour of the United States acting as mandatory at Constantinople. With regard to this, President Wilson had pointed out that the United States were extremely proud of their disinterested position in this War, and did not wish to be deprived of that pride. It would be difficult to persuade them that such a mandate was not a profit but really a burden. Altogether he had shown himself very much opposed to any intervention on the part of the United States in these territorial questions. To this Mr. Lloyd George and Mr. Balfour had replied by asking the question who was to undertake the burden

[4] Robert Henry Clive, First Secretary of the British legation at Stockholm.
[5] M. M. Litvinov to WW, Dec. 24, 1918.

of finding the two Divisions, or whatever troops might be required, to prevent the Armenians from being massacred. The President had not given a definite answer, but had certainly not yet reached the point of accepting the argument.

Lord Curzon said that he had put the same point to the President himself, to which the President had replied asking that we should lead him a little more slowly up to his fences; that if the League of Nations were once constituted and the Conference had been sitting some time, the United States might possibly be less reluctant to consider the question of mandatory intervention. As regards Constantinople, he reminded the Imperial War Cabinet that the Eastern Committee had only discussed the suggestion but had not actually recommended that it should be entrusted to the United States.

Mr. Lloyd George said that personally he considered it dangerous to give Constantinople and the Dardanelles to the United States. The suggestion had been made by Mr. Balfour; his own suggestion had been with regard to Armenia. He had not suggested the possibility of an American mandate for either Palestine, Mesopotamia, or East Africa, the first two of which had never in fact been referred to in their discussions.

As regards the German Colonies, the President agreed that they could not be returned to Germany, and that they should be put under some Power acting as a mandatory. Mr. Lloyd George had impressed upon him the distinction between the German Colonies conquered by the British Dominions and adjacent to them, and those in which the forces of the Empire as a whole had shared. He had expressed our willingness to leave German East Africa at the disposal of the League of Nations, and to accept all the conditions imposed by the League if we were entrusted with a mandate for its administration. In the other category he had put German South-West Africa as the strongest case, pointing out that it would be quite impossible to separate from the South African Union what was essentially part of the same country. The President did not seem prepared to contest that contention, but of his own accord retorted that the position of Australia with regard to the Pacific colonies was not quite the same. Mr. Lloyd George and Mr. Balfour had endeavoured to put the case as strongly as they could for Australia, on the grounds of security, but the President had answered that a case on similar grounds might be made for every other captured territory. In answer to the argument that we had definitely promised to Japan the Islands in the Northern Pacific, and that it would be impossible to deny to Australia and New Zealand what was given to Japan, the President had shown that he was by no means prepared to accept the Japanese Treaty, and was doubtful whether Japan could be admitted there even in the capacity of a mandatory Power. They had not succeeded in moving him from that position.

Mr. Bonar Law, who was present at that part of the discussion, said that President Wilson had remarked in that connection that he regarded it as his function to act as a buffer to prevent disagreeable things, such as the Japanese retention of the Islands, being carried out.

Lord Curzon suggested that President Wilson was not to be regarded as a sole arbiter in these matters; he would be only one of a party round the Conference Table.

Mr. Lloyd George agreed. He was only reporting the President's views, and had in no sense accepted them as final. With regard to the Colonies, he had left the matter by telling the President that the question would have to be fought out at the Conference, where the Dominions would be able to present their own case.

With regard to INDEMNITY, Mr. Lloyd George reported that he found the President, on the whole, stiffer than on any other question. The utmost concession he seemed inclined to make was that the claims for pure reparation should be tabled first, and that then other claims might possibly be considered afterwards. Mr. Lloyd George had pointed out that that practically ruled the British Empire out, in spite of the enormous burdens it had borne, and that France and Belgium, who had borne a lesser burden, would practically get everything. He had pointed out also that as a matter of fact our own burden of over six thousand millions to a population of 45,000,000 was much heavier than that of Germany with a similar debt distributed over 65,000,000 of people. Similarly, he had pointed out that Australia at this moment owed £75 for every man, woman and child of her population, a loss which was just as real as any loss represented by destroyed houses. He had, however, failed to make any impression upon the President.

In answer to a question by Mr. Hughes,[6] Mr. Lloyd George said that with regard to the question of economic barriers, raised in No. 3. of the President's Fourteen Points, the President had shown no inclination to raise the matter. His opinion was that President Wilson meant nothing particular by that Article anyhow, and since he had brought it forward he had lost the Election in the United States.

With regard to ITALY, Mr. Lloyd George reported that he found President Wilson distinctly anti-Italian, as the consequence of the

[6] That is, William Morris Hughes.

conversations he had had with Baron Sonnino. We had tried to do our best to state Baron Sonnino's case with regard to the strategical position of the Dalmatian Coast, but the President's only suggestion on that was that the Power to whom the Dalmatian Coast should be left should be forbidden to have a navy at all.

Mr. Hughes said that, in other words, the President held the view that those Powers which had ports should have no fleets, and that only those Powers which had no ports should be allowed to have them.

Mr. Lloyd George said that in any case it was clear that the President would strongly support the Yugo-Slavs against Italy.

With regard to FRANCE, he did not think the President was prepared to tolerate schem[e]s for the control of the West bank of the Rhine, though he might be prepared to accept the French annexation of the Saar Valley.

With regard to the proposed Inter-Allied Conference, they had found the President entirely opposed to holding such a Conference, at any rate formally. He considered that the general Peace Conference would be a sham if definite conclusions were simply arrived at beforehand and then presented to Germany. He was quite prepared to hold Inter-Allied discussions in Paris between the four Powers informally, and agreed that definite decisions would have to be arrived at there and presented to Germany at the Peace Conference. It really came to the same thing, but the President insisted definitely on his point of view.

Lord Curzon suggested that unless the President got beyond the very loose talks he had had with members of the British Government in this country, the Peace Conferences would be a dreary fiasco. In any case France had a very different conception of what was to be done, as was shewn by the French proposals for the representation of the smaller Allies at the Inter-Allied Conference.

With regard to the language to be used at the Peace Conference, Mr. Lloyd George mentioned that the President proposed to insist that English and French should both be the official languages, and that the reports of the Conference should be published in both languages.

> Lord Robert Cecil undertook to communicate with our Representatives abroad, with a view to their supporting Colonel House's attitude in this matter.[7]

With regard to the question of publicity, Mr. Lloyd George mentioned that President Wilson had been in favour of allowing the papers to publish what they liked, and to impose no restrictions.

---

[7] See EMH to WW, Nov. 20, 1918 (first telegram of that date).

Mr. Hughes said that if we were not very careful we should find ourselves dragged quite unnecessarily behind the wheels of President Wilson's chariot. He readily acknowledged the part which America had played in the War. But it was not such as to entitle President Wilson to be the god in the machine at the Peace Settlement, and to lay down the terms on which the world would have to live in future. The United States had made no money sacrifice at all. They had not even exhausted the profits which they had made in the first two and a half years of the War. In men their sacrifices were not even equal to those of Australia. Relatively their sacrifices had been nothing like as much as those of Australia. America had neither given the material nor the moral help which entitled her to come before France. If M. Clemenceau took the line which President Wilson seemed to be taking, he (Mr. Hughes) might be prepared to say "You have a right to speak." He hoped that Great Britain and France, which had both sacrificed so much, would defend their own interests and not let their future be decided for them by one who had no claim to speak even for his own country. Mr. Lloyd George had received an overwhelming vote from his fellow-countrymen, not only in recognition of what he had done, but because of their confidence that he would see to it that their sacrifices had not been made in vain. In taking up that line at the Peace Conference Mr. Lloyd George would have not only all England but more than half America behind him. He and M. Clemenceau could settle the peace of the world as they liked. They could give America the respect due to a great nation which had entered the War somewhat late, but it was intolerable for President Wilson to tell us that the world was to be saved on his terms. If the saving of civilization had depended on the United States, it would have been in tears and chains today. As regards the League of Nations, Mr. Hughes considered that a League of Nations which was to endure and weather the storms of time would have to be a thing like the British Empire, framed in accordance with historical associations and practical needs. President Wilson, however, had no scheme at all, and no suggestion that would bear the test of experience. The League of Nations was to him what a toy was to a child—he would not be happy till he got it. His one idea was to go back to America and say that he had achieved it, and that everything else could then be left for the League of Nations to complete. He (Mr. Hughes) did not consider that the peace of the world could be settled on the terms of "Leave it all to the schedule." Speaking for Australia, he wanted to know what Australia was to get for the sacrifices she had made. When he had secured what he wanted, the Freedom of the Seas as we knew it and meant to have it, and necessary guarantees for our security and development, then he would have no objection to handing over other matters to a League of Nations, properly constituted, and in which the British Empire enjoyed a part corresponding to its position in the world. He insisted that in any case we should not commit ourselves to the League of Nations until the Conference had completed its labours. To start with a League of Nations and then continually refer everything to this League would mean giving up the substance for the shadow. The League of Nations should be the gilded ball on the dome of the cathedral, and not the foundation-stone.

As regards the German Colonies in the Pacific, he thought that President Wilson was evidently talking of a problem which he did not really understand. New Guinea was only 80 miles from Australia. In any case, whatever else the people of Australia differed on, they were united on two things; firstly, their attitude towards Japan and the White Australia policy; and, secondly, the retention of these Islands.

Mr. Chamberlain[8] suggested that it might be made clear to President Wilson that there should be a British Monroe doctrine for the Southern Pacific.

Lord Curzon considered that Mr. Hughes' views were shared by many members of the Imperial War Cabinet. More particularly he thought it was felt that Mr. Lloyd George would remember the power he possessed not merely in virtue of the recent Election but of all sacrifices made by the British Empire and of the interests which it had at stake all over the world. While holding the opinion that the fortunes of the world would largely depend on co-operation between Mr. Lloyd George and President Wilson, he did feel that if President Wilson persisted in the line taken by him it might be necessary, on some issues, at any rate, for Mr. Lloyd George to work at the Conference in alliance with M. Clemenceau.

Mr. Long[9] agreed cordially with the views expressed by Lord Curzon, adding that he did not think that President Wilson realised what the conquest of German East Africa had meant, or the extent to which every part of the British Empire had been involved in it.

Lord Reading thought that it would be lamentable if the result of the friendly discussions which had taken place was to convey the impression that President Wilson and Mr. Lloyd George were acutely divided. He fully agreed that we could not give up our claims on any matter without fighting for it, but he did hope that we should

---

[8] That is, (Joseph) Austen Chamberlain.
[9] That is, Walter Hume Long.

not lightly abandon the position that, consistently with the maintenance of our rights, our main object was to bring about the closest co-operation between ourselves and the United States hereafter.

Lord Curzon explained that he placed as much reliance on the future co-operation of Great Britain and the United States as any member of the Imperial War Cabinet. All he had meant to imply was that at the Conference Mr. Lloyd George would go with an authority fully equal, and indeed superior, to that of President Wilson's.

Mr. Churchill[10] considered that the only point of substance was to induce the United States to let us off the debt we had contracted with them, and return us the bullion and script we had paid over, on the understanding that we should do the same to the Allies to whom we had made advances. If President Wilson were prepared to do that, we might go some way towards meeting his views in the matter of indemnity. For the rest, we should be civil and insist on our essential points.

Sir Robert Borden said that he would regret if we entered on the Peace Conference with any feeling of antagonism towards President Wilson or the United States. He considered that the recent conversations had, on the whole, been as favourable as he had anticipated. Future good relations between ourselves and the United States were, as he had said before, the best asset we could bring home from the war. With regard to the two points on which there had been a pronounced difference, namely, the Pacific Islands and Indemnity, there was no reason to conclude that we had yet got the President's final point of view. He agreed that with regard to these we should mantain our position strongly. He wished, however, to make clear that if the future policy of the British Empire was to work in co-operation with some European nation as against the United States, that policy could not reckon on the approval or the support of Canada. Canada's view was that as an Empire we should keep clear, as far as possible, of European complications and alliances. This feeling had been immensely strengthened by the experience of the War, into which we had been drawn by old-standing pledges and more recent understandings, of which the Dominions had not even been aware. He was in no sense reproaching the Imperial Government with regard to the past, and admitted—in answer to an interjection by Mr. Lloyd George—that the Dominions had not been committed to any Treaty binding upon them without their knowledge since the Imperial War Cabinet had been set up.

[10] That is, Winston S. Churchill.

With regard to RUSSIA, he did not see how the War could be regarded as terminated if we left the Peace Conference with five or six nations and Governments still fighting away in Russia. There were only two alternatives: one was to go and forcibly intervene in Russia itself; the other, which he preferred, was to get the Governments of the various States in Russia to come and be represented at the Peace Conference.

Lord Robert Cecil expressed his agreement with Sir Robert Borden's suggestion with regard to Russia. He admitted that there were certain difficulties in dealing with the Bolshevik Government, but thought they were not insuperable. He suggested that all parties in Russia should be told to stand fast where they were till the Peace Conference was over, and that meanwhile Allied Commissions might clear up many disputed points about the situation.

Lord Milner suggested that, if Lord Robert Cecil's proposal were accepted, there was no reason why all the Governments in Russia, including even the Bolsheviks, should not be invited to the Peace Conference. If the Bolsheviks really accepted the conditions and stopped their aggression upon their neighbours, they would in fact have begun to cease being Bolsheviks.

Mr. Lloyd George agreed, but pointed out that it would be necessary to stop aggression by General Denekin and the Siberian Government upon the Bolsheviks, and that measures might have to be taken at the Peace Conference to prevent the Bolsheviks using if for the purposes of propaganda.

Lord Robert Cecil said that he agreed with Mr. Hughes' view that the Empire would go into the Peace Conference in a position of enormous power, which, however, was also a position of prodigious responsibility. The vital thing was to secure a settled peace. The greatest guarantee of that was a good understanding with the United States, and that good understanding could not be secured unless we were prepared to adhere to the idea of the League of Nations. He agreed that the details of the League of Nations could not be settled at the beginning of the Peace Conference, but the general principles might be laid down as early as possible. His own idea would be that the Peace Conference should at the outset pass, say, three resolutions, laying down, firstly, the desirability of a League of Nations; secondly, the general functions of such a League; and, thirdly, the Powers which at present could be trusted to take part in it, referring the elaborating of these resolutions to a technical Commission, which could be working at the matter while the Conference was sitting. In answer to a question by Sir J. Cook, he agreed that Indemnity and other main terms of peace would have to be settled by the Peace Conference itself, and could not be left to the League of Nations.

T MS (W. Wiseman Papers, CtY).

From the Diary of Dr. Grayson

Tuesday, December 31, 1918.

The King and Queen accompanied the President to the Charing Cross Station, the start for Dover being made at 9:15 on the royal train. Their Majesties expressed deep regret because the President had to leave so soon and a very earnest hope that he would find time to return to London and again be their guests before he returned to the United States.

There was a really amusing incident in connection with our departure from Buckingham Palace, which gained notice all over the civilized world. In the hurry of getting ready for departure Brooks[1] had failed to turn down both legs of the bottom of the President's trousers. The result was he walked out with a cuff turned up, while the other leg was plain. The King and the Queen and the President and Mrs. Wilson with the Princess Mary posed for a photograph. This photograph showed the unusual character of the President's leg coverings. Another picture taken at the same time, which had only the King and the President included, emphasized again the one turned-up cuff on the trouser.[2] The British people, when the picture was published, felt very kindly towards the President and there were a number of editorial comments that this little freak of dress showed how little the President cared for personal appearances, and it strengthened him with people generally wherever the picture was printed. It made a particular hit with the man in the street.

On the way to Dover, the President sent a telegram of thanks to King George for the hospitality shown and best wishes for the New Year for himself, the Royal Family, and for peace, prosperity and happiness for Great Britain.

The authorities of Dover again met us at the station but this time our train was run well down on the pier so that it was only a short walk from the train to the Hospital Ship BRIGHTON, which again had been brought into service to carry us back to France. The Duke of Connaught was the last of the chief British officials to say goodbye to us at the Dover dock. Lloyd George and Balfour had been present at the station and said farewell on leaving London.

The trip across the Channel was uneventful. There was the same flotilla of destroyers—British to mid-channel, and then French; the overhead escort of aeroplanes and dirigibles, and the parting salute by the guns of Dover Castle. The weather was rainy and the Channel rather rough but none of the party suffered any discomfort from the trip.

The run from Calais to Paris was made without incident. We arrived at the French Capital at 9:30.

Among the guests of the President at luncheon while enroute from Calais to Paris was Viscount Acheson. The President told a number of good stories, and Viscount Acheson could not see the point of many of them and freely admitted it. The President said, "I will tell you one which I think you will understand, as it is an English story. A thoughtless gentlemen was at dinner, and while engaged in conversation he had a habit of rubbing his head with his hands. He put his hands in the asparagus and rubbed it in his hair. The hostess seeing that he had thoughtlessly made this mistake said, 'That is asparagus,' whereupon the guest replied, 'I beg your pardon, I thought it was spinach.' " The Viscount said, "I admit I don't see any point to that, except that it was a nasty performance."

[1] That is, Col. Arthur Brooks, Wilson's valet.
[2] See the illustration section.

Two Telegrams from Joseph Patrick Tumulty

[The White House] December 31, 1918

Number 1. Flood[, Foreign Relations,] called with reference to ——— [Irish resolution] pending before his committee providing for freedom and independence and self-determination for Ireland.[1] He says tremendous sentiment behind it and will pass House by big vote if committee reports it favorably. Flood willing to be guided by suggestion from you. He says resolution as drafted, if passed, might embarrass you. He thinks, however, if redrafted as expressing sense of House of Representatives that people of Ireland should have right of self-determination, might satisfy purpose(?) [advocates] of the resolution. Flood wishes to know if either resolution would be embarrassing. What do you think? Is there any action with reference to Ireland you would suggest that might strengthen your hand? He will act upon it.

Flood thinks House will pass resolution you wish favoring league of nations. Do you wish anything done?   Tumulty.

[The White House] December 31, 1918.

Number 2. Clemenceau's speech demonstrates necessity for and wisdom of your trip, and has set stage for final issue between balance of power and league of nations. If America fails now, Socialism rules the world, and if international fair play under democracy cannot curb —— [nationalistic] ambitions, there is nothing left but Socialism, upon which Russia and Germany have already embarked. You can do nothing more serviceable than, without seeming to disagree with Clemenceau, drive home in your speeches differences between two ideals: one, the balance of power, which means continuance of war; the other, concert of nations which means universal peace. One has meant great standing armies with larger armaments and burdensome taxation, consequent unrest and Bolshevism. If the statesmanship at Versailles cannot settle these things in the spirit of justice, Bolshevism will settle them in a spirit of injustice. The world is ready for the issue. Bolshevism [Clemenceau] has given you great chance; this country and whole world will sustain you. Country ready to back you up when you ask for its support. Everything fine here. Tumulty.

T telegrams (WP, DLC).

¹ About this resolution, see JPT to WW, Jan. 28, 1919, n. 1.

From Oscar Terry Crosby, with Enclosure

Dear Mr. President: Paris, le 31 December, 1918

Through oversight I find that memoranduma [memoranda] of the loans to Russia, Serbia, Cuba and Liberia were not included with my letter of December 23rd. These are now enclosed herewith.

Cordially yours, Oscar T. Crosby

TLS (WP, DLC).

E N C L O S U R E

LOANS TO RUSSIA

By the United States Treasury
  (As of November 15, 1918)
  Total credits established $325,000,000
Actual cash advanced 187,729,750

LOANS TO CUBA

By the United States Treasury
  (as of November 15, 1918)
  Total credits established $15,000,000.

LOANS TO SERBIA

By the United States Treasury
  (as of November 15, 1918)
  Total credits established $12,000,000

LOANS TO LIBERIA

By the United States Treasury
  (as of November 15, 1918)
  Total credits established $5,000,000

T MS (WP, DLC).

From Charles Prestwich Scott

Dear Mr Wilson,   Manchester. Dec: 31/18.

May I introduce to you my friend Dr Weizmann, of whom I spoke to you when you were in Manchester and whom you kindly said you would wish to see. He is the recognized leader of the Zionist movement and accepted as such by our Government under whose authority he has recently spent seven months in Palestine as head of the Jewish Mission which accompanied General Allenby. He is in complete possession of the facts in regard to the present position in Palestine, as it affects alike the Jews and the Arabs, and has studied comprehensively the whole problem of the conversion of Palestine into a home for the Jewish people. He is a chemist of distinction (before the war a professor in Manchester University) and has rendered important service during the war to the development of munitions. I am greatly impressed by his ability, his statesmanlike quality and his disinterestedness.

Mr Balfour and the Prime Minister have both been in communication with him and think highly of him.

Believe me   Yours very truly   C. P. Scott.

ALS (WP, DLC).

From Robert Lansing and Others

Dear Mr. President: Paris, December 31, 1918.

In view of certain recent developments, we feel that it is of importance to obtain from you a ruling as to the exact status in relation to the Commission of Mr. Hurley, Mr. Hoover, Mr. McCormick, Mr. Baruch and other similar advisors who have not been assigned as members of the Commission, but who will be in Paris during

the Peace Conference in association with the American representatives. It is, of course, the desire of the Commission to maintain
the closest cooperation with those officials in every way, in order
that their advice may be frequently sought upon matters relating
to the termination of the war, and with this end in view certain
conference rooms have been reserved for them at the Hotel Crillon.
But the inevitable tendency under these circumstances is that they
will wish to move their entire staffs to this hotel. Mr. Hoover has
already taken twelve rooms here for himself and his staff, while
Mr. McCormick has requested the assignment of accommodations
for himself and Mr. Hurley for himself and his wife.[1] The result is
that some of the personnel of the Commission itself, and officers
assigned to the Commission for essential duties, and who are daily
and hourly in conference with the Commissioners, are now obliged
to vacate their rooms in the Crillon and seek accommodations elsewhere in order to make room for those who are only occasionally
to be called upon for advice, as well as for their entire staffs.

We therefore recommend that these officials, while each keeping
one or two office rooms in the Crillon, should properly maintain
their general quarters, their families and their staffs elsewhere. Will
you be good enough to inform us if you concur in this view?

We are, dear Mr. President, Respectfully yours,
                    Robert Lansing.
                    Henry White.
                    E. M. House
                    Tasker H. Bliss.
                    Commissioners Plenipotentiary.

TLS (WP, DLC).
[1] Florence Agnes Amberg Hurley.

Edward Price Bell to Lawrence Lanier Winslow, with Enclosure

No. 719.   SECRET.

My dear Lanier: London, December 31, 1918

I obtained an interview for Frank Worthington, the Deputy Chief
Censor, with the President while the latter was in London, as Worthington next to Hall,[1] for whom I also obtained an interview, has
done more for us in the course of the war than probably any other
British official. I have not seen Worthington since the interview,
which lasted half an hour, but he has given me a memorandum
he has made of some of the President's remarks to him, which I

enclose herewith for your information and for that of Mr. Polk, who I make no doubt will also be interested. Needless to say the President's remarks should be treated in strict confidence.

Yours sincerely,   Edward Bell

TLS (SDR, RG 59, Office of the Counselor, Leland Harrison's General Corr., DNA).
¹ That is, Rear Adm. Sir William Reginald Hall.

E N C L O S U R E

STATEMENTS made by President Wilson to me on
the evening of Saturday, the 28th
December, 1918.

Speaking of closer relations between Great Britain and the United States, Mr. Wilson said, "You must not speak of us who come over here as cousins, still less as brothers; we are neither. Neither must you think of us as Anglo-Saxons, for that term can no longer be rightly applied to the people of the United States. Nor must too much importance in this connection be attached to the fact that English is our common language. The English language is a disadvantage to us as well as an advantage, because we can read in our books and newspapers what you say about us; for instance, it should not be said of us that we are building ship for ship against you. With French and German it is different, because much of what the French and Germans write does not reach the people, so less harm is done. No, there are only two things which can establish and maintain closer relations between your country and mine: they are community of ideals and of interests.

If I know anything of people, it is of the people of the United States. They cannot be said to be anti-British, but they are certainly not pro-British. If they are pro anything, it is pro-French."

"The war has helped American business men to make a discovery. They have found that they possess souls. They realise that business prosperity, wealth and power are not the only things worth having in the world. The sufferings of others have made them sympathetic. I do not mean to say that many have found their souls, but some certainly have and that is a national gain."

Speaking of Bolshevism, the President said, "No, I am not afraid of Bolshevism in America. It makes no appeal to the educated man. Moreover, it must be remembered that Bolshevism is no new thing. The present state of Russia is very much the same as that of France during the revolution. The acts of violence which are taking place in Russia now are as much to be deplored as were those which took place in France then. My own feeling is that Russia should be left to settle her own affairs in her own way so long as she does not become a menace to others. The phase of violence in France lasted for three years when Napoleon became the dominant figure, but the revolution can hardly be said to have been complete for close on 60 years. I do not mean to suggest that Russia will remain unsettled for so long: the means of communication are so much more rapid than formerly and the people of the world are much better educated. Again, the Russians are great organisers in their own way, organisers of village communities. It is wrong to think that Russia cannot organise.[1] She can, but not on a grand scale. Things must run their course, and it is for this reason that I am so much in favor of free speech and so much against secret diplomacy. Let the people know what is going on. If a man has beliefs and ideas, he should be encouraged to get up and expound his views in public. His audience will judge whether he is right or wrong.

I will not say that future wars are improbable, but what I have said is that if before the present war the situation had been freely discussed in public for even a week, this war would never have broken out.

I have promised to make public everything discussed at the Peace Conference. If I find anything going on in an underhand way I will publish it. This is the first time the people have ever had an opportunity of taking any share in a settlement of this sort and they shall not be baulked."

"If I find any tendency to grab, I shall make it known. For instance, I found the Italian statesmen quite incapable of taking a wide view of things. They demanded almost the whole of the Dalmatian coast and practically all the islands of the Adriatic. They based their claim on the necessity for adequate defence. From that point of view their argument is absolutely unanswerable, yet if you stand in front of a man with your fist in his face, it is of no use your explaining to him that it is there for defensive purposes only. Sooner or later your protective attitude will lead to a breach of the peace.

As regards the French, they are claiming nothing in the way of territory beyond that which the world has conceded to them.

Indemnity? Well, the sum Germany will have to pay is so vast in any case.

I have come to Europe to do the little I can, but I am under no delusion. Without the assistance of Divine Providence no man can effect anything which is lasting, anything which is great; no man of intelligence can deny the existence of a Divine Providence.

I hear to-night that the Ebert Cabinet has fallen and that the extremists are for the moment in power.[2] It is difficult to see with whom we shall make peace, but this confusion cannot last long in Germany, for the Germans are an educated people, and the Southern Germans in particular are very stable. It well may be that the Bolshevik movement is confined to Berlin. The Kaiser was always afraid of Berlin and expected a revolution there."

T MS (SDR, RG 59, Office of the Counselor, Leland Harrison's General Corr., DNA).
[1] On the following day, Wilson expressed similar views to Charles P. Scott of the *Manchester Guardian*. Scott recorded his remarks as follows: "As to any further invasion [of Russia] he [Wilson] was quite opposed to it, though if the Bolsheviks attacked on the Western front they must be repelled. I suggested that terms could probably be arranged with the Bolsheviks both in regard to the safety of those who had supported us in the Archangel and Murmansk districts and as to the Western border provinces but that we needed first of all much fuller information as to the facts, about which the [British] Government at present knew rather less than the Press, and secondly the opening of conversations with the Bolsheviks, whether we recognised them formally as a *de facto* Government or not. Their invasion was mainly an invasion of ideas and you could not defeat ideas by armies. He entirely agreed. We had no right to interefere with the internal affairs of Russia and, provided they did not attack their neighbours, they had a right to have what internal polity they liked. His policy all through had been not to attack Russia but to help her." Trevor Wilson, ed., *The Political Diaries of C. P. Scott, 1911-1928* (London, 1970), p. 365.
[2] There were news reports on December 28, apparently originating with the Berlin *Kreuz-Zeitung*, that the Ebert government had fallen in Germany. *New York Times*, Dec. 29, 1918. Actually, Ebert had formed a new government composed exclusively of Majority Socialists after the Independent Socialists withdrew from the government on December 28, 1918. See H. Sulzer to RL, Nov. 12, 1918, n. 1.

From the Diary of Colonel House

December 31, 1918.

Mr. Balfour has arrived from London and called this afternoon and spent nearly two hours with me. We went over every phase of the current situation and of all matters which might properly be brought before the Peace Conference.

I was interested to have him almost agree with my extreme views upon the freedom of the seas—views which if incorporated would allow ever [even] the belligerent commerce of the world go free, in time of war as well as in time of peace. He had obly [only] one argument to controvert what I said, that it would deprive England of the power to help right wrongs such as she has been able to do during the present war against Germany. I met this by saying there would be no objection to her having as large a navy as now, and that she could use it in the event the League of Nations undertook to discipline an outlaw nation.

He seemed to see as I do that Great Britain would fare better under my definition than she would under the definition of her extreme "Blue Water School."

He presented a very curious theory regarding Jews. Some told him, and he is inclined to believe it, that nearly all Bolshevism and disturbance of a like nature, are directly traceable to the Jews of the world. They seem determined either to have what they want or to upset present civilization. I suggested that we put them in Palestine, at least the best of them, and hold them responsible for the orderly behavior of the rest of the Jews throughout the world. Balfour thought the plan had many possibilities.

He told me of the conversation which he and Lloyd George had with the President and of their fairly general agreement. I outlined to him my plan for the League of Nations, which he seemed to accept as practical and satisfactory. He hoped Lord Robert Cecil and I would get together next week and work out something. He goes to the South of France tonight, intending to remain only four or five days. I urged him to remain until the tenth, promising to be responsible for his absence.

There is no one with whom I enjoy talking more than Balfour. He has one of the best, perhaps the best, mind I have ever come in contact with. He lacks decision and is too argumentative, nevertheless, the quality of his mind is nearly perfect. It is a pity that he has not some of the aggressive and popular qualities of Lloyd George. There is no comparison between the character and knowledge of the two, and it seems a tragedy to have the one Prime Minister and the other his Secretary of State for Foreign Affairs.

The President has returned and has just called me over the telephone. He told of his trip to England, how he and Lloyd George got on, and the kind of reception he received. Strangely enough, he said that if he could trust "The Little Man" he thought he could get along with him easier than he could with Balfour. He said they agreed more generally about things than he and Balfour.

He was disturbed over Clemenceau's speech in the Chamber. I took occasion to tell him that in my opinion we would have to work with England rather than with France if we hoped to get the things for which we were striving through. He needed some persuasion before he agreed with me, but finally di[d] so. I am to take lunch with him tomorrow and have a more general talk.

From the Diary of Dr. Grayson

Wednesday, January 1, 1919.

The President played his first game of golf on French soil during the morning on the St. Cloud links. He enjoyed the day very much. During the afternoon the President and Mrs. Poincaré made a formal call. This we returned later in the afternoon. The President went from this call to the Crillon Hotel where he held a conference with the members of the American Mission, discussing with them impressions of his trip to England. In the evening he departed for Rome. The Italian Government had insisted that the entire trip should be made on the Italian Royal Train, so the original plan for the President to proceed to Modane on the French train, there to change to the Italian Royal Train was abandoned. We were given the usual official "send-off" on our departure.

To Carter Glass

Paris. January 1, 1919.

127. For the Secretary of the Treasury from the President.

Extended investigation and consideration of the food situation in certain parts of Europe discloses that especially the urban populations in certain areas are not only faced with absolute starvation during the coming winter, but that many of these populations are unable to find immediate resources with which to purchase their food. These regions have been so subjected to destruction by war, not only of their foodstuffs but of their financial resources and their power of production and export, that they are utterly incapable of finding any resources that can be converted into international exchange for food purchases. While the Secretary of the Treasury can accept obligations of certain governments and through these measures their situation can be cared for tempor[ar]ily, there are still other areas through Eastern and Southeastern Europe where such arrang[e]ments cannot be made. This applies more particularly to the Liberated peoples of Austria, Turkey, Poland and Western Russia. In these countries freedom and government will slowly emerge from chaos and require our every assistance.

The total shipments of foodstuffs from the United States to all parts of Europe during the next seven months will be likely to exceed one and one-half billion dollars, and from our abundance we can surely afford to offer succor to these countries destitute of resources or credit. The minimum sum upon which this work can be carried on for the next six months in the countries above mentioned will amount to at least 100,000,000 dollars, for such services and supplies as we can render, and even this sum contemplates the finding of resources by so much of the populations as can do so and such assistance as can be given by the Allied Governments.

The high mission of the American people to find a remedy against starvation and absolute anarchy, renders it necessary that we should undertake the most liberal assistance to these destitute regions. The situation is one of extreme urgency, for foodstuffs must be placed within certain localities within the next 15 to 30 days if human life and order is to be preserved. I, therefore, request that you should ask Congress to make available to me an immediate appropriation of $100,000,000 for the broad purpose of providing foodstuffs and other urgent supplies, for the transportation, distribution, and administration thereof to such populations in Europe, outside of Germany, as may be determined upon by me from time to time as necessary.

I wish to appeal to the great sense of charity and good will of the American people toward the suffering, and to place this act upon a primarily humanitarian basis of the first magnitude. While the sum of money is in itself large, it is so small compared to the expenditures we have undertaken in the hope of bettering the world, that it becomes a mere pittance compared to the results that will be obtained from it, and the lasting effect that will remain in the United States through an act of such broad humanity and states-manlike influence. Ammission.

T telegram (WP, DLC).

To Robert Russa Moton

Dear Principal Moton: Paris, January 1, 1919.

I wish to express my appreciation for the service you have rendered during the past few weeks in connection with our colored soldiers here in France. I have heard not only of the very wholesome advice you have given regarding their conduct during the time they will remain in France, but also of your advice as to how they should conduct themselves when they return to our own shores.[1] I very much hope, as you have advised, that no one of them may do anything to spoil the splendid record that they with the rest of our American forces have made.

Cordially and sincerely yours, [Woodrow Wilson]

CCL (WP, DLC).
[1] Moton later summarized his standard speech to black soldiers as follows: "The record you have made in this war, of faithfulness, bravery, and loyalty, has deepened my faith in you as men and as soldiers, as well as in my race and country. You have been tremendously tested. You have suffered hardships and many privations. You have been called upon to make many sacrifices. Your record has sent a thrill of joy and satisfaction to the hearts of millions of black and white Americans, rich and poor, high and low. Black mothers and wives, sweethearts, fathers, and friends have rejoiced with you and with our country in your record. You will go back to America heroes, as you really are. You will go back as you have carried yourselves over here—in a straightforward, manly, and modest way. If I were you, I would find a job as soon as possible and get to work. To those who have not already done so, I would suggest that you get hold of a piece of land and a home as soon as possible, and marry and settle down. . . . Save your money, and put it into something tangible. I hope no one will do anything in peace to spoil the magnificent record you have made in war." Moton, *Finding a Way Out*, p. 263. Ellipses Moton's.

From Newton Diehl Baker

My dear Mr. President: Washington January 1, 1919.

I venture to send you a summary of conditions here, written with my own hand[1] and made up entirely of personal judgments and observations.

The doubt as to the wisdom of your going abroad, which was reflected in some of the newspaper comment before you left, continued for a few days and seemed to the Republicans to invite cutting up by them. Lodge, Knox and others less prominent made speeches and the newspapers of their persuasion began to praise their statesmanship. Very soon a noticeable reaction set in. At first it showed itself in a comical pride in the fact that you were "putting it over the Kings and Prime Ministers" and "telling Europe where to get off at" (both actual quotations). Then the tide of comprehension and approval set in strong and now the critics are explaining what they meant by what they said, and getting Mr. Taft to write articles in newspapers to prove that they really are patriotic and meant well. So far he has only appeared as advocatus diabolus for Lodge, but of course he will come to Mr. Roosevelt's assistance if anyone gives him a friendly shove in that direction. The motion picture theaters tell the story as your picture is tumultuously received and Mr. Roosevelt's is but faintly applauded.

The same fate has followed the League of Nations idea. There were all sorts of doubts at first, there were also numberless suggestions of better ways to do it. So far as I know Senator Reed is the sole survivor. All my letters from the West run in the phrase that it is a pretty hard job at best and safer in the President's hands than it would be in anyone else's. Meantime there is a growing resentment at the embarrassment planned for you by these orators. Mr. Roosevelt, who is now home from the hospital, is silent and Mrs. Longworth is "amazed at" your reception abroad. With regard to your whole trip and your objects abroad, home sentiment is rapidly becoming all you would have it; while, of course the people of France and England have plainly given you new credentials to the Peace Conference, which fill us all with delight and pride.

The situation in New York, with regard to Mr. Hearst's membership on the Mayor's Committee to welcome returning soldiers, grows daily more complicated.[2] Men of prominence are resigning

[1] Baker had the handwritten letter typed, signed the typed copy, and sent it to Wilson.
[2] Mayor John F. Hylan had appointed William Randolph Hearst as chairman of a committee to welcome homecoming soldiers. Because of the allegedly pro-German stance of Hearst and his newspapers during the war, the appointment created a furor. Many prominent citizens also appointed to the committee, such as Henry L. Stimson, Charles Evans Hughes, and Nicholas Murray Butler, refused to serve if Hearst remained a

and conducting acrimonious correspondence with the Mayor about it. I mention the matter only to ask you to consider the possibility of landing in Boston on your own return. I do not know that the Mayor of New York will attempt to organize a reception for you, though I have heard something to that effect, but for other reasons I think it would be wise. Boston would, of course turn out the Pilgrim Fathers to give you a worthy welcome, and I personally would enjoy having Senator Lodge witness the scene. Of course my feeling on this subject makes me untrustworthy, but you will know how to appraise the situation. Massachusetts has always seemed to me to be on the verge of being saved, perhaps some such opportunity would reveal the state to itself.

The situation in Congress is, I think distinctly better. No substantial progress has been made with legislation and a very great deal of talk has been going on in the "cloak room" (significant name) and some on the floor, but, as usual, that is beginning to moderate in response to the home papers, and a good many Senators and Representatives have expressed to me their growing displeasure at the past situation and their determination to insist on future pulling together. Senator Chamberlain yesterday made a three hour speech[3] on the unpreparedness of the War Department to deal with the problem of the returning sick and wounded, but the major part of the address was taken up with a reargument of the questions involved in the controversy which arose over his other speech.[4] I am told that there was much exaggeration and misinformation in what purported to deal with present conditions, and I shall supply the facts to Senator Thomas for the Record, as soon as I can get a correct copy of his address. As a matter of fact we have far more than enough bed capacity for all returning men, and I have twice personally inspected the arrangements for their reception, so that I know that they are adequate considerate and properly supervised against accidental breakdown.

In the meantime you will be interested to know that we have already demobilized about seven hundred thousand men out of the

---

member of the group. The legislatures of South Dakota and Pennsylvania and the state Senate of Ohio adopted resolutions urging the federal government to have the troops land at some port other than New York in order to avoid Hearst. An independent citizens' committee was formed to welcome the soldiers in place of or in competition with the Mayor's committee. Hearst refused to resign as chairman of the Mayor's committee, and Hylan stubbornly defended his selection. The excitement over the issue gradually died down in February and March 1919. See W. A. Swanberg, *Citizen Hearst: A Biography of William Randolph Hearst* (New York, 1961), pp. 317, 319-21, and the *New York Times*, Dec. 3, 1918-March 30, 1919, *passim*.

[3] George E. Chamberlain had addressed the Senate on December 30. See the *Cong. Record*, 65th Cong., 3d sess., pp. 869-83.

[4] See WW to G. E. Chamberlain, Jan. 20, 1918, n. 1, Vol. 46.

total million seven hundred thousand in our camps on November 11, and are progressing at the rate of about one hundred and seventy thousand per week. More than thirty five thousand officers have been released. All of this, of course, effects economies which are a relief to the Treasury and restores men to industry, but in addition to that it seems to be satisfying the restlessness of the men, who, on the signing of the armistice, became very impatient to return to their civilian status. The labor situation throughout the country is perhaps reported to you by Secretary Wilson, but we too are trying to keep in touch with it and so far, in spite of the demobilizations effected and the cancellations of war material contracts, which have been on a huge scale, there is no general surplus of free labor. Our latest reports show the situation in 114 industrial centres. Of these 23 report a labor shortage, 35 a labor surplus and 56 report demand for labor equal to supply. Of the places reporting surplus many are special and temporary, and centres reporting surplus one week frequently report normal the next, showing that adjustment is taking place. My own fear of disturbance in labor conditions has always more centred around the demobilization of war workers than of soldiers. The war workers are all industrials and are discharged in large groups in given localities. The soldiers, on the other hand are discharged from day to day in widely separated places and in very many places, so that no centre receives very many of them at a time, and the soldiers are about fifty per cent farmers who return naturally to their homes to await the routine of farm life. Of the remainder there are large numbers of men who either have their own business to return to, or are going to college, or to places which have been held for them, so that the total number who are to seek industrial opportunity on a competitive basis is really very small as compared with the number discharged.

The most delicate situation here just now is the retention of American troops in Russia. You will recall that before you went away I showed you a report from the commanding officer of the detachment at Archangel to the effect that his men became very restless immediately upon the signing of the armistice. I assume that some of the men in that force are writing home and some of them are being returned home to convalesce from illnesses of one kind and another. The result is that wild stories are afloat, particularly in Michigan, from which State most of the soldiers in Northern Russia come, to the effect that the men are ill provided and are exposed to conflict with Russian forces which outnumber them "fifteen to one." As a consequence both Michigan Senators have "addressed the Senate" demanding to know why the men are there and how long they are to stay and what the facts are about their outfits.[5] Meanwhile Senator Johnson of California has taken up the Vladivostock end of the inquiry and insists upon knowing whom we are proposing to fight and why we do not leave, now that the Czecho-Slovacs are safe.[6] So far as the equipment of the Archangel force is concerned, I feel sure that the arrangements will be found to be satisfactory. We instructed General Pershing to see that they were provided with everything, and when I was in London General Biddle[7] described to me in great detail the thoroughness with which the outfitting was done. The British helped and the men were provided with every necessity and every comfort which could be suggested by those who knew the climate and conditions. A carefully selected and adequate medical staff was sent with abundant hospital supplies. For the rest of the business of course your Aide Memoire[8] covers the reasons, and as the intervention of the armistice has been recent, there has not as yet been time to bring about the international adjustments which will ultimately be made to meet the new conditions. Polk and I have conferred and will make harmonious answers to the inquiries, should the Senate let the resolutions of inquiry pass. I give you the situation, however, as it may affect your conferences on the Russian situation.

The White House looks very deserted, but the sheep over there are not the only ones who have lost their shepherd by your absence. The Vice President is very much interested in the Cabinet Meetings[9] and enlivens them with yarns about Newt Plum, one of his Hoosier

[5] Senator Charles Elroy Townsend, Republican of Michigan, had briefly addressed the Senate on this subject on December 30. *Cong. Record*, 65th Cong., 3d sess., p. 864. The index to *ibid.* does not reveal any remarks on the subject by the other senator from Michigan, William Alden Smith, Republican.

[6] Senator Hiram W. Johnson, Republican of California, on December 12, had introduced Senate Resolution 384 which directed the Secretary of State "to send to the Senate, if not incompatible with the public interest, all data, documents, and information showing or bearing upon our present relations with Russia as to peace or war, so that the Senate and the Nation may know why and for what purpose our soldiers are in Russia and what is the policy of the Government in reference to Russia." The resolution also directed the Secretary of War "to advise the Senate of the number of United States soldiers in Russia and their location and of their operations, together with any lists of casualties which they may have suffered." Johnson declared that neither Congress nor the American people had any clear idea why American troops remained in northern Russia and Siberia. The conclusion of the war had removed the original rationale for sending these men to Russia. Why, then, were they still there, and why were they killing Russians and being killed by Russians in various unexplained clashes? Johnson quoted at length from various statements of President Wilson on Russian affairs, including his aide-mémoire of July 17, 1918, and asserted that they provided no real answers to these questions. He asked a number of other questions, such as the following: Was it true that the American government had rejected offers of military and economic cooperation from the Soviet government? Had the Department of State refused to permit the Red Cross to ship supplies to Moscow and Petrograd? Above all, was it the policy of the administration to destroy Bolshevism in Russia and, if so, what did the administration think should take its place? Johnson's resolution was referred to the Committee on Foreign Relations, whence it never emerged. *Ibid.*, pp. 342-46.

[7] That is, Maj. Gen. John Biddle.

[8] It is printed as an Enclosure with WW to FLP, July 17, 1918, Vol. 48.

[9] Wilson had asked Thomas R. Marshall to preside at cabinet meetings during his absence.

Justices of the Peace, who holds, as a matter of law that you have forefeited the Office but retain the salary, by going abroad; an opinion which the Vice President says robs the question of any interest for him!

We all miss you tremendously, but we are glad that none of our troubles are large enough to distract your mind from the important things pressing on you abroad.

Please permit me to wish for you, all the blessings of health and happiness the New Year can give, and to extend to Mrs. Wilson, the Greetings of the Season.

Respectfully yours,   Newton D. Baker

P.S. Since writing the foregoing I have received a cablegram from General Pershing, a copy of which he has sent to Mr. House and to General Bliss, with reference to the retention of American Divisions in France pending the signature of peace preliminaries. Marshall Foch seems to desire the retention of a very considerable number of Americans to enforce the performance of the terms. My own view is that Pershing's judgment is sound and that we must use all the available shipping, to the limit of its capacity, to bring our boys home. The best we can do will leave a large force in France until Summer, and any announcement now made of a policy of keeping them there for other reasons than the limitations of shipping would be unnecessary and cause great unrest and discontent here. I refer to the matter only because it is likely to be submitted to you and it clearly need not be decided now. Doing the best we can with the ships[,] we will still have in France in May a large enough force to meet any possible emergency. It is not impossible that the Marshall is somewhat influenced by a desire to have our troops remain for the incidental purpose of helping in the cleaning up process in the devastated regions.

TLS (WP, DLC).

From Eleanor Foster Lansing

My dear Mr. President   [Paris] Jan 1 1919

Your invitation to join your party going to Italy came to us late last night—too late to answer then, but I am sending this note as early as possible this morning to beg that you will excuse us from going—unless you think it absolutely necessary that we accompany you

Mr Lansing is far from well and I do not feel he is physically able to take the trip. You will realize, I am sure, that he is anxious to be in as good condition as possible, to do his work here, and we both feel this trip would be a most imprudent one for him to take

Of course Mr. Lansing will see you himself, and I know you will forgive my writing you, but I thought I might be able to explain a little better than he will our reason for not accepting your kind invitation.

We both send you and Mrs. Wilson our best wishes for a happy New Year.   Most cordially yours   Eleanor Lansing

ALS (WP, DLC).

The American Mission in Paris to John William Davis

[Paris] January 1, 1919.

Following letter handed today to Lord Derby from Colonel House:

"My dear Mr. Balfour: I enclose herewith a copy of a letter that I have this day sent to Monsieur Pichon in answer to his letter to me of December 23rd, a copy of which I understand that you have.

As the situation demands prompt action, I trust that the British Government will appoint its representatives at as early a date as possible. I am, my dear Mr. Balfour,"

Following is Colonel House's letter to Monsieur Pichon:

"I am in receipt of your letter of December 23rd, in reply to my letter of December 1st, relative to the European Relief Administration, and am glad to note that the French Government accepts in principle the plan proposed by me on behalf of the President.

The President is gratified that you desire that the United States Government should take the lead in this undertaking.

The President asks me to state that he accepts your suggestion that a special council of two members, representing each of the four Governments be substituted for the Supreme War Council.

In view of the urgent action required in some territories, the President suggests that it is most desirable that each of the Allied Governments designate its representatives at the earliest possible moment and that at the first meeting of the Council it would be desirable that the representatives of each Government be prepared to state what participation and resources they will be able and willing to contribute to the common object.

He has, therefore, appointed Mr. Herbert Hoover and Mr. Norman H. Davis as the American members on this Council, and has asked Mr. Hoover, as Director General of Relief, as soon as possible to call a meeting of the council.

With regard to the other considerations raised by you, it appears
to him that these are matters which will necessarily come before
the Council for consideration from time to time and that while none
of the Governments are releasing any freedom of action, all rec-
ognise that in setting up organizations of this kind there is a common desire to coordinate the activities of the different Governments
in the directions outlined by yourselves. I am, my dear Monsieur
Pichon."

Please hand the Foreign Office at once a memorandum obtaining
the above quoted letters.   Ammission.

T telegram (WP, DLC).

From the Diary of Colonel House

January 1, 1919.

I took lunch with the President and we discussed many matters
of importance. He is rather full of his trip to England and seems
to have had a thoroughly satisfactory time. Mrs. Wilson and the
others were startled when I told them they should have given the
Buckingham Palace entourage presents in the shape of cuff-but-
tons, scarf pins, etc. etc. They gave $750.00 to the servants and
thought that was the end of their obligations. I forgot to tell them
about this custom when they left and they had no one with them
who knew that these souvenirs should be provided for certain of
the gentlemen in waiting. I have told Frazier to see that it is properly
done when they visit Italy. I shall arrange to have these mememtoes
[mementoes] sent to England as soon as possible.

Mrs. Wilson said the Queen asked to be remembered to Loulie
and me. It is the general opinion that the banquet at Buckingham
Palace was the most elaborate effort that any of those attending
had ever witnessed.

The President told im [in] much detail of his conversation with
Lloyd George, Balfour, Bonar Law and others, and we discussed
Clemenceau's speech in the Chamber of Deputies. In my opinion,
it is the greatest diplomatic blunder that Clemenceau has made
since the famous Sixtus letter.[1] It may have the effect of cooling
our ardor and it may cost France many millions that she might
otherwise have had from us. After I read the speech I became
convin[c]ed that the United States and England should get together
closely and work to a common program in this Peace Conference,
rather than to depend upon France.

In accordance with this thought I went a long way with Balfour yesterday and I think I convinced the President this morning that it was the proper policy for us to pursue. Such blunders make me glad that I am not given to public speaking. It is a pleasant but dangerous pastime.

I asked the President why he appointed Glass instead of Houston to the Treasury. I thoroughly approve the appointment and told him so, but the last time it was discussed between us it was a question between Glass and Houston with Houston the favorite. His answer was that he thought Houston was not well enough known to the people to be an acceptable appointment. This I regard as nonsense, for Houston is as well or better known that [than] Glass. And this reminds me that I have just received a letter from Houston which is more like the old time letters and talks we formerly had than any since he has been in the Cabinet.

We discussed Gregory's successor.[2] I thought Sherman Whipple of Boston would be a good appointment. He said he was too reactionary. This, I replied, would be a great surprise to Massachusetts people who regard him as anything but safe and sane. He said Gregory wished him to appoint Todd,[3] but he gave no indication as to what he intended to do.

McAdoo has recommended Oscar Price to succeed himself as Director General of Railroads. I do not know enough about Price to give the President an opinion. I read Henry Frick's letter to the President advising that the Government retain the railroads for the present.[4] Coming from Frick this suggestion was interesting to both of us. I advised the President not to call an extra session of Congress after the Fourth of March. He said he had already had it in mind not to do so. I also advised him not to recommend any special legislation. This, too, corresponded with his own intentions. Where we differ is, he expressed a determination to veto any purely republican legislation that was put up to him. I am not certain in my own mind as to what I should do, but I have a feeling that I would let such legislation go through and explain to the people why I felt it my duty to do so, unless I considered the legislation was hurtful.

I am advising him to say to the American people that at the November elections they gave the Republican Party a mandate to legislate, and, yielding to their wishes as expressed at the polls, he would not make any recommendations regarding measures, but would leave them free to carry out the will of the people. I advised him to say this in a big and generous way and without the slightest tinge of bitterness. I want him to offer to help with advice and information when called upon, but I want him to drive it home again and again that the opposition have the legislative reins in their hands and must be responsible for results. I have several objects in mind. One is I am a believer in congressional government. By rights, the Republicans should now have both the executive and legislative departments of government in their hands, but since this is not quite possible under our Constitution, the next best thing is for the Executive to yield, as far as legislation is concerned.

I see difficult and dangerous times ahead and I do not believe any party can satisfy the people during the immediate after war period, therefore since the republicans have won, I want them to bear a large part of the blame which is certain to be heaped upon those in power. In theory the President seems to agree with my suggestions, but will he put it into practice? I doubt it for he has grown so accustomed to almost dictatorial powers that it will go hard to give them up.

The President returned with me to the Crillon. The other Peace Delegates were invited to my rooms where we held a meeting for nearly an hour. We discussed the League of Nations, and the President told the others something of his trip to England and of his conversations with those he met there.

We agreed to send W. H. Buckler to Copenhagen[5] to listen to what the representatives of the present Soviet Government of Russia had to say in their own behalf. Later, we will send Buckler to Lausanne to be present while the International Labor Congress sits. I took occasion to express my high regard for Buckler and the work which he had been doing since the beginning of the war.

[1] About which, see RL to WW, May 10, 1918, n. 1, Vol. 47 (first letter of that date).
[2] Gregory had conveyed his desire to resign to Wilson just before he, Wilson, left for Paris. See JPT to WW, Jan. 9, 1919 (third telegram of that date).
[3] That is, George Carroll Todd, Assistant Attorney General.
[4] It is missing.
[5] Actually, Buckler met Litvinov in Stockholm.

From the Diary of Edith Benham

January 2, 1919

Yesterday I didn't write because I was pretty busy the one day I was in Paris, and then getting ready for this trip to Rome. On the train last night there was such an awful shaking I couldn't make any characters. I really didn't have so very much to write either. Colonel House came to luncheon, and when he is there things conversationally are usually more interesting. The President read from quite an unusual paper, so far a confidential document of the

Peace Commission, written by the Boer general Smuts, who said that the under people of the world cannot be ignored, and the Commission must have the rights of the masses in mind, for a great unrest was stirring now in the world. The President said the King of Italy was very alive to that, but Sonnino did not seem to be alive to it in the conferences they had, and from Orlando they got no original expression. They spoke of the 14 points and the fact that the Governments had accepted that. Also that Lloyd George was so changeable, and though he might say in the morning that he would support a thing, he would change in the afternoon. The President also laughed and said he had not been able to congratulate him on his victory, in fact, had said nothing until the day he left London when something was said about it by the Queen at the platform, which gave him an opening, and he said, "I wish, sir, I could congratulate you on your recent victory without seeming to interfere in English politics."

From the Diary of Dr. Grayson

Thursday, January 2, 1919.

The first stop was made at Modane. Here the President left his car and walked up and down the platform. French, Italian and American officers and soldiers were congregated at this point to see what an American President looked like. All were extremely friendly. Leaving Modane additional engines were attached to haul the train up the grades and through the mountains. When the Italian border was reached the train was stopped and the Prince Udine[1] and aides, the Italian Ambassador to the United States, and Countess De Cellere boarded the train. Along the route crowds congregated who cheered the train as it passed. Arriving at Turin, Thomas Nelson Page, American Ambassador to Italy came on board with his aides. At one of the smaller stations en route, where the train halted the President acknowledged greetings of welcome from the platform, the Mayor compared the President's visit with "The second coming of Christ." This reference greatly pleased the Italian people who heard him.

[1] Ferdinand Humbert Philippe Adalbert, Prince of Udine, a second cousin of King Vittorio Emanuele.

From Thomas Garrigue Masaryk

Prague 2 January 1919

In the first new year in which after a long time of the darkness of war light of freedom and peace is beginning to glimmer over Europe and world I beg to greet you Mr. President on my own and our peoples behalf from the free capital of the free Czecho Slovak Republic. Our nation shall never forget that it was you Mr. President who by his kind sense of freedom and justice has brought about the disruption of the immoral state combination called Austria Hungary and it was you by his knowledge of our right in the most critical moment has made possible the revolution which brought us our national independence. We greet you the spokesman of the political ideals of the great American Republic of the ideals for which America in this war contested and conquered. These ideals are one with the ideals of our nation and will always find an enthusiastic defender in the free Czecho Slovak Republic.

President Masaryk

T telegram (WP, DLC).

Robert Lansing to Frank Lyon Polk

[Paris] January 2, 1919.

131, Your 92, December 21st 9 p.m. This was called to the President's particular attention before his departure for England. He is due back tonight and I hope to be able to take up the Siberian railway situation with him tomorrow before his departure to Rome.

Referring to your number 11 of December 28th and subsequent telegrams on the same subject, please realize that in addition to the absence of the President I am also handicapped by the fact that we have not as yet met the British and the French Commissioners and that no conferences have been held up to the present time. In view of the urgency of the matter and the impossibility of obtaining any action here, I would suggest that you continue to use the regular channels for presenting the matter to the Governments concerned. Lansing.

T telegram (WP, DLC).

Arthur James Balfour to Lord Derby

URGENT.   London, January 2. 1919.

Please suggest to Government to which you are accredited propriety of transmitting following message to Sovyet Government in Moscow, to General Kolchak at Omsk, to General Denikin at Ekaterinodar, to Monsieur Tschaikowsky[1] at Archangel and to Governments of ex-Russian States.

Begins. Great friendly Powers are about to assemble in Paris to work for a solution of problems arising out of war and to bring about a settlement of international and national controversies that still survive it.

One of their first tasks will be an endeavour to bring about peace in Russia, to reconcile conflicting nations, parties and peoples both in Russia and in adjacent States and territories and to bring succour to suffering populations.

Pending decisions that will be taken in this sense the great friendly Powers call upon all the Governments, parties and peoples in States and territories in question to abstain from further aggressions, hostilities and reprisals, and require them to keep the peace both at home and with their neighbours.

If the aforesaid Governments and parties will immediately suspend hostilities on all fronts for the duration of peace negotiations and then if they or any of them should desire to send representatives to Paris to discuss with Great Powers the conditions of a permanent settlement, the Great Powers would be prepared to enter on such a discussion with them. Message ends.

His Majesty's Government consider that some action of the kind must at once be taken before the Paris Conference meets, in view of the urgent appeals which they are receiving from the Esthonians and Lithuanians who are in danger of being exterminated within the next few weeks.

Addressed to Paris, Washington, Rome and Tokyo.[2]

TC telegram (WP, DLC).
   [1] That is, Nikolai Vasil'evich Chaikovskii.
   [2] About the fate of this suggestion, see the extract from the Diary of Lord Derby printed at Jan. 11, 1919.

Edith Bolling Galt Wilson to Her Family

Letter #3   On Royal Train en route to Rome.

Dearest Ones: Jan. 2nd 1919

The train shakes so I am afraid you will never read this, but I will begin another joint letter to you all. I sent a line yesterday to

Bert,[1] wishing you all a happy New Year, & we started at once for
the train leaving Paris at 7 last night. We slept pretty well as we
were all tired having reached there just 24 hours before from London. We had all longed for exercise, so we went out to St. Cloud
& played golf in the morning. Wilmer & Col. House came to lunch,
& afterwards the Pointcarés called on us at 2:15 & we returned the
call at 4. In the interval I had stacks of mail to look over & many
notes to write.

So many people sent me flowers for New Year & some candy &
fruit.

I began a letter to Mother in London but never had time to finish
it. Our visit there was perfect & I never saw such simplicity mingled
with beautiful state ceremony.

We reached London on the 26 of Dec. at 2. Found the King &
Queen & Princess Mary at the station together with most of the
Cabinet etc, we having been met at Dover by the Duke of Con-
naught, Mr. Davis, Lord Reading etc.

We lunched on the train & were waited on by one of the old
Servants of King Edward. At London we drove in State Coaches
drawn by 4 black horses with a groom in red coat & high hat
mounted on one of each pair, then 2 men up at the back. I never
saw denser crowds or a more whole-souled reception & welcome.

When we reached Buckingham Palace there was the inspection
of the guard of honor. Then we were taken to our own aptments
by the King & Queen & shown everything—just as one would do
in the most modest home. They then said if we would get ready it
would be nice if we would go & call on Queen Alexandra & all the
Royal family & they would send with us the King's Equerary
[Equerry]—Sir Charles Cust, a perfectly delightful person who took
complete charge of us from the time we left Calais until he returned
us there.

So we changed our clothes & with Sir Charles in the motor with
us & Gen. Harts & Adml. Grayson in another we started on our
round, going 1st to see the Queen Mother, who met us in the same
cordial unaffected friendship. Unfortunately she is now almost stone
deaf, so to hide this she talks most of the time, thus claiming the
Royal perogative of not listening.

The Princess Royal Victoria[2] was there, as was another daughter
now queen of Norway,[3] her daughter & little son.[4] Queen Alexandra

---

[1] Mrs. Wilson's sister, Bertha Bolling.
[2] Louise Victoria Alexandra Dagmar, Princess Royal of Great Britain and Duchess of
Fife.
[3] Maud Charlotte Mary Victoria, wife of Haakon VII of Norway.
[4] Mrs. Wilson was confused. The only child of the King and Queen of Norway was

introduced them this way "Oh, I want you to know Victoria, & this is Maud just come from Norway to make us a little visit, the 1st since this terrible war started. Maud tell them the names of the children." Thus we were at once made friends. They all keep beautiful leather books in which each one asks you to write your name, & thank you as though you had mentioned them in your will.

This was the only one of 7 calls we were to get out of the car [for;] the others were done by Sir Charles who wrote our names for us in more large books.

So we got back in about 30 minutes. I forgot to tell you about going on the Balcony at the Palace. Just after we arrived the crowd called for us, & the King and Queen appeared at our door to ask us to join them on the Balcony—which we were most interested to do. I never saw such a crowd. They said there were at least 30 thousand people in the square in front of the Palace & when Woodrow went out they cheered as with one throat—it was really wonderful. They insisted so that he made a little speech.

Well to go on, when we got back from the calls, W. had to have long conferences which kept him until just time to get ready for dinner which was at 8:30 This we had in a small dining room belonging to our suite, with only 8 in the Party—the King, Queen, Princess Mary, & the 2 young Princess Henry & George[5] home for the holidays, the old Duke[6] & ourselves. We had a really jolly party & at 10:30 when we got up from the table the queen invited me to go & see her own rooms & the King said he wanted to talk to W. So "the children" were told to entertain "Uncle Arthur." All of the rooms belonging to the queen are in exquisite taste & harmony & have been arranged entirely by her. There are about 10 & each one charming of its kind. There is a French one, an Empire, a Chinese etc.

The next day Miss Benham & I worked over mail in the morning & went to lunch with Lady Reading. She had Mrs. Lloyd George, Mrs. Asquith, Miss Bonar Law, Lady Wiseman, Lady Harcourt,[7] who is an American & ourselves.

Crown Prince Olav (born 1903), who did accompany his mother to London. London *Times*, Dec. 18, 1918. The "daughter" may have been one of the two daughters of the Princess Royal—Alexandra Victoria Alberta Edwina Louise or Maud Alexandra Victoria Georgia Bertha.

[5] That is, Princess Victoria Alexandra Alice Mary and Princes Henry William Frederick Albert and George Edward Alexander Edmund.

[6] That is, the Duke of Connaught.

[7] Margaret Owen (Mrs. David) Lloyd George; Emma Alice Margaret Tennant (Mrs. Herbert Henry) Asquith; Florence Marjorie Hulton Sams Wiseman, Lady Wiseman, wife of Sir William Wiseman; and Mary Ethel Burns Harcourt, Lady Harcourt, wife of Lewis Harcourt, 1st Viscount Harcourt. "Miss Bonar Law" was either Mary Law, sister of Andrew Bonar Law, or Isabel Law, his elder daughter.

From there we went home & had a call from Lady Brice[8] at 4.
Mrs Butler Wright[9] came for us & we went to the Americal [Amer-
ican] Club, where we met all the Americans in London, & from
there to the American Embassy for Tea, where all the wives of the
Cabinet Ministers were & all the Embassy staff & many English
Ladies.

This kept us until dark & at 8:30 was the State Banquet given
in our honor. All the gold plate had been brought up from Windsor,
& every thing on the table for every service was gold. The table
was brilliant with the tall gold candalabra & masses of Poinsettia
blossoms.

The old Beef Eaters in the costume worn by them since Henry
the 8th time were stationed like images every few feet around the
room. I know B.[10] will remember them at the Tower of London, &
the waiters were all in velvet shorts & gorgeous coats of crimson
with powdered hair—just as they were dressed in Queen Anne's
time. I will never forget the scene. At one end of the huge room is
a gallery where there is a great organ. Here they had the King's
Regiment Band, in splendid uniforms play mostly American music.

I wore my black velvet & every one liked it. The queen was in
Gold Brocade with her wonderful jewels & was splendid to look
upon. They had many more men than women, but among the latter
was the tall, slender "Princess Pat"[11] whom we all learned to know
so well when her father was Gov. Gen. of Canada. She was so happy
over her engagement[12] which was to be announced the next day,
but which she & the King confided to me that night. They all call
her "Patsy," & she said she had never been called "Pat" until she
went to America.

There was almost every interesting man there that figures in the
history of the day—certainly every one in London.

There were the Cabinet [—] Lloyd George, Balfour, Asquith, Bonar
Law, Marsh, Haig, Adtm Beaty,[13] Rudyard Kipling, Lord Curson,[14]
Sargent, the artist,[15] all the Ambassadors from Foreign Countries,
Marhahrahjah[16] from India—who spoke perfect English & invited

[8] That is, Elizabeth Marion Ashton Bryce, Lady Bryce.
[9] Maude Wolfe Wright, wife of Joshua Butler Wright, at this time Counselor of the American embassy in London.
[10] Again, Bertha Bolling, who had traveled in Europe with Mrs. Wilson before the war.
[11] Princess Victoria Patricia Helena Elizabeth, daughter of Arthur William Patrick Albert, Duke of Connaught.
[12] Comdr. Alexander Robert Maule Ramsay, R.N.
[13] That is, Vice-Adm. Sir David Beatty. Marsh, just mentioned, cannot be identified.
[14] That is, Lord Curzon.
[15] That is, John Singer Sargent.
[16] Shri Sir Ganga Singh Bahadur, Maharaja of Bikaner.

me to visit him. His own troop is mounted on Camels, & make a splendid sight.

The next day was the beautiful ceremony at the Guild Hall, & another wonderful procession & then to the Mansion House, which is the Official Residence of the Lord Mayor.

Then from there to No. 10 Downing Street to take tea with the Lloyd Georges who had just learned of his wonderful majority in the Elections, & were, naturally, very happy. Then W. dined there to meet some men, & I dined with the Davis's—going from there back to change my dress & then to the station to start at 11 for Carlisle. In the afternoon the queen came down to my room to say goodbye, as they were taking "Maud" to the Theatre, but they were going to see us on Monday, when we got back, that they were having just a little dinner of 35 for us on Monday, & as we got back at 7:30 they would dine at 8:30

AL (EBWP, DLC).

From the Diary of Dr. Grayson

Friday, January 3, 1919.

The special train reached the station in Rome at 9:30 in the morning. There was a great crowd in waiting together with a guard of honor. As the President descended from the train an Italian military band played the American National Anthem. President Wilson was greeted, as he stepped from his car, by King Victor Emanuel and his aides. The President inspected the guards, after which he passed through a double file of soldiers into the station then through to the great square beyond. Royal carriages were in waiting for the party. The first, in which the President and King rode immediately was surrounded by a troop of Royal Cavalry. They moved forward with the carriage enclosed in a hollow square. The entire route to the Quirinal Palace was lined with troops. At all street intersections the people were held well behind the house line. As far as the eye could see men, women and children were jammed in the roadways adjacent. The Rome reception was extremely enthusiastic so far as the people were concerned. In the big square around the Quirinal, every available inch of space was filled with an enthusiastic crowd of spectators. Entering the Palace, the President and King Victor, followed by Mrs. Wilson, the Queen,[1] and the other members of the party passed up the royal staircase between lines of Tuscan guards into the Swill room. These guards were selected from the grenadiers and were the largest men phys-

ically in Italy. Arriving in what is known as the Swill room the
members of the court were presented to the President by his Majesty. Following the presentation, on invitation of the King and Queen,
the President and his party inspected the wing of the Palace which
had been set aside for hospital purposes. In this section every patient had undergone a major operation. Those who were able to do
so stood at attention as the President went by. Some were without
arms, some without legs, but all apparently were very happy. On
many of the stands beside the beds were photographs of President
Wilson, showing the affection in which he was held by the wounded
soldiers. At the conclusion of the hospital inspection the King and
Queen invited the President and Mrs. Wilson to greet the crowd
from the little balcony. Not less than 25,000 people were gathered
in the square below. They cheered heartily. The President acknowledged their greeting by waving his hat and bowing. It was impossible to make a speech as he was too far removed above the heads
of the multitude.

This ceremony concluded, the President, Mrs. Wilson, myself,
General W. W. Harts and Miss Benham reentered carriages and
proceeded to the Royal Villa, where luncheon was served. In addition to the American guests there were present the King and
Queen, the Crown Prince[2] and the four little princesses.[3] The five
children spoke perfect English, but the Queen spoke only in French.
The King however spoke English. After luncheon the King entertained the President by showing him many war relics that he personally had collected on the battlefield, such as rifles, swords, gre-
nades, helmets, and many other German and Austrian souvenirs.
He offered to share with the President but the latter very courteously said that they mean so much to the King, owing to the fact
that he had personally collected them, that he did not feel that he
should take any of them from him. At this stage, Orlando, the Italian
Premier, arrived and said that the Italian newspaper men wanted
to see the President and that the President was expected to speak
to the crowd in the square in front of the Victor Emanuel Second
Memorial, but that Sonnino the Foreign Minister had sent word
that it was "impudent" for the newspaper men to expect to see the
President or for the crowd to expect a speech at this place, as the
officials had made no arrangements for such a meeting. The President did not agree with Mr. Sonnino and stated that he would see
the newspaper correspondents as soon as he returned to the Quirinal which he did. Following this talk he conferred with Sonnino
and Ex-Premier Salandra[4] separately. Previously, however, the representative of the American Committee on Public Information, Mr.
J. J. Hurley,[5] had announced through the afternoon newspapers

that the President would greet the populace from the Victor Emanuel Square. The President was promised by the Italian officials that he would be driven near enough to the court in the square so that he could see the people and they could see him and he could wave his hat to them on his way to the Parliament buildings. This promise was not kept and one of the largest crowds ever assembled to greet President Wilson was disappointed through no fault of his. The President was accompanied to the Parliament by the King, where he delivered an address.

A state dinner was given at the Quirinal at eight o'clock, about 150 guests attending. The King toasted the President while the President responded. At ten o'clock the President visited the capitol of the City of Rome, where he was made a citizen of the ancient municipality by the mayor. He made a speech. About 10,000 were in attendance.

[1] Queen Elena.
[2] Umberto, Prince of Piedmont.
[3] Princesses Jolanda Margherita Milena Elisabetta Maria, Mafalda Maria Elisabetta Anna Romana, Giovanna Elisabetta Antonia Romana Maria, and Maria Francisca Anna Romana. The spelling "Francisca" is from the *Almanach de Gotha* (Gotha, Germany, 1917), p. 50.
[4] Antonio Salandra, Prime Minister of Italy from March 1914 to June 1916.
[5] Actually, John Hearley.

An Address to the Italian Parliament[1]

January 3, 1919.

Your Majesty, Mr. President, Mr. President of the Chamber: You are bestowing upon me an unprecedented honor, which I accept because I believe that it is extended to me as the representative of the great people for whom I speak, and I am going to take this opportunity to say how entirely the heart of the American people has been with the great people of Italy. We have seemed no doubt indifferent at times, to look on from a great distance, but our hearts have never been far away. All sorts of ties have long bound the people of America to the people of Italy, and when the people of the United States, knowing this people, have witnessed its sufferings, its sacrifices, its heroic action upon the battlefield and its heroic endurance at home—its steadfast endurance at home touching us more nearly to the quick even than its heroic action on the battlefield—we have been bound by a new tie of profound admiration. Then, back of it all and through it all, running like the golden thread that wove it together, was our knowledge that the people of Italy had gone into this war for the same exalted principles of right and justice that moved our own people. And so I welcome this opportunity of conveying to you the heartfelt greetings of the people of the United States.

But we cannot stand in the shadow of this war without knowing that there are things awaiting us which are in some senses more difficult than those we have undertaken. While it is easy to speak of right and justice, it is sometimes difficult to work them out in practice, and there will require a purity of motive and disinterestedness of object which the world has never witnessed before in the councils of nations. It is for that reason that it seems to me that you will forgive me if I lay some of the elements of the new situation before you for a moment. The distinguishing fact of this war is that great empires have gone to pieces, and the characteristic of those empires was that they held different peoples reluctantly together under the coercion of force and the guidance of intrigue. The great difficulty among such states as those of the Balkans has been that they were always accessible to secret influence; that they were always being penetrated by intrigue of one sort and another; and that north of them lay disturbed populations which were held together, not by sympathy and friendship, but by the coercive force of a military power. Now the intrigue is checked and the bands are broken, and what are we going to do to provide a new cement to hold these people together? They have not been accustomed to being independent. They must now be independent. I am sure that you recognize the principle as I do that it is not our privilege to say what sort of government they shall set up, but we are friends of these people, and it is our duty as their friends to see to it that some kind of protection is thrown around them, something supplied which will hold them together. There is only one thing that holds nations together, if you exclude force, and that is friendship and good will. The only thing that binds men together is friendship and, by the same token, the only thing that binds nations together is friendship.

Therefore, our task at Paris is to organize the friendship of the world, to see to it that all the moral forces that make for right and justice and liberty are united and are given a vital organization to which the peoples of the world will readily and gladly respond. In other words, our task is no less colossal than this, to set up a new international psychology, to have a new atmosphere. I am happy to say that in my dealings with the distinguished gentlemen who lead your nation and those who lead France and England, I feel that atmosphere gathering, that desire to do justice, that desire to establish friendliness, that desire to make peace rest upon right; and with this common purpose no obstacle need be formidable. The only use of an obstacle is to be overcome. All that an obstacle does with brave men is, not to frighten them, but to challenge them. So that it ought to be our pride to overcome everything that stands in the way.

We know that there cannot be another balance of power. That has been tried and found wanting, for the best of all reasons that it does not stay balanced inside itself, and a weight which does not hold together cannot constitute a makeweight in the affairs of men. Therefore, there must be something substituted for the balance of power, and I am happy to find everywhere in the air of these great nations the conception that that thing must be a thoroughly united league of nations. What men once considered theoretical and idealistic turns out to be practical and necessary. We stand at the opening of a new age in which a new statesmanship will, I am confident, lift mankind to new levels of endeavor and achievement.

¹ Wilson spoke to a joint session of the Senate and the Chamber of Deputies, Adeodato Bonasi, President of the Senate, and Giuseppi Marcora, President of the Chamber, both read addresses of welcome. *New York Times*, Jan. 4, 1919, and London *Times*, Jan. 6, 1919.

Remarks to Press Representatives in Rome¹

[Jan. 3, 1919]

Let me thank you, gentlemen, very warmly, for this stirring address, because it goes straight to my heart as well as to my understanding. If I had known that this important delegation was coming to see me, I would have tried to say something worthy of the occasion. As it is, speaking without preparation, I can only say that my purpose is certainly expressed in that paper, and I believe that the purpose of those associated at Paris is a common purpose. Justice and right are big things, and in these circumstances they are big with difficulty. I am not foolish enough to suppose that our decisions will be easy to arrive at, but the principles upon which they are to be arrived at ought to be indisputable, and I have the conviction that if we do not rise to the expectation of the world and satisfy the souls of great peoples like the people of Italy, we shall have the most unenviable distinction in history. Because what is happening now is that the soul of one people is crying to the soul of another, and no people in the world with whose sentiments I am acquainted wishes a bargaining settlement. They all want settlements based upon what is right, or as nearly right as human judgment can arrive at, and with this atmosphere of the opinion of mankind to work in, it ought to be impossible to go very far astray. So that so long as the thought of the people keeps clear, the conclusions of their representatives ought to keep clear. We need the guidance of the people; we need the constant expression of the purposes and ideals of the people.

I have been associated with so many of your fellow countrymen in America, and I am proud to call so many of them my own fellow countrymen, that I would be ashamed if I did not feel the pulse of this great people beating in these affairs. I believe there are almost as many Italians in New York City as in almost any city in Italy, and I was saying today that in redistributing sovereignty we could hardly let Italy have these valued fellow citizens. They are men who have done some things that the men of no other nationality have done. They have looked after the people coming from Italy to the United States in a systematic way, to see that they were guided to the places and occupations for which they were best prepared, and they have won our admiration by this thoughtfulness for us. It is with a feeling of being half at home that I find myself in this capital of Italy.

> [1] Wilson received a delegation from the Italian press at the Quirinal. Andrea Torre, president of the Association of Italian Journalists, made a brief speech of welcome in which he stressed the necessity for a league of nations and for the settlement of all national and ethnic questions at the peace conference. *New York Times*, Jan. 4, 1919, and London *Times*, Jan. 6, 1919.

After-Dinner Remarks at the Quirinal

January 3, 1919.

Your Majesty: I have been very much touched by the generous terms of the address which you have just read.[1] I feel it would be difficult for me to make a worthy reply, and yet if I could speak simply the things that are in my heart I am sure they would constitute an adequate reply.

I had occasion at the Parliament this afternoon to speak of the strong sympathy that had sprung up between the United States and Italy during the terrible years of the war, but perhaps here I could speak more intimately and say how sincerely the people of the United States have admired your own course and your own constant association with the armies of Italy, and the gracious and generous and serving association of Her Majesty the Queen.

It has been a matter of pride with us that so many men of Italian origin were in our own armies and associated with their brethren of Italy itself in the great enterprise of freedom. These are no small matters, and they complete that process of welding together of the sympathies of nations which has been going on so long between our peoples. The Italians in the United States have excited a particular degree of admiration. They, I believe, are the only people of a given nationality who have been careful to organize themselves to see that their compatriots coming to America were from month to month and year to year guided to the places of the industries most suitable to their previous habits. No other nationality has taken such pains as that, and in serving their fellow countrymen they have served the United States, because these people have found places where they would be most useful and would most immediately earn their own living, and they have thereby added to the prosperity of the country itself. In every way we have been happy in our association at home and abroad with the people of this great state.

I was saying playfully to Mr. Orlando and Baron Sonnino this afternoon that in trying to put the peoples of the world under their proper sovereignties we would not be willing to part with the Italians in the United States. We would not be willing, unless they desired it, that you should resume possession of them, because we too much value the contribution that they have made, not only to the industry of the United States, but to its thought and to many elements of its life. This is, therefore, a very welcome occasion upon which to express a feeling that goes very deep. I was touched the other day to have an Italian, a very plain man, say to me that we had helped to feed Italy during the war, and it went to my heart, because we had been able to do so little. It was necessary for us to use our tonnage so exclusively for the handling of troops and of the supplies that had to follow them from the United States that we could not do half as much as it was our desire to do, to supply grain to this country, or coal, or any of the supplies which it so much needed during the progress of the war. And knowing as we did in this indirect way the needs of the country, you will not wonder that we were moved by its steadfastness. My heart goes out to the little poor families all over this great kingdom who stood the brunt and the strain of the war and gave their men gladly to make other men free and other women and children free. Those are the people, and many like them, to whom after all we owe the glory of this great achievement, and I want to join with you, for I am sure I am joining with you, in expressing my profound sympathy not only, but my very profound admiration as well.

It is my privilege and honor to propose the health of His Majesty the King and of Her Majesty the Queen, and long prosperity to Italy.

[1] The King had proposed a toast to Wilson in a brief speech which praised Wilson's dedication to international organization and peace and stressed the ties which bound Italy and the United States. One of the most important of these ties, he said, was the

one represented by Italians who had emigrated from Italy to the United States, many of whom had returned to fight in the Italian army during the war. His most significant sentence was the following: "Italy, having now gathered to her own bosom those brothers so long sorrowing under foreign oppression, and having reconquered the confines which alone can give her security and true independence, is preparing to co-operate with you in the most cordial manner to reach the most practical means for drawing into a single circle the civilized nations for the purpose of creating in the supreme form of a League of Nations the conditions most fitted to safeguard and protect each one's rights." An apparently complete English text of the King's remarks appears in the *New York Times*, Jan. 5, 1919.

Remarks at the Capitol

January 3, 1919.

You have done me a very great honor.[1] Perhaps you can imagine what a feeling it is for a citizen of one of the newest of the great nations to be made a citizen of this ancient city. It is a distinction which I am sure you are conferring upon me as the representative of the great people for whom I speak. One who has been a student of history cannot accept an honor of this sort without having his memory run back to the extraordinary series of events which have centered in this place. But as I have thought today, I have been impressed by the contrast between the temporary and the permanent things. Many political changes have centered about Rome, from the time when from a little city she grew to be the mistress of an empire. And change after change has swept away many things, altering the very form of her affairs, but the thing that has remained permanent has been the spirit of Rome and of the Italian people. That spirit seems to have caught with each age the characteristic purpose of the age. This imperial people now gladly represents the freedom of nations. This people which at one time seemed to conceive the purpose of governing the world now takes part in the liberal enterprise of offering the world its own government. Can there be a finer or more impressive illustration of the indestructible human spirit, and of the unconquerable spirit of liberty?

I have been reflecting in these recent days about a colossal blunder that has just been made—the blunder of force by the Central Empires. If Germany had waited a single generation, she would have had a commercial empire of the world. She was not willing to conquer by skill, by enterprise, by commercial success. She must needs attempt to conquer by arms, and the world will always acclaim the fact that it is impossible to conquer it by arms; that the only thing that conquers it is the sort of service which can be rendered in trade, in intercourse, in friendship, and that there is no conquering power which can suppress the freedom of the human spirit.

I have rejoiced personally in the partnership of the Italian and the American people, because it was a new partnership in an old enterprise, an enterprise predestined to succeed wherever it is undertaken—the enterprise that has always borne that handsome name which we call "Liberty." Men have pursued it sometimes like a mirage that seemed to elude them, that seemed to run before them as they advanced, but never have they flagged in their purpose to achieve it, and I believe that I am not deceived in supposing that in this age of ours they are nearer to it than they ever were before. The light that shined upon the summit now seems almost to shine at our feet, and if we lose it, it will be only because we have lost faith and courage, for we have the power to attain it.

So it seems to me that there never was a time when a greater breath of hope and of confidence had come into the minds and the hearts of men like the present. I would not have felt at liberty to come away from America if I had not felt that the time had arrived when, forgetting local interests and local ties and local purposes, men should unite in this great enterprise which will ever tie free men together as a body of brethren and a body of free spirits.

I am honored, Sir, to be taken into this ancient comradeship of the citizenship of Rome.

Printed in *Addresses of President Wilson on First Trip* . . .
   [1] Prince Prospero Colonna, Mayor of Rome, had presented Wilson with the citizenship of Rome. Tommaso Tittoni also spoke on behalf of the Provincial Council of Rome. London *Times*, Jan. 6, 1919.

Edgar Rickard to Herbert Clark Hoover

Washington Jan. 3, 1919.

98. For Hoover from Rickard. The following is a repeat of our 86. Facts as to wheat guarantee for 1919 have been submitted to Agricultural Committee Congress as directed by President through Secretary Houston. Lever now asking that bill be drawn. We suggest, to avoid discussion in Congress as to whether Department of Agriculture should be designated to carry out guarantees that a short bill be drawn making appropriation of 500 million to be used for that purpose and that power and authority be given the President to use such agency as he may select and under the supervision of such Department as he may designate. In our opinion we will stand much better chance of being relieved of this responsibility by the President than by Congress. Please advise your views, matter is pressing.

Edgar Rickard and William Anderson Glasgow, Jr.,
to Herbert Clark Hoover

Washington, Jan. 3, 1919.

RUSH. 99. Hoover from Rickard and Glasgow. Your number 127.

Houston reported that President had directed him to cooperate with us in statement to Congress as to wheat guarantee 1919. Combined meeting of Cabinet and War Council before President left which he attended urged same things. We submitted to Congress with Houston memorandum of facts giving provision of food acts on subject and various proclamations of President also showing crop conditions and prospects and stated: "The present agency will have to be convened or a new one created with power to buy stores and sell such wheat of the 1919 crop as may be offered to it and sufficient appropriation will have to be obtained to furnish such agency with ample funds to at all times purchase throughout United States at the guaranteed price such wheat of the 1919 crop as may be offered it and also to provide storage facility to take care the same by lease or purchase of facilities now in existence additional facilities or both. The appropriation will have to be on a basis to enable the guaranteed price to be maintained at all times by purchase of wheat with funds provided by the government and without relying upon outside credit." Lever now asks us to prepare and submit a bill and we propose for your approval a bill making appropriation of such sum as may be considered sufficient by the President for carrying out 1918 and 1919 guarantee and give him powers to select such agency as he may think desirable for maintaining the 1919 guarantee and put same under command of such permanent department of government as he may determine and also authorize the President to continue to exercise authority given him under food act for maintaining of guarantee alone and such other powers as may be found necessary until guarantee has been fully discharged. It is much better to have President select the agency than to have controversies in Congress in an effort to put this in Agricultural Department. It would do you and Barnes[1] great injury to announce to Congress that you would have nothing to do with it and yet you should be able to accomplish this with President. Have not discussed with Houston but do not believe he will allow this responsibility to be put upon his department unless by direct order from President. We would like to have your early approval of bills drawn on lines above indicated.

T telegrams (WP, DLC).
  [1] That is, Julius Howland Barnes, president of the United States Food Administration Grain Corp.

Frank Lyon Polk to Robert Lansing

Washington Jan. 3, 1919.

81. For Secretary of State. Secretary of War calls my attention to the fact that Polish troops are being enlisted in this country with the knowledge and consent of the War Department. This arrangement has also the approval of the Department. In view of the fact the Poles are apparently beginning hostilities against Germany, the Secretary believes the time has now come to refuse to permit any further enlistments in this country for foreign governments, particularly the new governments, as he believes that the troops may be used to enforce by arms claims of these new governments. Please take the matter up with the President and ask him to be good enough to instruct the Secretary of War as to the course he shall pursue.   Polk.

T telegram (WP, DLC).

From the Diary of Dr. Grayson

Saturday, January 4, 1919.

At 9:30 President Wilson visited the Pantheon, where he laid wreaths on the tombs of King Victor Emanuel, Third,[1] and King Humbert.[2] He spent half an hour inspecting the structure. The President was then driven to the Garibaldi monument, which he viewed, leaving his automobile to do so. He walked over to the side of the hill where he had a view of all the hills of Rome stretched in panorama beyond. The party proceeded to the Academy—where the President received a degree and made a response. An amusing incident of this visit was the attitude of a very elderly gentleman who during the entire visit rather rudely scrutinized Mrs. Wilson through opera glasses. Leaving the Academy the President visited the coliseum, baths and forum in turn. Luncheon was served at the American Embassy where the President was host to the King.

The luncheon was arranged at the Embassy by Thomas Nelson Page, the American Ambassador. The Ambassador "coached" the President as to how he should act as host, and among the things he said was this:

"You must toast the King as you are on American soil in the Embassy. The proper time to do so at this luncheon is immediately after they serve asparagus."

When the salad had been served, there being no asparagus, the President proceeded to give the toast to the King. After luncheon he said:

"Mr. Ambassador, if I had followed your instructions literally I would have failed to have given a toast."

The Ambassador said: "I do not understand, Mr. President."

To which the President replied: "Because we did not have any asparagus."

Whereupon Mrs. Page, the Ambassador's wife, said: "Oh, Mr. Page did not understand that; we found after making the menu card out that we could not buy any asparagus for the luncheon."

Among the notables present were General Diaz, Commander-in-Chief of the Italian Armies. Fifty-two guests in all were present. At 3:15 the President and party, in three automobiles, proceeded to the Vatican. Ambassador Page abandoned the party at the entrance to the Vatican. He was obliged to leave because of international etiquette, which prohibited him, an accredited ambassador to the Italian court visiting the Vatican in the company of an official mission. As the Presidential party entered the courtyard, the papal guard paid military honors while the band of papal gendarmes rendered the American National Anthem. The President was greeted by Mgr. O'Hearn,[3] an American prelate who was rector of the American College in Rome. He introduced the President to the Pope's Chamberlain and the latter in turn, introduced him to the Major Domo, who escorted the party up the stairs and through from thirty to forty rooms into the small room adjoining the little throne room. This is the room in which Leo XIII died. The procession traversed the entire distance through a line of Swiss guards while the papal guards accompanied the President. The Chamberlains of the Cape and Sword were dressed in the Elizabethan Court costume and the Vatican courtiers were garbed in the dress of Papal Rome. Among those in attendance on the Pope was the papal postmaster, a Roman Prince who traced his lineage to Fabius Maximus. Only lesser prelates of the church were present, among them three Americans. Formal ceremony was waived for the President and his party, they being escorted through the various chambers without the customary formalities. The President was ushered into the little throne room by Mgr. O'Hearn accompanied only by General Harts, an interpreter and myself. This room was that [in] which only reigning princes are received. The entrance of His Holiness was announced by the tinkling of a small bell. The Pope opened his study door himself entering the room unescorted. He greeted the President in French leading him alone by the hand into his study. They were accompanied by two interpreters. Following a brief private interview, Father O'Hearn opened the study door and called General

Harts and myself into the study, where we were presented to the Pope by the President. When I was presented to the Pope as the President's physician, the President said:

"This is the man who keeps me well." The Pope, addressing me in French said:

"You have done a good service and the world should be grateful to you."

Meanwhile the other members of the party had entered the little throne room. A small bell then tinkled to announce the reentry of the Pope and the President into the little throne room, where the President introduced the members of his party individually to his Holiness. The Pope was dressed in white, wearing the white cap, gold chain and cross, and red sandals. He was small of stature, not more than five feet four inches, and apparently weighed about one hundred and thirty pounds. He wore glasses. He blessed the members of the party with the sign of the cross saying:

"It is for you, your family and your dear ones."

Leaving the presence of the Pope we went down stairs where the President was introduced to Cardinal Gaspari,[4] Papal Secretary of State. From there we drove back to the American Embassy, which was American soil, leaving immediately afterward for the Quirinal, where the President held a number of conferences. At 5:30 the President visited the Parish House of Dr. Lowry, rector of the American Methodist College of Rome,[5] where he held a reception to the American Protestants of Rome. Following this the President returned a call to the King's Villa where he had a ten minute visit with the King and Queen and children. Dinner was served in the Quirinal Palace at 7:30. I sat beside an old Italian Duke who spoke English, but later proved to be very deaf. When I thought I was making fine headway, I remarked,

"I was delighted to see General Diaz." He replied: "Yes, the Alps were very beautiful but you had a poor opportunity to see them as you passed through ninety-two tunnels between Paris and Rome."

The King and Queen then accompanied the President and his party to the railroad station. A flash light photograph was taken of the King and Queen and the President and Mrs. Wilson. We departed at 9:30 for Genoa.

[1] Actually, Vittorio Emanuele II (1820-1878).
[2] Humbert I (1844-1900).
[3] That is, Msgr. Charles Aloysius O'Hern.
[4] That is, Pietro Cardinal Gasparri.
[5] Actually, the Rev. Walter Lowrie, rector of St. Paul's American Church in Rome.

Remarks to the Royal Academy of Science in Rome[1]

January 4, 1919.

Your Majesty, Mr. President, and Gentlemen of the Academy: I have listened, Sir, with the profoundest appreciation to the beautiful address which you have been kind enough to deliver, and I want to say how deeply I appreciate the honor you conferred upon me in permitting me to become a member of this great Academy, because there is a sense in which the continuity of human thought is in the care of bodies like this. There is a serenity, a long view on the part of science which seems to be of no age, but to carry human thought along from generation to generation, freed from the elements of passion. Therefore, it is, I dare say, with all men of science a matter of profound regret and shame that science should in a nation which had made science its boast have been put to such dishonorable uses in the recent war. Every just mind must condemn those who so debased the studies of men of science as to use them against humanity, and, therefore, it is part of your task and of ours to reclaim science from this disgrace, to show that she is devoted to the advancement and interest of humanity and not to its embarrassment and destruction.

I wish very much, Sir, that I could believe that I was in some sense a worthy representative of the men of science of the United States. I cannot claim to be in any proper sense a man of science. My studies have been in the field of politics all my life and, while politics may by courtesy be called a science, it is a science which is often practiced without rule and is very hard to set up standards for so that one can be sure that one is steering the right course. At the same time, while perhaps there is no science of government, there ought to be, I dare say, in government itself the spirit of science, that is to say, the spirit of disinterestedness, the spirit of seeking after the truth so far as the truth is ready to be applied to human circumstances. Because, after all, the problem of politics is to satisfy men in the arrangements of their lives, is to realize for them so far as possible the objects which they have entertained generation after generation and have seen so often postponed. Therefore, I have often thought that the university and the academy of science have their part in simplifying the problems of politics and therefore assisting to advance human life along the lines of political structure and political action.

It is very delightful to draw apart for a little while into this quiet place and feel again that familiar touch of thought and of knowledge which it has been my privilege to know familiarly through so great a part of my life. If I have come out upon a more adventurous and disordered stage, I hope that I have not lost the recollection and may in some sense be assisted by counsels such as yours.

Printed in *Addresses of President Wilson on First Trip* . . .
¹ Wilson was made a member of the Reale Accademia dei Lincei, or Royal Academy of Science, in an elaborate ceremony attended by the King and Queen, members of the diplomatic corps, and many prominent Italian officials and scientists. Senator Francesco D'Ovidio, Professor of Literature at the University of Naples and the President of the Academy, hailed Wilson as "the worthy representative of the culture of the New World, now revivifying the ancient culture of the Old." *New York Times*, Jan. 5, 1919.

Tasker Howard Bliss to Newton Diehl Baker

No. 42.

My dear Mr. Secretary: Paris, France, January 4, 1919.

The President came back from London on December 31st and had a meeting of the American Commission in Mr. House's apartments on the afternoon of January 1. He told us of the impressions which he had received at his various interviews with Mr. Lloyd George and Mr. Balfour. In general, he seemed very much pleased. He was surprised at the mildness of the attitude of Mr. Lloyd George and his substantial agreement with him (the President) on various important points. He confessed that he could not feel quite sure as to the permanence of Mr. Lloyd George's views. I think he will understand the man better after he has dealt with him a while in council.

He was very much impressed by a document which he described as thoroughly statesmanlike in character which had been prepared by General Smuts.¹ He had had time to study only part of this and intended to finish it on his way to Italy. He was struck by the extraordinary resemblance of General Smuts' views on such subjects as The League of Nations to the American views. In view of General Smuts' intimate relations with the British Government and the fact that he heard no criticism of the document, he hoped that these views might be more or less the governmental views.

The President left that same night at 7 o'clock for Italy. You have already read of his reception there, apparently as cordial and as enthusiastic as everywhere else here in Europe. What the reaction will be, should the American attitude oppose that of Italy or any of the points which now interest the latter so deeply, time alone will tell. The Italian Government has been conducting a tremendous and apparently highly successful propaganda in favor of their annexation schemes on the eastern coast of the Adriatic. Men like Bissolati who have constantly opposed the plans of annexation of alien races, seem now to be snowed under. An Italian sentiment of such intensity has been worked up in favor of such annexations that I am afraid that it is going to make trouble for the Peace Conference unless the latter plays entirely into Italian hands.

This matter of official propaganda is really, in my opinion, a very serious affair. The war time restrictions on the press still exists. Here in Paris the daily papers appear with white spaces in their columns indicating articles or news that have been censored. Nothing can be published that the Government does not approve. At the same time, the Government offers every inducement for the publication of articles which tend to lead public opinion in the channel desired by the Government. The press is venal everywhere outside of England. An atmosphere is being formed which completely distorts public vision.

Most thinking men here are looking with apprehension on the course being followed by the Allies with respect to Germany. The English view is coming to be more like that of the American; but the French view is little less than one of insanity. Neither England or France want to see German industrialism and commercialism revived until they themselves are well in the lead in the race. But the French want to bring complete and lasting ruin on Germany. At the same time, their propaganda has convinced their people that taxes will not have to be raised (they practically have not raised it during the war but have lived on borrowed money) and that they will live in ease on enormous indemnities to be squeezed out of Germany during many years to come. They cannot get a tithe of what they now expect except out of a Germany which is rich and prosperous. Their governmental organs are now demanding that German Austria shall not be permitted to join Germany or to remain as a confederated state with any of the former Austro-Hungarian states.

New problems for settlement are looming up every day. And the trouble is that if they are not settled before long, starvation with consequent Bolshevism and a general upheaval of all governmental systems may leave no one to do the settling. It seems to me that the United States has every possible interest in a speedy assembling of the Peace Conference and in a prompt adjustment of things that will permit us to withdraw. The mass of the common people here expect us and want us to direct the matter; their governments do not want this. I think that it is time that we were ranging ourselves more decidedly on the side of these common people.

There is still nothing definite to write to you about. No delegations but the Americans have arrived here. There is no one with whom to exchange views. There is nothing to tell you except the gossip and speculation which fill the newspapers. I hope matters will move more rapidly when the President returns from Rome next week.

Hastily but cordially yours,   T. H. Bliss.

CCL (T. H. Bliss Papers, DLC).
 [1] That is, Smuts' *The League of Nations. A Programme for the Peace Conference* . . . *16 December 1918.*

Ignace Jan Paderewski to Edward Mandell House

Copenhagen, January 4, 1919.

70. Urgent. Following written undated message received through British Legation addressed to Colonel House, Paris, signed Paderewski. "Situation most critical. Bolshevist invasion of former Polish territories still in progress.[1] Thousands of people tortured, murdered, many buried alive. Vilnaminsk[2] even Grodno menaced, huge population in danger of extermination. Invading army daily increased by prisoners of war returning from Germany. Starving veterans are fed by Bolshevist provided they join the ranks. Poland in assisting present Partisan Government, too weak to organize any resistance; human material still considerable but no arms, equipment, munitions. Disaster imminent. At this tragic hour my country appeals to her best, most generous friend asking for help for salvation. 50,000 Americans, one division of French and one of British troops if sent immediately with necessary material for a large Polish army will certainly stop further progress of this barbarous movement. If action is delayed our entire civilization may cease to exist. The war may result in establishment of barbarism all over Europe."

Osborne[3]

T telegram (WP, DLC).
 [1] The Soviet Western Army, following in the wake of the retreating German Army of the East, in late December 1918 and early January 1919 moved into the regions of Lithuania and Belorussia claimed by both Russia and Poland. The Bolsheviks captured Vilna on about January 8. *New York Times*, Jan. 10, 1919. This was a preliminary skirmish in what turned into the lengthy Polish-Soviet War of 1919-1920. For a detailed analysis of the origins of this conflict, see Norman Davies, *White Eagle, Red Star: The Polish-Soviet War, 1919-20* (London, 1972), pp. 19-38.
 [2] That is, Vilna and Minsk.
 [3] Lithgow Osborne, Chargé d'Affaires.

Edith Bolling Galt Wilson to Bertha Bolling

Continued

Rome Jan 4th 1918

Well Bert, who would ever have thought when we stayed at the little "Palais Hotel," that on my next visit I would stay at the "Palazzo

Quirinale" but here we are, and *how* I wish you were all with us! We arrived yesterday at 10, & nothing could have been more beautiful than these wonderful old buildings, with their windows flung wide open & from the sill of each one draped an old old banner in velvet or satin bearing either the Royal Arms or those of old families of Provinces and each in rich coloring softened by time.

Over these banners were the dark heads & brilliant dark eyes of men, women & children, crowded in to each until there was not an inch of space left, and each one crying Welcome & showering down baskets full of flowers, the lovely yellow mamosa & dark crimson roses—red as the blood Italy has shed for freedom, and the real Palma violet. The King & Queen met us & we went in open carriages just as we did in London.

The horses were not so fine, but the red Livery & gray wigs of the Flunkies were even more picturesque, & the Kings Guard was splendid to behold. We came straight to the Palais & the streets were indescribably beautiful & the crowds vast. When we arrived the Escort blew a blast of trumpets—which was deafening under those great stone arched gates, but inspiring never the less. We found all the Lords & Ladies in waiting lined up & each of the ladies wears a blue ribbon bow on the left shoulder pinned with a hugh diamond "E" with a coronet in diamonds over it. The "E" is for "Elanor" the Queen's name.

The King & Queen live in the Villa Savoyer outside the city & have given the Palais as a Hospital all during the War. So almost all of it is used still for that, they having had the furnature etc replaced for us in one side. I never saw more beautiful rooms— each one with wonderful Tapestrys, ceilings decorated by famous artists, magnificent furnature, Venetian chandeliers & mirrors. We each have 6 rooms, besides Miss Benham's, Margarets[1] & the servants.

Before coming to our rooms the K. & Queen took us through most of the Hospital which is filled with just boys pitifully wounded.

In one room the Dr. presented me with a Red Cross decoration for our help to Italy.

Paris Jan 8, 1918

I will have to leave this now for the next letter, for the Pouch goes today & I want you to be sure to get this. I had a lovely letter from Altrude[2] when I got back yesterday & a business line from Randolph,[3] both of which we thoroughly enjoyed. B's letter of the 10th of Dec. is the only other home news.

I sent a cablegram from Milan on the 5th to wish dear Mother many many more happy birthdays. We must have a celebration when we get back.

We reached here at 10 yesterday A.M. all of us tired out from 3 nights on the train & going hard each day at Genoa, Milan & Turin but are all well & join in love

happy New Year   Fondly   E.

ALI (EBWP, DLC).
  [1] That is, Margaret Woodrow Wilson.
  [2] That is, Alice Gertrude Gordon Grayson.
  [3] That is, John Randolph Bolling.

From the Diary of Dr. Grayson

Sunday, January 5, 1919.

At eight o'clock we arrived at Genoa, with rain falling in torrents. There was the usual local committee with open carriages, but I would not permit the President to ride in them. He with Mrs. Wilson and myself were furnished closed automobiles. Through well crowded streets, despite the rain, we proceeded to the statue of Mazzini, where the President laid a wreath at the base. Then we drove to the house wherein Christopher Columbus was born. This was located on a side street in what is now the poorer quarter of the city. In the room adjoining that in which Columbus was born is the wonderful statue known as "The Young Columbus." It represents a youth, sitting with legs crossed, chin resting on hand in an attitude of deep study, a beautiful type. Proceeding from this place we drove to the Town Hall, where the President delivered an address. En route to the railroad station we stopped at the Columbus Monument, at the base of which the President deposited another wreath. This monument was erected from money contributed by Italians in America. As the President laid the wreath at the base of the monument he said, "Columbus performed a great service to humanity when he discovered America."

We left Genoa at eleven o'clock arriving at Milan at three. Here the crowd was most enthusiastic, the President himself describing it as "Most superb, stupendous and overwhelming." The President drove from the station to the Royal Palace, where he addressed an enormous crowd from the balcony at four o'clock. None of the party could agree on the number in the crowd, the guesses ranging from 50,000 to 150,000. It was agreed, however by everyone, that it was the largest crowd they had ever seen gathered together. The American Consul at this place, whose name was Winship,[1] was by far the poorest and most inefficient we had yet seen. He proved much more of a hindrance than a help to us. As the President passed through the streets his automobile was deluged with papers hailing him as "Savior of humanity" and "God of Peace," "The Cavalier of Humanity," "The Moses from across the Atlantic." Members of the Italian party said that the population in this section are so enthusiastic about the President that they have burned sacred candles about his picture. At six o'clock the President visited the City Hall, where he was feted and made a citizen of Milan. The local committee tendered him a dinner at the Scala at 7:30. Here the President was asked to autograph many of the menu cards. I noticed that many of those to whom he gave them kissed the signature and pressed it to their hearts. The President then attended the opera, where the second act of Aida was given, with a cast of about four hundred. Before the opera he went out on the balcony and was heartily cheered by the crowd which filled the square below. At eleven o'clock we left for Turin in the special train.

[1] North Winship.

Remarks about Guiseppe Mazzini[1]

January 5, 1919.

I am very much moved, Sir, to be in the presence of this monument. On the other side of the water we have studied the life of Mazzini with almost as much pride as if we shared in the glory of his history, and I am very glad to acknowledge that his spirit has been handed down to us of a later generation on both sides of the water. It is delightful to me to feel that I am taking some small part in accomplishing the realization of the ideals to which his life and thought were devoted. It is with a spirit of veneration, Sir, and with a spirit I hope of emulation, that I stand in the presence of this monument and bring my greetings and the greetings of America with our homage to the great Mazzini.

[1] Wilson was responding to a brief speech by the Mayor of Genoa, one Signor Massone. An English translation of the mayor's remarks, T MS, is in WP, DLC. The Editors have been unable to learn the Mayor's given names.

Further Remarks in Genoa[1]

[Jan. 5, 1919]

Mr. Mayor: It is with many feelings of a very deep sort, perhaps too deep for adequate expression, that I find myself in Genoa. Genoa is a natural shrine for Americans. The connections of America with

Genoa are so many and so significant that there are some senses in which it may be said that we drew our life and beginnings from this city. You can realize, therefore, Sir, with what emotion I receive the honor which you have so generously conferred upon me of the citizenship of this great city. In a way it seems natural for an American to be a citizen of Genoa, and I shall always count it among the most delightful associations of my life that you should have conferred this honor upon me, and in taking away this beautiful edition of the works of Mazzini I hope that I shall derive inspiration from these volumes,[2] as I have already derived guidance from the principles which Mazzini so eloquently expressed. It is very inspiring, Sir, to feel how the human spirit is refreshed again and again from its original sources. It is delightful to feel how the voice of one people speaks to another through the mouth of men who have by some gift of God been lifted above the common level and seen the light of humanity, and therefore these words of your prophet and leader will, I hope, be deeply planted in the hearts of my fellow countrymen. There is already planted in those hearts, Sir, a very deep and genuine affection for the great Italian people, and the thoughts of my own nation turn constantly as we read our own history to this beautiful and distinguished city.

May I not thank you, Sir, for myself and for Mrs. Wilson and for my daughter, for the very gracious welcome you have accorded us and again express my pride and pleasure?

[1] Mayor Massone had just conferred upon Wilson citizenship of the city of Genoa in a brief address at the city hall. An English translation of his remarks, T MS, is in WP, DLC.
[2] Guiseppe Mazzini, *Scritti: Letterari, con un saggio di Enrico Neucioni* (2 vols., Milan, 1884). These volumes are in the Wilson Library, DLC.

Remarks about Christopher Columbus[1]

[Jan. 5, 1919]

In standing in front of this monument, Sir, I fully recognize the significance of what you have said. Columbus did do a service to mankind in discovering America, and it is America's pleasure and America's pride that she has been able to show that it was a service to mankind to open that great continent to settlement—the settlement of a free people, of a people, because free, desiring to see other peoples free and to share their liberty with the people of the world. It is for this reason no doubt, besides his fine spirit of adventure, that Columbus will always be remembered and honored, not only here in the land of his birth, but throughout the world as the man who led the way to those fields of freedom which, planted with a great seed, have now sprung up to the fructification of the world.

¹ Wilson was again responding to brief remarks by Mayor Massone. An English translation, T MS, is in WP, DLC.

Remarks at the Station in Milan¹

January 5, 1919.

Ladies and gentlemen: You make my heart very warm indeed by a welcome like this, and I know the significance of this sort of welcome in Milan, because I know how the heart of Italy and of the Italian people beats strong here. It is delightful to feel how your thoughts have turned towards us, because our thoughts first turned towards you, and they turn towards you from not a new but an ancient friendship, because the American people have long felt the pulse of Italy beat with their pulse in the desire for freedom. We have been students of your history, Sir. We know the vicissitudes and struggles through which you have passed. We know that no nation has more steadfastly held to a single course of freedom in its desires and its efforts than have the people of Italy, and therefore I come to this place, where the life of Italy seems to beat so strong, with a peculiar gratification. I feel that I am privileged to come into contact with you, and I want you to know how the words that I am uttering of sympathy and of friendship are not my own alone, but they are the words of the great people whom I represent. I was saying a little while ago at the monument to Columbus that he did a great thing, greater even than was realized at the time it was done. He discovered a new continent not only, but he opened it to children of freedom, and those children are now privileged to come back to their mother and to assist her in the high enterprise upon which her heart had always been set.

It is therefore with the deepest gratification that I find myself here and thank you for your generous welcome.

¹ Wilson had been greeted by many civil and military officials and by a large crowd. Senator Ludovico Gavazzi, a silk manufacturer of Milan, had delivered a speech of welcome in English. An Italian translation of his remarks is in the Milan *Corriere della Sera*, Jan. 6, 1919.

Remarks at the Royal Palace in Milan

[Jan. 5, 1919]

I cannot tell you how much complimented I am by your coming in person to give me this greeting. I have never known such a greeting as the people of Milan have given me on the streets. It has brought tears to my eyes, because I know that it comes from their hearts. I can see in their faces the same things that I feel towards them, and I know that it is an impulse of their friendship towards the nation that I represent as well as a gracious welcome to myself. I want to reecho the hope that we may all work together for a great peace as distinguished from a mean peace. And may I suggest this, that is a great deal in my thoughts: the world is not going to consist now of great empires. It is going to consist for the most part of small nations apparently, and the only thing that can bind small nations together is the knowledge that each wants to treat the others fairly. That is the only thing. The world has already shown that its progress is industrial. You cannot trade with people whom you do not trust, and who do not trust you. Confidence is the basis of everything that we must do, and it is a delightful feeling that those ideals are sustained by the people of Italy and by a wonderful body of people such as you have in this great city of Milan. It is with a sense of added encouragement and strength that I return to Paris to take part in the councils that will determine the items of the peace. I thank you with all my heart.

Remarks to the League of Mothers and Widows[1]

[Jan. 5, 1919]

I am very much touched by this evidence of your confidence, and I would like to express to you if I could the very deep sympathy I have for those who have suffered irreparable losses in Italy. Our hearts have been touched. And you have used the right word. Our men have come with the spirit of the crusades against that which was wrong and in order to see to it, if it is possible, that such terrible things never happen again. I am very grateful to you for your kindness.

[1] Wilson received a delegation from this organization at the royal palace in Milan. London *Times*, Jan. 7, 1919.

An Address at the City Hall in Milan[1]

January 5, 1919.

Mr. Mayor: May I not say to you as the representative of this great city that it is impossible for me to put into words the impressions I have received today? The overwhelming welcome, the spontaneous welcome, the welcome that so evidently came from the heart, has been profoundly moving to me, Sir, and I have not failed to see the significance of that welcome. You have yourself referred to it. I am as keenly aware, I believe, Sir, as anybody can be that the social structure rests upon the great working classes of the world, and that those working classes in the several countries of the world have by their consciousness of community of interest, by their consciousness of community of spirit, done perhaps more than any other influence has to establish a world opinion, an opinion which is not of a nation, which is not of a continent, but is the opinion, one might say, of mankind. And I am aware, Sir, that those of us who are now charged with the very great and serious responsibility of concluding the peace must think and act and confer in the presence of this opinion; that we are not masters of the fortunes of any nation, but that we are the servants of mankind; that it is not our privilege to follow special interests, but that it is our manifest duty to study only the general interest.

This is a solemn thing, Sir, and here in Milan, where I know so much of the pulse of international sympathy beats, I am glad to stand up and say that I believe that that pulse beats also in my own veins, and that I am not thinking of particular settlements so much as I am of the general settlement. I was very much touched today, Sir, to receive at the hands of wounded soldiers a memorial in favor of a league of nations, and to be told by them that that was what they had fought for; not merely to win this war, but to secure something beyond—some guarantee of justice, some equilibrium for the world as a whole which would make it certain that they would never have to fight a war like this again. This is the added obligation that is upon us who make peace. We can not merely sign a treaty of peace and go home with clear consciences. We must do something more. We must add, so far as we can, the securities which suffering men everywhere demand; and when I speak of suffering men, I think also of suffering women. I know that, splendid as have been the achievements of your armies, and tremendous as have been the sacrifices which they have made, and great the glory which they have achieved, the real, hard pressure of the burden came upon the women at home, whose men had gone to the front and who were willing to have them stay there until the battle was fought out. And as I have heard from your Minister of Food the story how for days together there would be no bread, and then know that when there was no bread the spirit of the people did not flag, I take off my hat to the great people of Italy and tell them that my admiration is merged into friendship and affection. It is in this spirit that I receive your courtesy, Sir, and thank you from the bottom of my heart for this unprecedented reception which I have received at the hand of your generous people.

¹ Wilson had just been presented with the freedom of the city of Milan. The Socialist Mayor of Milan, Emilio Caldara, in his speech of greeting, had stressed the adherence of the Italian working class to Wilson's fourteen points. In particular, he urged the right of self-determination for all peoples and called for the "end of all irredentisms." An English translation of Caldara's remarks, T MS, is in WP, DLC.

Remarks at La Scala Opera House¹

January 5, 1919.

Mr. Chairman: Again you have been very gracious, and again you have filled my heart with gratitude because of your references to my own country, which is so dear to me. I have been very much interested to be told, Sir, that you are the chairman of a committee of entertainment which includes all parties, without distinction. I am glad to interpret that to mean that there is no division recognized in the friendship which is entertained for America, and I am sure, Sir, that I can assure you that in America there would be a similar union of all parties to express friendship and sympathy with Italy. Because, after all, parties are founded upon differences of program and not often upon differences of national sympathy. The thing that makes parties workable and tolerable is that all parties love their own country and therefore participate in the general sentiments of that country.

And so it is with us, Sir. We have many parties, but we have a single sentiment in this war and a single sentiment in the peace; and at the heart of that sentiment lies our feeling towards those with whom we have been associated in the great struggle. At first the struggle seemed the mere natural resistance to aggressive force, but as the consciousness of the nations grew it became more and more evident to them that they were fighting something that was more than the aggression of the Central Empires. It was the spirit of militarism, the spirit of autocracy, the spirit of force; and against that spirit rose, as always in the past, the spirit of liberty and of justice. Force can always be conquered, but the spirit of liberty never can be, and the beautiful circumstance about the history of liberty is that its champions have always shown the power of self-sacrifice, have always been willing to subordinate their personal interests to the common good, have not wished to dominate their fellow men, but have wished to serve them. This is what gives dignity, this is what gives imperishable victory. And with that victory has come about things that are exemplified by a scene like this—the coming together of the hearts of nations, the sympathy of great bodies of people who do not speak the same vocabulary but do speak the same ideas. I am heartened by this delightful experience and hope that you will accept, not only my thanks for myself and for those who are with me, but also my thanks on behalf of the American people.

(On the balcony of La Scala)

I wish I could take you all to some place where a similar body of my fellow countrymen could show you their heart toward you as you have shown me your heart toward them, because the heart of America has gone out to the heart of Italy. We have been watchful of your heroic struggle and of your heroic suffering. And it has been our joy in these recent days to be associated with you in the victory which has liberated Italy and liberated the world. Viva l'Italia!

Printed in *Addresses of President Wilson on First Trip* . . .
    ¹ Wilson was responding to a toast by Riccardo Luzzatto, a lawyer of Milan who had been for many years a member of the Chamber of Deputies and who in his youth had been a soldier with Giuseppe Garibaldi in the campaigns for Italian unification. Luzzatto's remarks are printed in the Milan *Corriere della Sera*, Jan. 6, 1919. Among the many notable persons in attendance at the dinner were Senator Luigi Albertini, managing editor of the *Corriere della Sera*, and Benito Mussolini, then the editor of the Milan *Il Popolo d'Italia*. See Giuseppe Antonio Borgese, *Goliath: The March of Fascism* (New York, 1937), pp. 139-40.

From the Diary of Dr. Grayson

Monday, January 6, 1919.

We arrived at Turin at nine o'clock. A general holiday had been declared and the streets were black with people. The party proceeded to the City Hall, where the President was made a citizen of the municipality in a big reception room crowded with notables. The President was also made a citizen of the various municipalities comprising this state. Fourteen mayors had congregated to aid in the ceremony and all were personally presented. Many of these officials never had been in Turin before, some of them having had to ride horse back many miles down the mountain side to reach the city. Following the formal ceremony each mayor was presented individually while the President shook hands with them as they passed along the line. One of these officials greeted the President in English saying he had been a resident of the United States for twenty-five years. Another broke through the line and insisted upon shaking hands with me because I was in uniform and he thought I must be the President. From the City Hall the President went to the Philharmonic Club, formerly a royal palace. The President was very tired so I persuaded him to rest for a brief period although there were neither sofas nor beds in the building. However, I placed two chairs together and formed a fairly comfortable couch. Having no wraps I asked the American Consul, Morgan Havens,[1] whether he could get me a blanket. He said he would try and immediately returned with a heavy table cloth, which he asked me to use until he could secure more adequate covering. Later he returned with a blanket. Havens was the most efficient American official we met in Italy. Lunch was served at the club by the local committee and the President responded to the Mayor's toast. We left at four for Paris. We reached Modane about nine in the evening, and here the President received the sad word of the death of Theodore Roosevelt. He at once sent a message of condolence to Mrs. Roosevelt.

En route from Turin to Paris the President had a conference with Nevin, Probert and Bender,[2] at which he said, by way of opening, that he wished to match minds with them as to the impressions he got from the receptions on his Italian trip. The President said that he felt the people of the country were primarily interested in bringing about a peace which would insure them against another war, such as they had just gone through. He felt that they had hit upon the league of nations idea as the means to the end desired. Discussing the question of Italian territorial designs in Dalmatia, Fiume and elsewhere along the Adriatic the President mentioned his conference in Rome with Sonnino, saying the latter seemed determined to abide by the pact of London. He then told a little anecdote of his conversation with Sonnino, in which he informed the Italian Foreign Minister that if the right of possession he (Sonnino) advanced, prevailed, New York City had an Italian population which exceeded in number any city in Italy, but of course the United States could scarcely be expected to cede New York to Italy. It was called to the President's attention that during his trips through Genoa, Milan and Turin large numbers of propaganda leaflets demanding Dalmatia, Fiume, etc., were dropped on his carriage. The President said he had noticed this and was interested in it, but that he thought, regardless of the attitude of the statesmen, his talks with the common people indicated they were willing to make sacrifices if they felt it would insure a lasting peace.

Speaking of the pact of London, the President said that England and France were anxious to abrogate the agreement they had made and were "sort of looking to him" to help them. He declared that they were expecting him to haul their chestnuts out of the fire, which he said, "I will not do."

Questioned as to the League of Nations plans he said he had a definite program already formulated, but was at that time reading a League of Nations plan formulated by General Smuts of the British War Cabinet, who he said was one of the most able minded of British statesmen. The President thought it would be good politics to play the British game "more or less" in formulating the league covenant in order that England might feel her views were chiefly to be embodied in the final draft, thus gaining British support that would be withheld from a personal program.

Concerning the admission of Germany into the League, the President for the first time indicated that he did not believe Germany could be admitted at once but should participate in the league program during a period of probation.

¹ Actually, Joseph Emerson Haven.
² That is, John Edwin Nevin, Lionel Charles Probert, and Robert Jacob Bender.

An Address at the Philharmonic Club of Turin¹

January 6, 1919.

Mr. Mayor, Your Excellency, fellow citizens: You show your welcome in many delightful ways and in no more delightful way than that in which you have shown it in this room. The words which the mayor has uttered have touched me very much and I have been most touched and stimulated by the words which Signor Postorelli² has so kindly uttered in behalf of the government of this great kingdom. It is very delightful to feel my association with that government and with this city. I know how much of the vitality of Italian effort comes out of this great center of industry and of thought. As I passed through your streets I had this sensation, a sensation which I have often had in my own dear country at home—a sensation of friendship and close sympathetic contact. I could have believed myself in an American city. And I felt more than that. I felt, as I have also felt at home, that the real blood of the country flowed there in the street, in the veins of those plain people who more than some of the rest of us have borne the stress and burden of the war.

Because think of the price at which you and at which we have purchased the victory which we have won. Think of the price of blood and treasure not only, but the price of tears, the price of hunger on the part of little children, the hopes delayed, the dismay of the prospects that bore heavy upon the homes of simple people everywhere. That is the price of liberty. Those of us who plan battles, those of us who conceive policies, do not bear the burden of it. We direct and others execute. We plan and others suffer, and the conquest of spirit is greater than the conquest of arms. These are the people that hold tight. These are the people that never let go and say nothing. They merely live from day to day, determined that the glory of Italy or the glory of the United States shall not depart from her. I have been thinking as I have passed through your streets and sat here that this was the place of the labors of the great Cavour, and I have thought how impossible many of the things that have happened in Italy since, how impossible the great achievements of Italy in the last three years would have been, without the work of Cavour. Ever since I was a boy, one of my treasured portraits has been a portrait of Cavour; because I had read about him, of the way in which his mind took in the nation, the national scope of it, of the strong determined patriotic endeavor that never allowed obstacles to dismay him, and of the way he always stood at the side of the King and planned the great things which the King was enabled to accomplish.

And I have another thought. This is a great industrial center. Perhaps you gentlemen think of the members of your government and the members of the other governments who are going to confer now at Paris as the real makers of war and of peace. We are not. You are the makers of war and of peace. The pulse of the modern world beats on the farm and in the mine and in the factory. The plans of the modern world are made in the countinghouse. The men who do the business of the world now shape the destinies of the world, and peace or war is in large measure in the hands of those who conduct the commerce of the world. That is one reason why, unless we establish friendships, unless we establish sympathies, we clog all the processes of modern life. As I have several times said, you cannot trade with a man who does not trust you, and you will not trade with a man whom you do not trust. Trust is the very life and breadth of business; and suspicion, unjust national rivalry stands in the way of trade, stands in the way of industry. A country is owned and dominated by the capital that is invested in it. I do not need to instruct you gentlemen in that fundamental idea. In proportion as foreign capital comes in among you and takes its hold, in that proportion does foreign influence come in and take its hold. And therefore the processes of capital are in a certain sense the processes of conquest.

I have only this to suggest, therefore. We go to Paris to conclude a peace. You stay here to continue it. We start the peace. It is your duty to continue it. We can only make the large conclusions. You constantly transact the details which constitute the processes of the life of nations.

And so it is very delightful to me to stand in this company and feel that we are not foreigners to each other. We think the same thoughts. We entertain the same purposes. We have the same ideals; and this war has done this inestimable service—it has brought nations into close vital contact, so that they feel the pulses that are in each other, so that they know the purposes by which each is animated. We know in America a great deal about Italy, because we have so many Italian fellow citizens. When Baron Sonnino was arguing the other day for the extension of the sovereignty of Italy over Italian populations, I said, "I am sorry we cannot let you have New York, which, I understand, is the greatest Italian city in the world." I am told that there are more Italians in New York City than in any city in Italy, and I am proud to be President of a nation which contains so large an element of the Italian race, because, as a student of literature, I know the genius that has originated in this great nation, the genius of thought and of poetry and of philosophy and of music, and I am happy to be a part of a nation which is enriched and made better by the introduction of such elements of genius and of inspiration.

May I not again thank the representative of this great city and the representative of the government for the welcome they have given me, and say again, for I cannot say it too often, Viva l'Italia?

(On the Balcony at the Philharmonic Club)

It is very delightful to feel your friendship given so cordially and so graciously, and I hope with all my heart that, in the peace that is now about to be concluded, Italy may find her happiness and her prosperity. I am sure that I am only speaking the sentiments that come from the heart of the American people when I say, Viva l'Italia.

Printed in *Addresses of President Wilson on First Trip* . . .
    [1] Wilson was responding to toasts by Count Secondo Frola, the Mayor of Turin, and by Marquis Luigi Borsarelli di Refreddo, the Under Secretary of State for Foreign Affairs, who represented the Italian government at the ceremonies honoring Wilson in Turin. An English translation of Frola's remarks, T MS, is in WP, DLC.
    [2] That is, Marquis Borsarelli.

From Joseph Patrick Tumulty

[The White House, Jan. 6, 1919]

Colonel Roosevelt died this morning. Have ordered flags half mast. Suggest you designate Vice President your representative at funeral and send message of sympathy to Mrs Roosevelt. Polk advises he is cabling draft of proclamation for your signature.

                                        Tumulty

T telegram (WP, DLC).

To Edith Kermit Carow Roosevelt

[Modane?] 6 January, 1918 [1919]

Pray accept my heartfelt sympathy on the death of your distinguished husband, the news of which has shocked me very much.

Woodrow Wilson

T telegram (WP, DLC).

Three Telegrams from Joseph Patrick Tumulty

The White House, 6 January, 1919.

The attitude of the whole country toward trip has changed. Feeling universal that you have carried your self magnificently through critical situations, with prestige and influence greatly enhanced here and abroad. The criticisms of the cloak room statesmen have lost their force. I realize difficulties still to be met, but have no doubt of result. Trip admitted here by everybody to be wonderful success. Last week with perils of visit to Vatican most critical. The whole psychology favors the success of your trip. The peoples of Europe and the United States with you for League of Nations and against settlements based upon balance of power. Opinion here is that cards stacked against you. My own opinion your influence so great in Europe that European leaders cannot stand in your way. Now is the critical moment and there must be no wasting away of your influence by unnecessary delay of conference. Hearts of the peoples of the world for League of Nations and they are indifferent to its actual terms. They are against militarism and for any reasonable plan to effectuate peace.   Tumulty

TS telegram (J. P. Tumulty Papers, DLC).

The White House, 6 January, 1919.

Hope you will consider the suggestion for your return trip. Your personal contact with peoples of Europe has done much to help your program. Our people will be with your program, but it (the program) must be personally conducted. If you return here without reception or ovation, public opinion on other side liable to misunderstand. The time of your return (in my opinion) is the hour for you to strike in favor of League of Nations. Lodge and leading Republicans constantly attacking,[1] excepting Taft, who is daily warning them of political dangers of their opposition to your program. Could you not consider stopping upon your return at Port of Boston instead of at New York. The announcement of your stopping at Boston would make ovation inevitable throughout New England and would centre attack on Lodge. You have not been to New England in six years. It would be a gracious act and would help much. It would strengthen League of Nations movement in House and Senate and encourage our friends in Senate and House and throughout country. Our people just as emotional as people of Europe. If you return without reception, Lodge and others will construe *it as weakness*. If the people of our own country could have seen you as People of Europe, our situation would be much improved, especially result of last November would have been different. My suggestion would be speech at Fanueil Hall Boston; speech in Providence, New Haven, New York and reception upon return to Washington, to be participated in by returning soldiers.

T telegram (J. P. Tumulty Papers, DLC).
¹ Tumulty probably refers to the speeches by Henry Cabot Lodge in the Senate on December 21, 1918, and January 3, 1919, which were inspired by Philander C. Knox's resolution of December 3, 1918 (about which see n. 1 to the Enclosure printed with E. N. Hurley to WW, Dec. 23, 1918). Lodge presented a wide-ranging elaboration of the problems of the peace conference and of the projected league of nations which foreshadowed much of the later debate both inside and outside the Senate over the ratification of the Treaty of Versailles. Lodge suggested that a league, if it was to be anything more than a paper organization, had to have the power to enforce its decrees, and that this power would lead to much controversy both in the Senate and in the country at large. He also issued a blunt warning that, while Wilson might not want the Senate's advice on the peace settlement, both Wilson and the Allies would do well to remember that the Senate in the past had either rejected treaties outright or had strongly amended them. *Cong. Record*, 65th Cong., 3d sess., pp. 723-28, 972-74.

                              The White House, 6 January 1919.

My advice is that you take no part in present discussion as to extending Government control of railroads for five years. You will be better able to act when you return. Your attitude as stated in your message¹ leaves you in ideal position.

Paragraph. Do not accept Colby resignation until I can discuss it upon your return.   Tumulty.

T telegram (WP, DLC).
¹ That is, Wilson's Annual Message of 1918 printed at December 2, 1918.

From Carter Glass

                              Washington. January 6, 1919.

112. The President from Glass.

I fear there is great danger of confusion in regard to the matter of representatives of the Treasury in Europe. Colonel House has suggested that Norman Davis be appointed in connection with the armistice discussions at Spa¹ and I have recommended to you his appointment as such. Davis has also advised me of his appointment as one of the American representatives on special board created to deal with relief problem. Crosby hard to understand and I have left it to you for such action as you think proper. Secretary Lansing has cabled me saying that the peace commissioners wish to have financial trust from some one other than the Treasury's Representative and suggested Albert Strauss go over for that purpose if he approved. In view of these demands from various sources from the financial representation and the danger of conflicting councils and disorganization among his Treasury representatives I ask your approval of the creation of a Treasury Commission in Europe under the chairmanship of some one who will be my responsible representative if you approve. I plan to send Mr. Strauss over to head the Treasury's delegation at as early a date as possible.

I have concluded to ask your approval also of sending Thomas W. Lamont of New York. He would be particularly useful in connection with the armistice discussions at Spa. You know he is a member of the firm of J. P. Morgan and Company and the owner of the NEW YORK EVENING POST.   Polk.

T telegram (WP, DLC).
¹ Clause 34 of the Armistice Agreement provided for the creation of an International Armistice Commission to carry out the terms of the agreement. This commission, which included representatives of the United States, Great Britain, France, and Germany, met daily at the former German Supreme Headquarters in Spa, Belgium. *New York Times*, Nov. 26 and Dec. 9, 1918, and Harry R. Rudin, *Armistice, 1918* (New Haven, Conn., 1944), p. 432.

Three Telegrams from Frank Lyon Polk to Robert Lansing

Washington Jan. 6th, 1919.

111[110]. For the Secretary of State. Before you left Washington you discussed with the President a declaration by him of the attitude of the states towards the Bolshevik authorities in Russia and found that the President preferred to withhold any seperate stat[e]ment by himself until he could discuss the matter with the leaders of the associated Governments. The reports we receive and which are repeated to you by our embassies and legations show the growing menace of Bolshevism outside of Russia. In your opinion no one can take the lead so well as the President in defining the attitude of the associated Governments on this question, and would be glad to know what steps if any in that direction have been made.

Polk.

Washington. January 6, 1919.[1]

111. For Secretary of State. Following received from Carl Ackerman through Legation at Peking, dated January 2nd, 12 p.m. for the attention of Colonel House. I think it should also be considered by yourself as it further illustrates the difficulties of the existing situation in Siberia owing to lack of any concert of policy or action between the different governments who have sought in one way or another to render assistance in Russia. I wish you would also consider it in connection with the railway situation about which I am telegraphing you today. Congress is becoming extremely restive in regard to Russia, moreover, I find a general sentiment pauses on that element whose opinions are reflected by Raymond Robins that we should not withdraw but on the contrary take some positive measure to assist in restoring normal conditions of life and to do our part for Russia without becoming involved in controversies over political conditions.

"Having returned from an extensive visit in Siberia to Ekaterinburg, Omsk, and other cities I have the honor to submit this report covering our official relations towards Czech-Slovaks and the Russian political situation for the purpose of tendering the necessity of a definite and public decision regarding military intervention and also recommending assignment of responsible government official to Omsk as the head of all American activities and the sole authority in regard to our military, economic and political policies.

"During my visit I had opportunity of observing activities of our own representatives, conversing with them, and discussing with Czechs, Allies and Russian political and economic situation. I believe reason our policy of non-interference in internal affairs in some degree is not succeeding is because we have never corrected the initial mistakes which were made by official representatives of the United States. I believe the reason we do not have (?) Czechs in Russia is because we have not been open in announcing our attitude towards their activities.

"I believe the reason the intellectuals and liberals of Russia are turned against us is because we did not show an interest in the government which they tried to form, the All-Russian Government.[2] I believe the reason our Allies, especially Japan, England, and France, do as they please in Russia is because we do not show either by our actions or our attitude what our real intentions are. These criticisms I beg to submit with the evidence I possess in order that

[1] The Editors have been unable to find a copy of this telegram in the files of the State Department.
[2] About which see n. 2 to Enclosure I, printed with RL to WW, Sept. 24, 1918 (second letter of that date), Vol. 51.

it may be as clear in Washington as it is among our representatives in Vladivostok and Siberia why the United States must decide what its policy toward Russia is to be and act immediately accordingly.

"The initial move which was made in Russia was the pledging of military, political and economic aid to Czech-Slovak by Consuls General Poole and Harris.[3] I do not know what authority these men had for making the definite promises which they made. I do know that as a result supplemental promises transmitted from Moscow to Samara and from Irkutsk to Omsk, the Czechs maintain agreements with the Russian forces and jurisdiction of a certain front. These pledges by representatives our Government are known to all Czechs. Later, however, Ambassador Morris informed Gaida, General Graves informed General Syrorvy,[4] and Colonel Robinson[5] informed Girza of the Czech National Council in Vladivostok that American troops would not be sent to Czech front. None of these Czechs, however, transmitted this information to the Czech Army Staff or to the National Council. Neither the Vice Chairman and none of the members of the National Council in Ekaterinburg or in the United States has adopted this attitude.

"Gaida's and Syrorvy staffs were likewise ignorant. The result is that when I left Ekaterinburg every Czech with whom I spoke was certain that American troops would be sent to the interior because our government had never disavowed Poole and Harris messages. This belief of the Czechs was further substantiated by the receipt by the Czechs in Ekaterinburg on Thanksgiving Day of a message from Harris urging them to hold on which Gaida interpreted as meaning that America had finally decided to send her armed forces to assist them. Doctor Teusler who, because of his position with the Red Cross and his reliable service to the White House is considered by Czechs as a man with authority, told several Czech officers and councilmen in my presence and in the presence of our military observer on several occasions that 'If the Czechs shout loud enough for military aid, it will be forth-coming' and that 'I am doing everything I can to get American troops into Russia.' The attitude of both Harris and Teusler had by the time my Mission had (word omitted) Ekaterinburg completely nullified statements made by Ambassador Morris and Graves to Gaida and Syrovy.

[3] D. C. Poole, Jr., to G. W. Williams (Samara), June 18, 1918, which was repeated to Ernest L. Harris, Consul General at Irkutsk. Poole's message urged the Czechs in Siberia to hold their present positions, secure control of the Trans-Siberian Railway, and "retain control over the territory where they now dominate." George F. Kennan, *The Decision to Intervene* (Princeton, N. J., 1958), pp. 294-95. Poole's message was totally unauthorized.

[4] That is, Maj. Gen. Jan Syrovy.

[5] Lt. Col. Oliver Prescott Robinson, Graves' chief of staff.

"I submit that the United States cannot hope to succeed with any policy in Russia unless the officials representing different departments of the Government speak with unanimity or unless it is absolutely and publicly understood in Russia that such men do not speak with authority. By these mistakes of our officials we have lost the confidence of Czechs in Russia and by not keeping the promise which Poole and Harris made we have placed ourselves in the position of having betrayed Czechs.

"Today morale of the Czech Army is broken. During my stay in Ekaterinburg I learned from Czech official sources of mutinies in the various regiments and learned the political disagreements between the naval forces and the Czech military leaders. I fear reaction which is certain to come when the Czech soldiers learn that it is extremely doubtful the Americans are coming to support them and when Czech soldiers and all social revolutionists hear loose statements which the British Consul at Omsk[6] and other British and French representatives are instructed to pass out that the only reason for presence of an Allied Army in Russia is to save the British and French money invested in the country. I think patriotism and good will of the Czech is being taken advantage of by the Allies and I would not be surprised if the Czech soldiers decided from such observation to leave Russia and give up fight against the Bolsheviks. If they do the Allies will be in a most compromising position of affairs because it is extremely doubtful, whether any Army of Kolchak could meet them in battle and come out victorious.

"Neither the Czech soldiers, nor the National Council, nor the Russian people or Tchorlu[7] Soldiers sympathize with the Kolchak Government and I believe, judging by present indications, that there is more of a chance for the apparent opposition to gain control of all Russia than for the parties supporting Kolchak or by taking advantage of a favorable occasion after assuming another civil war contest. I think there will be an opportunity for the Democratic forces of Russia to come to the top. Our failure to show sympathy or interest in many activities of the all Russian Government is an event which cannot be remedied now.

"The Kolchak Government, I am convinced from the evidence which I obtained in Omsk and Ekaterinburg at the time of the change, was by the military parties encouraged and aided by Generals Knowgalitsen,[8] Gaida, McOroyouchf[9] and Kolchak for the purpose of establishing a strong military government. Considering the

[6] Sören Revsgaard Randrup.
[7] The Editors have been unable to determine the correct form of this garbled word.
[8] Gen. Vladimir Vasilevich Golitsyn, an associate of Adm. Kolchak.
[9] Leonid Aleksandrovich Ustrugov.

means by which the former government was overthrown, considering the men who took part in the coup, considered as of no importance in affairs, I do not see how the United States under any circumstances can support Kolchak Government, either morally, economically or militarily. If we were to take part in military intervention without defining our subject [object] at this stage of the Russian (omission) *slaughtered* we would be supporting the very class in Russia which corresponds to the class in Germany which we refused to deal with. On the other hand England and France, judging by the activities of their representative in Roumania, have no compunctions about the kind of government as long as it is Anti-Bolshevik.

"Today the United States is faced by this problem in Russia. There is no central de facto government or representative government with which the United States as a democratic nation can deal. There is grave danger of the Czechs withdrawing without notice which would (apparent omission) Russian management Kolchak and the allied armies in a dangerous position. The representative of the State Department in Omsk[10] is a person non grata with the Czechs. By refusing to confederate military operations along the Urals, we are antagonizing the Russians, we are being criticized by our Allies and are losing the respect of the Russians who for various reasons desired our participation in allied operations. If we continue our present policy of remaining in Vladimir [Vladivostok] and of not taking part in allied operations our presence is useless to Russia. If we invade Russia with the English and French, we will be supporting the monarchists, if we withdrew without cause we shall be in the position of breaking our public promises to the Russian people.

"Considering the Russian problem as a whole I beg to suggest that the best solution is for the Allies in Paris to decide upon a policy of either withdrawing together or intervening together. The present lack of unity among the Allies is not only destroying the faith of Russians in the Allies, but it is widening the gap which exists already between the representatives Allies in Russia and the Far East. Ambassador Morris and General Graves are doing their best in Virago [Vladivostok] and their splendid judgement and tact are the only things which prevent an open and serious break between America and the Allies and Russians but I am sure that they have reached the position where they realize that the United States and the Allies must decide to decide one thing or the other, either withdraw or intervene and if we intervene let it be publically under-

[10] That is, Ernest Lloyd Harris.

stood that our subject [object] is not to fight against or with any political faction of Russia but that our object is to establish order and make it possible for all factions in Russia to get together in a representative convention and determine the form and substance of their government.

Russia, the first great reconstruction problem, cannot be solved by divided councils."

Suggest you show this to McCormick.   Polk.

                          Washington, January 6, 1919.[1]

113. Shuetz [Siberian] railway negotiations between the Japanese Government and Mr. Morris[2] who is still at Tokyo and Mr. Stevens who is at (?) [Harbin] have reached a point which Mr. Stevens thinks will result favorably in a few days. The proposed plan provides for a special inter-allied committee with a Russian chairman which shall have under its control: first, a technical board with John F. Stevens as president of the technical operations of the railway and, second, a military transportation board for the purpose of coordinating military transportation. I believe the details, which I am hoping to hear prove acceptable to Stevens as well as to the Japanese Government, afford a working basis upon which we can make a start to relieve the present intolerable situation there. To make the plan effective will require the cooperation of General Graves with Mr. Stevens to assist in providing military protection to the different stations as railway guards in order to maintain the free movement of trains in cooperating with the power having military forces in Siberia. If the President will not authorize this cooperation on the part of General Graves with such portions of his forces as may be found requisite from time to time, I think we must withdraw and leave the solution of the railway transportation problem which, as you know, is vital to all economic assistance in Siberia, to others who will undertake the task.

If we withdraw from our effort to reorganize the railways, we leave it to others to effect the economic and other assistance in Siberia which we know to be essential. The several public statements made by this Government and also its general policy have all indicated the assumption of a responsibility to assist wherever it might prove possible to do so. This policy would have to be abandoned with its resultant effect on the morale of the general public in Russia who had looked to this country for aid.

Moreover, as suggested in my number 13, Dec. 27, 7:00 P.M.,[3] if we withdraw from Siberia, we tacitly consent to Japanese army control of the Chinese Eastern Railway as one of the direct results of our having agreed with Japan to send military assistance.

Furthermore, referring to the President's aide memoire of July 17th in which this Government expressed the opinion that military assistance is admissible in Russia only to assist the ? [Czecho-Slovaks consolidate their forces and get into successful cooperation with their Slavic kinsmen] or "to steady any efforts at self-government or self defense in which the Russians themselves may be willing to accept assistance," our agreement with Japanese, I believe, tends distinctly to unsteady such efforts as the Russians are now making. We must also keep in mind the fact that well over 200,000 enemy prisoners of war still remain in Siberia and that many of them who took active part with the Bolshevik Red army are now restrained only by the American, Russian, and other forces in Siberia.

Finally, I think you will agree with me that the present time would be hopeless as the question of Russia is one of such delicacy, and also under all the circumstances calls for a demonstration of our constancy of purpose. I hope you will see your way clear to bring the whole situation to the attention of the President very clearly and that you will let me know what decision you reach in conference with him on the points I have raised. McCormick who sailed January 1st is already informed fully of the situation. ? you may wish to confer with him and show him these telegrams.

Polk.

T telegrams (WP, DLC).
    ¹ There is apparently no copy of this telegram in the files of the State Department.
    ² About which see FLP to RL, Dec. 21, 1918, n. 1, and Dec. 30, 1918, n. 4.
    ³ Printed in *PPC*, II, 479-80.

Lord Derby to Arthur James Balfour

Confidential & Personal

My dear Arthur　　　　　　　　　　Paris. 6 January 1919.

I envy you very much indeed being in the sunshine at Cannes. I went up to Belgium and Brussels to see two Lancashire Divisions between the 1st and the 5th and came back here to find that it had rained the whole time. It poured all day yesterday and today is really about the first day that we have had without rain for 6 weeks.

I went to see House this morning and talked to him about various matters and to find out what opinion the President had formed of his visit to England. House tells me that he is enthusiastic about it. Delighted and suprised at his wonderful welcome but apparently the person who really impressed him the most was the King with whom he got on extraordinarily well. House tells me that the President feels more and more the necessity for working in close union with England and is determined to do so and in H's opinion he will allow no difficulties to stand in the way of such a union. The amusing thing is he apparently contemplates that the League of Nations shall begin by a joint agreement between England and America and that other Nations will then be told you must come into this or take the consequences. Of course there is no doubt if we can come to a satisfactory arrangement with America it would be everything and I am sure now is the time to do it, if it can be done, as the President is evidently annoyed at the grasping energies of the French especially in the direction of Tangier and Syria. . . .

Yours ever   D

TLS (A. J. Balfour Papers, Add. MSS 49744, British Library).

From the Diary of Dr. Grayson

Tuesday, January 7, 1919.

We arrived in Paris at ten o'clock in the morning. During the afternoon the President conferred with American members of the Peace Conference. In the evening the President read an article by A. G. Gardiner from the London News dealing with the peace precedents,[1] also from Gardiner's book on the King of Italy, Theodore Roosevelt and Lord Reading.[2] The State Department sent him a draft of a proclamation to be issued on the death of Colonel Roosevelt but the President rewrote it, in order to include mention of Colonel Roosevelt's Spanish war record. In his revision, the President credited Mr. Roosevelt with leadership in the awakening of the demand for public justice in America and paid tribute to his great work in the defense of the people's rights against large interests. This proclamation also declared a public holiday in the United States on the day of the funeral.

[1] Grayson meant Alfred George Gardiner, "The Peace President," London *Daily News*, Dec. 28, 1918. This article presented a brief sketch of both the life and thought of Woodrow Wilson. Gardiner wrote that Wilson's political career had been grounded throughout upon a well-thought-out philosophy.

[2] Grayson must have meant to say "Gardiner's books." The sketches of the King of Italy, Theodore Roosevelt, and Rufus Isaacs (the future Lord Reading) appeared, respectively, in *The War Lords* (London, 1915), *Pillars of Society* (London, 1913), and *Prophets, Priests, & Kings* (London, 1908).

A Proclamation[1]

[Jan. 7, 1919]

To the people of the United States:

It becomes my sad duty to announce officially the death of Theodore Roosevelt, President of the United States from September 14, 1901, to March 4, 1909, which occurred at his home at Sagamore Hill, Oyster Bay, New York, at four fifteen o'clock in the morning of January 6, 1919. In his death the United States has lost one of its most distinguished and patriotic citizens, who had endeared himself to the people by his strenuous devotion to their interests and to the public interests of his country.

As president of the police board of his native city, as member of the legislature and governor of his State, as Civil Service Commissioner, as Assistant Secretary of the Navy, as Vice President, and as President of the United States, he displayed administrative powers of a signal order and conducted the affairs of these various offices with a concentration of effort and a watchful care which permitted no divergence from the line of duty he had definitely set for himself.

In the war with Spain, he displayed singular initiative and energy and distinguished himself among the commanders of the Army in the field. As President he awoke the Nation to the dangers of private control which lurked in our financial and industrial systems. It was by thus arresting the attention and stimulating the purpose of the country that he opened the way for subsequent necessary and beneficent reforms.

His private life was characterized by a simplicity, a virtue, and an affection worthy of all admiration and emulation by the people of America.

In testimony of the respect in which his memory is held by the Government and people of the United States, I do hereby direct that the flags of the White House and the several departmental buildings be displayed at half staff for a period of thirty days, and that suitable military and naval honors under orders of the Secretaries of War and of the Navy be rendered on the day of the funeral.

Done this seventh day of January, in the year of our Lord one thousand nine hundred and nineteen, and of the independence of the United States of America the one hundred and forty-third.

Woodrow Wilson.

By the President:
Frank L. Polk,
Acting Secretary of State.

Printed in the *Official Bulletin*, III (Jan. 8, 1919), 4.

¹ The draft which Wilson emended is in WP, DLC, and a T draft of the final version of this proclamation is in the C. L. Swem Coll., NjP.

To Joseph Patrick Tumulty

Paris, January 7, 1919.

Number four. Answering your number three.¹ Sincerely hope passage of a resolution on Home Rule can be avoided. I would recommend passage by the House of a resolution approving League of Nations if it would be sure of a passage by a decisive majority. Letter to Secretary of Interior regarding oil situation being forwarded by pouch.   Woodrow Wilson.

T telegram (J. P. Tumulty Papers, DLC).
¹ It is missing.

To Thomas Riley Marshall

Paris, January 7, 1919.

Would appreciate it very much if you would act as my representative at the funeral of Colonel Roosevelt. Warmest regards.
                              Woodrow Wilson.

T telegram (WP, DLC).

To Franklin Knight Lane

My dear Mr. Secretary: Paris, January 7, 1919.

Because of the circumstances which have surrounded us during the last few weeks, I am sure you will pardon me for not having sooner answered yours of September 23rd, September 26th, and October 9th, in regard to the oil fields in Wyoming and California.¹ I still have under consideration the advisability of commandeering one or more of these fields, but have no intention of doing so in the immediate future.

In the meanwhile without regard to the question of commandeering, I feel that the following course should be pursued:

1. All operating agreements should provide for impounding or securing the net proceeds of production pending action on the applications for patents.

2. There should be eliminated from all operating agreements the clause which binds the Government to accept the amount impounded under them as liquidated damages in case of denial of the patents.

3. I see no objection to new operating agreements, provided they comply with 1 and 2.

4. I see no reason for discrimination between claimants in different fields, and my view is that the operating agreements in California should be on the same basis as those in Wyoming.

Cordially and faithfully yours, [Woodrow Wilson][2]

CCL (WP, DLC).
[1] FKL to WW, Sept. 23, 1918, enclosing Clay Tallman to FKL, Sept. 21, 1918; FKL to WW, Sept. 26, 1918, enclosing C. Tallman to FKL, Sept. 12, 1918; and FKL to WW, Oct. 9, 1918, enclosing C. Tallman to FKL, Oct. 8, 1918, all TLS (WP, DLC). Despite Wilson's reference to "oil fields in Wyoming and California," all of this correspondence concerned the proposed commandeering by the federal government of the Salt Creek oil field in Wyoming. Senator John B. Kendrick of Wyoming had written to Wilson in June 1918 and requested an investigation of the activities of the Midwest Oil Company in that field. He charged that the company had fraudulently laid claim to the public lands constituting the field and was making great profits on oil which rightfully belonged to the American people. The Justice Department subsequently recommended that the government regain control of the property. See J. Leonard Bates, *The Origins of Teapot Dome: Progressives, Parties, and Petroleum, 1909-1921* (Urbana, Ill., 1963), pp. 145-49. In the correspondence cited above, Lane and Tallman detailed the steps which had been taken to facilitate the proposed governmental takeover of the field. In the letter and enclosure of October 9, they were concerned to find out whether Wilson still proposed to carry out the seizure.
[2] This letter was based upon the legal advice given in TWG to WW, Nov. 22, 1918, TLS (WP, DLC).

From Carter Glass

Washington January 7, 1919.

131. For President from Glass. Transmitted to Congress your request for one hundred million dollar appropr[i]ation to relieve starvation in Europe. I took up matter in advance with Democratic leaders of Senate and House and am hopeful authority will be granted.[1]   Polk.

T telegram (WP, DLC).
[1] See WW to C. Glass, Jan. 1, 1919. Representative Sherley introduced the so-called Famine Relief bill (H.R. 13708) on January 7, 1919. *Cong. Record*, 65th Cong., 3d sess., pp. 1107-1109.

From Thomas Nelson Page

Rome, January 7, 1919.

57. Urgent for the President. Bissolati's having seen the President has made a profound impression here. I had a conversation with Baron Sonnino late this afternoon which indicates, as possible, important changes his position. Both he and Orlando, whom I had seen earlier in the day, were manifestly much impressed and even anxious over this situation. Sonnino reiterated his arguments as to the means of redeeming Italy from peril of menace from inner

waterway of Eastern Coast, and to my suggestion that provision might be made to prevent possibility of this menace and secure freedom of really Italian Cities under guarantees, he argued the impossibility of such a provision being effective and cited the present condition of terror in Montenegro, whose independence is being destroyed under a presumingly free choice by her people,[1] and added that the King had told the President something of the situation. On this I having first made plain that I had no part in the peace proceedings and no authority to speak for the President, or any one. I asked Sonnino why he did not give up his contention about Dalmatia, which does not appeal to others and try to secure the freedom of the really Italian Cities and the independence of Montenegro. I said "You are the one who can bring Italy and America together, and settle one of the most difficult obstacles to the peace." He appeared struck by this, and said that if Montenegro which has always been free and withstood the Turks so long were given independence, and were given Cattaro,[2] which is necessary to her, it would certainly make a difference to Italy. I told him I did not know the President's views on the present Montenegrin situation beyond the general sympathy with the aspirations of peoples to be free, but personally had much sympathy with Montenegro and believed the recent so called election in Montenegro to have been a sham.

I think Sonnino is ready in view of recent manifestations to concede much more than ever before.   Nelson Page.

T telegram (WP, DLC).
    [1] On November 26, 1918, a Montenegrin Skupština (Assembly), supposedly elected by democratic process, meeting in the city of Podgorica, had voted to abolish the monarchy of King Nicholas I and to seek union with the proposed Kingdom of Serbs, Croats, and Slovenes (often unofficially called Yugoslavia). The government of King Nicholas, then in exile in France, immediately declared that the so-called Podgorica Resolution was null and void because the Assembly had been fraudulently chosen and did not represent the people of Montenegro. By early January 1919, Serbian troops had occupied much of Montenegro in support of the group favoring union with Yugoslavia. The supporters of Nicholas in turn were attempting a "revolution" to preserve Montenegrin independence, or at least autonomy, under the old monarchy. Italy supported the latter movement in order to curb the Yugoslav nationalists, whose territorial claims conflicted with her own. Another reason for Italian support of Nicholas was the fact that he was the father of the Italian Queen, Elena: See Ivo J. Lederer, *Yugoslavia at the Paris Peace Conference, A Study in Frontiermaking* (New Haven, Conn., 1963), pp. 45, 113-16, and *PPC*, II, 347-72.
    [2] The Italian name for Kotor, or Kotoriba, a seaport of Croatia, located on the Gulf of Kotor, an inlet of the Adriatic Sea.

From Thomas Nelson Page, with Enclosure

Confidential

My dear Mr. President: Rome January 7, 1919.

We have followed you with keenest interest in your journey since you left Rome, and I was glad to see that you had a chance to speak directly to the Italian people before leaving Italy. I am sending telegrams to the Peace Commission giving summaries of what the principal papers say, but will not inflict them on you here save to say that every reference made by you to your sympathy with Italy has been published and greedily devoured by the people. I am enclosing herewith for yourself the only copy I have of the minute made by Lieutenant Lawrence G. White[1] of the conversation between Bisolatti and yourself. I suggested to him to show it to Bisolatti before sending it and this was done. It, therefore, expresses Bisolatti's mature presentation of his views as expressed on the occasion of the interview. As I saw him out of the room that evening after the interview he requested that what he said be kept entirely confidential.

The fact of his visit to you has, as I telegraphed this morning, made a deep impression here. A rumor reached me that it was thought that the French Embassy had brought this about. I, however, informed both Orlando and Sonnino that the French Embassy had nothing whatever to do with it and in fact had telephoned me to know if it were true that he had seen you.

I informed them further that you knew of his views before seeing him and wished to meet him, as you wished to meet all the leaders of Italian thought, and that I had sent for him.

As I have already telegraphed you to-day, I think that both Orlando and Sonnino appear somewhat anxious over the present political situation and I found Sonnino apparently readier to yield somewhat than he had been before. He is greatly interested in saving Montenegro from being absorbed in the Serbian Kingdom. I inquired if he wished Montenegro to be free and independent of every power, and he answered with great warmth that he did, and that he would himself give much of what belonged to himself to have it free. He said the King had spoken to you of it, and that Montenegro had been free for hundreds of years and had been the bulwark against the Turks for three centuries. Having stated to him that I did not know what your position was on this point, save in so far as your general principles in favor of the right of complete self-government might indicate it, & that I had no authority to speak for you or for anyone in the matter, I asked him why he did not give up his claims to Dalmatia and, accepting the modified programme of others in Italy and elsewhere, try to secure Montenegro's independence and right of uncoerced decision, and bring Italy to act with America in accordance with your principles. He replied that if Montenegro could have the Cattaro and be free it would make a great change for Italy and relieve her greatly from the peril of possible attack in the future from behind the islands on the Dalmatian side. This, as I understood it, was in connection with the guaranteed freedom of Fiume and Zara and possibly Sebenico[2] as Italian cities, that is, as cities of Italian population. I do not know what he may claim when he comes to the final discussion, but I felt that he was ready last night to yield much more that I had ever believed he would yield before, and I thought this due to your suggestion about the guarantees against the fortification of the islands and the possession of a war fleet by Jugo-Slavia.

I am sending you to-day a telegraphic report of a statement made to me by Signor Popovitch (my No. 57 to the Ammission) regarding the conditions in Montenegro.[3] He left there a week ago and reports that the whole country is in revolution and that all the cities have been captured by the Montenegrins who have overthrown the so-called Governments which the Serbs supported, and that the Montenegrins have requested of General Vinel,[4] the French Commander at Cattaro, that Allied troops be sent into Montenegro and have made the same demand of the Italian Government here. And further that a wireless received to-day by the Montenegrin Consulate General here states that American troops (probably the battalion from Cattaro) have been sent to Cetinje which both sides were struggling to obtain possession of. Popovitch, who was the representative sent by Montenegro before the Serbs set up the Government there recently to the Peace Conference, states that the revolutionary party comprise substantially the entire peasant population who constitute about four-fifths of the population of Montenegro, who have always been free and desire to remain so now, while the people in the cities rather desire to go in with the Serbs. He says further that they wish a Republican form of government and under such form to become a part of a federation something like that of Switzerland, in which Montenegro shall retain its individuality. He added that if Montenegro had to continue under a dynasty it preferred the old dynasty to any other and would not be willing to go under the Serbian dynasty. What they want, he says, is to have an opportunity accorded them by the Allies to decide freely without coercion or chicanery their own form of government and what disposition shall be made thereof when formed. This, I believe to be a pretty fair statement of what the Montenegrins are and wish.

I am enclosing herewith a summary of extracts from recent editorial comments in important papers regarding your visit, and the ideals which you represent.[5] I feel sure that they will interest you.

The whole world seems to me at this moment to hang on your decision. I believe the settlement of the Adriatic problem in such a way as to make the Italian people feel that you are in full sympathy with all their just claims and their desire to save from foreign oppression every considerable body of Italians wherever they may be in that region—I do not mean taking the cities as a part of Italian territory—will go far to solve the most difficult problem that will come before you at the Peace Conference.

Always, my dear Mr. President,

Your most sincerely, Thos. Nelson Page

TLS (WP, DLC).

[1] Lawrence Grant White, son of Stanford White; architect of the firm of McKim, Mead & White; secretary to Thomas Nelson Page, 1913-1914; recently executive officer of the United States Naval Air Forces in Italy. He had served as a personal aide to Wilson during the latter's visit to Italy.

[2] The Italian names for Rijeka, Zadar, and Sibenik, respectively, all Croatian seaports on the Adriatic.

[3] He meant No. 54, not 57: T. N. Page to Ammission, Jan. 7, 1919, PPC, II, 365-66. Page described "Monsieur Popovitch" as a "delegate from Montenegro to Peace Conference." However, he was not one of the Montenegrins who later appeared before the Council of Ten to urge the right of self-determination for Montenegro. Ibid., IV, 193, 207-11. He may have been Vladimir Popovitch, a lawyer and former president of the municipal council of Cetinje, who was one of the signers of a manifesto of "Certain Montenegrins Resident in France" presented to Robert Woods Bliss on January 10. Ibid., II., 368-70.

[4] Or Venel (Page so refers to him in the telegram citied in n. 3 above). He cannot be further identified.

[5] Not printed.

ENCLOSURE

Confidential/For the President

DIGEST OF THE PRESIDENT'S CONFERENCE WITH ON.[1] BISSOLATI.

The President received On. Bissolati in the private salon of the Quirinal Palace at 6.50 p.m. on January 4th., 1919. The American Ambassador arrived at 7.00 p.m. The conversation, which was carried on through the undersigned as interpreter, was about as follows:

THE PRESIDENT: I am very glad of this opportunity to meet you, and I regret that we have such a short time in which to exchange our ideas.

ON. BISSOLATI: I feel that it is a great privilege to be received by you, as I have always held the deepest admiration both for you and for your ideals.

THE PRESIDENT: I shall speak quite openly and ask you direct questions, and I hope that you will understand that your answers will be only for my own use.

ON. BISSOLATI: Yes, indeed.

THE PRESIDENT: What, in your opinion, is the heart of the Italian people towards the settlement of this war, as regards Italy?

ON. BISSOLATI: At the beginning of the war, the heart of the Italian people was set entirely upon national revendication; but lately they have been fighting in order to establish the peace of the world—to protect their descendants from the menace of another war. The mass of the people have very little conception of geographical questions; but they felt that the Trentino, the Carso, and Istria were justly Italy's heritage.

THE PRESIDENT: And what is your opinion in regard to Fiume?

ON. BISSOLATI: Fiume should be a free city, and a free port. Fiume, as you know, is divided by a canal, or narrow strait, from the adjacent city of Susac. While the former is entirely Italian in sentiment, the latter is entirely Slav. They should exist side by side, Fiume as a free city under Italian protection, and Susac a free city under Slavic protection; but both of them free ports, and entirely independent of each other.

THE PRESIDENT: Do you believe that they would be able to support themselves as free cities, from an economic standpoint?

ON. BISSOLATI: Yes indeed; with the removal of all customs duties and formalities, they would be sure to have a rapid economic development.

THE PRESIDENT: Just how much territory do you include in the peninsula of Istria?

ON. BISSOLATI: It is, properly speaking, the triangular peninsula which juts out into the Adriatic; but a certain amount of the Hinterland should be included in Italian territory.

THE PRESIDENT: Where, then, should the border line be?

ON. BISSOLATI: (taking an envelope and drawing a rough sketch map of the peninsula of Istria) It should start here, in the Carnic Alps; run along here, including Gorizia—

THE PRESIDENT: (interrupting) You mean that Gorizia should be Italian, do you not?

ON. BISSOLATI: Yes, but not Adelsberg, which is entirely Slav. The line should run close to Trieste; run through the mountains—which form a wild, uncultivated and thinly populated district—to Monte Maggiore; thence striking the Gulf at Punte Fianona.

THE PRESIDENT: (to the Ambassador) That is just about the line which was determined by our students. (To On. Bissolati) What is that line further South?

ON. BISSOLATI: That is an imaginary frontier line in the water.

THE PRESIDENT: Does it include the Islands?

ON. BISSOLATI: Perhaps the exterior ones. ((Cherso and Lussin))

THE PRESIDENT: I have had a conference with Mr. Sonnino, who assured me that the Dalmatian coast and islands were a vital military necessity to Italy for defensive purposes. This I could not grasp, perhaps because of my somewhat old-fashioned ideas.

ON. BISSOLATI: Their military value is not so much for defensive as for offensive purposes. Dalmatia is really a bridge-head, from which an army could strike to the north or south, as occasion demanded.

THE PRESIDENT: I had thought, however, that the Islands might be held by them, if the following conditions were observed: First, that the Jugo-Slav nation should not possess any war fleet; secondly, that all the fortifications on the coast be dismantled; and thirdly, that the Italian and Slav inhabitants be assured equality of treatment. What is your opinion?

ON. BISSOLATI: I believe in the immediate abandonment of all Italian pretentions to Dalmatia. I insisted upon this in the Council of Ministers, and it was because of this stand that I took, that I was obliged to resign from the government.[2] In September, Italy made a declaration of sympathy for the Jugo-Slav cause. In this declaration it was understood that the provisions of the Treaty of London would be used against Austria, but not against the nations which might arise from the wreck of Austria.

THE PRESIDENT: (To the Ambassador) That is very interesting; I had not fully understood that.

ON. BISSOLATI: Otherwise it would have been a very Platonic declaration; those provisions were clearly understood. As I have said, I believe that it would be a fatal mistake for Italy to seize Dalmatia and antagonize the Jugo-Slavs. It would throw them into the hands of the Germans, and speedily lay the foundations for another war. They should instead be won over by friendship, and allowed to achieve their national aspirations. As you have so often stated, boundary lines based upon the nationalities of peoples are the only ones which can ever be stable. In the Risorgimento, there was never any question of Dalmatia becoming a part of Italy. Zara might be said to be Italian, although even there there has been a large infiltration of the Slavic element. Even with the frontier which I have indicated, there would be many more Slavs in Italian territory, than Italians in Slav territory.

THE PRESIDENT: I quite agree with you; if Italy held Dalmatia, it would be a constant source of irritation to the Jugo-Slavs, and would lead to a new Pan-Germanism?

ON. BISSOLATI: A new Pan-Germanism, as you say. We are waiting for the word from you, to solve these problems. This program, which I have indicated to you, with which Italy would be freed from all Imperialism, would render her a stronger ally of yours, Mr. President, in the struggle which you may have to maintain against the excessive pretensions of French and English nationalism, and therefore better able to aid you in your attempt to found the League of Nations.

THE PRESIDENT: Do you think that the League of Nations is a popular idea in Italy, and that the Italian people have confidence in the practical application of the idea?

ON. BISSOLATI: I do, indeed. The Italian people are the most Wilsonian in Europe, the most adapted to your ideals. I myself am starting a series of lectures, beginning next Sunday in Milan, and then all over Italy, in order to expound your ideals.

THE PRESIDENT: I am very grateful to you, I am sure.

ON. BISSOLATI: Before leaving, I wish to express my great personal admiration for you, which is shared by all Italy—indeed, I might say, by all Europe.

THE PRESIDENT: I am very glad that I have had this opportunity to meet you. I have been most interested in what you have told me.

((They shake hands, and On. Bissolati leaves.))

The above digest was submitted to On. Bissolati by the writer on January 6 and was approved by him as it stands above. He also stated that he believed that Italy should abandon the Tirol and the Dodekanese as well as Dalmatia, as otherwise two national sentiments would be irrevocably offended. Dalmatia, he added, is only 6% Italian.   Lawrence Grant White

TS MS (WP, DLC).
    [1] That is, Onorevole (Honorable), the adjective used to describe a member of the Italian Parliament.
    [2] Bissolati had resigned as Minister for Military Aid and War Pensions on December 28, 1918.

From James Viscount Bryce

My dear Mr. President   Forest Row, Sussex. Jan. 7, 1919

As you were far too much occupied in London to permit my having any private conversation with you, I have put down a few notes[1] upon some of the matters which will arise at the Peace Conference and with which I happen, from my travels in the Near

East, to be personally conversant, in the hope that if you can find time to glance at them they may be of some use to you.

On the morning when you left London I came to see you off, but unfortunately went to the wrong station, having understood you were departing from Charing Cross. All I wished to do however was to tell you what you have since heard from many other quarters, how profoundly impressed our people were by your speeches, and what immense good seems to us to have been achieved by your visit. Your Manchester addresses were to me specially inspiring: and I earnestly trust that by your advocacy the League of Nations for Peace idea may take an onward step from which there will be no drawing back. If the principle, and a few of the essential points, can be definitely adopted at the Paris Conference, it will be possible to work them out in detail afterwards. There are many difficult problems of detail to be settled. But the main thing is to have the solid foundation laid before you are obliged to return to America. With heartiest wishes for you in this great work, and for your safe return,

I am   Very sincerely yours   James Bryce

ALS (WP, DLC).
¹ They are missing. See WW to Lord Bryce, Jan. 16, 1919.

The American Commissioners to Frank Lyon Polk

[Paris] January 7, 1919.

186, for Polk. The President has approved the following memorandum:¹ "1. As you are aware our government has been represented in Europe upon various Interallied Councils, relating to finance, food, shipping and raw materials, war trade measures, etc. The purpose of these councils is rapidly changing and the American attitude toward them and the problems they represent must change. The matters involved are much interlocked and up to the time of the armistice were co-ordinated through the Council sitting under your chairmanship. Messrs. Hoover, Hurley, Baruch and McCormick are, or will soon be, in Europe. The working of these bodies still needs co-ordination by the heads of the Departments concerned, who will be in Europe together with the chief representatives here of the departments whose heads are still in Washington. 2. This same group are essential in determination of policies to be pursued by our Government in the Peace negotiations. 3. It is recommended that a council be set up, comprising Messrs. Hoover, Hurley, Baruch, and McCormick and Davis, with a Treasury representative to be appointed by Mr. Glass, under your [Wilson's] chairmanship, to discuss and decide such joint policies as are necessary in both these phases and to co-ordinate it with the Peace Commission by inclusion of Colonel House, General Bliss, and Admiral Benson, Colonel House to act as Chairman in your absence or inability to find time." Inasmuch as Davis has been appointed Commissioner to represent the United States in matters pertaining to finance at Spa and has been instructed by Secretary Glass to hold himself in readiness to furnish such advice as the President may require in connection with Treasury matters during the coming conferences, it would seem to be proper that Davis should be the Treasury representative on this committee. Please show this telegram to Secretary Glass and request his approval for Davis to act on this committee as Treasury representative.

Ammission.

T telegram (WP, DLC).
    [1] The quoted text below reproduces a memorandum from Hoover, which House gave or sent to Wilson. T MS endorsed "Approved W.W." (E. M. House Papers, CtY).

Cary Travers Grayson to Joseph Patrick Tumulty

Paris, January 7, 1919.

Number five. All well. Reception in Italy greatest President has ever received anywhere. Pope received President in very democratic manner. Italian politicians tried to keep President from the people, but did not succeed. The Italian people worship him. Confidentially. For yourself and Mrs. Grayson. Plan here is to leave for home about the fifteenth of February. Many happy returns to Gordon[1] and love to his mother.   Grayson.

T telegram (J. P. Tumulty Papers, DLC).
    [1] That is, James Gordon Grayson.

William Gibbs McAdoo to Edward Mandell House

Washington Jan. 7, 1919.

134. For Colonel House from McAdoo "Please seek an early opportunity to bring the following to the President's attention. Have sent him two important telegrams on railroad situation both unanswered.[1] The point has now been reached where appointment of new director general is imperative. Senate Committe[e] holding important hearings on railroad question. I testified fully Friday and Saturday last. Railroad executives and various selfish interests are

fighting hard to secure legislation favoring their views. The President's policies which are the policies I have consistently carried forward in the railroad administration and which he and I both favor for the future are in danger. My waning authority and the daily expectation of announcement of my successor deprive me of the opportunity to lead the fight any further with effect. A neutral director general thoroughly familiar with the vast railroad problem in full sympathy with the President's policies and views and with the requisite ability not omitting loyalty should be appointed immediately. No man unfamiliar with this situation should be chosen in my opinion. It would be a grave risk. I have recommended Hines as the best qualified man within or without the railroad administration for the task. He is in full sympathy with the policies of the President and the railroad administration, has the ability to defend them, is loyal and dependable. I speak with absolute confidence because I have tested him in every conceivable way during the year that he has been my assistant. With the character of fight now being made upon the railroad administration and the President in connection with the railroad problem Hines is the best man for the job. Baruch will confirm this judgment. Consult him. Even Carter[2] my director of the division of labor and former chief of the Brotherhood of Locomotive Firemen who was skeptical at the outset approves Hines. I urge his prompt appointment. But as I have said to the President, if he prefers another I have a very high opinion of Chambers[3] director of the division of traffic, who is able, industrious, progressive, in full sympathy with the President and with the policies of the railroad administration and capable of defending them. He has an extremely pleasing personality and is universally popular. He has been not as well equipped all round as Hines especially for dealing with the complex legal questions constantly arising and would not be so effective a defender or advocate before congressional committe[e]s or public bodies. The only objection to Hines and Chambers is that they were former railroad men. Each would overcome this handicap I think in a short time. But if the President is unwilling to appoint any railroad man, then I believe that Oscar Price[4] who has been another one of my assistants from the beginning is the best man in sight. Price knows this job thoroughly, has been all over the country with me on railroad inspection trips, understands the problem, is popular with all classes including labor, is absolutely dependable, is a democrat with the public view of all questions strongly inborn in him. One of these men should be selected by the President immediately. I am obliged to leave tonight for California and shall direct the railroads by telegrams and mail as I have done on previous inspection trips until the

President acts. The whole situation however demands prompt action. Love for you and the President. We are glad to glory in the splendid things he is doing."   Polk.

This has just come from McAdoo. In my opinion Hines is the best of those suggested. E.M.H.

T telegram (WP, DLC).
    ¹ WGM to WW, Dec. 19, 1918, and Dec. 26, 1918, both T telegrams (WP, DLC).
    ² That is, William Samuel Carter.
    ³ Edward Chambers, formerly vice-president in charge of traffic of the Atchison, Topeka, and Santa Fe Railroad.
    ⁴ Oscar A. Price, assistant to the Director General of Railroads.

Lewis Strauss to Gilbert Fairchild Close, with Enclosures

My dear Close: Paris January seventh Nineteen nineteen.

In reply to yours of the seventh, relative to the cable from Senator Martin and Congressman Sherley, Mr. Hoover believes that the three cables (already sent) of which I am enclosing copies, so fully cover the matter that no point requires further illumination. I am sending a copy of this to Secretary Lansing.

Faithfully yours,   Lewis Strauss

TLS (WP, DLC).

E N C L O S U R E   I

[Paris] January 6, 1919

URGENT PLEASE RUSH

For FOOD ADMINISTRATION On area covered by new appropriation the general situation of these countries is that their animals are largely reduced their crops were far below normal due to man and animal shortage ravage and climatic conditions STOP The surplus harvest above peasants needs is now rapidly approaching exhaustion and consequently the towns and cities are in dangerous situation STOP Our reports show specifically Finland that food is practically exhausted in cities that while many of the peasants have some bread other sections are mixing large amount of straw they are exhausted of fats meats sugar and need help to prevent a renewed rise of Bolchevism Paragraph Baltic States food may last one or two months on much reduced scale they sent deputation our Minister Stockholm imploring food Paragraph Servia town bread ration down three ounces daily in north not accessible from Salonika in south where accessible British are furnishing food to civil population we are trying to get food in from Adriatic Paragraph Yugo Slavia bread ration in many towns three or four ounces in all cases short of fats milk and meat Paragraph Vienna Except for supplies furnished by Italians and Swiss their present bread ration of six ounces per diem would disappear large illness from shortage fats ration being one and one half ounce per week no coffee sugar eggs practically no meat Paragraph Tyrol is being fed by Swiss charity Paragraph Poland Peasants probably have enough to get through mortality in cities particularly among children appalling for lack of fats and milk meat bread situation in bread will be worse in two months Paragraph Roumania bread supply entire people estimated to last another thirty days short of fats and milk last harvest sixty per cent a failure Paragraph Bulgaria Harvest also a failure supplies available probably two or three months Paragraph Armenia already starving Paragraph Checko Slovacks large suffering lack of fats and milk have bread for two or three months have sugar six months STOP We have each country under investigation as to total amounts required to barely maintain life and their resources to pay STOP Preliminary investigation by Taylor[1] and staff in conjunction with Allied staffs show total above areas will require about one million four hundred thousand tons imported food to get through until next harvest costing say three hundred and fifty million dollars delivered.

                                                                Hoover

[1] That is, Alonzo Englebert Taylor.

E N C L O S U R E   I I

[Paris] January 5, 1919

141 Very Urgent. Rickard Food Administration. Food 173. Your 118. The British are already furnishing from army stocks food and clothing relief to Serbia and Syria, the Italians to South Austria, the British and French are advancing the money for transport Belgian Relief. Allies are willing and anxious to do all they can and have and will contribute to the full extent of their resources but must be borne in mind that most of the food must be purchased in the United States and American money would be used for such purchase and transportation. Yours 107 as to using this for revolving fund. It would in effect be such a fund but it must be borne in mind that it would ultimately be absorbed in giving credits possibly over long periods to such peoples and institutions as our Treasury could not properly advance under the law and some of it would be lost in sheer charity. This is not to replace Treasury advances to

England, Belgium, France, Italy, Serbia and Roumania Governments for the purchase of American food. The proposed appropriations would be entirely insufficient for these purposes. It might however later on be used to partially replace loans to Serbia and Roumania but their urgent needs must in any event be cared for by the Treasury pending this appropriation. The matter is most urgent and forms the foundation for any complete arrangement with the Allies fixing their participation. It would also furnish a large measure of relief to urgent surpluses if prompt enough. There needs be great emphasis to all American officials and Congress that the Armistice has left us large surplus of food that if we are to dispose of it we must give credits and that as the nation trying to put peace on high level ideals on which they went into war we cannot be niggardly in the world's greatest problem today, that is, how to get food. I need not repeat that strong liberal relief is today the only hope of stemming the tide of Bolshevism, without the expenditure of lives and vast sums on military action. While it is urgently necessary to dispose of our surplus foods in order to relieve congestion and protect the producers from disaster and the consequent chaotic results, it is most fortunate for the saving of human lives that we have this surplus and our country cannot afford to fail to meet both emergencies.   Hoover.

E N C L O S U R E   I I I

SECSTATE, WASHINGTON D. C.   [Paris] 7th January 1919

177. Replying your ninety eight of January fourth five p.m. See Hoover's one seventy three to Food Administration which explains situation rather fully. The relief for the Balkan States and other peoples of Europe is to be undertaken in cooperation with the Allies with American leadership, Hoover as Director General will be in charge of the undertaking and a Council composed of two representatives from each England, France, Italy and the United States which Council will decide all questions involving general policy such as to whom relief shall be furnished, the lifting of blockade, the amount of relief to be given and the manner of financing, as well as the contribution which each Government can make. The Allies are already furnishing relief but it is impossible to make any definite proposals or arrangements with them until we are in position to act. It is believed however that England, France and probably Italy would be willing to agree to participate in the relief for a fixed percentage of the whole contributing, to the extent of their available resources in transportation, clothing, expenses which can be paid in their currencies and such minor amounts of food as they

may have in surplus provided we are prepared to agree to advance any dollars required to complete their fixed contribution—but understand Secretary of Treasury does not favor advancing funds to Allies for payment of American food to be supplied by them to other countries. Investigations are being carried out now as to the actual requirements in the different areas for submission to the council but the actual Relief already carried out and information obtained thereby lead to the conclusion that the need will be great. It is also realized that the temporary and inadequate character of relief in progress will not be sufficient to meet the situation. There are urgent requests for help from dozens of sources, usually of the type of cables now in your hands. It would be well to impress upon Congress that there is in the United States at present a considerable stock of surplus food especially wheat and pork which was accumulated principally for supplying the Allies and which would have been required by them had the war continued but which must now be disposed of in order to relieve storage and financial facilities in the United States because the Allies are now able to purchase and transport food at lower prices from their own possessions. While it is most important for us to dispose of this surplus in order to avoid difficulties in the United States, it is most fortunate that we have this surplus which is necessary to save human lives and stem the tide of Bolshevism in Europe. The hundred million dollars fund asked for to be placed at the disposal of the President will in a way be a revolving fund. In most cases obligations of Governments or of the Municipalities or of institutions will be taken in payment of food and supplies furnished from the United States but in some cases to a minor extent food will be furnished on a strictly charitable basis. While none of this fund will be used for advance to Germany, assistance may be tendered Austria and food may be sold to Germany on a cash basis, and it is well to impress upon Congress the fact that entirely aside from a humanitarian standpoint it is necessary to feed even Germany in order to prevent starvation and anarchy and the necessity of an extended military occupation with consequent greater and more expensive problems to deal with. It is estimated that the total surplus food produced in United States will amount to about one billion five hundred million dollars on which there is a considerable profit to the country and the Congress is only being asked to appropriate one hundred million dollars or a portion of this profit with which to facilitate use of the balance of the food to be used for this humanitarian and expedient undertaking. The Relief organization, with the approval of the Council will only furnish supplies to such countries where after investigation it is found urgently necessary. 177   Ammission

TC telegrams (WP, DLC).

From the Diary of Colonel House

January 7, 1919.

This has been a most intense day. Pichon was my first caller. He desired to get my views regarding the calling of the Conference and the method of procedure.

Admiral Benson was next after my meeting with the Commissioners. We went over many phases of the naval situation.

Marechal Foch called while I was out and left word he would return at two o'clock. When he came at two we discussed the matters he had in mind. Our conversation is given in a memorandum together with one which he handed me and upon which he wished some action taken by our Government. I told him the French Prime Minister was to be here at five and that I would also see the President and discuss it with him. It is a larger matter than appears on the surface and needs much thought. I took occasion to congratulate the Marechal upon his perspicuity in advising as to the German Armistice terms. I intimated that if we had followed some of the other Generals instead of him, we would not have come out so well.

Clemenceau and the President both sent word they would call on me at five. The President came first. I brought him to my reception room and had the other Commisssioners meet him. We had hardly begun our conversation before the Prime Minister arrived. I asked President Wilson to excuse me and I took Clemenceau into another room where we had one of our heart to heart talks. I convinced him, I think, for the first time that a league of nations was for the best interests of France. I called his attention to the fact that before the war Germany was a great military power, but that to the east of her there was Russia, also a great military power. Today there was only one great military power on the Continent of Europe, and that was France. There was no balance of power as far as the Continent was concerned, because Russia had disappeared and both Germany and Austria had gone under. The thing that was apparent to me and to him must necessarily be apparent to England. The English had always thrown their weight first in the one direction and then in the other to establish an equilibrium. The English would not look with favor upon the present situation.

I brought to Clemenceau's attention the fact that England's and France's interests now touched here and there throughout the world. I recalled the Fashoda incident, an incident that brought the two countries to the verge of war.

In the present war England voluntarily came to France's aid. She was not compelled to do so. The United States did likewise without compulsion. I asked whether or not in the circumstances France would not feel safer if England and America were in a position where they would be compelled to come to the aid of France in the event another outlaw nation like Germany should try to crush her. France, after this peace, under our plan, would be always France as she will stand then. Under the old plan, the shadow and the spectre of another war would haunt her. If she lost this chance which the United States offered through the League of Nations, it would never come again because there would never be another opportunity. Wilson was an idealist but our people were not all of his mind. Wilson could force it through because with all the brag and bluster of the Senate they would not dare defeat a treaty made in agreement with the Allies, and thereby continue alone the war with Germany or make a separate peace.

The old man seemed to see it all and became enthusiastic. He placed both hands on my shoulders and said, "You are right. I am for the League of Nations as you have it in mind and you may count upon me to work with you."

I then took up the French economic problems. I told him I understood as well as he did the real difficulties that confronted him. A great debt hung over the nation—a debt, the interest of which could only be paid by excessive taxation. Wages must necessarily go down after war and taxation must necessarily go up. This would bring on a state of almost rebellion and I wanted him to know that speaking for myself alone, I was willing to formulate with him some plan by which the delicate and dangerous situation might be met. I told him of the foolish suggestions that were being made by Ribot and others, and urged him to use his influence to check such schemes. They were doing harm to France and would eventually prejudice the Americans against her. I told Clemenceau I was speaking as one brother to another and I hoped he would pardon me for bringing up the internal affairs of France with which I was only indirectly concerned. The old man replied, "I think of you as a brother and I want you to tell me everything that is in your mind, and we will work together just as if we were parts of the same government." In this spirit, I said, there could be no differences between France and the United States.

I then took Clemenceau into the room where the President and the other Commissioners were. They had a talk of some fifteen or twenty minutes. When Clemenceau left I returned to the conference with my colleagues.

I had a very long talk with the President today, over the private telephone, before he came to call, and I gave him pretty much of a resume of what had happened since he left Paris. He told me of his Italian trip with which he was very pleased. I think I have mentioned before that John Carty[1] has arranged a private wire between the President's study and mine. I also have a telephone at my bedside that connects with this wire. There is no intermediary. He rings and I answer and vice versa. The wire is constantly "covered" to see that it is not tapped.

I told Gordon not to allow the papers to announce that Pichon, Foch, Clemenceau, the President and Lord Robert Cecil had been my visitors during the day. I am afraid of hurt sensibilities.

[1] Col. John Joseph Carty, U.S.A., formerly chief engineer of the American Telephone & Telegraph Co., at this time in charge of communications for the American Commission to Negotiate Peace.

From the Diary of Dr. Grayson

Wednesday, January 8, 1919.

The President remarked that General Bliss had a more statesmanlike mind than any member of the American Commission. He called him the soldier-statesman. The President spent most of today conferring with the American peace delegates arranging the actual details of each member's work.

A Draft of a Covenant of a League of Nations[1]

[c. Jan. 8, 1919].

PREAMBLE

In order to secure peace, security, and, orderly government by the prescription of open _just_ and honorable relations between nations, by the firm establishment of the understandings of international law as the actual rule of conduct among governments, and by the maintenance of justice and a scrupulous respect _for_ all treaty obligations in the dealings of organized peoples with one another, the Powers signatory to this covenant and agreement jointly and severally adopt this constitution of the League of Nations.

ARTICLE I.

The action of the Signatory Powers under the terms of this agreement shall be effected through the instrumentality of a Body of Delegates which shall consist of the ambassadors and ministers of the contracting Powers accredited to H. and the Minister for Foreign Affairs of H. The meetings of the Body of Delegates shall be held at the seat of government of H. and the Minister for Foreign Affairs of H. shall be the presiding officer of the Body.

Whenever the Delegates deem it necessary or advisable, they may meet temporarily at the seat of government of B. or of S., in which

[1] The following document is called Wilson's first Paris draft of the Covenant of the League of Nations. Wilson composed this draft by editing, revising, and adding to what is called the Washington draft, which is printed as an Enclosure with WW to EMH, September 7, 1918, Vol. 49. The text in light ink in the document printed in camera copy below is that of the Washington draft; the handwritten and typed emendations and the text in heavy ink represent Wilson's retyping, changes, and additions. The printed copy of the first Paris draft in WP, DLC, which is printed as the following document, conforms to the camera-copy text when one follows Wilson in reconstructing

-2-

case the Ambassador or Minister to H. of the
country in which the meeting is held shall be
the presiding officer pro tempore.

Add A.

ARTICLE II.

The Body of Delegates shall regulate their
own procedure and shall have power to appoint
such committees as they may deem necessary to
inquire into and report upon any matters which
lie within the field of their action.·

They shall organize a Secretariat to act
as their ministerial agency, and the expenses
of the maintenance of the Secretariat shall be
borne as they may prescribe.

In all matters covered by this Article
the Body of Delegates may decide by a majority
vote of the whole Body.

Substitute B

ARTICLE III.

The Contracting Powers unite in guaranteeing to each other political independence and
territorial integrity; but it is understood between them that such territorial readjustments,
if any, as may in the future become necessary
by reason of changes in present racial conditions and aspirations or present social and political relationships, pursuant to the principle of self-determination, and also such territorial readjustments as may be in the judgment

the document. The one change is the deletion of Russia from the first supplementary agreement.

As the House Diary, January 8, 1919, reveals, Wilson had completed this draft by January 8. For the degree to which he incorporated Smuts' "proposals," see the memorandum printed at December 26, 1918. As future documents will reveal, Wilson soon distributed copies of the first Paris draft to the other American peace commissioners.

-3-

of three-fourths of the Delegates be demanded by
the welfare and manifest interest of the peoples
concerned, may be effected, if agreeable to those
peoples; and that territorial changes may in
equity involve material compensation. The Contracting Powers accept without reservation the
principle that the peace of the world is superior
in importance to every question of Political jurisdiction or boundary.

ARTICLE IV.

H. 21.   The Contracting Powers recognize the principle that the establishment and maintenance of
peace will require the reduction of national armaments to the lowest point consistent with domestic safety and the enforcement by common action of international obligations; and the Delegates are directed to formulate at once plans
by which such a reduction may be brought about.
The plan so formulated shall be binding when,
and only when, unanimously approved by the Governments signatory to this Covenant.

The Contracting Powers further agree that
munitions and implements of war shall not be
manufactured by private enterprise or for private profit, and that there shall be full and
frank publicity as to all national armaments
and military or naval programmes.

On page 1, "H," "B," and "S" refer to Holland, Belgium, and Switzerland. On page
3 and following, the notations in the margins are references to the articles of House's
draft of a Covenant printed at July 16, 1918, Vol. 48.

-4-

ARTICLE V.

~~The Contracting Powers agree that all dis-~~
~~putes arising between or among them, of what-~~
~~ever nature, which shall not be satisfactorily~~
~~settled by diplomacy,~~ shall be referred ~~for ar-~~
~~bitration~~ to three arbitrators, one of the three
to be selected by each of the parties to the dispute, when there are but two such parties, and
the third by the two thus selected. When there
are more than two parties to the dispute, one
arbitrator shall be named by each of the several
parties and the arbitrators thus named shall add
to their number others of their own choice, the
number thus added to be limited to the number
which will suffice to give a deciding voice to
the ~~added~~ arbitrators thus added in case of a tie
vote among the arbitrators chosen by the contending parties. In case the arbitrators chosen by
the contending parties cannot agree upon an additional arbitrator or arbitrators, the additional
arbitrator or arbitrators shall be chosen by the
Body of Delegates.

On the appeal of a party to the dispute the
decision of the arbitrators may be set aside by
a vote of three-fourths of the Delegates, in case
the decision of the arbitrators was unanimous, or
by a vote of two-thirds of the Delegates in case
the decision of the arbitrators was not unanimous,

-5-

but unless thus set aside shall be finally binding and conclusive.

When any decision of arbitrators shall have
been thus set aside the dispute shall again be
submitted to arbitrators chosen as heretofore
provided, none of whom shall, however, have previously acted as arbitrators in the dispute in
question, and the decision of the arbitrators
rendered in this second arbitration shall be
finally binding and conclusive without right of
appeal.

H. 14.

ARTICLE VI.

Any Power which the Body of Delegates shall
declare to have failed to submit any dispute to
arbitration under the terms of Article V of this
Covenant or to have refused or failed to carry
out any decision of such arbitration shall thereupon lose and be deprived of all rights of commerce and intercourse with any of the Contracting Powers.

ARTICLE VII.

If any Power shall declare war or begin hostilities, or take any hostile step short of war, a-
against another Power before submitting the dispute involved to arbitrators as herein provided,
or shall declare war or begin hostilities, or
take any hostile step short of war, in regard to

-6-

any dispute which has been decided adversely to
it by arbitrators chosen and empowered as herein
provided, the Contracting Powers hereby bind themselves not only to cease all commerce and intercourse with that Power but also to unite in blockading and closing the frontiers of that Power to
commerce or intercourse with any part of the
world and to use any force that may be necessary to
accomplish that object.

H. 5, 7, 8.   ARTICLE VIII.

Any war or threat of war, whether immediately affecting any of the Contracting Powers or not,
is hereby declared a matter of concern to the
League of Nations and to all the Powers signatory
hereto, and those Powers hereby reserve the right
to take any action that may be deemed wise and effectual to safeguard the peace of nations.

The Delegates shall meet in the interest of
peace whenever war is rumoured or threatened, and
also whenever the Delegate of any Power shall inform the Delegates that a meeting and conference
in the interest of peace is advisable.

The Delegates ~~shall~~ may also meet at such
other times and upon such other occasions as they
shall from time to time deem best and determine.

also

It is hereby declared and agreed to be
the friendly right of each of the nations signatory or adherent to this Covenant to draw
the attention of the Body of Delegates to any
circumstances anywhere which threaten to disturb international peace or the good understand
ng ~~upon~~ between nations upon which peace de-
ends.

-7-

H.16,17.   ARTICLE IX.

        In the event of a dispute arising between one
of the Contracting Powers and a Power not a party
to this Covenant, the Contracting Power involved
hereby binds itself to endeavour to obtain the submission of the dispute to judicial decision or to
arbitration. If the other Power will not agree
to submit the dispute to judicial decision or to
arbitration, the Contracting Power shall bring the
matter to the attention of the Body of Delegates.
The Delegates shall in such case, in the name of
the League of Nations, invite the Power not a party to this Covenant to become ad hoc a party and
to submit its case to judicial decision or to arbitration, and if that Power consents it is hereby
agreed that the provisions hereinbefore contained
and applicable to the submission of disputes to
arbitration or discussion shall be in all respects applicable
to the dispute both in favour of and against such
Power in al as if it were a party to this Covenant.

        In case the Power not a party to this Coven-
ant shall shall not accept the invitation of the Delegates to become ad hoc a party, it shall be the
duty of the Executive Council Delegates immediately to institute an
inquiry into the circumstances and merits of the
dispute involved and to recommend such joint action by the Contracting Powers as may seem best
and most effectual in the circumstances disclosed.

-8-

H.18.   ARTICLE X.

If hostilities should be begun or any hos-
tile action taken ~~on~~ _against_ the Contracting Power by the
~~other~~ Power not a party to this Covenant before a
decision of the dispute by arbitrators or before
investigation, report, and recommendation by the
~~Executive Council~~ _Executive Council_ in regard to the dispute, or contrary
to such recommendation, the Contracting Powers
shall thereupon cease all commerce and communication with that Power and shall also unite in
blockading and closing the frontiers of that
Power to all commerce or intercourse with any
part of the world, employing jointly any force
that may be necessary to accomplish that object.
The Contracting Powers shall also unite in coming
to the assistance of the Contracting power against
which hostile action has been ~~taking~~ taken, combining their armed forces in its behalf.

H.19.   ARTICLE XI.

In case of a dispute between states not
parties to this Covenant, any Contracting Power may bring the matter to the attention of the
Delegates, who shall thereupon tender the good
offices of the League of Nations with a view to
the peaceable settlement of the dispute.

If one of the states, a party to the dispute,
shall offer and agree to submit its interests and

-9-

cause of action wholly to the control and decision of the League of Nations, that state shall
ad hoc be deemed a Contracting Power. If no one
of the states, parties to the dispute shall so
offer and agree, the Delegates shall *through the Executive Council,* of their own
motion take such action and make such recommenda-
tion to their governments as will prevent hostilities and result in the settlement of the dispute.

H. 22.   ARTICLE XII.

whose government is based upon the principle of pop-
ular   Any Power not a party to this Covenant may
self-
gov-   apply to the Body of Delegates for leave to be-
ern-
ment   come a party. If the Delegates shall regard the
granting thereof as likely to promote the peace,
order, and security of the World, they may act
favourably on the application, and their favourable action shall operate to constitute the Power so applying in all respects a full signatory
party to this Covenant. **This action shall re-**
quire the affirmative vote of two-thirds of
the Delegates.
H. 23.   ARTICLE XIII.

The Contracting Powers severally agree that
the present Covenant and Convention is accepted
as abrogating all treaty obligations ~~inter se~~
inter se which are inconsistent with the terms
hereof, and solemnly engage that they will not
enter into any engagements inconsistent with the
the *terms* ~~terms~~ hereof.

A. (To be added to Article I as an additional
   paragraph.)

It shall be the privilege of any of the
contracting Powers to assist its representative
in the Body of Delegates by any method of conference, counsel, or advice that may seem best
to it, and also to substitute upon occasion a
special representative for its regular diplomatic representative accredited to H.

B. (To be substituted for Article II)

ARTICLE II.

The Body of Delegates shall regulate their
own procedure and shall have power to appoint
such committees as they may deem necessary to
inquire into and report upon any matters that
lie within the field of their action.

It shall be the right of the Body of Delegates, upon the initiative of any member, to
discuss, either publicly or privately as it may
deem best, any matter lying within the jurisdiction of the League of Nations as defined in
this Covenant, or any matter likely to affect
the peace of the world; but all actions of the
Body of Delegates taken in the exercise of the
functions and powers granted to them under this
Covenant shall be first formulated and agreed
upon by an Executive Council, which shall act
either by reference or upon its own ititiative,

-2-suplementary.

and which shall consist of the representatives
of the Great Powers together with representatives drawn in annual rotation from two panels
, one of which shall be made up of the representatives of the States ranking next after
the Great Powers and the other of the representatives of the minor States (a classification which the Body of Delegates shall itself
establish and may from time to time alter),
such a number being drawn from these panels
as as will be but one less than the representatives of the Great Powers; and three or more
negative votes in the Council shall operate
as a veto upon any action or resolution proposed.

All resolutions passed or actions taken
by the Body of Delegates ~~upon the initiative~~
upon the recommendation of the Executive
Council, except those adopted in execution of
any direct powers herein granted to the Body
of Delegates themselves, shall have the effect of recommendations to the several governments of the League.

The Executive Council shall apponit a
permanent Secretariat and staff and may appoint joint committees chosen from the Body
of Delegates or consisting of specially qualified persons outside of that Body, for the study and

-3-supplementary.

systematic consideration of the international
questions with which the Council may have to
deal, or of questions likely to lead to international complications or disputes. It shall
also take the necessary steps to establish and
maintain proper liaison both with the foreign
offices of the signatory powers and ~~but also~~ with
any governments or agencies which may be acting as mandatories of the League of Nations in
any part of the world.

C.   (To be inserted as the second and third paragraphs of
     Article IV.)

     As the basis for such a reduction of ar-
maments, all the Powers subscribing to the
Treaty of Peace of which this Covenant constitutes a part hereby agree to abolish conscription and all other forms of compulsory military service, and also agree that their future
forces of defense and of international action
shall consist of militia or volunteers, whose
numbers and methods of training shall be fixed,
after expert inquiry, by the agreements with
regard to the reduction of armaments referred
to in the last preceding paragraph.

     The Body of Delegates shall also deter-
mine for the consideration and action of the
several governments what direct military e-

-4- suplementary.

quipment and armament is fair and reasonable
in proportion to the scale of forces laid
down in the programme of disarmament; and
these limits, when adopted, shall not be exceeded without the permission of the Body of
Delegates.

D.   (To be the opening part of Article V.)
        The contracting Powers jointly and sever-
ally agree that, should disputes or difficulties arise between or among them which cannot
be satisfactorily settled or adjusted by the
ordinary processes of diplomacy, they will in
no case resort to/force without previously
submitting the questions and matters involved
either to arbitration or to inquiry by the
Executive Council of the Body of Delegates
or until there has been an award by the arbitrators or a decision by the Executive Council; and that they will not even then resort
to armed force as against a member of the
League of Nations who complies with the award
of the arbitrators or the decision of the
Executive Council.
        In case of arbitration, the matters at
issue The Powers signatory to this Covenant
undertake and agree that whenever any dispute or difficulty shall arise between or

-5- supplementary.

among them with regard to any question of the
law of nations, with regard to the interpretation of a treaty, as to any fact which would,
if established, constitute a breach of international obligation, or as to as to any alleged damage and the nature and measure of the
reparation to be made therefor, if such dispute or difficulty cannot be satisfactorily
settled by the ordinary processes of negotiation, to submit the whole subject-matter to
arbitration and to carry out in full good faith
any award or decision that may be rendered.

In case of arbitration, the matter or
matters at issue

E.   (To be inserted as an additional paragraph at
the end of Article V.)

If for any reason it should prove impracticable to refeh any maater in dispute to arbitration, either or any party to the dispute
may apply to the Executive Council to take the
matter under consideration for such mediatory
action or recommendation as it may deem wise
in the circumstances. The Council shall immediately accept the refrence and give notice
to the other party or parties, and shall make
the necessary arrangements for a full hearing,
investigation, and consideration. It shall

-6- supplementary.

ascertain all the facts involved in the dispute and shall make such recommendations as
it may deem wise and practicable based on the
merits of the controversy and calculated to secure a just and lasting settlement. Other
members of the League shall place at the disposal of the Executive Council any and all information that may be in their possession which
in any way bears upon the facts or merits of
the controversy; and the Executive Council
shall do everything in its power by way of
mediation or conciliation to bring about a
peaceful settlement. The decisions of the
Executive Council shall be addressed to the
disputants, and shall not have the force of a
binding verdict. Should the Executive Council
fail to arrive at any conclusion, it shall be
the privilege of the members of the Executive
Council to publish their several conclusions
or recommendations; and such publication shall
not be regarded as an unfriendly act by either
or any of the disputants.

Should any contracting Power break or disregard its covenants under thir ARTICLE, it
shall thereby _ipso_ _fact_o become at war with
all the members of the League, which shall immediately subject it to a complete economic
and financial boycott, including the severance

ARTICLE VI.

-7- supplementary.

of all trade or financial relations, the prohibition of all intercourse between their subjects and the subjects of the covenant-breaking
State, and the prevention, so far as possible,
of all financial, commercial, or personal intercourse between the subjects of the covenant-
breaking State and the subjects of any other
State, whether a member of the League of Nations or not.

It shall be the privilege and duty of the
Executive Council of the Body of Delegates in
such a case to recommend what effective military or naval force the members of the League
of Nations shall severally contribute, and to
advise, if it should think best, that the smaller members of the League be excused from making
any contribution to the armed forces to be used
against the covenant-breaking State.

The covenant-breaking State shall, after
the resoration of peace, be subject to perpetual disarmament and to the regulations with regard to a peace establishment provided for new
States under the terms of SPPLEMENTARY ARTICLE

At the top of next page, Wilson reverts to his regular pagination interrupted by the insertion of "supplementary" text on our pages 665-71.

-10-

In case any of the Powers signatory ~~heret~~ hereto or subsequently admitted to the League of Nations shall, before becoming a party to this Covenant, have undertaken any treaty obligations which are inconsistent with the ~~term~~ terms of this Covenant, it shall be the duty of such Power to take immediate steps to procure its release from such obligations.

SUPPLEMENTARY AGREEMENTS.

I.

In respect of the peoples and territories which formerly belonged to Russia, to Austria-Hungary, and to Turkey, and in respect of the colonies formerly under the dominion of the German Empire, the League of Nations shall be regarded as the residuary trustee with sovereign ~~so far as to be clothed with the~~ right of ultimate disposal or of continued administration in accordance with certain fundamental principles hereinafter set forth; and this reversion and control shall exclude all rights or privileges of annexation on the part of any Power.

These principles are, that there shall in no case be any annexation of any of these territories by any State either within the League or outside of it, and that in the future government of these peoples and territories the

-11-

rule of self-determination, or the consent of
the governed to their form of government, shall
be fairly and reasonably applied, and all
policies of administration or economic development be based primarily upon the well-consid-
ed interests of the people themselves.

II.

Any asthority, control, or administration
which may be necessary in respect of these
peoples or territories other than their own
self-determined and self-organized autonomy
shall be the exclusive function of and shall
be vested in the League of Nations and exercised or undertaken by or on behalf ot it.

It shall be lawful for the League of Nations to delegate its authority, control, or
administration of any such people or territory
to some single State or organized agency which
it may designate and appoint as its agent or
mandatory; but whenever and wherever possible
or feasible the agent or mandatary so appointed shall be nominated or approved by the autonomous people or territory.

III.

The degree of authority, control, or administration to be exercised by the mandatary
State or agency shall in each case be explicitly defined by the League in a special Act

-12-

or Charter which shall reserve to the League
complete power of supervision and of ultimate
control, and which shall also reserve to the
people of any such territory or governmental
unit the right to appeal to the League for the
redress or correction of any breach of the mandate by the mandatary State or agency.

The mandatary State or agency shall in all
cases be bound and required to maintain the
policy of the open door, or equal opportunity
for all the signatories to this Covenant, in
respect of the use and development of the economic resources of such people or territory.

The mandatary State or agency shall in no
case form or maintain any military/force in excess of definite standards laid down by the
League itself for the purposes of intehnal police.

IV.

No new State arising or created from the
old Empires of Russia, Austria-Hungary, or
Turkey shall be recognized by the League or
admitted into its mambership except on condition that its military/forces and armaments
shall conform to standards prescribed by the
League in respect of it from time to time.

As successor to the Empires, the League of
Nations is empowered, directly and without
right of delegation, to watch over the relation

-13-

relations <u>inter</u> <u>se</u> of all new independent S̶t̶a̶
States arising or created out of the Empires,
and shall assume and fulfil the duty of conciliating and composing differences between them
with a view to the maintenance of settled order
and the general peace.

V.

The Powers signatory or adherent to this
Covenant agree that they will themselves seek
to establish and maintain fair hours and humane
conditions of labour for all those within their
several jurisdictions who are engaged in manual
labour and that they will exert their influence
in favour of the adoption and maintenance of a
similar policy and like safeguards wherever
their industrial and commercial relations extend.

VI.

The Powers signatory or adherent to this
Covenant bind themselves, and the League of Nations shall require all new States to bind
themselves as a condition precedent to their
recognition as independent or autonomous States,
to accord to all racial or national minorities
within their several jurisdictions, exactly the same
a̶b̶s̶o̶l̶u̶t̶e̶l̶y̶ ̶
e̶q̶u̶a̶l̶ treatment and security, both in law and
in fact, that is accorded the racial or nation-

-14-

                    their
al majority of/its people.

-4-

ARTICLE XI.

House 19.

ARTICLE XII.

House 22.

ARTICLE XIII.

House 23.

This loose page accompanies Wilson's draft.

A Draft of a Covenant

[c. Jan. 8, 1919]

COVENANT

PREAMBLE

In order to secure peace, security, and orderly government by the prescription of open, just, and honorable relations between nations, by the firm establishment of the understandings of international law as the actual rule of conduct among governments, and by the maintenance of justice and a scrupulous respect for all treaty obligations in the dealings of organized peoples with one another, the Powers signatory to this covenant and agreement jointly and severally adopt this constitution of the League of Nations.

ARTICLE I.

The action of the Signatory Powers under the terms of this agreement shall be effected through the instrumentality of a Body of Delegates which shall consist of the ambassadors and ministers of the contracting Powers accredited to H. and the Minister of Foreign Affairs of H. The meetings of the Body of Delegates shall be held at the seat of government of H. and the Minister for Foreign Affairs of H. shall be the presiding officer of the Body.

Whenever the Delegates deem it necessary or advisable, they may meet temporarily at the seat of government of B. or of S., in which case the Ambassador or Minister to H. of the country in which the meeting is held shall be the presiding officer *pro tempore*.

It shall be the privilege of any of the contracting Powers to assist its representative in the Body of Delegates by any method of conference, counsel, or advice that may seem best to it, and also to substitute upon occasion a special representative for its regular diplomatic representative accredited to H.

ARTICLE II.

The Body of Delegates shall regulate their own procedure and shall have power to appoint such committees as they may deem necessary to inquire into and report upon any matters that lie within the field of their action.

It shall be the right of the Body of Delegates, upon the initiative of any member, to discuss, either publicly or privately as it may deem best, any matter lying within the jurisdiction of the League of Nations as defined in this covenant, or any matter likely to affect the peace of the world; but all actions of the Body of Delegates taken in the exercise of the functions and powers granted to them under this Covenant shall be first formulated and agreed upon by an Executive Council, which shall act either by reference or upon its own initiative and which shall consist of the representatives of the Great Powers together with representatives drawn in annual rotation from two panels, one of which shall be made up of the representatives of the States ranking next after the Great Powers and the other of the representatives of the minor States (a classification which the Body of Delegates shall itself establish and may from time to time alter), such a number being drawn from these panels as will be but one less than the representatives of the Great Powers; and three or more negative votes in the Council shall operate as a veto upon any action or resolution proposed.

All resolutions passed or action taken by the Body of Delegates upon the recommendation of the Executive Council, except those adopted in execution of any direct powers herein granted to the Body of Delegates themselves, shall have the effect of recommendations to the several governments of the League.

The Executive Council shall appoint a permanent Secretariat and staff and may appoint joint committees chosen from the Body of Delegates or consisting of specially qualified persons outside of that Body, for the study and systematic consideration of the international questions with which the Council may have to deal, or of questions likely to lead to international complications or disputes. It shall also take the necessary steps to establish and maintain proper liaison both with the foreign offices of the signatory powers and with any governments or agencies which may be acting as mandatories of the League of Nations in any part of the world.

ARTICLE III.

The Contracting Powers unite in guaranteeing to each other political independence and territoral integrity; but it is understood between them that such territorial readjustments, if any, as may in the future become necessary by reason of changes in present racial conditions and aspirations or present social and political relationships, pursuant to the principle of self-determination, and also such territorial readjustments as may in the judgment of three-fourths of the Delegates be demanded by the welfare and manifest interest of the peoples concerned, may be effected if agreeable to those peoples; and that territorial changes may in equity involve material compensation. The Contracting Powers accept without reservation the principle that the peace of the world is superior in importance to every question of Political jurisdiction or boundary.

ARTICLE IV.

The Contracting Powers recognize the principle that the establishment and maintenance of peace will require the reduction of national armaments to the lowest point consistent with domestic safety and the enforcement by common action of international obligations; and the Delegates are directed to formulate at once plans by which such a reduction may be brought about. The plan so formulated shall be binding when, and only when, unanimously approved by the Governments signatory to this Covenant.

As the basis for such a reduction of armaments, all the Powers subscribing to the Treaty of Peace of which this Covenant constitutes a part hereby agree to abolish conscription and all other forms of compulsory military service, and also agree that their future forces of defence and of international action shall consist of militia or volunteers, whose numbers and methods of training shall be fixed, after expert inquiry, by the agreements with regard to the reduction of armaments referred to in the last preceeding paragraph.

The Body of Delegates shall also determine for the consideration and action of the several governments what direct military equipment and armament is fair and reasonable in proportion to the scale of forces laid down in the programme of disarmament; and these limits, when adopted, shall not be exceeded without the permission of the Body of Delegates.

The Contracting Powers further agree that munitions and implements of war shall not be manufactured by private enterprise or for private profit, and that there shall be full and frank publicity as to all national armaments and military or naval programmes.

ARTICLE V.

The Contracting Powers jointly and severally agree that, should disputes or difficulties arise between or among them which cannot be satisfactorily settled or adjusted by the ordinary processes of diplomacy, they will in no case resort to armed force without previously submitting the questions and matters involved either to arbitration or to inquiry by the Executive Council of the Body of Delegates or until there has been an award by the arbitrators or a decision by the Executive Council; and that they will not even then resort to armed force as against a member of the League of Nations who complies with the award of the arbitrators or the decision of the Executive Council.

The Powers signatory to this Covenant undertake and agree that whenever any dispute or difficulty shall arise between or among them with regard to any question of the law of nations, with regard to the interpretation of a treaty, as to any fact which would, if established, constitute a breach of international obligation, or as to any alleged damage and the nature and measure of the reparation

to be made therefor, if such dispute or difficulty cannot be satisfactorily settled by the ordinary processes of negotiation, to submit
the whole subject-matter to arbitration and to carry out in full good
faith any award or decision that may be rendered.

In case of arbitration, the matter or matters at issue shall be
referred to three arbitrators, one of the three to be selected by each
of the parties to the dispute, when there are but two such parties,
and the third by the two thus selected. When there are more than
two parties to the dispute, one arbitrator shall be named by each
of the several parties and the arbitrators thus named shall add to
their number others of their own choice, the number thus added
to be limited to the number which will suffice to give a deciding
voice to the arbitrators thus added in case of a tie vote among the
arbitrators chosen by the contending parties. In case the arbitrators
chosen by the contending parties cannot agree upon an additional
arbitrator or arbitrators, the additional arbitrator or arbitrators shall
be chosen by the Body of Delegates.

On the appeal of a party to the dispute the decision of the arbitrators may be set aside by a vote of three-fourths of the Delegates,
in case the decision of the arbitrators was unanimous, or by a vote
of two-thirds of the Delegates in case the decision of the arbitrators
was not unanimous, but unless thus set aside shall be finally binding and conclusive.

When any decision of arbitrators shall have been thus set aside,
the dispute shall again be submitted to arbitrators chosen as heretofore provided, none of whom shall, however, have previously acted
as arbitrators in the dispute in question, and the decision of the
arbitrators rendered in this second arbitration shall be finally binding and conclusive without right of appeal.

If for any reason it should prove impracticable to refer any matter
in dispute to arbitration, the parties to the dispute shall apply to
the Executive Council to take the matter under consideration for
such mediatory action or recommendation as it may deem wise in
the circumstances. The Council shall immediately accept the reference and give notice to the other party or parties, and shall make
the necessary arrangments for a full hearing, investigation, and
consideration. It shall ascertain all the facts involved in the dispute
and shall make such recommendations as it may deem wise and
practicable based on the merits of the controversy and calculated
to secure a just and lasting settlement. Other members of the League
shall place at the disposal of the Executive Council any and all
information that may be in their possession which in any way bears
upon the facts or merits of the controversy; and the Executive
Council shall do everything in its power by way of mediation or

conciliation to bring about a peaceful settlement. The decisions of the Executive Council shall be addressed to the disputants, and shall not have the force of a binding verdict. Should the Executive Council fail to arrive at any conclusion, it shall be the privilege of the members of the Executive Council to publish their several conclusions or recommendations; and such publications shall not be regarded as an unfriendly act by either or any of the disputants.

ARTICLE VI.

Should any contracting Power break or disregard its covenants under ARTICLE V, it shall thereby *ipso facto* become at war with all the members of the League, which shall immediately subject it to a complete economic and financial boycott, including the severance of all trade or financial relations, the prohibition of all intercourse between their subjects and the subjects of the covenant-breaking State, and the prevention, so far as possible, of all financial, commercial, or personal intercourse between the subjects of the covenant-breaking State and the subjects of any other State, whether a member of the League of Nations or not.

It shall be the privilege and duty of the Executive Council of the Body of Delegates in such a case to recommend what effective military or naval force the members of the League of Nations shall severally contribute, and to advise, if it should think best, that the smaller members of the League be excused from making any contribution to the armed forces to be used against the covenant-breaking State.

The covenant-breaking State shall, after the restoration of peace, be subject to perpetual disarmament and to the regulations with regard to a peace establishment provided for new States under the terms SUPPLEMENTARY ARTICLE 3.

ARTICLE VII.

If any Power shall declare war or begin hostilities, or take any hostile step short of war, against another Power before submitting the dispute involved to arbitrators or consideration by the Executive Council as herein provided, or shall declare war or begin hostilities, or take any hostile step short of war, in regard to any dispute which has been decided adversely to it by arbitrators chosen and empowered as herein provided, the Contracting Powers hereby bind themselves not only to cease all commerce and intercourse with that Power but also to unite in blockading and closing the frontiers of that Power to commerce or intercourse with any part of the world and to use any force that may be necessary to accomplish that object.

ARTICLE VIII.

Any war or threat of war, whether immediately affecting any of the Contracting Powers or not, is hereby declared a matter of concern to the League of Nations and to all the Powers signatory hereto, and those Powers hereby reserve the right to take any action that may be deemed wise and effectual to safeguard the peace of nations.

It is hereby also declared and agreed to be the friendly right of each of the nations signatory or adherent to this Covenant to draw the attention of the Body of Delegates to any circumstances anywhere which threaten to disturb international peace or good understanding between nations upon which peace depends.

The Delegates shall meet in the interest of peace whenever war is rumored or threatened, and also whenever the Delegate of any Power shall inform the Delegates that a meeting and conference in the interest of peace is advisable.

The Delegates may also meet at such other times and upon such other occasions as they shall from time to time deem best and determine.

ARTICLE IX.

In the event of a dispute arising between one of the Contracting Powers and a Power not a party to this Covenant, the Contracting Power involved hereby binds itself to endeavour to obtain the submission of the dispute to judicial decision or to arbitration. If the other Power will not agree to submit the dispute to judicial decision or to arbitration, the Contracting Power shall bring the matter to the attention of the Body of Delegates. The Delegates shall in such a case, in the name of the League of Nations, invite the Power not a party to this Covenant to become *ad hoc* a party and to submit its case to judicial decision or to arbitration, and if that Power consents it is hereby agreed that the provisions hereinbefore contained and applicable to the submission of disputes to arbitration or discussion shall be in all respects applicable to the dispute both in favour of and against such Power as if it were a party to this Covenant.

In case the Power not a party to this Covenant shall not accept the invitation of the Delegates to become *ad hoc* a party, it shall be the duty of the Executive Council immediately to institute an inquiry into the circumstances and merits of the dispute involved and to recommend such joint action by the Contracting Powers as may seem best and most effectual in the circumstances disclosed.

ARTICLE X.

If hostilities should be begun or any hostile action taken against the Contracting Power by the Power not a party to this Covenant before a decision of the dispute by arbitrators or before investigation, report and recommendation by the Executive Council in regard to the dispute, or contrary to such recommendation, the Contracting Powers shall thereupon cease all commerce and communication with that Power and shall also unite in blockading and closing the frontiers of that Power to all commerce or intercourse with any part of the world, employing jointly any force that may be necessary to accomplish that object. The Contracting Powers shall also unite in coming to the assistance of the Contracting Power against which hostile action has been taken, combining their armed forces in its behalf.

ARTICLE XI.

In case of a dispute between states not parties to this Covenant, any Contracting Power may bring the matter to the attention of the Delegates, who shall thereupon tender the good offices of the League of Nations with a view to the peaceable settlement of the dispute.

If one of the states, a party to the dispute, shall offer and agree to submit its interests and cause of action wholly to the control and decision of the League of Nations, that state shall *ad hoc* be deemed a Contracting Power. If no one of the states, parties to the dispute, shall so offer and agree, the Delegates shall, through the Executive Council, of their own motion take such action and make such recommendation to their governments as will prevent hostilities and result in the settlement of the dispute.

ARTICLE XII.

Any Power not a party to this Covenant, whose government is based upon the principle of popular self-government, may apply to the Body of Delegates for leave to become a party. If the Delegates shall regard the granting thereof as likely to promote the peace, order, and security of the World, they may act favourably on the application, and their favourable action shall operate to constitute the Power so applying in all respects a full signatory party to this Covenant. This action shall require the affirmative vote of two-thirds of the Delegates.

ARTICLE XIII.

The Contracting Powers severally agree that the present Covenant and Convention is accepted as abrogating all treaty obligations *inter se* which are inconsistent with the terms hereof, and solemnly engage that they will not enter into any engagements inconsistent with the terms hereof.

In case any of the Powers signatory hereto or subsequently admitted to the League of Nations shall, before becoming a party to this Covenant, have undertaken any treaty obligations which are inconsistent with the terms of this Covenant, it shall be the duty of such Power to take immediate steps to procure its release from such obligations.

SUPPLEMENTARY AGREEMENTS.

I.

In respect of the peoples and territories which formerly belonged to Austria-Hungary, and to Turkey, and in respect of the colonies formerly under the dominion of the German Empire, the League of Nations shall be regarded as the residuary trustee with sovereign right of ultimate disposal or of continued administration in accordance with certain fundamental principles hereinafter set forth; and this reversion and control shall exclude all rights or privileges of annexation on the part of any Power.

These principles are, that there shall in no case be any annexation of any of these territories by any State either within the League or outside of it, and that in the future government of these peoples and territories the rule of self-determination, or the consent of the governed to their form of government, shall be fairly and reasonably applied, and all policies of administration or economic development be based primarily upon the well-considered interests of the people themselves.

II.

Any authority, control, or administration which may be necessary in respect of these peoples or territories other than their own self-determined and self-organized autonomy shall be the exclusive function of and shall be vested in the League of Nations and exercised or undertaken by or on behalf of it.

It shall be lawful for the League of Nations to delegate its authority, control, or administration of any such people or territory to some single State or organized agency which it may designate and appoint as its agent or mandatory; but whenever or wherever possible or feasible the agent or mandatory so appointed shall be nominated or approved by the autonomous people or territory.

III.

The degree of authority, control, or administration to be exercised by the mandatary State or agency shall in each case be explicitly defined by the League in a special Act or Charter which shall reserve to the League complete power of supervision and of intimate control, and which shall also reserve to the people of any such territory or governmental unit the right to appeal to the League for the redress or correction of any breach of the mandate by the mandatary State or agency or for the substitution of some other State or agency, as mandatary.

The mandatary State or agency shall in all cases be bound and required to maintain the policy of the open door, or equal opportunity for all the signatories to this Covenant, in respect of the use and development of the economic resources of such people or territory.

The mandatary State or agency shall in no case form or maintain any military or naval force in excess of definate [definite] standards laid down by the League itself for the purposes of internal police.

IV.

No new State arising or created from the old Empires of Austria-Hungary, or Turkey shall be recognized by the League or admitted into its membership except on condition that its military and naval forces and armaments shall conform to standards prescribed by the League in respect of it from time to time.

As successor to the Empires, the League of Nations is empowered, directly and without right of delegation, to watch over the relations *inter se* of all new independent States arising or created out of the Empires, and shall assume and fulfil the duty of conciliating and composing differences between them with a view to the maintenance of settled order and the general peace.

V.

The Powers signatory or adherent to this Covenant agree that they will themselves seek to establish and maintain fair hours and humane conditions of labour for all those within their several jurisdictions who are engaged in manual labour and that they will exert their influence in favour of the adoption and maintenance of a similar policy and like safeguards wherever their industrial and commercial relations extend.

VI.

The League of Nations shall require all new States to bind themselves as a condition precedent to their recognition as independent or autonomous States, to accord to all racial or national minorities within their several jurisdictions exactly the same treatment and security, both in law and in fact, that is accorded the racial or national majority of their people.

Printed copy (WP, DLC).

From Joseph Patrick Tumulty

The White House, January 8, 1919.

Great opposition to $100,000,000. relief appropriation by Democrats and Republicans. Suggest you send strong message to Sherley and Martin. Unless this done, think it in great danger.

Tumulty

T telegram (J. P. Tumulty Papers, DLC).

From Edward Mandell House, with Enclosures

Dear Governor,   [Paris, c. Jan. 8, 1919]

Hoover has asked me to send this to you after reading it. Before taking action I think it would be well to let me say a word to you.

E.M.H.

ALI (WP, DLC).

E N C L O S U R E   I

From Herbert Clark Hoover

My dear Mr. President: Paris, 8th January 1919.

I have cablegrams this morning, copies of which are enclosed,[1] stating that the whole of the customary monthly orders from the British buying organizations on behalf of the Allied Governments have been withdrawn. I am informed by the French and Italian officials that it is untrue, that they have not withdrawn their share of the orders, and I am endeavoring to restore them.

The Allied food necessities have been outlined from time to time by a series of programmes made up by the Inter-Allied Food Council, the latest of these programmes is as recent as the 15th of December and calls for our entire January surplus. Our manufacturers have provided the particular types of manufacture required by each of these Governments and have enormous stocks of these materials in hand ready for delivery in accordance with the indicated programmes above mentioned.

While we can protect our assurances given producers in many commodities, the most acute situation is in pork products which are perishable and must be exported. We have in January a surplus of about 400,000,000 pounds, and the French, Italian and Belgian Relief and other customary orders when restored will cover 60 percent of such. The British orders, at the rate indicated in their official programmes, would have been 140,000,000 pounds and covered our deficiency plus some help I am giving from the Relief. The British position is that they have sufficient supplies to last them for some weeks and that they wish to reduce their stocks.

If there should be no remedy to this situation we shall have a debacle in the American markets, and with the advances of several hundred million dollars now outstanding from the banks to the pork products industry we shall not only be precipitated into a financial crisis but shall betray the American farmer who has engaged himself to these ends. The surplus is so large that there can be no absorption of it in the United States and it, being a perishable, will go to waste.

You will recollect that measures are before the Congress providing for appropriations for further economic assistance to the Allied Governments and I am confident that with the disclosure of this situation and the apparent desire of certain parties in England to break the American market will cause a reaction in the United States that will destroy the possibility of this economic support. In the face of this, the demand of liberated, neutral and enemy populations in Europe as to fats is beyond the ability of the United States to supply, and the need from the point of view of preserving order and laying the foundation of peace is absolutely instant in its insistence.

Mr. Davis and I have endeavored for the last six weeks to arrange some co-operative action with the British agencies to forefend this situation and, as indicated above, the final result has been the refusal on their part to co-operate. We have suggested that the British Government should join with ourselves in the purchase of the necessary amounts of fats at our assured price to be resold to the liberated and enemy territories in order to prevent the above debacle, and in this they have finally refused. I wish to assure you again that the prices which we are maintaining are the very minimum on which our American producers can come out whole on the effort they have made in the Allied cause, and I cannot impress upon you too strongly the reaction that will arise in the United States if this situation falls to the ground.

With Mr. Davis I have prepared the attached memorandum which I would like to suggest should be presented by you to the Allied Premiers at the earliest possible moment, as I cannot conceive that men with their vision as to the present situation will tolerate for one moment the attitude taken.

                              Faithfully yours,   Herbert Hoover

TLS (WP, DLC).
¹ They are missing.

E N C L O S U R E   I I

MEMORANDUM FOR AGREEMENT WITH ALLIED PREMIERS,
TO COMPRISE A DIRECTION TO THEIR VARIOUS GOVERNMENT
DEPARTMENTS.

It is impossible to discuss the peace of the world until adequate measures have been taken to alleviate the fear of hunger, its attendant anarchy and its danger of possible further military operations. Therefore, before these peace negotiations can be opened auspiciously, it is essential to have the better feeding of the liberated, neutral and enemy territories of Europe in actual progress as the foundation of stability in government antecedent to the settlement of the great problems that will come before the Conference. It is therefore agreed by the Allied and the United States Governments that each shall, without further delay, furnish every possible assistance and facility required for carrying out the undertakings as to European Relief, which shall be carried out in the name of the Associated Governments.

The United States has, in order to support the Allied Governments in war, provided large supplies of foodstuffs, many of them perishable, which would have been required by the Allies had hostilities continued. In order to accumulate these supplies, the American Government has given assurances and guarantees to their producers. The Allied Governments, as the result of the cessation of hostilities and the opening of other markets, no longer require the same amount of supplies from the United States as they have from time to time indicated by their programmes.

This surplus is now required to meet the necessities of Europe and it is most fortunate that the surplus is available for these purposes. It would be a disaster to the objects of the Associated Governments if the congestion in the United States should not be relieved so as to save waste and to meet the assurances given by the United States Government, and the Allied Governments agree to at once direct their departments to co-operate with the United States Food Administration to support these assurances, and the application of these foodstuffs to the needs of liberated, neutral and enemy peoples.

Pending the more mature plans and settlements of the Relief Administration as to food, shipping and finance, it is directed that immediate provision should be made from any available source of food supplies for provisions to points of acute need in the Balkan States, the liberated peoples of Turkey, Austria, to Belgium and Poland, that such provision shall be retroactively the obligation of the four governments pending more definite arrangements.

It is desirable that the Associated Governments should show their good will towards the neutral countries of Europe by the immediate increase in the permitted importation of the surplus food commodities to these neutrals at once, being such amounts as the United States shall declare to be in surplus.

That it is necessary to at once give evidence of progress in the matter of food supplies to Germany and South Europe, and to this end the British, French and United States Governments will each at once give cabled orders for the shipment during the month of January of 30,000 tons of such fats (in addition to their orders for home consumption) as the United States shall declare available for these relief purposes. These foodstuffs shall be subsequently offered to Germany, subject to payment therefor and other conditions that the Associated Governments may impose. That the Allied Governments and the United States will co-operate in the securing of such payment in a manner acceptable to each of the Associated Governments, and for providing the transportation of such foodstuffs. Before these supplies can arrive, the Relief Administration is expected to be working and to decide the conditions of distribution of payment and of further supplies and shipping.

These arrangements are declared binding upon all departments of the Allied and the United States Governments and shall be given immediate execution.

CC MS (WP, DLC).

From John R. Shillady

New York 8 Jan 1919

Mass meeting January sixth Carnegie Hall New York under auspices of National Association for Advancement of Colored People greets the President of the United States and pledges him loyal support in his efforts toward establishment of a universal league of free nations which shall have among its central duties the protection and development of the peoples of middle Africa

John R Shillady

T telegram (WP, DLC).

The American Commissioners to Frank Lyon Polk

[Paris] January 8, 1919.

206. For your information and for the information of the Secretary of the Treasury. The President on January 7 wrote the two following letters to Norman H. Davis.

Letter No. 1. "Secretary Glass has recommended to me your appointment as commissioner in connection with the armistice discussion at Spa. He has also advised me that so far as your time is not occupied by this special mission you will be available to furnish general financial and economic advice as I may desire regarding questions which may arise at the peace conferences not directly touching our foreign loans.

I entirely agree with Secretary Glass that questions regarding our foreign loans such as the making of further loans the conversion of demand obligations dates of maturity interest rate and special receding long time obligations received by us in exchange and claims of one government against another for dollar reimbursements should be discussed and settled in Washington.

I shall take pleasure in following Secretary Glass's recommendation and I request that you act as United States Commissioner in connection with the armistice discussions at Spa and that you hold yourself available to furnish general financial and economic advice as I may desire from time to time during the Peace conference.

I have requested the Secretary of State to take the necessary steps to issue your commission in Washington. Until this is done this letter together with the enclosed letter of even date will serve as your credentials."

Letter No. Two. "I appoint you to act as United States Finance Commissioner and as such to take part on behalf of our government in the armistice discussion at Spa.

Your duties in connection with the armistice discussions will be to take up with the commission representing the German Treasury and the Imperial Bank questions of general financial and economic conditions in Germany with special reference to retiring German marks and controlling the exportation of German securities. You will sit with the representatives chosen by the British, French, Belgian and German Governments to consider these matters.

In addition to the above questions you will also consider and determine what expenses of our army of occupation are to be met by Germany and to make arrangements regarding same.

This letter will serve as your credentials to act for the United States with respect to these matters."   Ammission.

T telegram (WP, DLC).

Henry White to Henry Cabot Lodge

[Paris] January 8, 1919.

203. For Senator Lodge from Mr. Henry White.

Feel I should no longer delay laying before you condition which has been gradually forcing itself upon our Delegation and which now dominates entire European situation above all else: namely: steady westward advance of Bolshevism. It now completely controls Russia and Poland and is spreading through Germany. Only effective barrier now apparently possible against it is food relief, as Bolshevism thrives only on starvation and disorder. Consensus of opinion is that joint military occupation which has been suggested by France for Poland, even if practical would not solve problem. Confidentially Paderewski has sent us a most urgent appeal for assistance in Poland where conditions he says are desperate.[1] I consider it therefore of utmost importance that President's request for hundred million appropriation for relief be granted at once. Impossible to inaugurate Peace Conference under proper auspices without previous adequate provision to cope with situation. Aside from stoppage of Bolshevism, I understand there is in United States considerable surplus of food accumulated at high prices maintenance whereof guaranteed by our Government or assurance under its auspices and that it is necessary to dispose of this surplus in order to relieve warehouse and financial facilities as well as prevent serious fall in prices with radical break in market which would cost our country more than the appropriation asked for. The apropriation is not for the purpose of advancing money to Germany which will pay on a cash basis for any food sent there. It is too late I fear to stop Bolshevism in Russia and Poland, but there is still hope for making Germany, Roumania and certain other areas effective barriers. Allies are already furnishing relief to liberated territories and are disposed to assist otherwise to extent of their available resources but most of the food must come from the United States. I cannot too strongly impress upon you urgency of meeting situation herein described. Please communicate this to John Rogers, Gillett and Root[2] as a confidential message from me and of course you are welcome to do so to any of your colleagues to whom you think it will be interesting, also in confidence.

Signed   Henry White.

T telegram (WP, DLC).

[1] See I. J. Paderewski to EMH, Jan. 4, 1919.

[2] That is, John Jacob Rogers, Frederick Huntington Gillett, and Elihu Root. Rogers and Gillett were Republican congressmen from Massachusetts.

From the Diary of Colonel House

January 8, 1919.

David Miller and Herbert Hoover called immediately after breakfast. Lord Robert Cecil, Lansing and I had an hour's conference concerning the League of Nations. We found ourselves wide apart, Lansing and I desiring something stronger than Lord Robert.

Jusserand was also a caller. I had but scant time for him because the President was just about to arrive. The matter he had in mind was of no importance and had to do with something I had taken up with Marechal Foch and Clemenceau yesterday.

M. Transqui,[1] the Belgian Minister for Colonies, was another visitor. He told me the King was anxious that I should come to Belgium and I promised to do so in April.

We had a meeting of the Peace Delegates with the President presiding. We discussed the method of procedure for the informal conferences which are to come. We also discussed some of the covenants for the League of Nations. When we had finished, and while we were passing to the door, I told the President that I thought he ought to name a successor to Ambassador Sharp. Sharp wished to be relieved February first and that date was nearly upon us. He asked if I still thought Hugh Wallace would do. I replied in the affirmative and promised to guide him and to be responsible for him. The President put his name down and I take it he will appoint him. We did not talk about the matter more than two minutes, so casual does he do things.

Letters, cables and what not that have come in and gone out are parts of the record. I cannot go into details since my time is so completely absorbed.

Lansing and I had a talk with Lord Robert Cecil before lunch and made some progress. I invited Cecil to my rooms after lunch and we had a half hour of intense conversation. We got along because I opened up my mind to him and told the whole story of the League of Nations Covenant as the President and I had written it. It was something I could not explain to him before Lansing. I think there will now be but little difference between us.

Clemenceau came in the afternoon. He asked whether I could arrange with the President to have a meeting on Sunday at the Quai d'Orsay between the Prime Ministers and Foreign Secretaries in order to arrange a program. We agreed on 2.30 P.M. for this

---

[1] Miss Denton must have misheard or could not spell the name. The Belgian Minister for Colonies at this time was Ludwig Franck. House undoubtedly referred to Émile Francqui, a Belgian Minister of State.

meeting. We also agreed that there should be a general meeting called at the Quai d'Orsay at 3.30 Monday which would include the French, British, Italian and American Delegates in full. I confirmed this later after I had spoken with the President.

I had a heart to heart talk with Clemenceau about Bolshevism in Russia and its westward march. I made him confess that military intervention was impossible. I did not go into the remedy as I did not care to get into an argument with him about feeding the Central Powers, but I thought that since we were agreed that military intervention was impossible, then we should exert all the wisdom possible in order to devise some plan by which this critical and dangerous situation might be met. He assented.

Later in the afternoon when Orlando called, I gave him very much the same kind of talk, and he too, agreed with my conclusions. I am trying, and have partially succeeded, to frighten not only the President but the English, French and Italians regarding what might be termed "the Russian peril." Personally, I really do not believe there is as much danger as I make it to them. If I had the imper[i]alistic views that some of these people have who are at the heads of their governments, I would not confess that military intervention was an impossibility, because I believe that it could be successfully accomplished if gone about properly. A voluntary and a mercenary army of very small proportions, equipped with artillery and tanks, would in my opinion do the work. . . .

The President asked me to come to the Hotel Murat after dinner. He had finished another draft for the League of Nations, a copy of which he had sent me during the afternoon and which I had read hastily. The substance of the League was [the] covenant which I wrote at Magnolia in August, embellished with some of General Smuts' ideas and a paragraph or two of the President's own which he puts under "supplementary agreements." I am amused at his stanstant [constant] endeavor to bring everything within thirteen articles, thirteen being his lucky number.

I approved the draft as it now stands. It is much improved over the Magnolia document. I have suggested a way by which he might get it adopted and I shall hope for success.

I took up several matters with the President, all of which he approved without discussion. Before leaving the subject, I want to add that I suggested several corrections to this latest draft of the Covenant for the League of Nations which he readily adopted. These corrections are shown in his own handwriting in the copy of this date which is attached to the diary.

I do not know how I am to go through the many weeks ahead if matters are crowded upon me as they have been during the past few days. The other Commissioners are willing to help, but I am sorry to say are in fact a hindrance. So much time is taken up with them of a perfectly useless nature. The President seems to have no intention of using them effectively. It is the story of Washington over again. We settle matters between the two of us and he seems to consider that sufficient without even notifying the others. I feel embarrassed every day when I am with them. . . .

The President, at my suggestion, held the meeting of Commissioners in General Bliss' rooms. I have asked him to rotate from one Delegate's rooms to another in order that all may be complimented. Bliss and Lansing began the discussion of a draft of a treaty which Miller and Scott had drawn, largely under the direction of Lansing.[2] This draft included a Covenant for the League of Nations. The President spoke with some asperity and wanted to know why they had undertaken such a piece of work. As a matter of fact, I have been encouraging Lansing and the others to work out something so as to keep them contented, and I was more at fault than anyone. I did not know that Bliss and Lansing were to spring it on the President today, otherwise I should have prepared him.

The President was not feeling well, therefore our discussion did not continue more than fifty minutes. He had an engagement with Harry Davison on Red Cross matters, and he and I came up to my rooms where we talked to Davison for something over a half hour. It was agreed that I should write to the Prime Ministers of England, France and Italy in the name of the President and tell them that he thoroughly approved the plan to enlarge the scope of the Red Cross Organization.

There were several other matters to which I called the President's

---

[2] David Hunter Miller provides the following account of the origins of this draft in his diary entry of December 27, 1918: "Mr. Lansing sent for Dr. [James Brown] Scott and myself and told us that he wanted us to prepare a draft, or rather, he said, a skeleton treaty which would indicate the various subjects to be taken up in the treaty, and the difficulties connected therewith. The first part of the treaty he said should be the League of Nations, followed by the general particulars of the President's program, such as Freedom of the Seas, Limitation of Armaments, and economic matters. But the treaty he said should go on to questions of boundary and all other questions which might occur to us. He also told us to confer with him from time to time on the subject, as our work was more or less completed." David Hunter Miller, *My Diary at the Conference of Paris, With Documents* (21 vols., New York, 1924), I, 60.

On December 30, 1918, Scott and Miller submitted to Lansing a draft of a peace treaty in very sparse outline form. The only subjects covered in any precise detail were boundary and territorial questions and the problem of which nations should or should not be signatories to the treaty. See J. B. Scott and D. H. Miller to RL, Dec. 30, 1918, enclosing "Skeleton Draft of Peace Treaty" and an Appendix, "Signatories to the Treaty of Peace," *PPC*, I, 298-315. On January 9, 1919, Miller and Scott presented Lansing with a preamble and the first two articles of the proposed treaty. "Article B." was a detailed "Agreement," or covenant, for a league of nations. See D. H. Miller and J. B. Scott to RL, Jan. 9, 1919, enclosing "Draft Treaty," *ibid.*, pp. 316-24.

attention. Frazier had written letters to the different notables in Italy who he thought should be properly thanked by the President. Among them was a draft of a letter to the King which the President was supposed to either write with his own hand or have written by someone else. I was amused to hear the President say that he had dictated a letter to the King and had already sent it. I forgot to ask whether he had sent similar letters to the British officials. I shall do this tomorrow.

From the Diary of Dr. Grayson

Thursday, January 9, 1919.

The President had a two-hour conference with Premier Orlando of Italy who had come to Paris in order to press Italian claims in Dalmatia and secure for Italy control of the Adriatic. Orlando came to speak confidentially, not wishing Sonnino to know of his visit, because of the personal relations between them which were decidedly strained. Orlando gave many reasons for Italy's claims; among them that her boundaries should extend far to the north in order that she might never again be at the disadvantage of having a foe attack her from an elevated position and also because, he said, otherwise the Italian Army always would have the disadvantage of having the sun in their eyes. Orlando pushed Italy's claim to the whole eastern shore of the Adriatic, including the fortified islands, which are to be in the Yugo-Slavia Republic. The President, while having warm sympathy for Italy's ambitions, simply could not support this claim, because he felt that to give Italy a military control of the eastern shore of the Adriatic would be to create a serious military menace to the new governments coming into being in that region. The President's own idea at this stage was that Italy should have the Trentino and Trieste, but neither Polo[1] nor any material portion of the Dalmatian Coast. The President's idea was that the fortified islands on the eastern shore of the Adriatic should be dismantled and that, inasmuch as the Yugo-Slavia Republic would not have a Navy, therefore having no menace to the east of her, Italy would have no strategic claim to the territory. This proposal also took into consideration the internationalization of the straits of Otranto.[2] This was rather a bitter pill to the Italians, but I recalled an indication of how the people felt about it. When in Rome, Mr. Page, the Ambassasor, told the President that he had a conversation with an Italian, who asked him how much of this territory he thought Mr. Wilson would let Italy have and finished up by saying: "Well, I suppose if Mr. Wilson does not want us to have it, we should not get it." This was an indication of the popular confidence which the President had aroused in Italy. At this stage, however, the President was debating, "in his own mind," as he expressed it, how far he could disappoint the Italian popular ambitions and still get through an amicable settlement. There was one other incident which illustrated the way in which territorial ambitions were being carried out. In Rome, the President learned that the one regiment of American troops, which had been assigned to the Dalmatian territory, had been divided by the Italian Commander into platoons and used as a "cover" for the Italian advance into the disputed territory.[3] The President learned that the Italian military chiefs had found when they advanced into the towns of Dalmatia, Albania and Yugo-Slavia, rioting followed the appearance of Italian troops. The Italian commander then adopted the expedient of sending in small bodies of American soldiers. They were received with popular rejoicing. During the night however, the Americans would be withdrawn and replaced by Italian soldiers. In this way, the Italian commander had been using the popular esteem for the Americans to advance his own troops far across the armistice line. The President directed that the whole regiment should be assembled at once, under its own colonel. One young lieutenant in this regiment, who refused to take the American troops over the armistice line into Montenegro, when the Italian commander so directed, had made possible discovery of the plan. The President did not know his name, but remarked that he thoroughly appreciated his good sense.

[1] That is, Pola.
[2] Which connected the Adriatic Sea with the Ionian Sea, between Cape Otranto in southern Italy and Cape Linguetta in Albania.
[3] T. H. Bliss to WW, Dec. 23, 1918, discusses in general terms the use of the American regiment by the Italians for their own purposes.

To Vittorio Emanuele III

Your Majesty: Paris, 9 January, 1918 [1919].

The very delightful reception which you and your gracious Queen both accorded Mrs. Wilson and me in Italy will always remain in our hearts as a very delightful and fragrant memory. I tried to express to you when I was with you the sentiments of genuine friendship it had stirred in us. Nothing of any kind which could contribute to our comfort or enjoyment was overlooked, and it was delightful to us to get a glimpse of your life at the Villa Savoia, where everything was so genuine and gave evidence of the sort of family life which does everything for the heart and for the enoblement of life.

Mrs. Wilson joins with me in sending to you and the Queen our most cordial greetings and in expressing our heartfelt thanks for all your kindness.

Cordially and sincerely yours,   [Woodrow Wilson]

CCL (WP, DLC).

To Joseph Patrick Tumulty

Paris, January 9, 1919.

Replying to your number six. I am very much interested in suggestion of returning through New England and had myself been thinking out something equivalent. Shall be very glad to consider the whole thing. My chief difficulty just now is to get the heads of the governments together for genuine conference, the English particularly, but I think they will lose much more than they will gain by evident delays.   Woodrow Wilson.

T telegram (J. P. Tumulty Papers, DLC).

To Carter Glass

[Paris] January 9, 1919.

215. For the Secretary of the Treasury from the President.

Referring to cable from Davis to you relative to an advance of $5,000,000 to Roumania and the various communications to the State Department and Food Administration on Roumanian situation. The information from our authorities indicates an extremely dangerous situation which must be relieved in the next few days and one which, if cumulative, with others, may necessitate increased military effort on our part. In my opinion this would be in interest of National Defense and I strongly approve giving this advance so as to allow the shipment of urgent food pending the appropriation for relief now in Congress. The British are sending cargo of wheat and we must assist by forwarding cargoes now in the Mediterranean. I also wish to urge the desirability of the Treasury aiding in every way in the disposal of our surplus food products in order to prevent losses to our producers and to prevent consequent difficulties at home and disorder in Europe. Unless there is some legal obstacle I regard this of the highest importance.

Ammission.

T telegram (WP, DLC).

To Newton Diehl Baker

[Paris] January 9, 1919.

216. For the Secretary of War from the President.

The Food Administration will present to you the situation produced by army reductions in pork purchases and the situation generally arising out of changed currents of trade due to the Armistice and the action of the British authorities.

I have received the following letter from Hoover with its memorandum which latter I propose [to] present to early meeting with Allied premiers. As this latter may not succeed, I would like at once the views of yourself and colleagues as to whether, in the interest of peace, the safety of our army from rising anarchy, and the protection of our producers, the War Department should not make the necessary purchases to protect the American situation and ship the material to Europe for distribution under their direction as a military measure. . . .[1]   Ammission.

T telegram (WP, DLC).
[1] Here follow the texts of HCH to WW, Jan. 8, 1919, and the memorandum printed as Enclosure II with EMH to WW, Jan. 8, 1919.

Four Letters to Robert Lansing

My dear Mr. Secretary: Paris, 9 January, 1919.

I see no objection to this, and agree with Polk's judgment as to the course he ought to pursue.[1]

Cordially and sincerely yours,   [Woodrow Wilson]

CCL (WP, DLC).
[1] See FLP to RL, Jan. 6, 1919 (third letter of that date).

My dear Mr. Secretary: Paris, 9 January, 1919.

I doubt the wisdom of a Bolivian deputation either to the United States or to Paris at the present juncture.[1] They are apt to get lost in the mixup here anyway, and I should not like to have them come and feel more disappointed than if they had stayed at home.

Cordially and sincerely yours,   Woodrow Wilson[2]

TLS (SDR, RG 59, 723.2515/9, DNA).
[1] See RL to WW, Dec. 28, 1918.
[2] Wilson's message was conveyed to the State Department in RL to FLP, Jan. 10, 1919, T telegram (SDR, RG 59, 723.2515/2, DNA).

My dear Mr. Secretary: Paris, 9 January, 1919.

This communication concerns matters unhappily accumulating with which I confess I do not know how to deal.[1] It occurs to me that it might be wise for you to call the attention of Baron Sonnino, now that he is in Paris, to these particular statements, and then as a next step confer with the representatives of others whom he may think are involved.

> Cordially and faithfully yours,   [Woodrow Wilson]

¹ H. P. Dodge to R. W. Bliss, Dec. 31, 1918, *PPC*, II, 344-45. This telegram from Belgrade reported on further aggressive actions in Serbia by the Italian army and said that the Serbian authorities were deeply disappointed because the United States and the Allies seemed to be indifferent to the situation.

My dear Mr. Secretary: [Paris] 9 January, 1919.

Is there not in Paris some representative of the Polish Committee with whom you could have a frank talk about this?¹ It is clearly out of the question to allow Poles to be enlisted in the United States to fight against peoples with whom the United States is at peace and whose affairs the United States is trying to compose, but I think the representatives of the Poles should be told this before we take official action.

> Cordially and sincerely yours,   [Woodrow Wilson]

CCL (WP, DLC).
¹ See FLP to RL, Jan. 3, 1919.

To Robert Lansing, with Enclosure

My dear Lansing: [Paris] 9 January, 1918 [1919]

This is a very moving letter, and I would highly value your advice concerning it. I am inclined to advise and request that you have a very frank talk with the representative of Serbia and say how much distress and what serious questions are arising in our minds because of the dealings of Serbia with Montenegro. Undoubtedly the sympathies of the people of the United States are as much with Montenegro as with Serbia. Our people have always admired the sturdy independence of the little kingdom, and I feel that the whole cause of Jugoslavia is being embarrassed and prejudiced by the apparent efforts to decide by arms what ought to be decided by pacific arrangement and consent. I hope that this course will commend itself to you and that you will seek the earliest possible opportunity to express these sentiments to Mr. Vesnitch.

I am enclosing my reply to the King and hope, unless you see some diplomatic complication in it, you will be kind enough to have it delivered.

> Cordially and faithfully yours,   Woodrow Wilson

TLS (SDR, RG 59, 772.73/7, DNA).

From Nicholas I

Very dear and great Friend,   Paris. January 7, 1919.

You brought into the war the greatest and most pacific of the Republics in the name of outraged right and in the defence of the weak. You caused the Allies themselves to realize the true meaning of their heroic efforts and of the noble aims they were to strive for. You wished for victory in order that upon it peace might be fashioned by the hands of the just. You gave a definite form to the desire of all civilized peoples and to the principles on which perfectible humanity ought to build up its true happiness. In your person we are compelled to see the great conscience of our epoch.

It is because you are all this that to-day the oldest of the heads of States writes to you to appeal to your sense of equity.

My Government has already informed your Government of the facts which oblige me to break that reserve which I have perhaps too long observed.

On December 28, 1918, the Chargé d'Affaires of the Serbian Government near the Royal Government of Montenegro addressed to the latter the following note: "By order of the Royal Government I have the honor to inform the Royal Ministry that the diplomatic functions of the representative of the Royal Government near that ministry should be considered as at an end for the reason that on the 4th of this month the union of Montenegro to Serbia came into effect." These few words, this short, brutal sentence, have with cynicism put an end to the long and patient hypocrisy of official Serbia. Her tactics are revealed, her aims discovered, her greed avowed!

In 1914, when the ambition of Austria-Hungary threatened Serbia, Montenegro at once flew to arms. Nothing forced it so to act; it only obeyed a sentiment of fraternal solidarity. It fought courageously, not listening to offers made by the enemy, nor stipulating conditions for its Allies. At my desire the Montenegrin command was entrusted to Serbian officers. In 1915 our little Army sacrificed itself in order to cover the retreat of the Serbs, and thus saved them from disaster. This act of abnegation exhausted Montenegro. It was compelled to abandon the struggle. The brave Montenegrin soldiers were destined to die of cold and hunger in prison camps, and Austria occupied the whole of its territory.

Quickly lightened of its burden of gratitude, the Serbian Government at once sought to take advantage of the precarious situation of its unfortunate Ally and neighbor. It immediately saw the way to exploit the exile of the official representatives of unhappy Montenegro.

In spite of the hospitality extended by France, soon around us began to be heard the whisper of mischief-making, then the murmur of slander. Little by little rumours, at first of the vaguest kind, took shape and grew in volume; subterranean slander broke out into definite accusation. What had so far only been said soon began to appear in print; clandestine libel was replaced by widely distributed printed pamphlets; and these yet anonymous pamphlets were shortly followed by articles in publicly circulated newspapers. All and every means were good enough provided that the King of Montenegro, his family, his surroundings and his Ministers were cried down and vilified; every arm was legitimate if from the wound it made flowed some of the prestige of heroic Montenegro and its old sovereign.

To what end? It was necessary to cause a people to become disgusted with its dynasty, with its Government and even its independence. It was necessary to wear down the sympathy that the Allies were disposed to show towards the misfortunes of the smallest of their number. It was necessary to bring the minds of all thinking people to accept the absorption of one people by another.

Too soon the Serbian Government thought success won: and in 1917 came the declaration of Corfu, signed by the President of the Serbian Council.[1] It was attempted by this act to draw up a pure and simple declaration of the annexation of Montenegro to Serbia. Without its being a question of consulting a single Montenegrin subject, it pretended to place our people under the scepter of the Karageorgevitchs.[2] This attempt was in fact a failure, but a failure far from discouraging its authors. In November 1918 they imagined that they saw in the armistice another favorable opportunity. They hastened to smuggle Serbian troops into Montenegro as soon as the Austro-Hungarians had been evacuated therefrom, and then at once began armed propaganda.

The exploits of this propaganda are known to all. By clumsy artifice a "great Skouptchina" was created, while such an assembly is unprovided for in the Constitution of Montenegro, and while according to the laws of the country the national parliament cannot be legally called together when the King and his Government are on Allied territory and a number of its members are still interned or on their way home.

This assembly without a mandate was credited with authority. The result of a vote which was not even properly elaborated was trumped up—and throughout the world, thanks to the simplicity and cupidity of the Press, was spread the news of the union of Montenegro with Serbia and, at the same time, the deposition of Nicholas I.

The union of Montenegro with its Jugoslav brothers? But all my life I have been the most resolute and most listened to partisan of it! Only, I have always felt that it was necessary to leave to my people an independence which they have so dearly bought by five long centuries of strife, and I have always proclaimed that in the formation of a Jugoslav community each member ought to preserve its autonomy. This I re-stated in October 1918. No Jugoslavia is possible, in my opinion, without liberty and equality among its members.

To this conception what is the conception opposed by Serbia? Distinctly imperialist, the latter desires to see placed beneath the scepter of its King[3] the divers Jugoslav countries thus reduced to nothing more than docile provinces of an exacting and authoritative monarchy.

In this there is a danger which all the diplomats of Europe and of America must perceive. In this in any case there is a violation of those very principles to which it has rightly become a habit to give your name.

It is in the name of these principles and in the name of eternal justice that I raise my voice in complaint to-day. I complain that the Serbian Government ignores my acquired rights, and treats official Montenegro with ignominious disrespect. I complain that official Serbia has made an attempt on the sovereignty of the Montenegrin people. I complain that an attempt is made to cause the Allies to forget their formal promise to restore and reconstitute Montenegro on the same footing as Serbia and Belgium. I complain that by force and ruse one people is doing its utmost to annex another!

I protest with all my strength against this scandal.

If the methods of Prussia have not been for ever abolished by the war just brought to a close; if the old practices of imperialism are still exercised and honored; if Might is Right, then I am wrong to speak. I ought to resign myself to the silence of the weak and the vanquished!

But if the methods of a Bismarck have been uprooted from this world by the hand of the victors; if the will of nationalities and peoples is sacred; if Right is no longer a vain word; the United States and their associate, the Entente, will compel my adversaries to let go their prey and will not allow a political crime to be committed.

Je suis Très cher et Grand Ami

Votre sincère Ami   Nicholas.

TLS (SDR, RG 59, 772.73/7, DNA).
[1] Nikola Pašić.
[2] That is, the royal family of Serbia.
[3] Peter I.

To Nicholas I

My good friend: Paris, 9 January, 1919.

I have received your letter of January seventh and read it with considerable interest. I must at present content myself with a brief acknowledgment of it, but I beg that you will believe that the days will not be too crowded or too hurried for me to drive the interests of sturdy Montenegro out of my mind or to lessen in the least my sincere desire to do everything in my power to see that justice is done her. The matters to which you call my attention will have my most serious and sympathetic consideration.

Cordially and sincerely yours,   Woodrow Wilson.

TCL (SDR, RG 59, 772.73/7, DNA).

Five Telegrams from Joseph Patrick Tumulty

The White House, 9 January 1919.

[No. 8] Early action on appointment of director general of railways seems necessary to prevent disintegration of organization. Judge Lovett, Carl Gray[1] and other operating heads leaving. Hurley has been suggested as able business man, who would have the point of view of shippers and public, as well as approval of brotherhoods because of his early experience as fireman and engineer. If Hurley were named, double effectiveness could be achieved by simultaneous appointment of Homer Ferguson,[2] President of Newport News Shipbuilding Company, democrat and friend of Secretary Daniels, as Chairman of Shipping Board. It is essential that there should be in both places officials wholly sympathetic and upon whom you can rely in formulation of important policies. Suggestions made here are intended merely to supplement and not conflict with recommendation of Secretary McAdoo.   Tumulty.

T telegram (J. P. Tumulty Papers, DLC).
[1] Robert Scott Lovett was at this time director of the Division of Capital Expenditures of the United States Railroad Administration. Carl Raymond Gray was director of the Division of Operation.
[2] Homer Lenoir Ferguson.

The White House, January 9, 1919.

No. 9. Secretary Labor urgently recommends you authorize me to send following message in your name to Taft and Manly, National War Labor Board.[1] He says situation is desperate.

[1] It was sent with a few changes as WW to JPT, Jan. 10, 1919 (second telegram of that date). Basil Maxwell Manly was the new co-chairman of the Board.

Washington, D. C. [Jan. 9, 1919]

Number ten following from Gregory quote Dear President in accordance with the purpose expressed in our conversation just before you went abroad I tender my resignation. It has been not quite six years since I became connected with your administration and more than four years ago, a few days after war was declared by the European nations, I became a member of the cabinet. It can be fairly said that during no other six years in the history of our country have so many great problems been presented and solved. The reflection that at such a time I have been permitted to stand by your side and assist in a modest way in dealing with those national and international issues is now and will always be my greatest source of pride. No man ever served a leader who was more uniformly considerate, more kindly helpful, and more generously appreciative. No subordinate was ever more deeply grateful for the numberless friendly words and acts of his superior. Pecuniary responsibilities of a substantial nature rest upon me, and my private affairs have long demanded attention. During the continuance of actual warfare I did not feel at liberty to weigh these personal considerations in the balance against the public duties with which I was charged. By March fourth of the present year the Department of Justice will have substantially brought its war activities to a close and be working under normal conditions. I therefore ask that this resignation take effect on that date. Faithfully yours, T. W. Gregory unquote.[1]   Tumulty.

T telegrams (WP, DLC).
[1] The TLS of this letter is TWG to WW, n.d. (WP, DLC).

The White House, January 9, 1919

[No. 11] Am sending plain formal resignation Attorney General and in code personal note from him. Please cable this office your acceptance resignation as Attorney General wishes it given out at White House.   Tumulty

T telegram (J. P. Tumulty Papers, DLC).

Washington, January 9, 1919

[No. 12] Following from Atty Gen quote

Am today having Tumulty cable you letter containing my resignation effective March fourth. It is of some importance to me that it should be published within the next week. In our conversation you expressed a desire that it be not given out before January. If you see no objection to that course will you not kindly cable the White House such comments or letter as you think appropriate and authorize the release of same together with my letter to you of today. Matters on this side moving smoothly. Developments in Europe are daily strengthening your position on this side. T. W. Gregory. unquote   Tumulty

T telegram (WP, DLC).

From Robert Lansing

My dear Mr. President: Paris. 9th January, 1919.

You will perhaps recall that before our departure from Washington, you discussed with me the advisability of your making a declaration embodying a statement of the attitude of the Government toward the Bolshevik authorities in Russia, and at that time you decided to postpone any such statement until the opportunity had presented itself of discussing the matter with the leaders of the Governments associated with us in the war.

I have now received a cablegram from Mr. Polk[1] in which he refers to the reports from the American Representatives abroad, regarding the growing menace of the Bolshevik movement outside of Russia, and asks to be informed of the steps if any, which may have been taken with a view to defining the attitude of the associated governments toward the movement in general.

I shall be glad to be informed of any views which you may desire to have communicated to Mr. Polk in connection with the matter.

Faithfully yours,   Robert Lansing

TLS (WP, DLC).
[1] F. L. Polk to RL, Jan. 6, 1919, T telegram (first telegram of that date).

From the Diary of Dr. Grayson

Friday, January 10, 1919.

The President played his second game of golf since landing in France going to St. Cloud during the morning. He had a conference

with the American Delegation, at the Crillon Hotel during the afternoon. He also met Henry P. Davison, President of the American
Red Cross War Council, who presented his resignation and talked
over the selection of his successor. Davison discussed the internationalization of the Red Cross, a project conceived to unite the
Red Cross Societies of the world into one cohesive body. This step
was desirable, because the signing of the peace treaty involved a
revision of the Geneva convention, which had been so grossly violated by the Germans. The President told Davison that he would
appoint as his successor, any man that could be agreed upon by
Davison, Cleveland H. Dodge, Surgeon General Ireland, of the Army
and Franklin K. Lane, Secretary of the Interior.

Following a conference today, with Food Administrator Herbert
Hoover, at which he received a very full report showing that while
there was food enough on hand for the immediate present, there
were no reserves at all that could be utilized the President immediately sent cablegrams to the leaders of the House and Senate and
addressed a brief message to Congress, urging passage of the pending appropriation of $100,000,000, to finance the feeding of these
liberated peoples. In this message, among other things, he said:
"Bolshevism is steadily advancing westward, has overwhelmed Poland and is poisoning Germany. Force cannot stop it, but food can."

Henry White, the Republican member of the Peace Mission, sent
similar messages to Senator Lodge and other Republican members
of the conference [Congress], urging them to support the appropriation.

From the Diary of Edith Benham

Evening, January 10, 1919

Later, tonight at dinner, was Helen Bones' sister, Mrs. Brower,[1]
and a friend, Mrs. Stacy,[2] both of whom have come over to do
Y.M.C.A. work. Mrs. B. is about eight years younger than the President and after dinner she spoke of the lectures the Y.M.C.A. is
giving and one fact they are stressing that the Germans are being
particularly kind to our Army of Occupation and they are making
them very comfortable in houses so as to spread a good impression
in America. From there the discussion drifted into a discussion of
the Peace Congress and the President spoke more feelingly and at
more length than I have ever heard him on this subject. He said
that they were trying to force him to go to see the devastated regions
so that he might see red and play into the hands of the governments
of England, France and Italy. He had no words strong enough and

he was deeply moved and his voice trembled with indignation when he spoke of his contempt for them and the things for which they stood. He told her what I have already written that France wanted us to pay rent for the trenches she had dug and in which our men were fighting for her and that England wanted to charge $150 apiece for every soldier of ours she brought over here to fight for her and this did not include the food. He said he expected to speak of this in the Congress and expose England's violations of our rights at sea. He spoke of the peace and that there could be no lasting peace based on hate. If it were that and calculated on that there would be another and more terrible reckoning and the whole question of peace had to be approached in a perfectly cold blooded way to secure a just settlement.

He said that the people are for just settlements but the ruling classes are not and that the people are eager for peace and are resenting bitterly this delay. That Lloyd George is having trouble in England and that 10,000 British troops mutinied today on their own soil refusing to go abroad to replace other troops. This was probably in the paper which I have had no time to read. He drew a parallel between the Boxer case and the remission of that indemnity and what he hoped now, which is that we could exact an enormous sum from Germany but remit it as in that case. Mrs. Brower asked if he didn't believe in punishment and he said the German people had their own as they would be shunned and avoided like lepers for generations to come, and so far most of them had no idea of what other nations felt and didn't realize the coventry in which they would be put. He spoke again of the difficulties he had in getting people together; that Clemenceau said he needed ten day's rest and Lloyd George did and he was amused after getting Clemenceau to say he was willing to have informal conferences begin without him and getting Orlando and the Italians here, and then today Clemenceau appeared. He was afraid to go away. The President said he hoped to keep them here by "slipping something over on them when they were away." . . .

A man's mind is interesting. I have been particularly interested to find out the books he likes. He seems to have read everything and here he talks so much more of intellectual things than in Washington. His favorite author I would say is Walter Bagehot from whose writings he is constantly quoting. Night before last he read us A. G. Gardiner's sketch of Roosevelt in one of his books, "War Lords and Prophets."[3] Gardiner I didn't know of and I think is a semi-pacifist writer for the Daily News. The President wants very much to see him for he had a great opinion of his writings. He also read a study of himself by Gardiner which has come out recently and is very good. Colonel House gave the material for it.

[1] That is, Jessie Woodrow Bones (Mrs. Abraham Thew H.) Brower.
[2] She cannot be identified.
[3] As previously noted, Gardiner's sketch of Theodore Roosevelt appeared in his *Pillars of Society* (London, 1913).

To Robert Lansing

My dear Mr. Secretary: Paris, 10 January, 1919.

I must say that I still see no great advantage to be derived from words and public statements in the matter of Bolshevism. What I am at present keenly interested in is in finding the interior of their minds, and I hope that you have been able to get hold of Buckley [Buckler] and get him started to the interviews which we discussed the other day and which I regard as of capital importance.[1]

The real thing with which to stop Bolshevism is food.

Cordially and sincerely yours,   Woodrow Wilson

TLS (WP, DLC).
[1] About the Buckler mission, see the extract from the House Diary printed at Jan. 1, 1919. Buckler left London for Stockholm on or about January 9, 1919.

Three Telegrams to Joseph Patrick Tumulty

[Paris] 10 January, 1919.

Please convey following message to Senator Martin and Congressman Swager Sherley: quote. I cannot too earnestly or solemnly urge upon the Congress the appropriation for which Mr. Hoover has asked for the administration of food relief. Food relief is now the key to the whole European situation and to the solutions of peace. Bolshevism is steadily advancing westward, has overwhelmed Poland, and is poisoning Germany. It cannot be stopped by force but it can be stopped by food, and all the leaders with whom I am in conference agree that concerted action in this matter is of immediate and vital importance. The money will not be spent for food for Germany itself, because Germany can buy its food, but it will be spent for financing the movement of food to our real friends in Poland and to the people of the liberated units of the Austrian-Hungarian empire and to our associates in the Balkans. I beg that you will present this matter with all possible urgency and force to the Congress. I do not see how we can find definite powers with whom to conclude peace unless this means of stemming the tide of anarchism is employed. end quote.   Woodrow Wilson.

[Paris] 10 January, 1919.

Please send the following to Messrs. Taft and Manly National War Labor Board quote I have been informed by the Secretary of Labor as to the serious situation which has developed in the port of New York and the strike of Marine workers which seriously cripples the movements of troops and supplies. I consider this a very grave emergency and understand that it has arisen because the parties to the controversy failed to make a joint submission to the National War Labor Board. I earnestly request that you take up this case again and proceed to make a finding. I appreciate the honesty and sincerity of the board in announcing on Wednesday that it could not promise a final decision in the controversy without a formal submission from all parties but I am sure that the war and navy departments the shipping board and railroad administration and any other governmental agencies interested in the controversy will use all the powers which they possess to make your finding effective and I also believe that private boat owners will feel constrained by every consideration of patriotism in the present emergency to accept any recommendation which your board may make. Although the National War Labor Board upon [up] to the signing of the armistice was concerned solely with the prevention of stoppage of war work and the maintenance of production of materials essential to the conduct of the war I take this opportunity also of saying that it is my earnest hope that in the present period of industrial transition arising from the war the board should use all means within its power to stabilize conditions and to prevent industrial dislocation and warfare unquote

Woodrow Wilson

T telegrams (WP, DLC).

Paris, January 10, 1919.

Please inform Mr. Walker D. Hines that I request him to serve as Director General of Railroads and inform him that this cablegram will serve as authority for his appointment. Any papers that are necessary for me to sign I will be obliged if you will send to me, but in the meantime Mr. Hines may exercise the authority of the office by my commission.

Please also have made out and sent to me the nomination of Mr. Hugh C. Wallace as Ambassador of the United States to France, keeping the matter private until Sharp is ready to announce his resignation, which he feels obliged by private circumstances to insist on.

Is there anything else that I can do that might help to bring about the passage of the Suffrage Amendment?

Woodrow Wilson.

T telegram (J. P. Tumulty Papers, DLC).

To Thomas Nelson Page

My dear Mr. Ambassador: Paris, 10 January, 1919.

Thank you for your interesting and useful letter of January 7th. It contains a great deal that will be of real service in guiding my thought and action.

I am sorry to say that before I received it I had spoken to Mr. Orlando of my interview with Mr. Bisolatti and of his ideas with regard to a settlement, but apparently there was nothing new in it to Mr. Orlando, who referred to the published interview by Mr. Bisolatti to which you yourself had referred me.[1] I did not speak of the confidential memorandum which Mr. Bisolatti was kind enough to consent that I should have a copy.

In haste,

Cordially and sincerely yours,   Woodrow Wilson

TLS (T. N. Page Papers, NcD).
[1] Bissolati had given a lengthy interview to the Rome correspondent of the London *Morning Post* on December 29, 1918. It was published on January 6. Bissolati had set forth therein a territorial settlement for Italy similar to that given in the interview with Wilson, printed as an Enclosure with T. N. Page to WW, Jan. 7, 1919. In addition, he had urged that Italy promote friendly relations with Greece by not claiming thirteen islands in the southern Aegean Sea and with Germany by not claiming the German-speaking Tyrol north of Bolzano. He had also warned Baron Sonnino of the risk of incurring a serious diplomatic defeat at the peace conference, since Wilson, who was not bound by the Treaty of London, was unlikely to countenance annexationist claims. See the summary of the interview in Arno J. Mayer, *Politics and Diplomacy of Peacemaking*, p. 215.

To Thomas Garrigue Masaryk

My dear Mister President: [Paris] 10 January, 1919.

Your telegram of the second of January which was delayed in reaching me has given me the profoundest pleasure. It is deeply gratifying to me that the Czecho-Slovak peoples should recognize in me their friend and the champion of their rights and I beg you to believe that I shall be always happy to serve the Nation in any way that it is in my power to serve it. I hope that you will let me know from time to time what service of counsel or action you think I could render it. I rejoice in its establishment and hope for its permanent prosperity.   Woodrow Wilson

CC telegram (WP, DLC).

To Brand Whitlock

My dear Whitlock: Paris, 10 January, 1919.

Your letter of the thirtieth of December was not laid before me until my return from Rome the other day, and therefore I have not had an opportunity sooner to tell you how much it touched and pleased me. To have won your friendship and approval so entirely is a matter of real joy to me, and I know of no one whose approval and affection I more value. You may be sure that the feeling is reciprocal.

I wish that it were possible to fix now at least approximately the date of my going to Brussels, but it has been so hard to get even the preliminary conferences for the formulation of the peace started that now that they are started I dare not interrupt them or leave them at a standstill by absenting myself, and I must wait until I see a legitimate interval during which I can be away from Paris.

I rejoice to think of the Belgian government set up once more in Brussels and share in the happiness which the Belgian people must feel. Please convey to the King and Queen[1] my warm congratulations and assurances of my personal friendship, and tell them that it will be a very happy day for me when I can give them this greeting in person.

Cordially and sincerely yours,   [Woodrow Wilson]

CCL (WP, DLC).
[1] That is, Queen Elisabeth.

Maksim Maksimovich Litvinov to Ludwig Meyer[1]

Dear Comrade,   Stockholm, January 10th 1919.

Referring to your letter of the 30th December, we very much regret to be unable to share your opinion as to the desirability and expediency at the present moment of a declaration by the Soviet Government containing the terms on which it would be prepared to conclude peace with the Allies. We feel sure that if the Allies, as the attacking party, formulate their demands, the Soviet Government will not fail to state clearly and in unmistakable terms to what extend [extent] these demands could be satisfied. So far the peace objects of the Allies, as regards Russia, have never been made known to the Soviet Government, neither directly nor indirectly. Moreover, no reply whatever has been given to the many peace overtures made both by the Central Soviet Government and by their representatives abroad, although in the statement to President Wilson of December 24th[2] the possible changes in the external and internal policy of the Soviets were clearly outlined. The Soviet Government and ourselves are therefore of the opinion that as long as the Allies continue to show no sign of their willingness to enter into some kind of formal or informal negotiations, no useful purpose would be served by any further peace proposals or declarations on the part of Russia. However, we shall gladly recapitulate in this letter our views on the possible peace terms, as we expressed them during our conversation of December 25th.

Lord Milner has recently declared one of the reasons of Allied intervention in Russia to be the protection of the so-called "Russian friends of the Allies" who may be exposed to reprisals in case the Soviet regime reestablishes itself in parts of Russia now occupied by the Allies. This apprehension should certainly not be in the way of an understanding with the Soviets, since the latter would be willing to give the Allies' friends the necessary guarantees for their safety and an amnesty for their past offences. Irrespective of their line of policy in the past and of the social classes to which they previously belonged they would be given a fair chance of finding work within the Soviet System, according to their abilities, education and knowledge. It is our firm conviction that the discontinuance of foreign intervention would mean the cessation of civil war in Russia in its present forms, and that there would be no necessity for any press restrictions. We believe that when Russia is allowed to work under more normal conditions and the whole population has adapted itself to the new social system, an insignificantly small and ever diminishing part of the population will find itself excluded from active citizenship. But until this can take place the Soviet Republic must be allowed time and a fair chance to put into practice its principles and show what it can do for the Russian people.

With regard to Poland, Ukraine and similar parts of the former Russian empire, it is and will be the policy of the Soviet Republic to abstain from any violation of the right of these provinces to self-determination. The Soviet Republic must however at the same time insist on the non-interference with party or class strife in these provinces on the part of any other foreign powers. Pending a final settlement of the relations of these provinces with the Russian Republic, some arrangement should be secured regarding free railway, postal and telegraphic communications, exchange of goods, transit traffic, free use of ports, etc.

Russia needs for her economic reconstruction and development all the technical skill, experience and material support which can be obtained from other countries. For that purpose, should an understanding with the Allies be arrived at, the Soviet Government would be willing to reconsider some of its decrees affecting the financial obligations of Russia towards other countries, without infringing however the cardinal principles of its economic and financial policy. Special regard would be paid to the interests of small creditors abroad.

The Russian Government, as such, while anxious to continue to proclaim to the whole world its general principles and to combat the widely spread campaign of lies and calumnies directed against Soviets and their work, would certainly desist from carrying on any propaganda in the Allied countries, which could be construed as interference with their internal affairs. In connection with this, we must emphasise that no such propaganda has ever been carried on by the Soviets in any foreign country except, perhaps, Germany.

The only demand the Soviet Republic have to put to the Allies is that they should discontinue all direct or indirect military operations against Soviet Russia, all direct or indirect material assistance to Russian or other forces operating against the Soviet Government, and also every kind of economic warfare and boycott.

These, as far as we remember, are the chief points touched upon during our conversation. We believe these views to reflect those of our Government.

You are entitled to make of this letter any use you may find expedient in the interest of peace between the countries concerned.

Yours truly   [Maxim Litvinov][3]

CCL (W. H. Buckler Papers, CtY).
 [1] Advocate to the Supreme Court of Norway at Christiania. Meyer later stated that he had initiated this correspondence because of his longtime interest in Russia. L. Meyer to WW, Feb. 7, 1919, TLS (WP, DLC).
 [2] That is, M. M. Litvinov to WW, Dec. 24, 1918.
 [3] The Editors do not know whether Wilson saw this copy. However, L. Meyer to WW, Feb. 7, 1919, enclosed a printed copy.

To Herbert Clark Hoover

Dear Mr. Hoover: Paris 11 January 1919.

I desire to confirm your appointment as Director General of Relief in Europe, in accordance with the understandings with the Allied Governments with which you are familiar.

I also confirm your appointment as one of the representatives of the United States Government upon the Council of the Associated Governments which is to deal with the various questions involved in this matter.   Cordially yours,   Woodrow Wilson

TLS (Hoover Archives, CSt-H).

To Thomas Watt Gregory

My dear Mr. Attorney General: Paris, 11 January, 1919.

It is with profound reluctance and regret that I accept your resignation. I do so only because you have convinced me that it is necessary in your own interest for you to retire. There has been no one with whom I have been associated in Washington whom I have learned more to trust or to whose counsels I have attached more value and importance. Your administration of your office has been singularly able and singularly conscientious and watchful of the public interest, and I feel that it is a very serious loss indeed to the Nation that you should find yourself obliged to withdraw from public life. My best wishes not only, but my affectionate friendship will follow you into retirement, and I hope with all my heart that in some way and at some time I shall again have the privilege and benefit of being associated with you.

Cordially and faithfully yours,   [Woodrow Wilson]

CCL (WP, DLC).

To Carter Glass

Paris, January 11, 1919.

252. For the Secretary of the Treasury from the President.

1. With reference to the first four paragraphs of your No. 66 January 2nd 4 p.m.[1] I suggest that Crosby's resignation as Special Finance Commissioner be accepted and that he be told that I trust his plans will make it possible for him to hold himself available for consul[t]ation on financial matters as the occasion may arise during the Peace Conference.

2. As you know I am in entire agreement with you concerning the matters mentioned in paragraph No. 5 of your telegram No. 66 of January 2nd 4 p.m.

3. The Acting Secretary of State has been furnished by cable with the text of letters which I have written Mr. Norman Davis pursuant to the suggestion made in paragraphs Nos. 6 and 7 of your cable No. 66 of January 2nd 4 p.m.

4. I think it hardly necessary at present time to create a United States Treasury Commission in Europe as suggested in your No. 112 January 6th 6 p.m. Davis has entered upon his work in a manner entirely satisfactory to me and the other members of the Commission and as the official Treasury representative can I think give such advice on financial questions as we may require. He will

need assistants particularly in connection with the Armistice discussions and in handling Treasury problems and I am satisfied to
adopt your suggestion respecting Lamont to help in this work and
that the services of Goodhue Loree and Harris[2] as assistants should
be retained if possible.

5. I concur in the suggestion that Strauss should come to Europe
to advise with the Commission on general questions of International
finance as distinguished from Treasury matters. I believe however
that his services in connection with his work on the Federal Reserve
Board in Washington (on which there are only four members at
the present time) would not permit him remain here any length of
time. It seems to me that Strauss' wide knowledge of International
finance makes it desirable that he should return to the United States
at the earliest practical moment in order that the Federal Reserve
Board may avail itself in full of his services. Secretary Lansing and
Colonel House share my views.

6. I entirely agree with you that so far as the Peace Commission
or Mr. Hoover or others in Europe are in need of financial advice
they should obtain it from persons acting under your general direction and responsible to you.   Ammission.

T telegram (WP, DLC).
    [1] It is missing.
    [2] Francis Abbot Goodhue, vice-president of the First National Bank of Boston, member
for the United States of the Interallied Committee for War Purchases and Finance.
Wilson may have been thinking of Leonor Fresnel Loree, railroad executive and a
member of the National War Labor Board. However, there is nothing in the available
biographical sketches of Loree to indicate either that he was in Europe or that he even
contemplated going to Europe at this time. Harris cannot be identified.

To David Hunter Miller and James Brown Scott

My dear Friends: Paris, 11 January, 1919.

Thank you for the memorandum about the action of Congress
in authorizing and requesting the President to invite at an appropriate time the Governments of the World to send representatives
to a conference to consider a plan for a court of arbitration. I am
very glad indeed to have the full text of the law.[1]

Cordially and sincerely yours,   Woodrow Wilson

TLS (J. B. Scott Papers, DGU).
    [1] D. H. Miller and J. B. Scott to American Commission to Negotiate Peace, Dec. 27,
1918, TLS (WP, DLC). They quoted telegram No. 111 from Frank L. Polk, dated
December 23, 1918. Polk in turn called attention to the so-called Hensley resolution, a
section of the Naval Appropriations Act approved August 29, 1916. For Wilson's convenience, Miller and Scott quoted the section in full from 39 *Statutes at Large* 618. About
the Hensley resolution, see WW to C. H. Levermore, March 28, 1916, n. 1, Vol. 36.

To Sir George Paish

My dear Sir George: Paris, 11 January, 1919.

Your letter of December 26th to which I have not been able to turn sooner because I have been so much on the go, gave me deep and genuine pleasure. It gratifies me deeply that your thought should go with mine in the great matters now being handled and your letter will be a source of genuine strength and great encouragement to me.

Cordially and sincerely yours,   [Woodrow Wilson]

CCL (WP, DLC).

To Charles Prestwich Scott

My dear Mr. Scott: Paris, 11 January, 1919.

Thank you for your letter about Doctor Weismann. I shall certainly hope to have a real confidential talk with him. My thought certainly needs guidance in the complicated matters with which he is familiar.

It was a great pleasure to see you in Manchester and I shall hope that our conversation then was just the first of many.

Cordially and sincerely yours,   [Woodrow Wilson]

CCL (WP, DLC).

Two Telegrams from Joseph Patrick Tumulty

Washington, January 11, 1919 1 A.M.

No. 13. Best information Moses of New Hampshire will vote for suffrage. This makes one Democratic vote all the more necessary. Suggest cable from you to Trammel[l] of Florida will be helpful. Have it from inside sources that Trammel looking for excuse to jump our way. Would you consider a cable to John Sharp Williams?

Kitchin making winning fight with conferees on zone matter. Senators seem to be yielding to him. Only thing that can save situation is cable from you to Simmons expressing your interest.

Tumulty.

Washington, January 11, 6 P.M. [1919]

No. 14. Do you wish publicity given to your message to Martin and Simmons [Sherley] with reference to food legislation? I have asked them to regard message as confidential until word from you is received. I doubt the wisdom of giving it out. I can handle publicity with the White House correspondents without quoting you. Am afraid of the effect on the country of recognition in your message of the "rising tide of Bolshevism."   Tumulty.

T telegrams (J. P. Tumulty Papers, DLC).

From Frank Mason North[1]

My dear Mr. President: Paris, France, January 11, 1919.

I am the bearer of a message adopted by the Executive Committee of the Federal Council of Churches of Christ in America, which expresses the heartiest endorsement of the proposal for a League of Nations.

A commission was appointed to present this resolution for the consideration of the Peace Conference. Representing, as the action does, the undoubted sentiment of the great Protestant citizenship of our country, the presentation of it in some proper form at this time, it was hoped by the Committee and the Commission of which I have the honor to be chairman, might in some measure strengthen your own position and that of our American delegates.

Will you not indicate for the Commission the procedure you would desire to have followed in this matter?

With warmest personal regards,
                        Yours faithfully,   Frank Mason North

TLS (WP, DLC).
    [1] Wilson's old friend, at this time President of the Federal Council of the Churches of Christ in America.

Robert Lansing to Frank Lyon Polk

[Paris] January 11, 1919.

254. Urgent. L'HUMANITE published this morning alleged text of reply of French Government dated December 5th last to a proposal of the British Government[1] (which was claimed had also been addressed to the Italian, American and Japanese Governments) suggesting that the different governments in Russia, including the Soviet Government, be invited to cease hostilities between each other and with neighboring states during the Peace Conference. In that event British Government suggested that these governments, including the Soviet Government, should be permitted to send delegates to the Peace Conference. According to published

reply French Government refused to have any dealings with the Bolsheviki.[2]

Please inform me as soon as possible whether Department received any such proposal from the British Government and whether any reply was made thereto. Lansing.   Ammission.

T telegram (WP, DLC).
    [1] See A. J. Balfour to Lord Derby, Jan. 2, 1919.
    [2] About this matter, see the extract from the Derby Diary printed below.

Tasker Howard Bliss to Newton Diehl Baker

CONFIDENTIAL No. 43.

My dear Mr. Secretary:[1]   Paris, January 11th, 1919.

. . . At the same meeting[2] yesterday afternoon, the Secretary of State brought up for consideration a telegram received from Mr. Polk from which it appeared that some steps might be taken toward the withdrawal of American troops from Siberia, unless the President expressed a contrary wish.[3] It seemed to me that the telegram was somewhat blindly worded and gave a probably wrong impression of the intentions of the War Department. However, the President said that in view of the fact that the whole Russian question would undoubtedly be one of the very first for consideration by the Peace Conference, he thought it better to let the status quo remain unchanged for the present. He told Mr. Lansing to communicate his view to the State Department.

At six o'clock the President left the meeting of the Commission and went to Mr. House's rooms where he had an appointment with Mr. Davison. Immediately after he left, there came to me the translation of your confidential N.D.B. 4, dated January 9th, and sent to me "For the President."[4] I immediately delivered it in person to Mr. Auchincloss, who said that he would hand it to the President as soon as the latter's interview with Mr. Davison was finished.

In connection with an incident that occurred in my room yesterday, at the meeting of the Commission, I shall speak of another matter. At the previous daily meetings of the Commission in Mr. Lansing's apartment, I have constantly called attention to the unreadiness of the American Commission in regard to all of the important questions that are demanding attention. I have repeatedly called their attention to the fact that I did not know the views of a single member of the Commission on such questions as, what shall be our attitude in case France demands greater territorial cessions from Germany than Alsace-Lorraine; what is our view about the

Schleswig case; what are our views as to the boundaries of the New Poland and New Czecho-Slavakia; what are our views as to the frontiers that may be demanded by Italy, both on the north and on the Adriatic; what are our views in respect to the dispute between Italy and Greece as to Smyrna and the Dodekaneses; and so with no end of other questions. Each day the Commission agreed that we were in a state of unreadiness and that we ought to correct it. Finally, Mr. Lansing suggested that, as a good way to focus our attention on the individual points about which we must come to an agreement, it would be well if he were to appoint a committee to draw up a skeleton of a completed treaty covering all points that must be passed on by the Peace Conference. This was agreed to and in due time such a skeleton was submitted. It was then proposed and agreed to that the committee, enlarged for the purpose, should prepare for consideration the completed details of this treaty. As we were all agreed that the question of the League of Nations should be settled among the first by the Peace Conference, a proposed draft of an Agreement for a League of Nations was one of the first things prepared. Naturally enough this was promptly criticised with the result that several successive drafts were prepared. Only yesterday morning we received the latest one of them. I had supposed that, from various things that Mr. Lansing had said, the President fully understood what we were doing and that we were simply trying to formulate, if possible, ideas as a basis for subsequent discussion.

Yesterday afternoon, at our Conference, something was said about this draft for a League of Nations, at which the President expressed considerable surprise. He asked whether we did not know that he himself was preparing such a draft. Mr. Lansing told him that we did, but that we assumed that it was desirable that each one should focus his attention on this in order that we might come to an intelligent and common understanding. The President did not seem to like this, which naturally had a somewhat depressing effect. The situation is a somewhat difficult one. Of course I should not feel worried if I knew the President's exact views on all questions that are to come up; but I do not know them. If there be any other member of the Commission who does know them he apparently does not feel at liberty to take them up *seriatim* and explain them. The difficulty will come when our colleagues are all here and real work begins. Most of the real work will doubtless be done in quite informal conferences, in talks between two men lunching or dining together. But, suppose that on such an occasion Mr. Balfour, for example, were to ask us what was the view of the American delegation on such and such a subject; what reply could be given? We might be constantly contradicting each other and give the impression of lack of unanimity. It sometimes seems to me that it would be better if we had only one American representative.

Of course you will understand that I am naturally nervous about the outcome in some respects, although my nervousness may have no justification. The questions that come before the Peace Conference are not going to be settled "right off the bat." An important subject may be proposed today but may be held up for many days while each delegation is studying it and making up its own mind. That will give the Americans an opportunity and an obligation to come to a unanimous understanding and present a united front.

I have noted with the greatest interest what you say in the main part of your letter in regard to the underlying feeling, an unsympathetic feeling to say the least, between the British and the Americans. What you say in regard to the feeling of the Americans toward the British could be said also in some degree in regard to the feeling that appears to be growing up between the Americans and the French. I shall write to you of this another time; just now I shall say only that it makes me feel more strongly every day that perhaps the wisest thing for us to do is to get out of Europe, horse, foot and dragoons, as quickly as possible. We came into the war to help beat the Germans, which we have now done; we did not come into it with the idea of staying here indefinitely for the purpose of untangling every knot which has been and is being wantonly tied in the skein of European politics.

With kind regards, believe me

Cordially yours,   T. H. Bliss.

CCL (T. H. Bliss Papers, DLC).
    [1] The text omitted from the first part of this letter concerned the presence of American troops in Italy and Italy's use of them in an invasion of Montenegro.
    [2] Of the A.C.N.P.
    [3] FLP to A.C.N.P., Jan. 7, 1919, T telegram (SDR, RG 59, 861.77/611c, DNA).
    [4] The Editors have been unable to find this document, or a copy of it, in any collection.

From the Diary of Lord Derby

Saturday, 11th January 1919

During the day saw Admiral Fournier and Count Fels[1] with reference to a luncheon to be given by the Cercle Inter Allié for the Prince of Wales; and Vicomte D'Harcourt[2] in regard to a dinner at the Jockey Club. Both satisfactorily arranged.

Luncheon. The Pichons, Serbian Minister and his wife,[3] Madame Roger, Reading and Sir Eyre Crowe.

Pichon very depressed and upset by an incident which I will relate at length.

On January 2nd the Home Government telegraphed asking whether the French Government would be prepared to enter into some sort of negotiations with the Bolshevist Government to stop the reign of terror now going on. This telegram was communicated at once to Pichon and on January 7th he sent me an answer in which he categorically refused on behalf of the French Government to have anything to do with the Bolshevists and saying that to do so would be to act contrary to all our former policy. This letter appeared in L'Humanité this morning and has created a great sensation.

With regard to this publication there are two facts that require notice. One that the letter is dated December 5th, whereas the right date should have been January 7th and the second is that the text, although substantially the same, does not agree with the actual text of the letter as received by me and forwarded to the Home Government.

It appears that the Bureau de la Presse rang up Pichon at 1 o'c this morning to say this letter was going to be published in L'Humanité and in the Paris Daily Mail. Pichon communicated with Clemenceau and they sent a message to say that it was not to be published and that if it was L'Humanité would be suppressed. The Daily Mail (Paris Edition) agreed not to publish but at the same time said it was too late then to stop publication in the London edition. L'Humanité refused to accept the decision and said they would publish, their object being of course to damage in every way possible Clemenceau and to argue that a workmen's Government, which is what the Socialists persist in calling the Bolshevist Government, had been turned down by the free-thinking French Republic at Clemenceau's instigation and by altering the date to the 5th of December would make it appear that Clemenceau was actually in possession of the Home Government's message when he made his celebrated speech on the 30th December.[4]

Meanwhile I received a communication that House and Lansing were both very angry. They said that the telegram had never been communicated to them although in the telegram to me the Home Government said they were sending a similar telegram to Washington and Tokio. I therefore asked to see House but could not see him till late in the evening and meanwhile I made various further enquiries and got somebody in whom I had confidence (Capel)[5] to see Clemenceau. Clemenceau was furious about it and gives a very curious turn to the story. He says that he had told L'Humanité that he would suppress the paper if they published the letter but of course it was an impossible thing for him now to take any action as the Daily Mail in London had published it. With regard to the actual correspondence, he says that the telegram from the Home Government to me was sent when Arthur Balfour was in the South of France and when Bob Cecil was no longer functioning at the Foreign Office. That the telegram was sent at the instigation of somebody with Bolshevist tendencies. He would not say for the moment who it was but said that within 48 hours he would be able to give the name. This person had instigated the telegram making the proposal and had been shown the answer and had made use of this information by communicating it to the Daily Mail and to L'Humanité. That Pichon had sent the answer when he Clemenceau was away and that he entirely agreed with the line taken though not perhaps with the actual wording.

I went to see House only to have one minute with him as he came out from seeing the President. I told him I had come to clear myself and the Home Government from any idea of acting behind the American Government's back and I showed him the telegram as I had received it. He told me that I might make my mind quite easy about that but he himself was very much annoyed about the whole matter. That he had seen the American Press people and so had Lansing and they both said they knew nothing whatever about the telegram and it had never been received by the Americans. It now turns out that Jusserand the French Ambassador to the United States who is now in Paris had seen President Wilson and had handed the telegram direct.[6] That the President had taken no action on it and had told nobody of its receipt, hence the trouble.

Everybody was very upset about it. There is no doubt whatever that quite apart from the fact that it will make Clemenceau's position with the socialists even more difficult than it is at the present moment and will indeed make a certain amount of friction between our own Government and the French Government, there is also the fact that on the very eve of the Conference the publication of such an extremely confidential document is a bad augury for what will happen if the Press is to be allowed to publish what it likes without censorship.

T MS (A. J. Balfour Add, MSS 49744, British Library).

[1] Vice-Adm. François Ernest Fournier, retired, and Edmond, Count Fels, president of the board of the *Revue de Paris*.

[2] Emmanuel, Vicomte d'Harcourt.

[3] Milenko R. Vesnić and Blanche Ullman Vesnić.

[4] He meant Clemenceau's speech of December 29, about which see n. 1 to the extract from the Diary of Dr. Grayson printed at Dec. 30, 1918. Actually, Clemenceau did not mention

Russia in his speech. It was Pichon who had dealt with the problem of Russia earlier during the debate. See *Journal Officiel* . . . *1918*, pp. 3716-18.

⁵ He cannot be identified.

⁶ Again, the British memorandum (a copy of which *is* in the Wilson Papers) is A. J. Balfour to Lord Derby, Jan. 2, 1919. However, there is a copy of the memorandum in the files of the Department of State. It was conveyed in C. A. de R. Barclay to FLP, Jan. 3, 1919, and is printed in *FR Russia, 1919*, pp. 2-3. Polk did not relay it to the American mission on the assumption that the Foreign Office had sent a copy directly to Wilson or the A.C.N.P. See FLP to RL, Jan. 12, 1919.

INDEX

NOTE ON THE INDEX

THE alphabetically arranged analytical table of contents at the front of the volume eliminates duplication, in both contents and index, of references to certain documents, such as letters. Letters are listed in the contents alphabetically by name, and chronologically within each name by page. The subject matter of all letters is, of course, indexed. The Editorial Notes and Wilson's writings are listed in the contents chronologically by page. In addition, the subject matter of both categories is indexed. The index covers all references to books and articles mentioned in text or notes. Footnotes are indexed. Page references to footnotes which place a comma between the page number and "n" cite both text and footnote, thus: "418,n1." On the other hand, absence of the comma indicates reference to the footnote only, thus: "59n1"—the page number denoting where the footnote appears.

The index supplies the fullest known form of names and, for the Wilson and Axson families, relationships as far down as cousins. Persons referred to by nicknames or shortened forms of names can be identified by reference to entries for these forms of the names.

All entries consisting of page numbers only and which refer to concepts, issues and opinions (such as democracy, the tariff, and money trust, leadership, and labor problems), are references to Wilson's speeches and writings. Page references that follow the symbol Δ in such entries refer to the opinions and comments of others who are identified.

Three cumulative contents-index volumes are now in print: Volume 13, which covers Volumes 1-12, Volume 26, which covers Volumes 14-25, and Volume 39, which covers Volumes 27-38.

INDEX

WOODROW WILSON

Morgenthau dedicates book to, 3; impression
of as an "intellectual machine," 24; offered
honorary degree from Oxford, 27-28, 161,n1,
162,n1; receives congratulations on war's
end, 32, 34, 46, 46n1, 46-47, 50, 53-54,
126-27, 204, 246; on armistice acceptance,
34; address to Congress on peace terms,
35-43; remarks to state food administrators, 52; State of the Union message mentioned, 73, 217, 251n1; Thanksgiving Proclamation, 95-96; curtails all but necessary
appointments, 160-61; Red Cross appeal,
202-203; Baruch's praise of, 209; remarks
to B'nai B'rith, 239,n1, 239-40; State of the
Union message, 274-86; congressional reaction to WW's message, 301, 305, 310;
teller of stories and anecdotes, 332-33, 343,
366, 392, 424, 425, 552; and indemnity issue, 563; WW's appeal for a Democratic
Congress mentioned, 401; London *Times*
interview, 422-30; Christmas message, 491;
on European food crisis, 578-79; suggestion that WW return to Boston not N.Y.,
625-26, 698; proclamation on T. Roosevelt's death, 634, 635; indignation over
French and British claims, 707-708

APPEARANCE

321, 322, 460; The President did not like what
I said. His face assumed that harsh, obsti-